Multimodal AI in Healthcare

U. Venkatesh • Mamta Mittal
Jeetendra Kumar
Editors

Multimodal AI in Healthcare

Fusion Intelligence for Advanced Health Diagnostics

Springer

Editors
U. Venkatesh
Department of Community and Family Medicine
All India Institute of Medical Sciences
Gorakhpur, Uttar Pradesh, India

Mamta Mittal
Department of Data Analytics & Data Science
Delhi Skill & Entrepreneurship University
New Delhi, Delhi, India

Jeetendra Kumar
Department of Computer Science and Application
Atal Bihari Vajpayee University
Bilaspur, Chhattisgarh, India

ISBN 978-981-95-9026-1 ISBN 978-981-95-9027-8 (eBook)
https://doi.org/10.1007/978-981-95-9027-8

This Springer imprint is published by the registered company Springer Nature Singapore Pte Ltd.
The registered company address is: 152 Beach Road, #21-01/04 Gateway East, Singapore 189721, Singapore

Preface

The rise of Fusion Intelligence in healthcare marks a transformative shift in how medical systems understand, predict, and respond to human health needs. By integrating multimodal artificial intelligence (AI) with diverse data sources, including clinical records, medical imaging, genomics, geospatial intelligence, behavioural indicators, and population-level data—healthcare is moving towards a future of context-aware, patient-centred, and precision-driven diagnostics and treatment. This book, *Multimodal AI in Healthcare: Fusion Intelligence for Advanced Health Diagnostics*, provides a comprehensive and forward-looking exploration of how multimodal AI is reshaping modern medical science, clinical practice, public health, and population health management.

The book is organized into 17 chapters, each illustrating how multimodal AI frameworks unify heterogeneous data streams to enhance diagnostic accuracy, improve decision support, optimize resource allocation, and advance health equity.

Chapter 1 introduces the paradigm shift from single-modality AI systems to advanced multimodal frameworks capable of analysing imaging, EHR data, genomics, clinical notes, and physiological signals simultaneously. It discusses how this convergence enhances diagnostic precision, risk stratification, and the personalization of care pathways. The chapter highlights key technological architectures and emerging breakthroughs that position multimodal AI as the next frontier in clinical decision support.

Chapter 2 examines how demographic insights enable more equitable and context-aware AI systems. By integrating clinical, genomic, behavioural, environmental, and social data with demographic characteristics, multimodal AI can improve prediction accuracy and inclusiveness in health surveillance, chronic-disease forecasting, and epidemiological modelling. The chapter also addresses ethical challenges, emphasizing fairness, transparency, and privacy in demographic-driven algorithmic systems.

Chapter 3 explores the fusion of GeoAI, GIS, and multimodal AI to contextualize health outcomes within spatial and temporal environments. It details how spatial intelligence enhances disease surveillance, environmental risk mapping, infrastructure optimization, and precision public health. The chapter also evaluates technical and ethical challenges including data heterogeneity, scalability, privacy, and equity while underscoring the promise of GIS-enabled multimodal systems for population-level healthcare.

Chapter 4 highlights how multimodal AI can reduce long-standing inequities in global health. Drawing on examples from Ghana, Bolivia, India, and Bangladesh, the chapter explains how multimodal AI enhances early detection, intelligent resource allocation, and culturally adaptive care delivery. It examines critical governance considerations such as algorithmic bias, data colonialism, transparency, and digital divide, positioning multimodal AI as a key tool for equitable healthcare systems aligned with WHO and SDG goals.

Chapter 5 focuses on how AI transforms tuberculosis detection and management across India's healthcare system. It describes innovations in digital microscopy, chest-X-ray interpretation, molecular diagnostics, non-invasive screening, and clinical decision support. The chapter also discusses programmatic applications including surveillance, forecasting, hotspot identification, supply-chain optimization, and pharmacovigilance, while noting challenges in validation, ethics, and governance.

Chapter 6 presents AI as a pivotal force in advancing oncology, from early detection and screening to precision treatment planning, radiotherapy optimization, robotic oncosurgery, and population-level prediction. It highlights the expanding role of AI in drug discovery, epidemiological trend forecasting, and ethical data management, emphasizing how AI-driven tools improve outcomes across the cancer-care continuum.

Chapter 7 explores how AI-driven diagnostic and predictive tools support outbreak detection, drug discovery, digital microscopy, clinical imaging analysis, and multimodal monitoring. It highlights generative AI's role in vaccine design, clinical decision support, and treatment optimization, while addressing challenges in data privacy, modelling complexity, and real-world integration.

Chapter 8 examines applications of AI in dental public health, including imaging analysis, epidemiological modelling, teledentistry, predictive analytics, and personalized interventions. The chapter highlights AI's potential to reduce oral-health disparities through targeted prevention and improved access to care.

Chapter 9 discusses how integrating demographic, clinical, haematological, biochemical, imaging, and genomic data through fusion intelligence enhances anaemia diagnosis, classification, and personalized management. The chapter emphasizes explainability, ethical considerations, and translational challenges in operationalizing multimodal AI within haematology.

Chapter 10 analyses the legal, regulatory, and ethical challenges of deploying multimodal AI systems in intensive-care environments. It explores real-time data integration from sensors, imaging, laboratory tests, and health records to support critical-care decisions while addressing privacy, accountability, and medicolegal implications.

Chapter 11 highlights how multimodal predictive models can improve triage accuracy, sepsis detection, traumatic brain injury assessment, and workflow optimization in paediatric emergency settings. It outlines existing challenges, including data quality, ethical concerns, and real-world deployment barriers.

Chapter 12 explores AI-enhanced telemedicine systems capable of synthesizing biometric signals, clinical text, speech, and video data for remote diagnostics and monitoring. It presents global use cases, conceptual frameworks, architectural models, and ethical considerations for scaling multimodal telehealth systems.

Chapter 13 discusses the integration of AI in surgical planning, intraoperative imaging, robotic navigation, complication prediction, and postoperative rehabilitation. It describes advances across orthopaedics, gynaecology, obstetrics, pain medicine, and minimally invasive surgery, while highlighting persistent challenges related to transparency, bias, cost, and workforce readiness.

Chapter 14 offers an in-depth overview of how AI enhances diagnostic imaging, digital pathology, genomic interpretation, intraoperative guidance, robotic performance, postoperative monitoring, and surgical education. It also examines ethical challenges and future trends such as augmented-reality assistance, digital twins, and intelligent surgical ecosystems.

Chapter 15 explores how AI tools strengthen diagnostic, triage, screening, and decision-support capabilities in frontline healthcare settings, particularly in low-resource contexts. It highlights AI-supported imaging tools, symptom-assessment systems, workflow optimization, and patient-facing digital tools, while also addressing barriers relating to privacy, infrastructure, and algorithmic fairness.

Chapter 16 discusses how AI enhances community-based care delivery, early detection of infectious and chronic diseases, telemedicine expansion, supply-chain forecasting, and public-health surveillance. The chapter emphasizes the importance of ethical implementation, data governance, and equitable access.

Chapter 17 examines how multimodal AI systems integrate speech, facial cues, behavioural patterns, EHRs, psychometric data, and social-media signals to improve suicide-risk detection and intervention. It highlights modelling challenges, cultural variability, ethical concerns, and the importance of clinician oversight.

The interdisciplinary nature of this book reflects the rapid convergence of AI, clinical medicine, public health, geography, ethics, and digital technology. Together, these chapters demonstrate how Fusion Intelligence represents the next era of healthcare—one that integrates multimodal data, supports clinician expertise, strengthens health systems, and advances equitable, precise, and scalable medical care.

Gorakhpur, India — U. Venkatesh
New Delhi, India — Mamta Mittal
Bilaspur, India — Jeetendra Kumar

Contents

Editors and Contributors

About the Editors

U. Venkatesh, DMBBS, MD (Community Medicine) is a distinguished public health researcher, educator, and author with extensive experience in health policy, epidemiology, and data-driven decision-making. Currently serving as an Assistant Professor at AIIMS Gorakhpur, he is also the National Coordinator of the National Centre for Policy Research in Tobacco Control (NCPRTC) and the Centre for Policy Research & Data Analytics in Health and Environment (CePRAHE). He has led multiple ICMR-funded and internationally funded research projects, securing over ₹10 crores in research grants. His work has been published in top-tier journals, including *The Lancet Regional Health–Southeast Asia*, *Frontiers in Public Health*, and *Cambridge Prisms: Global Mental Health*. An accomplished author, he has written four books, including *Untold Stories of Tobacco (Youth Voices)* and *PSM Residency Made Easy*. As a National Trainer for Ayushman Bharat, he has contributed to capacity-building initiatives and the development of government policy documents and training manuals for healthcare professionals. Additionally, he is a peer reviewer for reputed medical and public health journals, influencing evidence-based policymaking in areas such as tobacco control, climate change, and health system strengthening.

Mamta Mittal is working as Associate Professor and Programme In-charge for Data Analytics and Data Science at Delhi Skill and Entrepreneurship University, New Delhi (under Government of NCT Delhi). She has received PhD in Computer Science and Engineering from Thapar University, Patiala; MTech (Honours) in Computer Science & Engineering from YMCA, Faridabad, and BTech in Computer Science & Engineering from Kurukshetra University Kurukshetra. For four consecutive years (2022 to 2025), Stanford University (USA) listed Dr Mamta Mittal in the world Top 2% Scientists list. She has been teaching for the last 22 years with emphasis on Data Mining, Machine Learning, DBMS, and Data Structures. She is a lifetime member of CSI and has published more than 100 research papers in SCI, SCIE, Scopus-indexed journals. She holds five patents and two copyrights in the area of Artificial Intelligence, IoT, and Deep Learning. She has edited/authored many books with reputed publishers like Springer, IOS Press, Elsevier, CRC Press, etc. and worked on a DST-approved project, "Development of IoT based hybrid navigation module for midsized autonomous vehicles", with a research grant of 25 lakhs. Currently, she is guiding PhD scholars in the field of Machine Learning and Deep Learning. She is Editor of the book series Edge AI in Future Computing with CRC Press, Taylor & Francis, USA. She is a member of editorial boards with InderScience, Bentham Science, Springer, and Elsevier and an Associate Editor with an SCIE-indexed journal of Springer.

Jeetendra Kumar holds a PhD degree in Computer Science from GLA University Mathura. Currently, he has been working as an Assistant Professor in the Department of Computer Science and Application at Atal Bihari Vajpayee University, Bilaspur, Chhattisgarh, India, for the last 12 years. He holds a master's degree (MSc) and a Master of Technology (MTech) in Computer Science. He has published various research articles in reputed journals and conferences, including topics such as sentiment analysis, fall detection using machine learning techniques, IoT applications, and automatic question generation. He has also contributed book chapters on topics related to neuroscience, smartphone applications, and fog computing in healthcare. He has edited one book with CRC Press, Taylor & Francis. He has completed two research projects sponsored by the State Planning Commission, C.G., Commonwealth Media Centre for Asia (CEMCA), New Delhi, and Atal Bihari Vajpayee University, Bilaspur. He is also a member of prestigious academic societies such as IEEE, the Indian Science Congress, the International Association of Engineers (IAENG), the International Computer Science and Engineering Society (ICSES), and the International Association of Academicians (IAASSE).

Contributors

Gaurav Aditya Department of General Surgery All India Institute of Medical Sciences, Gorakhpur, India

Dr. Rashmi Agarwalla, MD, Community Medicine Department of Community & Family Medicine, All India Institute of Medical Sciences, Guwahati, India

Arshad Ahmed Department of Community & Family Medicine, All India Institute of Medical Sciences, Gorakhpur, Uttar Pradesh, India

Mohd Rashid Alam Department of Psychiatry, All India Institute of Medical Sciences, Gorakhpur, Uttar Pradesh, India

Gopi Battineni Computer Science and Information Systems, University of Limerick, Limerick, Ireland

Clinical Research Centre, University Camerino, Macerata, Italy

Ajeet Singh Bhadoria Department of Community and Family Medicine, All India Institute of Medical Sciences, Rishikesh, India

Dr. Himashree Bhattacharyya, MD, Community Medicine Department of Community & Family Medicine, All India Institute of Medical Sciences, Guwahati, India

Naren Chandra Department of Pulmonary Medicine, VMMC & Safdarjung Hospital, New Delhi, India

Maurizio Di Masi University of Perugia, Perugia, Italy

Francesca Ferretti Scuola Superiore Meridionale di Napoli, Naples, Italy

Roberto Garetto International Legal Institute of Turin, Italy

Abhinav K. Gautam Department of Electrical & Electronics Engineering, S.R. Institute of Management & Technology, Lucknow, Uttar Pradesh, India

Arunagiri Gunasekar Government Medical College and Hospital, Thiruvallur, Tamilnadu, India

Shubham Gupta Department of Community Medicine, IMS, BHU, Varanasi, India

Jagani Harsha Sai Department of General Surgery All India Institute of Medical Sciences, Gorakhpur, India

Pranav Ish Department of Pulmonary Medicine, VMMC & Safdarjung Hospital, New Delhi, India

Krishna Jasani, MBBS, MD Department of Community and Family Medicine, All India Institute of Medical Sciences, Rajkot, India

Krupal Joshi, MBBS, MD, FIAPSM, FSPAAH, FCMA(UK), FIMSA, PGDHHM Department of Community and Family Medicine, All India Institute of Medical Sciences, Rajkot, India

Ankita Kabi Department of Anesthesiology, All India Institute of Medical Sciences, Gorakhpur, Uttar Pradesh, India

Kalaivane Kannadasan Public Health Medicine Specialist, Jempol Health District Office, Ministry of Health, Putrajaya, Malaysia

Rajesh Kannan Department of General and Minimal Access Surgery, All India Institute of Medical Sciences, Gorakhpur, India

Dr. Kanthakumar, MBBS Department of Community & Family Medicine, All India Institute of Medical Sciences, Guwahati, India

Venkatesh Karthikeyan Department of Community and Family Medicine, All India Institute of Medical Sciences, Patna, Bihar, India

Jeetendra Kumar Department of Computer Science and Application, Atal Bihari Vajpayee University, Bilaspur, Chhattisgarh, India

Manish Kumar Department of Paediatrics, All India Institute of Medical Sciences, Gorakhpur, India

Mamta Mittal Department of Data Analytics & Data Science, Delhi Skill and Entrepreneurship University, New Delhi, India

Aroop Mohanty Department of Microbiology, All India Institute of Medical Sciences, Gorakhpur, Uttar Pradesh, India

Ravindra Nath Department of Community Medicine, Autonomous State Medical College, Shahjahanpur, Uttar Pradesh, India

B. Nikhil Department of General and Minimal Access Surgery, All India Institute of Medical Sciences, Gorakhpur, India

J. P. Pandey Dr. A. P. J. Abdul Kalam Technical University, Lucknow, Uttar Pradesh, India

Sanjay Pandey Department of Community and Family Medicine, All India Institute of Medical Sciences, Patna, Bihar, India

Priyanka Parhad Centre for Community Medicine, All India Institute of Medical Sciences, New Delhi, India

Vineet Kumar Pathak Department of Community Medicine, IMS, BHU, Varanasi, India

Alan Phillip Department of General and Minimal Access Surgery, All India Institute of Medical Sciences, Gorakhpur, India

Dharmendra Kumar Pipal Department of General and Minimal Access Surgery, All India Institute of Medical Sciences, Gorakhpur, India

Rajendra Kumar Pipal Department of Orthopaedics, All India Institute of Medical Sciences, Gorakhpur, India

Vibha Rani Pipal Department of Obstetrics and Gynaecology, All India Institute of Medical Sciences, Gorakhpur, India

Swati Prasad Department of General and Minimal Access Surgery, All India Institute of Medical Sciences, Gorakhpur, India

Margubur Rahaman Department of Community & Family Medicine, All India Institute of Medical Sciences, Gorakhpur, Uttar Pradesh, India

Mahek Rai Department of Community Medicine, IMS, BHU, Varanasi, India

Vidushi Rathi Department of Pulmonary Medicine, VPCI, University of Delhi, New Delhi, India

Gupta Ravi Department of General Surgery All India Institute of Medical Sciences, Gorakhpur, India

Atul R. Rukadikar Department of Microbiology, All India Institute of Medical Sciences, Gorakhpur, Uttar Pradesh, India

Varkey Nadakkavukaran Santhosh Department of Community & Family Medicine, All India Institute of Medical Sciences, Gorakhpur, Uttar Pradesh, India

Sakshi Sharma Department of Microbiology, All India Institute of Medical Sciences, Gorakhpur, Uttar Pradesh, India

Shubham Department of Microbiology, All India Institute of Medical Sciences, Gorakhpur, Uttar Pradesh, India

Aradhana Singh Department of Obstetrics and Gynaecology, All India Institute of Medical Sciences, Gorakhpur, Uttar Pradesh, India

Raj Kishore Singh Department of Medicine, Nodal Officer, Multidisciplinary Research Unit & Clinical Trial Unit, BRD Medical College, Gorakhpur, Uttar Pradesh, India

Rujal Raj Singh Bachelor of Technology, Computer Science Engineering (Artificial Intelligence & Machine Learning), AKGEC, Ghaziabad, Uttar Pradesh, India

Shriyansh Srivastava Department of Pharmacy, School of Medical and Allied Sciences, Galgotias University, Greater Noida, India

Department of Pharmacology, Delhi Pharmaceutical Sciences and Research University (DPSRU), New Delhi, India

Richa Tripathi Department of Psychiatry, All India Institute of Medical Sciences, Gorakhpur, Uttar Pradesh, India

U. Venkatesh Department of Community & Family Medicine, All India Institute of Medical Sciences, Gorakhpur, Uttar Pradesh, India

Seema Yadav Department Anaesthesia, Critical Care and Pain Management, All India Institute of Medical Sciences, Gorakhpur, India

Part I

Foundations of Multimodal AI

The Rise of Multimodal AI in Healthcare: A New Frontier

1

U. Venkatesh, Varkey Nadakkavukaran Santhosh, and Mamta Mittal

1.1 Introduction

The intersection of multimodal data integration and artificial intelligence (AI) is poised to propel a technological revolution in the healthcare sector. A paradigm shift from conventional single-modality approaches to systems that can process, analyze, and synthesize data from multiple data sources at once is represented by multimodal artificial intelligence. Medical imaging, electronic health records (EHRs), pathology slides, clinical notes, genomic sequences, physiological signals, and even patient-reported outcomes are some examples of these sources. Unprecedented insights into disease mechanisms, diagnostic precision, treatment personalization, and patient outcomes could be unlocked through the integration of these diverse data types (Simon et al., 2025).

Conventional AI systems in healthcare have primarily concentrated on single-modality analysis, like radiology image classification or clinical note natural language processing. These methods do not fully capture the holistic complexity of human health and illness, despite their impressive success in some fields. When making decisions about diagnosis and treatment, human clinicians naturally combine a range of information sources, such as visual findings, laboratory results, patient history, physical examination findings, and contextual factors. Multimodal AI uses sophisticated machine learning architectures that can learn joint representations across various data modalities in an attempt to mimic and possibly surpass this integrative approach.

U. Venkatesh (✉) · V. N. Santhosh
Department of Community & Family Medicine, All India Institute of Medical Sciences, Gorakhpur, Uttar Pradesh, India

M. Mittal
Department of Data Analytics & Data Science, Delhi Skill and Entrepreneurship University, New Delhi, India

U. Venkatesh et al. (eds.), *Multimodal AI in Healthcare*,
https://doi.org/10.1007/978-981-95-9027-8_1

The rise of multimodal AI in healthcare is fuelled by a confluence of clinical, technological, and infrastructure factors. First, it is predicted that by 2020, the exponential growth in healthcare data generation will reach 2314 exabytes per year, resulting in an unprecedented accumulation of different types of data, including genomic sequences, medical imaging, electronic health records, physiological signals, and patient-reported outcomes. Multimodal learning, which is anticipated to incorporate complementary insights across modalities, is ideally positioned to benefit from this wealth of heterogeneous information.

Second, major breakthroughs in deep learning architectures, such as the emergence of transformer models, attention mechanisms, and large-scale pretraining strategies, have enabled the capabilities of extracting and aligning representations from multiple sources of data. These allow models to represent complex interdependencies between modalities, such as correlating radiological findings with genomic profiles or clinical narratives with laboratory results.

Third, recent advances in computational infrastructure have made large-scale training of multimodal AI systems increasingly practical. The availability of high-performance GPUs, TPUs, and distributed cloud computing platforms has dramatically reduced training time and cost, making it possible for researchers and clinicians to deploy sophisticated models to real-world healthcare environments. Moreover, recent progress on federated learning and privacy-preserving computation has further alleviated data sharing and patient confidentiality concerns.

Last but not least, the medical community is becoming more aware of the limitations of single-modality AI systems in numerous scenarios, which typically fail to capture the complex nature of the majority of disease processes. Integrating data from multiple sources is a natural part of clinical decision-making, and multimodal AI reflects this integrative reasoning process. AI has therefore sparked a paradigm shift towards multimodal approaches for diagnostics, prognosis, and customized treatment planning in response to the growing need for more comprehensive, context-aware, and explicable solutions.

This chapter discusses the theoretical underpinnings, technological advancements, clinical applications, difficulties, and potential future directions of multimodal AI, which is emerging as a new frontier in healthcare. After outlining the conceptual framework for multimodal learning in medical contexts, we go on to discuss current architectures and techniques. We go on to talk about its practical uses in various medical specialties, then move on to challenges in implementing it through data integration, model interpretability, regulatory considerations, and concluding remarks on potential future directions with views on its transformative potential (Simon et al., 2025).

1.2 Foundations of Multimodal AI in Healthcare

1.2.1 Definition and Conceptual Framework

Multimodal artificial intelligence refers to artificial intelligence systems capable of processing and integrating information from multiple data modalities to perform tasks for which cross-modal understanding is beneficial. Application contexts in health usually include medical imaging studies in the form of radiographs, computed tomography, magnetic resonance imaging, ultrasound, and positron emission tomography; pathology images; genomic and proteomic data; electronic health records; clinical notes; time-series physiological signals, such as electrocardiograms and electroencephalograms; laboratory values; and patient-reported outcomes (Schouten et al., 2025).

The underlying idea in multimodal AI is that the various data modalities reflect complementary aspects of biological reality. The medical images show anatomical structures and spatial patterns of disease, while genomic data shed light on molecular mechanisms and hereditary factors. Clinical notes contain rich contextual details and temporal disease evolution. Laboratory values quantify biochemical processes. Thus, by combining these partial perspectives, multimodal AI systems can form more complete representations of health states and disease processes than a single modality would allow (Schouten et al., 2025) (Fig. 1.1).

Multimodal learning can be categorized into several paradigmatic approaches. First, early fusion methods concatenate features from different modalities at the input level before joint processing. Second, late fusion techniques process each modality independently through specialized networks before combining predictions or representations at the output stage. Third, intermediate fusion strategies exchange information between modality-specific processing streams at multiple intermediate layers. Fourth, attention-based mechanisms dynamically weight contributions from different modalities based on their relevance to specific tasks or instances. Table 1.1 provides a comprehensive overview of common data modalities in multimodal healthcare AI systems (Schouten et al., 2025).

Fig. 1.1 Common data modalities in multimodal healthcare AI systems

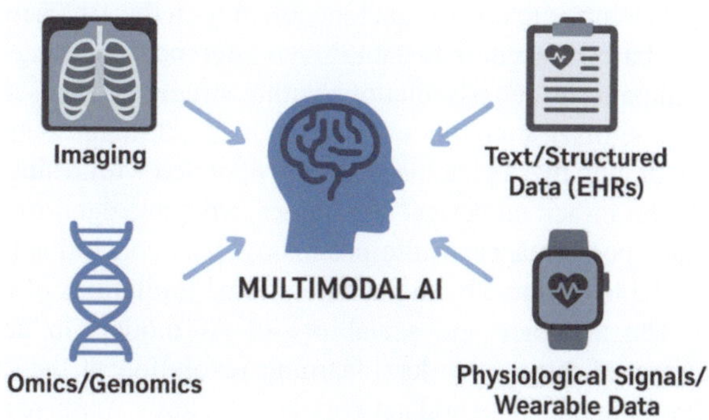

Table 1.1 Common data modalities in multimodal healthcare AI systems

Data modality	Characteristics	Examples	Primary applications
Medical imaging	High-dimensional, spatially structured, continuous-valued	Radiographs, CT, MRI, ultrasound, PET	Diagnosis, treatment planning, disease monitoring
Pathology images	Gigapixel resolution, cellular/subcellular detail	Whole-slide images, microscopy	Cancer diagnosis, prognostication, biomarker detection
Genomic data	Discrete sequences, expression levels, variable dimensionality	DNA sequences, gene expression, mutation profiles	Precision medicine, risk prediction, treatment selection
Electronic health records (structured)	Low-dimensional, categorical and numerical	Diagnostic codes, lab values, medications, procedures	Risk stratification, outcome prediction, clinical decision support
Clinical notes	Unstructured text, variable length and format	Progress notes, discharge summaries, radiology reports	Disease surveillance, phenotyping, temporal modeling
Physiological signals	Time-series data, specific temporal characteristics	ECG, EEG, vital signs	Monitoring, early warning, arrhythmia detection
Patient-generated data	Continuous, longitudinal, variable quality	Wearable sensors, smartphone data, patient-reported outcomes	Remote monitoring, early detection, personalized care

1.2.2 Evolution from Single-Modality to Multimodal Systems

The development of AI in healthcare has proceeded along a progressive path from narrow, single-task systems to integrated, multimodal frameworks with the capabilities to model complex clinical reasoning. Early efforts at medical AI in the 1970s, such as MYCIN and Internist-I, were rule-based expert systems whose purpose was to help clinicians arrive at a differential diagnosis by means of specific logic and symptom checklists. These systems constituted an early effort to codify medical knowledge into structured decision rules but were bound by the constraint of manually curated knowledge bases, an inability to learn from new data, and restricted adaptability to real-world clinical variability.

The introduction of machine learning in the 1990s marked a paradigm shift from rule-based reasoning to data-driven inference, enabling algorithms to identify statistical patterns and associations within structured datasets. Applications expanded to include disease prediction models, medical image segmentation, and signal analysis, though these systems generally operated within single-modality confines, focusing on either numerical lab values, imaging data, or text records independently. Their performance, while promising, was constrained by the quality and scale of available data and by the computational limitations of the time.

The accuracy and scalability of AI models in healthcare were significantly increased during the deep learning revolution of the 2010s, which was driven by developments in neural network architectures, massive annotated datasets, and GPU acceleration. For instance, RNNs and later transformer models improved the analysis of clinical text and temporal health data, while CNNs achieved expert-level performance in a variety of medical image analysis tasks, including tumor detection, lesion segmentation, and radiographic interpretation. Notwithstanding these advances, the majority of early deep learning systems were only capable of excelling in a single task or type of data, such as radiology, pathology, or genomics, and were unable to combine insights from other fields.

As the complexity of healthcare data grew and the limitations of siloed AI became apparent, the field began to transition toward multimodal AI systems that synthesize diverse data sources mirroring the integrative diagnostic reasoning used by clinicians. This evolution is more conceptual than technological, positioning AI as a collaborative and holistic decision-support tool rather than a narrow task executor.

Several milestone developments catalyzed this transition toward multimodal approaches. Medical image analysis, for instance, was revolutionized with the development of convolutional neural networks, executing some tasks at the level of a radiologist. Similarly, recurrent neural networks and transformer architectures allowed much more sophisticated analyses of sequential data, such as clinical notes or time-series signals. The critical breakthrough came when architectures that could learn joint representations across modalities became possible; examples include vision-language models that could relate images to textual descriptions (Hirani et al., 2024).

Modern multimodal AI systems rely on transfer learning from large-scale pretraining on diverse datasets. Models pretrained on large corpora of paired images and texts, such as CLIP, have shown impressive performance in learning generalizable cross-modal representations. Adaptation of these foundational models to medical domains through fine-tuning on healthcare-specific multimodal datasets has resulted in systems with unprecedented capabilities for integration of diverse medical information (Massimi et al., 2025).

1.2.3 Key Enabling Technologies

Several technological advances have enabled practical multimodal AI for healthcare. Deep neural network architectures provide a computational substrate for learning complex, high-dimensional mappings between modalities. Originally developed for natural language processing, transformer models have proven to be particularly effective for multimodal learning by virtue of their attention mechanisms that can dynamically focus on relevant information across different data types (Massimi et al., 2025).

Cross-modal attention mechanisms represent a critical innovation, enabling the model to learn which aspects of one modality are most relevant for interpreting another. For example, when analyzing a chest radiograph, the model may attend to mentions of cough or fever in clinical notes to better contextualize imaging findings.

These attention weights also confer interpretability by revealing which cross-modal relationships the model considers important for its predictions.

Contrastive learning methods have lately become powerful approaches to multimodal representation learning. These methods train models to produce similar embeddings for semantically related instances across modalities while producing dissimilar embeddings for unrelated instances. In medical contexts, contrastive learning can align representations of imaging findings with corresponding textual descriptions, pathology images with genomic profiles, or physiological signals with clinical outcomes.

Hardware acceleration through GPUs and specialized AI processors has made large-scale multimodal model training computationally feasible. The enormous parameter spaces in modern multimodal models, often consisting of hundreds of millions or billions of parameters, demand massive computational resources. Such distributed training across multiple processors is democratizing access via cloud computing platforms beyond elite research institutions (Hao et al., 2025).

1.3 Multimodal AI Architectures for Healthcare

1.3.1 Vision-Language Models for Medical Applications

The vision-language models are among the fastest-developing and transformative classes of multimodal AI in healthcare, with the potential to bridge the gap between visual perception and linguistic understanding. These models combine various medical imaging data, like X-rays, computed tomography (CT) scans, magnetic resonance images (MRIs), and histopathological slides, with textual information extracted from radiology reports, clinical notes, pathology descriptions, and structured entries in EHRs. By learning from these heterogeneous sources jointly, they capture complex relationships between the features of an image and clinical semantics, moving closer to what human experts do when interpreting and placing visual findings within a narrative and diagnostic context.

Fundamentally, vision-language models use bidirectional mappings between visual and textual modalities, which allow information to move both ways: from text to images, as in text-guided image retrieval or localization, and from images to text, as in automated report generation. For example, it creates a clinically coherent report of abnormalities, impressions, or differential diagnoses based on an image. Instead, it uses textual queries like "calcified thyroid nodule" or "ground-glass opacities in the right lower lobe" to retrieve pertinent images from large databases, allowing for extremely potent clinical search and decision support applications.

These models build upon the latest deep learning architectures, typically combining transformer-based language encoders such as BERT, GPT, or CLIP-style contrastive frameworks for textual understanding with CNNs or ViTs for feature extraction. Cross-modal reasoning and contextual awareness are made possible by the joint training, which aligns the textual and visual embeddings in a common latent space. On domain-specific datasets such as MIMIC-CXR, CheXpert, or

PadChest, vision-language models have proven to be highly effective in diagnostic interpretation. They frequently outperform unimodal systems and occasionally reach radiologist-level performance in specific tasks.

Beyond automated diagnosis, these systems are increasingly being explored for explainable AI and augmenting clinical workflows. Because they link visual evidence directly to descriptive language, they can generate human-interpretable explanations for their predictions, thus improving the transparency and trust in their predictions. What's more, they can enable educational tools, clinical triage, and longitudinal monitoring of diseases by enabling consistent interpretation across time and modalities. Taken altogether, vision-language models epitomize the trend toward context-rich, multimodal intelligence in healthcare, redrafting the contours within which clinical information is synthesized, communicated, and acted upon.

Medical vision-language architectures generally rely on separate image and text modality encoders, followed by fusion mechanisms that combine their representations. Image encoders often leverage convolutional neural networks or vision transformers pretrained on large-scale natural or medical image datasets. Text encoders rely on transformer-based language models such as Bidirectional Encoder Representations from Transformers (BERT) or its medical-domain variants. The cross-modal attention layers exchange information between the visual and linguistic representations in order to learn which textual concepts correspond to which image regions (Hao et al., 2025).

A typical example is the integration of chest radiographs with radiology reports. Large datasets of paired radiographs and reports can train models to produce correct textual descriptions of imaging findings, thus helping to decrease the workload for radiologists and increasing consistency in report generation. Conversely, such models can improve diagnostic accuracy by capturing relevant clinical context from text while interpreting images. This has been shown in studies where vision-language models outperform image-only models on a range of diagnostic tasks when textual clinical information is provided (Hao et al., 2025).

1.3.2 Image-Genomics Integration

Such integration of medical imaging phenotypes with genomic data represents a powerful multimodal approach called radiogenomics or imaging genomics. This paradigm considers that visible imaging features reflect underlying molecular and genetic alterations. Learning associations between imaging features and genomic profiles, for instance, can allow multimodal AI to predict molecular subtypes, genetic mutations, and treatment responses from noninvasive imaging with the potential to guide personalized therapy without the need for tissue biopsies.

Radiogenomics has shown particular promise in oncology, where tumor imaging characteristics correlate with genetic markers that influence prognosis and treatment selection. For example, in glioblastoma, certain magnetic resonance imaging features predict IDH1 mutation status, MGMT promoter methylation, and other molecular markers that inform treatment decisions. Such complex associations can be learnt by the multimodal AI models from paired imaging-genomics datasets and thus potentially enable noninvasive molecular profiling.

One of the main challenges faced during the development of architectures for the integration of images and genomics stems from the fact that the nature of these two types of data varies extremely. Imaging data is high-dimensional, spatially structured, and continuous-valued, while genomic data can be represented as either discrete sequences, expression levels, or mutation profiles with varying dimensionality and structure. The scheme for the successful integration of visual and genomic information must comprise the careful preprocessing, extraction, and fusion of features in such a manner as to consider the unique properties of each modality and their mutual interactions as well (Simon et al., 2025) (Fig. 1.2).

1.3.3 Multimodal Electronic Health Record Analysis

EHRs are inherently multimodal, involving structured data, such as diagnoses, procedures, laboratory values, and medications, unstructured text including clinical notes and discharge summaries, and increasingly images, genomics, and physiological signals. Indeed, comprehensive analysis of EHR data requires multimodal AI capable of jointly processing these diverse information types to support clinical decision-making, predict patient outcomes, and identify disease patterns.

Recent breakthroughs in EHR-based multimodal models are based on transformer architectures that encode temporal sequences of heterogeneous medical events. Each longitudinal record is represented by a sequence of multimodal tokens, including diagnostic codes, medication orders, laboratory results, and clinical note

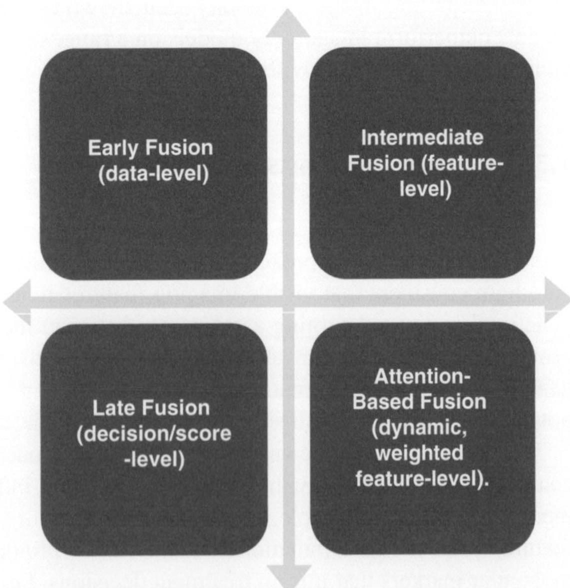

Fig. 1.2 Multimodal AI fusion strategies

embeddings. Self-attention mechanisms learn dependencies within and across modalities over time, capturing complex disease trajectories and treatment effects.

Applications of multimodal EHR analysis involve mortality prediction, readmission risk assessment, disease progression forecasting, and treatment response prediction. Multimodal models using different EHR data types have consistently been shown to outperform single-modality models. For example, models that combine structured codes with clinical note text achieve higher performance in predicting intensive care unit mortality compared to either data type alone, indicating that textual notes contain complementary information not captured in structured codes (Lee et al., 2023).

1.3.4 Pathology–Imaging–Clinical Integration

Digital pathology has become a rich source of high-resolution microscopic imaging data, providing cellular and subcellular detail that cannot be seen through radiological imaging. These whole-slide pathology images, integrated with radiological imaging and clinical data, form comprehensive multimodal representations at multiple biological scales, from molecular and cellular levels to tissue and organ levels. This multiscale integration opens perspectives for improved diagnostic accuracy, more robust prognostic assessment, and better treatment planning.

Computational pathology models typically use convolutional neural networks or vision transformers to analyze gigapixel whole-slide images, extracting features that reflect tissue architecture, cellular morphology, and spatial patterns. To integrate them with radiology imaging, alignment of information at various spatial scales and resolutions must be performed. Cross-scale attention mechanisms allow the model to relate microscopic pathology features to macroscopic imaging findings, while learning how cellular patterns appear as visible radiological signs.

Clinical applications of pathology–imaging–clinical multimodal AI include cancer diagnosis and prognostication. In breast cancer, integration of mammography, pathology images, and clinical factors improves prediction of lymph node metastasis and recurrence risk compared to any single data source. The multimodal approach captures complementary aspects of tumor biology: mammography reveals tumor size and morphology, pathology shows cellular grade and receptor status, and clinical data provides patient characteristics and treatment history (Peng et al., 2023).

1.4 Clinical Applications Across Medical Specialties

1.4.1 Oncology

The reasons for this are multifold: the complexity of cancer biology and the diversity of relevant data types have positioned oncology as a leading domain for multimodal AI applications. Multimodal approaches integrate medical imaging, pathology, genomics, clinical records, and treatment histories to enhance diagnosis, staging, treatment selection, and prognosis prediction. Heterogeneity in the type of cancer and the personalized nature of modern oncology has created a necessity for comprehensive multimodal analysis.

In lung cancer, AI multimodal systems combine computed tomography imaging with clinical risk factors, smoking history, and molecular biomarkers for improved early detection and decreased false positives in screening programs. It has been shown that the addition of clinical context to image-based analyses significantly enhances specificity without sacrificing sensitivity, with a potential decrease in unnecessary invasive follow-up procedures. Further, integration of imaging with genomic profiles allows the prediction of targetable mutations that guide the choice of precision therapies (Allon et al., 2021).

Radiotherapy planning is another oncology application in which multimodal AI is of use. Anatomical imaging for target volume and organs-at-risk delineation, functional imaging to detect metabolically active disease, and clinical factors all go into treatment planning. Multimodal AI can be used to automate organ segmentation, predict tumor response to radiation, and optimize treatment plans by considering multiple data sources simultaneously. This comprehensive approach has the potential to enhance efficacy and reduce toxicity.

1.4.2 Cardiology

ECG, echocardiography, cardiac magnetic resonance imaging, computed tomography angiography, laboratory biomarkers, and clinical risk factors are just a few of the data modalities that are intrinsically involved in the assessment of cardiovascular disease. By combining these various information sources, multimodal AI makes it possible for thorough cardiovascular risk stratification, disease diagnosis, and treatment optimization.

Electrocardiogram analysis has been revolutionized by deep learning, as different models have been able to use 12-lead recordings to diagnose arrhythmias, structural heart disease, and even potential negative events. The development of genuinely multimodal models with enhanced diagnostic and prognostic value is made possible by this integration of ECG data with imaging, biomarkers, and clinical history. For example, compared to a single modality, the combination of electrocardiogram features, echocardiographic measurements, and natriuretic peptide levels greatly improves heart failure diagnosis and risk stratification.

The assessment of coronary artery disease is a good example of the power of multimodal integration. Combining coronary computed tomography angiography with clinical risk scores, laboratory values, and patient characteristics allows superior predictions of obstructive coronary disease and future cardiovascular events compared to imaging alone. Quantitative imaging biomarkers, such as coronary calcium scores and plaque characteristics, can be combined by multimodal AI with nonimaging risk factors to provide comprehensive cardiovascular risk assessment for stratification of prevention strategies (Peng et al., 2023).

1.4.3 Neurology

Neurological applications of multimodal AI make use of the variety of data types relevant to brain health and disease, such as structural and functional magnetic resonance imaging, electroencephalography, cerebrospinal fluid biomarkers, neuropsychological assessments, and genetic information. The complexity of neurological disorders and the multifaceted nature of brain function create natural opportunities for multimodal approaches.

Multimodal AI has greatly advanced the diagnosis and prediction of Alzheimer's disease progression. The integration of structural brain imaging that reflects atrophy patterns, functional imaging showing metabolic changes, cerebrospinal fluid or blood biomarkers of pathological proteins, cognitive test scores, and genetic risk factors has led to comprehensive models that can predict the age of disease onset, rates of disease progression, and treatment responses. Such multimodal approaches outperform any one-modality approaches and much better reflect the multifactorial nature of neurodegenerative diseases.

Epilepsy management benefits from the multimodal integration of electroencephalography, magnetic resonance imaging, and clinical semiology. These multimodal AI will help in identifying the epileptogenic zone for surgical planning by relating seizure patterns on electroencephalography to both structural brain abnormalities visible on imaging and to clinical seizure characteristics. The said integration further improves localization accuracy and, as such, surgical outcomes compared to approaches depending on single data types alone. These multimodal models predict seizure likelihood by combining electroencephalography patterns with circadian rhythms, medication adherence data, and physiological signals (Sharma et al., 2021).

1.4.4 Emergency Medicine and Critical Care

In emergency and critical care situations, several data streams must be integrated as fast as possible to make choices with time pressure in conditions of uncertainty. Such a multimodal AI system can synthesize vital signs, laboratory results, imaging findings, clinical notes, and prior medical history toward supporting triage decisions, diagnosis, and the prioritization of treatments. The high-acuity, data-rich environment of critical care creates compelling use cases for multimodal approaches.

Sepsis prediction and management are the prime examples of multimodal AI in critical care. Early identification of sepsis requires the integration of the trends of vital signs, laboratory values demonstrating infection, organ dysfunction, clinical examination findings, and imaging. The many different types of multimodal models, continuously analyzing electronic health records, have shown early warning capabilities, informing clinicians about impending sepsis risk hours before conventional recognition may allow for earlier intervention and improved outcomes.

Trauma assessment at emergency departments involves rapid synthesis of mechanism of injury, physical examination findings, vital signs, bedside ultrasound, and radiological imaging. Multimodal AI can assist with injury severity scoring, predicting the need for specific interventions like surgery or blood transfusion, and identifying injuries that might be missed on initial evaluation. The integration of diverse information available during trauma resuscitation through these systems supports more comprehensive and timely assessment of the patient (Akramifard et al., 2021).

1.5 Technical Challenges and Solutions

1.5.1 Data Heterogeneity and Integration

Healthcare data is characterized by extreme heterogeneity along multiple dimensions and can pose significant integration challenges for multimodal AI. There are differences in modality dimensionality, temporal resolution, spatial scale, data type (continuous, categorical, sequential), and quality. For example, medical images contain millions of pixels; laboratory values are low-dimensional scalar measurements. Clinical notes are pieces of unstructured text of variable length and format. Physiological signals are time-series data with defined temporal characteristics.

Effective integration of multimodality requires preprocessing pipelines specific to the characteristics of each modality. Image preprocessing involves normalization, removal of artifacts, and augmentation in order to make a model robust. Text preprocessing may include tokenization, extraction of medical terms, and potentially embeddings from medical language models. Time-series data may require resampling, filtering, and feature extraction. Structured data benefits from handling missing values, outlier detection, and appropriate encoding of categorical variables.

It has also highlighted further challenges in the alignment of multimodal data in time and space. Different data types can be acquired at different times with different temporal resolutions. Spatial registration is needed when combining imaging modalities, such as computed tomography and positron emission tomography. Multimodal AI architectures must therefore consider these alignment issues through appropriate preprocessing or model designs that learn alignment implicitly during training (Caruso et al., 2022).

1.5.2 Limited Availability of Labeled Multimodal Datasets

Training effective multimodal AI models relies on large datasets with complete information across all modalities and high-quality labels for supervised learning. In healthcare, however, such completely multimodal datasets are extremely rare due to practical and privacy constraints. Often, different types of data are acquired at different times or institutions. Obtaining expert labels in several modalities is resource-intensive. Because of the privacy regulations, data sharing is limited, resulting in the fragmentation of multimodal data across institutions.

Limited labeled data is partially addressed by self-supervised learning approaches, which learn representations from unlabeled multimodal datasets. In particular, contrastive learning methods can learn to align representations across modalities with no explicit task labels by exploiting natural correspondences such as between radiological images and their reports. Large-scale pretraining on unlabeled multimodal datasets followed by fine-tuning on smaller labeled datasets has proved effective for various medical AI tasks.

Federated learning allows the training of multimodal models over multiple institutions without having sensitive patient data centralized. Each institution performs the local model training with its data, while sharing model parameters or gradients to find a global model. Therefore, it allows increasing the effective size of the training data by keeping privacy constraints. Federated multimodal learning is also facing extra challenges due to institutional heterogeneity of collection protocols and equipment; these call for robustness in model architectures and training strategies (Chen et al., 2024).

1.5.3 Model Interpretability and Clinical Trust

Clinical adoption of AI systems demands interpretability: it must be possible for clinicians to understand model reasoning and likely sources of errors. Multimodal AI compounds the challenges in interpretability because model predictions may depend on complex interactions across diverse data types. Whatever the predictive accuracy, black-box models that cannot explain their reasoning face huge barriers to clinical trust and regulatory approval.

Attention mechanisms, which indicate the input region or modality most influential in a prediction, provide crucial interpretability to multimodal models. By visualizing attention weights, one can see which regions in the image the model is focusing on, which phrases in the clinical note contribute to diagnosis, or which modality drives a particular prediction. However, attention itself may not completely explain the model's reasoning, especially for deep networks with multiple layers of attention, and possibly complex architectures.

Multimodal explanation techniques create human-interpretable justifications for AI predictions: gradient-based methods, such as Grad-CAM, highlight salient image regions; textual explanations describe model reasoning in natural language; and counterfactual explanations identify changes to inputs that would have changed the predictions, thereby helping clinicians understand decision boundaries. Developing explanation techniques that work across modalities remains a very active research area, critical to clinical deployment (Cui et al., 2022).

1.5.4 Computational Requirements and Scalability

Processing multiple types of high-dimensional data simultaneously, the computational requirements for multimodal AI models are, however, extremely high.

Medical imaging alone requires a lot of computations, especially in three-dimensional imaging or gigapixel pathology slides. This limits the accessibility for many health institutions since the training of large multimodal models might take days or weeks on powerful computing clusters (Tacelli et al., 2025).

These techniques for model compression reduce computational requirements while maintaining performance. Knowledge distillation trains smaller student models to mimic larger teacher models, achieving comparable accuracy with reduced parameters and computation. Pruning removes less important model parameters or channels. Quantization reduces numerical precision of model weights and activations. These techniques allow running multimodal models on resource-constrained platforms such as mobile systems or embedded systems.

Cloud AI platforms provide scalable computational resources for multimodal healthcare applications without requiring local infrastructure investments. Cloud services provide access to a range of specialized hardware accelerators, distributed training capabilities, and managed AI frameworks. However, cloud deployment increases data privacy vulnerabilities, which are critical in medical information. Hybrid approaches—preprocessing locally and performing model inference on the cloud, or edge computing architectures—leverage computational scalability with adequate privacy protection. Table 1.2 summarizes these fusion strategies, listing their advantages, disadvantages, and clinical applications.

1.6 Ethical, Legal, and Regulatory Considerations

1.6.1 Privacy and Data Protection

Because medical data is sensitive and any unauthorized disclosure could have major repercussions, privacy of healthcare data is a major concern. Because integrating various data sources results in more thorough patient profiles and a higher risk of re-identification, multimodal AI exacerbates privacy concerns. Patients can be uniquely identified across modalities even when individual modalities are de-identified.

Consent, access controls, and breach notification are just a few of the limitations on handling sensitive data in healthcare that are imposed by regulatory frameworks like the General Data Protection Regulation (GDPR) in Europe and the Health Insurance Portability and Accountability Act (HIPAA) in the United States. It is anticipated that such regulations will be taken into account during the entire life cycle of a multimodal AI system, from data collection and storage to model training and deployment. While still permitting the development of AI, privacy-preserving strategies such as secure multiparty computation and differential privacy offer improved protection options.

Frameworks for data governance establish guidelines and protocols for the conscientious handling of multimodal data. Statements about data ownership, consent procedures, quality assurance, access controls, retention guidelines, and audit trails ought to be included in the framework. While patients and clinicians develop trust,

Table 1.2 Multimodal AI fusion strategies and their applications

Fusion strategy	Description	Advantages	Disadvantages	Clinical examples
Early fusion	Concatenates features from different modalities at input level before joint processing	Simple architecture, learns interactions from raw data	Sensitive to missing modalities, assumes similar importance	Combining vital signs and lab values for sepsis prediction
Late fusion	Processes each modality independently through specialized networks, combines at output stage	Modality-specific optimization, robust to missing data	Limited cross-modal learning, ignores early interactions	Ensemble of image and text models for diagnosis
Intermediate fusion	Exchanges information between modality streams at multiple intermediate layers	Balances early and late fusion benefits, flexible architecture	Complex design, computationally intensive	Radiogenomics for tumor characterization
Attention-based fusion	Dynamically weights modality contributions based on relevance to specific tasks	Adaptive, interpretable, handles variable importance	Requires large datasets, computationally demanding	Vision-language models for radiology report generation

ethical multimodal AI development is made possible by clear governance. Informed consent is supported by data usage transparency and AI system capabilities, which also allay worries about algorithmic decision-making in the medical field.

1.6.2 Bias and Health Equity

These biases can be perpetuated or amplified in AI systems, further exacerbating healthcare disparities. Multimodal AI faces unique challenges in bias, given the presence of biases within individual modalities or in associations between modalities. Underrepresentation of demographic groups in training data leads to poor performance for those populations. AI systems can learn biased clinical practices represented in historical data and reinforce these practices.

If the training datasets are not diverse in terms of age, sex, race, ethnicity, or socioeconomic status, this will also show up as demographic bias. Due to trends in healthcare access, some populations may be over-represented in medical imaging datasets. The majority of genomic datasets, until recently, were centered on European ancestry, which restricts the studies' ability to be applied to a variety of populations. Biases are introduced into natural language processing components by the differences in clinical note language between providers and institutions. Evaluating model performance across pertinent demographic subgroups and modalities is necessary for a thorough assessment of bias.

Mitigating biases in multimodal AI requires intentional efforts throughout system development: diverse training datasets that represent target patient populations, fairness constraints incorporated during model training to ensure equitable performance across groups, regular bias audits to assess deployed systems for disparate impacts, clinical validation in diverse populations and settings, and transparency about model limitations and appropriate use cases helps prevent inappropriate deployment that could harm underrepresented groups (D'Souza et al., 2024).

1.6.3 Regulatory Pathways and Clinical Validation

Most jurisdictions regulate medical AI systems, including multimodal applications, as medical devices and require demonstration of their safety and effectiveness before clinical deployment. Regulatory bodies such as the FDA and the European Medicines Agency have designed frameworks for medical devices based on AI, considering some unique challenges that software may face because it could learn and evolve over time.

Clinical validation of multimodal AI involves several rigorous protocols for evaluating performance, safety, and clinical utility. Retrospective validation based on historical data gives initial evidence, but there are major problems with how representative it is in the real world. Prospective validation in routine clinical practice better captures practical impact but requires careful study design and protection of the patients. Randomized controlled trials comparing AI-augmented versus standard care provide the highest-quality evidence for clinical benefit but are resource-intensive and time-consuming.

Continuous monitoring of the deployed multimodal AI systems is necessary because performance may degrade over time due to data drift, changing clinical practices, or equipment upgrades. The postmarket surveillance mechanisms should track real-world performance, adverse events, and unintended consequences. There is an increasing recognition within regulatory frameworks for the requirement of adaptive pathways that allow AI systems to be updated with accumulating real-world evidence while ensuring proper oversight for safety (Fan et al., 2024).

1.7 Implementation Strategies and Clinical Integration

1.7.1 Clinical Workflow Integration

The incorporation of multimodal AI into clinical practice will require thoughtful integration with existing clinical workflows. AI systems should enhance and not disrupt clinical practice by delivering value at appropriate decision points and without excessive burden. Understanding the current workflow, pain points, and information needs is a crucial activity in the design of AI tools that clinicians would actually use.

User interface design plays a critical role in clinical utility and adoption. The interfaces should represent AI insights in a clear and concise way, outlining the actionable information without overwhelming the user with technical details. The visualizations should be intuitive, drawing on familiar clinical representations where possible. Interactive visualizations that allow clinicians to explore the AI reasoning or adjust parameters increase trust and utility. Designs are mobile-friendly, enabling use at point of care. Development is supported by usability testing with representative clinical users to ensure interfaces meet practical needs.

Alert fatigue stands as one of the greatest clinical AI adoption barriers. Systems that issue too many alerts (especially false positives) lead to clinicians becoming conditioned to ignore warnings, defeating safety. Multimodal AI systems should be tuned to only alert when predictions are highly confident and actionable. It is also a good practice to present the predictions as a continuous score or by risk category (e.g., high, medium, low) instead of binary alerts to give clinicians leeway in interpretation. Integrating such technologies into current clinical decision support infrastructure reduces alert load through notification consolidation (Gao et al., 2022).

1.7.2 Training and Change Management

Clinical staff need training in the effective use of multimodal AI tools and the understanding of their capabilities and limitations. Training should cover the technical functionality, appropriate use cases, interpretation of outputs, and recognition of possible errors. Hands-on practice with realistic scenarios builds confidence and competence. Ongoing education accommodates system updates and emerging evidence about AI performance.

Change management strategies help the organization to facilitate adoption of the multimodal AI. Engaging clinical champions who enthusiastically support and mentor colleagues in adopting AI tools can expedite adoption. Resistance to change emanates from concerns regarding AI taking the place of clinicians, increasing workload, or causing professional autonomy compromise. Being able to identify how AI is a tool that augments, rather than replaces, clinical expertise helps build acceptance. Showing key benefits measurable outcomes or efficiency fosters further adoption.

It requires interdisciplinary collaboration between clinicians, data scientists, informaticians, and administrators to enact successfully. Clinicians provide domain expertise by identifying valuable use cases and evaluating clinical validity. Data scientists create the models and develop technical infrastructure. Informaticians ensure appropriate data integration and embedding of workflows. Organizational, financial, and regulatory considerations come under the purview of the administrators. Communication across disciplines helps avoid misalignment; as noted, all perspectives need to inform implementation (Ghafoori et al., 2023).

1.7.3 Quality Assurance and Performance Monitoring

Quality assurance processes ensure that the performance of multimodal AI systems remains acceptable over time. This involves systematic monitoring of key performance metrics, such as accuracy, sensitivity, specificity, and positive predictive value during clinical use. Comparison of AI performance to clinical benchmarks or reference standards then serves to identify performance degradation requiring intervention.

Monitoring performance needs to be considered across many dimensions beyond standard metrics of accuracy. Clinical utility measures whether AI improves patient outcomes, workflow efficiency, or resource utilization in any way. User satisfaction surveys capture clinician and patient perspectives on AI tools. Safety monitoring tracks adverse events that may be related to AI errors or inappropriate reliance on AI. Equity assessments ensure performance remains fair across patient populations.

Continuous improvement processes utilize performance data in order to refine the performance of a multimodal AI system. Establishing modes of failure, in which AI performance is poor, drives selective improvements in either models or training data. The feedback from users points toward usability issues and feature requests. The updating of models with newer data keeps up the performance as clinical practices and patient populations evolve. However, the update of models needs validation and regulatory consideration a process of striking a balance between continuous improvement with the assurance of stability and safety (Hanley et al., 2017).

1.8 Future Directions and Emerging Opportunities

1.8.1 Foundation Models for Healthcare

Large-scale models that are pretrained on diverse data and can adapt to multiple downstream tasks by fine-tuning form a promising paradigm for multimodal healthcare AI. Medical foundation models pretrained on vast multimodal datasets provide general medical knowledge and multimodal reasoning capabilities, with the potential to be specialized for specific applications using limited task-specific data.

Compared to models of the general domain, developing medical foundation models presents certain challenges. First, health data is fragmented across institutions and cannot easily be pooled in bulk because of privacy constraints. Second, medical data often requires specialized preprocessing and quality control. Third, domain expertise is needed when identifying appropriate pretraining objectives that capture clinically relevant patterns. Despite the above difficulties, early medical foundation models have shown impressive capabilities in learning from multimodal pretraining.

Few-shot and zero-shot learning capabilities of foundation models could dramatically reduce data requirements for developing clinical AI applications. Instead of requiring thousands of labeled examples for every new task, a pretrained foundation model may learn new tasks from handfuls of examples or even task descriptions alone. This capability would reduce the development time of AI tools for rare diseases, emerging conditions, and specialized applications where large datasets are unavailable (Haque et al., 2023).

1.8.2 Integration of Real-World Evidence and Patient-Generated Data

Expanding the capabilities of multimodal AI beyond traditional clinical data to include real-world evidence and patient-generated data promises far more comprehensive health monitoring and truly personalized care. Wearables, smartphone sensors, patient-reported outcomes, social determinants of health, environmental exposures, and behavioral data provide continuous longitudinal information that complements episodic clinical encounters.

Integration of patient-generated data into clinical data provides several opportunities: the early detection of diseases, personalized risk prediction, and treatment monitoring. As a good example, wearable cardiovascular sensor data combined with electronic health records enable continuous heart failure monitoring and the early detection of decompensation. Integration of patient-reported symptoms and clinical assessments enhances patient-centered outcome measurement and treatment response evaluation.

Challenges in integrating patient-generated data include the variability of data quality, missing data patterns, and heterogeneity in measurement devices and protocols. Multimodal AI architectures must therefore be robust to such challenges. With continuous monitoring data, the considerations of privacy are heightened. Indeed, this requires trust, transparency, and perceived value by patients in their engagement and willingness to share data. Harnessing patient-generated data requires both technical solutions and, importantly, patient-centered design and governance (Huang et al., 2020).

1.8.3 Artificial General Intelligence in Medicine

Artificial general intelligence is an aspirational, long-term goal of AI that enables human-level reasoning across diverse domains. Medical AGI systems would have deep medical knowledge covering all specialties, integrate any data types available, reason over complex clinical scenarios, and communicate effectively with both patients and clinicians. While current multimodal AI systems have narrow intelligence for specific tasks, progress toward more general medical AI also continues.

Recent large language models are increasingly demonstrating general capabilities, including medical reasoning, question answering, and clinical decision support across diverse conditions. Multimodal extensions of these models that can also interpret images, genomic data, and other medical modalities bring AGI-level capabilities closer to reality. However, current systems still lack robust reasoning, common sense understanding, and adaptability to truly novel situations that characterize human intelligence.

Medical AGI holds great promise but comes with major questions on the role of human clinicians, accountability regarding AI decision-making, and societal implications related to granting machines medical judgment. Indeed, these are fundamental questions that thoughtful development of increasingly capable AI systems will need to come to terms with, ensuring that AI development is aligned with human values and serves the interests of both patients and society as a whole (Huang et al., 2020).

1.8.4 Explainable and Trustworthy AI

Reliability, robustness, safety, equity, and accountability are all aspects of trustworthy AI that go beyond explainability. AI systems for multimodal healthcare must function consistently in a range of clinical settings and patient demographics. They must be resilient to distributional changes, missing modalities, and problems with data quality. Thorough validation and monitoring are necessary for safety assurance. To be fair, all demographic groups must perform well. Structures for accountability must clarify who is responsible when AI causes unfavorable results (Watanabe et al., 2022).

This is significant because multimodal AI systems' explainability and reliability are becoming more and more crucial as they become more powerful and widespread in the medical field. The creation of explanation strategies that provide clinically significant insights into intricate multimodal model reasoning is required for future studies. Model confidence and uncertainty, as well as possible failure modes, must be included in explanations, along with the types of data and particular characteristics that influence predictions.

Emerging regulatory and technical frameworks guide the responsible development and deployment of trustworthy AI. Principles-based approaches articulate high-level values, such as transparency, fairness, and accountability, while technical standards detail specific requirements for documentation, testing, and monitoring. Certification schemes offer an independent assessment of AI systems against trustworthiness criteria. Adopting such frameworks supports the integration of multimodal AI into healthcare in a way that is both ethical and effective.

Table 1.3 summarizes the key categories of challenge, their manifestations, impact, solution status, and research directions toward the future.

1.9 Conclusion

With the potential to revolutionize how we diagnose illnesses, forecast their prognoses, tailor treatments, and provide care, multimodal AI is bringing about a revolution in the healthcare industry. Multimodal AI systems create more thorough representations of health and disease than can be created from any one of these

Table 1.3 Key challenges in multimodal healthcare AI and proposed solutions

Challenge category	Specific issues	Impact on development/ deployment	Current solutions	Future directions
Data heterogeneity	Variable dimensionality, temporal resolution, spatial scale, data types	Difficult integration, requires specialized preprocessing	Modality-specific preprocessing pipelines, learned alignment	Universal encoders, self-supervised alignment
Limited labeled data	Scarcity of complete multimodal datasets, expensive expert labeling	Restricted model training, generalization issues	Self-supervised learning, contrastive pretraining, transfer learning	Foundation models, few-shot learning
Privacy and security	Re-identification risk from multimodal integration, regulatory compliance	Data sharing barriers, institutional fragmentation	Federated learning, differential privacy, secure computation	Privacy-preserving multimodal architectures
Model interpretability	Complex cross-modal interactions, black-box predictions	Clinical mistrust, regulatory barriers	Attention visualization, gradient-based methods, counterfactual explanations	Multimodal explanation frameworks, causal reasoning
Computational requirements	High-dimensional data, large model parameters, training time	Limited accessibility, resource constraints	Model compression, knowledge distillation, cloud platforms	Efficient architectures, edge computing
Bias and fairness	Demographic underrepresentation, biased training data, disparate performance	Health equity concerns, potential harm to underrepresented groups	Diverse datasets, fairness constraints, bias audits	Algorithmic fairness frameworks, equitable validation
Clinical integration	Workflow disruption, alert fatigue, change resistance	Poor adoption, limited real-world impact	User-centered design, clinical champion engagement, training programs	Seamless workflow integration, adaptive interfaces
Regulatory approval	Evolving frameworks, validation requirements, post-market surveillance	Delayed deployment, compliance burden	Prospective validation, continuous monitoring, adaptive pathways	Standardized evaluation protocols, risk-based regulation

sources alone by combining various data modalities, including imaging, genomics, electronic health records, pathology, physiological signals, and patient-generated data. The integrative reasoning that distinguishes expert clinical decision-making is paralleled and possibly expanded by this holistic approach.

Over the past 10 years, these technological foundations of multimodal AI have advanced considerably. In particular, powerful deep learning architectures for learning joint representations of heterogeneous data types are now available thanks to transformer models with cross-modal attention mechanisms. The lack of fully labeled medical data is partially addressed by contrastive learning and self-supervised techniques, which allow efficient pretraining on sizable unlabeled multimodal datasets. Furthermore, large-scale multimodal model development is now possible outside of prestigious research institutions thanks to hardware acceleration and cloud computing infrastructure.

Multimodal AI has clinical applications in almost every area of medicine, with numerous areas showing distinct advantages. The integration of imaging, pathology, genomics, and clinical data improves prognosis estimation, therapy selection, staging, and diagnosis in oncology. Cardiovascular applications improve disease detection and risk stratification by combining imaging, biomarkers, risk factors, and electrocardiography. Multiple brain imaging modalities, biomarkers, and clinical evaluations are used in neurological applications to diagnose diseases like Alzheimer's disease earlier and more precisely. Applications for critical care and emergencies combine real-time multimodal data streams to facilitate snap decisions. In a variety of applications, multimodal approaches consistently outperform single-modality approaches.

However, there are important clinical, ethical, technical, and regulatory issues that must be resolved before multimodal AI in healthcare can reach its full potential. The data's heterogeneity makes it challenging to integrate modalities with disparate characteristics. Model development is hampered by the scarcity of complete, labeled multimodal datasets. Accessibility issues are brought up by the computational demands of large multimodal models. Although it is still difficult, model interpretability is crucial for both regulatory approval and clinical trust. To handle the increased re-identification risks resulting from multimodal data integration, privacy protection needs to be reinforced. To guarantee fair performance across a range of demographics, bias and fairness issues need close attention. In order to maintain safety and efficacy while accommodating the special features of multimodal AI, regulatory pathways must change.

Careful workflow embedding, user-friendly interfaces, suitable training, change management, and strong quality assurance are all necessary for successful clinical integration. By offering actionable insights at the right decision points without causing alert fatigue, multimodal AI systems should support clinical practice rather than interfere with it. At each stage of the development and implementation process, interdisciplinary cooperation between clinicians, data scientists, informaticians, and administrators is necessary. As clinical practices change, the system's quality and applicability must be maintained through ongoing performance monitoring and improvement procedures.

Even though each of these research avenues has made significant recent strides, several new avenues hold promise for further development of multimodal AI in healthcare. General medical reasoning could be provided by foundation models that have been pretrained on massive multimodal medical datasets. These models could then be tailored to specific applications using small amounts of task-specific data. Beyond sporadic clinical encounters, continuous health monitoring and individualized care are made possible by the integration of real-world evidence and patient-generated data from wearables and smartphones. Although these capabilities raise serious concerns about the future roles of human clinicians and the proper governance of increasingly autonomous AI systems, advancements toward more general artificial intelligence with human-level medical reasoning across diverse domains continue.

Explainability, reliability, robustness, safety, fairness, and accountability are all parts of trustworthy AI frameworks that provide necessary guardrails for the responsible deployment of multimodal AI. For multimodal AI to serve patient and societal interests while respecting basic values such as privacy, equity, and human dignity, technical standards, regulatory requirements, and ethical principles will have to keep pace with expanding technological capabilities.

The emergence of multimodal AI in healthcare represents a paradigm shift in how human health and illness are conceptualized and addressed, going beyond simple technological advancements. Multimodal AI reveals connections and patterns that are not visible to single-modality analysis or human cognition alone by combining data from various modalities, scales, and timepoints. Early disease detection, more accurate diagnosis, improved outcome prediction, and more individualized treatment are all possibilities presented by this all-encompassing viewpoint, which could ultimately lead to better patient outcomes and population health.

But technology is not a fate in and of itself. The wisdom with which we create, verify, control, and implement these potent instruments will determine the worth of multimodal AI. The realization of multimodal AI's transformative potential will be ensured by keeping a close eye on patient benefit, health equity, and clinical utility throughout the research and development phase. Responsible innovation that is in line with societal values is encouraged by the continuous discussion of appropriate AI development and use among a wide range of stakeholders, including patients, clinicians, researchers, ethicists, regulators, and policymakers.

The healthcare industry must continue to be both hopeful about AI's potential and cautious about its risks as it continues its swift transition from research labs to clinical settings. Unprecedented opportunities to enhance human health presented by this new frontier of multimodal AI in healthcare must be realized through a persistent dedication to patient-centered design, clinical validation, ethical rigor, and technical excellence. Multimodal AI has the potential to be a potent ally in the ongoing human endeavor to prevent illness, restore health, and lessen suffering if it is handled carefully.

Similar to the invention of antibiotics, vaccines, and medical imaging, the convergence of AI with multimodal medical data represents a turning point in medical history. Multimodal AI will transform clinical practice, medical education, and our very ideas of health and illness, much like these previous revolutions did. Although the journey is just getting started, it is already on a clear course: multimodal AI is a catalyst for rethinking healthcare rather than a technological advancement. The emergence of this new field challenges us to consider not just what AI can accomplish for medicine, but also what kind of medicine we hope to develop in collaboration with AI.

References

Akramifard, H., Balafar, M. A., Razavi, S. N., & Ramli, A. R. (2021). Early detection of Alzheimer's disease based on clinical trials, three-dimensional imaging data, and personal information using autoencoders. *Journal of Medical Signals and Sensors, 11*(2), 120–130. https://doi.org/10.4103/jmss.JMSS_11_20

Allon, R., Aronov, M., Belkin, M., Maor, E., Shechter, M., & Fabian, I. D. (2021). Retinal microvascular signs as screening and prognostic factors for cardiac disease: A systematic review of current evidence. *The American Journal of Medicine, 134*(1), 36–47.e7. https://doi.org/10.1016/j.amjmed.2020.07.013

Caruso, C. M., et al. (2022). A multimodal ensemble driven by multiobjective optimisation to predict overall survival in non-small-cell lung cancer. *Journal of Imaging, 8*(11), 298. https://doi.org/10.3390/jimaging8110298

Chen, Z., et al. (2024). Predicting gastric cancer response to anti-HER2 therapy or anti-HER2 combined immunotherapy based on multi-modal data. *Signal Transduction and Targeted Therapy, 9*(1), 222. https://doi.org/10.1038/s41392-024-01932-y

Cui, C., et al. (2022). Multi-modal learning with missing data for cancer diagnosis using histopathological and genomic data. *Proceedings of SPIE The International Society for Optical Engineering, 12033*, 120331D. https://doi.org/10.1117/12.2612318

D'Souza, N. S., et al. (2024). Fusing modalities by multiplexed graph neural networks for outcome prediction from medical data and beyond. *Medical Image Analysis, 93*, 103064. https://doi.org/10.1016/j.media.2023.103064

Fan, D., et al. (2024). Multimodal ischemic stroke recurrence prediction model based on the capsule neural network and support vector machine. *Medicine (Baltimore), 103*(35), e39217. https://doi.org/10.1097/MD.0000000000039217

Gao, R., et al. (2022). Reducing uncertainty in cancer risk estimation for patients with indeterminate pulmonary nodules using an integrated deep learning model. *Computers in Biology and Medicine, 150*, 106113. https://doi.org/10.1016/j.compbiomed.2022.106113

Ghafoori, M., et al. (2023). Predicting survival of Iranian COVID-19 patients infected by various variants including omicron from CT Scan images and clinical data using deep neural networks. *Heliyon, 9*(11), e21965. https://doi.org/10.1016/j.heliyon.2023.e21965

Hanley, D., et al. (2017). Emergency department triage of traumatic head injury using a brain electrical activity biomarker: A multisite prospective observational validation trial. *Academic Emergency Medicine, 24*(5), 617–627. https://doi.org/10.1111/acem.13175

Hao, Y., et al. (2025). Multimodal integration in health care: Development with applications in disease management. *Journal of Medical Internet Research, 27*, e76557. https://doi.org/10.2196/76557

Haque, M. I. U., Mukherjee, D., Stopka, S. A., Agar, N. Y. R., Hinkle, J., & Ovchinnikova, O. S. (2023). Deep learning on multimodal chemical and whole slide imaging data for predicting prostate cancer directly from tissue images. *Journal of the American Society for Mass Spectrometry, 34*(2), 227–235. https://doi.org/10.1021/jasms.2c00254

Hirani, R., et al. (2024). Artificial intelligence and healthcare: A journey through history, present innovations, and future possibilities. *Life (Basel), 14*(5), 557. https://doi.org/10.3390/life14050557

Huang, S.-C., Pareek, A., Zamanian, R., Banerjee, I., & Lungren, M. P. (2020). Multimodal fusion with deep neural networks for leveraging CT imaging and electronic health record: A case-study in pulmonary embolism detection. *Scientific Reports, 10*(1), 22147. https://doi.org/10.1038/s41598-020-78888-w

Lee, Y. C., et al. (2023). Multimodal deep learning of fundus abnormalities and traditional risk factors for cardiovascular risk prediction. *Npj Digital Medicine, 6*(1), 14. https://doi.org/10.1038/s41746-023-00748-4

Massimi, D., et al. (2025). Large language model for interpreting the Paris classification of colorectal polyps. *Endoscopy International Open, 13*, a27030209. https://doi.org/10.1055/a-2703-0209

Peng, Z., et al. (2023). Development and evaluation of multimodal AI for diagnosis and triage of ophthalmic diseases using ChatGPT and anterior segment images: Protocol for a two-stage cross-sectional study. *Frontiers in Artificial Intelligence, 6*, 1323924. https://doi.org/10.3389/frai.2023.1323924

Schouten, D., et al. (2025). Navigating the landscape of multimodal AI in medicine: A scoping review on technical challenges and clinical applications. *Medical Image Analysis, 105*, 103621. https://doi.org/10.1016/j.media.2025.103621

Sharma, D., Purushotham, S., & Reddy, C. K. (2021). MedFuseNet: An attention-based multimodal deep learning model for visual question answering in the medical domain. *Scientific Reports, 11*(1), 19826. https://doi.org/10.1038/s41598-021-98390-1

Simon, B. D., Ozyoruk, K. B., Gelikman, D. G., Harmon, S. A., & Türkbey, B. (2025). The future of multimodal artificial intelligence models for integrating imaging and clinical metadata: A narrative review. *Diagnostic and Interventional Radiology, 31*(4), 303–312. https://doi.org/10.4274/dir.2024.242631

Tacelli, M., Lauri, G., Tabacelia, D., Tieranu, C. G., Arcidiacono, P. G., & Săftoiu, A. (2025). Integrating artificial intelligence with endoscopic ultrasound in the early detection of biliopancreatic lesions: Current advances and future prospects. *Best Practice & Research. Clinical Gastroenterology, 74*, 101975. https://doi.org/10.1016/j.bpg.2025.101975

Watanabe, A., Ketabi, S., Namdar, K., & Khalvati, F. (2022). Improving disease classification performance and explainability of deep learning models in radiology with heatmap generators. *Frontiers in Radiology, 2*, 991683. https://doi.org/10.3389/fradi.2022.991683

Demography and Population Intelligence in Multimodal AI for Healthcare

2

U. Venkatesh, Margubur Rahaman, and Mamta Mittal

2.1 Introduction

Multimodal artificial intelligence (AI) underlines a paradigm shift both in health decision-making and planning. It includes diagnostic image, laboratory report, verbal clinical narratives, genomics, physiological aspects, and patient data in an integrated modeling framework. On another side, traditional statistical models in health decision-making and planning have often remained confined to only one mode. For example, radiographic images or tabulation of electronic health records talk about only single aspects. Whereas multimodal systems draw clinical reasoning from multiple datasets (Soenksen et al., 2022).

Contemporary research in healthcare puts increasing emphasis on demography for shaping disease patterns, choice, and demand for healthcare. By using AI, systematic cross-analyses can be conducted and models can be cross-validated using demographic data to strengthen the public health system. Demography is a scientific study that statistically analyzes age, sex, ethnicity, socioeconomic status, fertility, mortality, and migration of a population. Population intelligence extends this by leveraging large-scale analytics of demography to understand morbidity trends, disparities, and forecast healthcare needs (Lee et al., 2024). Integrating these dimensions into multimodal AI systems allows for reliable, cross-validated real-time

U. Venkatesh (✉) · M. Rahaman
Department of Community & Family Medicine, All India Institute of Medical Sciences, Gorakhpur, Uttar Pradesh, India

M. Mittal
Department of Data Analytics & Data Science, Delhi Skill and Entrepreneurship University, New Delhi, India

U. Venkatesh et al. (eds.), *Multimodal AI in Healthcare*,
https://doi.org/10.1007/978-981-95-9027-8_2

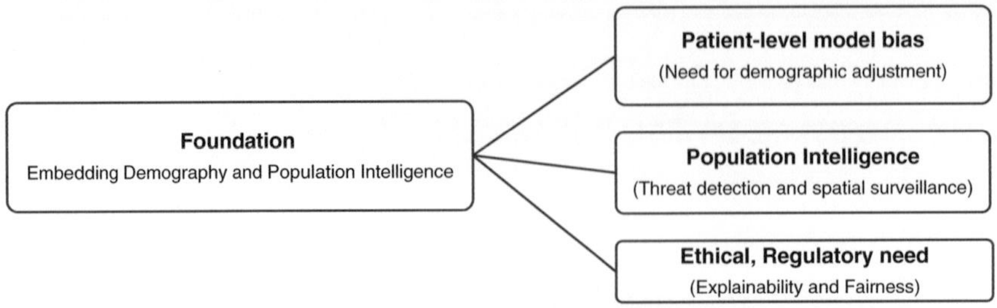

Fig. 2.1 Foundation for demography and population intelligence in multimodal AI

predictions and recommendations by considering diversity within a population. In particular, miscellaneous data-driven development of predictive models in multidomain AI assists evidence-based decision-making and strategic planning in clinical and public health domains. Inclusion of demography and population intelligence within multimodal AI is threefold (Fig. 2.1). First, patient-level models that are trained without adjusting demographic context may make biased estimations. Hence, integration of population-specific prevalence and incidence and distribution of risk factors will enable models to adjust for confounding and stratification of demographics both at training and inference. Second, population intelligence may enable the detection of emerging public health threats such as spatial epidemiological transitions by continuous monitoring of spatiotemporal patterns in multimodal networks. Third, ethical rules and regulatory frameworks increasingly require transparency and fairness of AI-driven decisions. Demographic explainability enhances clinician trust in models and helps adhere to guidelines set by recognized institutions (Colacci et al., 2025).

With a growing recognition of the critical role played by demography and population intelligence in shaping data-driven healthcare, this chapter aims to take a step further: carving out an analytically incisive and theoretically illuminated viewpoint concerning their integrated functioning within multimodal AI (Colacci et al., 2025; Kruk et al., 2024; Lee et al., 2024; Shaban-Nejad et al., 2018; Soenksen et al., 2022). This chapter describes the importance of demography, statistics, and multimodal analytics in healthcare decision-making. The two key points of the present chapter are, first, conceptual framework that links population science and AI-based health informatics. Second, the role of demographic indicators on AI models' accuracy.

2.2 Theoretical Foundations

2.2.1 Conceptualizing Demography in the Age of AI

The link between demography and AI introduces a characteristic shift in understanding and analyzing demographic and epidemiological transitions with associated health demands (Fig. 2.2). In simple words, modern-day demography extends

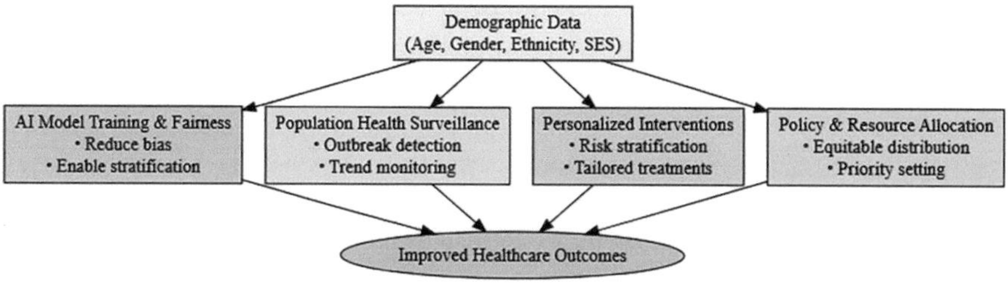

Fig. 2.2 AI-enhanced healthcare decision-making model using demographic data

from traditional statistics to a multimodel analytical approach. Additionally, AI-driven statistical analyses will make real-time population specialist care and analytical modeling easier. The shift marks credit that demographic indicators are not just descriptive but dynamic predictors of health status, demand and use of health system and resource provision (Duffy et al., 2022).

Application of AI in demography enhances traditional demographic indicators with digital footprints, behavioral patterns, and real-time health data streams. The Global Strategy on Digital Health 2020–2025 states that digital health results must talk about digital factors of health, including access to technology, digital literacy, and connectivity (Global Strategy on Digital Health 2020–2025, n.d.). Thus, demography meets digital accessibility and acceptance to accomplish digital health. AI applications within demography enhance the capacity for detecting understated demographic patterns that influence health outcomes across the spectrum of epidemiological transition. Recent literature highlights AI systems useful for capturing real-time demographic transitions beyond census-based approaches. This is a new development that holds potential to model these complex, nonlinear processes more accurately than conventional demographic methods can (Abidi & Filali, 2023).

2.2.2 Contextualizing Population Intelligence

Population intelligence is a disruptive innovation in health system management. The most evident change it brings to epidemiology is that data are now open in real time. Real-time data includes social media trends and compilation of daily health surveillance data (Şerban et al., 2019). Conventionally, most epidemiological analyses have been based on surveys or census data. Population intelligence, in contrast, uses diverse real-time data through continuous surveillance mechanisms. Application of this facilitates early detection of the emergence of health concerns to support timely public responses. AI-driven models using population intelligence predict shifts in population health trends.

Moreover, changes in demographics, lifestyle, experience of environments, and healthcare access influence transitions. In line with such a framework, it must be credited that population health is influenced by several factors (Non et al., 2025). Many factors affect health like social, behavioral, environmental, and digital. Recent

AI developments provide a means to bring these factors together through mobile health application, social media application, and telehealth engagement patterns. These newer sources reflect real-time health-seeking behaviors and patterns of technology adoption across diverse population groups. These advanced analyses improve traditional health management with an understanding of digital health trends. Because of this integrated approach, there is a more complete understanding of population exposures and of those factors that provide flexibility (Non et al., 2025; Rossi et al., 2025).

AI-enabled population insights into health demand inform healthcare systems in anticipation and thereby improve health policy and programs. The models can guide targeted prevention strategies and equitably allocate resources by stratifying the population's risk. This informs the organization of the delivery of healthcare by guiding the resourceful health infrastructure and workforce. In this respect, it is important to ensure data are representative to avoid biases and inequities. Assurance of transparency, algorithmic filtering, and accountability of performance of AI systems instills trust among a wide range of stakeholders. For this, regulatory guidelines and frameworks should be worked out urgently, ensuring that informed consent, data privacy, and equitable sharing are maintained. As populations continue through various demographic and epidemiological changes around the world, AI-enabled population intelligence offers an incomparable capacity to model and manage such complex diversities (Defo, 2014; Non et al., 2025). It thus converts health systems from inactive structures into proactive and sustainable healthcare solutions to meet the needs of populations (Fig. 2.3).

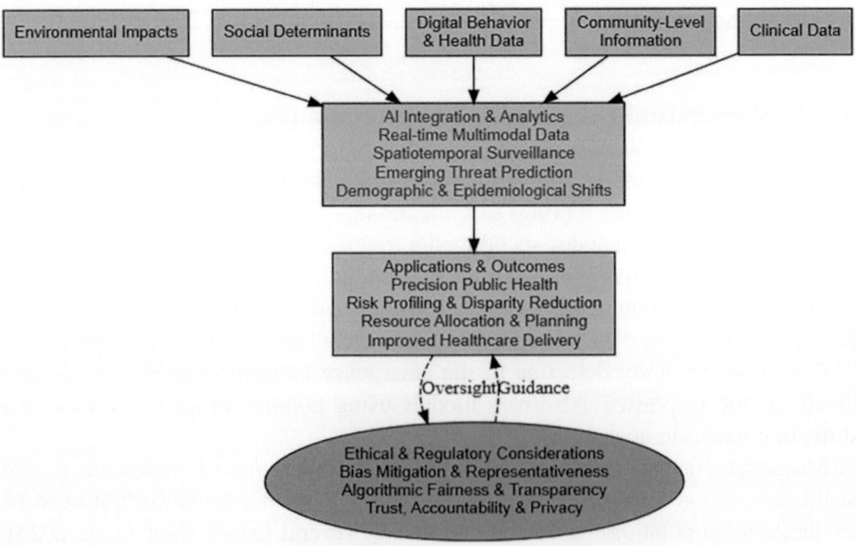

Fig. 2.3 Framework of population intelligence for AI-driven equitable healthcare

2.2.3 Theoretical Lenses for Integration

2.2.3.1 Systems Thinking Framework

Systems thinking framework offers basic theoretical characteristics of combining demography, population intelligence, and AI. Figure 2.4 presents six key features of the system thinking framework. The framework directly applies to AI-enabled population health systems, where demographic variables interact with health outcomes through complex paths. Health outcomes are the result of a complex interplay between individual, social, environmental, and health system responses. The framework has been highly relevant for feedback loops (Thelen et al., 2023).

2.2.3.2 Data Ecology Perspective

Data ecology outlines a theoretical framework of demographic data, health information, and algorithms that explain healthcare ecosystems. The Global Strategy on Digital Health pressures need to strengthen the safe digital ecosystem (Global Strategy on Digital Health 2020–2025, n.d.). However, data is not a neutral resource; it embeds social, political, and technological contexts. Integration of AI requires the association of data collectors, data processors, and data users. Furthermore, quality and representativeness of demographic data directly affect the ability of performance and outputs of AI systems. The context is relevant within population intelligence systems because several diverse sources of data require coherence within the integration process.

2.2.3.3 Population Informatics Framework

Population informatics provides a theoretical bridge between traditional approaches of public health and contemporary AI-driven population health management. The American Medical Informatics Association and Population Health Informatics agenda identifies four main areas: developing uniform collaborative frameworks,

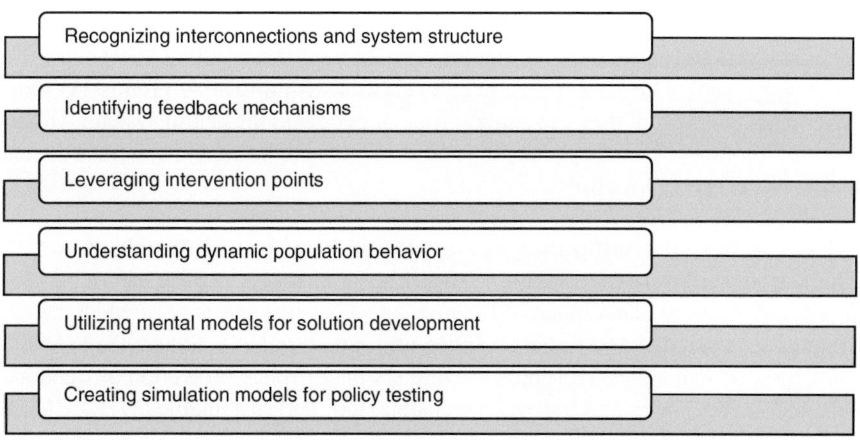

Fig. 2.4 Steps of the system thinking framework

advancing technical tools and methods, building scientific evidence bases, and creating appropriate policy and sustainability frameworks (Massoudi et al., 2012). This identified theoretical framework makes it clear that improvement in population-level health requires not only demographic intelligence and advanced computational methods, but technological capabilities, organizational capacity, and community engagement. Recent research has called for theoretical models that surpass and fit in health information science (Massoudi et al., 2012).

2.2.4 Population Dynamics, AI Applications, and Health Systems

2.2.4.1 Demographic, Epidemiological Transitions, and AI

The AI-driven health management system is founded on demographic and epidemiological transition frameworks. The classical transition model describes only the shift from infectious disease mortality to chronic disease. But it now needs a combination with digital health transitions that reflect changing patterns of technology adoption, health information seeking, and care delivery across population segments (Defo, 2014). AI systems combine to offer models of substantial regional variation in real-time epidemiological shifts. This is joined with demographic aspects for expecting health system needs and accurate allocating resources. The WHO emphasizes people-centered health systems with respect to this line (Zeng et al., 2021).

2.2.4.2 Health Systems Integration Framework

Understanding population change with AI requires ideas that connect big population trends to health patterns at an individual level. A theoretical background to a learning health system illustrates how data from populations informs improvement in personal care through continuous feedback. It also informs that population trends affect the function of health systems and health programs also shift health and structure of populations. Analyses of 15 countries' data show that people's trust in health system plays a big role in how well it works and how easily AI is accepted (Kruk et al., 2024). In order to link population change to health systems, a theory has to include social and cultural issues in its viewpoint. Such issues affect how people use technology, seek care, and utilize health services within diverse groups. AI tools have to be built so that they can support trust of people in the health system. All this calls for a community-engaged approach that makes sure the health system is trusted and works properly for all.

2.2.4.3 Artificial Intelligence as Population Health Infrastructure

This is a big shift from the thinking of AI as a separate tool to being a part of population health systems. That means AI is now understood as the way in which health systems are designed and function. Inherent in this thought is adherence to WHO guidelines on managing AI. It puts forward six major rules: protection of freedom, safe and healthy, open and honest, responsible, fair, and sustainable (WHO, 2023).

It is not easy to understand how AI systems influence and are inclined by shifting demography. This recognizes AI's usefulness in understanding population mobility patterns, health outcomes, and feedback loops to inform policy decisions from the World Health Organization (2023). The framework needs to make use of flexible models so that population intelligence systems can adapt to changing trends in population. A call to ensure that ethical standards are upheld in promoting health equity across all population segments is essential.

2.3 Overview of Multimodal AI in Healthcare

2.3.1 Understanding Multimodality: Data, Method, and Model

Current multimodal AI will learn patterns across different data types using shared common mathematical methods, while maintaining unique characteristics of each data type. Such systems make use of a great deal of AI machinery, including attention mechanisms, transformer models, and graph neural networks, which understand patterns not only within each type of data but also across diverse types of data. A good example can be the HAIM framework. Indeed, several studies have demonstrated the fact that HAIM outperforms single-modality systems by 6–33% consistently across a wide range of health analyses. (Petridis et al., 2025). The power of these systems emanates from their capability to handle complex challenges associated with healthcare data. Healthcare data is very varied; it is collected at different rates, sometimes with values missing and may not be recorded at the same time. These systems use specialized methods to clean, standardize, and fill in missing data.

2.3.2 Core Modalities in Healthcare AI

2.3.2.1 Clinical Data Integration

Clinical data is a fundamental modality in healthcare AI systems, with structured electronic health records, lab results, vital signs, and clinical notes. Advanced language processing tools can easily extract meaningful information from prescriptions and notes in modern multimodal systems. This enables them to integrate doctors' insights and patients' clinical history over time to improve their prediction models. This can be demonstrated by how well M2REMAP framework performed after learning from 12.6 million patient records, enhancing the accuracy of predictions by 23.6% for drug uses and 23.9% for drug side effects (Dou et al., 2026). Advanced clinical data processing includes bidirectional representation learning methods, which capture time dependence and patterns related to clinical progression. A good representative of these methods is Bidirectional Representation Learning from the Transformers model. It improves prediction of course of chronic diseases by using two main steps: pretraining and fine-tuning. The model features attention that helps explain which clinical factors are particularly important (Meng et al., 2021).

2.3.2.2 Integrating Genomic Data

The integration of genomic data can already be treated as one of the most advanced features of multimodal healthcare AI since this has to do with the need for specific methodological approaches that can work with high-dimensional genetic information besides clinical phenotypes. Whole-genome sequencing combined with large-scale population studies allows investigation of public health genomics in a far more holistic manner, thus unraveling the interaction of genetic risk factors with those of environmental and behavioral health-modulating factors. New approaches such as federated learning have overcome many obstacles regarding the sharing of genomic data. These approaches help researchers collaborate on questions while keeping data private and secure. Such approaches help multimodal AI systems make use of genetic information from various populations responsibly and safely, considering all rules for protecting sensitive genetic data (Alvarellos et al., 2023).

2.3.2.3 Behavioral and Environmental Data Streams

The integration of behavioral data and environmental information is a relatively new frontier in multimodal healthcare AI. It is faced with ever-increasing availability of wearable devices, mobile health applications, and environmental monitoring systems that provide streams of continuous real-time evidence regarding patient behaviors, activity patterns, and environmental exposures. Multimodal AI systems using such data are based on special time-based modeling, designed for dealing with irregularities of data collection, missing values, and complex links between behavior and health. A very good example is the MedFusionAI framework by Sun (2025), where LSTM networks process time-based behavioral data, while other types of data are kept separately encoded. This system achieved as high as 98.8% accuracy in predicting chronic disease risk. Integrating environmental data into this system would require even more advanced spatial and time-based modeling. These models involve a variety of factors—air quality, climate trends, and social or economic conditions—that influence health. One of the biggest challenges stands in connecting patient-level data with population-level environmental exposures while considering geography and time variations.

2.3.2.4 Demographic Data as a Contextual Framework

Demographic information provides a critical contextual framing in which interpretation and utilization of other modalities in multimodal AI take place. An increasing set of studies has shown that demographic factors are crucial for the performance of AI models across various population groups. It would, therefore, seem to indicate a need for special methods in making health AI systems representative and equitable for all people. Consequently, incorporating demographic data into AI systems should be treated with caution so as not to perpetuate bias or further entrench health inequalities. Attention mechanisms and tailored model architectures are some of the contemporary demographic-aware designs that modern multimodal AI models use to adapt to diverse population settings while sustaining high predictive accuracy.

2.3.2.5 Demographic Data as a Contextual Framework

Demographic information provides a critical contextual framework that informs interpretation and application of other modalities within the realm of multimodal AI. Recent studies show that demographic factors strongly affect the performance of AI models across different population groups (Gray et al., 2014; Zeng et al., 2021). This thus calls for special methods to be considered in ensuring healthcare AI systems are fair and representative for all people. Demographic information should be represented in AI systems with due care to avoid bias and prevent the continuation of existing health inequalities. Advanced demographic-aware designs, such as attention mechanisms and customized model structures, have been adopted by modern multimodal AI models to adapt to different population settings while maintaining high predictive accuracy (Bayoudh et al., 2022).

2.3.3 Advances in Deep Learning for Health Data Fusion

2.3.3.1 Fusion Architecture Innovations

Recent developments in deep learning for healthcare data fusion depend on three components: early fusion, intermediate fusion, and late fusion. The approach combines multiple input types into single-feature vectors. Such approaches are effective for discovering basic associations between different data modalities; however, they may fail to capture more complex patterns, which require separate learning of each data modality. The intermediate fusion models alleviate this limitation through the use of joint learning methods that process several data types while maintaining their distinctive characteristics. A typical example of such a model is the Multimodal Gated Contrastive Representation Learning framework. It employed graph-based fusion methods to handle missing or variable patient data and capture informative knowledge from different data sources effectively. Late fusion models merge outputs produced by separate models for each data type. This makes them faster and more interpretable but possibly causes loss of some advantages related to learning from data interactions. Hybrid fusion methods, mixing features of several fusion types, very often provide better scores, as leverage strengths of each approach and reduce its weaknesses, according to recent studies (Azevedo et al., 2024).

2.3.3.2 Representation Learning Methodologies

Advanced learning for integrating healthcare data now employs transformer-based models that utilize self-attention in search of complicated associations within and across diverse data types. It helps build a common information space where various types of data can be compared and merged even when very different data modalities are utilized. Contrastive learning methods have become particularly helpful for multimodal healthcare AI. They enable systems to learn strong features, indicative of key characteristics of each modality while effectively linking them across modalities. These approaches utilize advanced mathematical objectives that increase similarity between related and decrease similarity between unrelated data pairs, hence yielding informative and flexible representations. Graph-based learning methods are equally important as they can model complex relations among healthcare data types. It creates patient-specific graphs that demonstrate how clinical features are interrelated; this enables personalized data fusion methods that adapt to specific characteristics and data patterns of each patient.

2.3.3.3 Attention Mechanisms and Cross-Modal Learning

In multimodal healthcare AI, attention mechanisms have improved performance by allowing models to focus on the most important information from different data sources while keeping results interpretable. Cross-modal attention models help systems adjust the importance of each data type with respect to the clinical situation and the prediction goal. New advances in attention-based fusion have created attention networks for each data type that can make a decision on the usefulness of each data source for a specific medical decision. These models allow for combination in more flexible and precise ways to account for variability in data quality, availability, and importance across patient groups and healthcare environments (Azevedo et al., 2024; Gray et al., 2014).

2.3.4 Opportunities and Challenges in Multimodal Health Data Integration

2.3.4.1 Clinical Decision Support Opportunities

Multimodal AI brings new power into clinical decision support by providing a fuller picture of a patient's health. Various data types, such as images and medical records, combined in these systems, consistently outperform single-data methods and improve accuracy by 1.2–27.7% and AUROC by 0.02–0.16 across many healthcare tasks (Parvin et al., 2025). For example, linking radiology scans with patient history will enhance diagnosis and prognosis, particularly in cases that are complex and not diagnosable with images alone. For the diagnosis of Alzheimer's disease, multimodal models outperform models based only on scans or clinical data. Multimodal AI in precision medicine will combine genetic risk factors with clinical signs, behavior patterns, and environmental exposures to develop personalized treatments and better predict patient outcomes (Parvin et al., 2025).

2.3.4.2 Data Integration Challenges

Although there is a great deal of promise from multimodal health data, a number of significant technical and operational challenges must be overcome for clinical use. For data standardization, different formats, quality measures, and modes of collection used by individual health institutions make aggregation challenging to achieve. Health data variation is wide and creates complex preprocessing needs; therefore, advanced normalization and validation methods are imperative in maintaining the quality and integrity of data (Parvin et al., 2025). Missing data vary across modalities and, hence, strong imputation techniques must handle complex missingness while maintaining cross-modal relationships. Apart from this, there is another significant challenge regarding computational complexity: a multimodal AI framework requires high computational power, along with highly advanced infrastructure that may not be available within all healthcare settings to handle large-scale multimodal datasets.

2.3.4.3 Privacy and Security Considerations

Aggregation of these varied types of healthcare data introduces serious issues related to privacy and security. Moreover, an increase in risks from diverse sources increases the chances of compromising privacy. Such a result creates difficulty in regulatory compliance due to differing legal rules and protection standards. The trade-off therefore lies in developing secure ways of sharing data and anonymization techniques that enable multimodal research while protecting patient privacy. Federated learning, in this regard, holds much promise in letting institutions collaboratively build models without necessarily having to relocate sensitive data to one location. This approach allows healthcare organizations to participate in multimodal AI development while at the same time maintaining control of their patient information at their local levels (Krones et al., 2025).

2.3.4.4 Implementation and Scalability Barriers

Clinical translation of multimodal AI research faces many challenges in terms of integration into workflows, user acceptance, and interoperability of systems. Health systems need to adapt existing settings to handle new types of multimodal data without losing compatibility with established clinical practices (Krones et al., 2025). Training and change management are crucial to that end since healthcare professionals have to learn how to interpret and make use of the results provided by AI. Such systems can be so complex that they also reduce acceptance on the part of users, especially when systems are not interpretable or transparent. Scalability issues relate to the need for common frameworks for evaluation that can also validate performance in various healthcare settings and populations. Strong validation methods, accounting for complex interaction among data types, are important to ensure reliability and general use of such systems (Azevedo et al., 2024).

2.4 Role of Demography and Population Intelligence in Multimodal AI

2.4.1 Demographic Data

Previous large healthcare AI projects model performance can change by 15–20% across demographic groups if these factors are ignored (Sharma et al., 2023). For instance, during the COVID-19 pandemic, AI-based risk models considering rich demographic data provided better identification of high-risk groups compared to models leveraging only clinical data. The central place of demographic data is very prominent in precision medicine, where treatments should reflect group-specific risks, responses, and side effects. Demographic-aware attention mechanisms adjust the weight of clinical variables based on patterns learned from diverse population data and are being implemented in modern multimodal AI systems.

2.4.2 Population-Level Determinants in Health Models

These would encompass social, environmental, and structural factors involved. The understanding of these requires cross-model analyses that take into consideration both individual and population health. The addition of population-level factors in predicting health signifies a shift from sole concentration on individuals to the utilization of broad socioecological models that view health as an interaction of complex systems. In modern times, AI-based population stratification has come to use machine learning (Azevedo et al., 2024). Such applications use techniques like logistic regression, decision trees, and neural networks to handle complex data (Non et al., 2025). The rationale underlying population stratification in health models identifies various levels of determinants—from genetic to social community conditions. In this respect, social factors of health interact with individual risks in complex manners that often require special modeling (Gray et al., 2014). Such advanced stratification models make use of hierarchy techniques such as mixed-effects regression and multilevel structural equation modeling to quantify how individual and community factors each influence health outcomes. Incorporation of geospatial and environmental data facilitates the detailed development of population-based intelligence systems that forecast health risks geographically. Clinical testing has also shown these models to be more accurate and efficient. For instance, population stratification-driven AI analytics reported identification of 20–30% more high-risk patients compared to traditional methods. Their application has been particularly successful in chronic disease management, given their contribution to the development of personalized prevention and early treatment programs.

2.4.3 Enhancing Contextual Validity and Reducing Bias

Demographic data are used in two critical ways to enhance the performance of multimodal AI systems for healthcare. First, improving contextual validity of AI systems to the degree to which models reflect real-world situations and contexts across different groups. Second, mitigating risks of baked-in biases that make AI more likely to perpetuate or exacerbate healthcare disparities. Contextual validity indicates how well AI models understand and correct for social, cultural, and environmental context. For instance, ranges for normal tests and symptoms might vary between groups due to genetic, cultural, or economic reasons. Contemporary AI deploys demographic-aware methods that interpret results in a much fairer way, accounting for group-specific baselines and trends. Bias reduction is perhaps the most significant use of demographic data in health-related AI today. The accuracy of a model's predictions may decline significantly if its training datasets come from biased collections. Literature shows that accuracy may vary up to 10–15% across ethnic or racial groups. This gap can be mitigated by including more granular levels of demographic data, enabling AI developers to build fairness-aware models able to detect and correct these differences (Colacci et al., 2025). There are four main ways to reduce bias with the use of demographic information (Fig. 2.5).

2.4.4 Using Population Intelligence to Address Health Inequalities

Population health intelligence is a broad approach that integrates demographic data, social determinants, and community risks to equalize healthcare through AI technologies. It is based on the presumption that inequities in health occur as a result of active social, economic, and structural issues and do not happen randomly. Thus, successful solutions require multilevel data analyses: person-specific medical

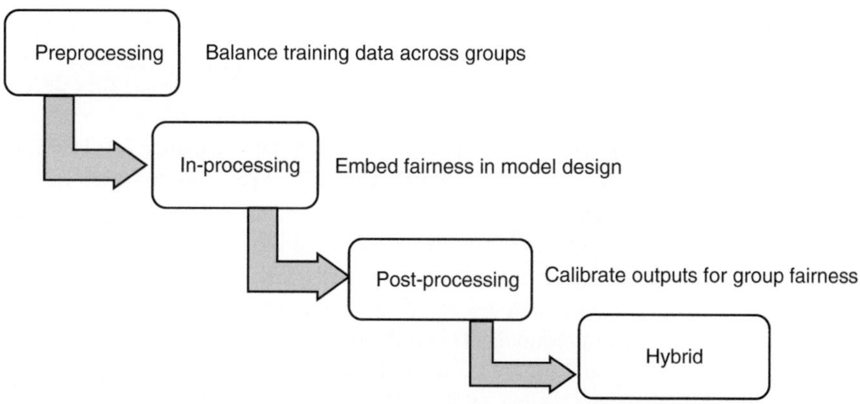

Fig. 2.5 Process of enhancing contextual validity and reducing bias

records, conditions within neighborhoods, and social determinants of health. The next level of population intelligence systems incorporates new sources of information beyond medical data: geographic, social media, economic, and environmental data. Natural language processing helps such systems extract social factors from unstructured information, such as clinical notes or messages involving public health. Such expanded analysis can disclose health risks that might not emerge from data within standard records (Colacci et al., 2025).

Population intelligence has been particularly valuable in crises, such as the COVID-19 pandemic, to identify high-risk populations and target support to the right places. Beyond crises, these systems assist long-term health challenges ranging from chronic disease to mental health to access to health (WHO, 2023).

2.5 Synthesis of Empirical Evidence and Emerging Trends

Put together, empirical evidence from diverse healthcare domains points out that demographic intelligence is one of the significant components to drive further performance improvements of multimodal AI systems (WHO, 2023). More than 300 studies conducted between 2018 and 2025 provide meta-analytical results that illustrate how AI models that include in-depth information about demographic profiles are improved in contrast to those not including information on demographic variation. Such findings indicate that with the addition of demographic context, models become more robust with increased performance and accuracy; fairness and generalization of AI solutions also improve in such cases for a diverse population.

2.5.1 Performance Patterns and Demographic Integration

The largest advantages in performance accrue for AI applications focused on health equity and resource optimization. Evidence from systematic reviews indicates that demographic-aware AI systems perform especially well in fields of maternal health surveillance, chronic disease prediction, and epidemiological forecasting (Non et al., 2025; WHO, 2023; Zeng et al., 2021). These findings indicate that demographic intelligence has the most value added in those domains where diversity of populations has a strong bearing on health outcomes and resource needs. More recent meta-analyses illustrate how different AI model types and contexts vary in how demographic integration impacts them (Colacci et al., 2025). Deep learning models, especially with attention mechanisms, are found to have the strongest capability for leveraging demographic information well. Transformer-based architectures achieve relative improvements of 15–20% higher than those obtained by traditional machine learning models. This reflects their advanced capacity for complex pattern recognition and modeling of relationships between demographic factors and clinical indicators (Krones et al., 2025).

2.5.2 Technological Trends

Integrating demographic data with AI requires strong collaboration across disciplines, drawing on expertise from demography and population studies, computer science, and health science. There is evidence to prove this: for example, interdisciplinary research groups produce more influential and highly cited work, such as collaborative projects attracting 23–35% more citations than single-discipline efforts. A diversified expert thus enables teams to gain access to wider knowledge and explore creative problem-solving approaches. Global collaboration provides important opportunities in the face of demographic challenges in the representation of AI. International research consortia on combining demographic insights with AI can be used to promote data sharing, standardize evaluation methods and coordinate capacity-building initiatives across regions. For example, large-scale partnerships can accelerate progress, as evidenced by the EuCanImage project for cancer imaging AI and AI for Health Imaging network, among others (Kondylakis et al., 2024). These new AI tools change with research teams to build and manage. This approach traces people with the right skills and helps in creating a network. AI tools help in linking experts from different fields. They also discover new links between population patterns and health outcomes. This technology helps in the formation of diverse and well-rounded teams that can tackle complex problems even more effectively. This, therefore, allows for building diverse teams that combine deep domain knowledge with sophisticated research techniques, fast-tracking innovation in demographic-AI applications. Another promising strategy pertains to participatory research methods that are integrated with AI development to drive demographic inclusivity (Duffy et al., 2022).

Recent studies highlight important new directions for improving AI systems that take demographic factors into account in healthcare (Lee et al., 2024). The first issue is consistency of collection of patient demographic data; this inconsistency is an obstacle to comparability and generalizability of AI tools across different health settings. Standardized ways to collect and represent demographic data hold the key to overcoming this challenge. From this perspective, global collaboration is needed to build datasets representing diverse populations that at the same time are aligned with specific regional health needs (Gray et al., 2014). Another critical area of research covers the intersection of social factors, such as living conditions, education, and income, with traditional demographic data. Evidence has shown that AI models based on this broader set of social and demographic information perform better in promoting health equity. However, clear and consistent methods for collecting and integrating such social data are so far lacking (Colacci et al., 2025).

2.6 Ethical, Equity, and Policy Considerations

2.6.1 Ethical Dimensions of Demographic Data Use in AI

Use of demographic data in AI-driven healthcare has far-reaching ethical implications, underlining issues of autonomy, privacy, and misuse of sensitive personal information. WHO's framework on Ethics and Governance of Artificial Intelligence for Health provides that, with respect to human autonomy, demographic data should be collected and used, subject to explicit consent mechanisms (WHO, 2023). AI systems should collect and use demographic data only with clear consent. Individuals also need to be informed about how their data is used for AI's predictions or to make health decisions. Demographic variables are inherently sensitive, including race, ethnicity, and socioeconomic status and thus require strict privacy protection against reidentification and unauthorized data linkage (Defo, 2014; Duffy et al., 2022). Ethical AI systems shall have privacy-preserving techniques: differential privacy and secure multiparty computation. This may support privacy while analyzing demographic data without exposure of individual identities. Beneficence requires that the use of demographic data in AI should generate concrete benefits for all rather than subjecting exposed groups to disadvantage (Defo, 2014).

2.6.2 Data Justice, Fairness, and Representation in Population Intelligence Systems

Data justice in population intelligence systems requires representativeness of all demographic groups across an AI's lifecycle. It means front and center presence through data collection, preprocessing, model training, and deployment. Literature has shown that AI models, trained on unrepresentative demographic datasets, can spread systemic disparities (Colacci et al., 2025). These lead to unequal health outcomes across racial and socioeconomic lines. Effective strategies in fairness incorporate demographic insights at multiple touchpoints (Fig. 2.6).

The Global Strategy on Digital Health 2020–2025 highlights the need for digital health ecosystems that are inclusive in advancing health (WHO, 2023). To make an inclusive digital ecosystem, representativeness across regions is important for quality demographic data. Comprehensive fairness metrics, including demographic parity difference and dissimilar impact ratio, should be followed by population intelligence systems to quantify inequities in model performance (Duffy et al., 2022).

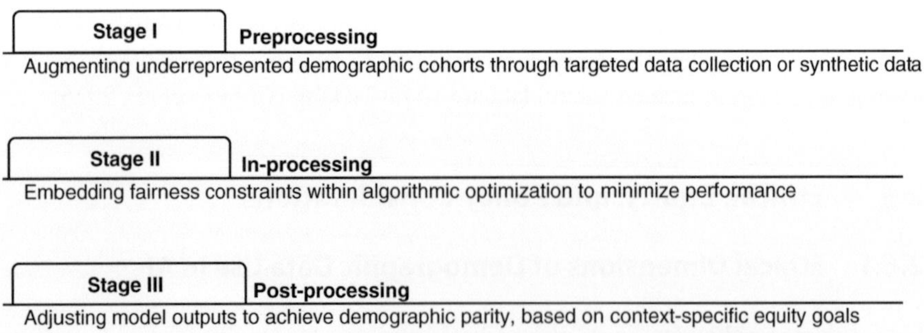

Fig. 2.6 Effective fairness strategies incorporate demographic insights at multiple stages

2.6.3 Governance Frameworks and Regulatory Challenges

Strong governance frameworks are required to ensure that demographic data in AI is used responsibly and ethically, balancing aspirations of new technology with imperatives of oversight. Data protection laws vary by region. For instance, the European Union's General Data Protection Regulation sets tight limits on the use of "special category" data such as race, health, and genetics, except when clear reasons can be demonstrated for public health research and with protections in place to ensure privacy (Roos, 2021). Under Article 9 of GDPR, an organization must demonstrate that demographic data is absolutely necessary for healthcare and that safeguards on privacy are in place. Similarly, India's proposed Digital Personal Data Protection Bill also requires persons to explicitly consent to the use of their sensitive personal data and prescribes penalties for noncompliance, casting a legal obligation upon organizations to ensure that the use of demographic data in AI is transparently made. On an international plane, WHO's AI for Health initiative advises the establishment of governance bodies comprising policy thinkers, doctors, patient groups, and technology experts (WHO, 2023). Such a body should ensure monitoring for compliance, auditing of AI systems for fairness, and management of data sharing across borders. It should establish a common framework for auditing whether AI conforms to ethical principles, laws, and equity objectives that provide certainty of ongoing monitoring after deployment. Monitoring real-world use of AI and rapid reporting of problems identifies new ethical issues and allows necessary corrections to be made.

2.6.4 Policy Implications for Inclusive and Responsible AI in Public Health

To use artificial intelligence for health, policies need to be inclusive and accountable. It begins with the national process for determining demographic data. Setting common benchmarks helps ensure that data from different sources can be compared and aggregated and helps identify who benefits from health services and who is left behind. This transformation requires a special role for the government. They can drive innovation through funding. Similar goals should include public–private partnerships and grant programs. India's national AI strategy, for example, could be aligned with Ayushman Bharat's digital mission to ensure that AI applications reduce health disparities among different social and regional groups.

At the global level, responsibility is shared. Global cooperation is needed so that the benefits of digital health reach everyone. Many LMICs lack the infrastructure and skills to use AI effectively. International bodies, such as the World Health Organization and World Bank, could create a Global Fund for AI and Health Equity. Such an initiative would center on country requests for strengthening their digital systems, training of health workers in new technologies, and developing data resources that represent their people (WHO, 2023). Without this type of shared investment, the digital divide will continue to widen, leaving much of the world behind. Equally important will be the question of openness. People have a right to know how an AI system reaches decisions, what kind of data shapes those choices. Developers should clearly mention model description, tested population, and reliability. Transparency builds trust, and trust is the foundation of ethical innovation.

2.7 Future Directions and Research Agenda

2.7.1 Gaps in Current Knowledge and Methodological Challenges

While demography and AI in health is a growing field, there are many gaps. First is the lack of clarity about what demographic data representation and usage is needed. Most AI systems are still being built from data belonging to high-income countries. When the same systems later get tested on LMICs, accuracy tends to drop. This underlines how much performance depends on the population one was trained on.

Another unresolved issue is that of fairness in AI. Most of the existing approaches to bias correction focus on a single variable, like gender, age, or income. However, people have complex and multiple identities (Krones et al., 2025). Not considering this intersection makes it difficult to determine how all these factors combine and interact with each other and result in health consequences. The so-called "frame problem" is also added to these problems. The AI systems perform well only in the particular context in which they were developed. When extended to new demographic groups, predictions tend to be unreliable. One important research need, therefore, is to identify algorithms that remain stable and accurate across population groups. Poor data quality and limited representativeness are other factors that continue to hinder progress. For example, in most LMICs, with general limited education and health data literacy, the way health information can be collected and used is curtailed. About 70% of children in these countries are affected by learning poverty; this leads to long-term impacts on how well data-driven systems can be implemented (Global Strategy on Digital Health 2020–2025, n.d.).

2.7.2 Emerging Technologies and Population-Level AI Innovations

Rapid technological development is fundamentally changing what population-level AI can achieve. In recent years, generative models—in particular, transformer and diffusion systems—have begun to fill historical gaps in demographic data. These models facilitate the study of diverse populations by creating realistic but fictional data that does not represent actual population data. For many researchers, this represents a major shift in the effort to balance innovation and privacy. In fact, some of these initiatives have produced methodological data for real populations, with data that is nearly 90% identical to the original categories (Sharma et al., 2023).

Another important change is the rise of progressive education. Instead of pulling sensitive data into a single database, this approach allows businesses in different environments to train a common AI model while keeping their data secure and local. Hospitals, clinics, or research institutions can contribute to the same goal without giving up control of their records. A broader collaborative approach has emerged, giving a voice to regions and populations that are often excluded from global health data while protecting privacy. Meanwhile, computing power is bringing AI closer to where it matters most: in places with weak Internet connections or infrastructure, systems running on local data can actually help healthcare professionals make faster, more meaningful decisions. For example, a tablet or phone analyzer can analyze symptoms and provide timely guidance. In community health centers or for professional teams, it can mean the difference between urgent and delayed care. Edge computing is bringing decision-making closer to the safety zone. In remote or poor infrastructure environments, AI tools running on local infrastructure can enable doctors to make more timely and automated decisions without relying on the power of the Internet. Technologies such as neuromorphic and quantum technologies are helping to change the way big tech works in the future. These systems promise significant increases in speed and efficiency, along with the ability to handle the complex, dynamic nature of population and health data. Cognitive computing, in turn, opens up new possibilities for modeling the interaction of social, biological, and environmental factors in real time. Adding another layer to this change is the increasing use of IoT devices. Wearables, health apps, and environmental sensors can continuously collect data about people's lifestyles and perceived behaviors. Combined with social intelligence systems, these tools reveal how health risks vary across different geographic, temporal, and geographical contexts.

2.7.3 Opportunities for Interdisciplinary Research and Global Collaboration

Interagency collaboration is key to the development of AI. Anthropologists, pathologists, computer scientists, ethicists, and social researchers can all play a role. This is reflected in the fact that such diverse teams can produce innovative and high-quality research results (Global Strategy on Digital Health 2020–2025, n.d.). Different perspectives help connect technological design with the real world. The same is true of international relations. International networks in the field of research on population-specific AI systems can agree on common standards of information, ethics, and diagnostic tools. Projects such as EuCanImage and the AI for Health Imaging Network have shown that collaborative efforts can accelerate the global development of AI and enhance its effectiveness (Kondylakis et al., 2024). New collaboration models driven by AI itself are changing the way research teams work together. This technology can streamline areas of expertise and connect researchers and specialists in related fields, thus fostering cross-disciplinary collaboration. This may also reveal previously unrecognized associations between population trends and health outcomes, opening new avenues for research (Soenksen et al., 2022).

Community involvement is equally important. Participatory research methods allow local residents to participate in the design, testing, and regulation of AI systems, ensuring that the technology reflects real-world needs. When communities have a voice, they are more trusting, receptive, and willing to use AI tools where needed. Evidence already exists that such partnerships can promote equitable and sustainable outcomes (Duffy et al., 2022; Kruk et al., 2024). The future of population convergence and AI is evolving rapidly and requires collaboration, empathy, and shared responsibility. This is not only about making machines smarter, but about building systems that understand and serve the diversity of human life (WHO, 2023).

2.8 Conclusion

Demography, population intelligence, and multimodal AI are highly intertwined elements of the modern approach to healthcare management. This approach transforms isolated data into unified and context-rich systems that understand and make better decisions. In addition, demographic variables have taken center stage in AI performance, health equity, and system effectiveness. Furthermore, demographic intelligence enhances predictability, contextual relevance, and fairness while enabling precise diagnosis, personalized treatment, and improved population health management. Moreover, demographic data in AI models are crucial stratification variables, confounders, and effect modifiers, and thus require a thoughtful model design and fairness-focused methods to ensure validity and equitability of outcomes. Their frameworks surpass mere descriptive analyses of demographic research and build dynamic, actionable insights for public health surveillance, prediction, and intervention planning. Especially in noncommunicable disease management and epidemiological forecasting, results have been much stronger than before with the integrated use of clinical, genomic, behavioral, environmental, and demographic data by multimodal AI systems.

Importantly, embedding demographic considerations helps to reduce algorithmic bias and supports equity of outcomes, particularly in vulnerable or underserved communities. Such efforts equally improve resource allocation, better target interventions, and allow expansion toward precision public health methods that address population needs. Ethical stewardship will be key to the success of these innovations, grounded in principles of transparency, privacy, and community engagement that make sure AI serves all populations equitably. Future systems must adopt inclusiveness in design and ensure international collaboration toward representative dataset development, standardized protocols, and capacity-building.

References

Abidi, J., & Filali, F. (2023). Real-time AI-based inference of people's gender and age in highly crowded environments. *Machine Learning with Applications, 14*, 100500. https://doi.org/10.1016/J.MLWA.2023.100500

Alvarellos, M., Sheppard, H. E., Knarston, I., Davison, C., Raine, N., Seeger, T., Prieto Barja, P., & Chatzou Dunford, M. (2023). Democratizing clinical-genomic data: How federated platforms can promote benefits sharing in genomics. *Frontiers in Genetics, 13*, 1045450. https://doi.org/10.3389/FGENE.2022.1045450/BIBTEX

Azevedo, B. F., Rocha, A. M. A. C., & Pereira, A. I. (2024). Hybrid approaches to optimization and machine learning methods: A systematic literature review. *Machine Learning, 113*(7), 4055–4097. https://doi.org/10.1007/S10994-023-06467-X/TABLES/3

Bayoudh, K., Knani, R., Hamdaoui, F., & Mtibaa, A. (2022). A survey on deep multimodal learning for computer vision: Advances, trends, applications, and datasets. *The Visual Computer, 38*(8), 2939–2970. https://doi.org/10.1007/S00371-021-02166-7/FIGURES/15

Colacci, M., Huang, Y. Q., Postill, G., Zhelnov, P., Fennelly, O., Verma, A., Straus, S., & Tricco, A. C. (2025). Sociodemographic bias in clinical machine learning models: A scoping review of algorithmic bias instances and mechanisms. *Journal of Clinical Epidemiology, 178*, 111606. https://doi.org/10.1016/J.JCLINEPI.2024.111606

Defo, B. K. (2014). Demographic, epidemiological, and health transitions: Are they relevant to population health patterns in Africa? *Global Health Action, 7*(Supp. 1). https://doi.org/10.3402/GHA.V7.22443

Dou, Y., Liu, Y., Zou, H., Zeng, W., Xu, K., & Peng, S. (2026). A survey on electronic health record driven multimodal representation learning. *Information Fusion, 127*, 103810. https://doi.org/10.1016/J.INFFUS.2025.103810

Duffy, G., Clarke, S. L., Christensen, M., He, B., Yuan, N., Cheng, S., & Ouyang, D. (2022). Confounders mediate AI prediction of demographics in medical imaging. *Npj Digital Medicine, 5*(1), 1–6. https://doi.org/10.1038/S41746-022-00720-8;SUBJMETA

Global Strategy on Digital Health 2020–2025. (n.d.). Retrieved 20 October 2025, from https://www.who.int/publications/i/item/9789240020924

Gray, S. W., Martins, Y., Feuerman, L. Z., Bernhardt, B. A., Biesecker, B. B., Christensen, K. D., Joffe, S., Rini, C., Veenstra, D., & McGuire, A. L. (2014). Social and behavioral research in genomic sequencing: Approaches from the clinical sequencing exploratory research consortium outcomes and measures working group. *Genetics in Medicine, 16*(10), 727–735. https://doi.org/10.1038/GIM.2014.26

Kondylakis, H., Catalan, R., Alabart, S. M., Barelle, C., Bizopoulos, P., Bobowicz, M., Bona, J., Fotiadis, D. I., Garcia, T., Gomez, I., Jimenez-Pastor, A., Karatzanis, G., Lekadir, K., Kogut-Czarkowska, M., Lalas, A., Marias, K., Marti-Bonmati, L., Munuera, J., Nikiforaki, K., et al. (2024). Documenting the de-identification process of clinical and imaging data for AI for health imaging projects. *Insights Into Imaging, 15*(1), 1–8. https://doi.org/10.1186/S13244-024-01711-X/TABLES/2

Krones, F., Marikkar, U., Parsons, G., Szmul, A., & Mahdi, A. (2025). Review of multimodal machine learning approaches in healthcare. *Information Fusion, 114*, 102690. https://doi.org/10.1016/J.INFFUS.2024.102690

Kruk, M. E., Kapoor, N. R., Lewis, T. P., Arsenault, C., Boutsikari, E. C., Breda, J., Carai, S., Croke, K., Dayalu, R., Fink, G., Garcia, P. J., Kassa, M., Mohan, S., Moshabela, M., Nzinga, J., Oh, J., Okiro, E. A., Prabhakaran, D., SteelFisher, G. K., et al. (2024). Population confidence in the health system in 15 countries: Results from the first round of the People's Voice Survey. *The Lancet Global Health, 12*(1), e100–e111. https://doi.org/10.1016/S2214-109X(23)00499-0

Lee, S. W., Morcos, M., Won Lee, D., & Young, J. (2024). Demographic representation of generative artificial intelligence images of physicians. *JAMA Network Open, 7*(8), e2425993–e2425993. https://doi.org/10.1001/JAMANETWORKOPEN.2024.25993

Massoudi, B. L., Goodman, K. W., Gotham, I. J., Holmes, J. H., Lang, L., Miner, K., Potenziani, D. D., Richards, J., Turner, A. M., & Fu, P. C. (2012). An informatics agenda for public health: Summarized recommendations from the 2011 AMIA PHI conference. *Journal of the American Medical Informatics Association, 19*(5), 688–695. https://doi.org/10.1136/AMIAJNL-2011-000507

Meng, Y., Speier, W., Ong, M. K., & Arnold, C. W. (2021). Bidirectional representation learning from transformers using multimodal electronic health record data to predict depression. *IEEE Journal of Biomedical and Health Informatics, 25*(8), 3121. https://doi.org/10.1109/JBHI.2021.3063721

Non, L. R., Marra, A. R., & Ince, D. (2025). Rise of the machines – Artificial intelligence in healthcare epidemiology. *Current Infectious Disease Reports, 27*(1), 1–8. https://doi.org/10.1007/S11908-024-00854-8/METRICS

Parvin, N., Joo, S. W., Jung, J. H., & Mandal, T. K. (2025). Multimodal AI in biomedicine: Pioneering the future of biomaterials, diagnostics, and personalized healthcare. *Nanomaterials, 15*(12), 895. https://doi.org/10.3390/NANO15120895

Petridis, P., Margaritis, G., Stoumpou, V., & Bertsimas, D. (2025). *Holistic artificial intelligence in medicine; improved performance and explainability*. https://arxiv.org/pdf/2507.00205.

Roos, A. (2021). The European Union's General Data Protection Regulation (GDPR) and its implications for South African data privacy law: An evaluation of selected 'content principles'. *Comparative and International Law Journal of Southern Africa, 53*(3). https://doi.org/10.25159/2522-3062/7985

Rossi, M., Rehman, S., Rossi, M., & Rehman, S. (2025). Integrating artificial intelligence into telemedicine: Evidence, challenges, and future directions. *Cureus, 17*(8). https://doi.org/10.7759/CUREUS.90829

Şerban, O., Thapen, N., Maginnis, B., Hankin, C., & Foot, V. (2019). Real-time processing of social media with SENTINEL: A syndromic surveillance system incorporating deep learning for health classification. *Information Processing & Management, 56*(3), 1166–1184. https://doi.org/10.1016/J.IPM.2018.04.011

Shaban-Nejad, A., Michalowski, M., & Buckeridge, D. L. (2018). Health intelligence: How artificial intelligence transforms population and personalized health. *Npj Digital Medicine, 1*(1), 1–2. https://doi.org/10.1038/S41746-018-0058-9;SUBJMETA

Sharma, A., Adekunle, B. I., Ogeawuchi, J. C., Abayomi, A. A., & Onifade, O. (2023). AI-driven patient risk stratification models in public health: Improving preventive care outcomes through predictive analytics. *International Journal of Multidisciplinary Research and Growth Evaluation, 4*(3), 1123–1130. https://doi.org/10.54660/.IJMRGE.2023.4.3.1123-1130

Soenksen, L. R., Ma, Y., Zeng, C., Boussioux, L., Villalobos Carballo, K., Na, L., Wiberg, H. M., Li, M. L., Fuentes, I., & Bertsimas, D. (2022). Integrated multimodal artificial intelligence framework for healthcare applications. *Npj Digital Medicine, 5*(1), 1–10. https://doi.org/10.1038/S41746-022-00689-4;SUBJMETA

Sun, J. (2025). MedFusion-TransNet: Multi-modal fusion via transformer for enhanced medical image segmentation. *Frontiers in Medicine, 12*, 1557449. https://doi.org/10.3389/FMED.2025.1557449/BIBTEX

Thelen, J., Sant Fruchtman, C., Bilal, M., Gabaake, K., Iqbal, S., Keakabetse, T., Kwamie, A., Mokalake, E., Mupara, L. M., Seitio-Kgokgwe, O., Zafar, S., & Cobos Muñoz, D. (2023). Development of the systems thinking for health actions framework: A literature review and a case study. *BMJ Global Health, 8*(3), 10191. https://doi.org/10.1136/BMJGH-2022-010191

WHO. (2023). *WHO releases AI ethics and governance guidance for large multi-modal models*. Retrieved 20 October 2025, from https://www.who.int/news/item/18-01-2024-who-releases-ai-ethics-and-governance-guidance-for-large-multi-modal-models

Zeng, D., Cao, Z., & Neill, D. B. (2021). Artificial intelligence–enabled public health surveillance—From local detection to global epidemic monitoring and control. In *Artificial intelligence in medicine: Technical basis and clinical applications* (pp. 437–453). https://doi.org/10.1016/B978-0-12-821259-2.00022-3

Geospatial Intelligence and GIS in Multimodal AI for Healthcare

3

U. Venkatesh, Arshad Ahmed, and Jeetendra Kumar

3.1 Introduction

In recent years, geospatial intelligence, artificial intelligence (AI), and geographic information systems (GIS) have integrated and transformed the way of acquiring and interpreting health data. What was once considered merely spatial mapping has become dynamic, data-driven, and is now commonly called GeoAI. It helps planners, clinicians, and public health professionals identify insights much deeper than conventional statistics based on spatial reasoning, predictive models, and multimodal data that may be from hospital records and wearable devices or from satellite imagery and sensors for environmental monitoring (Boutayeb et al., 2024). Another important novelty is the development of multimodal large language models. Such systems can combine text, images, and geographic information in one framework easily. This capability, when extended to healthcare, allows researchers and practitioners to connect medical information with environmental and social processes and conditions in order to reveal trends in health outcomes that are not only biology-based but also reflect a broader social and environmental context of communities (Nazi & Peng, 2024).

U. Venkatesh (✉) · A. Ahmed
Department of Community & Family Medicine, All India Institute of Medical Sciences, Gorakhpur, Uttar Pradesh, India

J. Kumar
Department of Computer Science and Application, Atal Bihari Vajpayee University, Bilaspur, Chhattisgarh, India

U. Venkatesh et al. (eds.), *Multimodal AI in Healthcare*,
https://doi.org/10.1007/978-981-95-9027-8_3

3.1.1 Why Spatial Intelligence Matters in Healthcare

Place is intimately linked to health. The air people breathe, the place they stay, and the ease with which they can get to clinics all have an effect on the disease and well-being. Localized intelligence introduces this spatial layer to the analysis, providing the policymakers with the opportunity to detect disparities that are sometimes difficult to see through traditional health statistics (Mennis & Yoo, 2018). Earlier uses of GIS mainly focused on plotting disease cases or facility locations on static maps. That helped with visualization, but it did not explain *why* certain areas suffered more. With better data and advanced AI tools, geospatial analysis can now move from describing to anticipating. GeoAI models process continuous streams from satellite feeds to mobility data to forecast outbreaks, detect pollution exposure, and estimate service demand (Boutayeb et al., 2024). The same technology originally developed for defense GEOINT is now being applied to environmental and public health emergencies. When AI analyzes satellite and demographic data together, it can flag hotspots or predict where medical supplies will be needed most. In effect, healthcare planning is shifting from reacting after crises to preparing ahead of them, guided by spatial intelligence (Soenksen et al., 2022).

3.1.2 The Role of Multimodal AI

Information used in medicine comes in many forms: laboratory readings, scans, notes, and increasingly, geographic layers. Traditional AI models that process only one kind of data miss important relationships between these sources. Multimodal AI fills this gap by merging varied data into a single interpretive system (Krones et al., 2025). A strong example is *OmniGeo*, which was trained to read remote-sensing images, urban databases, and descriptive text together. This helps systems think spatially, for example, linking pollution data to disease records or identifying land-use factors behind public health risks. Unlike older task-specific models, MLLMs transfer what they learn from one type of data to another, a skill that is particularly useful for health geography and environmental medicine. In fact, this type of AI has been used to combine hospital data with maps of air quality or green space to investigate how environmental exposures are linked to chronic diseases (Boutayeb et al., 2024). The result is a richer picture that connects individual-level care with community-level planning.

3.1.3 Combining Environmental and Biomedical Data

Understanding health from a holistic perspective means connecting what goes on inside the body with what goes on around it. GeoAI provides a technical foundation for doing this integrating data from molecular biology with local weather conditions. When analyzed together, these layers show subtle relationships between environmental stress and disease trends. Specific questions can be asked of their model in simple language and answered through automated GIS scripts, making the analysis non-expert-friendly. (Krones et al. 2025) further this idea with OmniGeo, which simultaneously learns from several geospatial and biomedical information. This will mark the beginning of an integrated, multimodal ecosystem that shifts away from data silos toward connected public health intelligence. But the more we combine data types, the more ethical issues there are around privacy, bias, and representation. If these tools are to be trusted in sensitive health domains, fair and transparent governance, as well as fair training data, must go hand in hand.

3.1.4 How GeoAI and GIS Have Evolved in Healthcare

Previously, GIS was mainly used as a mapping tool; now it acts as an analytical engine driven by AI. GeoAI combines machine learning with special science in cluster detection, exposure estimation, and simulation of the impact brought about by policy actions (Boutayeb et al., 2024). This moves epidemiological models from simple correlation to causal insights. Boutayeb et al. (2024) described how the roots of GeoAI in automation have grown into modern deep learning and basic models; its applications span from disaster management to precision agriculture, skills that easily could be applied to public health. (Sherman et al. 2025) used similar methods to study which populations lack dental access. His work shows how AI-assisted GIS can turn raw demographic and transport data into policy-ready information, helping health departments plan services with greater precision.

3.1.5 Current Relevance and Future Directions

Events such as the COVID-19 pandemic and climate-driven health crises have highlighted how crucial spatially linked data have become. Governments and health agencies are using GeoAI systems to monitor disease spread, model population mobility, and measure healthcare access in real time (Mir et al., 2022). At the same time, cheaper satellite imagery, IoT sensors, and open GIS platforms are expanding who can use such data. The next frontier is the merger of spatial reasoning with large multimodal foundation models. Systems like *OmniGeo* show that AI can now learn spatial relationships directly from mixed data sources, closing the gap between text-based and map-based reasoning. For health researchers, that means tools capable of both reading patient narratives and understanding the geography those stories describe. Ultimately, the merger of GeoAI with healthcare points toward the era of "spatially aware" medicine, not only a method for measuring inequality but also one for anticipating it. It is a more predictive, equitable, and contextual model for public health as location becomes an integral part of intelligent systems (Fig. 3.1).

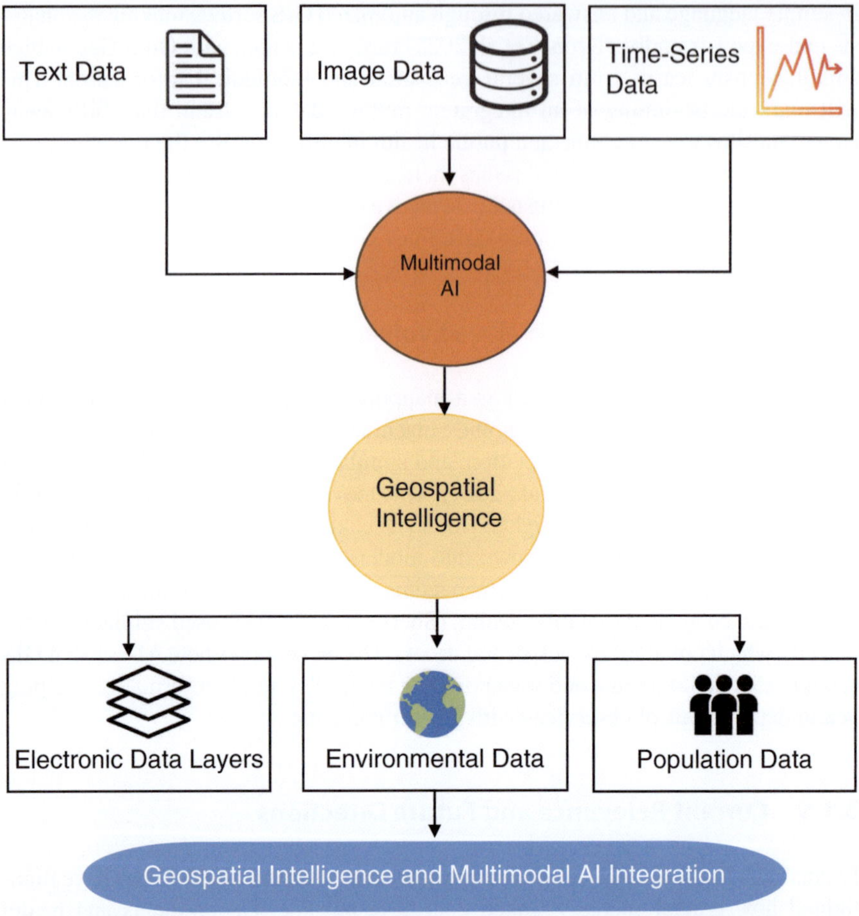

Fig. 3.1 Conceptual framework for integrating geographic intelligence and multimodal AI in healthcare

3.2 Fundamentals of Geospatial Intelligence and GIS

Before understanding how the multimodal AI connects to specialized analysis, one needs to first understand GEOINT and its roots in GIS. Stated simply, GEOINT is the process by which location-based data is transformed into actionable insight. GIS, on the other hand, provides the digital and analytical structure for capturing, storing, processing, and visualizing that information. When these two are brought together with AI, the result often called GeoAI becomes a toolkit for recognizing spatial patterns, forecasting outcomes, and improving decisions in domains ranging from climate monitoring to public health (Boutayeb et al., 2024).

3.2.1 Concept and Evolution of Geospatial Intelligence

Geospatial intelligence refers to the systematic gathering and interpretation of data tied to a particular place on Earth. It merges geography, remote sensing, and analytics to describe what is happening and why it matters. Although the field first took shape in defense and national security work, its reach has expanded into environmental studies, city planning, agriculture, and now healthcare. Ideas linking AI with geographic data actually go back several decades. During the 1980s and 1990s, researchers such as Boutayeb et al. (2024) and Herold et al. (2005) began exploring how computational intelligence could strengthen spatial reasoning.

However, the concept gained formal recognition much later around 2017, when the ACM SIGSPATIAL community defined GeoAI as "*the coupling of AI techniques with geospatial information or data.*" That workshop is often viewed as the point where GeoAI became its own research branch. Modern GEOINT now draws from a wide array of data sources: satellite imagery, UAV sensors, GPS devices, environmental monitors, and open datasets. Analysts use these feeds to detect change over time and to forecast likely outcomes. For example, AI applied to satellite data can track air quality trends, vegetation stress, or urban heat islands factors that strongly influence respiratory illness, vector-borne disease, and overall well-being.

3.2.2 GIS: Structure and Components

A geographic information system (GIS) is the technological backbone that makes spatial intelligence possible. It integrates hardware, software, data, people, and analytical methods to handle all types of location-referenced information. In essence, GIS helps users see *where* things happen, ask *why*, and model *what might happen next.*

3.2.2.1 Core Components of a GIS

1. *Spatial data acquisition*: Information is gathered from satellites, drones, mobile GPS devices, and environmental sensors. In health work, this may include hospital coordinates, patient distribution, and exposure levels to pollutants.
2. *Data storage and management*: Specialized databases such as PostgreSQL/PostGIS or ArcGIS geodatabases organize large volumes of spatial data and enable complex queries.
3. *Data processing and analysis*: Spatial operations buffering, overlay, interpolation—help identify exposure zones, detect clusters, or estimate service coverage.
4. *Visualization and mapping*: Finally, results are displayed through interactive maps and dashboards so planners can identify risk areas or resource gaps at a glance.

In this sense, GIS acts like the nervous system of GEOINT, transforming raw coordinates into information that decision-makers can actually use.

3.2.3 Relationship Between GeoAI, GIS, and AI

GeoAI is the connection between GIS infrastructure and modern AI methods such as machine learning, deep learning, and natural language processing.

Boutayeb et al. (2024) show that combining these fields makes it possible to automate complex tasks such as land-use classification, specific clustering, or time-varying forecasting. GIS provides a specific framework: coordinate systems, projection rules, and visualization tools. AI supports the reasoning layer, part that learns from examples and predicts new outcomes.

When combined, machine learning algorithms discover hidden geographic correlations; neural networks recognize complex features in imagery, including medical or satellite data; deep learning systems handle spatiotemporal sequences such as infections outbreaks or seasonal pollution patterns. A unique feature of GeoAI is its ability to work with Big Geodata large, mixed datasets that come from satellites, sensors, and even social media feeds. These datasets change rapidly, are highly variable, and grow rapidly, making AI essential for extracting useful signals from excessive noise (Li, 2020).

3.2.4 Types of Geospatial Data and Their Healthcare Needs

Geospatial information typically appears in three forms: raster, vector, and spatiotemporal, each of which plays a specific role in medical and public health research. Raster data includes satellite images of temperature or air pollution, while vector data describes discrete objects such as hospitals, roads, or administrative boundaries. In the case of spatiotemporal data, time is added as a dimension and consequently one can trace diseases over time or population movements. Jointly, these data types enable researchers to associate environmental conditions with clinical outcomes and allow health systems to predict rather than just respond to risk (Table 3.1).

Each data type provides a unique lens for understanding health determinants. Raster data highlight environmental gradients (e.g., air quality), vector data reveal healthcare infrastructure distribution, and temporal dimensions help trace evolving public health events.

Table 3.1 Major types of geospatial data and healthcare applications

Data type	Description and healthcare relevance
Raster data	Grid-based continuous data (e.g., satellite imagery, temperature, pollution). Used for mapping disease risk linked to environmental exposure
Vector data	Points, lines, and polygons representing discrete entities (e.g., hospitals, roads, administrative boundaries). Supports resource allocation and access analysis
Spatiotemporal data	Time-stamped spatial data, showing changes over time (e.g., outbreak progression, mobility patterns). Essential for pandemic modeling and surveillance

3.2.5 Applications of Geospatial Intelligence in Healthcare

The integration of GEOINT and GIS in healthcare serves multiple purposes, from epidemiological monitoring to policy-level planning. Below are some critical application areas derived from the recent literature.

3.2.5.1 Disease Surveillance and Epidemiology

GIS-based disease surveillance helps track and predict disease outbreaks by analyzing patterns in spatial data. For instance, during the COVID-19 pandemic, real-time dashboards combined satellite imagery, mobility data and case reports to map infection trends. AI-enhanced spatial models can now detect early signals of outbreaks through anomalies in healthcare utilization or environmental data.

3.2.5.2 Environmental Health Monitoring

Environmental exposures such as polluted air, extreme heat, or contaminated water remain among the strongest external factors shaping population health. When environmental data are layered with clinical or demographic information, GeoAI can begin to estimate where certain diseases are most likely to appear. For instance, models trained on satellite-derived pollution maps and hospital admission data have been used to forecast asthma or cardiovascular risks within specific neighborhoods. Because these systems learn from both spatial and temporal patterns, they can flag emerging "hot spots" before large numbers of people fall ill. The same logic applies to tracking mosquito-borne infections, where temperature and rainfall data are used as predictors. Maps are included to guide local health agencies in taking precautionary action.

3.2.5.3 Health Infrastructure and Access

GIS reveals differences in access to healthcare in ways that are simple and cannot do statistics. By mapping hospital density, travel times, and road or transit networks, planners can identify where services are lacking, are available, or not available. Such analyses help governments and other agencies decide where to open new clinics or improve transportation routes. Increasingly, geo-resolution models are also being used for practical tasks such as ambulance routing and emergency logistics. By simulating different scenarios of population growth or traffic, policymakers can test how the promised investments will fare in the coming years. How it might change access to care.

3.2.5.4 Disaster and Emergency Response

During a natural disaster or epidemic, timely specialized intelligence can save lives. High-resolution satellite images processed through AI-based classification help responders locate damaged infrastructure, flooded areas, or helps in locating temporary shelters. When these maps are combined with hospital capacity data and figures, officials can know in near real time which medical teams or where to send the goods? GEOINT has become a core part of emergency management frameworks worldwide, linking environmental observations with on-the-ground health information so that responses are better coordinated and resources are not wasted.

3.2.5.5 Precision Public Health

Precision public health aims to deliver the right intervention to the right population at the right moment. GeoAI supports this idea because it brings together multiple types of evidence, epidemiological surveys, environmental readings, genomic data, and demographic statistics in a single analytical space. Through such integration, health agencies can identify communities at particular risk and focus on vaccination drives or screening programs accordingly. Predictive risk maps created from these datasets help public health move from a reactive approach to a preventative one.

3.2.6 Challenges in Current GeoAI and GIS Applications

Despite rapid progress, there are still some persistent challenges in implementing GeoAI in healthcare: *Data quality and availability*. In many low- and middle-income areas, both clinical and medical datasets are incomplete or inconsistent, limiting analytical accuracy. *Scale and resolution*. Linking detailed patient records to larger environmental or regional data requires careful alignment across spatial and temporal scales. *Computational demand*. Handling vast, heterogeneous geospatial datasets calls for strong processing power and efficient AI architectures that not all institutions possess. *Ethical and privacy concerns*. Because health information is often location-specific, there is a real risk of exposing sensitive details about individuals or communities. *Interoperability*. A lack of standard formats and coordinate systems makes it difficult for AI models and GIS software to communicate seamlessly. Tackling these issues will require more than technical fixes. Collaborative efforts among data scientists, geographers, epidemiologists, and ethicists are essential to ensure that GeoAI in healthcare remains both analytically sound and socially responsible (Fig. 3.2).

3.3 Foundations of Multimodal AI in Healthcare

The arrival of multimodal AI has begun to change the way medical information is read and connected. Earlier AI systems usually depended on a single input such as a chest X-ray or an electronic health record field so that their view of a patient's condition was narrow. Multimodal AI instead tries to learn from several kinds of data at once, creating a shared analytical space where text, numbers, and images all contribute to the same decision. In medicine, that means a model can combine a doctor's written notes, laboratory values, imaging studies, physiological signals, and even spatial or environmental factors to form a fuller clinical picture. When these layers are fused, the algorithm gains a richer understanding of both individual health and population-level trends. One of the first structured attempts to make this idea work in real hospitals was the holistic AI in medicine (HAIM) framework,

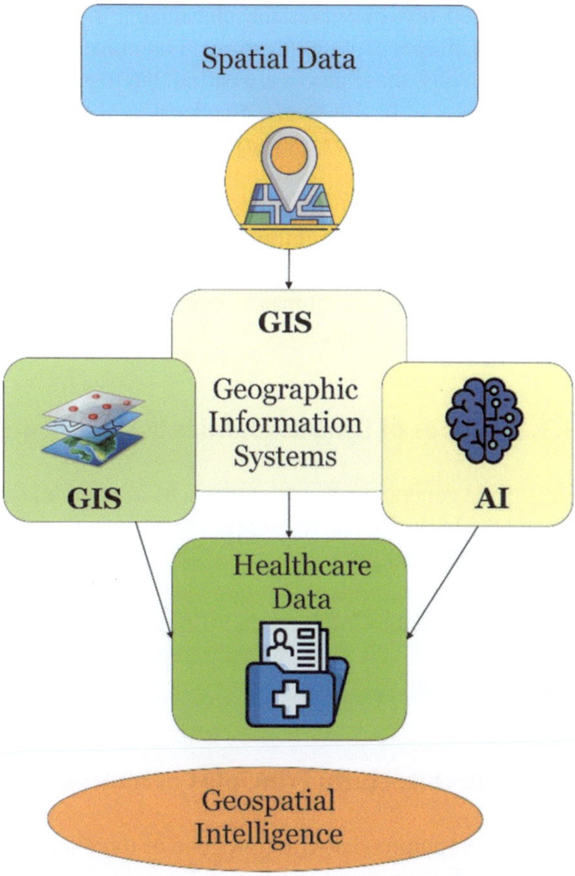

Fig. 3.2 Integration of GIS and AI for generating geospatial intelligence in healthcare

developed by Soenksen and colleagues at the Massachusetts Institute of Technology (Soenksen et al., 2022). Their work showed that blending multiple data sources improves the stability and interpretability of predictive models across many routine clinical tasks. The HAIM experiments illustrated that when AI learns from different types of evidence together, it performs more like a clinician who pieces information from many directions before reaching a judgment.

3.3.1 Concept and Motivation for Multimodal Learning

Doctors rarely base a diagnosis on one clue alone. They read the patient's history, look at physical exam findings, check lab reports, interpret scans, and often weigh environmental or lifestyle factors. Multimodal AI follows the same logic: it seeks to merge these heterogeneous signals into a single framework that captures the complexity of real clinical reasoning. Each form of data contributes something unique. Structured tables record measurable values such as blood pressure or glucose levels;

unstructured text preserves the physician's thought process and observed symptoms; and images capture the physical manifestation of disease.

Individually, these pieces are partial, but together they form a more coherent and realistic view of health status. Soenksen et al., 2022 observed that models trained with such joint inputs outperformed single-source systems in accuracy for six different prediction tasks. Their improvement ranging from roughly 6–33% is indicative not only of improved performance but also of robustness to missing or noisy data, hence showing flexibility (Soenksen et al., 2022). This evidence does more than just suggest that multimodal learning increases accuracy. It takes AI research one step closer to how human doctors actually think: by understanding signals in collaboration, not alone.

3.3.2 Types of Data Modalities in Healthcare

Healthcare generates a vast ecosystem of data. For clarity, these can be grouped into several modality classes, each requiring distinct preprocessing and feature-extraction strategies (Table 3.2).

Each modality presents unique challenges: different data formats, scales, and noise characteristics. Multimodal AI frameworks must therefore include robust preprocessing, normalization, and alignment mechanisms to harmonize them before learning begins.

3.3.3 Architectural Principles of Multimodal AI

At its core, multimodal AI follows one of three integration strategies: early fusion, intermediate fusion, and late fusion depending on when information from different modalities is combined within the learning pipeline.

Table 3.2 Common healthcare data modalities and illustrative applications

Modality	Typical examples and analytic purpose
Structured or tabular data	Laboratory results, demographics, billing codes, used for trend analysis and risk prediction
Unstructured text	Clinical narratives, discharge summaries, prescriptions, processed through NLP for entity recognition
Imaging data	X-ray, CT, MRI, histopathology slides, interpreted by convolutional networks for detection/classification
Signal data	ECG, EEG, wearable sensors, analyzed via temporal or frequency-domain models
Genomic or omics data	Gene expression, proteomics, used for personalized and precision medicine
Geospatial and environmental data	Residence, air quality index, climate, links environmental exposures to health outcomes

1. *Early fusion*: Raw or low-level features from all modalities are concatenated and fed into a single model. This allows joint feature learning but demands synchronized and complete datasets.
2. *Intermediate fusion*: Each modality is processed through its dedicated subnetwork (e.g., CNN for images, transformer for text) to create latent embeddings, which are then combined using attention mechanisms or cross-modal transformers.
3. *Late fusion*: Independent models produce separate predictions that are aggregated through weighted voting or meta-learning. This is useful when data availability differs across modalities.

The HAIM framework employs a *late-fusion* approach (Boulahia et al., 2021) with shared embedding layers that allow flexible integration even when certain modalities are missing. This adaptability is particularly important in healthcare, where data are often incomplete, for example, where imaging might be done on some patients and not others (Soenksen et al., 2022).

3.3.4 Benefits and Impact in Healthcare

Multimodal AI offers the following four advantages over unimodal systems:

1. Improved predictive accuracy: Because the signals are complementary in the different modalities, multimodal models have less uncertainty. In the HAIM study, the integrated model gave remarkably better AUROC scores for mortality and readmission predictions than the single-input baseline model.
2. *Enhanced generalizability*: Fusing diverse data sources makes models more resilient to noise or missing data in any single modality.
3. *Context-aware reasoning*: Inclusion of textual narratives and temporal signals allows algorithms to reason over contextual and causal factors.
4. *Interpretability*: Attention-based fusion enables visualization of which modality contributed most to a given prediction critical for clinical trust and accountability.

3.4 Clinical Use Cases of Multimodal AI

3.4.1 Diagnostic Support

Radiology and pathology have benefited most from multimodal integration. For instance, combining chest X-rays with electronic records improves pneumonia and COVID-19 detection accuracy. In oncology, models merging histopathology slides with genomic profiles predict tumor subtypes more precisely than imaging alone.

3.4.2 Prognostic and Operational Forecasting

Hospitals increasingly rely on multimodal AI to anticipate key operational metrics such as patient length of stay, likelihood of readmission, and overall resource demand. Instead of depending on a single dataset, these systems merge clinical notes, lab results, demographic factors, and sometimes environmental data to produce more practical forecasts. This means that, for example, hospital managers will get advance warning of bed occupancy or staff allocation needs. Multimodal forecasting tools, in some instances, have already been integrated with the scheduling systems of hospitals to enable managers to adjust workflows before disruptions occur.

3.4.3 Therapeutic and Precision Medicine

Personalized care has long been a goal, but multimodal AI has made it more achievable. By analyzing genetic profiles, drug-interaction data, and patient lifestyle factors together, these models can identify which subgroups are most likely to benefit or be at risk from a particular therapy. This capability advances precision medicine by moving beyond population averages toward treatments tailored to individual biological and social contexts. In oncology and pharmacogenomics, for example, multimodal systems are increasingly used to match patients with the right drug or dosage, taking into account genetic markers as well as lifestyle factors such as diet, age, and comorbidities.

3.4.4 Population Health and Epidemiology

At a larger scale, multimodal AI helps researchers understand how diseases spread across space and society. By combining geospatial layers like pollution maps, land-use data, or human mobility patterns with epidemiological and clinical information, these models can reveal environmental and socioeconomic influences on health outcomes.

3.4.5 Challenges and Barriers to Implementation

Despite their promise, multimodal AI systems face a set of persistent obstacles:

1. Heterogeneity of data: Medical and spatial data arrive in different formats and at different sampling rates.
2. Data scarcity and labeling costs: Some of these methods require expert annotation for training, which is very expensive, such as for medical imaging or pathology slides.

3. Computational demands: Training on large, complex datasets requires substantial computational resources and memory to train multimodal networks.
4. Ethical and privacy risks: Linking genomic, textual, and geographic data increases the potential for re-identification even when individual datasets have been anonymized.
5. Bias and fairness: Underrepresentation of some groups, whether demographic or regional, invites systematic errors that further increase inequality.
6. Model interpretability: More complex fusion architectures make the process leading to the model's conclusions harder to decipher.

Soenksen et al. highlighted that to address these challenges, open data standards, explainable model design, and close collaboration among clinicians, engineers, and regulators will be necessary to ensure that multimodal AI can be safely applied clinically (Soenksen et al., 2022).

3.4.6 Ethical and Regulatory Considerations

Since multimodal systems will be dealing with very sensitive information, ethics and regulation are a principal concern in their application. Laws such as HIPAA in the United States and GDPR in Europe set clear standards for consent, anonymization, and data security. Yet multimodal fusion introduces new challenges: information that seems anonymized under one modality for example, free-text notes—may become re-identifiable in conjunction with other kinds of data, such as geolocation or genetic data. A number of researchers are working to mitigate this risk by using federated learning and other approaches that preserve privacy. These involve models learning from distributed data without the need to transfer raw data off a local server. That enables secure cross-institutional and international research of particular importance when geospatial or environmental data is integrated with patient records and maintains confidentiality.

3.4.7 Relevance to Geospatial Integration

Although the original HAIM framework was focused mostly on clinical data, it inherently allows for spatial and environmental variables because of its modular design. Geographic context is an added modality for capturing health determinants externally, which the more traditional clinical record misses.

Environmental exposure: Satellite-based air quality measures combined with EHRs can refine asthma risk prediction and guide pollution control policies.

Accessibility and equity: Spatial data on hospital distribution or transportation networks help assess fairness in model predictions and service access.

Outbreak modeling: When mobility traces and clinical case reports are analyzed together, health agencies gain early warning of potential epidemics.

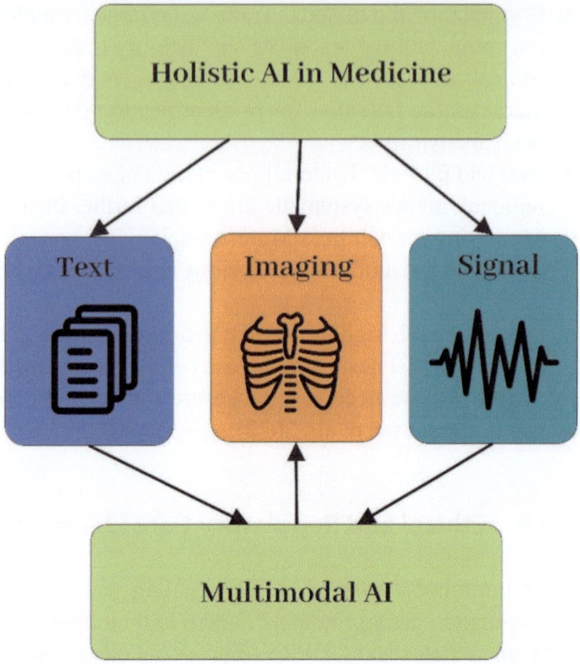

Fig. 3.3 Conceptual structure of a multimodal AI system for healthcare decision support

In this sense, multimodal AI provides a computational bridge to connect individual-level clinical reasoning with population-level specialized intelligence, laying the foundation for truly integrated precision public health (Fig. 3.3).

3.5 Integrating GIS and Multimodal AI: Frameworks and Methods

The integration of geospatial intelligence, GIS, and multimodal AI ushers in new frontiers within digital health analytics. It is widely referred to as GeoAI-driven multimodal healthcare. Its objective is to link the "where" and "why" of disease patterns in clinical data with the "how" and "who" of disease patterns. In other words, while considering lab results, medical notes, and imaging studies, it takes into account very specific information such as air quality in neighborhoods, land use, or proximity to healthcare facilities. These resulting models do not only predict risk for disease but also explain how local environments, socioeconomic factors, and individual differences impact health outcomes. The following section explains the conceptual architecture and computational workflow of this integration with a view to demonstrating how GIS analytics and multimodal learning can put forward actionable insights for healthcare planning.

3.5.1 Conceptual Overview of Geo-Multimodal Integration

Conventional healthcare AI relies on one common model to learn from relationships among all the different types of clinical data: imaging, lab values, and text notes. While powerful, these models often ignore the specific context that dictates where diseases occur and why they cluster. Incorporating GIS-based information adds this important geographic dimension to allow for precise localization of clinical data. As Boutayeb et al. explained, geospatial features such as terrain, land-use patterns, population density, and distance from infrastructure add depth not captured by clinical data alone (2024). When these specific layers are embedded in a multimodal AI pipeline, the model can shift scales from individual patients to whole communities in establishing connections between different health outcomes and broader population dynamics. This resulting framework is termed geo-multimodal AI (GMAI) and is hinged on the following three interconnected pillars:

1. Multimodal AI for fusion of disparate data: it fuses structured, unstructured, and visual data.
2. GIS-enabled specialized analytics that provides location-based variables and mapping capabilities.
3. Geospatial intelligence reasoning, where models learn to interpret how context and geography influence health phenomena.

Together, these components allow AI systems to "see" the patient not as an isolated data point but as part of a spatial network influenced by environmental, infrastructural, and social conditions.

3.5.2 Architectural Model for Geo-Multimodal Healthcare Systems

A practical architecture for integrating GIS and multimodal AI typically follows five stages (Fig. 3.4).

3.5.2.1 Stage 1: Data Acquisition

Data sources include both clinical and environmental origins: *clinical modalities*—electronic health records (EHR), imaging (CT, MRI), sensor signals, genomics. *Geospatial modalities*—remote sensing (satellite, UAV), environmental sensors (air quality, temperature), administrative maps, and social infrastructure data. Open datasets such as WorldPop, NASA Earth Observation, and WHO Health Mapper often provide foundational spatial layers.

3.5.2.2 Stage 2: Preprocessing and Geocoding

Health records are geocoded using patient residence or facility coordinates while ensuring privacy compliance through aggregation (e.g., block or district level). Spatial datasets are standardized to a common coordinate reference system (CRS)

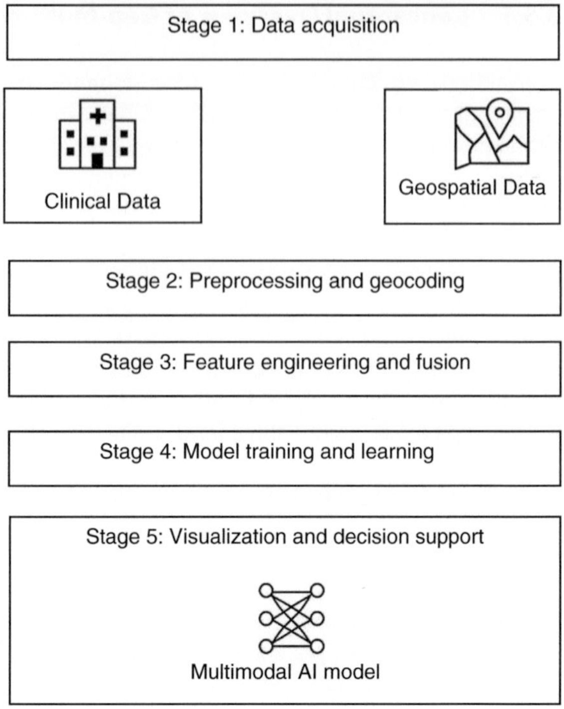

Fig. 3.4 Conceptual workflow showing stages from data acquisition to decision support in a geo-multimodal healthcare system

and temporal scale. Data normalization techniques ensure alignment between continuous (e.g., temperature) and categorical (e.g., land cover) features.

3.5.2.3 Stage 3: Feature Engineering and Fusion

Here, geospatial features are extracted distance to nearest healthcare facility, pollution index, green-space density, travel time, and merged with patient-level variables. Fusion strategies may follow: early fusion, concatenating raw features; intermediate fusion, embedding spatial data as latent vectors via graph or attention mechanisms; or late fusion, combining predictions from separate spatial and clinical models.

Demonstrated that *late fusion* designs, as used in HAIM, allow flexible inclusion of optional data types ideal for spatial variables that may be missing for certain samples (Soenksen et al., 2022).

3.5.2.4 Stage 4: Model Training and Learning

Machine learning algorithms such as random forests, gradient boosting, or deep architectures (CNNs, graph neural networks, transformers) can be trained on the integrated dataset. In spatial contexts, *graph-based neural networks* have shown strong performance, capturing spatial dependencies through adjacency relations between geographic entities. GeoAI models can also use *spatio-temporal attention networks* to model dynamic processes, such as disease spread over time. The combination of temporal patterns from clinical data and spatial proximity from GIS layers allows predictive modeling of regional outbreaks or healthcare demand surges.

3.5.2.5 Stage 5: Visualization and Decision Support

Results are visualized through GIS dashboards that display predictions on maps showing spatial distributions of risk, facility utilization, or environmental correlations. This makes outcomes interpretable and actionable for policymakers, clinicians, and public health authorities.

3.5.3 Computational Methods for Geospatial-Multimodal Learning

3.5.3.1 Spatial Feature Representation

Spatial data must be converted into machine-readable vectors. Methods include raster encoding, converting maps into pixel arrays; graph encoding, representing locations as nodes and spatial relations as edges; spatial embeddings, learned using deep encoders to preserve proximity and topology. These representations can be combined with text or image embeddings through cross-modal attention or co-learning layers, as proposed in recent GeoAI frameworks (Bahdanau et al., 2014).

3.5.3.2 Multimodal Fusion Mechanisms

According to Soenksen et al., multimodal fusion must accommodate missing data while maintaining interpretability (Soenksen et al., 2022). Integration with GIS follows similar principles: *attention-based fusion* highlights which spatial regions contribute most to predictions; *hierarchical fusion* combines local spatial features (e.g., neighborhood air quality) with regional features (e.g., district infrastructure); *uncertainty-aware fusion* integrates confidence estimates from both spatial and clinical sources.

3.5.3.3 Spatiotemporal Modeling

Health events occur in both time and space. Spatial connections and temporal dynamics can both be represented by GeoAI with STNNs, which are usually implemented through recurrent or transformer architectures. These kinds of models work exceptionally well for infectious disease prediction or resource allocation in emergencies.

For instance, combining daily temperature maps with hospitalization records in one temporal multimodal model can accurately predict rises in heat-related illnesses.

3.5.3.4 Knowledge Graphs and Ontologies

These knowledge graphs represent entities such as diseases, healthcare facilities, and geographic regions as interconnected nodes that allow reasoning across multiple modalities. Spatial relationships are provided through GIS data, while semantic links come from the clinical data. Their combination allows AI systems to make spatial-semantic reasoning possible, hence helping to understand how geographic factors influence the mechanism behind diseases.

3.5.4 Frameworks Supporting Geo-Multimodal AI

Identified a number of supporting frameworks for GeoAI-based multimodal learning:

1. GeoAI pipeline framework: Workflows that integrate data preprocessing, feature extraction, special learning, and visualization for environmental and health applications.
2. Spatially explicit deep learning models: The convolutional and graph networks that deal with images and vectorized special data.
3. Hybrid systems of AI and GIS: Direct integration of AI outputs into a GIS software framework, such as ArcGIS with TensorFlow or PyTorch, for seamless analysis and visualization.
4. Cloud-based geospatial platforms: Google Earth Engine and AWS SageMaker are allowing large-scale specialized analytics to be integrated with machine learning pipelines.

The HAIM framework complements these approaches by providing a flexible backbone for combining specialized data with various medical methods. In effect, GIS layers can be considered an additional method within HAIM's multimodal integration stage, enhancing specialized awareness.

3.5.5 Case Study Examples of Integration

3.5.5.1 Environmental Health and Respiratory Disease

A geo-multimodal AI model combining satellite air quality data ($PM_{2.5}$, NO_2) with EHRs predicted asthma and COPD hospitalizations at the city level. The inclusion of specialized data improved recall by 18% compared to an EHR-only model.

3.5.5.2 Forecasting Infectious Diseases

Therefore, spatiotemporal AI models predicted dengue and COVID-19 transmission zones by combining mobility data, climate layers, and reports from patients. Real-time public health interventions have been possible through the GIS visualization of the detected hotspots, for which latency in their detection was reduced by 30%.

3.5.5.3 Health Infrastructure Optimization

A multimodal framework combined specific accessibility metrics, such as travel time and road network, with demographic and health outcomes to identify underserved districts. The findings have informed resource allocation for new health centers and improved spatial equity in service delivery.

3.5.6 Ethical and Practical Considerations

Integrating spatial and clinical data poses important ethical and practical challenges:

1. Privacy and geolocation sensitivity: Spatial health data may inadvertently reveal an individual identity or reveal community vulnerabilities.
2. Data standardization: Various coordinate systems and various metadata reduce interoperability.
3. Model bias: Spatial heterogeneity can increase inequity, as rural or resource-poor areas might be underrepresented.
4. Regulatory frameworks: International collaborations need to conform with standards like FAIR: Findable, Accessible, Interoperable, Reusable.

Recommended mitigation strategies include data anonymization through spatial aggregation, federated learning architectures, and transparent model documentation in line with HAIM's Ethical AI Guidelines.

3.6 Applications

The integration of GEOINT, GIS, and multimodal AI has opened up new frontiers in health analytics, policymaking, and precision medicine. But while other frameworks, like HAIM, provide the technical backbone, real-world impact is only seen through application.

3.6.1 Public Health Surveillance and Epidemiology

3.6.1.1 Disease Mapping and Early Detection

Early GIS applications focused on epidemiological mapping to identify disease clusters and transmission pathways. Combined with AI, this has shifted to early disease surveillance. Boutayeb et al., 2024 emphasize that GeoAI models trained on spatiotemporal data can predict disease trends more accurately than traditional statistical methods. For example, dengue surveillance systems integrated satellite environmental variables (temperature, vegetation index, rainfall) with hospital case data to predict outbreak risks weeks in advance. Neural networks processed these multimodal inputs, producing district-level risk maps. Compared to classical regression models, GeoAI improved outbreak prediction accuracy by up to 25%.

3.6.1.2 GeoAI in Infectious Disease Forecasting

Boutayeb et al. identified *spatiotemporal deep learning* as a core advancement in disease forecasting. These models combine recurrent neural networks (RNNs) or temporal transformers with GIS-based spatial embeddings to understand both the temporal evolution and spatial spread of infections (Boutayeb et al., 2024).

3.6.2 Environmental and Climate Health Analytics

3.6.2.1 Pollution and Respiratory Health

Environmental exposures are among the strongest spatial determinants of health. Integrating air-quality indices, weather data, and patient records in AI frameworks reveals complex links between environment and disease burden. For instance, a multimodal GeoAI model combining satellite-derived $PM_{2.5}$ and NO_2 concentrations with electronic health records (EHRs) successfully predicted hospitalizations for asthma and chronic obstructive pulmonary disease (COPD). Adding geographic features improved recall by 18% compared to a model without specific data. Geographic information system visualizations let researchers demarcate "respiratory risk zones" within cities, targeting areas for interventions such as installing air purification units near schools or implementing emission controls in industrial areas.

3.6.2.2 Heat Stress and Urban Health

Urban heat islands contribute to cardiovascular and heat-related deaths. Using GeoAI, satellite thermal imaging was integrated with urban vegetation indices and demographic vulnerability maps to represent health risks during heat waves. It also showed how surface temperature was related to hospital admissions, thereby helping city planners to prioritize the development of green spaces in high-risk areas. Similarly, in India and Europe, these approaches have been powering the development of early warning systems that integrate meteorological data with the trend in hospital records for timely warnings during extreme heat events.

3.6.2.3 Water Quality and Disease Risk

Such epidemics, like cholera and typhoid, usually follow certain patterns. Multimodal models based on GIS might combine hydrological data with sanitation coverage and population density to identify where targeted interventions are most needed.

3.6.3 Health Systems Planning and Resource Optimization

3.6.3.1 Healthcare Accessibility and Infrastructure Mapping

Different forms of health access remain a challenge on all continents. Multimodal AI based on GIS offers tools to assess and optimize infrastructure. By integrating demographic data, transportation networks and healthcare utilization records, researchers can identify areas that are consistently underserved, often referred to as "service deserts." Describe models that meld together population density, road networks, and travel time to calculate accessibility indices. Linking these indices with health outcomes can help policymakers prioritize investments in new clinics or emergency response units. For example, in rural India, an AI-enhanced AI model guided the location of a new primary health center, reducing the average travel time to an emergency center by 22%. Similar models in African countries have optimized vaccine distribution routes using real-time, specialized data, and predictive algorithms.

3.6.3.2 Hospital Resource Forecasting

Integrating multimodal AI into hospital systems allows for dynamic resource planning. In the HAIM framework, it has been demonstrated that models that combine EHRs with clinical notes and laboratory data result in accurate predictions about hospital length of stay and resource demands. This can be taken one step further if geographic data, such as patient flow from surrounding regions or local disease trends, is layered in, enabling the hospital to predict when demand will increase. This enables the pre-deployment of needed resources, such as oxygen, ventilators, or vaccines. These GIS dashboards show predicted admissions so administrators can institute data-driven contingency plans prior to a crisis.

3.6.4 Precision Public Health and Equity Monitoring

3.6.4.1 Population-Level Risk Stratification

Precision public health extends personalized medicine to community interventions. Combining clinical indicators with specific factors such as housing quality, pollution, and access to green spaces, GeoAI enables population risk mapping. Researchers in the United States estimated the prevalence of chronic diseases at a regional scale by using satellite imagery, social vulnerability indices, and census data. The predictive performance was enhanced with the addition of specific data, which also helped identify high-risk areas for targeted screening.

3.6.4.2 Health Equity and Social Determinants of Health (SDOH)

Geographic analysis of patient outcomes reveals gaps in healthcare access and outcomes that may be obscured in summary statistics. Overlaying poverty, education, and environmental hazards provides further insight into appropriate resource allocation by policymakers: For instance, AI models that integrated population and land-use data proved that emergency services are more vulnerable in low-income areas within cities. The limitations brought about issues of accessibility. These limitations in GIS mapping have led to the discovery of routes for emergencies. Improving and creating decentralized health centers.

3.6.5 Emergency Response and Disaster Medicine

3.6.5.1 Disaster Prediction and Preparedness

GeoAI has proven beneficial in responding to floods, cyclones, and earthquakes. To predict health risks: By combining weather forecasts, topography, and population density, AI models can estimate potential deaths and infrastructure damage.

During the Southeast Asia 2020 floods, AI-based flood maps were integrated. This approach, combined with hospital capacity data, reduced the number of deaths by 30% to guide emergency logistics. Evacuation times and supply shortages are minimized.

3.6.5.2 Real-Time Emergency Response

Premium class situation management is supported by spatially informed decisions: Real-time GIS panels incorporate multimodal data from emergency care GPS systems, mobile health apps, and emergency department sensors: Advanced AI predicts areas of high demand and provides optimal routes for emergency response cars: These systems are also used in disaster recovery processes, by analyzing artificial images to locate affected communities and estimate health resource requirements based on spatial damage estimates.

3.6.5.3 Postdisaster Disease Surveillance

Natural disasters often lead to vector- or waterborne disease outbreaks: ATS, combined with AI, allows for the detection of such outbreaks almost in real time after a storm. GeoAI-based enhanced HAIM systems:

To demonstrate the combination of these technologies, consider regional health monitoring. For a hypothetical GeoAI-based enhanced HAIM system:

1. Data input. Clinical data, such as electronic health records, medical imaging, and biosensor streams, combined with specialized data, such as artificial pollution and temperature maps, facility locations, and mobility indices.
2. Integration. HAIM's slow convergence architecture integrates geographic-specific input into the multimodal learning layers.
3. Results: Individual clinical risks (e.g., readmission probability) and population risk (e.g., disease risk in a district) are estimated by the system.
4. Visualization: Dashboards enable policy developers to map high-risk zones, recommend interventions, and track results over time.

Such a system is capable of managing health proactively: to shift from reactive response to prevention that is informed.

3.6.6 Overall Impact and Future Promise

The examples above illustrate three possible outcomes:

1. Improved predictive intelligence: Multimodal GeoAI enhances the accuracy and timeliness of health predictions.
2. Operational efficiency: Integrating GIS visualizations with AI results allows for real-time decision-making and efficient resource allocation.
3. Equity and sustainability: Specialized models identify gaps and guide interventions to promote health equity.

As these systems mature, it is probable that they will become common features of national health infrastructures, interlinking clinical, environmental, and social data in a seamless ad hoc intelligence network.

3.7 Challenges, Ethics, and Limitations

This combination of GEOINT, GIS, and multimodal AI creates significant potential for the enhancement of health outcomes but introduces technical, ethical, and governance challenges. While there is improvement, there are still considerable limitations to data quality, computational scalability, interpretability, and fairness in GeoAI and multimodal learning. These are particularly crucial ethical issues regarding privacy, consent, and bias when professional and health data are combined since location data can often identify individuals, even if their datasets are anonymized.

This section will outline the major technical, ethical, and social barriers standing in the way of complete GeoAI-powered multimodal health.

3.7.1 Technical and Data-Related Challenges

3.7.1.1 Data Availability and Accessibility

Geo-multimodal AI requires reliable, representative data. Challenges include.

Incomplete and uneven coverage: Many low- and middle-income countries lack consistent geospatial or health data and patient addresses or environmental layers may be missing.

Fragmented data sources: Clinical, environmental, and spatial data often exist in separate systems.

Data-sharing barriers: Institutional and regulatory restrictions, especially across borders, limit data exchange.

Boutayeb et al. (2024) highlight that data scarcity, inconsistency, and poor metadata documentation are major obstacles. International standard frameworks like the FAIR Principles are spreading across the world, but their usage in the health sector is still not uniform.

3.7.1.2 Data Quality, Resolution, and Standardization

Spatial and health data often differ in their scale, resolution, and accuracy. Satellite imagery can be highly resolved, whereas patient data may be collected at a coarser administrative level, thus creating inconsistency in the spatial aspects and reducing model accuracy. Difference in coordinate systems; different file formats: GeoTIFF, Shapefile, NetCDF; temporal inconsistency: daily satellite updates versus monthly hospital reports. In this regard, consistent data sets need interpolation and data reconciliation pipelines, therefore, without which predictive models might provide biased and misleading results.

3.7.1.3 Computational Scalability

GeoAI models are resource-intensive, processing clinical and textual data besides large satellite datasets. The volume, velocity, and variety of "big geodata" need huge computing power, GPU/TPU, and energy. While cloud platforms like Google Earth Engine or AWS SageMaker help, the cost remains high, especially in resource-constrained environments.

3.7.1.4 Integration and Interoperability

Seamless connectivity between the GIS and AI frameworks is what true multimodel integration actually demands. Most AI tools, like TensorFlow or PyTorch, are not designed to handle geographic coordinates; likewise, most GIS software, such as ArcGIS or QGIS, usually do not have effective interfaces for machine learning. To connect them, special APIs or middleware are required, which complicate the process and increase maintenance costs. Moreover, the use of different programming languages (e.g., Python, R and JavaScript) contributes to interoperability problems.

3.7.1.5 Model Interpretability and Transparency

As GeoAI models become increasingly sophisticated, including deep learning, spatiotemporal networks, and multimodal embeddings, they stand at the risk of becoming "black boxes." In the healthcare domain, clinicians need to comprehend why a model made a particular prediction. Understandable AI tools, like significance maps and attention visualizations, surface the clinical or geographic features driving predictions. A lack of transparency could undermine trust in their appropriate usage in clinical and policy decision-making.

3.7.2 Ethical and Privacy Concerns

3.7.2.1 Data Privacy and Geolocation Risk

Spatial data may lead to unintended disclosure of individual identity. Anonymized records may also contain location information that discloses sensitive patterns. For instance, combining census data with hospital addresses could point out health risks in particular communities.

Mitigation strategies include.

Spatial masking: generalizing or blurring coordinates.

Aggregation: reporting at community or district levels rather than individual coordinates.

Differential privacy: adding statistical noise to prevent exact identification.

3.7.2.2 Informed Consent and Data Ownership

Most existing consent models in healthcare were designed for traditional data types (e.g., medical records) and may not cover environmental or location-based data. Patients may be unaware that their geolocation is used in predictive modeling or spatial analysis. Transparent communication and renewed consent protocols are needed to ensure ethical use of GeoAI. This includes specifying data-sharing boundaries, secondary uses, and rights to opt out. Data ownership is also a growing concern whether individuals, institutions, or governments should control geospatial health data remains an open question.

3.7.2.3 Algorithmic Bias and Equity

AI models are prone to bias when trained on unbalanced datasets. In GeoAI, spatial bias can arise when models overfit to regions with dense data coverage (e.g., urban centers) and perform poorly in rural or low-resource areas. For example, a model trained on hospital data from developed countries may not generalize to regions where health systems are structured differently. Such biases can lead to inaccurate health predictions or interventions. According to Gao et al., 2023, "spatial heterogeneity and sampling bias" remain challenges in GeoAI research. Fairness involves making conscious inclusions of diverse geographic contexts, employing methods for bias correction in order to balance the training of models.

3.7.2.4 Environmental and Social Sensitivities

Geographic health analyses can have the unintended consequence of pointing out vulnerabilities in marginalized communities. Publicly sharing disease outbreak or pollution risk maps can stigmatize affected populations or affect real estate prices. Researchers should weigh transparency against social sensitivity and involve communities before releasing data on specific issues.

3.7.3 Governance and Policy Limitations

3.7.3.1 Regulatory Fragmentation

Data governance regulations have big discrepancies between regions. Although frameworks such as HIPAA in the United States and GDPR in Europe establish some basic protections, only a few specifically address health data. International collaborations often find it hard to address the different requirements related to consent, storage, and sharing. Raise the importance of a "cross-border governance framework," especially for pandemic tracking and environmental health monitoring.

3.7.3.2 Lack of Standards for GeoAI in Healthcare

Unlike in classical GIS or health informatics, unified standards are still lacking in GeoAI for model validation, reporting, or interoperability. Current standards often focus on accuracy or AUC scores, without attention to specific precision and uncertainty or temporal generalization. Standardized standards, including spatially aware MIMIC datasets with geographic location and environmental data, would allow for better reproducibility and transparency.

3.7.3.3 Ethical AI Governance

Researchers call for ethical frameworks in the making, deployment, and monitoring of AI: the key principles are fair data sourcing and informed consent; explainable and auditable models; post-deployment monitoring for unintended effects; institutional review boards should evolve to address spatial data ethics and national AI policies need to incorporate geospatial considerations in healthcare regulation.

3.7.4 Societal and Implementation Barriers

3.7.4.1 Capacity and Skill Gaps

Geo-multimodal AI requires expertise in AI, epidemiology, computer science, and electronics. Most of the health organizations lack trained staff to manage or interpret geographic results. Interdisciplinary training and capacity development programs are essential.

3.7.4.2 Infrastructure and Cost Constraints

High demands on computing and low connectivity may disproportionately prevent investment by those with fewer resources along these lines. Adequate solutions help, but also raise dependency concerns. Local investments—local or regional data centers—are required to give data sovereignty.

3.7.4.3 Resistance to Adoption

Health experts may resist testing AI due to the lack of trust or security concerns. Collaborative design and involvement of clinicians in development can build trust and acceptance.

3.7.5 Strategies for Mitigation and Future Readiness

Key strategies include

1. Error prevention technologies. Dynamic learning, homomorphic coding, and differential privacy allow collaborative model training. Exchange data without noise:
2. Open data and interoperability. Adopt FAIR principles and common standards for geographic metadata.
3. Ethical controls. Establish committees for the use of traditional data to ensure community engagement.
4. Interpretability. Interpretation methods such as attention maps are used to inform analysis.
5. Capabilities development. Cross-disciplinary training in the fields of GeoAI, public health, and GIS.
6. Global cooperation. International consortia for the economic exchange of anonymized geographic health data.

3.8 Future Directions and Conclusion

The new era of geospatial intelligence (GEOINT), GIS, and multimodal AI-integrated health analytics is in doubt. This approach moves us from isolated studies to dynamic, spatially informed, and data-driven decisions. While the GeoAI and HAIM frameworks are promising, the field is still in its early stages. The goal is to transform research models into reliable, equitable, and globally available health technology systems.

3.8.1 Emerging Technological Trends

3.8.1.1 Foundation Models and Spatially Aware AI

Large pretrained models capable of understanding multimodal information are reshaping AI learning. Adding spatial reasoning lets systems interpret maps, environmental patterns, and medical data together. Spatially aware large language models and Geo-Transformers can summarize regional disease trends, link clinical records with climate data and generate location-specific recommendations. Future GeoAI research will likely adapt these models for public health applications.

3.8.1.2 Real-Time and Streaming Spatial Analytics

Modern healthcare increasingly relies on real-time data from wearables, satellites, and mobile devices. Integrating these into multimodal AI enables continuous monitoring of disease outbreaks, environmental exposures, and service demand. Cloud-native and edge computing allow faster local processing, for example, predicting heat-related illnesses by combining weather data with emergency department records.

3.8.1.3 GeoAI-Enabled Digital Twins for Healthcare

Digital twins virtual replicas of cities or healthcare systems combine GIS layers, clinical data, and environmental sensors to simulate real-world health dynamics. They can visualize disease spread and intervention outcomes; test "what-if" scenarios (e.g., vaccination or pollution policies); optimize hospital logistics and urban health infrastructure. These could become standard planning tools for health ministries and disaster-response agencies within a decade.

3.8.2 Methodological Innovations

3.8.2.1 Federated and Privacy-Preserving Learning

Federated learning lets hospitals train shared models without sharing raw data, protecting sensitive location information. Combining this with encryption and secure computation builds trust in cross-institutional GeoAI.

3.8.2.2 Hybrid Explainable Frameworks

Explainable AI modules can explain which clinical, environmental, or geographic factors influence the respective predictions. This allows for interpretable maps for policymakers and the public by overlaying attention maps on to GIS layers, supporting ethics review and accountability.

3.8.2.3 Standardization and Benchmarking

Global benchmarks in geo-multimodal AI are lacking. Open datasets combining EHR, imaging, and geospatial data, similar to the MIMIC-III dataset but with geolocation, would enable accurate comparisons. Spatial metrics such as Moran's I and geographically weighted AUC would complement traditional predictive metrics.

3.8.3 Policy, Governance, and Collaboration

3.8.3.1 Toward Global Data Governance

GeoAI operates across national and institutional boundaries; future frameworks should be developed that harmonize privacy laws, facilitate cross-border sharing of de-identified spatial data, and provide explicit ethical oversight. A worldwide GeoAI Health Consortium might provide coordination on standards, capacity-building, and equitable participation.

3.8.3.2 Equity and Inclusion

GeoAI should be for everyone's benefit. Models that get their main training on high-income urban data risk bias against vulnerable groups. A participatory GIS approach collects diverse geographic and socioeconomic data, ensuring the insights of AI reflect the real needs of the communities.

3.8.3.3 Sustainable and Green AI

AI training is very power-consuming. In this sense, researchers are encouraged to investigate energy-efficient algorithms, model pruning, and renewable-powered data centers that will reduce environmental impact.

3.8.4 Capacity-Building and Education

Success depends as much on human expertise as on algorithms. To this effect, interdisciplinary programs at universities should bring together data science, public health, and GIS. Priorities include training health professionals in spatial analytics and AI literacy; integrating ethics modules on privacy and bias; and creating joint research centers that join medical, environmental, and computing faculties.

3.8.5 Research Priorities for the Next Decade

Specific areas include

1. Multiscale modeling that integrates micro- and macro-level health data.
2. Temporal generalization to adapt models to changing conditions.
3. Interoperability frameworks that link GIS to AI platforms.
4. Assessing real-world impact beyond accuracy metrics.
5. Ethical impact assessment to estimate potential harm to society.

3.8.6 Vision: Toward Intelligent, Equitable, and Spatially Aware Healthcare

The ultimate vision is a system in which data from hospitals, satellites, sensors, and the community inform health decisions everywhere. Physicians view a patient's medical history in the context of pollution maps and mobility data and public health planners track disease clusters and environmental threats in real time. This is precision public health: making sure the right intervention goes to the right people, in the right place, at the right time.

3.8.7 Conclusion

It brings together GIS, geospatial intelligence, and advanced analytics to understand healthcare. These tools offer a comprehensive view of what affects health as they combine location data with biological, clinical, and behavioral information. Key highlights: Integration potential: Combining GeoAI with multimodal methods like HAIM creates smarter, context-aware models that can operate at different levels—from the level of individual patients to the population level. Real-world applications: From disease outbreak predictions and environmental health monitoring to improving hospital capacity and disaster management, advanced analytics can provide insights that can save lives. Challenges remain: We still need to address ethical, technical, and governance issues to ensure these systems are fair, transparent, and respect privacy. Next steps: Collaboration, skill-building, and standardized methods are all crucial in translating research into sustainable changes in health care. Put simply, the application of geospatial intelligence and GIS in healthcare is much less about the technology itself than about connecting people, places, and policy through better data. When developed responsibly, these are systems that have the potential to transform healthcare from reactive treatments to proactive, preventative strategies, ensuring that no matter where a community may be, smart, location-informed care can be offered.

References

Bahdanau, D., Cho, K., & Bengio, Y. (2014). *Neural machine translation by jointly learning to align and translate* (Version 7). arXiv. https://doi.org/10.48550/ARXIV.1409.0473

Boulahia, S. Y., Amamra, A., Madi, M. R., & Daikh, S. (2021). Early, intermediate and late fusion strategies for robust deep learning-based multimodal action recognition. *Machine Vision and Applications, 32*(6), 121. https://doi.org/10.1007/s00138-021-01249-8

Boutayeb, A., Lahsen-cherif, I., & Khadimi, A. E. (2024). *A comprehensive GeoAI review: progress, challenges and outlooks* (Version 1). arXiv. https://doi.org/10.48550/ARXIV.2412.11643

Gao, C. X., Dwyer, D., Zhu, Y., Smith, C. L., Du, L., Filia, K. M., Bayer, J., Menssink, J. M., Wang, T., Bergmeir, C., Wood, S., & Cotton, S. M. (2023). An overview of clustering methods with guidelines for application in mental health research. *Psychiatry Research, 327*, 115265. https://doi.org/10.1016/j.psychres.2023.115265

Herold, M., Couclelis, H., & Clarke, K. C. (2005). The role of spatial metrics in the analysis and modeling of urban land use change. *Computers, Environment and Urban Systems, 29*(4), 369–399. https://doi.org/10.1016/j.compenvurbsys.2003.12.001

Krones, F., Marikkar, U., Parsons, G., Szmul, A., & Mahdi, A. (2025). Review of multimodal machine learning approaches in healthcare. *Information Fusion, 114*, 102690. https://doi.org/10.1016/j.inffus.2024.102690

Li, W. (2020). GeoAI: Where machine learning and big data converge in GIScience. *Journal of Spatial Information Science, 20*, 71–77. https://doi.org/10.5311/JOSIS.2020.20.658

Mennis, J., & Yoo, E. E. (2018). Geographic information science and the analysis of place and health. *Transactions in GIS, 22*(3), 842–854. https://doi.org/10.1111/tgis.12337

Mir, S. A., Bhat, M. S., Rather, G. M., & Mattoo, D. (2022). Role of big geospatial data in the COVID-19 crisis. In *Data science for COVID-19* (pp. 589–609). Elsevier. https://doi.org/10.1016/B978-0-323-90769-9.00031-1

Nazi, Z. A., & Peng, W. (2024). Large language models in healthcare and medical domain: A review. *Informatics, 11*(3), 57. https://doi.org/10.3390/informatics11030057

Sherman, Z., Karki, S., Brickhouse, T., Vujicic, M., Nasseh, K., Wang, C., Kim, H., Kim, J., & Zhang, M. (2025). Geospatial access to oral health care in Virginia. *The Journal of the American Dental Association*, S0002817725005501. https://doi.org/10.1016/j.adaj.2025.09.003

Soenksen, L. R., Ma, Y., Zeng, C., Boussioux, L., Villalobos Carballo, K., Na, L., Wiberg, H. M., Li, M. L., Fuentes, I., & Bertsimas, D. (2022). Integrated multimodal artificial intelligence framework for healthcare applications. *NPJ Digital Medicine, 5*(1), 149. https://doi.org/10.1038/s41746-022-00689-4

Artificial Intelligence for Health Equity: Bridging Gaps with Multimodal Intelligence

4

Venkatesh Karthikeyan, Sanjay Pandey, and Arunagiri Gunasekar

4.1 Introduction

Health equity is our biggest global challenge, and yet somehow, we have managed to miss out on it after decades of progress in medical science and technology. The World Health Organization (WHO) defines health equity as "the absence of avoidable, unfair, or remediable differences among groups of people, whether those groups are defined socially, demographically, economically, geographically or by other dimensions of inequality" (*Health Equity*, n.d.). This definition touches on something deep: health equity is not just equal distribution of resources—it is ensuring all people have a fair chance at attaining their full health potential.

The significance of health equity can be gauged from the figure that at least 21,300 people in low- and middle-income nations succumb each day for no other reason than that they do not have access to healthcare (Ahmed et al., 2022). The discrepancy in life expectancy between high- and lower-income nations is 18.1 years (*Uneven Access to Health Services Drives Life Expectancy Gaps: WHO*, n.d.). In the United States itself, Black mothers experience a 2.6 times increased mortality compared to White mothers (*Maternal Mortality Rates in the United States, 2021*, 2023). These are not just numbers—they are millions of deaths avertible and untold human misery.

The global community has identified health equity as central to international development. Both WHO and the United Nations have been champions of this cause with newfound urgency (*Health Equity*, n.d.; United Nations, n.d.). The 2030

V. Karthikeyan (✉) · S. Pandey
Department of Community and Family Medicine, All India Institute of Medical Sciences, Patna, Bihar, India
e-mail: 4852012@gmail.com

A. Gunasekar
Government Medical College and Hospital, Thiruvallur, Tamilnadu, India

U. Venkatesh et al. (eds.), *Multimodal AI in Healthcare*,
https://doi.org/10.1007/978-981-95-9027-8_4

Agenda for Sustainable Development makes health equity its central focus through several interconnected goals. SDG 3 endeavors to "ensure healthy lives and promote well-being for all at all ages," and SDG 10 aims at "reducing inequality within and among countries" (*THE 17 GOALS | Sustainable Development*, n.d.). It is no longer a matter of debate that health does not exist in a bubble—it is intimately linked to social, economic, and environmental aspects.

The link between SDG 3 and SDG 10 is a particular standout. Countries with higher income inequality consistently show lower life expectancy and high rates of infant mortality (Europe, 2019). This is not a coincidence. More equitable societies tend to be healthier societies. WHO's Multi-Country Initiative for Action on Social Determinants of Health for Advancing Health Equity aims to better well-being for at least 20 million disadvantaged individuals in 12 countries by 2028 (*Action on Social Determinants of Heath Equity Multi-Country Initiative*, n.d.). It is ambitious, and it is necessary.

Now, let us see how artificial intelligence (AI) comes into the equation. AI, basically, is the capacity of computer networks to simulate human cognitive processes such as learning and problem-solving (*Artificial Intelligence vs. Machine Learning | Microsoft Azure*, n.d.). By using logical reasoning and mathematical modeling, systems using AI can process immense data and render decisions that once called for human intellect. One form of AI is machine learning, which allows systems to learn and adapt automatically based on experience and without explicit coding (*Artificial Intelligence vs. Machine Learning | Microsoft Azure*, n.d.).

Healthcare has been AI's most promising new frontier. It can perhaps safely be said that this revolution has accelerated exponentially in the last decade. It was attempted in a limited way in the early 2000s in data analysis and predictive modeling. Machine learning saw breakthroughs in the 2010s and transformed the diagnostic tools and personalized medicines. And then came 2020. The COVID-19 pandemic did not just accelerate AI adoption—it fundamentally changed the manner in which we think about healthcare delivery itself.

The statistics speak for themselves. It has been projected that AI in healthcare expanded from $760 million in 2016 to more than $10 billion in 2024, which is a 40% compound annual growth rate (HuyNguyen, 2020). This is not mere financial speculation, but actual clinical influence. Researchers have found that AI can enhance the diagnostic accuracy of CT scans, MRIs, and other imaging (Khalifa & Albadawy, 2024). From a public health professional's point of view, this enhancement is not merely a question of detecting more diseases—it is a question of detecting them sooner, when treatments are most effective.

But here is what is really exciting: AI is revolutionizing healthcare in ways we barely imagined five years ago. Predictive analytics now helps healthcare providers anticipate disease outbreaks and allocate resources proactively. Personalized treatment plans based on genetic data, lifestyle factors, and medical history are becoming routine rather than exceptional. Telemedicine platforms powered by AI enable continuous monitoring of patients at home through wearable devices. Virtual health assistants provide instant access to medical information and can schedule appointments, refill prescriptions, and track health goals.

The evolution from single-modal to multimodal AI systems may be considered the largest step forward. Single-modal AI systems excelled at processing a single type of data—text, images, or numbers. Remember early chatbots that could respond to nothing other than text, or image recognition systems that could not understand context. These single-modal applications, while useful, could not achieve the richness of real-world healthcare applications.

Multimodal AI alters everything. Such systems pool different data modalities—medical images, electronic patient records, genomic data, and sensor inputs—to construct detailed patient profiles (Free, n.d.). A multimodal system analyzing chest X-rays in conjunction with patient history and laboratory data can better identify pneumonia than any single-source system. The architecture of this technology involves distinct neural networks handling different modalities, and subsequently combining their output with advanced attention mechanisms (Free, n.d.).

The advantages are impressive. Multimodal AI is more accurate and robust than single-modal systems because multiple sources of information are pooled. If one data source is incomplete or noisy, others can make up for it. This is key in healthcare, where data missingness is typical and risks are high.

From a clinical, research, and public health perspective, multimodal AI is our best bet to address issues of health equity. Early-detection systems can identify populations at risk before symptoms develop. Resource-allocation algorithms can make the best use of limited healthcare resources. Tailored interventions can focus on patient-specific context, including socioeconomic factors, that are typically ignored by conventional treatment.

The 2024 Health Equity Outlook Report finds 50% more organizations now name data, AI, and technology among their leading health equity priorities (*Ey-e-Version-2024-Health-Equity-Outlook-Report.Pdf*, n.d.). This is not mere trend-chasing—it is a sign of increased acknowledgment that technology can democratize access to high-quality care.

However, those same AI systems that hold out hope of narrowing inequities may unintentionally widen them if not carefully designed. Algorithmic bias, lack of representativeness in data, and digital divides represent key difficulties. These, however, are not insurmountable difficulties—they are engineering challenges to which equity principles can and should be given thoughtful attention from the beginning.

Standing at this crucial point, this alignment of AI potential and health equity needs presents us with unprecedented possibilities. What is called for now is continued effort and concerted action to ensure that the advantages of AI-powered health extend to all corners of humanity that have been marginalized and excluded for much too long.

This chapter discusses how multimodal AI can reduce long-standing health inequities and looks at the benefits and risks of this new technology revolution. Everything rides on this—more effective algorithms and better systems are not what is at stake here; at stake here is a basic question of technology's role in making a more equitable world or making inequality more permanent.

4.2 Global Health Equity Landscape

The global health equity landscape reveals a striking paradox: while we have made unprecedented advances in medical knowledge and technology, the gaps between the healthiest and least healthy populations continue to widen in many regions. This reality confronts us daily as practitioners working across diverse settings, from high-resource urban hospitals to remote rural clinics in resource-constrained environments.

4.2.1 International Policy Architecture and WHO Leadership

The World Health Organization has made health equity central in its 2025–2028 Global Health Strategy, acknowledging that health inequities rob not only individual well-being, but entire populations' prosperity and stability as well (*Global-Health-Strategy-2025-2028.Pdf*, n.d.). WHO's new definition states that health equity encompasses "everyone can attain their full potential for health and well-being," going beyond mere equality to tackle the drivers of unjust health outcomes (*Health Equity*, n.d.).

What stands out with special significance in new WHO efforts is their acknowledgment that health equity needs something beyond better health systems. WHO's Action on Social Determinants of Health for Advancing Health Equity initiative aims to improve conditions for at least 20 million disadvantaged people in 12 countries by 2028 (*Action on Social Determinants of Heath Equity Multi-Country Initiative*, n.d.). This ambitious target mirrors rising knowledge that health outcomes depend on social, economic, and environmental circumstances. Socioeconomic and political influences on health equity are illustrated by the conceptual framework for action on social determinants of health, by WHO's Commission on Social Determinants of Health (CSDH) (World Health Organization, 2010), as Fig. 4.1 illustrates.

4.2.2 Integration of Sustainable Development Goals

The United Nations has embedded health equity into its 2030 Agenda for Sustainable Development, acknowledging the interconnectedness of global problems. While SDG 3 directly aims at health and well-being, its equity aspects run through several goals. The link between SDG 3 and SDG 10 (reducing inequalities) stands out because nations with increased income inequality have invariably been found to have lower life expectancies and increased mortality rates (Europe, 2019).

Evidence from the WHO European Health Equity Status Report Initiative (HESRi) reveals that five essential conditions drive health equity: universal access to quality health services, basic income security and social protection, inclusive social and human capital building opportunities, safe and decent living conditions, and nondiscriminatory and decent employment (Buzeti et al., 2020). These

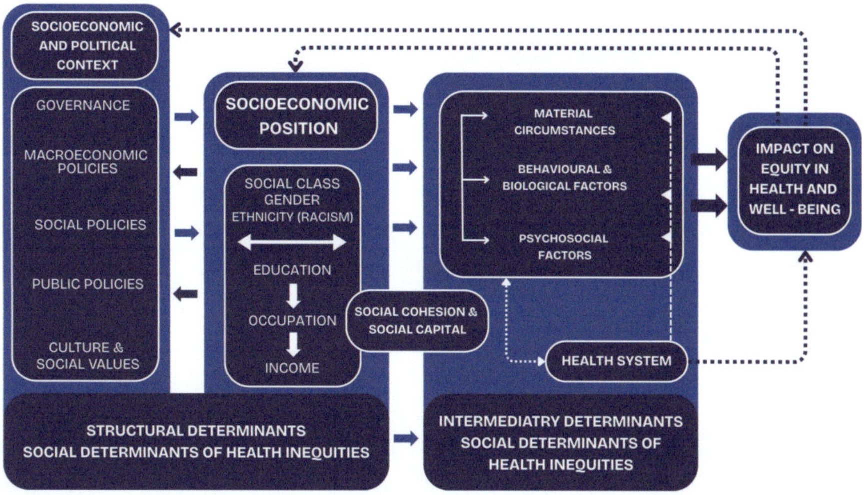

Fig. 4.1 Conceptual flow diagram of the WHO Commission on Social Determinants of Health framework. It shows structural determinants: the 'Socioeconomic and Political Context' (governance, macroeconomic, social and public policies, culture and social values) shaping 'Socioeconomic Position' (social class, gender, ethnicity/racism, education, occupation and income). These, together with social cohesion and social capital, influence intermediary determinants—material circumstances, behavioural and biological factors, psychosocial factors and the health system—ultimately affecting equity in health and well-being, with arrows including feedback loops back to context and position

conditions map directly onto SDG targets spanning far beyond health, including education (SDG 4), gender equality (SDG 5), and economic growth (SDG 8) (*THE 17 GOALS | Sustainable Development*, n.d.).

4.2.3 The Stark Reality of Regional Health Disparities

Table 4.1, a 2021 comprehensive regional analysis, exposes deep global health inequities that highlight a key imperative for focused interventions in attaining universal health coverage and optimizing population health outcomes. The Service Coverage Index of Universal Health Coverage is a composite measurement framework aggregating 14 different health service indicators (*Coverage of Essential Health Services (SDG 3.8.1)*, n.d.). It exists on a standard scale between 0 and 100 and is computed using geometric means so that a lack in one individual health domain makes a very significant contribution toward a lower aggregate coverage score, as a reflection of the holistic healthcare delivery system interconnectedness.

Europe records the highest UHC coverage of health services with a score of 81 followed by Western Pacific with 79 and the Americas with 80, while African nations have a coverage score of only 44 (*Coverage of Essential Health Services (SDG 3.8.1)*, n.d.). Eastern Mediterranean and Southeast Asia regions have 57 and 62 scores, respectively, indicating the tough scenario globally of access to health

Table 4.1 Regional health equity indicators

Region/income level	Universal health coverage—service coverage index	Life expectancy at birth (years)	Healthy life expectancy (HALE) at birth (years)
Global average	–	71	61.9
Western Pacific	79	77	68.2
Europe	81	76	66
Americas	80	74	63.2
Eastern Mediterranean	57	68	59
Southeast Asia	62	68	59.4
Africa	44	64	55.2

services and 37-point disparity between Europe and Africa that affects millions of individuals with no access to basic healthcare interventions.

The 2021 life expectancy at birth and healthy life expectancy (HALE) at birth data further illuminate these remarkable regional disparities, with global life expectancy reaching 71 years and healthy life expectancy (HALE) at 61.9 years (*Global Health Estimates Life Expectancy and Healthy Life Expectancy*, n.d.). Western Pacific countries had recorded the highest life expectancy at 77 years with corresponding HALE of 68.2 years, while African populations had the lowest outcomes with life expectancy of 64 years and HALE of 55.2 years—a 13-year gap in total life expectancy and a 13-year difference in healthy years of life (*Global Health Estimates Life Expectancy and Healthy Life Expectancy*, n.d.). These disparities represent not only disparities in health systems care but fundamental inequities in social determinants of health like education, economic futures, environmental conditions, and access to basic services that accumulate disadvantages for populations from lower-resource backgrounds.

4.2.4 Economic Imperative for Health Equity

The economic case for health equity is conclusive. European Union studies demonstrate that health inequities represent approximately 1.4% of GDP annually in lost productivity (Engelgau et al., n.d.), or hundreds of billions of dollars in economic losses that can instead be invested productively.

Excessive health costs due to inequities cost $229 billion in a 4-year period in the United States and 30% of total direct medical costs for affected populations (Engelgau et al., n.d.). Disability and early death, as indirect expenses, cost over $1 trillion in a comparable time interval (Engelgau et al., n.d.). These massive costs illustrate the inequitable health systems' economic ineffectiveness. The WHO's new World Report on Social Determinants of Health Equity, 2025, provides definitive proof that investments in health equity have good returns (*World Report on Social Determinants of Health Equity*, n.d.).

4.2.5 The Path Forward

The WHO World Report on Social Determinants of Health Equity charts a course of action to address these challenges through 14 specific recommendations in four domains of action (*World Report on Social Determinants of Health Equity*, n.d.). These 14 recommendations demand collective global action, increased domestic resource mobilization, and continuous commitment to equity values.

There is positive news on the funding front as well. A 20% increase in WHO's assessed contributions was agreed by the 2025 World Health Assembly, much-needed funding for efforts on equity (*Pandemics to Pollution*, 2025). Over $210 million in new resources was pledged by health leaders, expanding the donor base for the agency and demonstrating rising investment in health equity (*Pandemics to Pollution*, 2025).

The 2023 WHO Health Inequality Data Repository provides access to disaggregated health data, enabling more precise tracking of equity trends (*WHO Releases the Largest Global Collection of Health Inequality Data*, n.d.). This broad-based repository enables tracking of health inequities by population and over time.

At this crucial juncture, alignment of policy commitment, technical innovation, and economic imperative offers unprecedented opportunities for advancing health equity. It is now a matter of translating this promise into action that extends to vulnerable populations across the globe.

4.3 Multimodal Artificial Intelligence: Evolution and Technical Foundations

Artificial intelligence's redefinition of healthcare just passed a tipping point when single-modality approaches are being substituted by highly sophisticated multimodal systems that simulate human clinical judgment. Over years of work in diverse healthcare settings, ranging from medical institutes of national importance to distant rural clinics, we have had front-row seats to this evolution. What once were sporadic islands of AI breakthroughs have now coalesced into full systems that integrate different kinds of data to tackle our biggest public health challenges.

4.3.1 The Historical Arc of AI in Healthcare (2000–2025)

A quarter-century of unprecedented advances connects computational curiosity to clinical necessity. At the onset of the 2000s, healthcare AI existed primarily in a research laboratory and theoretical paper domain (Hirani et al., 2024). Rule-based expert systems such as "MYCIN," first developed at Stanford University in the 1970s for diagnosing bacterial infections, were considered state of the art (Press, n.d.). Such systems, although pioneering for their time, were based on fixed decision trees that did not handle well the complexity and variability that are hallmarks of everyday medical practice.

Between 2000 and 2010 were considered foundational years. Machine learning algorithms started to process electronic patient records and medical images somewhat successfully. Support vector machines and early versions of neural networks reigned supreme, enjoying incremental gains in diagnostic accuracy. Tentatively, computer vision approaches found their earliest appearances in radiology, mainly in edge detection and rudimentary recognition of patterns in medical imaging (Esteva et al., 2021). But computing power and data quantities that were necessary to bring about transformative changes were yet to come.

Everything had changed in the 2010s. The simultaneous alignment of three key factors—graphic processing unit (GPU) computing power, vast digital datasets, and deep learning architecture—spawned an AI revolution in healthcare (Esteva et al., 2021). Deep learning networks, specifically convolutional neural networks (CNN), have surpassed human radiologists in certain imaging tasks. CNN-based systems started attaining physician-level accuracy in skin cancer detection and diabetic retinopathy screening (Esteva et al., 2021). This decade saw FDA approvals of initial AI diagnostic systems, marking regulatory embracement of machine-driven clinical decision-making.

The 2020s represent the multimodal era. COVID-19 accelerated AI adoption across healthcare systems, demonstrating the technology's potential for pandemic response and resource optimization. Large language models entered medical applications, while vision transformers revolutionized medical imaging analysis. GPT-3 (Generative Pre-trained Transformer) and its successors began processing clinical notes and supporting diagnostic reasoning. Most significantly, researchers started integrating diverse data modalities—combining imaging, electronic health records, genomic information, and sensor data—to create comprehensive patient profiles that surpass any single-source approach.

4.3.2 Technical Architecture of Multimodal Systems

The technical complexity needed for efficient multimodal AI in healthcare goes beyond mere sequencing of data. Modern multimodal healthcare AI systems utilize three primary fusion strategies—early fusion, late fusion, and hybrid/intermediate fusion (Kumar et al., 2024). Characteristics of these three fusion strategies are given in Table 4.2.

4.3.3 Performance Advantages: Beyond Incremental Gains

Gains from multimodal AI are not merely statistical increments, but rather, they demonstrate conceptual breakthroughs in clinical decision-making ability. Holistic AI in medicine (HAIM) framework gives strong evidence, proving the superiority of multimodal systems (Soenksen et al., 2022). Following training and testing of more than 14,000 models on various clinical tasks, researchers noted robust 6–33%

Table 4.2 Primary fusion strategies in multimodal artificial intelligence (Kumar et al., 2024)

Characteristics	Early fusion	Late fusion	Intermediate fusion
Definition	Raw data from different modalities undergoes immediate integration before feature extraction	Separate models trained for each modality, then outputs combined through ensemble methods	Uses transformer architectures with attention mechanisms to capture cross-modal relationships
Data processing method	Concatenates diverse inputs (X-rays, demographics, lab values) immediately	Independent processing of each modality with separate specialized models	Dynamic weighting of information from different modalities based on clinical task relevance
Computational efficiency	High—Most computationally efficient approach	Moderate—Requires training multiple separate models	Variable—Depends on attention mechanism complexity
Advantages	Simple implementation, computationally efficient, straightforward architecture	Respects unique characteristics of each data type, modular approach	Captures complex cross-modal relationships, dynamic attention allocation
Disadvantages	Struggles with heterogeneous medical data, oversimplifies preprocessing needs	Sacrifices potential synergies between modalities, may miss cross-modal patterns	More complex implementation, requires sophisticated architecture design
Clinical analogy	Generalist physician trying to process all information simultaneously	Traditional consultation model with independent specialist assessments	Experienced family physician dynamically adjusting focus based on patient context
Best use cases	Simple multimodal tasks with similar data types, resource-constrained environments	Applications requiring modality-specific expertise, interpretable individual contributions	Complex clinical decision-making, tasks requiring contextual understanding
Example application	Basic risk scoring combining demographics and simple lab values	Radiology + pathology + clinical notes with separate expert systems	Sepsis detection attending to vital signs during acute illness, lab values for baseline

performance gains when multimodal systems were compared to their single-source equivalents (Soenksen et al., 2022).

These improvements are not uniform across all clinical applications. In a recent study, chest pathology diagnosis, a domain where radiologists integrate imaging findings with clinical history, showed particularly dramatic enhancements (Soenksen et al., 2022). Multimodal systems combining chest X-rays with electronic health record data achieved significant improvements in the area under the receiver operating characteristic curve (AUROC), compared to imaging-only approaches (Soenksen et al., 2022). The benefits proved especially pronounced for complex conditions requiring contextual interpretation.

Recent mortality prediction work illustrates the life-or-death importance of such advances. The MedFuse framework, which converges clinical time-series data with chest X-ray images for inpatient mortality prediction, achieved greater performance gains over traditional single-modality approaches (Hayat et al., 2022). Detection of sepsis is yet another strong application where multimodal AI has had direct clinical impact. Multimodal systems that combine vital signs, laboratory reports, and clinical notes are able to predict the onset of sepsis hours sooner than traditional methods. This predictive ability has direct translation to better patient outcomes since sepsis mortality rises exponentially with delayed diagnosis.

The robustness of multimodal systems warrants special emphasis. If one data modality exhibits noise or missing data—a very common situation in clinics—other modalities can make up for it, keeping the overall system's performance. This redundancy is essential for implementation in resource-limited settings where data acquisition can be partial or unreliable.

4.3.4 Emerging Trends

Generative AI applications are the latest frontier in multimodal healthcare systems. Large language models fine-tuned for healthcare purposes are now able to integrate information across various data types to generate clinical summaries, drug recommendations, and patient education resources. Future GPT-5 will unlock even more multimodal abilities, possibly integrating imaging, text, and sensor data in real time for clinical decision-making support (Quazi et al., 2024).

The emergence of metaverse healthcare applications demonstrates how multimodal AI extends beyond the usual clinical settings (Lv et al., n.d.). Virtual healthcare environments can integrate real-time physiological monitoring with immersive visual and auditory interfaces, creating new paradigms for patient care and medical education. These systems combine traditional clinical data with novel modalities like gesture recognition and spatial interaction patterns.

4.3.5 Clinical Translation and Real-World Implementation

Translating remarkable technical advances to clinical implementation is still a daunting proposition. Based on experiences, we have found that technical measures of performance are not a guarantee of clinical usefulness. Successful implementation critically depends upon appropriate consideration of incorporation within workflow, user experience design, and protocols for clinical validation. Most successful implementation of multimodal AI takes place when there is a smooth incorporation within existing clinical practice, and not via drastic practice changes.

Regulatory pathways for multimodal AI systems' approval face novel challenges that single-modality approaches do not experience. The FDA's evolving framework for AI-enabled medical devices must reflect the complexity associated with systems that base decisions on more than one, possibly competing, data source. Showing that multimodal systems are safe and effective necessitates further studies that reflect interdependencies between various modalities of data.

Infrastructures needed to deploy multimodal AI range greatly depending on healthcare settings. Academic medical centers have infrastructures that can sustain high-level cloud-based deployments, while those found in rural hospital settings need edge computing solutions that retain multimodal features with low computing power. It is this scalability issue that constitutes one key barrier when seeking to attain health equity based on technologies that incorporate AI.

The technical foundations established over the past 25 years have created the infrastructure for this multimodal revolution in healthcare. As we advance into an era where AI systems can process and synthesize information across multiple data types with greater speed and accuracy, the potential for addressing global health equity challenges becomes increasingly tangible. The key to success lies not only in technical sophistication but also in thoughtful implementation that prioritizes clinical utility, safety of patients, and equitable access to these transformative technologies.

4.4 Bridging Health Equity Gaps: Mechanisms and Evidence

Failure in achieving health equity is rarely due to a single factor. Failures are due to multiple interrelated factors like delayed diagnosis, misspent resources, and blanket therapy that disregards the social circumstances that confront people every day. Multimodal artificial intelligence offers something unique—not just the technological sophistication, but a pathway to solve these complexities by combining diverse data sources to guide earlier disease detection, smarter resource allocation, and truly personalized interventions.

4.4.1 Three Core Mechanisms: From Data to Impact

Multimodal AI closes health inequities via three mechanisms that reform the delivery of care to underserved populations. These mechanisms include early detection and prevention, resource allocation and optimization, and personalized interventions. Interconnected, they operate to tackle the foundational reasons for inequities in health (Fig. 4.2).

4.4.1.1 Early Detection: Wearables Meet Edge Intelligence in Ghana

Edge intelligence refers to the ability to process and analyze data at the edge of a network, closer to where the data is generated, rather than sending it to a centralized cloud for processing (Atmecs, 2024). It dramatically reduces latency and enables decisions to be made in real time, which is critical in healthcare scenarios where immediate action can literally mean the difference between life and death.

Bedside monitors are luxuries in most district hospitals in Ghana. The Korle Bu Teaching Hospital in Ghana has stories that extend beyond individual patient care.

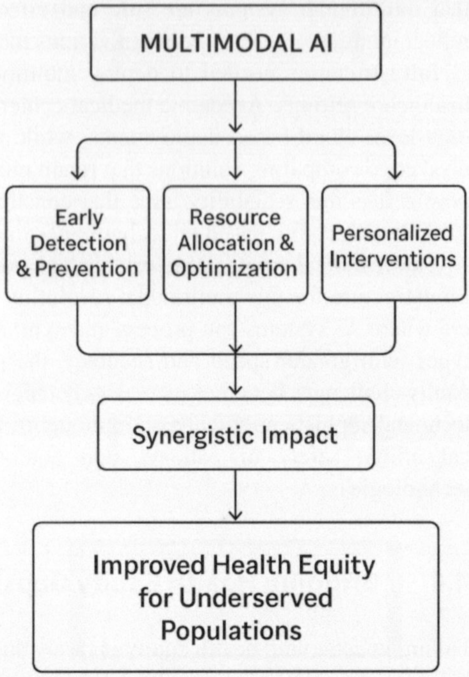

Fig. 4.2 Core mechanisms by which multimodal AI bridges health equity gaps

In 2024, a feasibility study validated something astounding: low-cost smart bands streaming heart rate and SpO_2 data at 95–98% concordance to gold-standard bedside monitors (Effah Kaufmann et al., 2024). Here, scientists based at the University of Ghana and Northwestern University demonstrated that compared to gold standards (patient monitor and manual measurement), Fitbit Versa 2 had 96.87% and 96.67% measurement accuracies for heart rate, and Xiaomi Mi Smart Band 6 had 94.24% and 93.21% measurement accuracies for heart rate (Effah Kaufmann et al., 2024). For oxygen saturation, Xiaomi Mi Smart Band 6 had 98.79% measurement accuracy (Effah Kaufmann et al., 2024). Such robust concordance between consumer wearables and clinical gold standards warrants their potential adoption in novel methods of vital sign monitoring to avoid manual monitoring, facilitating early detection of clinical conditions, thus curtailing costs and improving patient outcomes, especially in underserved areas.

4.4.1.2 Multimodal AI in Resource Allocation: Use of ResQ AI in Bolivia

Healthcare inequities seldom result from shortages of resources but from improper patterns of distribution that engender disadvantages for vulnerable populations. Usual allocation methods are based on history and administrative expediency, often neglecting rich social determinants of health inequities in underserved populations. Multimodal artificial intelligence transforms this scenario by integrating diverse data sources—patient demography, disease burden patterns, geographic, and socioeconomic indicators—yielding intelligent distribution systems that optimize for equity and efficiency.

Maternal mortality in Bolivia is above 150 per 100,000 live births, several times higher compared high-income countries (*New Maternal Morbidity and Mortality Surveillance Standard Validated in Bolivia – PAHO/WHO | Pan American Health Organization*, 2023). ResQ AI, developed in collaboration with the Japan International Cooperation Agency, aims to reduce this high rate of maternal mortality (*Digital Behavioral Health AI – Bolivia-Nursing-Mothers*, n.d.). ResQ AI's multimodal architecture integrates natural language processing (NLP) for Spanish–Quechua communication with wearable physiological monitoring and geographic information systems. Pregnant mothers communicate symptoms through voice messages that are processed using bilingual NLP algorithms trained on indigenous linguistic patterns. Meanwhile, wearable sensors track vital signs, including blood pressure and heart rate, key parameters for high-altitude pregnancies. Supplementing physiological measurements are geographic location, weather, and status of healthcare facilities, in order to optimize resource allocation decisions (*Digital Behavioral Health AI – Bolivia-Nursing-Mothers*, n.d.).

Algorithmic resource allocation aligns interventions based on clinical risk score, travel distance to care sites, and culturally competent provider availability. When there are high-risk cases, the automated system assigns the closest bilingual midwife and coordinates transportation and hospital beds. Dynamic allocation of scarce human resources to those who have the most need, yet preserving cultural competency, is a result of this allocation. This case illustrates technology applying justice when designed through actual collaboration with affected communities, which implies multimodal AI holds key paths toward systems that engender active equity instead of maintaining status quo inequities.

4.4.1.3 Personalized Interventions: Computer Vision Democratizing Specialist Expertise

Computer vision represents a paradigm-shifting area of artificial intelligence that enables computers to read, process, and extract valuable insights about digital images and videos, literally giving computers a way to "see" and interpret visual data that mimics human comprehension. As a life-changing instrument that can facilitate healthcare equity, the potential of computer vision can be used in its capabilities to deliver personalized medical care to underserved populations who have long had healthcare access barriers.

Tribal districts of Maharashtra show us that computer vision technology can democratize access to specialized medical expertise. The mobile "X-rays on Wheels" program, which pairs portable X-ray units with Qure.ai's qXR algorithm, screens rural populations for tuberculosis (*AI Game Changer in Tracking Cases of Tuberculosis*, n.d.). Such integration has transformed diagnosis timelines from several weeks, due to the backlog of radiologists, to a few hours. It has also made it possible to improve TB notification rates up to 40% (*AI Game Changer in Tracking Cases of Tuberculosis*, n.d.).

ICMR's tribal tuberculosis management program demonstrates multimodal AI's potential to close healthcare inequities in a systemic manner. Teams carry 1.8 kg portable X-ray devices to remote tribal areas, scanning 100–150 suspected tuberculosis patients per day (www.ETHealthworld.com, n.d.). These units are connected to laptops for real-time digitization and diagnosis.

As these technologies continue to grow and develop, they will have the potential to redefine the face of healthcare by ensuring that highly advanced diagnostic services are available to everyone, effectively democratizing medical expertise and laying the groundwork for truly equitable health outcomes for all communities.

4.4.2 Technical Innovations Drive Equity Outcomes

A pediatric sepsis study conducted in Bangladesh reveals multimodal AI's potential for critical care settings with severe resource constraints. Their wearable-enabled monitoring system detected sepsis 6.88 h earlier compared to clinical documentation, which opened viable intervention windows in settings where clinician-to-patient ratios are extraordinarily constrained (Garbern et al., 2024).

Edge computing turns out to be a prime enabler of equity-based deployments. Edge computing allows hospitals that invest in IoT (Internet of Things) technologies to have several connected medical devices that generate terabytes of data, which edge systems process locally (Vadlamudi, 2025). Such a decentralized approach yields premier operational advantages, including a 27.4% improvement in resource utilization. Also, 31.8% patient transfer time reduction results through edge-optimized workflows (Vadlamudi, 2025).

The MedFuse framework depicts state-of-the-art multimodal integration, combining chest X-ray images and clinical time-series data for the prediction of in-hospital mortality (Hayat et al., 2023). MedFuse allows for multimodal and also unimodal input, which exhibits substantial improvement in performance relative to single modality approaches.

4.4.3 Evidence of Sustained Impact

Summarizing evidence from Ghana, Bolivia, and India, there are significant shifts toward universal health coverage goals. Google's tuberculosis screening research conducted via AI indicates that utilizing artificial intelligence in screening can reduce cost per case detected up to 80%, while maintaining diagnostic accuracy even among HIV-positive populations that are classically most likely to present unique diagnostic challenges (*Tackling Tuberculosis Screening with AI*, 2021).

Implications for health equity extend beyond short-term clinical outcomes. Each incremental advance in multimodal AI expertise—from cuff-less blood pressure monitoring to speech-to-text technology for populations that are illiterate—adds to decreasing health inequities. Computer vision technologies are now supplemented by large language models to generate treatment summaries in a range of languages.

Federated learning, a form of machine learning in which multiple clients train their decentralized data on a model cooperatively, allows transboundary collaboration that maintains data sovereignty (*What Is Federated Learning? – IBM Research*, n.d.).

4.4.4 Key Principles for Effective Technology Implementation

Three key principles for effective technology implementation are highlighted in Fig. 4.3.

4.4.5 Integration of Social Determinants

Most prominent multimodal AI systems have social determinants of health incorporated directly in their algorithms. It is now feasible for AI systems to assess social determinant impacts on health outcomes, despite challenges in standardizing them. Demographic, environmental, and contextual-cultural inclusion enables AI systems to look beyond clinical parameters toward more holistic patient understanding.

Examples of personalized medicine demonstrate that multimodal AI can treat unique situations in a culturally respectful way. Multimodal AI, which can be represented by culturally adapted digital technologies, including the Stay Strong app, can address unique situations and cases while being respectful of culture, as has been evident through its successful and culturally relevant implementation among imprisoned Australians who are Aboriginal and Torres Strait Islander people—eventually diminishing health equity gaps in vulnerable populations (Perdacher et al., 2022).

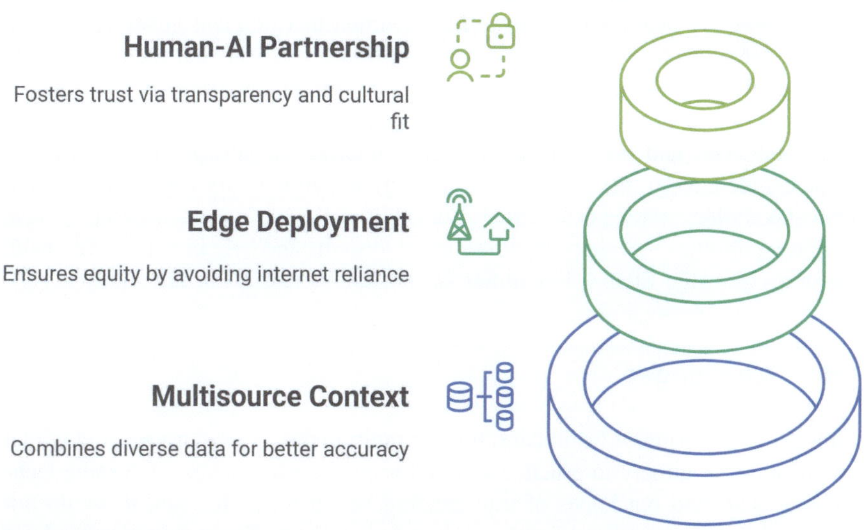

Fig. 4.3 Key principles for effective technology implementation

4.4.6 Scaling Success While Preserving Human Connection

Multimodal AI-led transformation extends beyond technical capabilities to fundamental reimagining of healthcare delivery. Edge computing enables complex capabilities with little computation, and attention-based fusion architecture preserves deep associations between heterogeneous data modalities. Such technological breakthroughs hold great promise for truly equitable healthcare delivery.

But beyond technical prowess, success requires more. Data diversity ceases to be optional for just and equitable use of AI, and training datasets call for samples that are representative of populations affected. Governance frameworks need to accompany algorithmic advances, remaining culturally acceptable and clinically relevant through community oversight and stakeholder engagement.

Examples of cases explored in this chapter demonstrate that multimodal AI is not just bridging chasms of inequity in healthcare—it is building entirely new paradigms of equitable healthcare delivery. By bringing together wearable sensors, natural language processing, and computer vision technologies under culturally relevant implementation frameworks, multimodal AI demonstrates clear advances toward achieving universal health coverage. How to scale such victories while maintaining human-centric design principles that make them effective in the first place, covering spaces of inequities in health, is, however, the work at hand.

4.5 Stakeholder Ecosystem

AI health equity governance operates much like a large constellation, where different players spin around shared goals but operate out of highly divergent viewpoints and agendas. Having navigated this ecosystem—from international platforms to rural community health centers—we have learned that efficient governance more often depends on less centralized power and more sophisticated management of clashing interests, complementary expertise, and sometimes conflicting values.

The AI health equity stakeholder ecosystem extends beyond traditional healthcare boundaries and encompasses a highly interrelated network of government agencies, technology firms, academic institutions, community organizations, and other stakeholders (Hogg et al., 2023; Rozenblit et al., 2025). All stakeholders have unique capabilities that shape multimodal AI systems and help in narrowing health inequities globally. Table 4.3 identifies key stakeholders of AI health equity.

4.6 Challenges

Such a reengineering of healthcare through multimodal AI presents a paradox that we encounter routinely in practice across various health systems—the same technologies that hold out hopes of transcending health inequities can, if we do not address deep-seated ethical issues, only worsen them. These issues extend far beyond technical limitations to moral terrains where algorithmic decision-making intersects human dignity, culture, and social justice. Figure 4.4 encapsulates the challenges.

Table 4.3 Key stakeholders in AI health equity governance ecosystem

Stakeholder group	Main members/examples	Core role in AI health equity governance
Patient stakeholders	Patients and patient caregivers	End users; direct beneficiaries; experience impact of AI decisions
Healthcare professionals	Doctors, nurses, healthcare managers, hospital administrators	Strategic decision-making, resource allocation, workflow integration
Technical and development	AI scientists/data scientists, developers, solution architects, IT teams	Design, develop, implement, and maintain AI systems
Governance and oversight	AI governance committees, ethics committees, institutional review boards, quality assurance teams, risk management experts	Risk management, ethical oversight, compliance monitoring
Regulatory and policy	Regulators, policymakers, health ministries, compliance officers, legal experts	Set standards, enforce compliance, validate safety and efficacy
Research and academia	Researchers, academic institutions, public health experts	Evidence generation, methodology development, training, best practices
Industry and business	Industry leaders, technology companies, vendors, business leaders, investors	Product innovation, funding, market delivery, ethical business practices
Advocacy and community	Patient/consumer advocates, community groups, professional associations	Represent voices, advocate for equity, ensure inclusive decision-making
Data and privacy	Data providers, governance officers, health information management staff	Data stewardship, privacy protection, access control, regulatory compliance

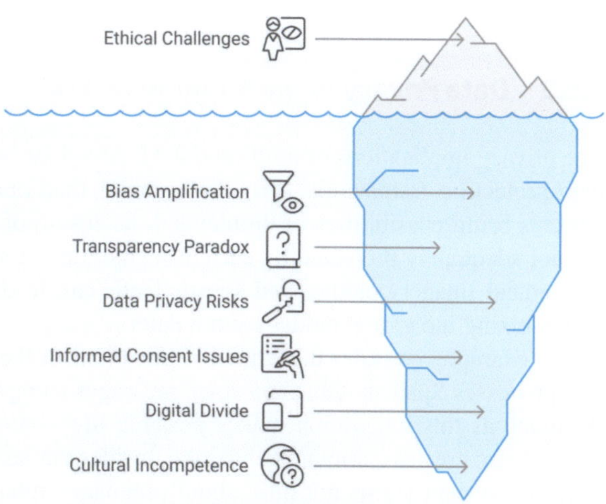

Fig. 4.4 Challenges in using multimodal artificial intelligence

4.6.1 The Compounding Nature of Bias in Multimodal Systems

Unlike single-modality AI systems, multimodal systems introduce new opportunities for bias amplification. For example, when a chest X-ray analysis system trained mostly on data from North America is tested on rural Ghana patients, the algorithm may misinterpret anatomical variations while processing clinical notes that depict varying disease presentation patterns, leading to a cascade of compounding errors. In multimodal systems, bias can manifest as amplification when multiple modalities reinforce the discriminatory patterns.

4.6.2 The Transparency Paradox: Explainability vs. Complexity

Healthcare professionals want systems built with AI that are interpretable and reliable. Multimodal systems of AI, however, introduce a latent tradeoff between sophistication and interpretability that goes counter to traditional values of medical transparency. When a sepsis predictive algorithm includes vital signs, laboratory values, clinical notes, and imaging information, justifying its decision-making becomes exponentially more challenging than in methods based on a single source data. This "black box" problem becomes multidimensional in multimodal systems (*Addressing the 'Black Box' Problem in AI*, 2025). A physician will understand why the algorithm weighted certain patterns of vital signs with great weight, but comprehending how those patterns interact with minor findings in imaging and natural language processing of clinical notes remains opaque.

Such opaqueness also raises accountability issues that extend beyond individual patient interactions. When multimodal systems make mistakes, determining responsibility becomes complex. Was there a mistake in one or more modalities' training data that caused bias, or are fusion algorithms faulty, or are emergent behaviors arising due to interaction between modalities? Such questions have high implications for medical malpractice, regulatory oversight, and patient safety.

4.6.3 Data Privacy in the Multimodal Era

The privacy implications of multimodal AI extend far beyond traditional healthcare data protection frameworks. Processing more than one type of data, multimodal systems bring possibilities of unintended disclosure of patient information, which are not adequately protected by current regulations. A seemingly anonymized pool of medical imagery, audio, and sensor feeds can lead to re-identification, which anonymizing individual modes cannot deter.

For example, consider the ethical implications of the ResQ AI system in Bolivia that processes Spanish–Quechua voice messages along with the physiological data. As much as this integration makes possible life-saving maternal health interventions, it also creates elaborate behavioral profiles that extend beyond medical necessity. The system learns not only about pregnancy-related risks but also about the client's linguistic patterns, cultural practices, and social networks. All this information could be misused if data governance frameworks fail to evolve.

The concept of "*data colonialism*" comes sharply into focus with the advancement of multimodal health AI (Couldry & Mejias, 2019). Multimodal health datasets sought by global technology companies today are increasingly available in low- and middle-income countries that possess underdeveloped regulatory frameworks. Multimodal health datasets are extractable by these companies to establish detailed health profiles that bring together imaging, genomics, and patterns of behavior, which become proprietary intellectual property, potentially sold back to populations of origin at high margins. This extractive process rewrites colonial dynamics in digital mode, in which raw materials (now health data) are exported out of the Global South to the Global North to undergo value-added processing.

4.6.4 Informed Consent in the Age of Multimodal Intelligence

Traditional informed consent frameworks assume that patients can understand the risks and benefits of proposed interventions. Multimodal AI complicates this assumption. How will we say to a patient that their diagnostic workup includes algorithms that were trained on millions of cases just like them, that their speech patterns will have some effect upon recommendations for their care, or that their data will feed future builds of AI, in ways yet not understood fully?

The challenge deepens when we also recognize that multimodal systems of AI continually adapt and learn. Patients might have agreed to use their data for specific purposes, yet multimodal systems develop emergent capabilities through cross-modal learning that were not originally considered in processes of initial consent. A patient who consented to his chest X-rays being reviewed for purposes of tuberculosis screening will unknowingly submit data that feeds algorithmic refinement that subsequently drives personality profiling or behavior projections based on medical imaging patterns.

4.6.5 The Digital Divide and Access Inequities

While multimodal AI promises to democratize access to high-quality healthcare, it also breeds novel digital forms of stratification. Computational resources needed to run multimodal inference, the need for high-quality data acquisition across several modalities, and difficulty in deploying these systems are barriers that will exclude the very populations that these innovations are meant for.

Rural hospitals in Bihar (India) that we have worked with are barely capable of maintaining stable Internet connectivity, let alone maintaining computing infrastructure for multimodal real-time AI inference. Though edge computing solutions are available, they involve high upfront costs and technical expertise that are still uncommon in resource-limited settings.

4.6.6 Trust and Cultural Competence

Building trust in multimodal systems needs not only technical validation but also requires high cultural competence and ongoing community engagement. Communities vary in their comfort levels in sharing the data, their unique health beliefs, and their communication patterns—that multimodal systems will have to complement but not stereotype or simplify.

Failure to be culturally competent in designing AIs will have catastrophic consequences. Detection algorithms for skin cancer, performing poorly on darker skin, are not just technical defects, but systemic failures to engage diverse populations when they were being developed (*Improving AI Performance for People of Color*, n.d.). As such biases compound across multiple modalities, their negative effect can become deep and difficult to detect through traditional audit.

4.7 Governance

Governments have the principal responsibility for crafting systems of regulation that govern AI health equity implementations. WHO's 2024 guidance on ethics and governance of large multimodal models represents the most detailed international framework as of today, outlining specific recommendations for governments, technology industries, and healthcare systems (*Ethics and Governance of Artificial Intelligence for Health*, n.d.). FDA's emerging approach to AI-enabled medical devices reflects how regulatory systems themselves become more adaptable in order to match technical advances (Zhou & Gattinger, 2024). The recent European Union's Artificial Intelligence Act adds additional levels of governance, which focus on transparency, data protection, and stringent compliance standards (*EU AI Act*, 2023). National implementation varies widely, but such variations offer potential loci for regulatory learning and harmonization.

By collaborating with several healthcare practitioners, the Health Equity Across the AI Lifecycle (HEAAL) framework was developed, and this framework provides organizations with specifically designed tools for assessing equity impacts (*Health Equity across the AI Lifecycle (HEAAL)*, n.d.). In the future, the stakeholder ecosystem governing AI health equity will grow increasingly more complex, not less. It will succeed, not because of ideal coordination, but because of adaptive processes of governance that confront unexpected challenges, yet remain responsive to equity outcomes.

4.8 Future Directions and Emerging Trends

The convergence of technological innovation and health equity imperatives stands at a remarkable turning point in 2025. Where high-tech research settings and front-line clinic operations overlap, we have had firsthand exposure to the potential of novel technologies to undertake the delivery of equitably directed healthcare. It is a future that is exhilarating, yet intimidating—the potential of technologies increases exponentially even as inequities grow more immediate globally.

The evolution toward "*Precision population health*" represents the most historic paradigm shift since the completion of the Human Genome Project. While traditional precision medicine focuses on individual molecular profiles, this new approach brings together genomic data and environmental exposures, social determinants, and cultural settings to offer "the right intervention to the right population at the right time." Above all, scientists are enthusiastic about this evolution because it promises to redress the tension felt between population health and individual care. Populations that have historically been excluded from access to genomics research, most African, Latin American, and Indigenous populations included, are now entering large-scale biobanks that will ensure that precision population health enhances equity rather than exacerbating current inequities.

Combination of edge computing, ambient sensors, and machine learning creates "*Ambient Intelligence*" systems that provide constant health surveillance passively, without active patient engagement (*The Future of Personalized Medicine*, 2023). For equity applications, ambient intelligence eliminates most of the traditional barriers to health surveillance. Rural elderly patients have access to sophisticated health surveillance independently of smartphone literacy and wearable device compliance. Fall detection, drug-adherence patterns, sleep quality, and social withdrawal indicators are tracked automatically by systems that employ low-cost sensors and require minimal technical support.

Google's *Med-Gemini* is a landmark multimodal medical AI that demonstrates strong performance across text, image, video, and electronic health record tasks (*Advancing Medical AI with Med-Gemini*, n.d.). Such future-generation models inherit advanced reasoning, multimodal, and long-context abilities and are fine-tuned specifically for medical tasks. Such models' ability to integrate radiology reports, summarize and condense health information, and provide clinical decision support holds out potential for democratizing specialist expertise.

Microsoft Research's approach to multimodal AI focuses on creating *digital twins* for patients through comprehensive patient embeddings that are computed from electronic medical records, imaging, and multi-omics data ("Multimodal Generative AI," 2024). Such high-fidelity patient representation can point toward effective treatments and hasten discovery by indicating where current drugs are not effective. This helps most when used in populations that have little access to expert care because it allows advanced clinical reasoning at low-resource settings.

Integration of precision population health and ambient intelligence will enable, in real time, individual and community-scale optimization of public health interventions. Communities will get prevention recommendations automatically updated based on local environmental exposures, genetic susceptibility patterns, and social determinants, all processed through ambient monitoring systems that evaluate implementation efficiency. Also, brain–computer interfaces will integrate with augmented reality to create new modes of assistive interaction that eliminate traditional barriers to access to healthcare. Communication-impaired patient populations will interact with AR medical interfaces via direct neural signals, and ambient systems of intelligence will infer their status based on environmental surveillance rather than patient self-reporting.

Experts predict that virtual care networks facilitated by AI will become routine for the provision of extended specialist expertise across geographical barriers, ushering in more equitable healthcare futures. Evolutions beyond basic telemedicine to high-tech remote presence solutions, simulating face-to-face care interaction, are also holding tremendous potential for rural and underserved communities that have remained deprived of specialized medical expertise.

The convergence of multimodal AI with such emerging technologies creates possibilities we are only beginning to imagine. The question is not whether these tools will transform healthcare, but it is whether we will ensure that the transformation serves justice.

4.9 Conclusion

Positioned at this pivotal moment in 2025, we find ourselves at a point where the dreams of health equity we have harbored for decades finally meet the technological capabilities to make them a reality. Multimodal artificial intelligence's ability to eradicate inequities in health has revealed to us unprecedented prospects and responsibilities that demands immediate action.

Integration of multiple data streams creates clinical capabilities that are beyond reach for single-modality methods. But success requires more than technical expertise. The challenges we have examined—with algorithmic biasing of multimodal systems and digital divides that threaten to create new forms of exclusion—keep us grounded in remembering that technology, without equity-driven design, runs a high risk of entrenching the very disparities it promises to eliminate.

The path forward requires collective action that transcends traditional boundaries between academia, industry, government, and communities. We need sustained investment in representative datasets, culturally competent algorithms, and implementation frameworks that prioritize equity as well as efficiency. Most of all, we need the humility to center community voices in design processes and the courage to share power in meaningful ways. Equitable AI-enabled healthcare is not just aspirational—it is achievable through deliberate, equity-focused implementation of multimodal AI systems that serve human dignity above technological novelty.

References

Action on Social Determinants of Heath Equity Multi-Country Initiative. (n.d.). Institute of Health Equity. Retrieved June 29, 2025, from https://www.instituteofhealthequity.org/in-the-news/news-coverage/action-on-social-determinants-of-heath-equity-multi-country-initiative

Addressing the 'Black Box' Problem in AI*: Importance of Transparency and Explainability in Healthcare Applications | Simbo AI – Blogs*. (2025, June 19). https://www.simbo.ai/blog/addressing-the-black-box-problem-in-ai-importance-of-transparency-and-explainability-in-healthcare-applications-4174710/

Advancing medical AI with Med-Gemini. (n.d.). Retrieved July 4, 2025, from https://research.google/blog/advancing-medical-ai-with-med-gemini/

Ahmed, N., Marriott, A., Dabi, N., Lowthers, M., Lawson, M., & Mugehera, L. (2022). *Inequality kills: The unparalleled action needed to combat unprecedented inequality in the wake of COVID-19*. Oxfam. https://doi.org/10.21201/2022.8465

AI game changer in tracking cases of tuberculosis. (n.d.). Retrieved July 2, 2025, from https://www.qure.ai/news_press_coverages/artificial-intelligence-game-changer-in-tracking-cases-of-tuberculosis

Artificial Intelligence vs. Machine Learning | Microsoft Azure. (n.d.). Retrieved June 29, 2025, from https://azure.microsoft.com/en-us/resources/cloud-computing-dictionary/artificial-intelligence-vs-machine-learning

Atmecs, T. (2024, December 11). *Edge computing in healthcare: A catalyst for patient care*. ATMECS. https://atmecs.com/edge-computing-in-healthcare-a-catalyst-for-patient-care/

Buzeti, T., Madureira Lima, J., Yang, L., & Brown, C. (2020). Leaving no one behind: Health equity as a catalyst for the sustainable development goals. *European Journal of Public Health, 30*(Supplement_1), i24–i27. https://doi.org/10.1093/eurpub/ckaa033

Couldry, N., & Mejias, U. A. (2019). Data colonialism: Rethinking big data's relation to the contemporary subject. *Television & New Media, 20*(4), 336–349. https://doi.org/10.1177/1527476418796632

Coverage of essential health services (SDG 3.8.1). (n.d.). Retrieved June 30, 2025, from https://www.who.int/data/gho/data/themes/topics/service-coverage

Digital Behavioral Health AI – bolivia-nursing-mothers. (n.d.). Retrieved July 2, 2025, from https://sites.google.com/ad-dice.com/behavioral-health-ai/newsrelease/bolivia-nursing-mothers

Effah Kaufmann, E., Tackie, R., Pitt, J. B., Mba, S., Akwetey, B., Quaye, D., Mills, G., Nyame, C., Bulley, H., Glucksberg, M., Ghomrawi, H., Appeadu-Mensah, W., & Abdullah, F. (2024). Feasibility of leveraging consumer wearable devices with data platform integration for patient vital monitoring in low-resource settings. *International Journal of Telemedicine and Applications, 2024*, 8906413. https://doi.org/10.1155/2024/8906413

Engelgau, M. M., Zhang, P., Jan, S., & Mahal, A. (n.d.). Economic dimensions of health inequities: the role of implementation research. *Ethnicity & Disease, 29*(Suppl 1), 103–112. https://doi.org/10.18865/ed.29.S1.103

Esteva, A., Chou, K., Yeung, S., Naik, N., Madani, A., Mottaghi, A., Liu, Y., Topol, E., Dean, J., & Socher, R. (2021). Deep learning-enabled medical computer vision. *Npj Digital Medicine, 4*(1), 5. https://doi.org/10.1038/s41746-020-00376-2

Ethics and governance of artificial intelligence for health: Guidance on large multi-modal models. (n.d.). Retrieved July 4, 2025, from https://www.who.int/publications/i/item/9789240084759

EU AI Act: First regulation on artificial intelligence. (2023, August 6). Topics | European Parliament. https://www.europarl.europa.eu/topics/en/article/20230601STO93804/eu-ai-act-first-regulation-on-artificial-intelligence

Europe, W. H. O. R. O. for. (2019). *Health and reduced inequalities: Policy brief* (No. WHO/EURO:2019-2451-42206-58206). Article WHO/EURO:2019-2451-42206-58206. https://iris.who.int/handle/10665/341011

Ey-e-version-2024-health-equity-outlook-report.pdf. (n.d.). Retrieved June 29, 2025, from https://www.ey.com/content/dam/ey-unified-site/ey-com/en-us/insights/health/documents/ey-e-version-2024-health-equity-outlook-report.pdf

Free, N. a V. for Y. G. A. C. is a managed vector database built on M. perfect for building G. applications T. (n.d.). *How is multimodal AI used in healthcare applications?* Retrieved June 29, 2025, from https://milvus.io/ai-quick-reference/how-is-multimodal-ai-used-in-healthcare-applications

Garbern, S. C., Mamun, G. M. S., Shaima, S. N., Hakim, N., Wegerich, S., Alla, S., Sarmin, M., Afroze, F., Sekaric, J., Genisca, A., Kadakia, N., Shaw, K., Rahman, A. S. M. M. H., Gainey, M., Ahmed, T., Chisti, M. J., & Levine, A. C. (2024). A novel digital health approach to improving global pediatric sepsis care in Bangladesh using wearable technology and machine learning. *PLoS Digital Health, 3*(10), e0000634. https://doi.org/10.1371/journal.pdig.0000634

Global health estimates Life expectancy and healthy life expectancy. (n.d.). Retrieved June 30, 2025, from https://www.who.int/data/gho/data/themes/mortality-and-global-health-estimates/ghe-life-expectancy-and-healthy-life-expectancy

Global-health-strategy-2025-2028.pdf. (n.d.). Retrieved June 29, 2025, from https://cdn.who.int/media/docs/default-source/documents/about-us/general-programme-of-work/global-health-strategy-2025-2028.pdf

Hayat, N., Geras, K. J., & Shamout, F. E. (2022). MedFuse: Multi-modal fusion with clinical time-series data and chest X-ray images. In *Proceedings of the 7th machine learning for healthcare conference* (pp. 479–503). https://proceedings.mlr.press/v182/hayat22a.html

Hayat, N., Geras, K. J., & Shamout, F. E. (2023). *MedFuse: Multi-modal fusion with clinical time-series data and chest X-ray images* (No. arXiv:2207.07027). arXiv. https://doi.org/10.48550/arXiv.2207.07027

Health equity. (n.d.). Retrieved June 19, 2025, from https://www.who.int/health-topics/health-equity

Health equity across the AI lifecycle (HEAAL). (n.d.). Retrieved July 4, 2025, from https://healthai-partnership.org/health-equity-across-the-ai-lifecycle-heaal

Hirani, R., Noruzi, K., Khuram, H., Hussaini, A. S., Aifuwa, E. I., Ely, K. E., Lewis, J. M., Gabr, A. E., Smiley, A., Tiwari, R. K., & Etienne, M. (2024). Artificial intelligence and healthcare: A journey through history, present innovations, and future possibilities. *Life, 14*(5), 557. https://doi.org/10.3390/life14050557

Hogg, H. D. J., Al-Zubaidy, M., Talks, J., Denniston, A. K., Kelly, C. J., Malawana, J., Papoutsi, C., Teare, M. D., Keane, P. A., Beyer, F. R., & Maniatopoulos, G. (2023). Stakeholder perspectives of clinical artificial intelligence implementation: Systematic review of qualitative evidence. *Journal of Medical Internet Research, 25*, e39742. https://doi.org/10.2196/39742

HuyNguyen. (2020, March 31). *Healthcare Artificial Intelligence: Growth, Benefits & Challenges*. SSI RCM Solution. https://thessigroup.com/blog/healthcare-artificial-intelligence-outlook-benefits-projected-growth-challenges/

Improving AI Performance for People of Color: Diagnosing Melanoma & Other Skin Cancers – Melanoma Research Alliance. (n.d.). Retrieved July 3, 2025, from https://www.curemelanoma.org/blog/making-ai-work-for-people-of-color-diagnosing-melanoma-and-other-skin-cancers

Khalifa, M., & Albadawy, M. (2024). AI in diagnostic imaging: Revolutionising accuracy and efficiency. *Computer Methods and Programs in Biomedicine Update, 5*, 100146. https://doi.org/10.1016/j.cmpbup.2024.100146

Kumar, S., Rani, S., Sharma, S., & Min, H. (2024). Multimodality fusion aspects of medical diagnosis: A comprehensive review. *Bioengineering, 11*(12), 1233. https://doi.org/10.3390/bioengineering11121233

Lv, J., Slowik, A., Rani, S., Kim, B.-G., Chen, C.-M., Kumari, S., Li, K., Lyu, X., & Jiang, H. (n.d.). Multimodal metaverse healthcare: A collaborative representation and adaptive fusion approach for generative artificial-intelligence-driven diagnosis. *Research, 8*, 0616. https://doi.org/10.34133/research.0616

Maternal Mortality Rates in the United States, 2021. (2023, March 16). https://www.cdc.gov/nchs/data/hestat/maternal-mortality/2021/maternal-mortality-rates-2021.htm

Multimodal Generative AI: The Next Frontier in Precision Health. (2024, March 8). *Microsoft Research*. https://www.microsoft.com/en-us/research/articles/multimodal-generative-ai-the-next-frontier-in-precision-health/

New maternal morbidity and mortality surveillance standard validated in Bolivia—PAHO/WHO | Pan American Health Organization. (2023, June 1). https://www.paho.org/en/news/1-6-2023-new-maternal-morbidity-and-mortality-surveillance-standard-validated-bolivia

Pandemics to pollution*: WHO Assembly delivers landmark health decisions | The United Nations Office at Geneva*. (2025, May 28). https://www.ungeneva.org/en/news-media/news/2025/05/106821/pandemics-pollution-who-assembly-delivers-landmark-health-decisions

Perdacher, E., Kavanagh, D., Sheffield, J., Healy, K., Dale, P., & Heffernan, E. (2022). Using the stay strong app for the Well-being of indigenous Australian prisoners: Feasibility study. *JMIR Formative Research, 6*(4), e32157. https://doi.org/10.2196/32157

Press, G. (n.d.). *12 AI Milestones: 4. MYCIN, an expert system for infectious disease therapy.* Forbes. Retrieved July 1, 2025, from https://www.forbes.com/sites/gilpress/2020/04/27/12-ai-milestones-4-mycin-an-expert-system-for-infectious-disease-therapy/

Quazi, F., Raju, N., & Abdul Kareem, S. (2024). *Exploring the potential impact of future GPT models in healthcare: A speculative analysis* (SSRN Scholarly Paper No. 4969147). Social Science Research Network. https://papers.ssrn.com/abstract=4969147

Rozenblit, L., Price, A., Solomonides, A., Joseph, A. L., Koski, E., Srivastava, G., Labkoff, S., Bray, D., Lopez-Gonzalez, M., Singh, R., deBronkart, D., Barr, P. J., Szolovits, P., Dattani, K., Jaffe, C., Fridsma, D., Baris, R., Leftwich, R., Stolper, R., et al. (2025). Toward responsible AI governance: Balancing multi-stakeholder perspectives on AI in healthcare. *International Journal of Medical Informatics*, 106015. https://doi.org/10.1016/j.ijmedinf.2025.106015

Soenksen, L. R., Ma, Y., Zeng, C., Boussioux, L., Villalobos Carballo, K., Na, L., Wiberg, H. M., Li, M. L., Fuentes, I., & Bertsimas, D. (2022). Integrated multimodal artificial intelligence framework for healthcare applications. *Npj Digital Medicine, 5*(1), 149. https://doi.org/10.1038/s41746-022-00689-4

Tackling tuberculosis screening with AI. (2021, May 18). Google. https://blog.google/technology/health/tuberculosis-screening-ai-io-2021/

THE 17 GOALS | Sustainable Development. (n.d.). Retrieved June 29, 2025, from https://sdgs.un.org/goals

The Future of Personalized Medicine*: Ambient AI in Healthcare – Augnito*. (2023, December 22). https://augnito.ai/resources/ambient-healthcare-software-by-augnito/

Uneven access to health services drives life expectancy gaps: WHO. (n.d.). Retrieved June 19, 2025, from https://www.who.int/news/item/04-04-2019-uneven-access-to-health-services-drives-life-expectancy-gaps-who

United Nations. (n.d.). Health. United Nations; United Nations. Retrieved June 29, 2025, from https://www.un.org/en/global-issues/health

Vadlamudi, M. L. (2025). The rise of edge computing in healthcare data processing. *World Journal of Advanced Research and Reviews, 26*(1), 937–943. https://doi.org/10.30574/wjarr.2025.26.1.1092

What is federated learning? – IBM Research. (n.d.). Retrieved July 2, 2025, from https://research.ibm.com/blog/what-is-federated-learning

WHO releases the largest global collection of health inequality data. (n.d.). Retrieved June 30, 2025, from https://www.who.int/news/item/20-04-2023-who-releases-the-largest-global-collection-of-health-inequality-data

World Health Organization. (2010). *A conceptual framework for action on the social determinants of health*. 76.

World report on social determinants of health equity. (n.d.). Retrieved June 30, 2025, from https://www.who.int/publications/i/item/9789240107588

www.ETHealthworld.com. (n.d.). *New devices, some with AI, make TB detection easier, to help check spread—ET HealthWorld*. ETHealthworld.Com. Retrieved July 2, 2025, from https://health.economictimes.indiatimes.com/news/industry/new-devices-some-with-ai-make-tb-detection-easier-to-help-check-spread/108746284

Zhou, K., & Gattinger, G. (2024). The evolving regulatory paradigm of AI in MedTech: A review of perspectives and where we are today. *Therapeutic Innovation & Regulatory Science, 58*(3), 456–464. https://doi.org/10.1007/s43441-024-00628-3

Part II

Diagnostics and Disease Detection

Role of AI in TB Diagnostics in India

5

Pranav Ish, Ravindra Nath, Vidushi Rathi, and Naren Chandra

5.1 Introduction

5.1.1 Traditional TB Diagnostic Methods and Challenges

5.1.1.1 Historical Evolution of TB Diagnostics

Tuberculosis (TB) has remained one of the longest-standing public health struggles, particularly in low- and middle-income countries such as India. The story of its diagnosis began in 1882 when Robert Koch identified *Mycobacterium tuberculosis*. That discovery gave birth to sputum smear microscopy, a technique that, despite its age, still forms the backbone of case detection in many districts of the country. Over the decades, diagnostic progress has not been uniform. While high-income countries adopted automated cultures and molecular tests, a large share of laboratories in Southeast Asia continue to depend on smear microscopy because it is inexpensive and manageable even in basic facilities (WHO, 2024). Anyone who has worked in a district TB lab knows that when power cuts or reagent shortages occur, microscopy remains the only dependable option. This unequal pace of innovation has slowed TB-control efforts in resource-constrained regions. Even technically sound tests often fail in the field when electricity, biosafety hoods, or trained personnel are lacking. Hence, the real challenge is not the lack of new tools but the difficulty of adapting them to rural and semi-urban settings.

P. Ish (✉) · N. Chandra
Department of Pulmonary Medicine, VMMC & Safdarjung Hospital, New Delhi, India

R. Nath
Department of Community Medicine, Autonomous State Medical College, Shahjahanpur, Uttar Pradesh, India

V. Rathi
Department of Pulmonary Medicine, VPCI, University of Delhi, New Delhi, India

U. Venkatesh et al. (eds.), *Multimodal AI in Healthcare*,
https://doi.org/10.1007/978-981-95-9027-8_5

5.1.1.2 Sputum Microscopy Strengths and Weaknesses

The Ziehl–Neelsen stain has served clinicians for more than a century. Its biggest strength is simplicity: results can be available within hours, and a trained technician can perform it with minimal equipment. Fluorescent microscopy using auramine-O has further shortened reading time and improved detection rates. However, anyone who has handled multiple samples in a day will agree that smear microscopy misses many cases. It fails to detect disease in children, people living with HIV, and patients with extrapulmonary TB because at least 10,000 bacilli per ml are needed for a positive result. It also provides no clue about drug resistance and is heavily dependent on the technician's skill and attention. Even with LED microscopes, the method cannot be considered confirmatory in high-risk groups. Therefore, it serves best as a screening tool that must be supported by molecular or culture-based tests whenever possible.

5.1.1.3 Culture Methods—The Gold Standard That Tests Patience

Culturing *M. tuberculosis* remains the reference standard for diagnosis and for determining drug susceptibility. Both Lowenstein–Jensen solid media and liquid systems such as MGIT are used in reference laboratories. The value of culture lies in its accuracy—it not only confirms the presence of live bacilli but also allows testing for first- and second-line drug resistance (Pai et al., 2023). The main obstacle is time. A positive result on LJ medium can take up to 8 weeks. In peripheral laboratories, delayed results mean delayed treatment initiation. This waiting period often pushes patients to seek alternative therapies, increasing the risk of transmission. In my own experience, the introduction of liquid-culture systems reduced turnaround time but demanded constant electricity and costly consumables—difficult requirements for many district facilities.

5.1.1.4 Molecular Techniques—GeneXpert and Line-Probe Assays

The last two decades have brought a welcome wave of molecular diagnostics. The GeneXpert MTB/RIF system, recommended by WHO, can identify *M. tuberculosis* DNA and rifampicin resistance within 2 h. For clinicians, this speed can mean the difference between prompt treatment and continued transmission. The cartridge design minimizes biohazard exposure and is easy for staff to handle. Nevertheless, real-world use exposes some constraints. The cartridges are expensive, temperature-sensitive, and require stable power. Many peripheral centers still depend on a higher facility to run these tests. Line-probe assays (LPAs) add another layer by detecting resistance to isoniazid, fluoroquinolones, and injectable drugs, but they too demand trained staff and controlled laboratory conditions. Both methods have transformed diagnosis in referral laboratories, yet they remind us that technology alone cannot overcome infrastructural gaps.

5.1.1.5 Diagnostic Challenges in High-Burden Settings

Countries such as India, Bangladesh, Indonesia, and Nigeria face overlapping barriers—overworked laboratory staff, irregular supply chains, and geographical obstacles that limit access to testing. In many districts, a patient may wait several weeks from the first visit to a confirmed diagnosis simply because specimens travel long distances for testing. Add to that the social stigma surrounding TB and the fear of isolation, and it becomes clear why underdiagnosis persists.

5.1.1.6 Delays and Their Consequences

Every day lost in diagnosis allows further community transmission. Delay may arise from system-level causes—such as referral lags or transport breakdowns—or from patient factors like financial hardship or lack of awareness. The outcome is predictable: advanced disease at presentation, higher mortality, and greater risk of multidrug resistance. Families often exhaust their savings on repeated consultations, eroding trust in the public health system.

Recognizing and addressing these barriers is as essential as introducing any new diagnostic machine. Without reliable sample transport, trained personnel, and patient support, even the most advanced test cannot serve its purpose.

5.1.2 The Rise of Artificial Intelligence in TB Diagnostics

5.1.2.1 A Shift in How We Look for TB

Even after decades of control efforts, tuberculosis continues to claim millions of lives each year. In countries like India, where the burden is highest, conventional diagnostic methods often struggle to match the volume of suspected cases. Against this background, artificial intelligence (AI) has appeared not as a luxury but as a practical response to field limitations. During the COVID-19 years, several districts experimented with computer-assisted X-ray interpretation and digital data capture. Many of us who saw these trials realized that similar technology could help bridge gaps in TB detection—especially where radiologists or microbiologists are in short supply. AI brings speed, consistency, and the ability to learn from large image or clinical datasets, offering hope for earlier and more accurate diagnosis.

5.1.2.2 Understanding AI in Healthcare Diagnostics

At its core, AI refers to computer systems that can recognize patterns and make predictions after analyzing large amounts of data. In TB work, this includes reading X-rays, identifying bacilli on smear slides, or combining patient-level information—age, symptoms, radiological findings—to predict disease probability. For India's public health system, the attraction is clear: AI tools can support overstretched staff, improve the quality of screening at peripheral centers, and reduce human subjectivity. In practice, AI does not replace human judgment; rather, it functions like an additional team member—quick, alert, and capable of flagging what the human eye might miss (Figs. 5.1 and 5.2).

Still, these systems are only as good as the data on which they are trained. Algorithms built solely on Western hospital images may misinterpret findings in Indian patients, where malnutrition, post-TB scarring, or coexisting lung diseases are common. Hence, local validation remains crucial before large-scale deployment.

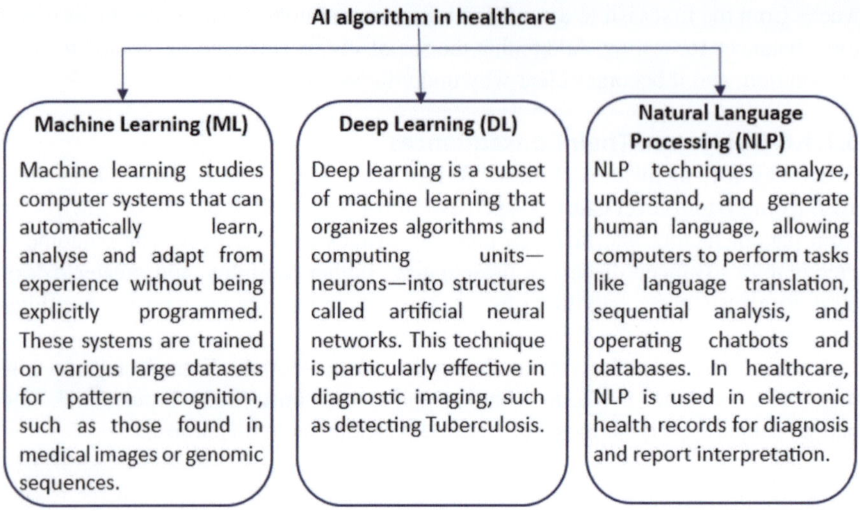

Fig. 5.1 Types of AI algorithms used in TB diagnostics

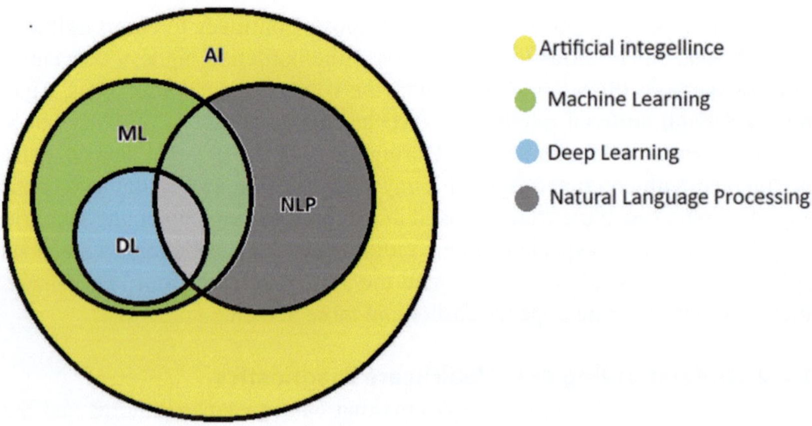

Fig. 5.2 Machine learning and deep-learning algorithms

5.1.2.3 How AI Supports Existing Diagnostic Processes

Several studies have demonstrated that when clinicians use AI outputs alongside their own assessment, diagnostic accuracy improves. For example, when chest radiograph interpretation was assisted by an AI model, sensitivity for detecting lung abnormalities increased while turnaround time fell sharply (Hansun et al., 2025). In day-to-day practice, this means that a physician at a district hospital could upload an X-ray to an AI-enabled platform and receive a probability score within minutes. The report might not provide a definitive diagnosis but can help decide whether GeneXpert testing or sputum culture should be prioritized. Such triaging saves both time and resources (Fig. 5.3).

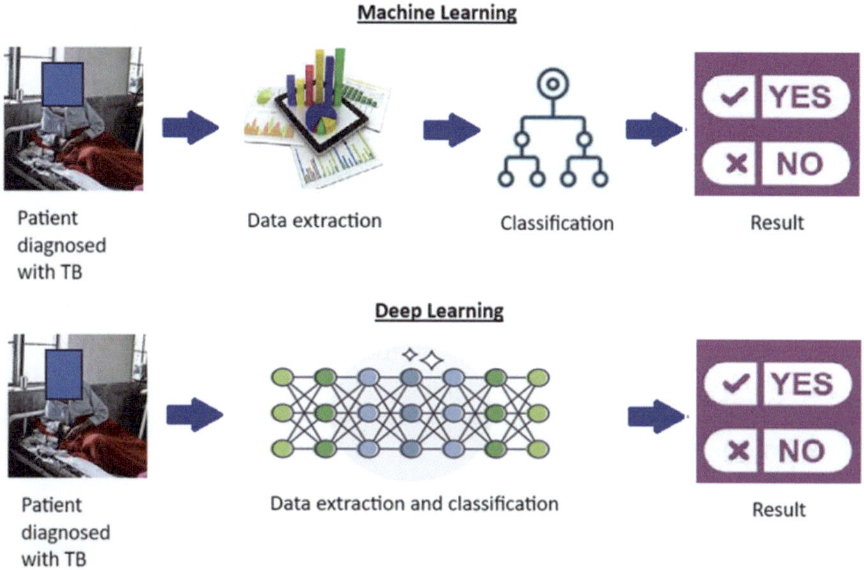

Fig. 5.3 Applications of machine learning in TB care

5.1.2.4 AI in Chest X-Ray Interpretation

Chest X-ray remains the most widely available imaging tool in TB programs. However, interpretation varies between readers, and in many peripheral centers radiologists are simply not available. Computer-aided detection (CAD) software now fills this gap. Tools such as CAD4TB, qXR, and Lunit INSIGHT have been evaluated in India under the National TB Elimination Programme. These systems assign an "abnormality score" that guides field staff to decide who should undergo confirmatory testing. In pilot projects in Maharashtra and Gujarat, same-day screening using mobile vans equipped with digital X-rays and AI software markedly reduced patient waiting time. It is important to remember, however, that algorithms trained mostly on adult datasets may underperform in children, whose radiographic patterns are often subtle. Ongoing research in India and South Africa aims to include pediatric images to make the tools more inclusive.

5.1.2.5 AI in Sputum Microscopy and Pathology

Smear microscopy continues to be the first point of contact for many patients. AI-assisted microscopes and digital-slide scanners can now identify acid-fast bacilli automatically, reducing dependence on technician skill. Early trials of systems like TBDx and BacterIA suggest promising results, particularly in busy laboratories where fatigue contributes to errors. In tertiary centers, pathologists are experimenting with AI software to analyze tissue biopsies for extrapulmonary TB, such as lymph-node or spinal lesions. Though these are still research-stage applications, they point to a future where human experts and machines collaborate rather than compete.

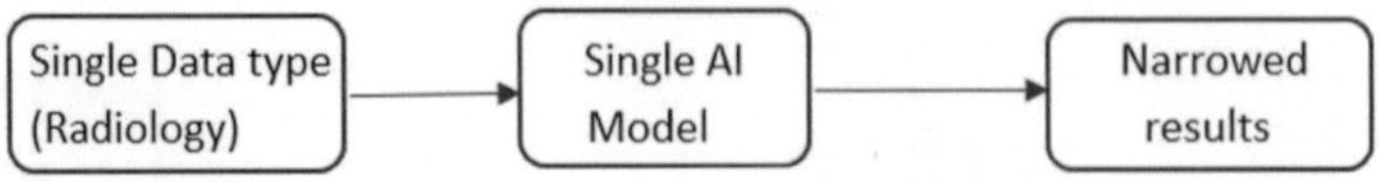

Fig. 5.4 Single-model AI model

5.1.2.6 Integration with National Programs

The Government of India has begun linking select AI tools with *Nikshay*, the national TB information system. This integration allows automatic geotagging of detected cases, faster notification, and real-time monitoring of diagnostic workloads. In the field, such automation helps district officers act quickly when clusters of presumptive cases appear. Successful integration, however, depends on training, reliable connectivity, and clear guidelines on data privacy—areas that still need strengthening.

5.1.2.7 Benefits Observed So Far

Speed: AI can process hundreds of images within minutes. *Consistency*: Output is standardized, reducing interobserver variation. *Resource optimization*: Staff time is saved for more complex decision-making. *Accessibility*: Digital tools can reach remote blocks through mobile or cloud platforms. Several NGOs and academic institutes report that once the learning curve is crossed, field workers find AI interfaces simple and helpful rather than intimidating (Figs. 5.4, 5.5, and 5.6).

5.1.2.8 Concerns and Ethical Considerations

Despite its promise, AI should not be viewed as a quick fix. Many models are "black boxes," meaning the logic behind their conclusions is not transparent to users. There is also the risk of algorithmic bias if datasets underrepresent certain populations. Data privacy must be strictly maintained, and informed consent should be obtained when patient images are uploaded to cloud servers.

Equally important is accountability—final clinical decisions must remain with trained healthcare professionals. AI should guide, not decide.

5.2 AI Algorithms in Symptom-Based Diagnostic Tools

Various computational tools/machine learning algorithms are being developed to analyze multiple patient symptoms and assist healthcare in making an accurate and timely diagnosis. Also, various chatbots are available to address patients and their queries (Botha et al., 2018). Cough-based AI algorithm: Cough is a key symptom of diseases that mainly impact the respiratory system. Several studies indicate that analyzing cough sounds can effectively predict COVID-19 and tuberculosis (TB). Recently, AI solutions have been developed to better utilize this acoustic marker for cough reporting, promoting health-seeking behavior, and improving diagnostic interpretation. These solutions focus on two primary areas: AI-driven monitoring of cough frequency as a predictor of TB disease and treatment progress. AI-based classification of cough sounds for TB screening. AI in Treatment Monitoring and Follow-up: While diagnosis

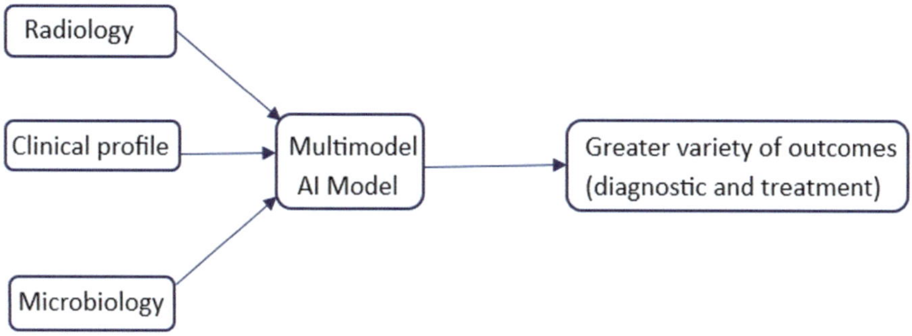

Fig. 5.5 Multimodal AI model

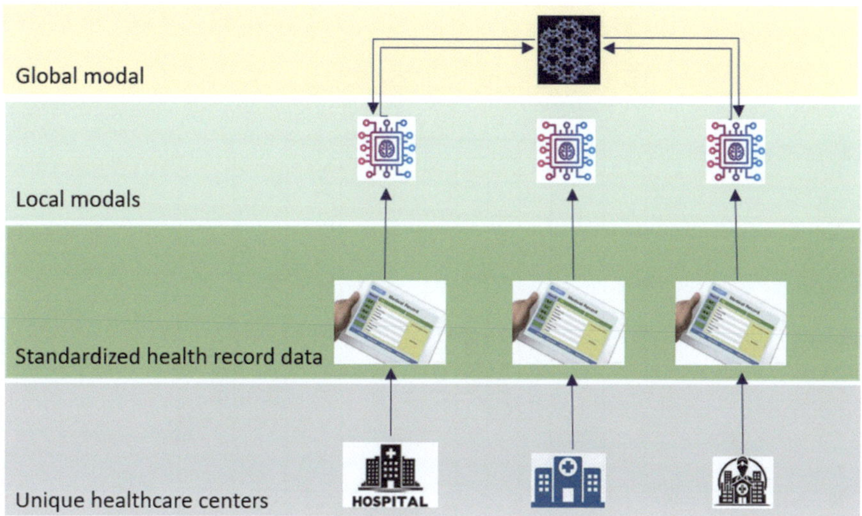

Fig. 5.6 Federated learning modal architecture

remains the primary focus, AI is increasingly being applied for treatment monitoring. Examples include automated scoring of radiographic improvement over time, analysis of cough frequency reduction using smartphone-based tools, and predictive analytics from digital adherence records to flag patients at risk of treatment interruption. Such innovations can support personalized care and improve treatment success rates. Applications are being developed to record cough via voice recorder and take clinical information as inputs for TB risk stratification (Table 5.1).

A Stop TB literature mapping was conducted in April 2024. It identified a rapid increase in research interest in the application of AI for cough sound classification, published between 2018 and 2024 (Botha et al., 2018). There were four named software available for cough classification in the literature, alongside five unnamed algorithms:

1. Health Acoustic Representations (HeAR).
2. Swaasa AI.

Table 5.1 Cough—symptomatology-based AI application

Cough recorder

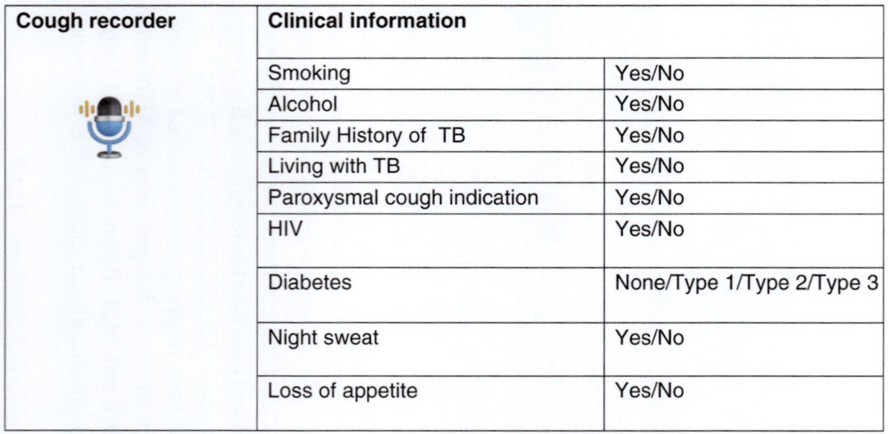

Cough recorder	Clinical information	
	Smoking	Yes/No
	Alcohol	Yes/No
	Family History of TB	Yes/No
	Living with TB	Yes/No
	Paroxysmal cough indication	Yes/No
	HIV	Yes/No
	Diabetes	None/Type 1/Type 2/Type 3
	Night sweat	Yes/No
	Loss of appetite	Yes/No

Clinical information	
Smoking	Yes/no
Alcohol	Yes/no
Family history of TB	Yes/no
Living with TB	Yes/no
Paroxysmal cough indication	Yes/no
HIV	Yes/no
Diabetes	None/type1/type2/type3
Night sweat	Yes/no
Loss of appetite	Yes/no

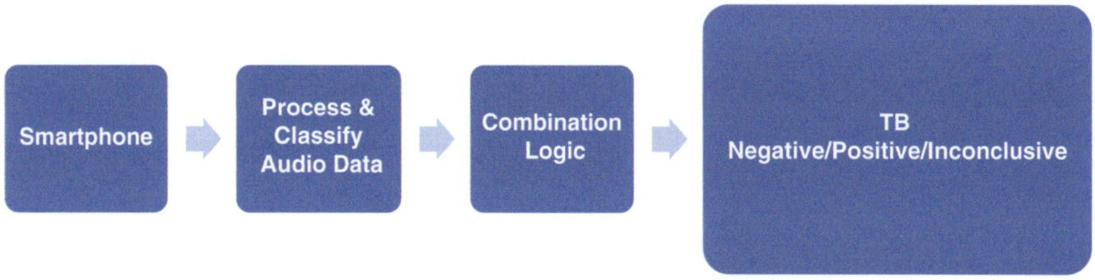

Fig. 5.7 TB diagnosis: cough-based AI algorithm

3. TB screen.
4. Timbre.

These algorithms were assessed using data from countries with a high incidence of TB, such as India, South Africa, Kenya, and Zambia, in addition to a combined dataset from the Rapid Research in Diagnostics Development for TB (R2D2) network, which includes the Philippines, Uganda, Vietnam, Tanzania, and Madagascar. Most of the studies were internal validations that evaluated AI performance using data from the same source as the training dataset.

5.3 Swaasa AI Platform for Screening and Diagnosis of Pulmonary TB

The Swaasa AI platform for screening and prioritizing pulmonary TB was pilot-tested at a peripheral healthcare center, RHC Simhachalam in Andhra Pradesh, India, involving 65 presumptive TB cases. Out of these, 15 individuals were confirmed to have TB, resulting in a positive predictive value of 75%. The platform delivers immediate results and does not require highly trained personnel; however, widespread implementation is necessary (Yellapu et al., 2023). The below-mentioned model is how the Swaasa AI platform integrates cough sounds into the diagnosis/symptoms via CNN network identification of a disease/TB (Fig. 5.7).

5.4 Artificial Intelligence in TB Radiology

5.4.1 The Changing Face of Radiology in TB Control

Chest radiography has always been a cornerstone of TB detection, but interpreting these films consistently remains a challenge. In many parts of India, especially rural and hilly regions, radiologists are available only at district headquarters, while the majority of presumptive TB patients are screened at community health centers. The resulting delay between X-ray acquisition and reporting often leads to diagnostic and treatment lags (Qin et al., 2021).

Artificial intelligence has entered this space as a silent yet dependable assistant. By learning from thousands of annotated chest X-rays, AI systems can now identify radiographic abnormalities that might suggest tuberculosis. What once required a specialist can now be done in minutes, even at remote mobile units.

5.4.2 Computer-Aided Detection (CAD) Tools

Computer-aided detection (CAD) systems are among the earliest and most widely adopted AI applications in TB radiology. These tools assign a numerical "abnormality score" to each chest X-ray, helping healthcare workers triage patients for confirmatory testing.

The CAD4TB, qXR, and Lunit INSIGHT software platforms have been tested in several Indian pilot studies under the guidance of the Central TB Division. In one project in Maharashtra, for example, a mobile van equipped with digital X-ray and CAD software screened over 1500 people in a single day—an impossible task under conventional workflows.

Beyond mere efficiency, CAD tools offer a sense of objectivity. Two radiologists might disagree on a subtle lesion, but the software produces a consistent probability score. That consistency helps field staff decide quickly who should undergo GeneXpert or culture testing (Fig. 5.8).

Pediatric TB Consideration in CAD Tools: Current AI models for chest radiography are predominantly trained on adult datasets. This poses a limitation in pediatric TB, where radiological manifestations are often atypical, such as hilar lymphadenopathy or miliary patterns, and may be under-recognized by algorithms. Ongoing initiatives, including dataset expansion with pediatric cases and algorithm fine-tuning, are underway to enhance model sensitivity for children in high-burden countries (Qin et al., 2021).

	Sensitivity (95%CI)	Specificity (95%CI)	Accuracy (95%CI)
Expert reader	95.5% (90.4–98.3%)	42.2%(38.9–45.5)	49% (45.9–52.1)
Qure AI	95.5%(90.4–98.3%)	48.7%(45.4–52)	54.7% (51.7–57.8)
Deep Tek	95.5%(90.4–98.3%)	46.3%(43.0–49.6)	52.6% (49.5–55.7)
Delft imaging	95.5% (90.4–98.3%)	45.3%(42.0–48.6)	51.7% (48.7–54.8)

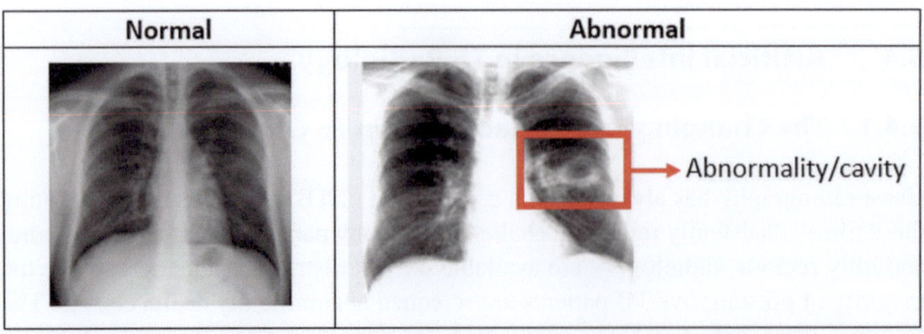

Fig. 5.8 Chest X-ray-based AI algorithm

5.4.3 Integration with Existing Workflows

AI-driven radiology systems are most useful when they complement, not replace, human expertise. The best results come from "hybrid reading," where the AI generates a preliminary interpretation and a human expert verifies or refines it. This arrangement is already in practice in some district hospitals where radiologists supervise multiple mobile screening vans.

A radiographer can upload the X-ray, receive an instant report, and send the flagged cases to a remote radiologist through the cloud. This reduces reporting time from days to hours and helps prioritize high-risk cases. The integration of AI interpretation into Nikshay also ensures that positive findings are automatically notified within the TB surveillance network.

5.4.4 Field Experiences and Lessons Learned

In many of the early pilot projects, staff members expressed initial hesitation toward AI systems, fearing that they might be replaced. With proper training, however, the attitude shifted. Once they realized that AI simply lightened their workload and reduced fatigue-related errors, acceptance grew rapidly (Jayaraman et al., 2025). A recurring field lesson is that image quality matters. AI models trained on clear, well-exposed X-rays can misread images taken under poor lighting or with improper positioning. Consequently, ensuring standard protocols for image capture is just as important as deploying the software itself. Another practical insight is the value of local calibration. Algorithms trained in other countries sometimes misclassify healed lesions or fibrotic scars as active disease in Indian patients. Local retraining of models using indigenous datasets has significantly improved accuracy.

5.4.5 Special Applications and Limitations

AI in radiology has shown potential in detecting extrapulmonary manifestations, though its role remains exploratory (Liu et al., 2024). Deep-learning models can now assess CT scans of the spine and lymph nodes for TB-related changes, but these require much larger datasets to become reliable (Codlin et al., 2021). Limitations persist: AI cannot replace the clinical judgment required to differentiate TB from other lung diseases like silicosis or lung cancer. Many algorithms struggle with pediatric X-rays, where patterns differ markedly from adult lungs. Connectivity issues and high licensing costs restrict access in peripheral areas. Despite these barriers, the trajectory is clearly forward. Every evaluation has demonstrated time savings and improved screening coverage, particularly in mass-screening programs.

5.4.6 Ethical and Operational Considerations

With growing use of digital images and cloud storage, data privacy and patient consent are gaining attention. Field teams must ensure that identifiable information is masked before uploading to cloud platforms. Additionally, AI models should undergo independent validation by government-approved institutions to avoid commercial bias. An operational challenge is maintaining hardware and Internet connectivity in rural areas. Experience from the National TB Elimination Programme shows that even a few hours of power outage can disrupt automated screening. Therefore, backup systems and periodic audits are vital to sustain confidence in the technology.

5.5 AI in Laboratory Diagnostics: Smear, Culture, CBNAAT, and LPA, and the Role in Detecting Drug-Resistant TB

5.5.1 A Practical Introduction

Laboratory tests form the backbone of TB diagnosis and drug-resistance detection. In everyday practice, however, labs in many districts face heavy workloads, intermittent supplies, and staff shortages. These realities slow diagnosis and sometimes force clinicians to make treatment decisions before confirmatory results arrive. Artificial intelligence offers ways to speed up routine tasks, reduce human error, and triage samples more intelligently—but it must be applied with pragmatic safeguards (Venkatesh et al., 2023).

5.5.2 AI for Sputum Smear Microscopy

Smear microscopy is still widely used because it is cheap and simple. Yet it is tiring work: scanning slides for acid-fast bacilli (AFB) can be monotonous and error-prone, especially in high-volume labs. AI-assisted microscopy changes that routine. Systems that digitize slides and run convolutional neural network models can flag fields with likely bacilli, provide counts, and suggest a smear grade. In practice, this means a junior technician can focus on validating the AI's flagged areas rather than scanning hundreds of fields manually. In a few pilot sites, automation reduced turnaround time and improved consistency between readers. Still, image quality matters: poorly stained or damaged slides limit AI performance, so simple quality checks at the staining step remain essential.

5.5.3 Culture Workflows and Early Detection

Culture remains the diagnostic gold standard and is indispensable for drug susceptibility testing. The problem, of course, is time: solid media may take weeks to grow. AI can help here too. By analyzing time-lapse images of culture media or liquid culture growth curves, machine-learning models can detect subtle early growth patterns and predict positivity before colonies are visible to the naked eye. For reference laboratories handling large batches, such early alerts can prioritize confirmatory testing and speed reporting. That said, these systems require good imaging hardware and regular calibration; in resource-poor labs the initial investment is nontrivial.

5.5.4 CBNAAT (GeneXpert): Optimizing Interpretation and QA

CBNAAT platforms like GeneXpert provide rapid molecular confirmation and rifampicin resistance screening. Their output is largely automated, but borderline or invalid runs still need interpretation. AI approaches that analyze raw fluorescence curves and machine logs can flag suspicious runs, predict likely indeterminate outcomes, and recommend repeat testing (Nurzynska et al., 2023). Programmatically, such dashboards have been useful for large networks: they reduce wasted cartridges, flag machines needing maintenance, and help managers spot sites that need training. For clinicians, the benefit is fewer false alarms and more reliable early decisions.

5.5.5 Line-Probe Assays (LPAs)—Standardizing Band Interpretation

LPAs remain critical for detecting key resistance mutations, but manual band reading is subjective—faint bands or smudges cause disagreement. Image-based AI tools can standardize band interpretation by measuring intensity, position, and pattern against validated thresholds. In labs where technicians struggle with faint bands, these tools cut variability and speed up reporting. However, success depends on consistent image capture—good lighting, steady imaging rigs, and standard strip orientation. Many pilot projects show excellent concordance with expert readers when these preconditions are met (Lewis et al., 2012) (Fig. 5.9).

5.5.6 Whole-Genome Sequencing (WGS) and Resistance Prediction

WGS offers the most detailed picture of resistance mechanisms, but interpreting genomic variants requires complex bioinformatics. AI and machine-learning models help translate sequence data into clinically meaningful resistance predictions.

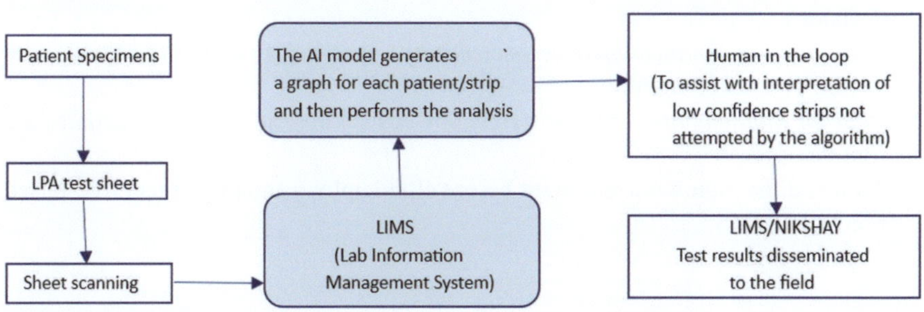

Fig. 5.9 LPA AI reader

When models are trained on high-quality datasets with linked phenotypic DST, they can predict resistance to multiple drugs rapidly, helping guide individualized therapy. Yet the bottlenecks here are more than algorithmic: sequencing costs, computing infrastructure, and curated databases are often limiting factors in routine program use. Where WGS is available, AI helps triage that strains need urgent public health attention—for example, possible transmission clusters or emerging resistance patterns.

5.5.7 Cross-Modality Benefits and Laboratory Information Systems

A practical strength of AI is its ability to combine inputs—microscopy images, GeneXpert outputs, LPA images, and basic clinical data—to generate an integrated risk score. Smart LIMS (laboratory information management systems) that incorporate these scores can prioritize samples, suggest confirmatory tests, and create alerts for public health action. For programs, this reduces backlog and focuses scarce resources where they matter most.

5.5.8 Limitations, Biases, and Quality Safeguards

AI is not a silver bullet. Models trained on high-quality reference datasets may underperform on local samples that differ in staining quality, prevalent comorbidities, or strain diversity. There is also a risk of over-reliance: automation should augment, not replace, human judgment. Data privacy, secure storage of diagnostic images, and informed consent must be built into any deployment plan. Regular local validation and periodic retraining of models prevent drift and reduce bias.

5.5.9 Practical Recommendations for Deployment (Field-Tested)

1. *Start small*—pilot in one lab, iron out imaging and workflow issues first.
2. *Maintain staining and image-capture standards*—AI works poorly on substandard inputs.
3. *Use hybrid review*—have AI flag results but retain human sign-off for critical decisions.
4. *Monitor performance metrics*—sensitivity, specificity, and turnaround time should be tracked monthly.
5. *Plan for maintenance*—imaging rigs, power backups, and software updates are routine costs.
6. *Protect data*—anonymize images before cloud upload and implement role-based access in LIMS.

5.5.10 Concluding Note

When used thoughtfully, AI can shave days off diagnostic timelines, reduce technician fatigue, and standardize interpretations across districts. The real gains come when algorithms are married to sound laboratory practice: clean slides, good imaging, and trained staff who trust but verify the machine output. In the end, the goal is practical—faster, fairer, and more reliable diagnosis so patients begin the right treatment sooner.

5.6 Clinical Decision Support Systems (CDSS) in Tuberculosis Care

5.6.1 Introduction—From Records to Real-Time Guidance

Clinical decision support systems (CDSS) represent the next step in digitizing TB care. In simple terms, these are software platforms that assist clinicians by offering prompts, treatment suggestions, or alerts based on patient data. Many Indian physicians first encountered CDSS indirectly—through electronic Nikshay notifications, automated regimen reminders, or sputum follow-up alerts. Although not always labeled “AI,” these systems already influence daily decision-making by translating raw data into actionable insights (Fig. 5.10).

5.6.2 Why CDSS Matters in TB Management

Tuberculosis treatment is long and often complicated by comorbidities, drug toxicity, and social factors (Dugdale et al., 2025). A missed drug interaction or an incomplete follow-up can undo months of effort. CDSS tools help clinicians manage this complexity by reminding staff of pending sputum conversions or due follow-ups. Checking prescriptions against national guidelines. Flagging potential adverse drug reactions or contraindications. Tracking adherence through digital pillboxes or SMS feedback loops. When used consistently, these systems act like a silent colleague—organized, patient, and impossible to tire.

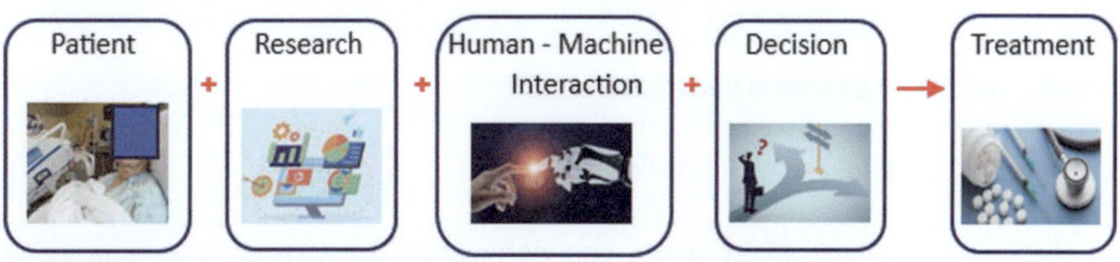

Fig. 5.10 CDSS integrated system

5.6.3 How CDSS Works in Practice

Modern CDSS platforms rely on a mix of structured patient data, treatment algorithms, and, increasingly, machine-learning modules. For example, when a new patient is registered in Nikshay, the system cross-checks demographic details, prior history, and lab reports. It can automatically suggest the appropriate regimen, generate dosing schedules, and schedule sputum follow-ups. Some state TB cells have piloted mobile applications that integrate decision support prompts for peripheral medical officers. A notification might read: "*Patient due for follow-up sputum examination—Day 60*." Another may warn: "*Potential hepatotoxicity risk—ALT >3 × ULN; consider drug substitution*." Such contextual guidance reduces errors and strengthens adherence to the National TB Elimination Programme (NTEP) standards.

5.6.4 Examples from the Field

In 2023, pilot CDSS modules were tested in selected districts of Uttar Pradesh and Maharashtra. Clinicians reported that automated prompts cut down manual register checking and improved follow-up rates. Pharmacists used digital alerts to monitor MDR-TB drug stocks, ensuring fewer treatment interruptions. Field supervisors noted that dashboards displaying "missed visits" helped target home-based counseling more effectively. However, the success of these pilots depended heavily on staff familiarity with smartphones and stable network access—two factors that still vary across regions.

5.6.5 Advantages Observed

- *Consistency*: ensures uniform adherence to NTEP guidelines.
- *Efficiency*: saves time otherwise spent on manual paperwork.
- *Accountability*: every action leaves a digital footprint, improving program transparency.
- *Patient-centric care*: facilitates timely reminders and early identification of treatment default.
- *Data-driven insight*: aggregated reports highlight trends in drug resistance or adherence lapses.

5.6.6 Challenges and Caution

Despite clear benefits, several hurdles remain.

- *Data overload*: too many alerts can desensitize users; relevance filtering is essential.
- *Connectivity gaps*: offline functionality is vital in remote settings.
- *User training*: without orientation, staff may bypass prompts or enter incomplete data.

- *Ethical issues*: automated recommendations must never override clinical judgment.
- *Privacy*: patient identifiers stored on shared devices require strict safeguards and consent mechanisms.

A clinician's intuition—built from experience—remains irreplaceable; CDSS should inform, not dictate.

5.6.7 Integrating CDSS into the Health-System Fabric

The most promising direction is integration. Linking CDSS modules with Nikshay, laboratory information systems, and pharmacy databases can create a seamless care continuum. For instance, when a GeneXpert result flags rifampicin resistance, the system can automatically generate an MDR-TB referral ticket and alert the district DR-TB Centre. Public–private partnerships are beginning to explore voice-based CDSS assistants for community health workers, enabling verbal updates in local languages—an innovation that may improve inclusivity.

5.6.8 The Road Ahead

For India to meet its 2025 TB-elimination target, CDSS adoption must move beyond pilots. Investments in digital literacy, power reliability, and secure cloud infrastructure are equally critical. Future systems will likely integrate predictive analytics—estimating a patient's default risk or forecasting drug stock-outs before they occur. As with any tool, sustainability will depend on trust. When clinicians see that digital recommendations genuinely save time and prevent mistakes, acceptance will grow naturally. The ultimate aim is straightforward: to let technology handle routine precision so that humans can focus on compassion and clinical judgment.

5.7 Artificial Intelligence in Drug-Resistance Surveillance and Pharmacovigilance

5.7.1 Introduction: The Growing Challenge of Resistance

Drug-resistant tuberculosis (DR-TB) remains one of the toughest obstacles in achieving a TB-free India. While diagnostic capacity has improved, the challenge now lies in detecting resistance early and ensuring that patients receive the right drugs safely. Artificial intelligence has begun to play a useful role in this space—helping predict resistance trends, detect early warning signals, and monitor adverse drug reactions in real time. Traditional surveillance depends on periodic culture or line-probe assay data, often arriving weeks late. AI systems, in contrast, can scan multiple data streams simultaneously—laboratory results, pharmacy inventories, and patient treatment logs—to highlight unusual patterns much sooner.

5.7.2 Predicting and Mapping Resistance

Machine-learning models can analyze thousands of past laboratory results to predict where new resistant strains are likely to emerge. For example, if multiple rifampicin-resistant cases appear within a short radius, the algorithm can alert program managers to investigate possible transmission links. Some pilot studies in India have combined GeneXpert results with patient addresses and demographic data from Nikshay to produce resistance heat maps. These maps allow district TB officers to focus contact tracing and community screening in high-risk pockets rather than scattering resources thinly across blocks. When combined with genomic data from reference laboratories, AI can even cluster isolates by genetic similarity, suggesting whether cases share a transmission chain or represent independent resistance events.

5.7.3 AI in Genomic and Molecular Surveillance

With the introduction of whole-genome sequencing (WGS) at national reference labs, the data volume has exploded. Each isolate yields thousands of genetic variants, many with uncertain significance. AI tools help make sense of this complexity by matching variant patterns with known resistance phenotypes. Globally, models such as *DeepAMR* and *GenTB* have demonstrated promising accuracy in predicting resistance to isoniazid, fluoroquinolones, and bedaquiline. In India, researchers are working toward locally trained models that account for regional strain diversity. Such integration will allow faster detection of emerging mutations before they translate into widespread treatment failure.

5.7.4 Pharmacovigilance: Monitoring Safety Through Data

The second major domain where AI is proving valuable is pharmacovigilance. Newer anti-TB drugs like bedaquiline, delamanid, and pretomanid have transformed DR-TB management but come with potential cardiac, hepatic, and neurological side effects. AI-driven pharmacovigilance systems can process data from Nikshay Aushadhi, electronic medical records, and even SMS-based patient feedback. They flag abnormal ECG readings, prolonged QT intervals, or clusters of adverse event reports from specific centers. Instead of waiting for monthly summaries, safety officers can act within days. Some pilot apps now allow patients to self-report side effects in simple vernacular prompts; algorithms then triage these reports by severity for clinician follow-up. This not only increases patient engagement but also builds real-world safety databases—something manual systems have long struggled to maintain.

5.7.5 Strengthening Supply-Chain and Adherence Monitoring

Resistance can also emerge from erratic drug supply or poor adherence. AI models that analyze pharmacy stock data can forecast shortages weeks in advance, allowing timely redistribution between centers. Similarly, digital adherence technologies linked to CDSS modules can predict which patients are at higher risk of default based on missed calls, SMS patterns, or irregular refill dates. By catching these early warning signs, program managers can intervene before partial treatment leads to resistance amplification.

5.7.6 Ethical and Operational Considerations

Using AI for surveillance and pharmacovigilance raises familiar but serious questions about privacy and data ownership. Patient identifiers, genomic information, and treatment history must be handled under strict confidentiality. Any AI platform integrated into public health programs should undergo independent auditing for bias, data security, and accuracy. Operationally, systems must be user-friendly and provide interpretable outputs. A red-flag dashboard without explanation can overwhelm rather than assist. Training field epidemiologists to interpret alerts correctly is therefore just as important as the algorithm itself.

5.7.7 Early Lessons from Indian Experience

Districts that have experimented with AI-based resistance dashboards report quicker detection of local MDR clusters and faster initiation of contact tracing. Pharmacovigilance cells using automated text-mining tools have identified adverse event trends that previously went unnoticed. However, most success stories share two features: human oversight and phased deployment. Algorithms work best when supervised by experienced microbiologists, pharmacologists, or public health officers who can validate each alert and fine-tune thresholds to local conditions.

5.7.8 Future Prospects

The near future may see integrated national dashboards where genomic data, drug stocks, and pharmacovigilance reports flow into a single platform. AI could automatically rank risks, trigger supply corrections, and alert field teams—all in near real time. The ambition is not to replace epidemiologists but to make their work faster and more precise. With careful validation, strong ethical safeguards, and sustained training, AI-assisted surveillance could turn today's reactive system into a proactive one—spotting resistance before it spreads widely and ensuring that every patient receives effective and safe therapy.

5.8 Artificial Intelligence in TB Epidemiology and Public Health Modeling

5.8.1 Why Modeling Matters

Epidemiology gives programs their direction: It tells us where infection spreads, who is at risk, and what interventions may work best. In tuberculosis control, good modeling can save years of trial and error. Yet traditional epidemiologic models depend heavily on complete, timely data—something most high-burden countries struggle with (Al-Antari, 2023). Artificial intelligence now offers a way to bridge these gaps by recognizing patterns within fragmented datasets and projecting scenarios far more quickly than manual analysis ever could.

5.8.2 Data Sources and the Indian Context

In India, epidemiological information flows from a patchwork of systems—Nikshay, laboratory registers, district TB offices, and national surveys. Each has its own structure and lag time. AI-driven analytic tools can merge these data streams, clean inconsistencies, and produce real-time dashboards showing incidence trends, diagnostic delays, and treatment outcomes. For example, when district data from Uttar Pradesh and Bihar were combined, algorithms detected subtle seasonal spikes in case notifications coinciding with labor-migration cycles. Such insights help program managers anticipate surges and plan mobile diagnostic units before case loads peak.

5.8.3 Forecasting Incidence and Evaluating Interventions

Machine-learning models excel at forecasting. By analyzing historical notification data, demographic variables, and socioeconomic indicators, they can project likely future caseloads under different policy scenarios. When districts introduced active case-finding through community camps, AI models estimated the number of additional cases likely to surface and the resources required to manage them. This predictive capacity transforms planning from reactive to proactive, allowing authorities to pre-position GeneXpert cartridges, drugs, and staff.

5.8.4 Contact-Tracing Optimization

Traditional contact tracing is labor-intensive and depends on accurate recall by patients. AI tools simplify this by integrating GPS data, electronic treatment records, and even anonymized mobility data from mobile networks to map potential exposure clusters.

In a few urban pilot projects, AI-generated "risk circles" around index cases helped field teams prioritize households for screening. Instead of visiting every contact, they began with those most likely to be infected, saving time without compromising coverage.

5.8.5 Understanding Social and Behavioral Patterns

TB transmission does not occur in isolation from social realities. AI text-mining of counseling notes, social media discussions, or community health worker reports can highlight emerging barriers—fear of stigma, drug-stock rumors, or treatment-fatigue trends.

Such soft data insights are difficult to capture through conventional surveys but can guide health education strategies. During one campaign in Delhi slums, AI-supported sentiment analysis helped redesign posters and radio messages, resulting in better participation in screening camps.

5.8.6 Modeling Health System Performance

Beyond patient-level analysis, AI can assess how the health system itself performs. Predictive models can simulate the effect of adding laboratories, redistributing staff, or changing diagnostic algorithms. For instance, an NTEP-supported modeling exercise suggested that deploying one additional GeneXpert machine per 100,000 population could cut diagnostic delay by nearly 20% in high-burden districts. By turning routine program data into dynamic simulations, managers can test interventions virtually before investing resources on the ground.

5.8.7 Challenges and Ethical Safeguards

While powerful, AI epidemiology raises important concerns:

- *Data quality*: incomplete or biased inputs can lead to misleading forecasts.
- *Transparency*: many AI models act as "black boxes," offering predictions without clear reasoning.
- *Equity*: algorithms trained mostly on urban data may under-represent rural and tribal populations.
- *Privacy*: location-based analyses must anonymize data to protect individuals and communities.

Hence, any deployment should include human oversight, open-source validation, and clear accountability for decisions derived from model outputs.

5.8.8 From Numbers to Policy

Epidemiological models are only useful if they influence decisions. AI-generated forecasts should feed directly into district microplans, budget allocations, and contingency strategies for outbreaks. When planners can visualize how delayed contact tracing increases projected incidence curves, resource prioritization becomes evidence-driven rather than intuition-based. Some state TB cells now use AI dashboards during monthly review meetings, turning raw numbers into actionable tasks—a small but meaningful cultural shift toward data-centered governance.

5.8.9 The Road Ahead

The future of TB epidemiology will likely blend classical statistics with adaptive AI. Hybrid models combining machine learning with established epidemiologic equations (like SEIR frameworks) can deliver both transparency and flexibility.

India's vast TB dataset provides fertile ground for such innovation, provided data sharing remains secure and ethical. With continued collaboration between data scientists, epidemiologists, and public health officers, AI-supported modeling could help anticipate outbreaks, optimize resource distribution, and bring the nation closer to its 2025 elimination goal.

5.9 Artificial Intelligence in Program Monitoring and Evaluation

5.9.1 Introduction: From Data Collection to Intelligent Insight

Monitoring and evaluation (M&E) have always been the backbone of public health programs. In tuberculosis control, thousands of data points—ranging from sputum test results to treatment outcomes—are generated daily across the country. The challenge has never been collecting data; it has been turning that data into actionable insight.

Artificial intelligence is now helping bridge this gap by analyzing vast datasets in real time and highlighting patterns that human reviewers might miss. Instead of waiting for quarterly reports, program managers can receive timely alerts on performance bottlenecks, regional disparities, or sudden changes in case trends.

5.9.2 The Traditional Bottleneck

Under the National TB Elimination Programme (NTEP), information from laboratories, treatment centers, and pharmacies converges at district and state levels through platforms like Nikshay. While comprehensive, the volume of data often overwhelms human analysts. Errors in entry, duplication, and delayed uploads dilute the usefulness of reports.

AI tools trained on these databases can automatically flag inconsistencies, detect missing fields, and even estimate probable values based on historical trends. This reduces clerical burden and allows officers to focus on interpretation and decision-making rather than endless verification.

5.9.3 Real-Time Dashboards and Predictive Analytics

Modern M&E increasingly relies on dynamic dashboards that update automatically. AI enhances these by generating predictive insights—not just what has happened, but what is likely to happen next.

For instance, if notification rates in a district suddenly drop, an AI model can correlate it with laboratory downtime or stock-out data, prompting early investigation. Similarly, algorithms can estimate treatment-outcome probabilities based on adherence patterns and sociodemographic variables. Such early warnings enable proactive supervision instead of post-facto correction.

5.9.4 Measuring Program Efficiency and Equity

Beyond counts and percentages, AI tools can evaluate efficiency and equity in service delivery. Heat maps generated from Nikshay and logistics data can show whether diagnostic resources are equitably distributed or clustered around urban centers.

During a pilot in Madhya Pradesh, AI-assisted spatial analysis revealed that mobile X-ray vans were disproportionately covering easily accessible blocks. After redeployment guided by these findings, case detection increased in previously underserved tribal regions. These experiences highlight how analytics can support fairer allocation of limited resources.

5.9.5 Evaluating Interventions and Policy Impact

Program evaluation often suffers from long feedback cycles—by the time a new intervention is reviewed, circumstances have changed. AI-based models shorten this loop by continuously analyzing inputs and outputs. For example, when a new incentive scheme for treatment adherence was launched, the system tracked changes in default rates week by week. Early dips signaled that field staff needed additional counseling sessions, allowing course correction without waiting for an annual review.

Similarly, AI can conduct *counterfactual analysis*—comparing what actually happened with what would likely have happened without the intervention. This provides policymakers with quantitative justification for scaling or modifying programs.

5.9.6 Supporting Supervision and Accountability

AI-enabled dashboards can assist supervisors by automatically ranking facilities or districts according to performance metrics—case detection, conversion rates, follow-up completion, or data quality scores. Instead of uniform monitoring visits, officers can prioritize poorly performing sites.

Some states are experimenting with automated feedback reports where AI systems draft concise summaries highlighting each facility's strengths and areas for improvement. Supervisors then validate these drafts and issue actionable recommendations. This saves valuable time and brings greater objectivity to evaluations.

5.9.7 Integrating Patient Feedback and Community Data

Program monitoring cannot rely solely on facility data. AI-driven text-mining and sentiment analysis tools are now being explored to capture community feedback from helplines, grievance portals, and social media. These analyses can identify emerging concerns—medicine shortages, rude behavior at centers, or stigma incidents—and flag them for corrective action. Such community-sensitive analytics help make programs more responsive and patient-centric, aligning with the NTEP's vision of compassionate care.

5.9.8 Challenges and Safeguards

Like any technology, AI in monitoring brings both promise and pitfalls:

- *Data privacy* must be upheld; individual-level data should always be anonymized before analysis.
- *Algorithmic transparency* is critical—users need to understand why the model is raising a flag.
- *Capacity building* remains a priority; staff must be trained to interpret dashboards meaningfully.
- *Infrastructure reliability* (Internet, power) continues to determine success in rural areas.

Ultimately, AI is a support system, not a substitute for human oversight. Its outputs must always be reviewed in context before policy decisions are made.

5.9.9 Future Directions

The next generation of program monitoring will likely move toward adaptive learning systems that refine their own models as new data arrive. AI could automatically identify underperforming regions, suggest targeted microplans, and simulate outcomes of proposed interventions.

With India's large and diverse TB dataset, the potential for such evolution is enormous. As these systems mature, the role of field officers will shift from data entry to intelligent data interpretation—exactly where human insight matters most.

AI, when integrated responsibly, can turn monitoring from a bureaucratic formality into a real-time decision support mechanism—helping ensure that no patient, district, or demographic group is left behind.

5.10 Ethical, Legal, and Social Implications (ELSI) of Artificial Intelligence in Tuberculosis Care

5.10.1 Introduction: The Dual Edge of Innovation

Artificial intelligence promises speed, consistency, and precision in tuberculosis care, but these very strengths raise new ethical and social questions. In the excitement of adopting advanced tools, it is easy to forget that healthcare is built on trust, confidentiality, and equity. When technology enters this space, the responsibility to safeguard human values becomes even greater. For countries like India, where public health systems are diverse and populations are vulnerable, ethical governance of AI is not an afterthought—it is a necessity.

5.10.2 Data Privacy and Patient Confidentiality

AI systems thrive on data. Each X-ray, GeneXpert result, or Nikshay entry contributes to model training and prediction. However, patient records often include sensitive identifiers—address, HIV status, or socioeconomic details—that must remain confidential. Ethical deployment requires data anonymization before uploading to cloud platforms and clear consent from patients for secondary data use. Hospitals and laboratories must maintain encrypted storage and restricted access. Unfortunately, many healthcare workers are unaware of the digital trails they create. Awareness sessions on data ethics should therefore accompany every AI rollout. In practice, "data safety" should be treated as seriously as infection control: both protect patients, just in different ways.

5.10.3 Algorithmic Bias and Fairness

AI learns from existing data, which means it inherits existing biases. If most training datasets come from urban hospitals, algorithms may underperform in tribal or rural populations. Similarly, a model trained largely on adult chest X-rays might miss pediatric TB. Ensuring fairness requires diverse and representative training data, continuous validation across regions, and transparency about model limitations. Policymakers should insist on public documentation of algorithm performance before approving its use in national programs. Bias in AI is not merely a technical flaw—it can translate into real harm for patients left undiagnosed.

5.10.4 Accountability and Decision Ownership

AI recommendations can influence treatment decisions, but the final accountability must always rest with qualified health professionals. A misinterpreted AI suggestion—say, an incorrect radiological classification—cannot justify clinical negligence. Therefore, every AI system used in healthcare should clearly specify its role: *"decision support," not "decision making."* This principle protects both patients and practitioners. Legal frameworks must define liability boundaries so that clinicians remain in charge while developers remain responsible for algorithm integrity.

5.10.5 Informed Consent and Patient Autonomy

Patients deserve to know when AI is involved in their diagnosis or treatment planning. A simple, understandable explanation builds trust and transparency. Informed consent forms should include a short statement such as: "*Your medical data may be analysed by computer software to assist doctors in making decisions. All results will be reviewed by qualified medical staff.*" In community settings, especially among low-literacy groups, such disclosure may require verbal communication through community health workers rather than written forms. Ethical governance is not achieved through signatures alone—it requires comprehension and respect.

5.10.6 Data Ownership and Intellectual Property

A less-discussed issue in public health is who owns the data used to train AI systems. If a private company develops an algorithm using government program data, does the government retain partial ownership? Can the data be exported or monetized? These are important legal questions that India's digital health framework must clarify. National guidelines should ensure that datasets generated through public programs remain public goods, accessible for noncommercial research under strict ethical supervision.

5.10.7 Social Acceptance and Trust

Even the best technology fails if people do not trust it. Field experiences show that patients and health workers are often skeptical of AI tools—either fearing job loss or doubting accuracy. Transparent communication and user involvement in system design can ease these fears. When radiographers or lab technicians understand *how*

AI supports rather than replaces them, they tend to use it more confidently. Similarly, patients reassured that human doctors remain the final decision-makers are more likely to cooperate with AI-supported screening.

5.10.8 Legal and Regulatory Frameworks

India is taking initial steps toward regulating AI in healthcare through policies under the National Digital Health Mission (NDHM) and Digital Information Security in Healthcare Act (DISHA) (proposed). However, specific clauses addressing algorithm transparency, data sharing, and redress mechanisms are still evolving. A national certification process—similar to drug approval—could ensure that only validated and bias-tested algorithms enter clinical use. Independent ethics committees and data protection officers should oversee compliance within both public and private sectors.

5.10.9 Ethical Use in Research and Publications

Researchers using AI-generated analysis must disclose it clearly in their manuscripts. Journals increasingly require statements specifying the extent of AI assistance used for writing, analysis, or image interpretation. Honesty here protects scientific credibility and prevents allegations of academic misconduct. AI can assist in data analysis or writing clarity, but the researcher must take full intellectual responsibility for interpretation and conclusions. Ethical transparency, not avoidance, is the hallmark of credible scholarship.

5.10.10 Moving Toward Responsible AI

The path forward lies in "responsible AI"—technology that advances health goals without compromising dignity or fairness. Each AI project in TB care should be guided by four ethical principles:

1. *Autonomy*: respect for patient rights and informed consent.
2. *Beneficence*: maximizing patient and public health benefit.
3. *Non-maleficence*: preventing harm through bias or misuse.
4. *Justice*: ensuring equitable access and representation across populations.

When these principles guide innovation, AI can strengthen—not threaten—the human core of medicine. The challenge for our generation is to ensure that in the rush toward digital precision, we do not lose empathy, accountability, and trust.

5.11 The Future Roadmap: Integrating Artificial Intelligence into the National TB Elimination Program

5.11.1 Introduction: A Turning Point for Public-Health Technology

India's ambition to eliminate tuberculosis by 2025 demands not only human commitment but also intelligent use of data and innovation. Artificial intelligence, once limited to research laboratories, is now mature enough to be woven into the daily machinery of the National TB Elimination Programme (NTEP). The question is no longer *whether* to use AI, but *how* to use it responsibly, equitably, and sustainably.

5.11.2 Building Digital Infrastructure as the Foundation

For AI systems to work reliably, basic digital plumbing must be strong. This includes stable Internet connectivity at peripheral health centers, interoperable data formats between Nikshay, laboratory information systems, and drug supply portals, and adequate hardware maintenance budgets.

The Government's Ayushman Bharat Digital Mission (ABDM) already provides a framework for health data integration; aligning NTEP within this architecture will allow smoother data exchange and reduce duplication of effort.

5.11.3 Establishing National AI Governance Standards

AI tools used in public health should meet uniform benchmarks for accuracy, bias testing, and data protection compliance. A dedicated AI in TB Task Force under the Central TB Division could evaluate, certify, and periodically audit algorithms before their program-level use.

Such a mechanism would ensure that only validated, open-documentation models—preferably trained on Indian data—enter the national system.

5.11.4 Phased Integration and Capacity-Building

Rather than a single nationwide rollout, AI adoption should follow a phased approach: pilot → evaluate → expand. Each phase should include orientation for field staff and district officers so that technology complements existing workflows instead of disrupting them.

Training modules in the modular NTEP curriculum can include short sessions on AI literacy, ethical data handling, and interpretation of AI-based dashboards. Empowered users are the best defense against misuse or misunderstanding.

5.11.5 Strengthening Local Innovation and Public–Private Partnerships

India's startup ecosystem offers tremendous potential for home-grown AI solutions. Encouraging collaborations between government institutions, IITs, medical colleges, and startups can foster low-cost, field-ready applications—from smartphone-based X-ray readers to AI-supported adherence tracking. Public–private partnerships should, however, operate under transparent contracts that guarantee data ownership remains with public authorities and that all patient data are anonymized.

5.11.6 Integrating AI Across the TB Care Cascade

AI can contribute meaningfully at every step:

- *Screening*: CAD-enabled mobile vans for community X-rays.
- *Diagnosis*: automated smear and GeneXpert interpretation.
- *Treatment*: CDSS-guided regimen adjustments and adverse-event alerts.
- *Surveillance*: real-time dashboards mapping resistance clusters.
- *Monitoring*: predictive analytics for adherence and supply management.

A unified data pipeline connecting these modules will allow smoother patient tracking from detection to cure, reducing losses along the continuum of care.

5.11.7 Policy Alignment and Resource Allocation

To sustain innovation, AI activities must be reflected in annual program implementation plans (PIPs) and budget lines. Dedicated funding for software licenses, hardware maintenance, and training should be routine, not ad hoc. Inclusion of AI indicators—such as "percentage of districts using validated CAD software" or "average turnaround time reduction through AI tools"—within the national monitoring framework will also institutionalize accountability.

5.11.8 Ethical and Legal Readiness

As integration advances, NTEP should align with India's evolving digital health laws and data protection policies. Each AI deployment must undergo ethical review covering consent, privacy, and fairness. Establishing a Data Ethics and Governance Unit within NTEP could oversee compliance, manage grievances, and guide safe data sharing with research partners.

5.11.9 Community Engagement and Communication

Sustained success depends on public trust. Community leaders, NGOs, and patient support groups should be briefed on how AI contributes to faster diagnosis and safer treatment.

When patients understand that technology assists—not replaces—their doctor, resistance declines and cooperation increases. Transparency and dialogue will prevent misconceptions about "machines deciding care."

5.11.10 Vision for 2030: Human Intelligence with Machine Support

By the end of this decade, India could operate an adaptive, AI-assisted TB-control system that learns continuously from every case reported. Health workers might use handheld devices for instant radiographic triage; district officers could monitor outbreaks through predictive dashboards; and policymakers could model funding scenarios with near-real-time accuracy.

Yet amid this technological leap, the human element must remain central. AI should free clinicians and public health workers from repetitive tasks so they can spend more time listening to patients—the very heart of medicine. The roadmap ahead must therefore balance innovation with empathy, precision with participation, and automation with accountability.

5.12 Conclusion: Balancing Technology and the Human Touch in TB Care

5.12.1 The Essence of Balance

As tuberculosis care enters a new technological era, the real challenge is not only developing smarter tools but also ensuring that these tools strengthen human compassion rather than replace it. Artificial intelligence has proven its ability to speed up diagnosis, improve accuracy, and streamline program operations. Yet, numbers and algorithms alone cannot capture the lived realities of a person facing months of treatment, stigma, or financial hardship (Al-Antari, 2023).

A strong TB program will always rest on both pillars—data-driven precision and empathetic human connection**.** One without the other cannot achieve elimination.

5.12.2 Reflecting on the Journey So Far

The introduction of AI into TB care in India has moved rapidly from pilot projects to programmatic discussions at the national level. From AI-assisted radiology and laboratory diagnostics to predictive dashboards and decision support systems, the possibilities are expanding every year. Each advancement demonstrates that technology can make healthcare more efficient, but it also reminds us of the need for thoughtful design, continuous validation, and careful ethical governance. At its best, AI has allowed overburdened doctors, technicians, and program managers to see patterns that once took months to recognize. At its worst, when poorly implemented or uncritically trusted, it risks turning patient care into a mechanical process devoid of empathy.

5.12.3 Lessons Learned from the Field

The most valuable lesson from early pilots is that AI works best when people remain in charge. District TB officers who treat AI-generated alerts as supportive tools—not final verdicts—achieve better outcomes. Field workers trained to interpret AI outputs with curiosity rather than fear become partners in innovation. Another key lesson is the importance of local validation. Algorithms trained elsewhere must learn to understand Indian data, patient behavior, and disease presentation. Ground truth must come from the field, not from the cloud.

5.12.4 The Road Toward Sustainability

Integrating AI sustainably into the National TB Elimination Programme (NTEP) will require investment not just in technology but also in people—training them, listening to their challenges, and adapting tools to their workflow. Clear guidelines on data sharing, privacy, and ethical use will help maintain public trust. Strengthening digital infrastructure and promoting Indian-led AI research will make innovation both cost-effective and contextually appropriate. The next few years will determine whether AI becomes a short-lived trend or a lasting instrument of change. Sustainability will depend on continuous learning, transparent governance, and shared accountability between technologists and health professionals.

5.12.5 Looking Ahead: A Vision Beyond 2025

As India approaches its TB elimination target, AI can play a pivotal role in reaching the "last mile." Predictive models can identify unreached populations; AI-driven adherence tools can support patients through difficult phases of therapy; and automated dashboards can provide early warnings for emerging resistance or stock-outs. However, the ultimate victory will not be measured only in algorithms deployed or dashboards built—but in patients cured, lives restored, and trust strengthened. Technology should make the healthcare system more humane, not more mechanical. The goal is simple yet profound: to ensure that every innovation serves the person, not the other way around.

5.12.6 Final Words

AI offers us an unprecedented opportunity to rethink tuberculosis care—faster, fairer, and more inclusive. But as we embrace this revolution, we must remember what makes healthcare meaningful: empathy, listening, and the human bond between a healer and a patient.

When technology and humanity move together, TB elimination becomes not just a policy target but a collective moral commitment.

The future of TB control, therefore, lies not in replacing the doctor or the health worker—but in empowering them. Artificial intelligence should remain a tool in our hands, never the mind behind our decisions.

References

Al-Antari, M. A. (2023). Artificial intelligence for medical diagnostics—Existing and future AI technology! *Diagnostics, 13*(4), 688. https://doi.org/10.3390/diagnostics13040688

Botha, G. H. R., et al. (2018). Detection of tuberculosis by automatic cough sound analysis. *Physiological Measurement, 39*(4), 045005. https://doi.org/10.1088/1361-6579/aab6d0

Codlin, A. J., et al. (2021). Independent evaluation of 12 artificial intelligence solutions for the detection of tuberculosis. *Scientific Reports, 11*(1), 23895. https://doi.org/10.1038/s41598-021-03265-0

Dugdale, C. M., et al. (2025). TB or not TB? Development and validation of a clinical decision support system to inform airborne isolation requirements in evaluating suspected tuberculosis. *Infection Control and Hospital Epidemiology, 46*(2), 1–9. https://doi.org/10.1017/ice.2024.214

Hansun, S., et al. (2025). Diagnostic performance of artificial intelligence-based methods for tuberculosis detection: Systematic review. *Journal of Medical Internet Research, 27*, e69068. https://doi.org/10.2196/69068

Jayaraman, P., et al. (2025). Artificial intelligence as a proficient tool in detecting pulmonary tuberculosis in massive population screening programs: A case study in Chennai, India. *Journal of Rural Medicine, 20*(1), 13–19. https://doi.org/10.2185/jrm.2024-015

Lewis, J. J., et al. (2012). "Proof-of-concept" evaluation of an automated sputum smear microscopy system for tuberculosis diagnosis. *PLoS One, 7*(11), e50173. https://doi.org/10.1371/journal.pone.0050173

Liu, Y., Wu, Y.-H., Zhang, S.-C., Liu, L., Wu, M., & Cheng, M.-M. (2024). Revisiting computer-aided tuberculosis diagnosis. *IEEE Transactions on Pattern Analysis and Machine Intelligence, 46*(4), 2316–2332. https://doi.org/10.1109/TPAMI.2023.3330825

Measuring the impact of AI in the diagnosis of hospitalized patients: A randomized clinical vignette survey study. (2025, June 22). *PubMed.* Retrieved June 22, 2025, from https://www.pubmed.ncbi.nlm.nih.gov/38112814/

Nurzynska, K., Li, D., Walts, A. E., & Gertych, A. (2023). Multilayer outperforms single-layer slide scanning in AI-based classification of whole slide images with low-burden acid-fast mycobacteria (AFB). *Computer Methods and Programs in Biomedicine, 234*, 107518. https://doi.org/10.1016/j.cmpb.2023.107518

Pai, M., Dewan, P. K., & Swaminathan, S. (2023). Transforming tuberculosis diagnosis. *Nature Microbiology, 8*(5), 756–759. https://doi.org/10.1038/s41564-023-01365-3

Qin, Z. Z., et al. (2021). Tuberculosis detection from chest X-rays for triaging in a high tuberculosis-burden setting: An evaluation of five artificial intelligence algorithms. *The Lancet Digital Health, 3*(9), e543–e554. https://doi.org/10.1016/S2589-7500(21)00116-3

Venkatesh, N., Rajani, G., & Basapur, S. (2023). BacilliFinder: Revolutionizing tuberculosis detection with computer vision. *Indian Journal of Tuberculosis*. https://doi.org/10.1016/j.ijtb.2023.12.005

World Health Organization. (2024). *Global tuberculosis report 2024* (1st ed.). World Health Organization.

Yellapu, G. D., et al. (2023). Development and clinical validation of Swaasa AI platform for screening and prioritization of pulmonary TB. *Scientific Reports, 13*(1), 4740. https://doi.org/10.1038/s41598-023-31772-9

Role of Artificial Intelligence in Cancer

6

Himashree Bhattacharyya, Rashmi Agarwalla,
and Kanthakumar

6.1 Introduction

Cancer has been emerging as one of the major killer diseases in the present century. As per the statistics, 16.8% of all causes of deaths and 22.8% of deaths from non-communicable diseases (NCDs) worldwide are attributable to cancer.

In many countries, cancer accounts for a significant proportion of premature deaths due to noncommunicable diseases (30.3%) among individuals aged 30–69 years. Globally, in 2022, cancer was responsible for an estimated 20 million new cases and 9.7 million deaths. In 2022, Asia accounted for the majority of global cancer deaths, representing approximately 56.1% of the total. Lung cancer emerged as the most prevalent malignancy, with an estimated 2.5 million new cases, followed by breast cancer (2.3 million), colorectal cancer (1.9 million), prostate cancer (1.5 million), and stomach cancer (0.97 million). There are significant disparities in the mortality burden globally, with mortality being disproportionately higher in African and Asian regions. It is estimated that 1 in 5 people residing in Africa and Asia develop cancer in their lifetime (Bray et al., 2024b). As per the predictions, by the year 2050, cancer cases will be over 35 million, with a 77% increase since 2022. The Southeast Asia region, which represents 9% of the global population, is one of the fastest-growing regions globally. Annually more than 2.3 million people are diagnosed, and 1.4 million succumb to cancer from this region alone. Cancers of the lungs, breast, and cervix together cause more than 400,000 deaths annually. Breast, followed by cervical, cancer still remains the topmost cause of cancer in women. In the Southeast Asia region, lung cancer among men and breast cancer among women are the principal contributors to cancer incidence and mortality. The case fatality rates are high as most cases present late and also due to difficult access to treatment

H. Bhattacharyya (✉) · R. Agarwalla · Kanthakumar
Department of Community & Family Medicine, All India Institute of Medical Sciences, Guwahati, India

U. Venkatesh et al. (eds.), *Multimodal AI in Healthcare*,
https://doi.org/10.1007/978-981-95-9027-8_6

in many regions that are not yet equipped with proper diagnostic and treatment facilities. Liver cancers are also seen to be most common in Cambodia, Laos, Thailand, and Vietnam of the South East Asia region (*Management of Cancer*, 2024).

The National Cancer Registry Programme (NCRP), launched by the Indian Council of Medical Research in 1981, has played a pivotal role in generating comprehensive data on cancer patterns and burden across different regions of India. Currently, the NCRP covers 16.4% of the national population and comprises 38 Population-Based Cancer Registries (PBCRs) and 215 Hospital-Based Cancer Registries (HBCRs) throughout the country.

In 2022, India recorded a crude cancer incidence rate of 100.4 per 100,000 population. Among males, the most common cancer sites were the lung (10.6%), mouth (8.4%), prostate (6.1%), tongue (5.9%), and stomach (4.8%). In females, the predominant cancer types included breast (28.8%), cervix (10.6%), ovary (6.2%), corpus uteri (3.7%), and lung (3.7%). The cumulative lifetime risk of developing cancer among people of both sexes for all sites between 0 and 74 years was one in every nine persons. Among children aged 0–14 years, lymphoid leukemia was the most common cancer in both sexes, followed by malignancies of the brain and nervous system. In the productive age group of 40–64 years, the predominant cancer sites among males are the lung, mouth, and tongue, while among females, they are the breast, cervix, and ovary. This age group exhibits a higher overall cancer incidence compared to other age groups. In the elderly population (above 65 years), lung cancer remains the most common malignancy in males, followed by prostate cancer.

According to projected estimates, the number of cancer cases in India is expected to rise from 1.46 million in 2022 to 1.57 million by 2025. This may be attributed to the improved cancer diagnostic facilities and robust capturing of data on cancer over the last few years. Also, the population being in the state of epidemiological transition is overtly exposed to the various risk factors related to diet, physical activity patterns, tobacco, and alcohol consumption that have resulted in an increase in cancers like lung, breast, head and neck, and colorectum. Given the increasing cancer burden in India in the coming decades, there is a pressing need to enhance diagnostic facilities and develop more effective algorithms for the timely detection of cancer.

The rising magnitude of cancer cases, along with the diversities of cancer profiles observed across regions, warrants an extraordinary response from the medical community and the need to focus on cancer control measures with high impact (Sathishkumar et al., 2022). Infections due to certain viruses like the *Helicobacter pylori*, human papilloma virus (HPV), hepatitis B and C virus, and Epstein–Barr virus are the causes of approximately 13–15% of cancers.

Early detection through screening is a cornerstone of cancer control strategies, aiming to identify malignancies at asymptomatic stages when treatment is more effective and outcomes are improved. Early detection of cancer can significantly reduce mortality rates by enabling interventions before the disease progresses to advanced stages. Even a 4-week treatment delay increases the chance of death for cancer patients by 6–13% (Lynge et al., 2012).

Different screening approaches are utilized based on the specific type of cancer and the characteristics of the target population. Common screening modalities include

- *Mammography*: Advised for breast cancer screening, especially for women between 50 and 74 years of age.
- *Colonoscopy*: Used for colorectal cancer screening, with recommendations suggesting a screening interval of every 10 years for individuals aged 50–75 years.
- *Pap smear and HPV testing*: Considered the standard for cervical cancer screening, with updated guidelines allowing extended screening intervals for women aged 25–49 years who test negative for HPV.
- *Low-dose CT scan*: Employed for lung cancer screening in high-risk individuals (Tun et al., 2025).

Artificial intelligence (AI) is transforming oncology by enhancing cancer screening, enabling early detection, supporting precision treatment, and improving prognosis prediction.

Artificial intelligence (AI) is defined as the capability of a machine to perform tasks that involve learning, reasoning, and problem-solving, mimicking intelligent human behavior. Two fundamental components of AI are machine learning (ML) and deep learning (DL). Machine learning involves algorithms that learn patterns from data without explicit programming, while deep learning consists of multilayered algorithmic networks, similar to the human brain, capable of analyzing and interpreting complex data. The algorithms may be either predictive or generative. Predictive AI tools feed on data to predict possible outcomes, whereas generative AI creates new outputs that were not explicitly fed in training data. The use of algorithms to make predictions through the usage of exhaustive data is one of the characteristic features of AI. AI has the capability to analyze vast amounts of data, uncovering patterns and correlations that are challenging for humans to detect. Recent progress in AI model training algorithms, the availability of advanced computing hardware, and access to diverse cancer-related data—including imaging, genomics, and clinical records—have collectively opened new opportunities for applying AI in cancer research. The extensive use of AI in predicting biological mechanisms for early diagnosis, interpretation of complex epidemiological and real-world data has helped in improvement of patient outcomes in this field with greater prospects in the near future (*AI and Cancer - NCI*, 2024).

AI research first evolved as a concept at a conference in 1956 in Dartmouth. Machine learning has increasingly been applied across academic and industrial settings to tackle complex tasks—such as decision-making, language interpretation, and visual perception—that traditionally relied on human intelligence. The ways in which AI can contribute to cancer care are varied, ranging from mechanisms to enhance cancer screening and diagnosis to precision therapy, immunotherapy, drug discovery, and cancer surveillance. A brief overview of these has been highlighted in this chapter.

6.2 Accelerating the Processes of Cancer Screening, Detection, and Diagnosis

Early detection through screening is a cornerstone of cancer control strategies, aiming to identify malignancies at asymptomatic stages when treatment is more effective and outcomes are improved. Early detection of cancer can significantly reduce mortality rates by enabling interventions before the disease progresses to advanced stages. For instance, colorectal cancer screening has been shown to reduce mortality by 43%. These statistics underscore the critical role of screening in cancer prevention and control. Detecting cancer early—frequently before any symptoms appear—allows for treatments that are more effective, less invasive, and can improve patient outcomes.

Cancer screening plays a crucial role in public health efforts to lower cancer-related illness and death. Continuous research, technological progress, and revised guidelines are constantly evolving the field of cancer screening. Addressing challenges such as overdiagnosis, access disparities, and ensuring the inclusivity of screening programs remains crucial for their success. As the field evolves, a balanced approach that considers scientific evidence, patient preferences, and healthcare capabilities will be key to optimizing cancer screening efforts globally. AI-based imaging algorithms are increasingly aiding the early detection of cancers, such as breast and prostate cancer. Machine learning (ML) and AI are also being applied to genomics data for predictive modeling and precision oncology. These technologies not only enhance the accuracy and speed of cancer detection but also have the potential to extend high-quality cancer care to underserved populations. ML plays a significant role in multi-omics approaches, integrating genomic, proteomic, and metabolomic data to provide a deeper understanding of cancer biology. Advanced sequencing technologies enable oncologists to develop targeted therapies tailored to specific genetic mutations and cancer subtypes, thereby making treatment more personalized and precise. For instance, the AI model Sybile, developed at the Massachusetts Institute of Technology, can detect abnormal lung growths and pinpoint cancerous regions with up to 90% accuracy, allowing clinicians to concentrate their screening efforts more effectively Goel et al., 2025).

In India, the most prevalent cancers are those of the breast, cervix, oral cavity, and lung. The following section provides a brief overview of how AI can enhance the screening and detection of these cancers.

6.2.1 Role of AI in Breast Cancer Screening

Breast cancer, now the most commonly diagnosed cancer in women, has seen a rising incidence, overtaking lung cancer. Advances in AI technology play a crucial role in facilitating early detection and in creating personalized treatment strategies. Computer algorithms for automated breast cancer diagnosis in mammograms have been studied, developed, and used in clinical settings for many years (Sechopoulos et al., 2021). The majority of breast cancer screening is still done by radiologists, who even with the best of intentions may miss some apparent cancerous lesions (false-negative assessments) and choose to recall healthy women for more testing (false-positive assessments) (Schünemann et al., 2020). The application of deep learning-based AI systems in breast cancer screening has been widely researched and remains a topic of active discussion. These artificial intelligence (AI) algorithms have received recognition for helping radiologists identify breast cancer more precisely either in digital mammography or digital breast tomosynthesis and thereby lowering false-positive and false-negative results (Díaz et al., 2024). The detection of breast cancer has been improved with deep learning-based AI systems. AI algorithms can detect tumors in mammography with accuracy, and in ultrasound and MRI they can assist in detecting subtle patterns that may indicate cancer, reducing false positives and unnecessary biopsies. AI models can analyze biopsy slides (digital pathology) to identify malignant cells, assess tumor grade, and quantify hormone receptor expression. AI can evaluate personal health information—such as genetic makeup, family history, and lifestyle factors—to estimate an individual's likelihood of developing breast cancer. Polygenic risk scores (PRS) combined with AI can improve predictive accuracy. Wearable AI tools track vitals and symptoms for early detection of recurrence. Digital health apps powered by AI offer symptom tracking, medication reminders, and virtual follow-ups. AI provides decision support tools to assist oncologists in evaluating treatment options, predicting side effects, guiding surgical decisions (e.g., breast-conserving surgery vs. mastectomy) (Ahn et al., 2023).

6.2.2 AI in Lung Cancer Screening

Lung cancer is the second most common cancer in both males and females, and is one of the leading causes of cancer-related deaths, causing 21% of total deaths (Jacobs & van Ginneken, 2019). The majority of lung cancers are diagnosed late. It is necessary to look for diagnostic tools for lung cancer, which are highly sensitive and specific and facilitate early detection (Gandhi et al., 2023). AI models can provide a number of advantages and are now a crucial component of the lung cancer screening procedure. These include reducing radiation exposure, correctly identifying and classifying lung nodules, customizing screening plans, and offering low-dose CT interpretation in areas where qualified radiologists are in short supply (Ladbury et al., 2023). AI applications that are FDA approved in clinical oncology are available. Due to its heterogeneity, lung cancer is a strong candidate for artificial intelligence applications (Jacobs & van Ginneken, 2019; Chiu et al., 2022). Numerous AI-based technologies have been developed to assist in lung segmentation, nodule detection, and characterization.

Using clinical data and visual imagery taken from electronic medical records (EMRs), convolutional neural networks (CNNs), a type of deep learning artificial neural networks, have demonstrated encouraging outcomes in predicting the risk of lung cancer (Jacobs & van Ginneken, 2019). CT scan analysis and computer-aided design systems that are AI-driven image recognition excel at detecting small lung nodules, their characterization, and segmentation. AI-powered tests such as EPIC-Seq and CAPP-Seq examine circulating tumor DNA (ctDNA) to enable early detection, classify subtypes (e.g., adenocarcinoma versus squamous cell carcinoma), and predict relapse, often before tumors become visible on imaging.

AI algorithms can analyze various imaging modalities (CT, PET/CT, etc.) and integrate clinical data to provide a comprehensive diagnostic assessment. AI can extract radiomic features from medical images to characterize lesions, effectively providing a "virtual biopsy" without needing invasive procedures. Deep learning models can analyze biopsy slides to classify tumors, identify driver mutations, and predict the best treatment outcomes. Advanced transformer-based AI models yield 94–97% accuracy in lung tumor classification and nodule detection, integrating with CNNs for high-quality results. AI-guided radiotherapy auto-contouring tools can dramatically cut planning time from 20 to 150 minutes, improving accuracy and reducing wait times. AI-powered 3D reconstructions in robotic systems can enhance tumor localization, margin assessment, and surgical precision and thereby reducing complications and operative time by 25–30% (Cellina et al., 2023).

6.2.3 AI in Oral Cancer

Oral and maxillofacial cancer is among the most common types of head and neck cancers, encompassing various conditions that affect the jaws, oral cavity, and other facial structures. Early detection of oral cancers is vital to increase the chances of survival and lower the rates of mortality and morbidity (Khanagar et al., 2023).

However, diagnosis is sometimes challenging due to the variability of such pathological conditions, as well as potential observer variability among clinicians and pathologists. The gold standard for identifying and classifying oral cancer is tissue sample histopathological analysis performed under a microscope. However, the clinical utility of this method may be limited due to its slowness and error-proneness. Moreover, outcomes may vary, and interpretations can be subjective. The course of treatment may then be impacted by this (Santana & Ferreira, 2017). There is a need for diagnostic techniques that can provide higher accuracy, speed, and consistency to minimize the occurrence of errors and improve patient outcomes.

AI's primary benefit is that it lessens the workload that is there with manually visualizing slides. AI models (especially deep learning like CNNs) can analyze intraoral photos, radiographs, or histopathology slides to detect precancerous and cancerous lesions. In oral photographs, AI models exceed 90% accuracy and over 85% sensitivity. AI can help interpret cytology smears with higher accuracy and consistency. AI-enabled mobile screening tools are being created to enable point-of-care detection—particularly in low-resource environments—offering early identification of oral cancers and improving access to screening (Al-Rawi et al., 2022; Abdul et al., 2024).

6.2.4 AI in Cervical Cancer

One of the biggest causes of cancer-related deaths among women is still cervical cancer, which poses a major risk to their physical and emotional well-being. It is the only cancer that can be eradicated through primary prevention measures, which include early identification, prompt treatment, and a completely effective human papillomavirus (HPV) vaccine (Brisson et al., 2020).

One economical method of preventing cervical cancer in women is to screen for and treat precancerous lesions. Although improvements in screening have boosted detection and reduced mortality for cervical cancer, the vast majority of deaths still occur in low- and middle-income countries. Challenges like weak health infrastructure and not-so-accurate manual screening make cancer screening difficult. The application of AI in the early screening and diagnosis of cervical cancer is ideal in the settings where the at-risk population is large but human resources are limited.

AI-powered image recognition systems can automatically detect abnormal cervical cells from pap smear slides. Smartphone-based AI apps analyze cervix images that are captured via mobile colposcopes or VIA to identify suspicious lesions, especially useful in low-resource settings. AI algorithms are being developed to correlate HPV genotyping data with patient demographics and history to predict risk stratification. AI assists in confirming cancer presence, grading severity, and planning biopsy. AI models can interpret colposcopy images and highlight areas of concern, reducing subjectivity and variability among clinicians. AI-driven digital pathology tools analyze biopsy samples to classify lesion grades (CIN1, CIN2, CIN3), predict tumor aggressiveness or potential for progression. AI models can synthesize patient histories, test results, and risk factors to suggest diagnostic pathways or flag high-risk individuals. In the field of histopathology, convolutional neural networks in AI can augment early detection and classification of cancerous tissue in whole-slide images, enabling real-time analysis with minimum intraobserver variability.

AI aids in personalized treatment planning, prognosis, and therapy optimization. AI can extract quantitative features from imaging modalities (MRI, CT) to predict tumor response to chemoradiation, guide radiation therapy planning, and monitor treatment progress. Machine learning models can also help tailor treatments based on the stage of cancer, genetic and molecular markers, and prior treatment responses. AI systems can predict recurrence risk, overall survival, or treatment toxicity, supporting long-term follow-up care and patient counseling.

Cancer screening plays a critical role in public health efforts to reduce cancer-related illness and death. With continuous advances in research, technology, and evolving guidelines, the screening landscape is being transformed. In this evolving environment, the potential for artificial intelligence (AI) to aid in the early detection of less common malignancies—such as glioblastomas, thyroid cancers, and sarcomas—is significant, as numerous models and algorithms continue to mature. The potential of AI to facilitate the early detection of several rare cancers like glioblastomas, thyroid cancers, and sarcomas cannot be undermined as several models and algorithms continue to evolve. Addressing challenges such as overdiagnosis, access disparities, and ensuring the inclusivity of screening programs remains crucial for their success. As the field evolves, a balanced approach that considers scientific evidence, patient preferences, and healthcare capabilities will be key to optimizing cancer screening efforts globally (Hou et al., 2022).

Beyond screening and early detection, AI plays a crucial role across multiple domains, supporting comprehensive cancer care and management.

6.2.5 AI in Precision Treatment

When it comes to precision treatment, its aim is not only to reduce side effects to patients but also maximize the therapeutic efficacy. Also, it involves tailoring the treatment as per the individual's specific cancer and genetic makeup. An AI algorithm developed by Hu et al. helps in accurately identifying the precancerous lesions in cervix in cervical cancer so as to precisely target the lesions. The study by Bahl et al. explores the effectiveness of digital breast tomosynthesis done on 1000 women and the validation of such AI tool was also done by two radiologists. They worked completely on detecting interval breast cancers that develop between screening periods. Use of AI tools can help to accurately predict how individual cells would respond to cancer chemotherapy. Precision oncology is a new approach that often involves analyzing a large amount of data to help physicians predict responses of individual cancer cells to a single drug or drug combinations. For example, genetic subtyping of brain tissue can be done with the use of AI during a complex brain surgery, giving faster and more accurate results that can help to take treatment decisions during the course of the surgery. AI tools can help to combine molecular and histopathological data of many patients that can help the physicians to predict survival outcomes and personalize the treatment regimen accordingly (Dlamini et al., 2020; Wang et al., 2025). Clinical decision support systems also work on the mechanism of deep learning technology that can help physicians to generate evidence-based treatment options by evaluating large amounts of data (Liao et al., 2023).

6.3 AI in Cancer Care: Oncosurgery, Cancer Chemotherapy, Radiotherapy, and Immunotherapy

AI can help surgeons to make effective decisions during all stages of cancer surgery. Preoperatively it aids surgeons by providing insights into the patient profiles, tumor characteristics, and predicting surgical outcomes in terms of effective prediction of lymph node metastasis. A deep learning model was used by Song JH et al. with stained endoscopic resection specimens to predict metastasis to lymph nodes that performed better in prediction compared to traditional models (Liang et al., 2020). The prediction of lymph node metastasis can be enhanced by combining with other parameters like radiological and histopathological data. AI models show great potential in application for other solid tumors like thyroid, breast, lung, and other endometrial tumors.

The IDEAL framework developed by Hani J Marcus explores the use of surgical robotics in four different stages. Early stages (stages 0–2a) evaluate the safety and feasibility while the last three stages (2b, 3, 4) monitor the intervention against a current standard and long-term monitoring for future adoption. Computer-assisted surgery (CAS) plays a crucial role in onco-surgery with enhanced efficiency and effectiveness. Computer vision (CV) is extensively used in image-guided navigation by which the surgeon can make effective and prompt decisions during surgery. Their methodology includes four key stakeholders (clinician perspective, patient perspective, device perspective, and system perspective) who bring out the current implementation of AI in practice and possible solutions to improve the efficiency of care (Marcus et al. 2024).

Similarly, the work by Dorman, S.N. et al. on the breast cancer treatment with machine learning tools like support vector systems showed that paclitaxel has 82% accuracy while gemcitabine had 85% efficacy. Numerous research studies have also demonstrated that AI models outperform the Epstein–Barr virus DNA-based model in determining treatment choices and risk assessment for nasopharyngeal cancer. AI's potential to effectively treat colon and rectal tumors has recently come to light. When it came to choosing treatment plans and assessing prognoses for patients with colorectal cancer, machine learning and deep learning approaches demonstrated promising outcomes. The effectiveness of AI in forecasting treatment responses in patients with metastatic colorectal cancer was evaluated in a systematic review. With an accuracy of up to 99% for responders and 100% for nonresponders, they discovered that the AI algorithms were highly effective at predicting the results of therapy (Yang et al., 2024; Lin et al., 2019).

AI is being used in cancer treatment in a very specialized and advanced way. AI can allow radiologists to map out the target area, identify the organs at risk, and so develop an effective radiation plan targeting the malignant lesions. AI systems' capacity to recognize intelligent image delineation automatically without the need for human intervention reduces error and time while improving precision, which is crucial for cancer treatment. When it came to defining the lesions of nasopharyngeal cancer, an AI contouring tool created by Lin et al. showed a 79% accuracy rate that was on par with radiation specialists. Another predictive model combining deep learning technology with radiomics that could evaluate the response to bladder cancer treatment was developed by Cha et al. An automation software developed by Babier et al. greatly reduced the time required in planning radiation therapy with equivalent results compared to conventional treatment plan (Lin et al., 2019).

At present, radiotherapists frequently ascertain the dosage of radiotherapy in accordance with established protocols, which are subsequently modified on multiple occasions, thereby significantly constraining the efficacy and accuracy of radiotherapy. Artificial intelligence-driven algorithmic systems have achieved substantial advancements in enhancing the precision of dosage predictions. Furthermore, the integration of AI-based radiomics with dosimetry data has been extensively employed in the prediction of treatment response and associated toxicities. A deep learning multitask imaging-based model developed by Jin C et al. can predict solid tumor radiotherapy dose prediction and substantially improves radiotherapy dose accuracy when combined with blood-based tumor markers (Zhang et al., 2022).

AI can augment the development process of nanomedicines by adjusting and refining their properties and minimizing toxicity. This helps in enhancing the efficacy of nanomedicines by making it more precise and personalized. Nanomedical products have been proficiently employed in the therapeutic management of various malignancies, including but not limited to ovarian carcinoma, breast carcinoma, lung carcinoma, pancreatic carcinoma, acute myeloid leukemia, among others. Several factors, however, need to be considered during delivery of nano medicines like internalization, responses within the tumor microenvironment, distribution in the affected cells, and their therapeutic actions. AI can even estimate drug release kinetics from nanocarriers using advanced algorithms. Thus, AI-driven nanotechnology can play a vital role in cancer care in the near future (Sorrentino et al., 2024).

Another innovative methodology in oncological treatment is the utilization of the patient's immune system in the fight against malignancies, referred to as immunotherapy. This approach encompasses the enhancement or restoration of the organism's immune response to modulate the proliferation of neoplastic cells. It necessitates the activation of effector T lymphocytes, followed by the ensuing identification and eradication of malignant cells by these activated T lymphocytes. Numerous biomarkers are examined prior to the commencement of therapy to ascertain associations with the responsiveness of cancer patients.

In the evolving field of cancer immunotherapy, artificial intelligence (AI) plays a pivotal role in guiding physicians to tailor and refine treatment strategies based on individual patient responses. By leveraging predictive scoring systems such as the immunoscore and immunophenoscore—tools specifically designed to anticipate outcomes of immune checkpoint blockade (ICB) therapy—AI enhances the ability to forecast therapeutic efficacy. Through sophisticated analysis of high-throughput genomic data and medical imaging, AI facilitates optimal patient selection, timely initiation of treatment, and accurate prognosis prediction. Notably, a platform developed by Sun et al. demonstrated significant effectiveness in evaluating immunotherapy outcomes among patients with advanced solid tumors, particularly those responsive to inhibitors targeting programmed cell death protein-1 (PD-1). AI can also lead to uniformity in assessments and decision-making process instead of relying on pure subjectivity of clinicians. Some limitations hereby exist like unknown predictive power of individual biomarkers and difficulty in combining multiple biomarkers into one model. By identifying the molecular intricacies of tumors, cancer immunotherapy has emerged as a pivotal component of systematic cancer treatment (Xu et al., 2021).

AI has been extensively used to extract data from large sources for understanding the fundamental mechanisms of cancer initiation, progression and metastasis. AI helps experts to develop computational tools from large data sets to improve and further knowledge and research on cancer biology. AI models help scientists to simulate the atomic behavior of proteins commonly mutated in cancer and find new avenues to target these mutations [6]. AI algorithms and machine learning offer a great opportunity to process the humongous amount of data generated during the process of drug development to make evidence-based decisions that would otherwise require tedious years of experimentation and prediction. Artificial intelligence algorithms are increasingly being employed to model drug responses and predict how cancer cell lines react to various therapeutic agents using vast datasets to enhance precision and personalization in treatment outcomes. One of the transformative applications of AI in oncology is drug repurposing—identifying novel therapeutic roles for existing medications. Notable examples of AI-assisted drug development include BPM 31510 and EXS-21546. BPM 31510, created by Breg, functions by reprogramming cancer cells, enabling their natural elimination without the need for conventional chemotherapy. Another innovation, PHI-101, is an orally administered selective inhibitor of checkpoint kinase 2, developed through an AI-powered drug discovery framework. Additionally, researchers have harnessed AI to analyze extensive datasets on human and murine T cell activation, enabling more accurate predictions of T cell behavior and thereby enhancing the effectiveness of immunotherapy strategies. Predictive AI models may be used to design maps of common drug response pathways (Weerarathna et al., 2023).

Limited access to adequate healthcare remains a significant contributor to elevated cancer mortality rates, particularly in developing and underdeveloped regions. However, the growing integration of artificial intelligence in medical practice, along with the expansion of telemedicine services, is helping bridge this gap. These technologies enable patients in resource-constrained environments to receive expert consultations from oncology specialists, thereby promoting more equitable healthcare delivery and reducing disparities in cancer outcomes. By gathering a huge amount of evidence-based information, AI can help to make a personalized treatment plan for a particular patient, thus making cancer treatment choices more evidence-based and intelligent. Cancer surveillance through the use of cancer registries is the ongoing collection of patient information and cancer statistics. It can be either hospital based or population based. Designing deep learning algorithms based on population-level data has been used to predict a person's risk of various types of cancer, thus facilitating early detection. AI facilitates the extraction of population-level cancer data to identify prevalence and patterns of cancer across regions and surveillance reporting. Even patient outcomes may be predicted using this approach. By collating data of sociodemographic variates of cancer patients, researchers are able to better understand social determinants and risk factors for certain cancers that is very crucial for cancers linked to lifestyle factors (Kolla & Parikh, 2024) (Fig. 6.1).

6.4 Challenges and Opportunities for AI in Cancer Research

Artificial intelligence, with its sophistication and precision, has extensive scope for use in cancer care. The recent years have witnessed the rapid acceleration in AI research in cancer care and to mitigate the suffering due to it. Researchers are revolutionizing cancer care by integrating AI-driven imaging technologies—such as MRI and CT scan analysis—with advanced machine learning and mathematical models. These tools are being employed not only to detect malignancies at earlier

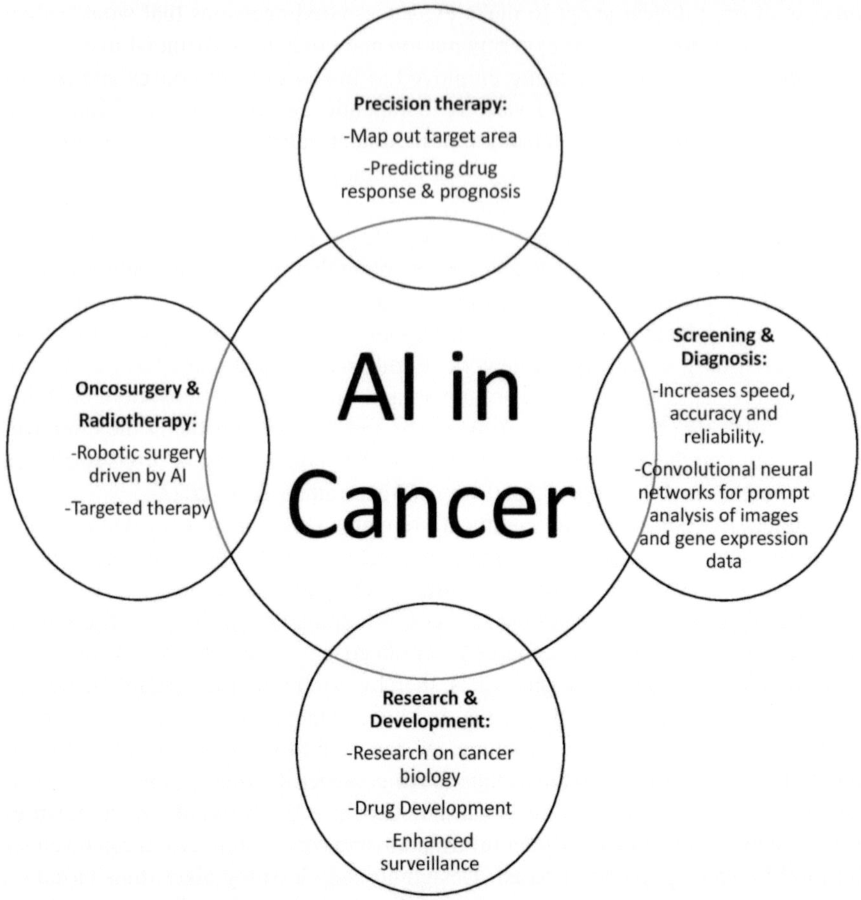

Fig. 6.1 Role of AI in cancer research

stages but also to forecast treatment responses and tailor therapies to individual patient profiles, marking a new era in precision oncology.

Use of AI-based algorithms has been helpful in correctly predicting anticancer drug sensitivity as well as toxicity of anticancer drugs (Rosen-Zvi et al., 2023). However, there is always a flip side that needs to be considered. Data privacy and security concerns are an important concern in healthcare when it pertains to patients' health data. Data confidentiality and sharing of patients' personal data to build AI-based algorithms without the patient's knowledge can lead to a breach of confidentiality. Also, there still remains a huge challenge in the aspect of interoperability and refinement of data quality. AI models can also be subject to bias based on those who create them or suffer from errors of poor sampling quality that might alter the analytics. This can lead to unfair or discriminatory outcomes in diagnosis or treatment. For example, some countries are leading the race in AI development, contributing to a huge chunk of global AI investments. The models created by them are based on data from their people that may not be representative of ethnic compositions or genetic diversity of other regions. This can result in flaws in treatment doses, SOPs, and plans, thereby increasing inequities in cancer care globally, which is a cause of grave concern. These models are expensive and complicated, making it difficult for use by most mid-level scientists and operators. AI solutions in healthcare require significant investment in data infrastructure and computing power and have to undergo a rigorous process of quality control before it could be finally accepted as in healthcare the stakes are very high. Also, there is a question of accountability. It is very difficult to trace the source of the originator from AI-based technologies. So if it goes wrong, therein comes the question of accountability. Also, being overdependent on AI, especially by the healthcare professionals, can lead to a potential decline in clinical decision–making, which is of pivotal importance in healthcare … the so-called human touch.

Ensuring that AI technologies adhere to the complex regulatory frameworks and standards within the healthcare sector presents a significant challenge. Moreover, the integration of AI into clinical practice often encounters resistance from healthcare professionals, stemming from concerns about its reliability, insufficient training, and a general lack of trust. Compounding these issues is the limited public understanding of how AI can enhance healthcare delivery, which further hinders widespread acceptance and utilization. To ensure accuracy and fairness in AI-driven healthcare applications, it is essential that the datasets used for training are inclusive and reflective of the wider population. This helps mitigate bias and reduces the risk of misleading outcomes. The development of machine learning models must follow established protocols and regulatory standards. Additionally, healthcare institutions must implement secure data management practices, including strong encryption, controlled access, and routine audits, to safeguard patient information and maintain the integrity of AI systems. Fostering collaborations between healthcare institutions to share data responsibly can help overcome the problem of poor quality or inadequate data. Adhering to ethical standards, transparency in data sharing, and decision-making with regular auditing mechanisms need to be in place so there is accountability for the outcomes of AI-driven models. To overcome the financial issues, AI-driven systems need to be backed up with innovative financial models. Government support with strong public–private partnerships can help in making the benefits of AI in healthcare and cancer care reach out to the masses in an equitable manner. Training programs for the staff and promoting a culture of innovation and improvement primarily involving the frontline staff can overcome the resistance to adoption in healthcare organizations. Keeping in view the rising ethical and confidential concerns in the use of personalized and health data, it is important that organizations need to stay up to date with latest regulatory requirements and ensure measures to ensure compliance to regulatory standards. A need for further research to validate the applications of AI and machine learning technologies in cancer care is the need of the hour (Kolla & Parikh, 2024; Sebastian & Peter, 2022).

References

Abdul, N. S., et al. (2024). Applications of artificial intelligence in the field of oral and maxillofacial pathology: A systematic review and meta-analysis. *BMC Oral Health, 24*(1). https://doi.org/10.1186/s12903-023-03533-7

Ahn, J. S., Shin, S., Yang, S. A., Park, E. K., Kim, K. H., Cho, S. I., Ock, C. Y., & Kim, S. (2023). Artificial intelligence in breast cancer diagnosis and personalized medicine. *Journal of Breast Cancer, 26*(5), 405–435. https://doi.org/10.4048/jbc.2023.26.e45. PMID: 37926067; PMCID: PMC10625863.

Al-Rawi, N., et al. (2022). The effectiveness of artificial intelligence in detection of oral cancer. *International Dental Journal, 72*(4), 436–447. https://doi.org/10.1016/j.identj.2022.03.001

Artificial Intelligence and Cancer. (2024). National Cancer Institute, NIH. https://www.cancer.gov/research/infrastructure/artificial-intelligence

Bray, F., Laversanne, M., Sung, H., Ferlay, J., Siegel, R. L., Soerjomataram, I., & Jemal, A. (2024a). Global cancer statistics 2022: GLOBOCAN estimates of incidence and mortality worldwide for 36 cancers in 185 countries. *CA: A Cancer Journal for Clinicians, 74*(3), 229–263. https://doi.org/10.3322/caac.21834. Epub 2024 Apr 4. PMID: 38572751.

Bray, F., Ferlay, J., Soerjomataram, I., Siegel, R. L., Torre, L. A., & Jemal, A. (2024b). Global cancer statistics 2018: GLOBOCAN estimates of incidence and mortality worldwide for 36 cancers in 185 countries. *CA: A Cancer Journal for Clinicians, 74*(3), 229–263. https://doi.org/10.3322/caac.21834. Epub 2024 Apr 4. PMID: 38572751.

Brisson, M., et al. (2020). Impact of HPV vaccination and cervical screening on cervical cancer elimination: A comparative modelling analysis in 78 low-income and lower-middle-income countries. *The Lancet., 395*(10244), 575–590. https://doi.org/10.1016/S0140-6736(20)30068-4

Cellina, M., Cacioppa, L. M., Cè, M., Chiarpenello, V., Costa, M., Vincenzo, Z., Pais, D., Bausano, M. V., Rossini, N., Bruno, A., & Floridi, C. (2023). Artificial intelligence in lung cancer screening: The future is now. *Cancers, 15*(17), 4344. https://doi.org/10.3390/cancers15174344. PMID: 37686619; PMCID: PMC10486721.

Chiu, H. Y., Chao, H. S., & Chen, Y. M. (2022). Application of artificial intelligence in lung cancer. *Cancers, 14*, 1370. https://doi.org/10.3390/cancers14061370

Díaz, O., Rodríguez-Ruíz, A., & Sechopoulos, I. (2024). Artificial Intelligence for breast cancer detection: Technology, challenges, and prospects. *European Journal of Radiology, 175*, 111457., ISSN0720 048X. https://doi.org/10.1016/j.ejrad.2024.111457

Dlamini, Z., Francies, F. Z., Hull, R., & Marima, R. (2020). Artificial intelligence (AI) and big data in cancer and precision oncology. *Computational and Structural Biotechnology Journal, 28*(18), 2300–2311. https://doi.org/10.1016/j.csbj.2020.08.019. PMID: 32994889; PMCID: PMC7490765. https://pubmed.ncbi.nlm.nih.gov/32994889/.

Gandhi, Z., Gurram, P., Amgai, B., Lekkala, S. P., Lokhandwala, A., Manne, S., Mohammed, A., Koshiya, H., Dewaswala, N., Desai, R., Bhopalwala, H., Ganti, S., & Surani, S. (2023). Artificial intelligence and lung cancer: Impact on improving patient outcomes. *Cancers, 15*(21), 5236. https://doi.org/10.3390/cancers15215236. PMID: 37958411; PMCID: PMC10650618.

Goel, I., Bhaskar, Y., Kumar, N., Singh, S., Amanullah, M., Dhar, R., & Karmakar, S. (2025). Role of AI in empowering and redefining the oncology care landscape: Perspective from a developing nation. *Front Digit Health, 7*, 1550407. https://doi.org/10.3389/fdgth.2025.1550407. PMID: 40103737; PMCID: PMC11913822 https://pmc.ncbi.nlm.nih.gov/articles/PMC11913822/

Hou, X., Shen, G., Zhou, L., Li, Y., Wang, T., & Ma, X. (2022). Artificial intelligence in cervical cancer screening and diagnosis. *Frontiers in Oncology, 12*. https://doi.org/10.3389/fonc.2022.851367

Jacobs, C., & van Ginneken, B. (2019). Google's lung cancer AI: A promising tool that needs further validation. *Nature Reviews. Clinical Oncology, 16*, 532–533. https://doi.org/10.1038/s41571-019-0248-7

Khanagar, S. B., et al. (2023). Application and performance of artificial intelligence (AI) in oral cancer diagnosis and prediction using histopathological images: A systematic review. *Biomedicine, 11*(6), 1612. https://doi.org/10.3390/biomedicines11061612

Kolla, L., & Parikh, R. B. (2024). Uses and limitations of artificial intelligence for oncology. *Cancer, 130*(12), 2101–2107. https://doi.org/10.1002/cncr.35307. Epub 2024 Mar 30. PMID: 38554271; PMCID: PMC11170282. https://pubmed.ncbi.nlm.nih.gov/38554271/

Ladbury, C., Amini, A., Govindarajan, A., Mambetsariev, I., Raz, D. J., Massarelli, E., Williams, T., Rodin, A., & Salgia, R. (2023). Integration of artificial intelligence in lung cancer: Rise of the machine. *Cell Reports Medicine, 4*, 100933. https://doi.org/10.1016/j.xcrm.2023.100933

Liang, G., Fan, W., Luo, H., & Zhu, X. (2020). The emerging roles of artificial intelligence in cancer drug development and precision therapy. *Biomedicine & Pharmacotherapy, 128*, 110255. https://doi.org/10.1016/j.biopha.2020.110255. Epub 2020 May 20. PMID: 32446113. https://pubmed.ncbi.nlm.nih.gov/32446113/

Liao, J., Li, X., Gan, Y., Han, S., Rong, P., Wang, W., Li, W., & Zhou, L. (2023). Artificial intelligence assists precision medicine in cancer treatment. *Frontiers in Oncology, 12*, 998222. https://doi.org/10.3389/fonc.2022.998222. PMID: 36686757; PMCID: PMC9846804.

Lin, L., Dou, Q., Jin, Y. M., Zhou, G. Q., Tang, Y. Q., Chen, W. L., Su, B. A., Liu, F., Tao, C. J., Jiang, N., Li, J. Y., Tang, L. L., Xie, C. M., Huang, S. M., Ma, J., Heng, P. A., Wee, J. T. S., Chua, M. L. K., Chen, H., & Sun, Y. (2019). Deep learning for automated contouring of primary tumor volumes by MRI for nasopharyngeal carcinoma. *Radiology, 291*(3), 677–686. https://doi.org/10.1148/radiol.2019182012. Epub 2019 Mar 26. PMID: 30912722. https://pubmed.ncbi.nlm.nih.gov/30912722/

Lynge, E., Törnberg, S., von Karsa, L., Segnan, N., & van Delden, J. J. M. (2012). Determinants of successful implementation of population-based cancer screening programmes. *European Journal of Cancer, 48*(5), 743–748. https://doi.org/10.1016/j.ejca.2011.06.051

Marcus, H. J., Ramirez, P. T., Khan, D. Z., Layard Horsfall, H., Hanrahan, J. G., Williams, S. C., Beard, D. J., Bhat, R., Catchpole, K., Cook, A., Hutchison, K., Martin, J., Melvin, T., Stoyanov, D., Rovers, M., Raison, N., Dasgupta, P., Noonan, D., Stocken, D., Sturt, G., Vanhoestenberghe, A., Vasey, B., McCulloch, P., & IDEAL Robotics Colloquium. (2024). The IDEAL framework for surgical robotics: development, comparative evaluation and long-term monitoring. *Nat Med, 30*(1), 61–75. https://doi.org/10.1038/s41591-023-02732-7. Epub 2024 Jan 19. Erratum in: Nat Med. 2024 Apr;30(4):1213. https://doi.org/10.1038/s41591-024-02836-8. PMID: 38242979.

Rosen-Zvi, M., Mullen, L., Lukas, R. J., Guindy, M., & Gabrani, M. (2023). Editorial: Explainable multimodal AI in cancer patient care: How can we reduce the gap between technology and practice? *Frontiers in Medicine, 10*, 1190429. https://doi.org/10.3389/fmed.2023.1190429. PMID: 37122326; PMCID: PMC10133714.

Santana, M. F., & Ferreira, L. C. L. (2017). Diagnostic errors in surgical pathology. *Jornal Brasileiro de Patologia e Medicina Laboratorial, 53*(2). https://doi.org/10.5935/1676-2444.20170021

Sathishkumar, K., Chaturvedi, M., Das, P., Stephen, S., & Mathur, P. (2022). Cancer incidence estimates for 2022 & projection for 2025: Result from National Cancer Registry Programme, India. *The Indian Journal of Medical Research, 156*(4&5), 598–607. https://doi.org/10.4103/ijmr.ijmr_1821_22. PMID: 36510887; PMCID: PMC10231735.

Schunemann, H. J., Lerda, D., Quinn, C., Follmann, M., Alonso-Coello, P., Rossi, P. G., Lebeau, A., Nystrom, L., Broeders, M., Ioannidou-Mouzaka, L., et al. (2020). Breast cancer screening and diagnosis: A synopsis of the european breast guidelines. *Annals of Internal Medicine, 172*(1), 46–56.

Sebastian, A. M., & Peter, D. (2022). Artificial intelligence in cancer research: Trends, challenges and future directions. *Life (Basel), 12*(12), 1991. https://doi.org/10.3390/life12121991. PMID: 36556356; PMCID: PMC9786074. https://pubmed.ncbi.nlm.nih.gov/36556356/

Sechopoulos, I., Teuwen, J., & Mann, R. (2021). Artificial intelligence for breast cancer detection in mammography and digital breast tomosynthesis: State of the art. *Seminars in Cancer Biology (Elsevier), 72*, 214–225.

Sorrentino, C., Ciummo, S. L., Fieni, C., & Di Carlo, E. (2024). Nanomedicine for cancer patient-centered care. *MedComm(2020).*, *5*(11), e767. https://doi.org/10.1002/mco2.767. PMID: 39434967; PMCID: PMC11491554. https://pmc.ncbi.nlm.nih.gov/articles/PMC11491554/

Tun, H. M., Rahman, H. A., Naing, L., & Malik, O. A. (2025). Artificial intelligence utilization in cancer screening program across ASEAN: A scoping review. *BMC Cancer, 25*(1), 703. https://doi.org/10.1186/s12885-025-14026-x. PMID: 40234807; PMCID: PMC12001681.

Wang, J., et al. (2025). The clinical application of artificial intelligence in cancer precision treatment. *Journal of Translational Medicine, 23*(1), 120. https://doi.org/10.1186/s12967-025-06139-5

Weerarathna, I. N., Kamble, A. R., & Luharia, A. (2023). Artificial intelligence applications for biomedical cancer research: A review. *Cureus, 15*(11), e48307. https://doi.org/10.7759/cureus.48307. PMID: 38058345; PMCID: PMC10697339. https://pmc.ncbi.nlm.nih.gov/articles/PMC10697339/

World Health Organization. (2024). *Management of Cancer-South East Asia*. https://www.who.int/southeastasia/activities/management-of-cancer

Xu, Z., Wang, X., Zeng, S., Ren, X., Yan, Y., & Gong, Z. (2021). Applying artificial intelligence for cancer immunotherapy. *Acta Pharmaceutica Sinica B, 11*(11), 3393–3405. https://doi.org/10.1016/j.apsb.2021.02.007

Yang, J., Huang, J., Han, D., & Ma, X. (2024). Artificial intelligence applications in the treatment of colorectal cancer: A narrative review. *Clinical Medicine Insights: Oncology, 18*, 11795549231220320. https://doi.org/10.1177/11795549231220320. PMID: 38187459; PMCID: PMC10771756. https://pubmed.ncbi.nlm.nih.gov/38187459/

Zhang, X., Zhang, Y., Zhang, G., Qiu, X., Tan, W., Yin, X., & Liao, L. (2022). Deep learning with radiomics for disease diagnosis and treatment: Challenges and potential. *Frontiers in Oncology, 17*(12), 773840. https://doi.org/10.3389/fonc.2022.773840. PMID: 35251962; PMCID: PMC8891653.

Intelligent Diagnosis: Leveraging Artificial Intelligence to Detect and Manage Infectious and Noninfectious Diseases

7

Aroop Mohanty, Shubham, Sakshi Sharma,
Atul R. Rukadikar, Ankita Kabi, and Shriyansh Srivastava

7.1 Introduction

The healthcare industry is entering a new age when large amounts of medical data will become increasingly crucial. For example, healthcare accuracy considers a variety of patient data, including variations in routine, atmosphere, Electronic Health Records (EHRs), and biological traits. This ensures that the proper medication is promptly given to the right patient (Hampel et al., 2017; Hossain et al., 2021). Despite the great potential of current models, technique-based prediction tools like Deep Learning (DL) and Machine Learning (ML) have not been extensively used in the healthcare sector (Nienhold et al., 2017; Bhardwaj et al., 2017).

An increasingly common tool in many industries, including healthcare, is Artificial Intelligence (AI). The field of AI known as "Generative AI" has drawn interest lately due to its capacity to create new data, including writing, images, and music, using machine learning techniques (Kothari, 2023; Jadon & Kumar, 2023). Computer science, linguistics, neuroscience, cognitive psychology, theory of decisions, neurology, statistics, logic, and cybernetics are all examples of the wide-ranging and diverse discipline of artificial intelligence (Jain et al., 2024). There have

A. Mohanty (✉) · Shubham · S. Sharma · A. R. Rukadikar
Department of Microbiology, All India Institute of Medical Sciences,
Gorakhpur, Uttar Pradesh, India

A. Kabi
Department of Anesthesiology, All India Institute of Medical Sciences,
Gorakhpur, Uttar Pradesh, India

S. Srivastava
Department of Pharmacy, School of Medical and Allied Sciences, Galgotias University,
Greater Noida, India

Department of Pharmacology, Delhi Pharmaceutical Sciences and Research University
(DPSRU), New Delhi, India

U. Venkatesh et al. (eds.), *Multimodal AI in Healthcare*,
https://doi.org/10.1007/978-981-95-9027-8_7

been notable developments in AI; two examples are ChatGPT and Alphafold. Numerous fields are impacted by it, including biotechnology, pharmacology, genetics, pathology, drug safety, and drug discovery (Li et al., 2024).

Many industries, including healthcare, use AI as a tool. One branch of AI that has recently gained interest is Generative AI, which uses algorithms to create new data, including writing, pictures, and music (Kothari, 2023; Jadon & Kumar, 2023). A type of machine learning technology called generative AI uses training data to learn how to create new data (Epstein et al., 2023). The possible applications of generative AI in healthcare include: it has become a potent instrument for improving patient care because it can analyze large datasets and produce insightful results, transforming the diagnosis of illness and increasing the range of available treatments (Suthar et al., 2022; Kanjee et al., 2023; Vert, 2023).

By using this cutting-edge technology's potential, medical professionals may now accomplish what was previously unheard-of degrees of precision, effectiveness, and creativity in business processes. The usefulness and effects of generative AI in healthcare are still not well known (Zohny et al., 2023). Generative AI in medical fields brings moral and medical-legal concerns (Duffourc & Gerke, 2023). It is uncertain how the healthcare staff can effectively use generative AI technologies and how they may be included in the delivery of healthcare services (Stokel-Walker & Van Noorden, 2023).

The healthcare industry uses generative AI for image and voice synthesis, and unsupervised computing enables it to learn from information without explicitly classifying it. When obtaining labeled information is difficult or excessively costly, understand the fundamental foundation of data collection, create fresh samples similar to the original data, and create artificial information through discovering the fundamental information distributions from actual data. After that, new information is created mathematically comparable with the exact information (Brynjolfsson et al., 2025).

To make predictions or take actions using the already available data, generative AI models emphasize classification, regression, or reinforcement learning. Unlike other machine learning prototypes, generative prototypes are centered on enabling machines to produce new things (Brynjolfsson et al., 2025).

7.1.1 Artificial Intelligence and Health Diagnosis

DL and ML offer an intriguing and modern paradigm with potential for biomedical informatics. It has proven its efficacy in various domains (including voice recognition, machine learning, and spontaneous activities involving language processing) and the rapid rate of methodological innovations (Kamath et al., 2019).

The application of DL and ML skills in medicine is either already being used or is being suggested. International Business Machines, or IBM, Watson Health, for example, focuses on providing a large population with cheap medical treatment by using this technology to connect with patients and healthcare professionals; Google DeepMind has proposed to use the knowledge it has to improve healthcare and

Enlitic uses deep neural networks and X-rays to determine whether computed tomography (CT) scans reveal any health issues (Bali et al., 2019; Hsu, 2016). A summary of the major AI applications across infectious and noninfectious diseases is presented in Table 7.1.

7.1.2 AI in Noninfectious Diseases Diagnosis and Surveillance

7.1.2.1 Machine Learning in Noninfectious Diseases Diagnosis

- *Disease Identification and Diagnosis*: This covers everything from other inherited diseases to early-stage cancers that are hard to detect (Rahman et al., 2024).
- *Engineering and Medical Innovation*: The main clinical education programs for robots are part of the new era of medicine manufacturing. This also includes research and development capabilities that might be used to discover alternative therapies for complex diseases, such as next-generation genetic sequencing and precision medicine (Rahman et al., 2024).
- *Examination of Medical Imaging*: DL and AI have enabled a technological breakthrough in computer visualization. This is acknowledged by the Inner Eye activity developed by Microsoft, which focuses on image diagnostic tools for image analysis. The goal of understanding new information based on changing

Table 7.1 Key applications of artificial intelligence across infectious and noninfectious disease diagnosis

AI application area	Key functions	Examples
Machine learning (ML)	Disease identification, prediction, EHR optimization, OCR (optical character recognition)-based data processing	Early cancer detection, alternative therapy discovery, integrated health records (Rahman et al., 2024)
Deep learning (DL)	Image analysis, automated detection, segmentation, enhanced radiology outputs	MRI with reduced GBCAs, low-dose CT, automated malignant cell detection (Rahman et al., 2024)
AI in infectious diseases	Early outbreak detection, digital surveillance, modeling spread patterns	ProMED, HealthMap, MRIIDS, EWARS, mobile-based dengue monitoring (Li et al., 2024)
Generative AI	Synthetic medical images/text, data augmentation, clinical support	ChatGPT, Alphafold, diagnostic support tools (Kothari, 2023)
AI in vaccine & drug development	Antigen prediction, mRNA optimization, protein structure prediction	Random forest classifiers, interaction prediction, escape mutation modeling (Li et al., 2024)
AI for antimicrobial resistance	Drug repurposing, protein structure modeling, rapid AMR detection	Protein-based drug design, disk-diffusion zone quantification (Parums, 2023)
AI in public health	Policy modeling, outbreak forecasting, RL (reinforcement learning)-based decision support	COVID-19 forecasting, risk mapping, RL for scenario evaluation (Kraemer et al., 2025)

clinical symbols is revealed to include this AI-driven symptomatic interaction as machine learning becomes more open and approaches its informative limit (Rahman et al., 2024).

- *Personalized Medicine*: It's possible that prognostic analysis and personal fitness don't result in tailored treatment. More devices and biosensors with sophisticated health assessment capabilities will be released in the coming years, making getting data for innovative ML-based medical treatment simpler (Rahman et al., 2024).
- *Integrated Health Records*: Keeping a contemporary medical record is complex and time-consuming. While this is true for most cycles, technological advancements have helped the information section measure. The primary function of machine learning in the medical field is to expedite processes to save money, time, and effort. Using ML-based optical character recognition (OCR) and vector technology (Rahman et al., 2024).

7.1.2.2 Deep Learning in Noninfectious Diseases Diagnosis

- *Deep Learning in MRI*: Gadolinium-based contrast agents (GBCAs) are increasingly used in conventional magnetic resonance imaging (MRI). GBCAs have been connected to nephrogenic systemic fibrosis, a serious and progressive condition. Using less gadolinium is probably going to lessen this testimony. It may surprise you that low-partition contrast-enhanced MRI usually provides poor presentation images (Rahman et al., 2024).
- *DL-Enabled CT Scan*: CT techniques provide a radioactive risk, even though they are often used in medical treatments. The people would be exposed to 200 chest X-rays of radiation (the radioactive component of a CT scan) when they are diagnosed using a CT scan for more than 7 years. DL-enabled body scanning will facilitate more precise scanning with decreased chances of radiation exposure by prompt detection (Rahman et al., 2024).

7.1.2.3 Combining the Role of ML-DL in Noninfectious Diseases Diagnosis

- *Identifying Brain Hemorrhage Signs*: The speed at which a brain hemorrhage is identified determines the likelihood that a patient will recover. According to analysis, these bleedings may be explained in between 12% and 51% of cases, and brain bleeding-related illnesses claim the lives of about six million people annually (Rahman et al., 2024).
- *Surgery that Is Robotic or Robotically Assisted*: In conclusion, combining data from robotic systems and AI integration with surgical robots may characterize the period of surgical development we are currently accomplishing. This automated skill-enabled technology can change the treatment delivery. Three important AI systems—Alpha Go, IBM Watson, and machine learning algorithms—can be incorporated in the surgical robots when AI and big data analytics propel the next generation of surgical robots (Rahman et al., 2022a, b).
- *Cancer Diagnosis*: Most cancers are diagnosed using Ultrasonography, MRI, CT scans, and X-rays. Sadly, current tools cannot sufficiently identify certain malig-

nancies to save lives reliably. Another method is to examine microarray sequencing profiles; however, unless the study is AI-enabled, this requires many processing hours. AI-enabled diagnostic algorithmic principles have proven effective in identifying potential skin cancers (Rahman et al., 2024).

7.1.3 DL and ML Integration in Noninfectious Diseases Diagnosis

Businesses, industries, educational institutions, healthcare systems, and more have all seen notable transformations due to DL and ML. We may state that more modifications are being found in the medical field due to the abundance of online and offline resources (Rahman et al., 2020, 2022a, b). DL is necessary for the automated identification of malignant cells. While ML can handle various problems, it requires human involvement; in contrast, DL operates independently. Compared to ML, DL resolves the entire issue right away. When diagnosing cardiac problems, DL can be pretty helpful for elderly patients, coma patients, and young children (Wang et al., 2019).

7.1.4 AI in Infectious Diseases Diagnosis and Surveillance

Evidence of newly identified infections that might lead to widespread epidemics may be present. It is nearly impossible to raise the alarm about emerging illnesses because infectious disease experts struggle to sift through this deluge of information and uncover crucial insights. In these circumstances, the availability of algorithms developed by AI is advantageous (Gawande et al., 2025). The Program for Monitoring Emerging Diseases is one of the first organizations to use digital disease surveillance. Major epidemics, like the development of Zika and the early discovery of SARS, have prompted prompt warnings from ProMED scientists and analysts. For the first thorough analysis and risk analysis of a group of coronavirus patients with an unclear etiology, China, in 2019, which eventually sparked the pandemic COVID-19, ProMED garnered international recognition (Li et al., 2024; Carrion & Madoff, 2017).

For over a decade, HealthMap (www.healthmap.org) has shown efficacy in detecting markers of the incidence of infectious diseases. It was essential to track the 2019 US lung disease outbreak linked to e-cigarettes and provide early warning indicators of the development of H1N1 influenza in Mexico (Li et al., 2024; Freifeld et al., 2008). These early-warning systems are combined in a web-based application called "Mapping the Risk of International Infectious Disease Spread" (MRIIDS) (Bhatia et al., 2021). A global positioning system (GPS) enabled mobile application for dengue monitoring may be made possible using AI technology. For successful and economical local responses to the management of the Zika, dengue fever, and chikungunya outbreaks, the early warning and response system (EWARS) tools can also be useful (Rahman et al., 2022a, b; Ningrum et al., 2024).

Since mobile phones are so widely used, IoT-equipped healthcare systems that rely on mobile computing may be able to obtain patient data quickly. Since there is presently no trustworthy way to identify or track Aedes mosquitoes that directly carry arboviruses, IoT-enabled fog safety monitoring devices can be utilized to monitor Aedes mosquito outbreaks in vulnerable locations and help government agencies with prevention and control (Olmo et al., 2023; Dey et al., 2024).

7.1.5 AI to Diagnose Infectious Illnesses

Auxiliary diagnosis is greatly impacted by AI, as was evident in China at the beginning of COVID-19 (Asada et al., 2021). In Wuhan, the outbreak expanded swiftly, placing a heavy burden on healthcare facilities nationwide. AI is a valuable diagnostic tool. After being trained on an extensive database, the AI system correctly detects pneumonia caused by coronavirus and differentiates it from common pneumonia and similar lung diseases (Li et al., 2024; Zhang et al., 2020). It expedites initial examination, streamlines diagnostic procedures, cuts down on patient wait times, reduces the workload of radiologists, and improves emergency response. Supporting healthcare providers in their battle against COVID-19. Estimate the risk of a significant illness early in the patient's hospital stay based on their clinical characteristics. The hunt for molecular markers of infectious disorders has been significantly sped up by developments in spatial transcriptomics and single-cell sequencing technologies (Shubham & Kandasamy, 2023).

7.1.6 AI in the Development of Communicable Illness Treatments and Vaccines

mRNA technology has rapidly created potential booster treatments that target troublesome variants. AI and ML models will enhance the technology of mRNA vaccines, boosting their effectiveness against infectious diseases. ML includes random forest classifiers and complicated language models, which were used to identify genes and protein-protein interactions linked to alterations in host cells (Li et al., 2024). Interactions between genes and proteins connected to changes in the host have been found using machine-learning techniques like random forest classifiers and complex language models. These models have shown promise in forecasting immunogenicity and evaluating variables including pathogenicity, host cell adaptability, and pathogen death (Li et al., 2024; Okuyama, 2022).

Furthermore, by anticipating and selecting antigens and optimizing gene expression, supervised models have been essential in directing the creation of vaccinations and pharmaceuticals (Weerarathna et al., 2024). The amino acid sequence data developed models for the virus-associated proteins of the influenza virus, the HIV-1 virus, and SARS-CoV-2. Many models accurately anticipated the escape tendencies of many pathogens, allowing them to evade the immune system of humans. The body is protected from infectious diseases by cellular immunity (Fischer et al., 2021).

7.1.7 AI in Antimicrobial Resistance

Multidrug-resistant organisms resistant to traditional antibiotics have become more common over time. Conventional drug discovery methods are daunting since they need new compounds with particular features. This strategy has a poor success rate and is expensive and lengthy. Drug development has been revolutionized by AI/ML-based algorithms to deal with these issues. Machine learning has become a sought-after method for drug research, combination selection, and drug dosage optimization (Fanelli et al., 2020).

AI technologies provide rapid and economical treatment development possibilities and enable drug repurposing. Repurposing existing medications enables more rapid and economical distribution of drugs than developing new ones, since their safety has been shown in clinical studies for other purposes. This strategy works really well in treating recently reported infectious illnesses. Protein-derived drugs, such as peptides and monoclonal antibodies, have been essential in treating contagious disorders. Even without a comparable structure, AI can predict protein structures at the atomic level. This finding would greatly benefit the development of protein-based medications to treat infectious disorders (Li et al., 2024; Cesaro et al., 2025).

7.1.8 AI in Nonpharmaceutical Procedures

Nonpharmaceutical therapies like contact tracing and tactics like mask wearing and movement restrictions to reduce transmission have extensively used AI and ML applications. Health codes have been integrated into popular mobile applications like WeChat during the COVID-19 epidemic, allowing for the real-time evaluation of transmission hazards in public areas. India's pandemic has drastically decreased due to the COWIN platform and the AI-powered Arogya Setu App. These apps also provide consumers access to AI-powered medical chatbots that comprehensively explain disease prevention and treatment, control strategies, and epidemic prevention (Ganapathy, 2024).

AI has responded to the monkeypox outbreak with better scientific reasoning because of the insights gained from COVID-19. Significant improvements have been made in scientific extension, pathogen analysis, auxiliary diagnostics, precise medical therapy, and follow-up formulation. Other cutting-edge AI devices, including brilliant masks (temperature monitoring and breathing detection), have used the original online dynamic forecasting and precision medical guidance (Li et al., 2024). They all demonstrate how AI epidemic prevention significantly improves the medical system's capacity to control the outbreak and expands how individuals can prevent it independently (Hirani et al., 2023).

Based on epidemiological characteristics, Eva, an AI system, may detect a substantially greater proportion of subclinical infected passengers during COVID-19 than conventional testing techniques. Our system's constant learning allows it to recognize more scenarios than previous methods. Furthermore, AI approaches are crucial in locating epidemic sites by analyzing regions where many people exhibit symptoms. Mask-wearing compliance may be tracked using closed-circuit television and image recognition technologies (Li et al., 2024; Chirigati, 2021). ChatGPT can provide accurate information on public health knowledge and prevent and control infectious diseases. Chatbots, virtual assistants, and automated communication systems are used to do this (Li et al., 2024). These innovative AI apps have the potential to lower high mental stress during pandemics by debunking beliefs and promoting preventative measures (Cheng et al., 2023).

7.2 Challenges in Using AI for the Diagnosis and Monitoring of Infectious Diseases

Given how profoundly learning algorithms rely on massive datasets, data availability is critical to the efficacy of AI in treating infectious illnesses. The advancement of transfer learning technology is one possible remedy for this issue. If several data sources are accessible, the output results may suffer since they can be irrelevant or low-quality. AI also frequently struggles to distinguish between several viral illnesses with comparable symptoms during the identification phase. Additional algorithm optimization is needed to address these issues (Kumar et al., 2023).

Individual privacy issues are increasingly crucial as surveillance models integrate data from linked health devices and wearable technologies. The need for superior freely accessible information to support future research, the possibility of the intrusive nature of AI technology, and individual confidentiality concerns must all be carefully balanced (Li et al., 2024; Canali et al., 2022). Infectious disease monitoring techniques that detect diseases and their variations and enable the prompt administration of the best therapies or public health initiatives have been aided by AI. However, surveillance information that relies solely on syndromic data—clinical symptoms and indicators—may not always be accurate. Monitoring infectious diseases also includes detecting antibiotic resistance. Like histopathology image analysis, AI image analysis has been used to identify antibiotic resistance (Parums, 2023).

Subjective analysis is used in microbiology disk-diffusion experiments to evaluate the antibiotic susceptibility of microorganisms. One aspect of infection surveillance is identifying bacteria that are antibiotic-sensitive or resistant. Small-budget labs might be unable to purchase automated readers due to their high cost. By using the image processing algorithms on the disks to evaluate the antibiotic sensitivity of bacteria, AI algorithms can now quantify the growth inhibition zones and determine the type of antibiotic required (Parums, 2023).

Language barriers, a lack of human interaction, false information about illnesses, and accessibility are potential issues with utilizing AI modalities like ChatGPT. ChatGPT is trained on data. Hence, it may generate inaccurate information. The responses are incorrect if there is erroneous information in the input data. Accessibility is another issue with AI, including the incapacity of patients and medical professionals to utilize the Internet, especially in places with inadequate connections. Another drawback of AI tools is the language barrier; patients and doctors may find it challenging because these tools are only available in a few languages (Parums, 2023).

Additionally, it has been demonstrated that doctors may gain a great deal from using AI in imaging; yet, several scientific challenges remain to be solved. These include a lack of illness specificity, spectrum bias, and unavailable data. Concerns over spectrum bias have also been raised by the AI models in the healthcare sector, since this may affect the models' performance based on factors like age, sex, or membership in an ethnic minority (Sarantopoulos et al., 2024).

There is a significant risk of bias when using AI in research. If the AI software creates the research question, the algorithm may favor particular population subgroups based on demographic information and the condition's occurrence. This might lead to selection bias, including discrimination based on gender or race. Furthermore, the bias may arise in sampling as AI models cannot determine if the cohorts used are representative of the population. When AI research software generates a model that works well on one dataset but cannot reproduce the same results when applied to other datasets, this is referred to as "overfitting" (Sarantopoulos et al., 2024).

7.3 AI Tools, Applications, and Prospects

Infectious disease researchers use ARIMA, three-step floating catchment area, random forest, unsupervised modeling, and supervised learning to decode pathogen mutation, diagnosis, zoonotic disease outbreak, infection origin, resistance prediction, pandemic prediction, epidemic prediction, drug discovery, host genetics, pathogen-host interaction, therapy compliance, and data gaps by concentrating on decisions. Promote outcomes, cut down on time spent on diagnosis, drug development, and epidemic forecasting, and find ways to prevent the spread of disease. AI should be ready to help underdeveloped nations, save money, save lives, and enhance people's quality of life—customized medications and a forensic approach (Agrebi & Larbi, 2020). Figure 7.1 illustrates the key roles of AI in infectious disease research.

7.4 Outlook for the Future

AI boosts the healthcare system by transforming sickness diagnosis, treatment, and management (Faiyazuddin et al., 2025). AI outperformed traditional techniques in several scenarios. By enabling the discovery of more powerful active medicinal molecules that may be used to cure or prevent ailments, artificial intelligence (AI) could benefit the pharmaceutical sector in the future (Rabaan et al., 2023). Additionally, it shortens the period between diagnosis and therapy (Faiyazuddin et al., 2025).

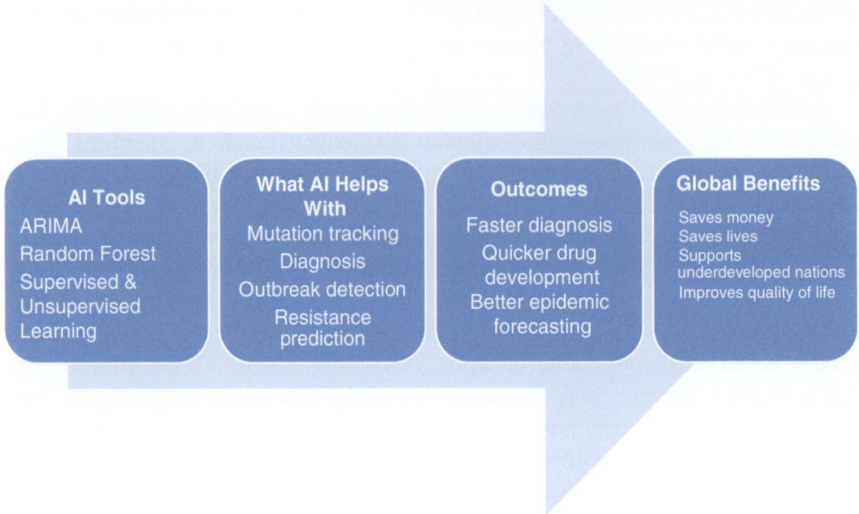

Fig. 7.1 Representation of how AI tools support infectious disease research, improve diagnosis and forecasting, and enhance global health outcomes. (Agrebi & Larbi, 2020)

It also reduces the time between diagnosis and treatment. Al can also assist physicians in modifying current treatment regimens. Analytics based on previously saved data may allow for the customization of medical therapies (Kraemer et al., 2025). In the upcoming years, AI will transform healthcare through hybrid models that will increase clinicians' diagnostic, risk factor, and treatment planning abilities while beginning to show quantifiable gains in patient outcomes and operational effectiveness. Furthermore, the increasing incidence of infectious illnesses raises the possibility of a variety of potential worldwide transmissions. As a result, AI techniques must adjust their algorithms appropriately (Faiyazuddin et al., 2025).

7.4.1 AI Ethics: Utilizing AI to Diagnose and Monitor Infectious Diseases

Despite its enormous promise for advancement, the application of AI in healthcare poses serious ethical issues. Some of these difficulties are getting informed permission for data use, maintaining safety and openness, safeguarding data privacy, and addressing algorithmic biases and fairness (Weerarathna et al., 2024). Protecting patient data and maintaining equality are crucial as AI is used increasingly in personalized medicine. Data theft prevention by encryption and restricted access is required due to the large gathering of sensitive health data to avoid unauthorized usage (Cesaro et al., 2025). Government representatives, developers, and medical professionals must keep working together to create precise guidelines for the moral and secure application of AI to manage its increasing role in medicine (Rabaan et al., 2023).

Two regulatory agencies that monitor AI's application in healthcare and ensure that safety, privacy, and quality criteria are met are the Food and Drug Administration (FDA) in the USA and the Medicines and Healthcare Products Regulatory Agency (MHRA) in the UK. They conduct audits and inspections to ensure stakeholders follow the applicable requirements. While the European Data Act governs equitable access to and use of healthcare data, the General Data Protection Regulation (GDPR), in January 2024, establishes strict criteria for data protection (Weerarathna et al., 2024). At the same time, by emphasizing transparency, security, and equality, the WHO promotes frameworks for supervision and responsibility and helps nations create laws to guarantee the ethical application of AI.

7.4.2 AI in the Context of Public Health

During global health emergencies, such as introducing a novel infectious disease, countries must make tough choices in several sectors, such as health, economics, education, and social well-being, to control and prevent the spread of sickness (Kraemer et al., 2025; Ellwanger et al., 2021). The disease spreads among close-knit populations due to urbanization and international travel, and within weeks of their 10% debut, they might turn into pandemics. Decision-makers must balance the benefits and drawbacks of policies with severe uncertainty to protect health by maximizing their efficacy and limiting unintended and negative consequences. All methods may focus on developing generalized systems that enable decision assistance. As a result, advanced AI might drastically change how public health policy choices are made and how data and models are interpreted (Kraemer et al., 2025; Reyes et al., 2012).

Policymakers and infectious disease modelers frequently interact, with scientific advisory committees occasionally serving as a conduit for the modeling community to receive questions and feedback from policymakers. Since decision-makers are usually presented with a large amount of data and conclusions that aren't always directly relevant to the decision and might not be adequately summarized at the appropriate level, time is of the essence in these interactions. Meanwhile, modelers have to develop more intricate models to address various questions, for which it might occasionally be challenging to specify a clear objective (Kraemer et al., 2025; Hadley et al., 2021).

To speed up modeling and use it to guide policy decisions, artificial intelligence is likely to be a key tool. The runtime of epidemiological models may be significantly decreased by new ML and AI techniques, allowing for a more in-depth analysis of circumstances and the statistical uncertainty that goes along with them. Furthermore, since not everyone likes graphs, Large Language Models (LLMs) may offer customized explanations of intricate quantitative models based on a decision-maker's preferences (Kraemer et al., 2025; Gawande et al., 2025).

The theoretical frameworks of Reinforcement Learning-based Interaction (RLI) and Markov decision processes may be extended to include more data kinds, prediction models, and expert input to enable rational and efficient decision-making during epidemics (Kraemer et al., 2025). Enhancing the speed at which models may be updated and executed has made this feasible. Reinforcement learning (RL) frameworks are appealing for dealing with disease outbreaks in several countries. Still, they require explicit goals and a list of the advantages and disadvantages of policy options (RL is beneficial in robotics) (Kraemer et al., 2025).

Future connections between research and societal policy may be encouraged by including public health goals, which are frequently dynamic and less likely to be quantifiable, into adaptable models that can take human input into account. To create sociotechnical decision-making frameworks that might demand solid confidence and trust among the public for epidemiology in the case of a probable global pandemic, stakeholders, members of civil society, and the scientific community must work closely together. The reaction will rely on how timely and high-quality the data is, and it remains to be seen if today's RL models (or other decision-making algorithms) can reconstruct and anticipate outbreak trajectories with sufficient precision to be practical. Unintended and often unexpected effects from treatments, like the emergence of medication resistance for infection risks, were not yet included in epidemic models before their application in decision frameworks (Kraemer et al., 2025).

7.5 Future Scope

Accuracy in illness diagnosis is essential for treatment planning, patient well-being, and effective therapy. AI is an amalgamation of data, algorithms, analytics, DL, and neural networks that is growing and changing to cater to the demands of the health sector. All methods are crucial in the healthcare system, especially when identifying illnesses. To diagnose various disease conditions, the AI intends to clarify how DL and ML work in many fields of illness detection.

An assessment of the quality of work, AI's methods and applications came after the introduction and contribution were discussed in the first part. Additional topics included a theoretical AI framework for identifying illness models, various AI applications for medical care, and various illness signs and diagnostic difficulties.

Overall, medical experts are more knowledgeable about the potential applications of AI in disease diagnosis, which leads to better recommendations for developing AI models in the future. Despite tremendous advancements in recent years, there are still a number of issues with trustworthy clinical diagnostics that need to be resolved in order to effectively treat emerging illnesses and diseases. Even medical professionals agree that challenges need to be overcome before AI and sickness may be detected together. Even doctors do not fully rely on AI-based techniques since they are uncertain of their ability to forecast illnesses and the symptoms that go along with them.

Therefore, it is needed to train AI systems to enhance the recognition ability of diagnostic technology. The partnership approach and continuous research in the field of emerging AI-enabled future can benefit both AI and clinicians. Additionally, a single training framework for disease records at remote sites should be developed using a distributed, federated learning approach for early sickness diagnosis (Kumar et al., 2023).

7.6 Conclusion

Utility of innovation equipped with DL and ML can address emerging issues in epidemiology and healthcare. With increase in the rate of mortality due to increased prevalence of diseases globally. AI-enabled innovation including DL can solve the majority of these issues by complimenting the healthcare system. ML and DL technology can deliver healthcare in the time of increasing population, shortage of healthcare infrastructure and resources. This innovation can predict probable outcomes with less error. This can fasten the action implementation which can reduce time and resources. Utilization of virtual assistant technology is cost-effective in the clinical setting. This can ease the employability of these innovations without extra expanses.

Although the use of sophisticated technology that could put people responsible for making important decisions regarding people's lives is restricted, it may be difficult to replace all of the antiquated or conventionally used scientific technology in healthcare. These issues can be fixed by improving infrastructure including healthcare workers and technical resources. Integration of DL- and ML-enabled technology can solve many urgent issues present in the healthcare sector. As these technologies develop, a plethora of fascinating medical applications becomes possible, which could improve the caliber and efficacy of healthcare delivery. To fully realize the potential of the technology, however, a great deal more research in this area is still required. Furthermore, the need for a large dataset is one of the primary difficulties and barriers to doing it.

Digital disease monitoring networks with artificial intelligence (AI) have proven effective in predicting infectious disease outbreaks. These systems require ongoing development and substantial learning to enable precise and timely detection of hotspots. This facilitates early human intervention to curb the outbreak. AI has aided in laboratory analysis and auxiliary clinical diagnosis, which is why medical personnel have handled the situation more deftly and effectively. Lastly, artificial intelligence set the standard in invention to battle against infectious diseases. They are essential for improving the production of protein-based medications, speeding up drug development, facilitating drug repurposing, and improving vaccinations. These developments provide encouraging approaches to dealing with both current and new infectious dangers. We expect AI automation solutions that cover every facet of infectious disease prevention to proliferate quickly. This pattern suggests an impending revolution in the use of AI to the study of infectious illnesses, which will present both possibilities and difficulties.

References

Agrebi, S., & Larbi, A. (2020). Use of artificial intelligence in infectious diseases. In *Artificial intelligence in precision health* (pp. 415–438). Academic.

Asada, K., Komatsu, M., Shimoyama, R., Takasawa, K., Shinkai, N., Sakai, A., et al. (2021). Application of artificial intelligence in COVID-19 diagnosis and therapeutics. *Journal of personalized medicine, 11*(9), 886.

Bali, J., Garg, R., & Bali, R. T. (2019). Artificial intelligence (AI) in healthcare and biomedical research: Why a strong computational/AI bioethics framework is required? *Indian Journal of Ophthalmology, 67*(1), 3–6.

Bhardwaj, R., Nambiar, A. R., & Dutta, D. (2017, July). A study of machine learning in healthcare. In *2017 IEEE 41st annual computer software and applications conference (COMPSAC)* (Vol. 2, pp. 236–241). IEEE.

Bhatia, S., Lassmann, B., Cohn, E., Desai, A. N., Carrion, M., Kraemer, M. U., et al. (2021). Using digital surveillance tools for near real-time mapping of the risk of infectious disease spread. *NPJ Digital Medicine, 4*(1), 73.

Brynjolfsson, E., Li, D., & Raymond, L. (2025). Generative AI at work. *The Quarterly Journal of Economics, 140*(2), 889–942.

Canali, S., Schiaffonati, V., & Aliverti, A. (2022). Challenges and recommendations for wearable devices in digital health: Data quality, interoperability, health equity, fairness. *PLOS Digital Health, 1*(10), e0000104.

Carrion, M., & Madoff, L. C. (2017). ProMED-mail: 22 years of digital surveillance of emerging infectious diseases. *International Health, 9*(3), 177–183.

Cesaro, A., Hoffman, S. C., Das, P., & de la Fuente-Nunez, C. (2025). Challenges and applications of artificial intelligence in infectious diseases and antimicrobial resistance. *NPJ Antimicrobials and Resistance, 3*(1), 2.

Cheng, K., Li, Z., He, Y., Guo, Q., Lu, Y., Gu, S., & Wu, H. (2023). Potential use of artificial intelligence in infectious disease: Take ChatGPT as an example. *Annals of Biomedical Engineering, 51*(6), 1130–1135.

Chirigati, F. (2021). Eva to the rescue. *Nature Computational Science, 1*(10), 633–633.

Dey, N., Misra, B., & Chakraborty, S. (Eds.). (2024). Smart medical imaging for diagnosis and treatment planning. CRC Press.

Duffourc, M., & Gerke, S. (2023). Generative AI in health care and liability risks for physicians and safety concerns for patients. *JAMA, 330*(4), 313–314.

Ellwanger, J. H., Veiga, A. B. G. D., Kaminski, V. D. L., Valverde-Villegas, J. M., Freitas, A. W. Q. D., & Chies, J. A. B. (2021). Control and prevention of infectious diseases from a One Health perspective. *Genetics and Molecular Biology, 44*(1 Suppl 1), e20200256.

Epstein, Z., Hertzmann, A., Investigators of Human Creativity, Akten, M., Farid, H., Fjeld, J., et al. (2023). Art and the science of generative AI. *Science, 380*(6650), 1110–1111.

Faiyazuddin, M., Rahman, S. J. Q., Anand, G., Siddiqui, R. K., Mehta, R., Khatib, M. N., et al. (2025). The impact of artificial intelligence on healthcare: A comprehensive review of advancements in diagnostics, treatment, and operational efficiency. *Health Science Reports, 8*(1), e70312.

Fanelli, U., Pappalardo, M., Chinè, V., Gismondi, P., Neglia, C., Argentiero, A., et al. (2020). Role of artificial intelligence in fighting antimicrobial resistance in pediatrics. *Antibiotics, 9*(11), 767.

Fischer, W., Giorgi, E. E., Chakraborty, S., Nguyen, K., Bhattacharya, T., Theiler, J., et al. (2021). HIV-1 and SARS-CoV-2: Patterns in the evolution of two pandemic pathogens. *Cell Host & Microbe, 29*(7), 1093–1110.

Freifeld, C. C., Mandl, K. D., Reis, B. Y., & Brownstein, J. S. (2008). HealthMap: Global infectious disease monitoring through automated classification and visualization of Internet media reports. *Journal of the American Medical Informatics Association, 15*(2), 150–157.

Gawande, M. S., Zade, N., Kumar, P., Gundewar, S., Weerarathna, I. N., & Verma, P. (2025). The role of artificial intelligence in pandemic responses: From epidemiological modeling to vaccine development. *Molecular Biomedicine, 6*(1), 1.

Hadley, L., Challenor, P., Dent, C., Isham, V., Mollison, D., Robertson, D. A., et al. (2021). Challenges on the interaction of models and policy for pandemic control. *Epidemics, 37*, 100499.

Hampel, H., O'Bryant, S. E., Durrleman, S., Younesi, E., Rojkova, K., Escott-Price, V., et al. (2017). A precision medicine initiative for Alzheimer's disease: The road ahead to biomarker-guided integrative disease modeling. *Climacteric, 20*(2), 107–118.

Hirani, R., Noruzi, K., Iqbal, A., Hussaini, A. S., Khan, R. A., Harutyunyan, A., et al. (2023). A review of the past, present, and future of the monkeypox virus: Challenges, opportunities, and lessons from COVID-19 for global health security. *Microorganisms, 11*(11), 2713.

Hossain, M. J., Wadud, M. A. H., Rahman, A., Ferdous, J., Alam, M. S., Bhuiyan, T. A. U. H., & Mridha, M. F. (2021, August). A secured patient's online data monitoring through blockchain: An intelligent way to store lifetime medical records. In *2021 international conference on science & contemporary technologies (ICSCT)* (pp. 1–6). IEEE.

Hsu, J. (2016). For sale: Deep learning [News]. *IEEE Spectrum, 53*(8), 12–13.

Jadon, A., & Kumar, S. (2023, July). Leveraging generative AI models for synthetic data generation in healthcare: Balancing research and privacy. In *2023 international conference on smart applications, communications and networking (SmartNets)* (pp. 1–4). IEEE.

Jain, M., Vats, S., Pahwa, C., Chahal, A., & Ali, K. (2024). Past, present and future perspective of artificial intelligence in healthcare and nanotechnology: A communication. *Journal of Clinical and Diagnostic Research, 18*(11), KM01–KM03.

Kamath, U., Liu, J., & Whitaker, J. (2019). *Deep learning for NLP and speech recognition* (Vol. 84, p. 1). Springer.

Kanjee, Z., Crowe, B., & Rodman, A. (2023). Accuracy of a generative artificial intelligence model in a complex diagnostic challenge. *JAMA, 330*(1), 78–80.

Kothari, A. N. (2023). ChatGPT, large language models, and generative AI as future augments of surgical cancer care. *Annals of Surgical Oncology, 30*(6), 3174–3176.

Kraemer, M. U., Tsui, J. L. H., Chang, S. Y., Lytras, S., Khurana, M. P., Vanderslott, S., et al. (2025). Artificial intelligence for modelling infectious disease epidemics. *Nature, 638*(8051), 623–635.

Krishnan Ganapathy, M. N. (2024). A glimpse into the deployment of digital health in India. *Telehealth and Medicine Today, 9*(1).

Kumar, Y., Koul, A., Singla, R., & Ijaz, M. F. (2023). Artificial intelligence in disease diagnosis: A systematic literature review, synthesizing framework and future research agenda. *Journal of Ambient Intelligence and Humanized Computing, 14*(7), 8459–8486.

Li, C., Ye, G., Jiang, Y., Wang, Z., Yu, H., & Yang, M. (2024). Artificial intelligence in battling infectious diseases: A transformative role. *Journal of Medical Virology, 96*(1), e29355.

Nienhold, D., Dornberger, R., & Korkut, S. (2017, August). Pattern recognition for automated healthcare assessment using non-invasive, ambient sensors. In *2017 IEEE international conference on healthcare informatics (ICHI)* (pp. 189–197). IEEE.

Ningrum, D. N. A., Li, Y. J., & Hsu, C. Y. (2024). Artificial intelligence approach for severe dengue early warning system. *Studies in Health Technology and Informatics, 310*, 881–885.

Okuyama, R. (2022). Nurturing deep tech to solve social problems: Learning from COVID-19 mRNA vaccine development. *Pathogens, 11*(12), 1469.

Olmo, R. P., Todjro, Y. M., Aguiar, E. R., de Almeida, J. P. P., Ferreira, F. V., Armache, J. N., et al. (2023). Mosquito vector competence for dengue is modulated by insect-specific viruses. *Nature Microbiology, 8*(1), 135–149.

Parums, D. V. (2023). Infectious disease surveillance using artificial intelligence (AI) and its role in epidemic and pandemic preparedness. *Medical Science Monitor: International Medical Journal of Experimental and Clinical Research, 29*, e941209–e941201.

Rabaan, A. A., Bakhrebah, M. A., Alotaibi, J., Natto, Z. S., Alkhaibari, R. S., Alawad, E., et al. (2023). Unleashing the power of artificial intelligence for diagnosing and treating infectious diseases: A comprehensive review. *Journal of Infection and Public Health, 16*(11), 1837–1847.
Rahman, A., Sara, U., Kundu, D., Islam, S., Islam, M. J., Hasan, M., et al. (2020). Distbsdoindustry: Enhancing security in industry 4.0 services based on distributed blockchain through sdn-iot enabled architecture. *International Journal of Advanced Computer Science and Applications, 11*(9).
Rahman, A., Chakraborty, C., Anwar, A., Karim, M. R., Islam, M. J., Kundu, D., et al. (2022a). SDN–IoT empowered intelligent framework for industry 4.0 applications during COVID-19 pandemic. *Cluster Computing, 25*(4), 2351–2368.
Rahman, M. S., Safa, N. T., Sultana, S., Salam, S., Karamehic-Muratovic, A., & Overgaard, H. J. (2022b). Role of artificial intelligence-internet of things (AI-IoT) based emerging technologies in the public health response to infectious diseases in Bangladesh. *Parasite Epidemiology and Control, 18*, e00266.
Rahman, A., Debnath, T., Kundu, D., Khan, M. S. I., Aishi, A. A., Sazzad, S., et al. (2024). Machine learning and deep learning-based approach in smart healthcare: Recent advances, applications, challenges and opportunities. *AIMS Public Health, 11*(1), 58.
Reyes, R., Ahn, R., Thurber, K., & Burke, T. F. (2012). Urbanization and infectious diseases: General principles, historical perspectives, and contemporary challenges. In *Challenges in infectious diseases* (pp. 123–146). Springer New York.
Sarantopoulos, A., Mastori Kourmpani, C., Yokarasa, A. L., Makamanzi, C., Antoniou, P., Spernovasilis, N., & Tsioutis, C. (2024). Artificial intelligence in infectious disease clinical practice: An overview of gaps, opportunities, and limitations. *Tropical Medicine and Infectious Disease, 9*(10), 228.
Shubham, S. S., & Kandasamy, R. (2023). Enigma to artificial intelligence.
Stokel-Walker, C., & Van Noorden, R. (2023). What ChatGPT and generative AI mean for science. *Nature, 614*(7947), 214–216.
Suthar, A. C., Joshi, V., & Prajapati, R. (2022). A review of generative adversarial-based networks of machine learning/artificial intelligence in healthcare. In *Handbook of research on lifestyle sustainability and management solutions using AI, big data analytics, and visualization* (pp. 37–56).
Vert, J. P. (2023). How will generative AI disrupt data science in drug discovery? *Nature Biotechnology, 41*(6), 750–751.
Wang, N., Zhao, X., Zhao, P., Zhang, Y., Zou, Z., & Ou, J. (2019). Automatic damage detection of historic masonry buildings based on mobile deep learning. *Automation in Construction, 103*, 53–66.
Weerarathna, I. N., Doelakeh, E. S., Kiwanuka, L., Kumar, P., & Arora, S. (2024). Prophylactic and therapeutic vaccine development: Advancements and challenges. *Molecular Biomedicine, 5*(1), 57.
Zhang, K., Liu, X., Shen, J., Li, Z., Sang, Y., Wu, X., et al. (2020). Clinically applicable AI system for accurate diagnosis, quantitative measurements, and prognosis of COVID-19 pneumonia using computed tomography. *Cell, 181*(6), 1423–1433.
Zohny, H., McMillan, J., & King, M. (2023). Ethics of generative AI. *Journal of Medical Ethics, 49*(2), 79–80.

8 Revolutionizing Oral Healthcare: Artificial Intelligence as a Paradigm Shift in Public Health Dentistry

Varkey Nadakkavuakran Santhosh

8.1 Introduction

The interconnection between AI technology and dental public health marks an important point in the development of new ways to provide oral healthcare. There is an increase in the global burden of oral diseases as well as a continuous imbalance in the accessibility of quality dental care. Nevertheless, the use of AI technologies opens up new horizons to create different ways of tackling population-level oral health issues (Petersen et al., 2005). According to the World Health Organization, about 3.5 billion individuals all over the globe are affected by oral diseases. In fact, dental caries is the most commonly found disease in the world among noncommunicable diseases. These facts highlight the necessity for innovative measures directed towards improving prevention and early detection, access to treatment, and the social determinants that lead to oral health inequities.

Public health dentistry is typically characterized by the systematic, scientific speaking method of preventing oral disease, promoting oral health and improving the quality of life through organized population-based community action. Thus, public health has until now mainly used epidemiological monitoring, population interventions, health promotion campaigns and policy advocacy (Watt, 2005) as its means to tackle the oral health problems of the population. But this whole picture has changed completely with the introduction of AI technologies, machine learning, deep learning, natural language processing, computer vision, and modern health systems in the area of health recording, documentation, monitoring and analysis as well as the ability to get people to participate in their own health and well-being. Consequently, public health dentistry has encountered new challenges which are

V. N. Santhosh (✉)
Department of Community and Family Medicine, All India Institute of Medical Sciences, Gorakhpur, Uttar Pradesh, India

U. Venkatesh et al. (eds.), *Multimodal AI in Healthcare*,
https://doi.org/10.1007/978-981-95-9027-8_8

manifested by the evolving needs in clinical practice and public health initiatives that could not be possibly addressed by old methods.

The effect of AI on dental public health is not the sole reason for the new technology's acceptance; instead, it is the very reason for the change in how we understand, scheme, and carry out oral health interventions. The traditional method of classifying diseases according to the degree of treatment where an attempt to completely eradicate the disease is the last resort has been replaced in some cases and replaced in others by a predictive and more proactive approach that targets the definition of at-risk populations, the resource allocation being optimized, and the personalization of interventions at the population level (Olawade et al., 2023). The changes come at a great cost to health disparities which AI technologies make more visible and thus easier to mitigate by ensuring the fair distribution of limited healthcare resources.

8.1.1 Historical Context and Evolution

The various phases of development track the evolution of AI integration in public health dentistry. AI applications in simple computer-aided diagnostic systems for interpreting radiographs were initiated as early as the 1980s. Although the limitations in features and accuracy of these systems were disappointing, these applications nevertheless marked an important milestone that paved the road to providing even more robust AI applications.

Digital imaging was progressing in the 1990s and early 2000s, as was the development of expert systems for dental diagnosis in dental public health. It was during this developmental period that researchers began to investigate the possibilities offered by neural networks and pattern recognition algorithms to analyze dental radiographs and clinical images. However, there were limitations associated with computational resources and availability of digital images and large datasets of health data which prevented these applications from being moved from the theoretical to practical experimentation and application in public health dentistry.

Beginning in the 2010s and continuing today, the embedding of big data and cloud computing reached full fruition to enter a new era for AI applications in health, including dentistry. Mass use of electronic health records, digital imaging systems, and mobile health technologies have created an unprecedented level of data generated in the field of dental health. Technology on the side of machine learning algorithms, in particular deep learning algorithms are strong means of deriving meaningful findings from these complex data.

Today, we are at the threshold of a new era when AI technologies are at once becoming more sophisticated, accessible, and practical for real-world implementation in public health dentistry settings. The COVID-19 pandemic accelerated the adoption of digital health technologies, including teledentistry and AI-powered diagnostic tools, which have accentuated their potential for maintaining and improving oral healthcare delivery even during difficult times (Kshirsagar et al., 2021).

8.1.2 Scope and Objectives

The aim of this chapter is to provide a comprehensive overview of how artificial intelligence is revolutionizing dental public health practice. Our analysis encompasses current applications, emerging technologies, implementation challenges, and future prospects of AI integration in population-level oral healthcare delivery. Our key objectives will be:

1. Identify the current landscape of AI applications in public health dentistry, including those for diagnosis, epidemiological surveillance systems, and population health management platforms
2. Analyzing the impact of AI technologies on oral health disparities and access to care
3. Assessing the evidence base for the effectiveness of AI at improving clinical outcomes and population health metrics
4. New and emerging AI technologies and their application in preventive dentistry and health promotion
5. Discussion of implementation challenges: technical, regulatory, and ethical considerations.
6. Providing insights into the future direction and recommendations for successful AI integration in public health dentistry practice

The chapter is designed to progress from basic concepts through current applications to future possibilities in a manner that provides readability to both technical and nontechnical readers without sacrificing scientific rigor or practical applicability.

8.2 Fundamentals of Artificial Intelligence in Healthcare

8.2.1 Core AI Technologies and Methodologies

AI in health involves a broad range of technologies and approaches, each with different capabilities to address unique challenges for public health dentistry. Fully understanding the fundamental technologies provides an important perspective on applications and potential impacts on oral healthcare delivery. Machine learning undergirds many modern applications of artificial intelligence and describes computational methods that provide systems with the ability to learn from experience automatically without explicit programming for every eventuality. In the context of public health dentistry, machine learning algorithms analyze multi-thousand data points consisting of individual demographics, clinical findings, treatment, and outcomes to identify patterns informing clinical decision-making and population health strategies (Gómez-Ríos et al., 2025).

The algorithms of support vector machines, random forests, and neural networks are highly useful for classification and prediction tasks in which the algorithms have been previously trained on labeled datasets. These algorithms have been of particular value in diagnostic applications, whereby the algorithms can learn to identify healthy/pathological conditions from clinical images, radiographs, or other diagnostic data. For example, convolutional neural networks have shown very good performance in the detection of dental caries, periodontal disease, and oral pathologies from radiographic images. Unsupervised learning methods, including clustering algorithms and dimensionality reduction techniques, represent important approaches to exploratory data analysis and pattern discovery with population health datasets. These methods can identify previously unknown subpopulations, uncover hidden relationships between risk factors and oral health outcomes, and help identify targeted intervention strategies (Lee et al., 2018).

Deep learning is a subclass of machine learning, drawing inspiration from the structure and functionality of neural networks. It has become an especially powerful tool for complex pattern recognition tasks. A deep neural network architecture with multiple hidden layers can automatically learn hierarchical features from raw data. This makes them exceptionally well-suited to analyze medical images, process natural language, and handle other high-dimensional healthcare data (Lee et al., 2018).

8.2.2 Computer Vision and Image Analysis

Computer vision technologies are one of the most promising applications of artificial intelligence in public health dentistry. The practice of dentistry is visual in nature, relying heavily on radiographic imaging, intraoral photography, and clinical examination in diagnosis and treatment. Therefore, computer vision solutions are obviously relevant. Convolutional neural networks have changed the medical image analysis field by automatically learning relevant features from large numbers of annotated images. In dental applications, CNNs have been shown to outperform traditional approaches in tasks such as caries detection, tooth segmentation, and identification of pathology. CNNs can recognize a number of images modal together, periapical radiographs, bitewing radiographs, panoramic images and intraoral photographs all can be processed simultaneously (Lee et al., 2018).

Object detection and semantic segmentation algorithms allow AI systems to identify and precisely locate both anatomical structures and pathological features in dental images. Advanced architectures, such as YOLO and Mask R-CNN, have been adapted for dental applications, accomplishing real-time performance both in detecting and classifying various oral conditions. The development of 3D imaging technologies, including cone-beam computed tomography and intraoral scanners, opens new possibilities regarding the use of AI-powered three-dimensional dental anatomy. Advanced algorithms can process volumetric information for the assessment of bone density, surgical procedure planning, and monitoring of treatment processes with precision not previously possible (Yilmaz et al., 2024).

8.2.3 Natural Language Processing in Dental Records

Natural language processing technologies, therefore, provide the AI system with the ability to understand, interpret, and generate human language-openings for new ways in which unstructured textual data in dental health records could be analyzed. The information contained in electronic health records, clinical notes, patient communications, and research literature exists in forms that are not easily extracted or utilized through conventional analytical techniques. Named entity recognition algorithms can automatically identify and classify medically significant concepts, such as diagnoses, treatments, medications, and anatomical structures mentioned in clinical notes. This capability enables large-scale analysis of clinical documentation to identify trends, assess treatment patterns, and monitor population health indicators (Pethani & Dunn, 2023).

Sentiment analysis and patient experience mining techniques make it possible to analyze patient feedback, reviews, and communications to identify satisfaction levels, recognize service gaps, and improve patient-centered care delivery. These insights are more valuable to public health programs interested in understanding the needs and preferences of the community. Powered by NLP, the clinical decision support systems can analyze patient records in real time to offer evidence-based recommendations, alert clinicians about potential complications, and ensure that care is delivered per clinical guidelines. These can very much enhance the quality and consistency of the care provided across diverse settings (Chen et al., 2021).

8.2.4 Predictive Analytics and Population Health Modeling

Predictive analytics is one of the revolutionary uses of AI in dental public health, moving from reactive to proactive oral health management. By analyzing trends and patterns in historical data, demographic changes, and risk factors, AI systems can predict future oral health outcomes, identify high-risk populations, and optimize intervention strategies. Time series analysis and forecasting algorithms could predict disease outbreaks or estimates of treatment demand and resource allocation decisions. This is especially valuable for public health programs that work with limited resources, and serve diverse populations with varying oral health needs (Olawade et al., 2023).

Risk stratification models, applying machine learning algorithms, estimate individual and population-level risk factors for oral diseases. These can combine various sources of data, including clinical findings, socioeconomic indicators, behavioral factors, and environmental conditions, to produce detailed risk profiles that can aid in the targeting of prevention strategies. The population health simulation models, driven by AI, can be used to examine the probable impact of various intervention scenarios, thus aiding policymakers and public health professionals in evidence-based decisions concerning program design and implementation. Agent-based models and system dynamics approaches can capture the complex interaction between individual behaviors, social factors, and healthcare system characteristics (Olawade et al., 2023).

8.3 Current Applications of AI in Public Health Dentistry

8.3.1 AI-Powered Diagnostic Systems

Implementation of AI-powered diagnostic systems is one of the most significant advances in modern public health dentistry practice. Sophisticated algorithms are used by these systems to enhance diagnostic accuracy, reduce interpretation variability, and extend access to specialist expertise in a wide variety of healthcare settings. Deep learning algorithms used in radiographic analysis systems have shown outstanding performance in the detection and classification of oral pathologies. AI systems have been proven to offer diagnostic accuracy that is equal to, or sometimes surpasses, that of experienced dental practitioners in the identification of dental caries, periodontal disease, and endodontic pathology. DIAGNOCAT is one example of such a system that has been validated across multiple populations and consistently performs well in detecting more than 30 different oral conditions from panoramic radiographs. These include highly prevalent conditions such as dental caries and periodontal bone loss, which constitute significant public health concerns due to their overall global impact on oral health (Table 8.1).

Intraoral imaging analysis platforms leverage computer vision to evaluate soft tissue conditions, detect oral lesions, and monitor the progression of diseases. These systems are of great importance, especially in community health settings where access to specialist expertise may be limited. Real-time diagnostic support during clinical examinations improves confidence and competence for general practitioners while delivering oral health care (Bayrakdar et al., 2022).

Multimodal AI systems allow for the integration of multiple imaging modalities that make comprehensive diagnostic assessments, taking into consideration both hard and soft tissue conditions. These systems can correlate radiographs with intraoral photographs and clinical examinations for holistic diagnostic insights that support evidence-based treatment planning. Quality assurance and standardization are other benefits of AI diagnostic systems in public health settings. By providing consistent standards of interpretation and reducing inter-examiner variability, these systems help ensure quality of care is equitably distributed across different practitioners

Table 8.1 AI diagnostic systems in oral healthcare

Diagnostic task	AI system
Caries detection (bitewing)	CNN-based
Periodontal disease (panoramic)	Deep learning
Oral cancer screening	Vision transformer
Endodontic pathology	Ensemble methods
Wisdom tooth assessment	Object detection

and healthcare facilities. The key reason this is very important is that this standardization is crucial for population health surveillance and epidemiological research (Ali et al., 2025) (Fig. 8.1).

8.3.2 Epidemiological Surveillance and Disease Monitoring

In public health dentistry, AI technologies are transforming epidemiological surveillance to identify, in real time, patterns of oral disease, monitor for outbreaks of disease, and perform comprehensive analyses of population health trends. These capabilities are important for informing public health policy, developing effective resource allocation, and targeting interventions. An automated data collection and analysis system can evaluate large amounts of clinical data within electronic medical records, insurance claims, and public health data to observe emerging oral health trends. Machine learning algorithms can identify anomalous patterns that suggest an outbreak, changes in treatment patterns, or changes in the population's risk profile (Tiwari et al., 2023).

Platforms for geospatial analysis that are powered by AI can detect the areas where oral diseases are more prevalent, the geographic concentration of negative oral health outcomes, and can quantify the impact of environmental and social factors on the oral health of the population. These discoveries will lead to more effective initiatives in the community that is at risk and give guidance on the best location for healthcare facilities and how to allocate resources efficiently. To monitor social media, digital surveillance systems depend on natural language processing in order to analyze online discussions, get anecdotal evidence from patients, and assess community health indicators to detect oral health problems early. This approach not

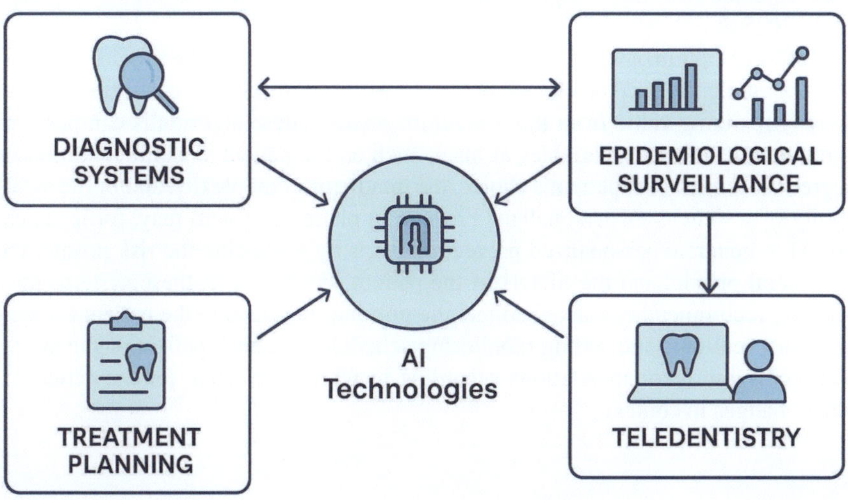

Fig. 8.1 AI-powered public health dentistry ecosystem

only provides extra data but also supports traditional surveillance systems and helps in recognizing problems that are just starting to occur and in time before they become too serious (Tiwari et al., 2023).

Predictive modeling in disease forecasting allows public health officials to anticipate future oral health challenges and prepare appropriate responses. These models incorporate historical disease data, demographic trends, environmental factors, and social determinants, generating probabilistic forecasts of disease incidence and healthcare demand.

8.3.3 Treatment Planning and Clinical Decision Support

The use of Artificial Intelligence (AI) in treatment planning systems signifies a major step in the direction of accepting evidence-based dental practice. The dentist receives a recommendation based on data, which includes the best treatment outcomes considering patient factors and public health goals. These systems use clinical practice guidelines, outcome data, and patient characteristics to aid in complex decision-making. An AI-CDSS can do various things such as analyzing the patient's medical history, taking into account the radiographic impressions, assessing the risk factors, proposing possible medical treatments, forecasting the patient's future, recognizing, and identifying the complications. The AI-CDSS can be extremely beneficial, particularly in community health centers and government-funded clinics where access to specialized consultations is often not readily available (Chen et al., 2021).

Machine learning algorithms used in treatment outcome prediction models estimate the probability of successful outcomes, the duration for healing, and the considerations that may influence treatment outcomes. This predictive capacity can then help clarify realistic expectations, inform optimized protocols, and guide clinician suspicion that might require additional support or alternative strategies (Feher et al., 2025).

Resource optimization algorithms have been developed for the providers to prioritize treatments based on clinical necessity, expected result, and cost-effectiveness thereby realizing value from the limited resources. These algorithms can perform computations of many variables at once, such as the patient's health condition or degree of sickness, the patient's choice, the treatment's complexity, and/or the availability of resources. A personalized prevention planning system may, for instance, use AI to generate personalized prevention plans by evaluating the risk profile, the behavioral profile, and the SDOH of the patient. Furthermore, these systems may not only recommend but also facilitate the provider in selecting the patient for specific interventions, and setting monitoring schedules to check patient engagement, and modifying recommendations according to what is effective for the patient or other changes in context.

Table 8.2 Teledentistry AI applications and outcomes

Application	Technology	Population served	Implementation challenges
Remote screening	Mobile App + AI	Rural communities	Internet connectivity limitations
Virtual consultations	Video + NLP	Elderly patients	Technology literacy barriers
Emergency triage	Chatbot + ML	Urban underserved	Integration with existing systems
Follow-up monitoring	Image analysis	Postsurgical patients	Device availability issues

8.3.4 Teledentistry and Remote Care Delivery

The application of AI technologies to teledentistry platforms opens up new avenues for improved access to oral health care among underserved populations and remote communities. The system integrates the capabilities of remote consultation with AI-powered diagnostic support to ensure quality of care, regardless of the geographical constraints. The remote diagnostic platforms allow patients to capture images of their oral health status with the use of smartphones or portable devices; these are further analyzed by the AI algorithms for the identification of possible problems and advice on appropriate routes for care. These systems can immediately flag cases for professional evaluation and provide feedback to patients. AI-powered triage and referral systems enable assessments of dental problems reported through teledentistry platforms for urgency and route patients to appropriate levels of care. This functionality ensures that emergency cases receive timely intervention, while routine issues are managed in an efficient manner via community health resources (Kshirsagar et al., 2021). In particular, these platforms are highly effective in the early detection of dental caries, thus allowing noninvasive treatments that prevent pain, infection, and complex procedures (Table 8.2).

Patient engagement and education platforms deploy AI to provide personalized oral health information, remind patients of preventive care appointments, and support longer-term behavior modification. Communication style and content can be tailored according to patient preference, literacy level, and cultural background. Quality monitoring and continuous improvement systems analyze interactions occurring in teledentistry to understand opportunities for quality improvement, evaluate provider performance, and ensure consistency in the quality of care offered via virtual platforms. Machine learning algorithms identify patterns across patient-provider interactions associated with positive outcomes and automatically suggest best practices.

8.4 Advanced AI Technologies in Preventive Dentistry

8.4.1 Predictive Risk Assessment Models

Predictive risk assessment is a cornerstone of modern preventive dentistry, and AI technologies allow the identification of individuals and populations with an increased risk of oral diseases well before the disease shows up clinically. These advanced models integrate multisource data into a comprehensive risk profile to give reason to appropriate, targeted prevention strategies and effective resource allocation in public health programs. Multifactorial risk prediction models use ensemble learning techniques that combine various risk indicators, such as demographic factors, medical history, behavioral patterns, socioeconomic status, and environmental exposure. These models can process not only structured data from electronic health records but also unstructured information from clinical notes and patient questionnaires in order to provide an even more nuanced risk assessment (Feher et al., 2025).

The CAMBRA system of Caries Management by Risk Assessment has been augmented by artificial intelligence which now automatically gives risk stratification and certain intervention recommendations. Machine learning algorithms can update risk assessment constantly, incorporating new clinical findings, responses to treatment, and patient conditions, and so the care process can remain agile and adaptive. One of the topics currently being explored is the AI-driven risk assessment being fed with genetic and genomic data. The polygenic risk scores that come from genome-wide association studies can be utilized to create accurate predictive models that spot individuals with a genetic history of susceptibility to oral diseases. The method allows for developing ultra-early interventions that focus on the prevention of the disease rather than the mere delaying of its progression. A typical case may be that of applying very early and targeted preventive care if a high genetic risk to periodontitis is identified, many years before the active disease shows any clinical signs and symptoms (Fries et al., 2024).

The modeling of social determinants of health utilizes geospatial analysis along with demographic data in order to assess the risk factors affecting oral health at the community level. AI algorithms are employed to analyze factors such as the status of water fluoridation, availability of healthy foods, level of education, and access to healthcare, in order to predict the trends of oral health in the population and direct public health actions. Temporal risk modeling applies time-series analysis and longitudinal data to foresee the changes in an individual's risk profile through time. These models are dynamic and can therefore reveal the periods when interventions are most likely to be effective and also modify prevention measures to the changing risk factors and life circumstances (Tiwari et al., 2023).

8.4.2 Personalized Prevention Protocols

Developing individualized prevention protocols using AI signifies a shift from a public health intervention framework to a personalized care framework, whereby each patient's characteristics, preferences, and circumstances are factored in. In a sense, these systems optimize prevention by making interventions as effective as possible for each individual while still prioritizing population health outcomes. In the context of oral health, optimization for behavioral intervention leverages reinforcement learning algorithms to generate the best personalized strategies to improve oral health behaviors. These systems can assess how individuals behave under various intervention strategies and subsequently adapt generated recommendations towards the most effective behavior change. Such mobile health technologies have the capability to deliver personalized supportive coaching in real time, based on algorithms described above (Snider et al., 2023) (Table 8.3).

AI can assist with precision fluoride therapy protocols to determine optimal fluoride exposures including the caries risk of the individual, dietary habits, water fluoridation status, and previous compliance. Machine learning algorithms assess the protection of categories to be protective against dental fluorosis risk that can lead to a recommendation process that provides personalized fluoride therapy with maximum protection and minimum risk. AI is also used to support dietary counseling systems and nutrition interventions. AI analyzes dietary patterns, creates personalized recommendations on nutrition, and identifies cariogenic risk factors. The dietary factors could include, but are not limited to, food diaries, mobile phone applications, and wearables. A system like this would produce comprehensive assessments of dietary risks and practical intervention strategies (Liang et al., 2025).

Recall and maintenance scheduling optimization relies on predictive algorithms to assess the individual patients' risk profiles, disease progression rates, and treatment response patterns and, consequently, to recommend the best appointment intervals for them. The systems are capable of modifying recall schedules in real time to enhance preventive effectiveness as well as to cut down on unnecessary visits and healthcare expenses. Health behavior change support systems harness natural language processing and conversational AI to dispense continuous motivation, education, and problem-solving support to patients aiming to improve their

Table 8.3 Personalized prevention protocol components and outcomes

Protocol component	AI technology	Personalization factors	Measured outcomes
Oral hygiene coaching	Reinforcement learning	Behavioral patterns, preferences	Plaque reduction
Fluoride optimization	Predictive modeling	Risk factors, exposure history	Caries prevention
Dietary intervention	Pattern recognition	Food preferences, habits	Sugar reduction
Recall scheduling	Optimization algorithms	Risk level, compliance	Appointment attendance

oral health. These systems are able to vary their style, content, and communication timing according to each patient's learning preferences and motivation factors.

8.4.3 Community Health Program Optimization

AI technologies facilitate the next phase of optimizing community health programs through population needs assessment and intervention effectiveness prediction, subsequently advancing program design and implementation over time. These features are essential for optimizing scarce public health resources and addressing long-standing oral health disparities. In this scenario, population needs assessment is premised on data clustering and density of demographic analysis to reveal specific subgroups with specific oral health needs and characteristics in a community. This approach would help to uncover the unobserved patterns of disease, risk factors, and service use prevalence that would inform design for targeted interventions. The intervention effectiveness prediction models use machine learning to predict the likely impact of different prevention programs prior to implementation in order to address intervention design, community characteristics, and implementation resources and setting conditions as factors into estimating effectiveness and costs (Sadegh-Zadeh et al., 2024).

8.4.4 Health Promotion and Education Innovation

AI, which stands for artificial intelligence, is going to revolutionize health promotion and education in dental public health by making possible personalized, adaptive, and culturally relevant approaches for behavior change and knowledge dissemination. The new technology will offer a vast improvement over the previous situations where educational methods suitable for all were used. For instance, adaptive learning systems will use AI and adjust the delivery of educational content according to individual students and their learning styles, knowledge levels, and engagement patterns in real time. They will be able to increase or lower the difficulty level, change the format, and control the speed of educational materials in order to make maximum learning achievable, regardless of whether it is given to students or to the general public.

Gamification platforms powered by AI can be specifically designed to provide engaging interactive experiences aimed at stimulating oral health behavior through game mechanics and social interaction. Machine learning algorithms can be used to optimize game design components to maximize engagement and effectiveness of behavior change in various demographic populations. Similarly, AI-enhanced virtual and augmented reality applications have the opportunity to provide immersive educational experiences to demonstrate oral health concepts and consequences in an interesting and memorable way. This makes the technologies particularly effective and broad applicability for younger audiences, and those communities with lower literate levels (Table 8.4).

Table 8.4 AI-enhanced health promotion innovations

Innovation	Technology	Target audience
Adaptive learning	Machine learning	School children
Gamified apps	Reinforcement learning	Adolescents
VR experiences	Computer vision	Community groups
Cultural adaptation	NLP + translation	Immigrant communities

Cultural adaptation algorithms leverage community characteristics, preferences, and communication patterns to automatically tailor health promotion materials for culturally diverse and linguistically different groups. This capability makes certain that health messages are relevant, respectful, and effective across diverse populations (Livingstone et al., 2023).

Social media optimization and digital outreach systems use AI to help analyze social media trends, identify influential community members, and optimize the timing of health promotion messages. Such a system can maximize reach and impact of public health communications and ensure message accuracy and appropriateness.

8.5 Addressing Health Disparities Through AI

8.5.1 Identifying and Analysing Disparities

Artificial intelligence presents entirely new opportunities for the identification, analysis, and understanding of oral health disparities among populations. Conventional means of identifying and analyzing disparities involve simply comparing demographic variables that can mask disparities and create missed opportunities for specifically targeted interventions. AI allows for much more advanced analyses to identify both hidden disparities and their causalities. Multidimensional disparity detection algorithms utilize unsupervised learning approaches to identify patterns of inequality that may be undetectable using other traditional analysis methods. These algorithms can analyze multiple variables simultaneously, such as race, ethnicity, socioeconomic status, location, insurance, and various others, to identify the complex intersection patterns that influence oral health outcomes (Snider et al., 2023).

Machine learning-based statistical modeling can manage several confounding variables simultaneously and provide a Bayesian estimation of the independent contribution of social determinants to oral health disparities. By employing these models, it becomes possible to differentiate between the disparities that are linked with varying degrees of exposure to risk factors and the ones that are due to different treatment or access to care. Disparity trend analysis applies time series analysis and longitudinal modeling which is a great way to see if and how disparities are changing over time and to measure the effects of policy shifts and social changes on health equity. Disparity trend analysis can indicate when oral health disparities occur or getting worse thereby allowing the planners to select the optimal time for preventive measures (Kshirsagar et al., 2021).

Through AI-assisted GIS, one can chart the oral health discrepancies in the neighborhoods or regions, for example, and reveal the spatial patterns that can assist in the allocation of resources and the selection of interventions. Such systems can integrate the environmental, demographic, and health data to provide a more comprehensive view of where the oral health needs might be the most significant. The sophisticated machine learning algorithms will not only automate but also improve the overall quality of the intersectionality research that examines the interplay of varied identity categories in producing distinct and intricate patterns of disadvantage and privilege. This allows us to move along to more complex viewpoints instead of working with the traditionally additive ones by analyzing the interrelations of race, gender, socioeconomic status, and age to produce particular oral health experiences (Fries et al., 2024). As an illustration, it could involve the establishment of a model that enables the pinpointing and determining the much larger share of the low-income populations with untreated periodontal disease and then, as a consequence, having the public health officials directing their efforts more accurately (e.g., through better targeting of resources), and also enforcing screening programs.

8.5.2 Targeted Intervention Development

AI technologies enable the development of precisely targeted interventions that serve the specific needs and situations of various population groups, taking into consideration the complex interacting causes of health disparities. This precision approach is a big improvement over classical population-wide interventions that may not be similarly effective across heterogeneous communities. Community-specific intervention design makes use of clustering algorithms and community profiling in order to create tailored interventions that meet the specific characteristics, needs, and assets of different communities. These systems can analyze demographic data, social networks, cultural factors, and resource availability in the design of culturally appropriate and practically feasible interventions (Ali & Marhazlinda, 2023).

Personalization of behavioral intervention utilizes reinforcement learning and behavioral modeling to provide individualized strategies for promoting oral health behaviors among the members of disadvantaged groups. These systems can consider cultural factors, economic constraints, and social influences on changing behavior in different populations. Identification and mitigation systems for access barriers use pattern recognition algorithms to determine which access barriers prevent various groups from accessing oral health services. The findings from these analyses can be used to formulate specific strategies that address access impeding factors such as transport problems, communication barriers, inability to pay, among others (Table 8.5).

AI-driven cultural competency enhancement can enable healthcare providers to build the knowledge and competencies required to effectively provide care to

Table 8.5 AI-targeted interventions for health equity

Population	Primary barriers	AI intervention type	Key features
Rural communities	Geographic access	Mobile health platforms	Teledentistry + AI diagnosis
Low-income families	Financial barriers	Predictive resource allocation	Optimized clinic placement
Elderly populations	Mobility limitations	Home-based AI tools	Portable diagnostic devices
Immigrant communities	Language barriers	Multilingual AI systems	Cultural adaptation algorithms

diverse populations. The system can provide real-time guidance on culture, language support, and communication recommendations at the point of care. Social Network Intervention Optimization: Network analysis algorithms identify influential community members and optimal communication pathways for health promotion messages. This strategy leverages existing social structures to maximize the reach and impact of interventions within specific communities.

8.5.3 Resource Allocation and Service Delivery Optimization

AI-powered resource allocation systems can help ensure equity in the distribution of limited healthcare resources across disparate populations while optimizing overall population health impact. These systems represent a quantum leap beyond legacy practices in resource allocation, which often inadvertently perpetuate or worsen existing disparities. An equity-constrained optimization algorithm can consider multiple objectives—such as health improvement, cost-effectiveness, and equity—all at once in making resource allocation decisions. Such systems can ensure that interventions reach underserved populations even when they may not represent the most cost-effective targets for intervention.

Healthcare demand through predictive modeling might reveal future healthcare requirements across different population groups for an active resource planning that would support the service needs of the less fortunate communities. The computations may include the prevalence of diseases, the difficulty of treatments, and other accessibility elements that influence the user's pattern of service. The mobile health platform optimization uses AI in the process of creating and executing mobile health programs that will be directed to the individuals with difficult accessibility to regular health care. The different technological skills and/or the different users' choices can be taken into account for different platforms by adjusting their functionalities, content, and user interfaces.

Systems that monitor and improve quality through AI can guarantee that the healthcare quality is the same across different populations and locations. Not only that, but they will also be able to detect and bring up the unequal quality of care to the management for quick solutions to fill in the gaps in service delivery. Just-in-time transportation and logistics-optimizing algorithms, for instance, can help in the

Table 8.6 AI-supported policy development tools

Tool type	AI technology	Primary function	Stakeholder benefits	Implementation challenges
Impact simulators	Agent-based modeling	Policy outcome prediction	Evidence-based decision-making	Model validation complexity
Evidence synthesizers	NLP + meta-analysis	Research integration	Rapid evidence reviews	Quality assessment automation
Message optimizers	Sentiment analysis	Communication enhancement	Persuasive advocacy	Cultural sensitivity
Monitoring systems	Predictive analytics	Policy tracking	Real-time feedback	Data integration issues

redesign of service systems that make access to healthcare less difficult for the underprivileged. Clinic sites, mobile service routes, and appointment timetables can be perfected to lighten the traveling load and make the service more accessible (Chinta et al., 2025).

8.5.4 Policy Development and Advocacy Support

AI technologies have become powerful tools to support evidence-based policy development and advocacy in efforts to reduce disparities in oral health. In addition, such capabilities allow for more advanced policy impact analysis and better presentation of evidence to policymakers and other stakeholders. Policy impact simulation models use agent-based modeling and system dynamics to predict the potential impacts of various policy interventions on oral health disparities. These can help policymakers to understand the complex interactions between policy changes and population health outcomes (Feng et al., 2022).

AI-driven evidence synthesis and meta-analysis systems can rapidly analyze large volumes of research literature to identify effective interventions for reducing disparities. Algorithms for natural language processing can do the extraction of key findings from research papers and synthesize evidence across multiple studies. Advocacy messaging optimization applies both sentiment analysis and communication research to construct compelling messages that resonate with a variety of different stakeholder groups. These systems analyze successful advocacy campaigns and identify strategies in communications most effective for different audiences (Chinta et al., 2025) (Table 8.6).

Real-time policy monitoring systems can monitor the implementation and effects of policy interventions through continuous data collection and analysis. These can give early warnings on unintended consequences and provide opportunities to refine policies. AI-powered stakeholder engagement platforms facilitate meaningful participation of affected communities in policy development processes. Such a platform analyzes the input of the community, identifies the emergence of common themes and concerns, and ensures that the various voices are heard in policy debates (Ali & Marhazlinda, 2023).

8.6 Future Directions and Emerging Technologies

8.6.1 Next-Generation AI Technologies

The future of AI in public health dentistry will be shaped by a set of emerging technologies that promise to further extend the capabilities and applications of artificial intelligence in oral healthcare delivery. These next-generation technologies represent important steps beyond current AI systems, offering new possibilities for addressing persistent challenges in population oral health.

Federated learning is an emerging field of AI model development in which multiple healthcare organizations can collaborate in training AI systems without sharing sensitive patient data. This technology can be used to develop robust and more generalizable AI models with the assurance of data privacy and security. In public health dentistry, federated learning will facilitate the development of AI systems that have been trained on diverse populations and clinical settings, further improving their performance across communities (Chinta et al., 2025).

8.6.2 Integration with Emerging Healthcare Technologies

The merging of AI with other up-and-coming healthcare technologies creates new avenues for creativity in public health dentistry. The combination of AI with robotics, nanotechnology, biomaterials, and biotechnology could result in the changes that will be made in the delivery and outcomes of oral healthcare. The systems with AI-enhanced robotics could be providing the highest possible accuracy in dental procedures which is the goal of reducing human error and having a very high standard of care. The AI-powered robots could be doing the simple tasks, the helping hands in the very hard surgeries, and the partners in the very gentle interventions. In the public health area, the robot system could deal with the problem of shortage of staff and make the specialist skills available to the communities deprived of expert care.

Nanotechnology applications, being AI-assisted, could make it possible to achieve precise drug delivery, better diagnosis, and innovative treatment. AI could perform the functions of the design of nanoparticles, the prediction of drug release patterns, and the treatment protocols based on the individual patient's traits. Therefore, AI-informed smart biomaterials would render adaptive treatments that can adjust with the different conditions (Mazumdar et al., 2025).

3D printing and additive manufacturing along with AI might change the whole game regarding the production of dental devices, prosthetics, and treatment materials. The application of AI algorithms comes in handy through the optimization of design parameters, the prediction of material properties, and the personalization of the manufacturing process for each patient. This interaction could lead to the opening up of a new era in which even the most sophisticated dental treatments would be placed within the reach and accessibility of a large variety of the population. AI-powered wearable devices and IoT technologies might enable the continuous consumption of the state of oral health and the early detection of issues through monitoring. Smart toothbrushes, oral sensors, and other connected devices might provide the necessary input for the implementation of prevention and intervention strategies by monitoring the real-time oral health behaviors and conditions while giving valuable insights (Tiwari et al., 2023).

The application of AI in biotechnology could offer regenerative treatments, personalized therapeutics, and novel diagnostics. AI algorithms might optimize protocols in tissue engineering, predict treatment outcomes, and create personalized biological interventions based on unique genetic and biological profiles.

8.6.3 Global Health Applications and Scalability

In the case that AI technologies are utilized to tackle the global oral health problems, a unique chance will be presented to eliminate the long-standing disparities in health outcomes among different population groups. AI systems' potential will improve and their increasing availability will also contribute to the power of responding to dental issues in poor and middle-income countries. On the other hand, the use of AI technologies in less fortunate areas will have to deal with various obstacles such as unreliable Internet, low-tier hardware, and lack of tech support. Technologies used for global health must be tough, efficient, and capable of operating in unfavorable conditions with minimal maintenance (Livingstone et al., 2023).

Mobile health platforms augmented by Artificial Intelligence (AI) could provide sophisticated diagnostic and treatment assistance to vulnerable populations around the world. Low-cost smartphones and tablets could be used to implement these platforms, creating opportunities for advanced AI functionalities to be used in resource-limited settings without large investments in infrastructure. Capacity building and technology transfer programs will be fundamental when it comes to adapting AI technologies to manage them well within a single geographic and socioeconomic area across multiple global settings. International partnerships between developing and developed countries may facilitate this sharing of knowledge, channeling resources, and the opportunity to use the technology sustainably (Farzandipour et al., 2025).

Cultural adaptation and localization of the AI system are viewed as driving factors to successful use of the technology around the globe. The AI system must be designed to factor in language, different cultures, healthcare systems, and social contexts. Training of machine learning algorithms must reflect diverse datasets concerning the populations they plan to serve. Any use of AI in global health must consider sustainability and the long-term impact of the systems design. Implementation strategies should address how the system would be maintained and updated over time to ensure AI functionality. Local capacity strengths and knowledge transference will be an important component to create impact in a sustainable way (Livingstone et al., 2023).

8.6.4 Research and Innovation Opportunities

Identifying areas of research and innovation within the intersection of AI and public health dentistry can generate new developments to move the field forward and influence population health. The areas of research and innovation include, but are not limited to: basic research, translational studies, implementation science, and policy research. Basic research includes innovation of new AI algorithms developed for dental contexts, new data or biomarkers to measure oral health, and addresses biological evidence for the phenomenon seen in oral health data the AI has detected. This very area of research may lead to significant findings that subsequently lead to reconceptualizing our ideology and preventative actions towards oral disease (Chinta et al., 2025).

Translational research aimed at developing and validating AI applications for clinical practice is a major focus of investment efforts. Research should investigate issues around the performance of the AI system, clinical effectiveness, cost-effectiveness, and feasibility of implementation in different healthcare contexts and populations. Implementation science research is necessary to understand how AI technologies can be incorporated into an existing healthcare system and work patterns. Research here should identify facilitators and barriers of AI adoption, strategies to overcome implementation barriers, and strategies to scale effective AI applications.

Health services research can also look to understanding how AI impacts quality, access, and equity in healthcare, as well as studying the economic implications of AI adoption in healthcare systems for investment purposes and policy development. Health services research will guide policy decisions and help prioritize investment. It will also be important to investigate policy research that examines the regulatory, ethical, and social implications of AI in healthcare more broadly. These investigations can focus on important questions related to what constitutes an appropriate governance framework, how liability and responsibility should be determined, and how best to ensure that AI-enabled healthcare services, including those developed using the principles of EDI, are equitably accessible (Tiwari et al., 2023).

8.7 Conclusion and Recommendations

As the detailed examination of the issue presented in this chapter will show, artificial intelligence is a revolutionary factor in public health dentistry and it gives unparalleled chances for resolving the long-standing issues concerning the delivery of oral healthcare, disease prevention, and population health management. AI technologies have definitely moved their position from being merely experimental to being very useful and practically applicable tools that are, moreover, able to enhance the whole clinical practice, improve the outcomes of the population's health, and even speed up the achievement of health equity.

AI applications in public health dentistry have promised to deliver good results in the areas of diagnostic accuracy, epidemiological surveillance, treatment planning, and prevention measures' optimization. Thus, they have made it easier for healthcare providers, who have been very precise and efficient in delivering care, to deal with complex population health management issues by making use of machine learning algorithms, computer vision systems, and predictive analytics technology. One of the most significant potentials of AI in public health inequalities is the ability of AI to detect hidden trends in inequality. This detection can support the formulation of strategic interventions towards the deprived populations along with the equitable distribution of resources that would grant access to high-quality oral health. The reduction of health inequalities can be achieved by AI systems that analyze various data sources and give insights based on the simultaneous analyses and the provision of actionable insights.

In order to encourage healthcare delivery powered by AI rather than drive it underground, reimbursement and payment policies always have to be modified. At present, the prevailing payment models may not give the right value to AI-enhanced care or even possibly make it harder for AI to be applied. It will be necessary for the regulators too.

References

Ali, N. I. M., & Marhazlinda, J. (2023). Geo-mapping of the spatial accessibility to public Oral health facilities among schoolchildren in Selangor, Malaysia. *Healthcare (Basel), 11*(10), 1405. https://doi.org/10.3390/healthcare11101405

Ali, M., Irfan, M., Ali, T., Wei, C. R., & Akilimali, A. (2025). Artificial intelligence in dental radiology: A narrative review. *Annals of Medicine and Surgery, 87*(4), 2212–2217. https://doi.org/10.1097/MS9.0000000000003127

Bayrakdar, I. S., Orhan, K., Akarsu, S., Çelik, Ö., Atasoy, S., Pekince, A., Yasa, Y., Bilgir, E., Sağlam, H., Aslan, A. F., & Odabaş, A. (2022). Deep-learning approach for caries detection and segmentation on dental bitewing radiographs. *Oral Radiology, 38*(4), 468–479. https://doi.org/10.1007/s11282-021-00577-9

Chen, Q., Zhou, X., Wu, J., & Zhou, Y. (2021). Structuring electronic dental records through deep learning for a clinical decision support system. *Health Informatics Journal, 27*(1), 1460458220980036. https://doi.org/10.1177/1460458220980036

Chinta, S. V., Wang, Z., Palikhe, A., Zhang, X., Kashif, A., Smith, M. A., Liu, J., & Zhang, W. (2025). AI-driven healthcare: Fairness in AI healthcare: A survey. *PLOS Digital Health, 4*(5), e0000864. https://doi.org/10.1371/journal.pdig.0000864

Farzandipour, M., Sharif, R., & Anvari, S. (2025). Effects of mhealth applications on military personnel's physical and mental health: A systematic review. *Military Psychology, 37*(3), 199–207. https://doi.org/10.1080/08995605.2024.2336640

Feher, B., de Souza Oliveira, E. H., Mendes Duarte, P., Werdich, A. A., Giannobile, W. V., & Feres, M. (2025). Machine learning-assisted prediction of clinical responses to periodontal treatment. *Journal of Periodontology*. https://doi.org/10.1002/JPER.24-0737

Feng, Y., Liang, S., Zhang, Y., Chen, S., Wang, Q., Huang, T., Sun, F., Liu, X., Zhu, H., & Pan, H. (2022). Automated medical literature screening using artificial intelligence: A systematic review and meta-analysis. *Journal of the American Medical Informatics Association, 29*(8), 1425–1432. https://doi.org/10.1093/jamia/ocac066

Fries, N., Haworth, S., Shaffer, J. R., Esberg, A., Divaris, K., Marazita, M. L., & Johansson, I. (2024). A polygenic score predicts caries experience in elderly Swedish adults. *Journal of Dental Research, 103*(5), 502–508. https://doi.org/10.1177/00220345241232330

Gómez-Ríos, I., Saura-López, V., Pérez-Silva, A., Serna-Muñoz, C., & Ortiz-Ruiz, A. J. (2025). Application of machine learning for data analysis in paediatric dentistry: A systematic review. *European Journal of Paediatric Dentistry, 1*. https://doi.org/10.23804/ejpd.2025.2288

Kshirsagar, M. M., Dodamani, A. S., Dodamani, G. A., Khobragade, V. R., Garg, Y., & Deokar, R. N. (2021). Teledentistry: A new horizon in COVID-19 pandemic for oral health. *International Journal of Clinical Pediatric Dentistry, 14*(3), 441–442. https://doi.org/10.5005/jp-journals-10005-1970

Lee, J.-H., Kim, D.-H., Jeong, S.-N., & Choi, S.-H. (2018). Detection and diagnosis of dental caries using a deep learning-based convolutional neural network algorithm. *Journal of Dentistry, 77*, 106–111. https://doi.org/10.1016/j.jdent.2018.07.015

Liang, Y., Li, D., Deng, D., Chu, C. H., Mei, M. L., Li, Y., Yu, N., He, J., & Cheng, L. (2025). AI-driven dental caries management strategies: From clinical practice to professional education and public self care. *International Dental Journal, 75*(4), 100827. https://doi.org/10.1016/j.identj.2025.04.007

Livingstone, K. M., Love, P., Mathers, J. C., Kirkpatrick, S. I., & Olstad, D. L. (2023). Cultural adaptations and tailoring of public health nutrition interventions in Indigenous peoples and ethnic minority groups: Opportunities for personalised and precision nutrition. *The Proceedings of the Nutrition Society, 82*(4), 478–486. https://doi.org/10.1017/S002966512300304X

Mazumdar, H., Khondakar, K. R., Das, S., Halder, A., & Kaushik, A. (2025). Artificial intelligence for personalized nanomedicine; from material selection to patient outcomes. *Expert Opinion on Drug Delivery, 22*(1), 85–108. https://doi.org/10.1080/17425247.2024.2440618

Olawade, D. B., Wada, O. J., David-Olawade, A. C., Kunonga, E., Abaire, O., & Ling, J. (2023). Using artificial intelligence to improve public health: A narrative review. *Frontiers in Public Health, 11*, 1196397. https://doi.org/10.3389/fpubh.2023.1196397

Oral Health. (n.d.). Retrieved July 1, 2025, from https://www.who.int/news-room/fact-sheets/detail/oral-health

Petersen, P. E., Bourgeois, D., Ogawa, H., Estupinan-Day, S., & Ndiaye, C. (2005). The global burden of oral diseases and risks to oral health. *Bulletin of the World Health Organization, 83*(9), 661–669.

Pethani, F., & Dunn, A. G. (2023). Natural language processing for clinical notes in dentistry: A systematic review. *Journal of Biomedical Informatics, 138*, 104282. https://doi.org/10.1016/j.jbi.2023.104282

Sadegh-Zadeh, S.-A., Bagheri, M., & Saadat, M. (2024). Decoding children dental health risks: A machine learning approach to identifying key influencing factors. *Frontiers in Artificial Intelligence, 7*, 1392597. https://doi.org/10.3389/frai.2024.1392597

Snider, V., Homsi, K., Kusnoto, B., Atsawasuwan, P., Viana, G., Allareddy, V., Gajendrareddy, P., & Elnagar, M. H. (2023). Effectiveness of AI-driven remote monitoring technology in improving oral hygiene during orthodontic treatment. *Orthodontics & Craniofacial Research, 26*(Suppl 1), 102–110. https://doi.org/10.1111/ocr.12666

Tiwari, A., Ghosh, A., Agrawal, P. K., Reddy, A., Singla, D., Mehta, D. N., Girdhar, G., & Paiwal, K. (2023). Artificial intelligence in oral health surveillance among under-served communities. *Bioinformation, 19*(13), 1329–1335. https://doi.org/10.6026/973206300191329

Watt, R. G. (2005). Strategies and approaches in oral disease prevention and health promotion. *Bulletin of the World Health Organization, 83*(9), 711–718.

Yilmaz, S., Tasyurek, M., Amuk, M., Celik, M., & Canger, E. M. (2024). Developing deep learning methods for classification of teeth in dental panoramic radiography. *Oral Surgery, Oral Medicine, Oral Pathology and Oral Radiology, 138*(1), 118–127. https://doi.org/10.1016/j.oooo.2023.02.021

Fusion Intelligence for Anemia Diagnosis: Multimodal AI Approaches for Early Detection and Integrated Management

9

Raj Kishore Singh, Rujal Raj Singh, Aradhana Singh, J. P. Pandey, and Abhinav K. Gautam

9.1 Introduction

9.1.1 Burden of Anemia

One quarter of the world's population is suffering from anemia, making it the most important global health issue. Anemia affected about 1.92 billion people in 2021 (GBD 2021 Anaemia Collaborators et al., 2023). A modest reduction in global prevalence of anemia was noted from 28.2% in 1990 to 24.3% in 2021. Despite this the absolute number of anemia sufferers continue to rise due to population expansion. Anemia, once known as a disease of lower socioeconomic status, became prevalent in upper socioeconomic status due to nutritional changes, e.g., use of tea, coffee, & junk food (GBD 2021 Anaemia Collaborators et al., 2023). The Global Burden of Disease study estimated that anemia leads to substantial morbidity with over

R. K. Singh (✉)
Department of Medicine, Nodal Officer, Multidisciplinary Research Unit & Clinical Trial Unit, BRD (Baba Raghav Das) Medical College, Gorakhpur, Uttar Pradesh, India

R. R. Singh
Batchlor of Technology, Computer Science Engineering (Artificial Intelligence & Machine Learning), AKGEC, Ghaziabad, Uttar Pradesh, India

A. Singh
Department of Obstetrics and Gynaecology, All India Institute of Medical Sciences, Gorakhpur, Uttar Pradesh, India

J. P. Pandey
Dr. A. P. J. Abdul Kalam Technical University, Lucknow, Uttar Pradesh, India

A. K. Gautam
Department of Electrical & Electronics Engineering, S.R. Institute of Management & Technology, Lucknow, Uttar Pradesh, India

U. Venkatesh et al. (eds.), *Multimodal AI in Healthcare*,
https://doi.org/10.1007/978-981-95-9027-8_9

520 million years lived with disability (YLDs) attributed to it (GBD 2021 Anaemia Collaborators et al., 2023).

Anemia disproportionately affects most vulnerable population groups. Across South Asian and sub-Saharan African, low- and middle-income countries, anemia prevalence exceeds 50% among pregnant women, 70% among young children, and from 50% to 90% among toddlers (GBD 2021 Anaemia Collaborators et al., 2023). In India there are high interstate variations where eastern states report anemia prevalence of around 87%, while that in northern regions is approximately 50% (Jeevan et al., 2025). This disparity is due to varying etiologies of anemia. Nutritional deficiencies, chronic infections, hemoglobinopathies, bone marrow suppression, malignancy associated anemia, and significant blood loss may present separately or coexist in varied combinations as a cause of anemia. Its presentation and management are further complicated by socioeconomic inequities, food insecurity, gender inequality, and healthcare access inequality.

9.1.2 Current Gaps and Diagnostic Challenges in Anemia

Significant progress in laboratory diagnostics has been achieved over the years, but evaluation of anemia continues to pose challenges due to its multifactorial etiology and overlapping phenotypic manifestations. Conventional diagnostic approaches such as hemoglobin concentration and red blood cell indices are not sufficient for etiological diagnosis (Sonia et al., 2025). Moreover, threshold values for hemoglobin and red blood cell indices established from reference populations may fail to adequately represent a varied population (Williams et al., 2023). Pre-analytical sampling factors, including differences between capillary, arterial and venous sampling, hydration status and instrument calibration inconsistencies, also contribute to measurement variability and misclassification of anemia status (Williams et al., 2023).

One of the most common drawbacks of current general clinical practice is the presumption of iron deficiency as the etiology in almost every patient. This leads to under diagnosis of other important etiologies such as chronic inflammation, parasitic infections, hemoglobinopathies, bone marrow failure syndromes, micronutrient deficiencies or a combination of factors (Sonia et al., 2025). Even at higher centers clinicians most commonly use hemoglobin and red blood cell morphological indices for diagnosis. This results in inaccurate etiological diagnosis and wrong therapeutic interventions in a significant number of the patients, decreasing the overall effectiveness of anemia control programs (Sonia et al., 2025; Williams et al., 2023).

An integrated diagnostic approach including demographic variables, clinical assessments, red blood cell morphological assessment, reticulocyte indices, biochemical parameters, and inflammatory markers can increase diagnostic accuracy. The use of clinician supervised machine learning and artificial intelligence (AI) as an integrated diagnostic approach will provide personalized diagnostic profiles differentiating between overlapping etiologies with precision and clinical relevance

Table 9.1 Multimodal data sources used in fusion intelligence for anemia diagnosis

Data modality	Examples of parameters/inputs	Diagnostic contribution
Hematological data	Hemoglobin, RBC indices (MCV (mean corpuscular volume), MCH (mean corpuscular hemoglobin), RDW (red cell distribution width)), reticulocyte indices, scattergrams	Morphological + quantitative assessment; subtype classification
Biochemical biomarkers	Ferritin, CRP (C-reactive protein), transferrin saturation, vitamin B12, folate, hepcidin	Distinguishes nutritional vs inflammatory vs mixed etiologies
Imaging data	Conjunctival/palmar images, retinal fundus images, digital blood smears	Detects pallor, vessel changes, dysmorphia, microvascular patterns
Genomics / proteomics	Thalassemia/SCD (sickle cell disease) mutations, G6PD (glucose 6 phosphate dehydrogenase) variants, protein biomarkers	Identifies hereditary anemia; detects enzymopathies & hemoglobinopathies
Clinical & demographic data	Age, sex, pregnancy status, symptoms, comorbidities	Contextual classification; improves precision of etiological diagnosis
EHR & clinical notes (NLP)	Symptoms (pica, fatigue), diet, bleeding history, medication records	Converts unstructured text into structured predictors using NLP (Natural Language Processing)

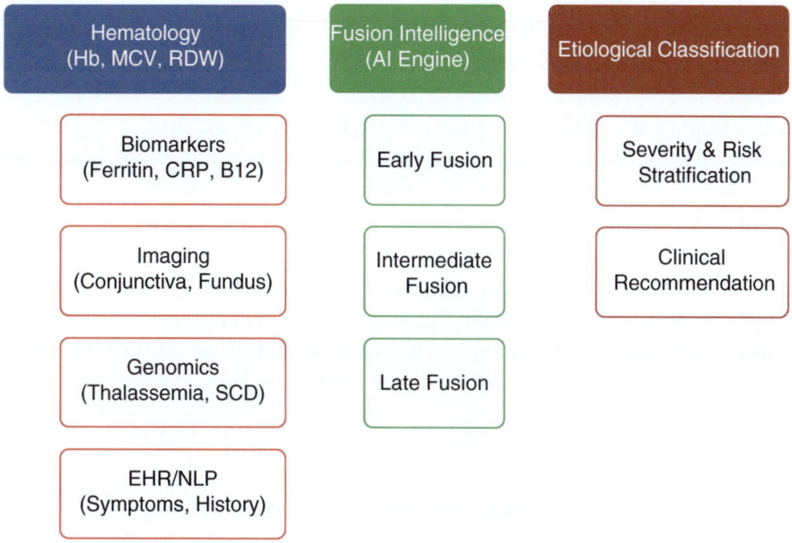

Fig. 9.1 Multimodal fusion architecture for anemia diagnosis

(Sonia et al., 2025; Williams et al., 2023). A consolidated overview of the multimodal data sources used in fusion-intelligence-based anemia diagnostics is presented in Table 9.1 and Fig. 9.1. Multimodal data fusion framework for anemia diagnosis hematology, biochemistry, imaging, genomics, and EHR (electronic health record) inputs are fused by the AI engine to produce etiological classification, severity stratification, and clinical recommendations.

9.1.3 Objective and Scope of the Chapter

This chapter aims to provide a comprehensive and systematically organized understanding of how fusion intelligence (the integration of multimodal artificial intelligence techniques) can transform diagnosis and management of anemia. Drawing on peer reviewed empirical studies, meta-analyses, and systematic reviews published between 2020 and 2025, the chapter pursues four primary objectives:

Critical appraisal of AI methodologies: Evaluate current machine learning and deep learning architectures relevant to automated, high precision etiological diagnosis of anemia (Liao et al., 2025).

Architectural design for multimodal fusion: Examine data fusion strategies that integrate diverse modalities like complete blood count parameters, morphological imaging, biochemical markers, and genomic information into unified diagnostic systems (Liao et al., 2025; Williams et al., 2023).

Translational implementation and scalability: Develop operational frameworks for the application of fusion intelligence across different tiers of healthcare from tertiary hospitals to resource limited primary settings. The goal is to support maternal and child health targets by enabling evidence-based policy and equitable access to advanced diagnostics (GBD 2021 Anaemia Collaborators et al., 2023; Liao et al., 2025; Sonia et al., 2025; Williams et al., 2023).

Strategic trajectories for future research: Identify opportunities for innovation in AI-driven hematology, including real-time monitoring, continuous multimodal data integration, and explainable AI (XAI) systems to enhance clinical trust and accelerate adoption.

Together, these objectives define the scope of this chapter; to elucidate scientific principles, technical architectures, and translational pathways through which multimodal fusion intelligence can bridge current diagnostic gaps and promote precision hematology.

9.1.4 The Future of Fusion Intelligence in Hematology

Currently clinicians diagnose anemia by looking at one or more pieces of information at a time, e.g., a hemoglobin level, red cell indices from CBC (complete blood count) etc. in the background of demographic characteristics and clinical presentations of the patient. In resource poor, overcrowded rural primary healthcare settings clinicians face the challenge of long patient queue, limited time and lack of team support. This often leads to presumptive diagnosis of iron deficiency anemia in most of the patients. Thus patients having thalassemia trait or anemia from chronic inflammation or other anemias are wrongly prescribed iron therapy causing more harm (Liao et al., 2025). Fusion intelligence changes this completely and merges all available data instead of analyzing them in isolation. It brings together and analyze patients' demographic data, electronic health record (EHR), clinician note, imaging data, hematology analyzer data, biochemistry analyzer data of iron profile, hormonal analyzer results of vitamins, thyroid hormone, hepcidin, data of genetic study etc. all at once. All this information flows into a multi-modal AI system simultaneously and the clinician gets an answer with a confidence score to guide their next steps (Gómez et al., 2025; Liao et al., 2025; Young, 2024).

For successful implementation of fusion intelligence in clinical practice, three things matter the most. First, rigorous supervised validation testing in real-world settings. Second, they must explain their decisions with logic so that doctors can understand why the AI is recommending something with a provision of real-time feedback from the clinician. Third, the systems must be trained on diverse patient populations from different countries and backgrounds.

In busy hospitals with limited resources, fusion intelligence becomes a game changer. It can quickly identify patients at highest risk, even when team support from different specialties is not available. It predicts who might need blood transfusions, who will respond to treatment, and who might relapse. This transforms anemia management from reactive to predictive and doctors can act before problems get worse.

The future of anemia diagnosis lies in fusion intelligence that sees patients as whole, think faster than humans, and make fairer decisions than any single clinician. It prevents misdiagnosis, stops harmful presumptive treatment, and ensures every patient, whether in a tertiary hospital or a remote village clinic will receive the right diagnosis and treatment from day one.

9.2 Anemia: A Complex Multidimensional Health Disorder

There are many diseases leading to anemia, such as defective erythrocytes production, maturation, and their decreased survival. The overlap of etiologies has been commonly faced in clinical settings, such as coexistence of iron deficiency with chronic kidney disease or systemic inflammation which leads to diagnostic challenges. Such overlap in etiologies cannot be identified by conventional diagnostic methods. The recent advancements in the fusion models of artificial intelligence which are trained with bulk of biochemical, imaging and molecular data offers the promise of identifying such overlaps in etiologies.

9.2.1 Morphological and Etiological Classification of Anemia

Knowing the morphology of red blood cells (RBCs) is very crucial for diagnosing anemia, because morphology of RBCs provides the key information about the main cause by revealing the size, shape, and color of the RBCs. Based on morphology, anemia can be microcytic anemia (iron deficiency, thalassemia trait, and chronic blood loss), normocytic anemia (anemia of chronic disease, acute hemorrhage, and hemolysis), and macrocytic anemia (vitamin B12, folate deficiency, and bone marrow dysplasia).

To determine a definitive diagnosis, morphological data of RBCs must be combined with the etiological data. The etiology of anemia has six major domains, and these are, blood loss related, chronic disease related, genetic, hemolytic, nutritional, and bone marrow or neoplasia related. Each of these domains represents a different mechanism that impairs erythropoiesis, reduces erythrocyte survival, and disrupts hemoglobin synthesis.

Blood loss anemia can be caused by either acute or chronic hemorrhage. Acute hemorrhage, such as bleeding from surgery or trauma leads to normochromic, normocytic anemia whereas chronic hemorrhage, such as gynecologic or gastrointestinal bleeding leads to progressive iron depletion and microcytic anemia. AI-based predictive analytics can detect subtle progressive declines in hemoglobin levels allowing for the early detection of occult bleeding and timely intervention.

Chronic disease anemia is linked to persistent inflammation, infection, autoimmune disorders, and renal conditions. Elevated hepcidin levels inhibit erythropoietin responsiveness, resulting in normocytic normochromic anemia profile (Asare et al., 2023a; Williams et al., 2023). This type of anemia reflects impaired iron utilization rather than absolute iron deficiency.

Genetic anemia can be caused by the inherited defects affecting hemoglobin production, red blood cell membrane integrity, and enzyme activity. Major examples of the inherited defects include glucose 6 phosphate dehydrogenase (G6PD) deficiency, sickle cell disease, and thalassemia. Advancements in carrier screening, molecular diagnostics, and prenatal interventions helped early detection and planning of the prevention strategies (Gómez et al., 2025).

Hemolytic anemia is caused when red blood cells are destroyed faster than they can be replaced. The diagnosis of hemolytic anemia is based on the laboratory parameters, such as increased indirect bilirubin, lactate dehydrogenase (LDH), reticulocyte count and decreased haptoglobin. Integration of biochemical, morphological, and genetic data in fusion intelligence using machine learning algorithms can predict hemolytic anemia (Asare et al., 2023b; Gómez et al., 2025).

Nutritional anemia is the most widespread form of anemia globally and is caused largely by the deficiency of iron, folate, vitamin A, vitamin B12, and riboflavin, which are needed for the maturation of erythrocyte, production of hemoglobin, and synthesis of DNA (Brittenham et al., 2023).

Bone marrow-related anemia may be nonneoplastic anemia such as aplastic anemia or neoplastic anemia such as myelophthisic anemia or cytotoxic therapy-induced bone marrow failure. The diagnosis of nonneoplastic and neoplastic anemia requires bone marrow aspiration and biopsy supplemented with cytogenetic analysis and flow cytometry. Integration of morphological, cytogenetic, and molecular data in fusion intelligence using machine learning algorithms can increase diagnostic precision and improve prognosis assessment.

9.2.2 Diagnostic Parameters: Hemoglobin, RBC Indices, and Biomarkers

Diagnostic parameters for anemia include hemoglobin level, and various hematological indices, such as mean corpuscular volume (MCV), mean corpuscular hemoglobin (MCH), mean corpuscular hemoglobin concentration (MCHC), and red cell distribution width (RDW) and specific biomarkers, such as serum iron, serum ferritin, and transferrin saturation. Interpretation of hemoglobin values must be based on the age, sex, altitude, and physiological status of the individual. Error in the interpretation of hemoglobin values can occur due to the differences in capillary and venous sampling and during the device calibration that compromise accuracy. Hematological indices help in the morphological classification of anemia whereas reticulocyte count demonstrates bone marrow compensation. Reliable measures of body iron storage are serum ferritin adjusted for the inflammatory markers such as a-1 acid glycoprotein (AGP) and C-reactive protein (CRP). Transferrin saturation, soluble transferrin receptor, and hepcidin are examples of complementary assays that aid in distinguishing iron deficiency anemia from chronic disease-related anemia.

Hemoglobinopathies and enzymopathies can be diagnosed with the aid of molecular diagnostics, such as hemoglobin electrophoresis, High Performance Liquid Chromatography (HPLC), and DNA-based testing. Artificial intelligence-based conjunctival or palmar colorimetry analysis, hyperspectral imaging, and smartphone-based photoplethysmography are examples of emerging noninvasive diagnostic technologies that provide inexpensive tools for screening anemia, enabling early detection and clinical decision-making (Asare et al., 2023b; Vohra et al., 2022).

9.2.3 Clinical Presentations and Overlap Syndromes

Fatigue, exertional dyspnea, cognitive impairment, pallor, and tachycardia are some of the signs of anemia. The rate, amount, and duration of hemoglobin loss are directly related to the severity of these symptoms. Mixed presentations are common and pose serious diagnostic difficulties.

In order to simplify the overlapping etiologies by the probabilistic classification, recent developments in fusion intelligence have assisted in combining hematological, biochemical, and genetic datasets (Asare et al., 2023a, b; Brittenham et al., 2023). By objectively quantifying pallor and morphological abnormalities, convolutional neural networks (CNNs) trained on peripheral blood smear and conjunctival image datasets have demonstrated better diagnostic precision. By incorporating such AI-based technologies, etiology-specific treatment methods can be developed, improving therapy efficacy and maximizing resource use.

9.2.4 Limitations of Conventional Diagnostic Approaches Versus Fusion Intelligence

Traditional methods for diagnosing anemia present certain limitations: for instance, the manual evaluation of pallor is inherently subjective, resulting in low sensitivity, especially when identifying mild cases of anemia (Williams et al., 2023). Factors occurring prior to analysis, including sample degradation, humidity exposure, and improper collection or handling practices, can lead to inaccuracies in measurement. Advanced biochemical assays offer improved diagnostic precision. However, their use is frequently limited in healthcare environments with scarce resources due to financial constraints, infrastructural challenges, and technical requirements.

Fusion intelligence mitigates these limitations by combining hematological parameters with noninvasive optical and digital imaging techniques, such as smartphone-based photoplethysmography. Deep learning algorithms have shown clinically acceptable levels of accuracy in estimating hemoglobin concentrations, and multimodal artificial intelligence frameworks assist in the detection and management of anemia (Jayakody & Edirisinghe, 2020). Consequently, artificial intelligence is effectively bridging the gap between centralized laboratory services and community-based healthcare delivery.

9.3 Fusion Intelligence and Multimodal AI: Concepts and Frameworks

Recent advances in artificial intelligence (AI) and data integration have fundamentally transformed the principles of biomedical diagnostics, particularly for complex, multi-etiologic diseases such as anemia. Continuous improvements in computational power, biomedical instrumentation, and data capture now permit the seamless integration of heterogeneous information into cohesive analytical frameworks. This fusion-intelligence paradigm aims to emulate and extend the holistic reasoning of expert clinicians by drawing simultaneous inferences from multiple, complementary data modalities (Chen et al., 2025; Teoh et al., 2024).

Whereas conventional single domain algorithms function within limited scopes, fusion intelligence constructs intrinsic links between biological systems across molecular, cellular, and physiological levels. The sections below delineate its conceptual principles, levels of data fusion, and modality-specific applications relevant to anemia diagnosis.

9.3.1 Definition and Principles of Fusion Intelligence

Fusion intelligence extends beyond classical machine learning models. It integrates diverse data modalities, computational techniques, and hierarchical knowledge to form unified diagnostic systems that may surpass physician level accuracy.

Anemia's etiology involves intertwined nutritional, genetic, and inflammatory factors. Therefore, multimodal models are essential for accurate classification. Morphological features convey cellular structure, biochemical assays quantify iron and nutrient status, genomic data identify hereditary variants, and clinical narratives document symptoms and comorbidities. Together, these data generate a layered etiopathogenic profile that far exceeds the resolution of unimodal approaches (Chen et al., 2025; Teoh et al., 2024).

Fusion intelligence surpasses simple ensemble models by employing graph-based knowledge representations and attention-driven neural mechanisms that dynamically adjust the weight of each modality based on diagnostic reliability. Importantly, such systems quantify uncertainty, enabling clinicians to gauge confidence intervals for both individual predictions and aggregated outputs. This interpretive transparency links AI-generated results to clinical reasoning and supports evidence-based decision-making.

Through this architecture, fusion models can concurrently assess disease presence, severity, and underlying cause.

9.3.2 Levels of Data Fusion: Early, Intermediate, and Late Fusion

Multimodal data integration in AI systems is commonly organized into three hierarchical levels. These are early, intermediate, and late fusion, depending on the stage at which information from various modalities is combined.

9.3.2.1 Early Fusion (Feature-Level Fusion)

Early fusion merges raw or minimally processed data from multiple modalities into a single composite feature space before model training. This unified dataset exposes cross-modal dependencies and hidden relationships. In anemia diagnostics, early fusion may integrate reticulocyte counts, red cells indices (MCV, MCH, RDW), biochemical parameters (transferrin saturation, ferritin, CRP, vitamin B12), and demographic variables (age, sex, pregnancy status) into one learning matrix. Algorithms such as gradient boosted trees or deep neural networks can then learn complex nonlinear relationships, enabling simultaneous classification of microcytic, normocytic, and macrocytic subtypes (Chen et al., 2025; Teoh et al., 2024).

9.3.2.2 Intermediate Fusion (Model-Level Fusion)

Intermediate fusion maintains separate computational pipelines for each modality before merging them at hidden layers. At this junction, cross-modal attention filters emphasize context relevant information. For example, when evaluating hereditary spherocytosis, the system places greater emphasis on genomic variant data, whereas for anemia of chronic disease, it gives more weight to inflammatory biomarkers. This approach offers flexibility and adaptive learning even when datasets are heterogeneous or partially missing.

9.3.2.3 Late Fusion (Decision-Level Fusion)

Late fusion, also known as decision fusion, aggregates the independent outputs of separate models through ensemble techniques such as weighted averaging, stacking, or meta-learning. Each modality-specific model contributes a partial decision, and the ensemble synthesizes them into a final diagnostic consensus. Late fusion frameworks are transparent and modular, allowing new data types or algorithms to be incorporated without retraining the entire system.

Empirically, early fusion performs best when modalities are strongly correlated; intermediate fusion suits architecturally diverse datasets; and late fusion excels when data availability varies among patients. In anemia diagnosis, red cell indices and biochemical markers lend themselves to early fusion, gnomic and imaging data to intermediate fusion, and clinical narratives from EHRs to late fusion. Combined, these strategies deliver robust, scalable, and flexible multimodal solutions (Chen et al., 2025; Teoh et al., 2024).

9.3.3 Modalities Used in Anemia Diagnostics

Given the intricate pathophysiology of anemia, no single dataset captures the entire disease spectrum. A multimodal fusion framework therefore integrates multiple information sources to construct a comprehensive diagnostic representation (Chen et al., 2025; Teoh et al., 2024). The primary modalities include hematological, imaging, genomic/proteomic, and electronic record data.

9.3.3.1 Hematological Data

The complete blood count (CBC) remains the cornerstone of anemia diagnosis. Parameters such as hemoglobin concentration, RBC concentration, RBC indices (MCV, MCH, and RDW), platelet and leukocyte counts, and reticulocyte indices offer quantitative insight into erythropoiesis. Modern analyzers additionally generate high-dimensional scattergrams and flow cytometric features (50–100 variables per sample) that capture cellular granularity and hemoglobinization patterns. Machine learning models can exploit these complex numerical profiles to uncover subtle diagnostic correlations (Chen et al., 2025; Teoh et al., 2024).

Integration of biochemical markers further refines characterization of iron metabolism and inflammatory burden. With advances in microfluidics and smartphone linked point of care devices, hematologic profiling can now be performed rapidly from a single drop of blood, enabling real-time fusion AI analysis even in resource limited settings.

9.3.3.2 Clinical Imaging

Noninvasive imaging modalities supplement hematologic data by visualizing physiological correlations of anemia. Calibrated smartphone cameras can estimate hemoglobin concentration via conjunctival, palmar, or nail-bed color analysis, achieving mean absolute errors of 1.0–1.5 g/dL in validation studies. Deep convolutional networks trained on retinal fundus images can detect microvascular alterations like tortuosity, caliber narrowing, or hemorrhage which are linked to chronic anemia.

Advanced optical technologies such as hyperspectral imaging, optical coherence tomography (OCT), and photoacoustic imaging allow continuous, noninvasive monitoring of hemoglobin and tissue oxygenation, correlating strongly with invasive measurements (Chen et al., 2025; Teoh et al., 2024). Together, these imaging methods complement hematology by revealing systemic and microcirculatory effects of anemia.

9.3.3.3 Genomics and Proteomics

Omics-based modalities add molecular depth to anemia diagnostics. Genomic sequencing distinguishes hereditary disorders such as thalassemia, sickle cell disease, hereditary spherocytosis, and G6PD deficiency (Chen et al., 2025; Teoh et al., 2024). When combined with CBC indices and biochemical data, genomics enables discrimination between phenotypically similar conditions (e.g., thalassemia trait versus iron deficiency anemia).

Proteomic profiling, including mass spectrometry-based quantification of plasma proteins, provides insights into inflammation, oxidative stress, and nutrient status. Network-based multi-omics integration connects gene-protein-metabolite pathways, advancing a mechanistic understanding of anemia and supporting development of targeted therapies.

9.3.3.4 Electronic Health Records (EHRs) and Natural Language Processing (NLP)

EHR systems accumulate extensive patient data across structured and unstructured formats. Structured fields contain laboratory values and medication records, while free text notes capture nuanced clinical observations. Transformer-based NLP models (e.g., BERT, GPT architectures) can extract entities such as "pallor," "splenomegaly," or "pica" from narrative text and link them to ontologies within knowledge graphs.

Temporal modeling of EHR data enables tracking of longitudinal hemoglobin patterns and treatment responses. Privacy preserving federated learning frameworks allow cross institutional model training without sharing raw data, addressing ethical and regulatory constraints while enhancing model generalizability (Chen et al., 2025; Teoh et al., 2024).

9.3.4 AI Techniques: Machine Learning, Deep Learning, and Hybrid Models

Fusion-intelligence frameworks for anemia leverage complementary strengths of traditional machine learning, deep learning, and hybrid reasoning architectures

(Chen et al., 2025; Teoh et al., 2024). Traditional machine learning algorithms (logistic regression, random forests, gradient-boosted machines such as XGBoost and LightGBM) handle structured tabular data efficiently and provide interpretable feature-importance outputs. Gradient-boosted trees have achieved 90–95% classification accuracy for anemia subtype and severity even on modest datasets.

Deep-learning architectures (CNNs for images, RNAs and transformers for sequential data, graph neural networks for relational data) automatically extract hierarchical features from raw inputs. CNN-based models applied to conjunctival or palmar images achieve 85–92% binary-classification accuracy, while recurrent or transformer models trained on longitudinal lab data can predict anemia onset weeks before clinical manifestation.

Hybrid models combine statistical learning with rule-based reasoning. Bayesian networks update diagnostic likelihoods as new data appear, while physics-informed neural networks embed physiological constraints ensuring biological plausibility and reducing overfitting.

Multitask learning architectures further enhance efficiency by sharing representations across related objectives (e.g., hemoglobin estimation, subtype classification, and treatment-response prediction). Continuous learning frameworks permit adaptation to evolving clinical data without loss of prior knowledge, a requirement for sustainable deployment in dynamic healthcare settings.

9.4 Applications of Multimodal AI in Anemia Detection

Multimodal AI can revolutionize anemia detection and management approaches. This system integrates different data types like laboratory tests, medical images, genetic information, and clinical documentation to identify anemia earlier, determine underlying causes, and predict at-risk populations. The following subsections detail five major AI applications in anemia care.

9.4.1 AI-Augmented Hematology Analyzers

Modern blood analyzers measure not only hemoglobin but also detailed red blood cell characteristics like size, shape, hemoglobin content, generating 50–100 data points per sample. Machine learning models can process these features to classify anemia severity (mild, moderate, severe) and suggest probable causes (iron deficiency, chronic inflammation, inherited disorders). For example, by combining basic blood counts (MCV, RDW, reticulocyte count) with iron and inflammation markers (ferritin, CRP), AI can distinguish iron deficiency from thalassemia trait with over 90% accuracy. When model uncertainty exceeds thresholds, cases are manually reviewed. The model is trained collaboratively across many laboratories to help maintain accuracy without sharing patient data (Parvin et al., 2025; Simon et al., 2025).

9.4.2 Retinal Image-Based Anemia Screening with Deep CNNs

Retinal microvasculature reflects overall blood health. High-resolution fundus images are captured using ultra-wide-field or smartphone fundus cameras. These images show blood vessels, optic disc, vessel thickness, and conjunctival color which are linked to low hemoglobin levels. Deep neural networks trained on retinal photographs can detect anemia indicators with 85–92% accuracy. The system combines image features with patient information like age, sex, and symptoms using attention layers and classify anemia severity and type. The model decides who needs more blood tests, making decisions more accurate and personalized. Highlighted areas on the retinal images show doctors where the AI is focusing. This makes the system easier to trust and also helps it adapt to images taken from different camera types through transfer learning.(Obeagu, 2025; Parvin et al., 2025).

9.4.3 Genomic Variant Integration for Thalassemia and Sickle Cell Screening

Inherited disorders like thalassemia and sickle cell disease alter hemoglobin genes. AI models merge genetic variants (from targeted panels or exome sequencing) with blood counts to identify carriers and affected individuals. Deep learning models like convolutional neural networks (CNNs) or vision transformers (ViTs) learn which genetic changes matter most, for inherited anemia. CNNs capture local spatial patterns in images such as vessel caliber or papillary pallor that may reflect phenotypic manifestations of genetic variations. Vision Transformers (ViTs) extract global relationships between different retinal regions and analyze how vessel color relates to other parts of the retina.

Thus, these architectures integrate learned image features, genomic signatures, and clinical inputs into a unified deep model for genetic variants integration for anemia (Obeagu, 2025; Simon et al., 2025).

9.4.4 NLP Extraction of Diagnostic Clues from Clinical Notes

Clinical documentation contains valuable information like symptoms (fatigue, pica), examination findings (pallor, splenomegaly), bleeding risks, dietary habits, family history etc. These data are often absent from structured laboratory fields. Transformer-based NLP models automatically extract these clinical details and convert them into structured data. When combined early with laboratory, clinical and imaging data, AI learns patterns such as pica indicating iron deficiency or inflammatory bowel disease linked to chronic anemia. Knowledge graphs in healthcare link extracted medical terms (like diseases, genes, drugs, or symptoms) to standardized ontologies allowing consistent and intelligent interpretation of data across systems. By doing this, they convert raw or unstructured information into structured, interconnected knowledge that machines can reason about (Obeagu, 2025; Parvin et al., 2025; Simon et al., 2025).

9.4.5 Predictive Modeling for At-Risk Groups

AI can predict anemia development or transfusion needs by combining multiple data types over time. Temporal models track how a patient's medical values (like hemoglobin) change over time. Tracking symptom changes over time can help identify treatment response and need for clinical review. They use past and present data points such as laboratory trends, retinal images, genetic risk scores, and clinical values to recognize improvements, or warning patterns. Survival analysis predicts when anemia or complications might appear.

Temporal models and survival analysis prove valuable for pregnant women where anemia affects maternal and fetal outcomes, children in low-resource settings in whom poor nutrition and infection are prevalent, elderly patients who suffer from chronic diseases and kidney disease patients where reduced erythropoietin production is a cause for anemia.

Fairness audits verify prediction consistency across ages, genders, and ethnicities. Mobile applications powered by these models can guide community health workers in screening programs (Asare et al., 2023a, b; GBD 2021 Anaemia Collaborators et al., 2023; Obeagu, 2025; Parvin et al., 2025).

9.4.6 Case Studies and Clinical Implementations

A smartphone app developed at Brown University, USA, analyzed images of the palpebral conjunctiva in 435 emergency department patients, to estimate hemoglobin levels in real time. The model predicted hemoglobin concentration with accuracy of 75.4% (95% CI 71.3, 79.4%) for all categories of anemia. The Noninvasive Anemia Detection App (NiADA) used advanced image-processing AI to analyze over 50,000 eyelid images with corresponding lab-confirmed hemoglobin values. The mean difference between NiADA-V2 and laboratory-estimated hemoglobin values was −0.11 g/dL, and it outperformed medical professionals, showing a mean difference of 0.07 g/dL compared to medical professionals' 0.42 g/dL. Apps using eye, nail, or facial images enable low-cost, needle-free screening in remote or resource-limited areas. AI models spot subtle physiological or visual symptoms before clinical diagnosis, facilitating early detection and continued monitoring. AI-based apps can support public health programs targeting maternal, pediatric, and geriatric anemia control, aligning with WHO's 2030 anemia reduction goals (An et al., 2021; Parvin et al., 2025; Sharma et al., 2024; Simon et al., 2025).

9.5 AI-Based Anemia Screening and Diagnostics Across Three Major Settings

9.5.1 Rural and Resource Limited Settings

The first part in AI-based screening in rural areas with resource limited settings is community screening and smartphone imaging. Health workers use smartphones to take photos of the inside of the person's eyelid, or their palm called conjunctival and palmar images, respectively. The inbuilt CNN analyzes these images to estimate hemoglobin levels, with an error margin of plus or minus 1.0–1.5 g/dL. The system now classifies the patients by comparing their risk score to a set level and automatically refers them for follow up in case the risk score is higher than the set level. By fusing information from the photos with other patient data like age and any reported symptoms such as fatigue, shortness of breath (dyspnea) and strange cravings (pica) we can improve the system's accuracy. This approach will be better to detect medium to severe anemia while also preventing false positives in villages where anemia is rare. This method has reported to have over 85% sensitivity for detecting "actionable anemia" (cases needing treatment) in LMIC (low- and middle-income countries) (An et al., 2021; Parvin et al., 2025; Perez et al., 2025; Simon et al., 2025).

The second part of this system is low-cost paper or chip-based tests (microfluidic tests), these measure hemoglobin and they work with a phone camera or a small scanner. These tests provide the exact readings of hemoglobin and other red blood cell data. When the information from these tests is fed into a gradient boosted AI model which has been trained on the local population, it examines a combination of all the results like Hb, MCV, RDW, ferritin, and CRP and differentiated between iron deficiency and thalassemia trait with about 90% accuracy. This process plays a crucial role in stopping thalassemia carriers from getting iron supplements which could otherwise be harmful for them. This device is both cost-effective and economical as it costs less than 1$ per test and they run on solar batteries. Another benefit is that these use an offline app which synchronizes the data with central registries when Internet is available (An et al., 2021; Parvin et al., 2025; Perez et al., 2025; Simon et al., 2025).

The third part of this system is the tele-referral which enables the doctor to get a second opinion. A feature called store and forward, allows the nurses to send the difficult cases to nearby hematologists. This is done whenever the AI model is not sure about the result. Another feature called federated improvement uses federated learning methods to update the AI models at the local clinic itself without exporting raw patient data at all. Using offline workflows, just-in-time training, and bulk purchasing can help solve problems when AI systems are used at places with inadequate Internet connections or where users have low levels of digital literacy. The system's success is evaluated by its sensitivity (how well it detects anemia), positive predictive value (how many positive results are real), turnaround time (how fast is it), and referral completion (if patients finish their follow up) (Perez et al., 2025; Simon et al., 2025).

9.5.2 Hospital-Based Multimodal Integration

Analyzer native fusion is used in core labs, and it works in the following steps. Firstly, data like CBC features, cell data/scattergrams, and reticulocyte metrics are streamed by the modern blood analyzer into an inbuilt AI which classifies the severity of the condition and suggests probable causes. The second step or intermediate fusion merges analyzer's output with parameters like ferritin-CRP, transferrin sTfR, B12, and hepcidin giving us a ranked list of possible diagnoses which have uncertainty bands. Uncertainty bands help the doctors decide if more reflex tests are required (tests like electrophoresis or molecular panels). To make the oversight and audits easier the lab's main software called LIS/EMR middleware logs the AI's reasoning which includes feature importance and attention maps. In addition to that there is a real-time quality control software constantly running which monitors for sample issues like hemolysis, delays, or temperature problems and evaluates "model drift" (AI readings are less accurate) (An et al., 2021; Parvin et al., 2025; Simon et al., 2025).

When imaging and cytology are co-read it means AI CNNs are used to analyze images like retinal fundus or eye scans, conjunctival or eyelid photos and digital blood smears. The CNN gives visual scores for attributes like pallor (paleness), caliber change (vessel size), hemorrhages (bleeding), or dysmorphia (abnormal cell shape) which are combined with lab-based classifiers to improve calibration (accuracy) for tricky decision thresholds (cutoff points for diagnosis). It also reduces the number of discordant cells or disagreements. The automated workflow triggers confirmatory tests for any of these discordant cases which shortens the time to diagnosis and reduces unnecessary transfusions for borderline cases (Obeagu, 2025; Perez et al., 2025; Simon et al., 2025).

A new variant aware pathway is being used in regions with frequent thalassemia or sickle cell disease (SCD). An AI method called joint embeddings is used to combine two sets of data namely, targeted genetic variants like HBA1/2, HBB and microcytosis profiles like MCV, RBC count, and the Mentzer index. Better cascade screening (testing family members) and improved iron therapy can be achieved via this system as looking at two sets of data helps the front-line clinics separate a genetic trait from simple iron deficiency. On top of that it flags potential carriers who are then directed to counselling and prenatal pathways. To implement this special emphasis must be given to patient consent along with ancestry aware validation and equitable performance monitoring across all language and socioeconomic groups, this is important to prevent algorithmic disparities or bias in detecting carriers (Obeagu, 2025; Simon et al., 2025).

Implementing this system leads to visible gains in capacity and stewardship. Analyzing a patient's longitudinal labs, medications, and comorbidities to anticipate the need for transfusion 48–72 hours in advance via the predictive model provides a big help in streamlining crossmatch workflows and reducing emergency requests. Simultaneously, dashboards track Hb trajectories after a patient receives ESA (Erythropoiesis Stimulating Agent)or IV iron which helps in optimizing their dosing and clinic visit rhythm. To ensure safety, institutional governance codifies rules for model versioning, regular bias audits, and mandatory human verification for any high-risk task hence ensuring the system's alignment with safety and medicolegal requirements (Perez et al., 2025; Simon et al., 2025).

9.5.3 Telehematology and Edge-AI for Point of Care Diagnostics

Earlier, we stated that the inbuilt AI will run on a smartphone and how the systems do not need a cloud connection. This is made possible with something called edge inference. This feature increases speed and enhances privacy, as the AI models (AI models and tabular transformers) can run directly on the device itself like a portable analyzer like smartphones (Cai et al., 2024). This makes delivery of Hb estimates anemia classifications and potential causes in a matter of few minutes. The most prominent advantage is that this system works without an Internet connection which immediately reduces lag while protecting patient privacy. This feature is perfect for clinics with poor Internet connectivity. This is possible because techniques such as knowledge distillation and pruning make the AI models smaller and more efficient, allowing them to run directly on a smartphone using its built-in Advanced RISC Machine (ARM) processor and to continue operating on battery power throughout the day (An et al., 2021; Parvin et al., 2025; Perez et al., 2025; Simon et al., 2025).

To improve agreement between the reviewers and effectively reduce the turnaround time of the process of getting a sample to issuing a report we use features like remote microscopy and expert support. Digital smear attachments can be used to take pictures of white blood cell fields and red blood cell fields. To enable prompt expert inspection, the AI examines the photos and flags in any questionable areas, such as schistocytes, blasts or parasites. Additionally, it comes with a tool called bidirectional annotation tools that serves the dual functions of continuously updating the AI's dataset and assisting in the development of local abilities. AI triage saves specialized capacity by giving referral transport priority for suspected marrow failure or hemolysis wherever marrow access is restricted.

This approach allows for proactive care and ongoing monitoring. To anticipate when hemoglobin may drop, it combines data from wearables such as smartwatches (PPG or photoplethysmography) with the patient's electronic health record patterns. Preemptive iron/ESA changes or day care transfusions are made possible by these early predictions, which lowers the expense of ED visits. The AI creates a risk score and attaches brief excerpts to it, which are then sent straight to patient applications and clinician inboxes. By distributing federated updates to every site without centralizing any private health information (PHI), further improvement is achieved. A procedure known as "site level calibration" is used to maintain equity across various age, sex, pregnancy, and ancestry groups.

Programs must adhere to minimum operational standards, such as external validation, ablation tests, calibration curves, and decision curve analysis, for the system to be sustainable. Key operational metrics (KPIs) are also monitored by the system. Monitoring the KPIs makes it easier to keep an eye on events, such as the average time for treatment, instances of preventable iron therapy, and the missed anemia rate. To identify any injustice or model drift, opinions from various patient groups are also taken into consideration. These initiatives may receive funds from a variety of sources, including device leasing, diagnostic tariffs, and governmental financing. This method ensures sustained operation in low-resource scenarios and maintains reagent supply and device maintenance contracts.

9.6 Challenges and Considerations

While multimodal fusion intelligence offers transformative potential for anemia diagnostics, several technical, clinical, ethical, and logistical challenges must be addressed before large-scale implementation. Ensuring data quality, algorithmic transparency, equity, and regulatory compliance is critical for sustainable deployment. The following subsections discuss these key considerations in detail.

9.6.1 Data Quality, Standardization, and Interoperability

The diagnostic performance of AI systems depends directly on the quality and representativeness of training data. Anemia datasets often originate from heterogeneous laboratory platforms that vary in calibration standards, reference intervals, and reporting units. Even minor inconsistencies in hemoglobin estimation, mean corpuscular volume (MCV), or ferritin values can introduce systematic bias.

Data standardization is thus essential. Harmonization requires adoption of global laboratory norms (e.g., WHO reference ranges, International Council for Standardization in Hematology guidelines) and unified metadata schemes for demographic, clinical, and environmental variables.

Interoperability among hospital information systems enables seamless integration of structured and unstructured data, including laboratory results, genomic sequences, and imaging outputs. Interoperability also ensures that models trained in one region can be validated and recalibrated elsewhere without extensive manual reconfiguration (Boehm et al., 2022; Ogut, 2025).

Additional challenges include limited data availability in rural or underrepresented populations. Synthetic data generation and transfer learning may mitigate this limitation but must be used cautiously to avoid overfitting or amplification of bias. Rigorous external validation remains indispensable before clinical deployment.

9.6.2 Algorithmic Bias and Fairness

Bias can infiltrate AI systems through unbalanced training data, subjective labeling, or population homogeneity. For anemia, sex-, age-, ethnicity-, and pregnancy-related physiological variations complicate algorithm design. Models trained primarily on data from one demographic group may perform poorly in others, leading to misclassification and inequitable care.

Fairness-aware AI methodologies apply re-weighting, stratified sampling, and counterfactual testing to reduce such disparities. Federated-learning frameworks also help by drawing on diverse multicenter datasets without centralizing sensitive information. Continuous bias auditing, outcome monitoring, and inclusion of stakeholder feedback are critical to maintaining fairness and reliability (Boehm et al., 2022; Yang et al., 2025).

9.6.3 Interpretability and Explainability

Clinicians must understand AI recommendations to trust and act upon them. Black-box algorithms, particularly deep neural networks, can produce accurate but opaque results. Explainable AI (XAI) methods bridge this gap by visualizing how features such as MCV, ferritin, or retinal-vessel tortuosity contribute to diagnostic outcomes. Attention heatmaps, Shapley additive explanations (SHAP), and feature-importance rankings clarify the reasoning behind predictions.

In hematology, transparent algorithms enable correlation of computational decisions with known physiological mechanisms. For example, a model that attributes anemia classification primarily to low ferritin and high RDW aligns with established iron-deficiency physiology, reinforcing clinician confidence. Combining human interpretive judgment with algorithmic insights yields optimal diagnostic performance and fosters ethical accountability (Boehm et al., 2022; Dychiao et al., 2024).

9.6.4 Validation, Calibration, and Generalizability

Robust validation ensures that AI systems maintain accuracy across populations, instruments, and institutions. This involves internal validation (cross-validation within the training set), external validation (testing on independent datasets), and prospective clinical validation in real-world workflows. Models must be recalibrated periodically to account for demographic shifts, laboratory upgrades, or evolving clinical guidelines.

Generalizability requires diverse, high-quality datasets. Without such diversity, models risk overfitting specific instruments or populations. External validation across continents, such as testing Indian-developed models on African or South American datasets, enhances adaptability and global applicability (Boehm et al., 2022; Dychiao et al., 2024).

9.6.5 Regulatory, Ethical, and Legal Frameworks

The use of AI in healthcare invokes regulatory oversight and ethical scrutiny. Data privacy, informed consent, and algorithmic accountability must conform to national and international standards (e.g., GDPR, ICMR, and WHO AI ethics frameworks).

Ethical considerations include ensuring transparency in decision-making, maintaining confidentiality, and enabling user autonomy.

Regulatory frameworks should mandate risk-based classification of AI systems: diagnostic-support tools (low–moderate risk) versus autonomous decision-makers (high risk). Periodic review by multidisciplinary ethics boards ensures adherence to safety, equity, and patient-rights principles. Additionally, manufacturers and researchers must guarantee post-deployment monitoring, incident reporting, and continuous model evaluation (Boehm et al., 2022; Dychiao et al., 2024).

9.6.6 Cost, Infrastructure, and Sustainability

Implementation cost remains a major barrier to adoption, particularly in low-income settings. Infrastructure constraints such as unstable electricity, limited Internet bandwidth, and shortage of trained personnel, affect reliability. Cost–benefit analyses indicate that AI-assisted diagnostics become economically viable only when scaled across large populations and integrated into national screening programs.

Cloud-computing and edge-AI models can reduce dependency on expensive servers. Open-source frameworks lower software costs, while microfinance and government partnerships can subsidize hardware acquisition. Training local technicians and clinicians to operate AI tools fosters capacity building and long-term sustainability (Dychiao et al., 2024; Ogut, 2025).

9.6.7 Ethical Use of Patient Data and Privacy Protection

Large-scale data aggregation poses inherent privacy risks. De-identification, encryption, and differential-privacy algorithms must be applied throughout data life cycles. Federated learning offers a powerful alternative by training models locally without transferring raw data. Combining this with blockchain-based audit trails ensures traceability, consent management, and tamper-proof record keeping.

Continuous patient engagement is vital, individuals must understand how their data are used, stored, and protected. Transparent communication enhances trust and supports long-term participation in AI-based research (Boehm et al., 2022; Dychiao et al., 2024).

9.6.8 Human-AI Collaboration and Clinical Acceptance

AI tools are designed to augment, not replace, clinicians. Successful adoption depends on how effectively human expertise and algorithmic intelligence complement each other. Training programs should familiarize healthcare professionals with AI concepts, strengths, and limitations. Interactive dashboards displaying confidence intervals and reasoning trails help clinicians interpret model recommendations.

Collaborative decision-making models, where AI provides probabilistic suggestions and physicians make final judgments, yield higher diagnostic accuracy and safety than either approach alone. Integrating clinician feedback into model retraining cycles ensures continuous improvement and fosters mutual trust (Dychiao et al., 2024; Ogut, 2025).

9.7 Future Directions and Innovations

The field of fusion intelligence in anemia diagnostics is rapidly evolving. Continuous advances in computational modeling, sensor technology, and biomedical data integration promise to revolutionize how anemia is detected, classified, and managed. Future research will emphasize scalability, interpretability, personalization, and ethical governance to ensure equitable deployment across healthcare systems worldwide.

Emerging trends in multimodal AI point toward three overarching trajectories: (i) enhanced data integration and interpretability through explainable fusion models, (ii) personalized predictive systems leveraging longitudinal and wearable data, and (iii) translation of fusion intelligence from research to real-world implementation.

9.7.1 Explainable and Transparent Fusion Models

The next generation of multimodal AI systems must incorporate explainable-AI (XAI) principles that make diagnostic reasoning visible and auditable.

Hybrid systems combining symbolic reasoning (medical ontologies, decision rules) with data-driven deep learning represent a key innovation frontier. These hybrid architectures can link AI outputs directly to diagnostic criteria from WHO or the International Council for Standardization in Hematology (ICSH), ensuring consistency and transparency (Dychiao et al., 2024; Ogut, 2025; Yang et al., 2025).

9.7.2 Personalized and Predictive Anemia Management

The future of anemia care will move from episodic diagnosis to continuous, personalized management supported by AI-driven analytics. Predictive and preventive fusion frameworks will integrate longitudinal laboratory data, dietary patterns, wearable sensor outputs, and environmental information (altitude, pollution, infection exposure).

Machine-learning models can dynamically predict anemia onset or relapse weeks before laboratory confirmation, enabling early intervention (Dychiao et al., 2024; Yang et al., 2025).

Reinforcement learning could further optimize therapeutic pathways by simulating outcomes for various treatment strategies and selecting those with maximal benefit and minimal side effects. These personalized systems will promote proactive management, supporting the global transition from disease correction to health maintenance.

9.7.3 Integration of Multi-omics Data

Beyond conventional genomics, multi-omics integration, including transcriptomics, proteomics, metabolomics, and microbiomics offers unprecedented insights into the molecular underpinnings of anemia. Fusion-intelligence platforms will merge these data layers with traditional hematological indices and clinical imaging to create a multidimensional disease signature.

Such insights will facilitate discovery of novel biomarkers and therapeutic targets for specific anemia subtypes, including unexplained refractory or mixed-etiology anemia (Dychiao et al., 2024; Yang et al., 2025). Open-access global omics repositories, combined with ethical data-sharing frameworks, will accelerate knowledge transfer between institutions and reduce disparities in genomic research participation.

9.7.4 Portable, Real-Time, and Noninvasive Diagnostics

Advancements in edge computing, wearable sensors, and miniaturized optical systems are driving the emergence of portable, real-time anemia diagnostics. Smartwatches equipped with reflective photoplethysmography (PPG) and multispectral sensors can estimate hemoglobin levels continuously, while compact spectrometers quantify hemoglobin absorption signatures at multiple wavelengths.

When combined with contextual inputs such as pulse rate, oxygen saturation, and hydration status, these signals feed into multimodal AI algorithms that monitor hemoglobin trends and alert clinicians to early anemia onset. The convergence of Internet of Medical Things (IoMT) infrastructure with secure cloud databases will enable population-scale, noninvasive screening programs.

Edge-AI frameworks ensure these devices can function offline, providing point-of-care diagnostics in remote regions. Such integration will democratize access to advanced hematological surveillance globally (Dychiao et al., 2024; Yang et al., 2025).

9.7.5 Federated and Collaborative Learning Networks

To ensure privacy and inclusivity, federated-learning models allow decentralized training across institutions without centralizing patient data. This approach promotes equitable AI development by including data from underrepresented regions while adhering to data-protection laws such as GDPR and India's Digital Personal Data Protection Act. Federated learning, coupled with transfer-learning mechanisms, allows models trained in high-resource laboratories to adapt efficiently to low-resource environments with minimal retraining. Collaborative research consortia are essential to establish standardized protocols, interoperability formats, and ethical oversight structures for these networks (Dychiao et al., 2024; Yang et al., 2025).

9.7.6 Integration with Digital Health Ecosystems

Fusion intelligence will increasingly interact with electronic health records (EHRs), clinical-decision-support systems (CDSS), and national digital-health infrastructures. Integration of anemia prediction models into patient portals and mobile applications will allow continuous engagement, real-time feedback, and remote monitoring.

Automated alerts to physicians and patients can prompt early testing or therapy adjustments, reducing delays in care. Data from nutrition programs, antenatal services, and community health initiatives can be ingested by AI systems for longitudinal tracking and outcome evaluation. This holistic digital-health ecosystem will align with Sustainable Development Goal (SDG) 3.4 reducing premature mortality from noncommunicable diseases through early detection and management (Dychiao et al., 2024; Yang et al., 2025).

9.7.7 Ethical, Regulatory, and Societal Outlook

The exponential growth of medical AI demands robust governance. Ethical frameworks must evolve alongside technology, emphasizing transparency, inclusivity, accountability, and environmental sustainability. Life-cycle assessments should quantify the carbon footprint of AI infrastructures, encouraging the use of green data centers and low-power hardware.

International collaboration between policymakers, clinicians, engineers, and ethicists is essential to harmonize guidelines on clinical validation, algorithmic auditing, and post-market surveillance. Public engagement initiatives should foster awareness of both the benefits and limitations of AI-based diagnostics, preventing overreliance or misuse.

Ultimately, the success of fusion intelligence in anemia care will depend not solely on algorithmic accuracy but on the creation of trustworthy, human-centered systems that respect privacy, equity, and societal values (Boehm et al., 2022; Dychiao et al., 2024; Ogut, 2025; Yang et al., 2025).

9.8 Conclusion

9.8.1 Summary of Key Insights

Anemia continues to be a global health challenge, predominantly in low- and middle-income countries where nutritional deficiencies, inherited hemoglobinopathies, and chronic diseases coexist. Usual diagnostic methods based on isolated laboratory parameters are insufficient for precise etiological purposes.

Fusion intelligence will enhance diagnostic accuracy, accelerate decision-making and support personalized care by merging biochemical, morphological, genomic and imaging modalities into unified analytical models. On the other hand, fusion intelligence mitigates the lack of team support from other specialties like hematologists, biochemists, etc.

The translation of these technologies across diverse health settings, such as rural, hospital-based, and telemedicine networks demonstrate their potential and adaptability for the global equity in diagnostics. Noninvasive, real-time, and predictive models enable early detection, proactive intervention, and resource optimization. The following four major conclusions were highlighted in a summary of current and ongoing research.

First, by quickly and precisely recognizing and analyzing a large dataset from many streams and resources, multimodal AI systems with hybrid early, intermediate, and late fusion methods may achieve an incomparable diagnostic accuracy.

Second, in resource-poor environments where anemia is most common, automated point-of-care devices empowered by scalable fusion intelligence will democratize access to high-quality diagnoses.

Third, explainable AI (XAI) with uncertainty quantification will support the development of physicians' confidence in and utilization of fusion AI.

Fourth, federated learning of fusion AI-empowered devices will support global relevance, accuracy, and acceptability by ethical learning models based on a range of datasets from various communities and geographical areas.

In both individual and community health contexts, early detection, accurate etiological diagnosis, and adequate management of anemia depend on fusion intelligence. Integration of fusion intelligence into hematology is not a technological luxury but rather a therapeutic need.

It's time for medical professionals to shift their perspective and see AI as a cognitive partner in diagnostic reasoning rather than an auxiliary tool. Clinicians will focus on synthesis, empathy, and ethical judgment qualities that are specific to humans and cannot be replicated by artificial intelligence. Precision and equity in medical practice will be redefined by human-machine collaboration. Doctors won't be replaced by it, but those who don't employ AI will soon be replaced.

Acknowledgments The authors acknowledge the support of the Department of Health Research, Government of India and Multidisciplinary Research Unit (MRU), Baba Raghav Das (BRD) Medical College, Gorakhpur, Uttar Pradesh, India, for providing the institutional resources essential for the successful completion of this work. We thank Aditya Kumar, Scientist-2, MRU, BRD

Medical College; Maitree Upadhyay, MSc in Stem Cell and Regenerative Medicine from Manipal University and Abhinav Raj Singh, Class 12th student, Excellence Academy, Bargadahi, Gorakhpur, Uttar Pradesh, for thoughtful feedback that enhanced the clarity of this chapter.

References

An, R., Patel, S. K., O'Connor, M. J., & White, L. R. (2021). Emerging point-of-care technologies for anemia detection. *Lab on a Chip, 21*(10), 1843–1865. https://doi.org/10.1039/d0lc01235a

Asare, J. W., Appiahene, P., & Donkoh, E. T. (2023a). Detection of anaemia using medical images: A comparative study of machine learning algorithms—A systematic literature review. *Informatics in Medicine Unlocked, 40*, 101283. https://doi.org/10.1016/j.imu.2023.101283

Asare, J. W., Appiahene, P., Donkoh, E. T., & Dimauro, G. (2023b). Iron deficiency anemia detection using machine learning models: A comparative study of fingernails, palm and conjunctiva of the eye images. *Engineering Reports, 5*(12), e12667. https://doi.org/10.1002/eng2.12667

Boehm, K. M., Aft, E. F., Miller, R. N. G., & Thomas, S. P. (2022). Harnessing multimodal data integration to advance precision oncology. *Nature Reviews Cancer, 22*(2), 114–126. https://doi.org/10.1038/s41568-021-00408-3

Brittenham, G. M., Grosse, S. K., Beard, J. L., & Huang, R. Y. (2023). Biology of anemia: A public health perspective. *Journal of Nutrition, 153*(Suppl. 1), S7–S28. https://doi.org/10.1016/j.tjnut.2023.07.018

Cai, Z. X., Zhang, L. M., Wang, S. R., & Li, H. J. (2024). Paper-based microfluidic analytical device patterned by label printer for point-of-care blood glucose and hematocrit detection using 3D-printed smartphone cassette. Sensors, 24 (15), 4792. https://doi.org/10.3390/s24154792.

Chen, Y. M., Hsiao, T. H., Lin, C. H., Lee, W. C., & Huang, S. J. (2025). Unlocking precision medicine: Clinical applications of integrating health records, genetics, and immunology through artificial intelligence. *Journal of Biomedical Science, 32*(1), 16. https://doi.org/10.1186/s12929-024-01110-w

Dychiao, R. G., Santos, M. P., Fernandez, A. L., & Tanaka, K. J. (2024). Artificial intelligence and global health equity. *BMJ (Clinical Research Ed.), 387*, q2194. https://doi.org/10.1136/bmj.q2194

GBD 2021 Anaemia Collaborators, et al. (2023). Prevalence, years lived with disability, and trends in anaemia burden by severity and cause, 1990–2021: Findings from the Global Burden of Disease Study 2021. *The Lancet Haematology, 10*(9), e713–e734. https://doi.org/10.1016/S2352-3026(23)00160-6

Gómez, J. G., Parra Urueta, C., Álvarez, D. S., Hernández Riaño, V., & Ramirez-Gonzalez, G. (2025). Anemia classification system using machine learning. *Informatics, 12*(1), 19. https://doi.org/10.3390/informatics12010019

Jayakody, J. A. D. C. A., & Edirisinghe, E. A. G. A. (2020). HemoSmart: A non-invasive, machine learning based device and mobile app for anemia detection. In *Proceedings of IEEE region 10 conference (TENCON)* (pp. 1401–1406). IEEE. https://doi.org/10.1109/TENCON50793.2020.9293903

Jeevan, J., et al. (2025). Prevalence of anemia in India: A systematic review, meta-analysis and geospatial analysis. *BMC Public Health, 25*, 1270. https://doi.org/10.1186/s12889-025-22439-3

Liao, H., Zhang, S., Chen, M., & Wang, L. (2025). Application of artificial intelligence in laboratory hematology: Advances, challenges, and prospects. *Acta Pharmaceutica Sinica B*. https://doi.org/10.1016/j.apsb.2025.05.036

Obeagu, E. I. (2025). Revolutionizing hematological disorder diagnosis: Unraveling the role of artificial intelligence. *Annals of Medicine and Surgery, 87*(6), 3445–3457. https://doi.org/10.1097/MS9.0000000000003227

Ogut, E. (2025). Artificial intelligence in clinical medicine: Challenges across diagnostic imaging, clinical decision support, surgery, pathology, and drug discovery. *Clinical Practice, 15*(9), 169. https://doi.org/10.3390/clinpract15090169

Parvin, N., Joo, S. W., Jung, J. H., & Mandal, T. K. (2025). Multimodal AI in biomedicine: Pioneering the future of biomaterials, diagnostics, and personalized healthcare. *Nanomaterials, 15*(12), 895. https://doi.org/10.3390/nano15120895

Perez, K., Rodriguez, M. L., Kim, S. H., & Johnson, A. B. (2025). Investigation into application of AI and telemedicine in rural communities: A systematic literature review. *Healthcare, 13*(3), 324. https://doi.org/10.3390/healthcare13030324

Sharma, V., Mehta, P. K., Singh, R. N., & Gupta, S. (2024). Enhancing anemia detection with non-invasive Anemia Detection with AI (NiADA): Insights from clinical validations and physician observations. *Cureus, 16*(12). https://doi.org/10.7759/cureus.76369

Simon, B. D., Ozyoruk, K. B., Gelikman, D. G., Harmon, S. A., & Türkbey, B. (2025). The future of multimodal artificial intelligence models for integrating imaging and clinical metadata: A narrative review. *Diagnostic and Interventional Radiology, 31*(4), 303–312. https://doi.org/10.4274/dir.2024.242631

Sonia, R., Verma, D., Chopra, R., Singh, V., & Goswami, D. (2025). Demystifying intricate factors of nutritional anemia beyond iron deficiency—A narrative review. *Clinical Nutrition ESPEN, 69*, 745–764. https://doi.org/10.1016/j.clnesp.2025.08.034

Teoh, J. R., Dong, J., Zuo, X., Lai, K. W., Hasikin, K., & Wu, X. (2024). Advancing healthcare through multimodal data fusion: A comprehensive review of techniques and applications. *PeerJ Computer Science, 10*, e2298. https://doi.org/10.7717/peerj-cs.2298

Vohra, R., Hussain, A., Dudyala, A. K., Pahareeya, J., & Khan, W. (2022). Multi-class classification algorithms for the diagnosis of anemia in an outpatient clinical setting. *PLoS One, 17*(7), e0269685. https://doi.org/10.1371/journal.pone.0269685

Williams, A. M., Brown, K. H., Allen, L. H., Dary, O., Moorthy, D., & Suchdev, P. S. (2023). Improving anemia assessment in clinical and public health settings. *Journal of Nutrition, 153*(Suppl. 1), S29–S41. https://doi.org/10.1016/j.tjnut.2023.05.032

Yang, H., Zhang, L. Q., Kumar, P. R., & Li, S. M. (2025). Multimodal deep learning approaches for precision oncology: A comprehensive review. *Briefings in Bioinformatics, 26*(1), bbae699. https://doi.org/10.1093/bib/bbae699

Young, M. F. (2024). Time for conceptual advancement in anemia assessment? *Advances in Nutrition, 15*(10), 100293. https://doi.org/10.1016/j.advnut.2024.100293

Part III

Clinical Intelligence & Critical Care

Legal and Ethical Dimensions of AI-Driven Multimodal Treatment Response Systems in the Intensive Care Units

10

Francesca Ferretti, Roberto Garetto, Maurizio Di Masi, and Gopi Battineni

10.1 Introduction

The use of artificial intelligence (AI) in intensive care units (ICUs) has changed dramatically in the last few decades. In real time, clinical decision-support systems using AI integrate and analyze multiple data sources like electronic health records (EHRs), imaging, lab results, and physiological signals (Song et al., 2024). It promises to improve diagnostic precision, personalize treatment strategies, and improve patient outcomes. Despite these advances, ICU workflows with AI present complex legal and ethical challenges. When AI systems make clinical decisions or influence them, it's hard to determine responsibility. Human agency-based legal frameworks can't accommodate distributed responsibility among clinicians, developers, and institutions (Committee on Federal Research Regulations and Reporting Requirements, 2016). As a result of many AI models' opacity, particularly deep learning systems, patients and providers may not be able to explain how decisions are made, which leads to questions about explainability and informed consent, which leads to a lot of questions (Mir & Rizvi, 2025).

In addition, there are ethical considerations, and AI systems can inadvertently perpetuate or amplify existing biases, especially if they're trained on

F. Ferretti
Scuola Superiore Meridionale di Napoli, Naples, Italy

R. Garetto
International Legal Institute of Turin, Turin, Italy

M. Di Masi
University of Perugia, Perugia, Italy

G. Battineni (✉)
Computer Science and Information Systems, University of Limerick, Limerick, Ireland

Clinical Research Centre, University Camerino, Macerata, Italy
e-mail: gopi.battineni@ul.ie

U. Venkatesh et al. (eds.), *Multimodal AI in Healthcare*,
https://doi.org/10.1007/978-981-95-9027-8_10

nonrepresentative data (Ferrara, 2024). Therefore, marginalized populations may get different treatment recommendations. Additionally, using sensitive patient data for training and operating these systems raises privacy, governance, and consent concerns, especially in jurisdictions with inconsistent or evolving laws. Additionally, there's a problem with human values being undermined in clinical care (Johnson et al., 2021). AI systems may lose their nuanced, empathic, and context-sensitive judgments as they become more autonomous. It's been argued that AI enhances decision-making but shouldn't replace clinicians' roles in interpreting patient values, preferences, and social contexts. Healthcare values like beneficence, nonmaleficence, autonomy, and justice must be aligned with AI deployment.

These challenges require a multidisciplinary approach when developing and implementing AI in ICUs. To make sure innovation in critical care doesn't compromise trust, equity, or human dignity, we need robust legal frameworks, ethical guidelines, and technical standards. The purpose of this chapter is to examine the legal and ethical implications of implementing AI-driven multimodal treatment response systems in ICUs. Specifically, the study aims to provide a balanced analysis of the benefits and risks of critical care technologies and make recommendations for responsible development, deployment, and governance.

10.2 Benefits and Challenges of AI in ICUs

Considering ICUs are the most data-rich and high-stakes environments in medicine, integrating AI into them makes a lot of sense. Critical care could be revolutionized with AI's enhanced diagnostics, personalized treatments, and improved ICU operations. However, to unlock the potential of multimodal AI systems, we need to figure out how to integrate data, make models transparent, and deploy them ethically. By combining clinicians and AI tools, we may be able to deliver safer, faster, and more effective care to the sickest patients in the future. For this vision to come true, data scientists, clinicians, ethicists, and policymakers must work together continuously. It's possible to improve patient outcomes, optimize workflows, and reduce clinician workload with AI, especially through multimodal systems. In this section, we'll talk about definitions, types, applications, and challenges of AI-driven multimodal systems.

10.2.1 Definition and Types of AI-Driven Multimodal Systems

AI-driven multimodal systems use computational models to integrate and interpret data from multiple sources. Critical care can use structured EHRs, imaging technologies like computed tomography (CT), magnetic resonance imaging (MRI), X-rays, waveform data (ECG, EEG), laboratory results, and clinician notes. These systems make it possible to synthesize heterogeneous data types, which is why they're so powerful. AI in critical care includes rule-based expert systems, machine learning (ML), natural language processing (NLP), and multimodal fusion systems.

Initially, rule-based systems used predefined "if-then" rules to make clinical decisions, but they couldn't handle complex, nonlinear relationships in datasets.

Predicting outcomes is easier with data-driven models like logistic regression (LR), decision trees, support vector machines (SVMs), and random forests. Although deep learning (DL) models can learn hierarchical representations of data, this is especially useful when analyzing unstructured data, like medical images. Besides being able to analyze unstructured texts like clinical notes, radiology reports, and other unstructured texts, NLP can also be used to develop context-aware tools for healthcare. In a simulated ICU environment, reinforcement learning (RL) is used to teach optimal treatment strategies through trial-and-error interactions. In medicine, it's a great tool for managing dynamic treatment protocols, like sepsis. By integrating structured and unstructured data streams, these solutions can provide holistic insights based on radiological images, lab values, clinical notes, and more.

10.2.2 AI Role in ICUs

AI is used extensively in critical care, including real-time monitoring, predictive analytics, and treatment optimization. Using AI systems to prioritize patients based on risk scores can help allocate resources and provide timely intervention (Carroll et al., 2022). Using AI, it is possible to predict adverse events such as sepsis, acute kidney injury (Cheungpasitporn et al., 2024), respiratory failure, and cardiac arrest well before they occur. ICU mortality or organ failure can be predicted with models such as DeepSOFA (Shickel et al., 2019) or InSight (Patel, 2025) hours before symptoms appear. Based on the risk scores of patients, these systems help allocate resources more efficiently and provide timely interventions.

Diagnoses, treatment plans, and medication dosing can be improved by AI-driven clinical decision support systems. IBM Watson is aimed at a broad audience, but it illustrates how clinical decision support systems (CDSS) are relevant to intensive care units and suggests differential diagnoses based on EHR and imaging data, as well as warns of potentially harmful drug interactions. CT, X-ray, and ultrasound images can be analyzed using deep learning algorithms to detect pneumothorax, pulmonary edema, and hemorrhage (Horng et al., 2021). Using these models, diagnostic delays are reduced, and seizure and arrhythmia detection can be accomplished in real time (Muzammil et al., 2024). Like early sepsis detection, AI in ICUs can detect subtle changes in temperature, heart rate, and lab results indicative of sepsis onset, allowing clinicians to initiate treatment sooner (Haas & McGill, 2022).

AI algorithms can suggest personalized ventilator settings by modeling lung compliance and oxygenation response (Stivi et al., 2024). Like sedation, AI can optimize analgesia regimens by analyzing patient-specific responses. Furthermore, AI can facilitate the management of ICUs by predicting demand for beds, supply shortages, and staff workloads, which can be especially helpful during pandemics or mass casualties (Gonzalez et al., 2024). Planning discharge and counseling for patients can be helped by predicting ICU mortality, readmission, and stay length

(Luo et al., 2025). Using historical ICU data, AI models provide more accurate estimations than traditional scoring methods.

10.2.3 Benefits and Challenges

AI can identify complications early and support personalized treatment, which reduces mortality and morbidity. Studies show AI-based alerts can lower mortality by 15% in intensive care units (Aakula, 2025; Gonzalez et al., 2024; Singh et al., 2025). Routine tasks like chart reviews, documentation, and preliminary diagnostics can be automated with AI to reduce clinician workload and burnout. The patient-centered care provided by healthcare providers can be improved as a result. Through real-time analysis of patient data and alert generation, AI can respond sooner to deteriorating patients' conditions, and continuous monitoring ensures no critical changes are overlooked (Cho et al., 2020). By comparing patient data and historical patterns, AI can identify inconsistencies or dangerous decisions, such as making errors or contraindications. In addition to reducing inter-physician variability and ensuring uniform care quality, these models can help implement evidence-based guidelines consistently.

While AI has many potential applications in critical care, its adoption faces several challenges. The data collected in ICUs is often noisy, incomplete, and stored across multiple systems in a variety of formats. Bringing multimodal data together into a unified platform can be resource-intensive and challenging. Most AI models are trained on data from specific hospitals and may not generalize well across different patient populations or clinical settings without external validation and calibration. Clinicians may hesitate to trust AI systems with unknowable inner workings when they use black-box models, especially deep learning algorithms. To ensure compliance with these systems that influence medical decisions, regulations such as the Health Insurance Portability and Accountability Act (HIPAA), the General Data Protection Regulation (GDPR), and the Food and Drug Administration (FDA) are essential. Additionally, algorithmic bias and patient consent must be addressed. Due to significant investments in hardware, software, and cybersecurity, many healthcare facilities are not equipped to implement AI solutions. It will be easier for humans and machines to collaborate if workflows and training paradigms are adapted for AI.

10.3 Legal and Ethical Infrastructures for AI in Healthcare

This section examines the legal frameworks shaping the AI integration into healthcare, highlighting their strengths and limitations in addressing the normative challenges posed by algorithmic systems. These analyses call for a legal paradigm capable of governing AI not merely through compliance, but through equity, accountability, and structural awareness.

10.3.1 Regulatory Frameworks and Compliance

The AI incorporation into healthcare systems marks a disruptive transformation that challenges not only traditional clinical practices but also the legal foundations upon which those practices rest. Regulatory frameworks, especially those developed within the EU, are attempting to catch up with the rapid evolution of AI technologies by adopting a risk-sensitive, sector-specific approach. However, from a critical legal perspective, this adaptation often reveals the limitations of liberal legalism in adequately addressing the socio-technical complexities and distributive consequences of AI in medicine. In the context of the European Union, Regulation (EU) 2024/1689, introduces a "risk-based" model—originally set out in the European Commission's 2021 proposal for an Artificial Intelligence Act—distinguishing AI systems based on their potential impact on safety and fundamental rights. In this hierarchy, healthcare-related AI systems, such as diagnostic algorithms, robotic surgery platforms, and clinical decision support tools, are classified as "high-risk," subjecting them to strict requirements around transparency, documentation, human oversight, and conformity assessments. At first glance, this approach seems prudent: it prioritizes the protection of individuals and the minimization of harm. However, an informed critique reveals its limitations. First, the concept of "risk" is itself historically contingent and institutionally constructed. It can be observed that the law's emphasis on technological safety can obscure more fundamental political questions, such as who benefits from AI implementation in healthcare? Who bears the cost of algorithmic failures or of overregulation that stifles access to innovation (Allegranti et al., 2023).

Moreover, the AI Regulation maintains an anthropocentric and arguably anachronistic vision of legal subjectivity and responsibility. Autonomous systems that make clinically significant decisions or recommendations remain legally invisible as actors. Instead, liability and regulatory obligations are imposed exclusively on human developers, providers, and users. This tension is particularly evident in the notion of "human oversight," which the AI Regulation elevates to a central pillar of legitimacy for high-risk systems. Yet, in practice, oversight is often formal, superficial, or structurally impossible. Clinical staff may lack the time, expertise, or access to interrogate the logic of an opaque algorithm embedded in an electronic health record system. As a result, the legal insistence on human control risks becoming a symbolic gesture, serving the function of legitimizing technological expansion rather than protecting patient autonomy.

From a critical viewpoint, this exposes the ideological function of legal form as the AI Regulation appears to potentially radical technology by translating it into familiar categories including risk, compliance, conformity thereby neutralizing its challenge to existing distributions of power within healthcare. AI systems are not neutral tools but embedded political actors that reflect the values, biases, and priorities of those who design and implement them (Farhud & Zokaei, 2021). A regulatory framework that fails to interrogate these socio-technical dynamics risks legitimizing inequality under the guise of risk management. Finally, the AI Regulation's harmonization objective—i.e., ensuring legal certainty across the

Digital Single Market—must be assessed critically. While harmonization may facilitate innovation and cross-border deployment, it also imposes uniformity on diverse healthcare contexts. What is deemed an acceptable risk in a well-resourced urban hospital may be intolerable in a rural or underfunded healthcare setting. Without meaningful space for local adaptation, the regulatory framework may entrench systemic disparities rather than correct them.

10.3.2 Data Privacy and Security

The digital transformation of healthcare has radically reframed the question of medical confidentiality, shifting it from the ethical terrain of professional secrecy to the legal architecture of data protection. Within this shift, the GDPR (Reg. EU 2016/679) represents not merely a normative safeguard, but a paradigmatic moment in the juridification of informational subjectivity. In its treatment of health data defined in Article 9 as a "special category of personal data" the GDPR constructs a regime of heightened protection premised on consent, purpose limitation, data minimization, and accountability. However, from a critical legal standpoint, this regime is as much a site of tension and structural opacity as it is of protection. First, the GDPR enshrines a model of informational self-determination that presumes an autonomous, rational, and digitally literate data subject. This liberal subject is expected to navigate privacy notices, exercise granular control over consent, and understand the complex flows of their medical data across cloud infrastructures, health platforms, and AI diagnostic systems. In practice, this subject does not exist. As several empirical studies show, patients particularly those in vulnerable positions rarely have the resources, knowledge, or negotiating power to make informed decisions about their data (Ocloo et al., 2021). The critical gap between normative ideal and structural reality renders much of the GDPR's protective promise illusory.

Secondly, the regulation's emphasis on individual consent as the main lawful basis for data processing in healthcare contexts is profoundly ambivalent. On one hand, it empowers patients to refuse the commodification or misuse of their medical information; on the other, it shifts the burden of risk and responsibility from institutions to individuals. Consent, when required for accessing essential services or when obtained through opaque interfaces, risks becoming a formalistic ritual what some scholars have called "privacy theatre" (Kitkowska et al., 2023). This is especially problematic in AI-driven environments where secondary data use (e.g., algorithm training, model refinement) are difficult to anticipate and explain now of data collection. Moreover, the GDPR's data security provisions (Articles 32–34) obligate data controllers and processors to adopt "appropriate technical and organizational measures." While this sounds robust, the regulation does not prescribe specific encryption standards, architectural safeguards, or audit protocols—leaving a broad zone of discretion that often privileges efficiency and cost-saving over patient safety. In the context of AI, where large-scale data aggregation, cloud storage, and automated processing are routine, such ambiguity becomes fertile ground for systemic under protection. As noted in legal analyses of digital health systems, compliance with formal security checklists often masks underlying vulnerabilities, especially in decentralized or fragmented health networks.

Further critique concerns the transnational dimension of patient data management. The GDPR formally forbids transmissions of personal data to third countries that do not guarantee "adequate" protection. Yet in practice, exceptions are common, particularly under mechanisms like standard contractual clauses or public interest derogations. This flexibility motivated by the globalized nature of the health tech market risks exposing EU health data to surveillance, misuse, or commercial exploitation by actors in jurisdictions with weaker legal safeguards. The uneven global governance of digital health data thus replicates postcolonial asymmetries, where the Global North extracts informational value from populations in the Global South under the banner of innovation and research. Finally, from a critical legal perspective, privacy and security should not be treated merely as compliance issues, but as sites of distributive justice. Data protection laws must not only prevent unauthorized access but also resist the concentration of informational power in the hands of a few dominant tech-health actors. Many scholars—most notably Shoshana Zuboff—have argued that the commodification of personal data, especially in the health sector, reconfigures the relationship between citizens and institutions, creating new forms of informational asymmetry and surveillance capitalism. The GDPR, while formally resisting this dynamic, has yet to meaningfully address its structural drivers (Zuboff, 2019).

10.3.3 Intellectual Property Issues

The use of AI in healthcare introduces complex questions concerning intellectual property (IP), particularly relating to the entitlement over algorithms, data, and AI-generated outputs. These issues are amplified by the convergence of public and private interests, the growing role of proprietary software in clinical decision-making, and the dependence of many AI systems on large-scale health data collected in public institutions. At the core of the intellectual property debate is the ownership and control of the AI models themselves. Many advanced systems used in diagnostic imaging, patient monitoring, and predictive analytics are developed by private companies using proprietary algorithms. These models are often protected by copyright, trade secrets, or patents, which may limit transparency and hinder the ability of healthcare professionals and regulators to fully understand or audit how decisions are made. This can become especially problematic in critical clinical scenarios where explainability and traceability are essential for ensuring safety, fairness, and patient consent.

Another central issue involves the training datasets for AI systems. While healthcare data are often generated within public hospitals and through publicly funded research, access to these datasets is frequently granted to private entities under licensing agreements. Questions arise over who holds the rights to these datasets, how value is extracted from them, and whether patients whose data underpin the system should be recognized as stakeholders in the innovation process. Furthermore, the reuse of patient data for secondary purposes, such as training commercial AI models, must be carefully evaluated from both legal and ethical perspectives, particularly when patients have not explicitly consented to such uses.

AI-generated outputs also present legal uncertainty. In contexts such as personalized treatment recommendations or drug discovery, AI systems may generate results that carry significant clinical or commercial value. However, it remains unclear under current legal frameworks who can claim rights over these outputs—whether the developer of the AI system, the healthcare provider deploying it, or the institution hosting the data infrastructure. Traditional IP regimes, which were not designed for autonomous or semi-autonomous systems, may struggle to allocate rights in a way that reflects the complexity and interdependence of the actors involved. Additionally, there is growing concern that IP protections may restrict interoperability and collaboration. Closed, proprietary systems may impede integration with other digital health technologies, limit innovation, and create dependencies on a small number of dominant providers. Promoting open standards, open-source solutions, and collaborative models of innovation could help address these risks, while still ensuring that developers are appropriately incentivized and recognized.

10.3.4 Case Studies and Legal Precedents

Legal systems across Europe have only begun to confront the implications of AI in healthcare through litigation and policy reforms. While judicial engagement with fully autonomous AI systems remains limited, existing legal frameworks (particularly those regulating telemedicine, informed consent, and healthcare documentation) offer a valuable foundation for understanding how law mediates the rise of algorithmically supported clinical decision-making. Yet these frameworks, as recent European developments illustrate, are marked by conceptual inertia: they struggle to accommodate the epistemic and distributive shifts introduced by AI, particularly within more rigid or path-dependent regulatory environments. In contrast, smaller jurisdictions—benefiting from more agile and centralized legal structures—may be better positioned to adapt swiftly and proactively to the evolving demands of AI governance (Vujičić, 2024).

A prominent area of legal reflection has emerged around the notion of informed consent in digitally mediated care. Italian scholarship has emphasized that, within telemedicine, consent must not be reduced to a procedural signature on a precompiled form. Instead, it must be reconstructed as a substantial expression of the patient's autonomy and self-determination. This includes full awareness not only of the medical risks and benefits of a given procedure, but also of the technological infrastructures—AI systems, smart interfaces, data flows—that shape how information is delivered, and decisions are taken. In particular, the implementation of the Fascicolo Sanitario Elettronico (FSE)—Italy's electronic health record system—exemplifies how documentation practices are evolving under digital and algorithmic pressure. The FSE falls within the scope of concurrent competences in healthcare, being managed by the regions within a national regulatory and infrastructural framework. This regional dimension may, as pointed out above, enable more agile responses and allow local systems to engage dynamically with emerging challenges in AI governance. The FSE not only archives clinical acts but also interacts with decision-support tools and predictive analytics. Although it expands informational continuity, it also risks codifying patient identity into data architectures that are inaccessible, opaque, and difficult to contest. The tension between documentation and discretion becomes more acute when clinicians rely on algorithmically produced outputs whose reasoning is not fully comprehensible, neither to the professional nor to the patient (Guarda & Ducato, 2016).

Within the Italian legal framework, telemedicine has been further institutionalized through national guidelines and digital health strategies. A recurring factor across areas situated in diverse geographical contexts—yet sharing a demographic structure characterized by a highly aged population and rural dispersion—is the pronounced legal significance of telehealth infrastructures (Gajarawala & Pelkowski, 2020). As noted in the collaboration between the regional government and the Istituto Nazionale di Ricovero e Cura per Anziani (INRCA), AI-supported telemedicine is framed not only as a service enhancement, but as a tool for implementing the constitutional right to health under Article 32 of Italian Constitution, operating at the regional rather than national level. This implementation, however, depends on complex institutional mediation and is shaped by asymmetric access to technological infrastructures (Garetto et al., 2022).

In contexts where care is mediated by AI, responsibility tends to be framed through conventional categories of physician negligence, equipment failure, or institutional liability. Yet such framings obscure the collective and infrastructural nature of harm in algorithmic environments. The "delegation" of care to digital infrastructures—when not accompanied by new norms of transparency, explainability, and auditability—risks undermining the very conditions of legal responsibility (Garetto et al., 2022). From a critical legal standpoint, these dynamics suggest that existing legal institutions are insufficiently equipped to manage the distributive and epistemic complexity of AI-driven healthcare. The tendency to personalize liability, in a system increasingly governed by collective machine-human assemblages, reveals a deeper reluctance of law to engage with the social embeddedness of technological decision-making. What is needed is not merely doctrinal adjustment, but a reorientation of legal reasoning toward models of co-responsibility, infrastructural transparency, and participatory design.

10.3.5 Ethical Challenges: Autonomy, Bias, and Algorithmic Justice

The implementation of AI in healthcare raises a cluster of interconnected ethical and legal challenges, especially concerning patient autonomy, algorithmic bias, and the uneven distribution of harms and benefits. At the core of this debate lies a structural asymmetry between those who design and control AI systems, and those often patients in vulnerable or marginalized positions who are subjected to their outputs.

A critical legal approach reveals that current frameworks of consent, fairness, and risk mitigation often operate as formal abstractions, detached from the lived realities of digital healthcare. AI systems promise to enhance diagnostic accuracy, optimize workflows, and personalize care. Yet these benefits are not neutral. They are embedded in socio-technical infrastructures shaped by historical inequalities, institutional priorities, and commercial interests. For example, algorithmic bias resulting from skewed training datasets or socially encoded assumptions can lead to discriminatory outcomes, particularly against racialized groups, women, and persons with disabilities. Such bias is not a technical glitch but a distributive injustice, one that law often fails to name, let alone address. Legal systems tend to individualize faults, ignoring the collective processes through which algorithmic discrimination is produced and sustained.

The same limitations apply to the principle of patient autonomy. While informed consent is widely recognized as a cornerstone of medical ethics, its application in AI-mediated contexts remains largely underdeveloped. Patients are rarely informed of the role played by automated decision systems, nor of the limitations and uncertainties they carry. Even when consent is formally obtained often via digital interfaces this does not guarantee comprehension, nor empower genuine choice and in such cases, risks becoming a ritualized practice of institutional legitimacy rather than a tool of emancipation (Abujarad et al., 2021). Furthermore, the lack of transparency in AI systems can complicate efforts to detect and correct bias. If a patient is denied access to treatment or misdiagnosed based on an algorithmic prediction, they may lack the means to understand why, let alone to challenge it. Explainability often invoked as a solution—remains a contested and underregulated domain. The law, in its current state, offers little in the way of substantive rights to explanation, appeal, or redress for algorithmic harms.

10.3.6 Transparency and Explainability

Transparency and explainability are key conditions for ethical and lawful AI deployment in healthcare. As AI systems increasingly support clinical decisions—ranging from diagnostics to treatment recommendations their ability to offer clear, understandable justifications for their outputs becomes crucial. Without this, patients, practitioners, and regulators are left in a position of epistemic dependence on systems they cannot scrutinize or contest. Explainability refers to the capacity of an AI system to make its decision-making processes interpretable to human users. In healthcare, this is particularly important because clinical decisions can have life-altering consequences. When a diagnostic algorithm suggests a course of action, both the clinician and the patient must be able to understand the reason behind it, whether to validate the decision, reject it, or integrate it into a broader treatment plan. The absence of this transparency undermines trust, impedes accountability, and poses risks to both clinical safety and legal compliance.

From a legal standpoint, the right to explanation, especially in data protection frameworks may be difficult to guarantee when the model cannot be unpacked.

From an ethical perspective, lack of transparency compromises the informed consent process and may leave patients unaware of how their data has been used or why a particular clinical path was chosen. To address this, efforts have been made to develop explainable AI (XAI) systems specifically tailored for healthcare (Mir & Rizvi, 2025). These models prioritize interpretability, often using simpler algorithms, visualization tools, or feature attribution methods that allow users to see which data inputs contributed most significantly to a given outcome. While there may be trade-offs between explainability and performance, especially in complex clinical scenarios, a balance must be struck to ensure that accuracy does not come at the cost of clarity. Transparency also relates to broader questions of system design and governance. Developers and healthcare institutions must clearly document how AI models are trained, what data they use, what assumptions are embedded in their architecture, and how they are validated and updated over time. This documentation should be made accessible not only to technical experts but also to clinicians, patients, and oversight bodies. Transparency in this sense is not only a technical requirement but also a democratic one: it enables public scrutiny and supports collective trust in the deployment of AI in healthcare.

10.4 Legal Responsibility in Multimodal AI Systems in ICUs

This section explores the evolution of legal liability frameworks in relation to the integration of AI into clinical decision-making, with a particular focus on high-risk settings such as intensive care units.

10.4.1 The Crisis of Traditional Attribution Models: Who Decides, Who Is Liable?

The high performance of data-driven systems in critical settings like ICUs produces ambivalent effects. On the one hand, it entails a problematic reduction of qualitative, patient-centered medicine and on the other, it brings a marked improvement in the accuracy, timeliness, and precision of clinical decisions, thanks to the capacity of multimodal AI to integrate heterogeneous data from various sources into a unified decision-making synthesis. However, these improved clinical outcomes are grounded in statistical and aggregated evidence: they do not automatically translate into better quality of individual medical acts, nor do they strengthen the personal doctor patient relationship, an area where a proper legal framing of responsibility remains crucial. A broader concept of responsibility is therefore needed, understood not merely as the ex post attribution of errors, but as the capacity to make decisions under uncertainty and to bear the consequences of those decisions. In clinical settings, this corresponds to assuming full ownership of diagnostic and therapeutic choices.

When algorithmic output decisively influences or determines the final decision, identifying the actual decision-maker and thus the legally responsible subject becomes significantly more complex. While the physician formally retains decision-making authority, they may find themselves in a position of cognitive or epistemic dependence on the AI system, ultimately reduced to a mere technical executor of its outputs. Such delegation is legally inadmissible: it not only violates the principle of human-in-the-loop oversight but also undermines professional competence, fostering processes of deskilling. Some scholars have invoked a model of physician–machine co-decision, inspired by actor-network theory, that interprets interaction with AI as a cooperative process. However, even this reading proves misleading, as the physician is required to retain final evaluative control. In these scenarios, the intelligent device remains purely instrumental in nature, and legal responsibility lies entirely with the physician, who must reclaim the decision by filtering, contextualizing, or if necessary, disregarding the algorithmic recommendation. Subjective (negligence-based) liability may therefore arise both when the physician unjustifiably deviates from a correct AI recommendation, and when they adhere to it uncritically, without clinical validation. The claim that a physician who relies on the machine should not be held liable, as they did not truly participate in the decision-making process, is thus incorrect. Such a position would imply a form of automatic legitimization of the algorithm—one as uncritical as it is dangerous—which risks dissolving the centrality of human responsibility in future medicine (Schwartz, 1983).

Nevertheless, the described model of liability for medical negligence does not exhaust all legally relevant hypotheses. Consideration must be given to cases in which multimodal AI is embedded in automated devices capable of directly executing therapeutic interventions. In such contexts, the physician's decision-making space is drastically reduced, giving rise to new profiles of liability, beyond professional responsibility alone. At that point, institutional and corporate liability come into play, namely, the responsibility of the healthcare facility as owner and operator of the system, and of the manufacturer for placing a potentially defective device on the market. The American legal system offers illustrative examples, having addressed these issues through specific tools of product liability, including the malfunction doctrine and the learned intermediary doctrine, originally developed for medical robotics and now applied to AI-based technologies (Beglinger, 2019).

The malfunction doctrine eases the burden of proof on the claimant by allowing the inference of a defect from the mere malfunction of the device, provided it was used correctly and no alternative causes exist. However, this presumption does not apply if the physician is a co-defendant and fault can be demonstrated, in which case the human conduct absorbs the technical fault. Moreover, its probative value in AI cases remains controversial, as illustrated by a well-known case involving the Da Vinci robot, where a display error alone was deemed insufficient by the court to clearly demonstrate a product defect. This has led to doctrinal proposals to update the theory, introducing a presumption of defects in the event of malfunction under proper conditions of use, with a reversal of the burden of proof placed on the manufacturer, who would then be required to demonstrate the presence of external factors excluding their presumed liability.

The learned intermediary doctrine, which imposes a duty on the manufacturer to inform the qualified end user, typically the physician, has been extended by

American case law to include the healthcare institution, recognized as a central actor in the care process. From this perspective, the manufacturer is obliged to train not only physicians but also the healthcare organization, which may be held liable for the proper integration and management of the devices, even in the absence of individual medical negligence. This marks a shift toward objectivizing liability: the mere presence and use of the device within the institution, in the absence of adequate oversight, verification, or training, may trigger institutional liability. In such cases, error does not stem from a clinical act, but from systemic failures in the governance of innovation. However, this delicate equilibrium of responsibilities is now increasingly unstable, challenged by the emergence of AI systems that are more autonomous, opaque, and deeply integrated into the operational and decision-making structures of critical care. In a context where roles blur and decisions are automated, the distribution of liability along the chain of actors becomes more complex, making a normative and conceptual revision of existing legal models both urgent and necessary.

10.4.2 The Chain of Responsibility: Physician, Institution, Manufacturer

The adoption of multimodal AI systems in clinical settings requires a deep reconfiguration of the traditional liability paradigm, which has historically been centered exclusively on the use phase and the conduct of medical personnel. Legal responsibility can no longer be confined to the final moment of care delivery but must extend retroactively along the entire lifecycle of the intelligent device, encompassing the stages of design, development, training, validation, and assembly. This shift in perspective moves the legal focus away from the clinical use of the device and toward the prior phases of production and integration of AI systems into medical technologies. As a result, the range of potentially liable parties expands, including but not replacing the physician and the healthcare institution.

What distinguishes AI systems from other technologies used in medicine is the depth of their production chain, determined by their composite and layered nature. Embedded AI systems do not merely support medical decision-making but are capable of autonomously executing therapeutic interventions, significantly narrowing the scope of human intervention. This technical complexity corresponds to an organizational complexity, in which the system's development is entrusted to multiple actors, each responsible for a specific segment: functional design, software coding, preparation of training data, algorithmic training, hardware manufacturing, final assembly, testing, and distribution. Given this fragmentation, harm to the patient is rarely attributable to a single direct cause but usually results from the interaction between human conduct and technological malfunction giving rise to a multi-agent tort involving a plurality of potentially jointly liable actors (Widder & Nafus, 2023).

While this scenario may appear advantageous to patient multiplying the number of actors against whom a claim can be brought, it also carries a structural risk: the fragmentation of the decision-making and production chain may serve as a mechanism for systemic de-responsibilities, allowing blame to shift endlessly among parties and ultimately leaving the harm without a clearly identifiable legal subject. Hence the urgent need—already recognized in comparative legal practice—to clearly define the duty-bearing roles and structurally responsible actors within the clinical innovation chain.

EU law has responded significantly to this need, updating its liability framework through the new rules on defective products. One of the most important developments is the inclusion, among the relevant components of a product, of associated digital services that are essential to its functioning. This overcomes the outdated distinction between product and service, which under the previous directive 85/374/EEC excluded from the scope of product liability all intangible activities, even when indispensable to AI functionality. Under the new EU directive 2024/2853, any provider of digital services that are functionally incorporated into the system and constitute a condition for its operation is also to be considered as a producer. In data-driven systems, this specifically concerns the trainer, who provides the training data and supervises the system's learning process. These actors perform critically, not merely auxiliary functions and must therefore be included among those potentially liable in the event of harm caused by system malfunction (Buiten, 2024).

From a practical standpoint, the legal relevance of the multiple actors involved emerges only when these activities are performed by independent entities, rather than within a single integrated organization. However, even in the latter case, liability is not simplified: the final producer who assembles and places the AI-powered device on the market remains liable for the entire process, albeit with the possibility of seeking contractual redress from internal or external parties involved in the system's design. In the case of embedded AI, the chain becomes even more extended: in addition to the previously mentioned actors, hardware manufacturers enter the picture, responsible for building the mechanical body into which the intelligent software is integrated. Here too, the same fragmentation applies to design, production, and testing may be internal or outsourced.

At the top of the chain is the company that markets the finished product, often acting as integrator and orchestrator of a complex system. This entity may have directly developed one or more components or merely assembled them, but in either case it retains the status of "producer." This central role entails a duty of vigilance and verification over the system's overall reliability and represents the legal interface between manufacturing liability and enterprise accountability. In a regulatory framework that tends to assign risk to those who derive economic benefit from placing the product on the market, the lead enterprise becomes the primary legal point of contact for the harmed patient, who retains the right to pursue direct action.

10.4.3 Reconstructive Approaches: Joint Liability Versus One-Stop-Shop

A possible solution to the issue of multi-agent torts—frequently encountered in the use of multimodal AI systems in intensive care—is the adoption of the principle of joint liability. In this context, the medical act often constitutes only the causal antecedent that enables the malfunction or unpredictable behavior of the intelligent device to materialize. When patient harm arises from a combination of human and technological actions, the joint liability model enables responsibility for the same event to be assigned to multiple actors, without the need to prove coordination or a shared intent.(Custers et al., 2025).

Across European legal systems, the principle of joint liability provides a legally meaningful solution when several actors, though acting independently, causally contribute to the same clinical harm. Table 10.1 presents the comparative overview of legal provisions in the EU and associated nations.

The underlying rationale is to guarantee the injured party a reliable compensation channel without requiring them to disentangle the specific shares of responsibility of each actor in the chain. In this context, joint liability serves not only a compensatory function but also a systemic one: it helps prevent the ping-pong of blame between physicians, institutions, and manufacturers, which could otherwise leave the patient without effective redress. Though it results in a more onerous risk distribution for the economic operators involved, the joint liability model adheres to principles of substantive justice and efficiency, especially in the presence of opaque technologies and multifactorial causal processes.

However, joint liability is not the only possible solution to multi-agent harm. While it provides an effective remedy for the injured party, it also presents structural challenges, particularly in technologically complex fields such as the clinical use of

Table 10.1 Comparative overview different jurisdictions

Jurisdiction	Legal provision	Summary
Italy	Article 2055 Civil Code	Establishes joint liability for parties contributing to the same harm, even if they acted independently or without coordination; applies to both tort and contract
Spain	Article 1137 Civil Code	Excludes presumption of joint liability for concurrent obligors, but courts/doctrine extend joint liability in tort law based on distributive fairness
France	Articles 1310, 1313, 1317 Code civil	No explicit joint liability, but judicial doctrine (solidarité fautive) permits shared liability among co-authors of harm, even without coordination
Germany	840 BGB	Provides automatic joint liability for multiple individuals liable for the same event, regardless of joint action
European Union	Article 5, Directive 85/374/EEC	Recognizes joint liability in the supply chain for damage from defective products
European Union	Article 12, Directive (EU) 2024/2853	Expands joint liability to include digital services and complex intelligent products (e.g., AI systems)

multimodal AI. First, joint liability implies that each actor involved—physician, hospital, manufacturer, developer is liable for the entire damage amount, even if their causal contribution was marginal. This may lead to disproportionate deterrent effects, disincentivizing innovation or penalizing smaller actors with limited contractual leverage and encouraging overcompliance and defensive medicine.

Second, there is a risk of conflating distinct forms of liability, placing on the same level professional medical negligence, product defects, and informational or training obligations even though these are governed by different legal regimes. Third, from a procedural standpoint, joint liability can complicate litigation, with heavily responsible manufacturers attempting to shift blame onto clinicians or institutions leading to cross-claims and delaying effective compensation. Considering these issues, an alternative has been proposed in the recent AI report and Civil Liability (Bertolini, 2025), which advocates for a unitary model of liability centered on a key factor in the chain. This model is inspired by the "one-stop-shop" approach already known in EU data protection law (GDPR, Article 56). According to this logic, the goal is not to analytically divide responsibility shares but to identify a central legal entity (lead entity) to whom primary liability is assigned, leaving that actor free to seek recourse or indemnification from other contributors.

In the healthcare context, this model could translate into assigning liability to the producer of the AI system understood as the actor exercising functional and organizational control over the algorithm's lifecycle, including training, validation, maintenance, and updating activities. Centralizing risk at the level of the producer responds not only to efficiency but also to fairness, as the producer is typically the party that derives the most economic benefit from the system's commercialization. The "one-stop" model does not aim to exempt other parties from liability, but to simplify the patient's path to compensation by providing a single legal interlocutor without precluding subsequent determinations of contributory fault within the chain. From this perspective, harm caused by AI is not treated as a fragmented tort to be distributed, but as a centralized organizational risk for which the actor with technical and managerial control over the intelligent system bears initial responsibility. This model, already under discussion in the European legal sphere, deserves careful consideration within comparative civil law, particularly considering the limits of traditional frameworks and the growing causal opacity of AI systems.

10.4.4 Accountability as Legal Risk Governance: From Reaction to Design

In the evolving regulatory landscape of AI applied to healthcare, a fundamental distinction emerges between safety rules and liability rules, a dichotomy that continues to shape, among other areas, the European framework for product regulation. This distinction is embodied in two complementary legal instruments: Regulation (EU) 2023/988 on general product safety and Directive (EU) 2024/2853 on liability for defective products (Gikay et al., 2023). A central legal question concerns whether compliance with statutory safety requirements is sufficient to classify a product as "non-defective," or whether such compliance should be regarded as a necessary but not sufficient condition to exclude the manufacturer's liability toward private users.

A comparison with the U.S. model provides a useful point of reference. Under the so-called preemption doctrine, product compliance with federal safety standards is treated as a complete defense: once conformity is established, tort actions under state law are, in principle, precluded. In this configuration, regulatory compliance is not merely probative but operates as a substantive limitation on civil liability. As a result, any harm suffered by the patient would fall on the user of the device, namely, the healthcare professional rather than on the manufacturer. This framework, however, remains a minority position in the European context. While there is a broad consensus that noncompliance with safety standards automatically renders a product defective, the inverse that compliance alone suffices to exclude defectiveness is neither valid nor symmetrically sustainable. In other words, asserting that a compliant product is not necessarily defective is very different from claiming that compliance alone guarantees its safety.

Safety law refers to a set of predominantly public obligations and requirements aimed at the formal approval of a product through tests, inspections, and predefined technical criteria. These are static parameters, applicable to the technical abstraction of the product and geared toward an ex ante assessment of its fitness for commercialization or use. By contrast, civil liability rules are triggered ex post, upon the occurrence of actual harm, and require a concrete assessment of a causally relevant defect. This results not only in a conceptual distinction between safety and defectiveness, but also in a structural divergence in their logic and temporal application.

Assuming that civil liability rules are merely derivative of safety regulations, that liability could automatically be excluded based on compliance would lead to a problematic outcome: the proliferation of sector-specific liability regimes, each based on mutable technical standards subject to frequent revision. Such a configuration would create a normative framework inherently unstable, constantly exposed to the risk of legal obsolescence due to the high speed of technological progress (the pacing problem). In this scenario, the legislator would be perpetually trailing behind innovation, thereby undermining the effectiveness and predictability of the legal system in protecting users' rights. This distinction between regulation and liability is also reflected in the European approach to AI. While the adoption of the AI Regulation (EU) 2024/1689 represents a major step toward regulatory harmonization, efforts to align civil liability rules have proven less successful. The withdrawal in February 2025 of the proposed directive on AI liability (COM (2022) 496 final) confirms the structural difficulties in formulating a common framework for noncontractual actions based on faults. That proposal, which, in Article 1(2), would have extended its scope to claims against healthcare professionals not contractually bound to the patient would have directly impacted medical liability regimes.

The regulatory phase has taken a different path. The AI Regulation adopts a risk-based approach, under which most healthcare AI applications are classified as "high-risk systems." This classification rests on two elements: first, the inclusion of Regulation (EU) 2017/745 on medical devices among the harmonization laws referenced in Annex I; second, the explicit mention in Annex III of AI systems used in healthcare assistance and emergency patient triage (points 5(a) and (d)). These provisions underscore the sensitivity of the clinical context and the need for reinforced safeguards. The regulatory emphasis based on harmonized standards and ex ante conformity assessments marks a paradigm shift: from a reactive logic of post hoc liability to a preventive logic of protection. The legal framework aims to embed accountability into the very design of AI systems, making it an integral part of their operation. In this perspective, risk governance is no longer limited to attributing fault after the fact but extends to shaping obligations of transparency, oversight, and responsible design. Legal accountability, thus reconceptualized, becomes a proactive tool for risk management, capable of aligning technological innovation with the protection of fundamental rights and the dignity of the individual (Novelli et al., 2024).

10.5 Autonomy and Risk Management in AI-Driven Critical Care

This section addresses the legal reconfigurations brought about by the integration of multimodal AI into ICUs, focusing on how it reshapes foundational notions of autonomy, liability, and risk governance. It calls for a doctrinal renewal capable of adapting legal categories to the hybrid logic of human-algorithmic decision-making in contemporary critical care.

10.5.1 The Concept of Patient Autonomy in ICUs

Patient autonomy is a cornerstone of contemporary health law, premised on the subject's capacity for informed and voluntary decision-making. However, this legal conception encounters significant limits in the context of critical care. In the ICU, patients are frequently sedated or cognitively incapacitated, rendering the formal requirements of informed consent disclosure, comprehension, voluntariness—largely inapplicable. National laws typically respond through advance directives, proxy consent regimes, and shared care planning instruments. Yet these mechanisms, while normatively important, often prove insufficient in practice due to their proceduralizing, limited accessibility and weak integration into clinical governance (Garetto et al., 2022).

Legal systems across Europe provide for a range of formal instruments meant to safeguard autonomy ex ante or ex post: from statutory frameworks for living wills to procedural guarantees for proxy decision-making. Nonetheless, the effectiveness of such instruments is often constrained by their practical marginality in ICU routines and by the inadequacy of their doctrinal assumptions. Advance directives, for instance, tend to reduce the complexity of autonomy to a fixed, anticipatory expression of will, which does not accommodate the dynamic and relational nature of identity and preference formation under clinical distress.

From a critical legal perspective, this crisis of autonomy reveals the fragility of the liberal legal subject under conditions of clinical vulnerability (Marini, 2010). The ICU becomes a space where legal subjectivity is suspended and where decision-making shifts from the patient to institutional actors. The legal figure of the autonomous patient is replaced by procedural substitutes: next of kin, guardians, or clinical ethics committees. However, these proxies are governed by formalistic rules that fail to reflect the sociocultural and relational embeddedness of care decisions.

This limitation is accentuated by the lack of legal attention to the communicative infrastructure of autonomy. ICU contexts are often marked by temporal compression, emotional crisis, and epistemic asymmetry, all of which challenge the feasibility of deliberative processes (Pioggia, 2021). The law's reliance on binary distinctions—capacity/incapacity, consent/refusal—collides with the fluid reality of decision-making in intensive care. Jurisprudence has yet to systematically address how autonomy can be meaningfully operationalized in such contexts without reducing it to either bureaucratic formality or clinical paternalism.

Considering these tensions, some jurisdictions have begun experimenting with enriched legal models, such as relational or supported decision-making frameworks. These models seek to expand the legal meaning of autonomy beyond individual will to encompass dialogic processes of recognition and assistance. While promising, they remain largely absent from mainstream ICU regulation. Therefore, a reconfiguration of legal doctrine is necessary: one that reconceives autonomy not as an isolated capacity but as a legally mediated relation situated in time, context, and care. This shift would entail revisiting the legal taxonomy of incapacity, revising informed consent doctrine to account for narrative and collective elements, and embedding patient voice through structured participatory mechanisms within critical care governance (Pioggia, 2021). Such a move would not only realign legal norms with clinical realities but also reaffirm the foundational commitment to patient dignity. As Rodotà argued, the law must confront the techno-clinical challenges of biomedicine not by retreating to procedural abstractions, but by generating new forms of legal recognition capable of honoring vulnerability without extinguishing agency (Rodotà, 2020). Table 10.2 provides legal tools for patient autonomy in ICUs among different nations in EU frameworks.

10.5.2 The Legal AI Impact on Patient Autonomy

The AI integration into intensive care settings generates a profound reconfiguration of patient autonomy, not merely as a clinical matter, but as a legal construct. AI-driven systems—ranging from decision-support algorithms to automated diagnostic and triage tools—reshape the decisional ecology of the ICU and introduce normative opacity into the heart of medical judgment. From a legal standpoint, this development raises urgent questions concerning the right to informed consent, the intelligibility of risk, and the accountability for decisions mediated through nonhuman agency (Solaiman & Malik, 2025).

Table 10.2 Legal tools for patient autonomy in ICUs

Country	Legal instruments for advance directives	Proxy/Surrogate decision-making	Integration in ICU practice
Italy	Law No. 219/2017 on informed consent and DAT (advance treatment directives); allows binding advance expressions of will	The patient may designate a fiduciary (trusted person); default to close relatives if no appointment made	Implementation remains limited; poor dissemination and training; strong emphasis on formal documentation
Germany	Patient enverfügung (Binding advance directives, Civil Code §1901a); requires written form and specific content	Legal guardianship (Betreuung) or Vorsorgevollmacht (power of attorney) regulates substitute consent	Strong legal enforceability; hospital ethics committees active in conflict resolution
France	Loi Leonetti (2005, revised in 2016—Claeys-Leonetti); recognizes advance directives and limits therapeutic obstinacy	Mandataire de confiance (trusted person) can be appointed; default to family if absent	Broad legal framework but underused in ICU; physicians retain decisional primacy in case of doubt
Spain	Ley 41/2002 on patient autonomy; regional registries for advance directives; binding if clear and applicable	Possibility to appoint a representante legal; default to relatives in order of preference	Heterogeneous implementation; better integration in autonomous regions with established registries

At the core of legal concern lies the challenge of transparency. Most AI systems used in clinical contexts, particularly those based on deep learning, operate as so-called "black boxes" whose internal logic remains obscure even to the developers themselves. This lack of explainability fundamentally undermines the legal condition for informed consent as it is defined across European legal traditions: not merely the act of agreeing to treatment, but the capacity to understand the grounds, risks, and alternatives involved. Where neither clinicians nor patients can access the rationale of the AI's recommendation, the basis for valid consent collapses into a fiction. Regulatory frameworks have attempted to address these concerns through layered protection. The GDPR gives people rights when it comes to automated decision-making. This includes the right to refuse a decision that's made by a computer without human involvement if it has a significant impact on them. They also have the right to get clear information about how the automated system arrived at that decision. However, these provisions are limited in scope, primarily designed for consumer contexts and often inapplicable to complex clinical decision-making scenarios where human oversight is formally retained but substantively minimal (Blinick, 1968–1969).

The AI Regulation (EU) 2024/1689 classifies AI systems used in healthcare as "high-risk" and subjects them to stringent requirements of conformity assessment, risk management, and post-market monitoring. However, the AI Regulation reflects a predominantly technocratic and product-centric perspective: it prioritizes safety, robustness, and accuracy of systems, while failing to explicitly confront the ethical and legal dimensions of patient self-determination (van Kolfschooten, 2022). Critically, the Regulation does not embed enforceable rights tailored to the clinical setting, such as the right to contest algorithmic outputs that affect diagnosis, prognosis, or triage decisions. This omission is more concerning given that AI-driven decision-making often occurs within asymmetric power structures, where patients are structurally vulnerable, dependent and frequently excluded from meaningful participation in the decisional process (Pioggia, 2021). The AI Regulation's risk-based approach, while harmonizing market access and ensuring compliance with technical standards, displaces the normative centrality of patients' rights as rooted in the EU Charter and Member State constitutional traditions. The substitution or integration of clinical judgment with opaque algorithmic reasoning problematizes the attribution of liability: traditional fault-based legal models presuppose a chain of human decisions, yet when clinicians act upon AI-generated outputs—whose logic may be inscrutable or proprietary—liability becomes fragmented, diffuse, and legally elusive (Solaiman & Malik, 2025).

From a distributive standpoint, AI systems may encode structural biases inherited from their training datasets. If deployed uncritically, such systems can replicate or exacerbate health disparities, thereby violating principles of equality and nondiscrimination protected under both the charter of fundamental rights of the EU (Arts. 20–21) and domestic constitutional norms. The absence of mandatory bias audits or algorithmic impact assessments in patient-specific terms leaves a regulatory gap. Moreover, the relational fabric of autonomy—its dependence on dialogue, trust, and shared understanding—is further eroded by the automation of decision-making. Legal regimes have yet to incorporate safeguards that preserve the communicative dimensions of care in AI-mediated environments. Without such measures, there is a risk that patient autonomy will be reduced to passive acquiescence to algorithmically pre-structured options.

Consequently, a reorientation of legal regulation is required: one that acknowledges the qualitative shift introduced by AI into the structure of medical knowledge and the condition of legal subjectivity. In the age of AI-driven healthcare, especially in critical care environments like ICUs, a robust and integrated legal strategy is essential to maintaining autonomy. Assuring both clinicians and patients can understand, and question algorithmic decisions will require embedding explainability requirements as enforceable conditions for the lawful use of AI in clinical practice. A legal framework must also guarantee rights like human override, second opinions, and algorithmic transparency, reinforcing the primacy of human judgment. In addition, clinically specific interpretations of GDPR rights should consider the principle of informational self-determination, giving patients more control over how their data is used. Both healthcare providers and institutions must assess and mitigate algorithmic bias, both at the individual patient level and across systems. The only way to resuscitate patient autonomy as a substantive right grounded in intelligibility, contestability, and accountability is through such a comprehensive and proactive legal approach.

10.5.3 Reframing Legal Balances Between Autonomy and Clinical Governance

The rise of AI technologies in critical care settings compels a reconsideration of how law balances the principles of autonomy, beneficence, and clinical necessity. Traditional medicolegal doctrine relies on a model in which the physician is the central decision-maker, accountable through professional standards and subject to fiduciary duties toward the patient. This architecture is now destabilized by the insertion of algorithmic intermediaries, which simultaneously augment and displace clinical judgment.

From a legal standpoint, the delegation of decision-making authority to AI systems raises new forms of normative tension. When clinical choices are informed—or even dictated—by opaque predictive models, the question arises as to who exercises agency and who bears responsibility. Courts and legislature must grapple with this dispersion of authority and its implications for fundamental rights. This uncertainty is compounded in triage situations, where AI tools may be used to prioritize patients based on survival probabilities or resource optimization. In such contexts, decisions acquire not only clinical but distributive dimensions, touching on rights to equal treatment, nondiscrimination, and access to care. If AI systems produce de facto exclusions from intensive treatment without transparent justifications or recourse mechanisms, they may run afoul of constitutional and human rights guarantees (Flynn, 2018).

Moreover, legal systems must now contend with a deeper epistemic transformation: the shift from interpretive, narrative-based decision-making to data-driven computation. Law has traditionally mediated clinical discretion through principles of proportionality, reasonableness, and accountability. These principles require adaptation to a regime in which the basis of medical action is not human reasoning but algorithmic inference. To restore coherence and legitimacy, a rebalancing of clinical governance must occur on legal terrain. Legal and ethical frameworks for AI integration in clinical settings need to be clarified, as well as professional and institutional responsibilities. When AI tools are used, it's important to delineate the scope and limits of clinical discretion, emphasize independent verification and engage critically with algorithmic results. For clinicians to interpret and challenge AI recommendations, professional standards need to include algorithmic literacy and accountability. AI-influenced decisions should be protected by procedural safeguards, including rights to explanation, refusal, and appeal. Likewise, institutions need to be obligated to be transparent about the deployment, calibration, and ongoing updates to clinical AI. It's also important to recognize and scrutinize the legal significance of algorithmic thresholds and cutoffs, which are often used as proxies for eligibility in care pathways. In healthcare, these measures form the foundation for a rights-based, ethically sound approach. Importantly, courts and regulators must develop interpretive doctrines capable of addressing hybrid human-machine decisions. Doctrines of fault and causation, informed by evolving understandings of technological mediation, must reflect the shared nature of clinical agency in AI-integrated environments.

10.5.4 Legal Strategies for Enhancing Patient Autonomy

In the face of increasingly complex and technologically mediated care environments, especially within ICUs, legal systems must move beyond traditional notions of autonomy understood as static, individual choice. Instead, enhancing patient autonomy requires a multilayered legal approach that supports agency through relational, procedural, and structural safeguards.

One central strategy is the legal reinforcement of shared decision-making (SDM). While SDM has been ethically endorsed and clinically promoted, its legal status remains fragile. Embedding SDM into statutory and regulatory frameworks—by codifying duties of dialogic engagement, mutual information exchange, and collaborative deliberation—can shift autonomy from a one-off event to an ongoing process. In jurisdictions such as Germany and Spain, preliminary steps toward formalizing these obligations exist, but comprehensive implementation remains lacking. Second, the law must strengthen procedural rights that empower patients in algorithmically shaped decisions. These include:

- The right to be informed about the use of AI in clinical decisions, including the function, limitations, and implications of such systems.
- The right to refuse AI-supported recommendations or demand human-centered alternatives.
- The right to a second opinion in cases where decisions are heavily influenced by automated scoring or triage tools.
- The right to access, interpret, and contest the data that informs algorithmic risk assessments.

These rights, while partly derived from data protection regimes like the GDPR, require targeted extension and operationalization in health-specific legislation. Importantly, they should be enforceable in real time, not only retrospectively through litigation. Third, legal mechanisms should promote institutional duties of facilitation. Hospitals and health authorities must be obligated to: ensure that advance directives and care plans are systematically solicited, recorded, and respected; provide infrastructure and training for clinicians to meaningfully communicate AI outputs to patients and families; establish patient advisory boards and ethics committees with formal consultative roles in the deployment of high-impact AI tools; implement language-accessible and culturally appropriate materials explaining AI tools and patient rights.

Fourth, the protection of autonomy must extend to collective and structural dimensions. Vulnerable populations—such as persons with disabilities, migrants, or individuals with low digital literacy—require enhanced legal protections to ensure that autonomy is not exercised merely under conditions of formal equality, but in terms of genuine accessibility and inclusion. This calls for an intersectional legal approach, capable of recognizing how multiple forms of disadvantage—including gender, ethnicity, social class, age, or legal status—intersect to shape experiences of exclusion, both within human systems and algorithmic ones (Kennedy, 2017). A truly effective right to health and self-determination cannot disregard this critical awareness (Pioggia, 2021).

Finally, courts and regulatory bodies should develop interpretive doctrines that affirm a thicker concept of autonomy: not merely the right to choose, but the right to participate, understand, dissent, and be recognized. This includes doctrinal evolution in areas such as informed consent, standard of care, and institutional accountability. For example, failure to disclose algorithmic mediation in clinical decision-making should be treated as a breach of both informational and decisional rights.

In sum, enhancing patient autonomy in the ICU in the era of AI requires a convergence of legal instruments: individual rights, institutional obligations, procedural guarantees, and equality-oriented safeguards. Only through such an integrated framework can autonomy retain its critical function as a principle of legal personhood, even in the technologically complex and emotionally charged landscape of critical care.

10.5.5 Rethinking Risk and Ethical Governance Through Legal Frameworks

The integration of AI technologies in intensive care not only challenges traditional notions of clinical discretion but also transforms how law conceptualizes and regulates risk. Historically, medical risk has been assessed and managed through a combination of professional standards, evidentiary thresholds, and doctrines of liability. However, AI systems introduce a computational paradigm in which risk is expressed as a statistical output derived from population-level data, often divorced from contextualized patient narratives. This shift complicates the legal identification, communication, and distribution of risk in critical care (Solaiman & Malik, 2025).

From a legal standpoint, two major concerns arise. First, AI-driven risk assessments may obscure or distort individual patient needs, especially when algorithmic outputs are treated as prescriptive rather than probabilistic. Second, the use of risk stratification tools—particularly in triage scenarios—can lead to discriminatory exclusions from care if not properly constrained by legal safeguards. These concerns intersect with core principles of constitutional law and human rights, including equality, proportionality, and the right to health.

As Alessandra Pioggia has noted in her critical reflections on healthcare organization, risk governance in the medical context cannot be disentangled from the institutional responsibility to safeguard fundamental rights, first among them, the right to self-determination (Pioggia, 2021). When an individual chooses to entrust their health to a medical institution, they do not thereby relinquish their autonomy regarding how, when, and under what terms they are to be treated. The absence of an organizational infrastructure that actively protects such rights leads not only to their practical erosion, but to their unequal realization across different social and clinical contexts. Risk governance, in this light, is not only a matter of managing clinical uncertainty or technological complexity; it also entails designing care environments capable of recognizing and enabling individual subjectivities, especially when patients are at their most vulnerable.

A critical legal approach to risk insists on reclaiming its normative dimension. Risk is not merely a quantitative metric but a distributional decision that determines who is exposed to harm, under what conditions, and with what recourse. Accordingly, ethical risk management in the ICU must be governed by law in a way that embeds procedural fairness, transparency, and contestability. To this end, several legal strategies are necessary which are mentioned below:

- *Mandatory risk disclosure*: Legal norms should require that patients or their proxies be informed when decisions are based on AI-generated risk scores. This includes disclosure of the system's role, logic, and limitations.
- *Algorithmic impact assessments*: Healthcare institutions should be subject to legal obligations to conduct and publish assessments of how algorithmic tools affect different patient populations, especially in terms of access, outcomes, and disparities.
- *Procedural safeguards in triage*: The use of AI in triage must be regulated to ensure that algorithmic classifications do not become opaque justifications for exclusion. Legal mechanisms such as appeal rights, independent reviews, and clinical overrides are essential to preserving substantive fairness.
- *Integration of fundamental rights*: Risk governance must be explicitly aligned with constitutional and supranational rights, such as those enshrined in the EU Charter of Fundamental Rights. This includes safeguarding dignity (Art. 1), protection of personal data (Art. 8), and nondiscrimination (Art. 21).
- *Legal responsibility and accountability*: When algorithmic recommendations lead to adverse outcomes, it is essential that legal doctrines of causation and fault are adapted to reflect shared agency between clinicians, developers, and institutions. Without clear attribution of responsibility, patients are left without effective remedies.

The normative horizon for such legal reform can be drawn from Stefano Rodotà's vision of the "homo dignus" (Rodotà, 2010) which resists the reduction of the person to a technical or managerial object. In this framework, risk management is not an exercise in optimization, but an ethical and legal task grounded in human dignity, relational recognition, and democratic accountability. Legal governance must therefore move beyond risk as a managerial category and reclaim it as a site of legal subjectivity. Through enforceable rights, institutional duties and constitutional principles, the law must ensure that the digital architecture of ICU care remains answerable to the people it serves. In this sense, the governance of risk becomes a litmus test for the legal system's capacity to preserve justice, agency and human value in the age of medical AI.

10.5.6 AI and the Doctor–Patient Relationship: Lessons from the EU Council

A recent report (Kingsford & Ambrose, 2024) offers a comprehensive and authoritative reflection on the shifting dynamics of clinical care in the age of algorithmic medicine. While not focused exclusively on intensive care, the findings are highly relevant for understanding how the deployment of AI technologies affects fundamental legal values particularly autonomy, trust and human dignity, within critical care settings. The report emphasizes that the integration of AI into clinical workflows does not merely alter the tools of medical practice but reconfigures the normative structure of the doctor–patient relationship itself. This transformation carries profound implications for legal frameworks governing informed consent, patient participation and ethical oversight (Cohen, 2019). Below are the key concerns that are highlighted:

- *Erosion of interpersonal trust*: The opacity of AI systems and the potential substitution of human judgment with machine-generated outputs risk undermining the foundational trust that patients place in their physicians. In ICU contexts, where patients are often incapacitated, the legal principle of substituted or relational autonomy becomes especially fragile in the face of black-box decisions.
- *Shift in professional responsibility*: The report raises important questions about how legal systems can or should attribute responsibility when decisions are jointly or opaquely mediated by AI. In critical care, this issue is compounded by the urgency and gravity of decisions made—often in life-or-death circumstances—under uncertain conditions.
- *Informational asymmetry and consent*: The Council underscores the inadequacy of current informed consent models in capturing the complexities introduced by AI. Patients and their surrogates may not be equipped to understand or question algorithmic reasoning, thereby risking a reduction of consent to formalistic compliance.
- *Risk of dehumanization*: There is concern that an overreliance on algorithmic tools could erode the humanistic foundations of medicine. For ICU patients, whose care is deeply dependent on relational attention and contextual judgment, this risk is legally relevant to the interpretation of dignity-based rights under both national constitutions and the European Convention on Human Rights.

The report thus calls for a recalibration of legal and ethical frameworks to safeguard the irreplaceable value of human relationships in medical decision-making and it recommends:

- Embedding rights to transparency and explainability in health-specific legislation.
- Establishing enforceable safeguards for shared and participatory decision-making in AI-mediated care.
- Promoting professional training on ethical use and communication of AI tools.
- Ensuring that patient-facing digital systems preserve space for empathy, narrative, and dignity.

In sum, the Council of Europe's contribution reinforces the thesis that autonomy in the age of AI must be defended not only through technological standards or data protection regimes, but through a legal reconstruction of the doctor–patient relationship as a space of care, accountability and mutual recognition.

10.6 Conclusions

In this chapter, we discuss the challenges that arise when technology, law, and ethics are combined. Multimodal AI systems integration into intensive care settings raises immediate legal and ethical concerns. To address the limitations of current regulatory frameworks, we need a more inclusive and accountable governance framework. As a result of the EU's AI Regulation, standardized processes, risk management, and procedural compliance are emphasized. Even though such measures provide regulatory infrastructure, they don't address the broader normative and distributive implications of AI. A focus on participatory and reflexive models that emphasize the voices and needs of patients, frontline healthcare workers, and marginalized communities is urged by critical legal perspectives. In clinical settings, the implementation of AI must be aligned with principles of justice and care, recognizing the technology's inherent political nature.

Additionally, GDPR's individualistic and proceduralist assumptions limit its potential for transformation, even as it provides a foundation for data privacy and security. Health data protection needs to be reframed as a collective, democratic practice, which considers the socio-technical realities of data production, sharing, and contestation. Patients should be empowered and have meaningful control over their medical data, not just follow the rules. It is important to view the process as an ongoing, dynamic process of co-governance. A legal framework in the field of intellectual property needs to strike a balance between incentivizing innovation and promoting transparency, equity, and public interest. Due to this, ownership models and benefit-sharing mechanisms need to be reevaluated, especially when AI systems are trained with data from vulnerable populations.

The concept of fairness in AI cannot be reduced to checking regulatory checklists or technical debiasing. We must examine the issue from a structural and distributive perspective—asking who defines system objectives, who achieves efficiency gains, and who risks exclusion or harm. In the absence of this critical inquiry, AI risks reinforcing existing hierarchies under the guise of innovation. A clinical AI system is not an isolated tool, but rather a distributed socio-technical assemblage shaped by decisions made throughout the design, development, and deployment processes. Therefore, the responsibility cannot be limited to clinical settings where the product is used. It is essential that legal frameworks evolve so patients have access to timely, enforceable remedies throughout the lifecycle of AI systems. The goal isn't to slow down technology, but to embed it within legal and ethical frameworks that respect human dignity, institutional responsibility, and equitable treatment. In the AI era, clinical governance required more than simply adapting existing norms. It calls for revised legal frameworks reflecting a reconfigured landscape of healthcare decision-making. Intensive care can only be improved by using AI in this way to ensure justice, safety, and patients' well-being.

References

Aakula, R. (2025). Real-time AI dashboards for ICU monitoring and alerting. *European Journal of Computer Science and Information Technology, 13*(12), 15–23. https://doi.org/10.37745/ejcsit.2013/vol13n121523

Abujarad, F., Peduzzi, P., Mun, S., et al. (2021). Comparing a multimedia digital informed consent tool with traditional paper-based methods: Randomized controlled trial. *JMIR Formative Research, 5*(10), e20458. https://doi.org/10.2196/20458

Allegranti, I., Battineni, G., & Garetto, R. (2023). The use of artificial intelligence and mixed reality in preventing natural disasters: Practical and legal issues. In *Springer series on cultural computing* (pp. 349–368). Springer. https://doi.org/10.1007/978-3-031-27166-3_19

Beglinger, C. (2019). A broken theory: The malfunction theory of strict products liability and the need for a new doctrine in the field of surgical robotics. *Minnesota Law Review, 104*, 1041–1111.

Bertolini, A. (2025, July). *Artificial intelligence and civil liability: A European perspective.* European Parliament. https://www.europarl.europa.eu/RegData/etudes/STUD/2020/621926/IPOL_STU(2020)621926_EN.pdf

Blinick, M. (1968–1969). Mental disability, legal ethics, and professional responsibility. *Albany Law Review, 33*, 92–93.

Buiten, M. C. (2024). Product liability for defective AI. *European Journal of Law and Economics, 57*, 239–273. https://doi.org/10.1007/s10657-024-09794-z

Carroll, N. W., Jones, A., Burkard, T., Lulias, C., Severson, K., & Posa, T. (2022). Improving risk stratification using AI and social determinants of health. *American Journal of Managed Care, 28*(11), 582–587. https://doi.org/10.37765/AJMC.2022.89261

Cheungpasitporn, W., Thongprayoon, C., & Kashani, K. B. (2024). Artificial intelligence and machine learning's role in sepsis-associated acute kidney injury. *Kidney Research and Clinical Practice, 43*(4), 417–424. https://doi.org/10.23876/j.krcp.23.298

Cho, K. J., Kwon, O., Kwon, J. M., et al. (2020). Detecting patient deterioration using artificial intelligence in a rapid response system. *Critical Care Medicine, 48*(4), e285–e289. https://doi.org/10.1097/CCM.0000000000004236

Cohen, I. G. (2019). Informed consent and medical artificial intelligence: What to tell the patient? *Georgetown Law Journal, 108*, 1425–1470.

Custers, B., Lahmann, H., & Scott, B. I. (2025). From liability gaps to liability overlaps: Shared responsibilities and fiduciary duties in AI and other complex technologies. *AI & SOCIETY, 40*, 4035–4050. https://doi.org/10.1007/s00146-024-02137-1

Farhud, D. D., & Zokaei, S. (2021). Ethical issues of artificial intelligence in medicine and healthcare. *Iranian Journal of Public Health, 50*(11), i. https://doi.org/10.18502/ijph.v50i11.7600

Ferrara, E. (2024). The butterfly effect in artificial intelligence systems: Implications for AI bias and fairness. *Machine Learning with Applications, 15*, 100525. https://doi.org/10.1016/j.mlwa.2024.100525

Flynn, E. (2018). Legal capacity for people with dementia: A human rights approach. In S. Cahill (Ed.), *Dementia and human rights* (pp. 157–159). Bristol University Press. https://doi.org/10.2307/j.ctt22h6q92

Gajarawala, S. N., & Pelkowski, J. N. (2020). Telehealth benefits and barriers. *The Journal for Nurse Practitioners, 17*(2), 218–221. https://doi.org/10.1016/j.nurpra.2020.09.013

Garetto, R., Allegranti, I., Cancellieri, S., Coscarelli, S., Ferretti, F., & Nico, M. P. (2022). Ethical and legal challenges of telemedicine implementation in rural areas. In *Telemedicine and E-health: Ethical, legal and social implications* (pp. 31–60). Springer. https://doi.org/10.1007/978-3-031-05049-7_3

Gikay, A. A., Lau, P. L., Sengul, C., Miron, A., & Malin, B. (2023, November 2). High-risk artificial intelligence systems under the European Union's Artificial Intelligence Act: Systemic flaws and practical challenges. *SSRN Electronic Journal*. https://doi.org/10.2139/ssrn.4621605

Gonzalez, F. A., Santonocito, C., Lamas, T., et al. (2024). Is artificial intelligence prepared for the 24-h shifts in the ICU? *Anaesthesia Critical Care & Pain Medicine, 43*(6), 101431. https://doi.org/10.1016/j.accpm.2024.101431

Guarda, P., & Ducato, R. (2016). From electronic health records to personal health records: Emerging legal issues in the Italian regulation of e-health. *International Review of Law, Computers & Technology, 30*(3), 271–285. https://doi.org/10.1080/13600869.2016.1189738

Haas, R., & McGill, S. C. (2022). *Artificial intelligence for the prediction of sepsis in adults* (CADTH Horizon Scan). Canadian Agency for Drugs and Technologies in Health. https://www.ncbi.nlm.nih.gov/books/NBK596676/

Horng, S., Liao, R., Wang, X., Dalal, S., Golland, P., & Berkowitz, S. J. (2021). Deep learning to quantify pulmonary edema in chest radiographs. *Radiology: Artificial Intelligence, 3*(2), e190228. https://doi.org/10.1148/ryai.2021190228

Johnson, J. C., Kim, H., & Johnson, P. A. (2021). Pedagogy in perspective: Ethical erosion and effects on empathy levels in healthcare education. *Medical Science Educator, 31*(3), 1173–1181. https://doi.org/10.1007/s40670-021-01273-3

Kennedy, D. (2017, August 6). *Intersectionality and critical race theory: A genealogical note from a CLS point of view*. SSRN. https://ssrn.com/abstract=3014312

Kingsford, P. A., & Ambrose, J. A. (2024). Artificial intelligence and the doctor–patient relationship. *American Journal of Medicine, 137*(5), 381–382. https://doi.org/10.1016/j.amjmed.2024.01.005

Kitkowska, A., Karegar, F., & Wästlund, E. (2023, September 20–22). Share or protect: Understanding the interplay of trust, privacy concerns, and data sharing purposes in health and well-being apps. In *15th Biannual Conference of the Italian SIGCHI Chapter (CHItaly 2023)* (pp. 1–14). ACM. https://doi.org/10.1145/3605390.3605417

Luo, X., Li, B., Zhu, R., et al. (2025). Development and validation of an interpretable machine learning model for predicting in-hospital mortality for ischemic stroke patients in ICU. *International Journal of Medical Informatics, 198*, 105874. https://doi.org/10.1016/j.ijmedinf.2025.105874

Marini, G. (2010). Il consenso. In S. Rodotà & M. Tallacchini (Eds.), *Trattato di biodiritto, vol. I: Ambito e fonti del biodiritto* (p. 361). Giuffrè.

Mir, A. N., & Rizvi, D. R. (2025). Advancements in deep learning and explainable artificial intelligence for enhanced medical image analysis: A comprehensive survey and future directions. *Engineering Applications of Artificial Intelligence, 158*, 111413. https://doi.org/10.1016/j.engappai.2025.111413

Muzammil, M. A., Javid, S., Afridi, A. K., et al. (2024). Artificial intelligence-enhanced electrocardiography for accurate diagnosis and management of cardiovascular diseases. *Journal of Electrocardiology, 83*, 30–40. https://doi.org/10.1016/j.jelectrocard.2024.01.006

National Academies of Sciences, Engineering, and Medicine. (2016, July 27). *Ethical, legal, and regulatory framework for human subjects research*. National Academies Press. https://www.ncbi.nlm.nih.gov/books/NBK373547/

Novelli, C., Taddeo, M., & Floridi, L. (2024). Accountability in artificial intelligence: What it is and how it works. *AI & SOCIETY, 39*(4), 1871–1882. https://doi.org/10.1007/s00146-023-01635-y

Ocloo, J., Garfield, S., Franklin, B. D., & Dawson, S. (2021). Exploring the theory, barriers and enablers for patient and public involvement across health, social care and patient safety: A systematic review of reviews. *Health Research Policy and Systems, 19*(1), 1–21. https://doi.org/10.1186/s12961-020-00644-3

Patel, M. (2025, May 21). *The INSIGHT-ICU study: Illuminating neuropsychological dysfunction and systemic inflammatory mechanisms gleaned after hospitalization in trauma-ICU study.* https://grantome.com/grant/NIH/R01-GM120484-02

Pioggia, A. (2021). Administrative citizenship and public services: Is the constitutional project still possible in the perspective of the union? In D. Sorace, L. Ferrara, & I. Piazza (Eds.), *The changing administrative law of an EU member state* (pp. 117–130). Springer Nature Switzerland. https://doi.org/10.1007/978-3-030-50780-0_7

Rodotà, S. (2010). Antropologia dell'homo dignus. *Rivista Critica del Diritto Privato, 4*, 547.

Rodotà, S. (2020). Of machines and men. The road to identity: Scenes for a discussion. *Comparative Law Review, 11*(2), 29–43.

Schwartz, G. T. (1983). *New products, old products, evolving law, retroactive law*. New York University Law Review.

Shickel, B., Loftus, T. J., Adhikari, L., Ozrazgat-Baslanti, T., Bihorac, A., & Rashidi, P. (2019). DeepSOFA: A continuous acuity score for critically ill patients using clinically interpretable deep learning. *Scientific Reports, 9*(1), 1–12. https://doi.org/10.1038/s41598-019-38491-0

Singh, S., Singh, S., & Raghuvanshi, C. S. (2025). Generating synthetic medical data using GAI. In *Generative artificial intelligence for biomedical and smart health informatics* (pp. 51–71). IEEE. https://doi.org/10.1002/9781394280735.ch3

Solaiman, B., & Malik, A. (2025). Regulating algorithmic care in the European Union: Evolving doctor–patient models through the Artificial Intelligence Act (AI-Act) and the liability directives. *Medical Law Review, 33*(1), fwae033. https://doi.org/10.1093/medlaw/fwae033

Song, J., Wang, X., Wang, B., et al. (2024). Learning implementation of a guideline-based decision support system to improve hypertension treatment in primary care in China: Pragmatic cluster randomised controlled trial. *BMJ, 386*. https://doi.org/10.1136/BMJ-2023-079143

Stivi, T., Padawer, D., Dirini, N., Nachshon, A., Batzofin, B. M., & Ledot, S. (2024). Using artificial intelligence to predict mechanical ventilation weaning success in patients with respiratory failure, including those with acute respiratory distress syndrome. *Journal of Clinical Medicine, 13*(5), 1505. https://doi.org/10.3390/jcm13051505

van Kolfschooten, H. (2022). EU regulation of artificial intelligence: Challenges for patients' rights. *Common Market Law Review, 59*(1), 81–112. Amsterdam Law School Legal Studies Research Paper No. 2022-60; Law Centre for Health & Life Research Paper No. 2022-01. https://ssrn.com/abstract=3997366 or. https://doi.org/10.2139/ssrn.3997366

Vujičić, J. (2024). Strategic legal frameworks for artificial intelligence: Why smaller countries must act now. *World Journal of Advanced Engineering Technology and Sciences, 12*(2), 953–972.

Widder, D. G., & Nafus, D. (2023). Dislocated accountabilities in the "AI supply chain": Modularity and developers' notions of responsibility. *Big Data & Society, 10*(1). https://doi.org/10.1177/20539517231177620

Zuboff, S. (2019). *The age of surveillance capitalism*. Hachette.

Multimodal Artificial Intelligence in Pediatric Emergency and Critical Care

11

Manish Kumar

11.1 Introduction

Pediatric emergency and critical care require time-critical decision-making in the face of extraordinary complexity emanating from the nonspecific nature of presenting symptoms, the dynamism of an evolving physiology across different age groups, and the potential for rapid deterioration owing to the minimal homeostatic reserves in children. In case of nonverbal or preverbal young patients' clinical data is often ambiguous, warranting greater reliance on indirect signs and caregiver reports. Optimal morbidity and mortality outcomes depend on the clinician's ability to perform accurate assessment and initiate appropriate interventions.

However, such decision-making is often clouded by cognitive biases—such as anchoring on an initial diagnosis, availability bias favoring recent or dramatic cases, or confirmation bias reinforcing preexisting beliefs (Kunitomo et al., 2022). These heuristics can often mislead clinicians in high-stakes acute care scenarios which require serial monitoring of vitals and other clinical parameters.

Modern healthcare can inundate clinicians with multiple data streams from monitors, laboratory systems, imaging studies, and electronic health records, often causing information overload. According to Miller's law most humans can process seven (plus or minus two) discrete pieces of information (Miller, 1994). This cognitive limitation which impairs the ability of healthcare providers to synthesize complex data from multiple streams, worsens further in high pressure environs of acute care which requires balancing competing priorities in extreme time constraints while processing heterogenous and at times high volume of information.

In this background, multimodal artificial intelligence (AI) promises a paradigm shift as a clinical decision support tool in acute pediatric care settings. Multimodal

M. Kumar (✉)
Department of Paediatrics, All India Institute of Medical Sciences,
Gorakhpur, Uttar Pradesh, India

U. Venkatesh et al. (eds.), *Multimodal AI in Healthcare*,
https://doi.org/10.1007/978-981-95-9027-8_11

AI employs advanced machine learning architecture to extract latent patterns, prioritize salient information and present contextualized insights from diverse data streams. These capabilities can be useful for rapid triage, real-time monitoring of clinical trajectories, anticipation of organ dysfunction and need for intensive interventions, thus guiding individualized therapeutic strategies based on integrated data analytics.

This chapter aims to comprehensively explore the role of multimodal AI in pediatric emergency and critical care. After an initial overview of technical modalities and machine learning architecture, the subsequent sections delve into specific case applications of multimodal AI ranging from triage optimization to early warning systems. Subsequently, the technical challenges of integrating multimodal AI into existing healthcare systems along with the multifaceted ethical and regulatory concerns involved in the operationalization of multimodal AI are elaborated upon. Finally, a sneak peek into future advances of multimodal AI and its transformative potential is described.

11.2 Foundations of Multimodal AI

11.2.1 Definition

Multimodal AI refers to machine learning systems that can simultaneously process and integrate information from multiple data modalities (Soenksen et al., 2022). In pediatric emergency and critical care, data emanates from multiple sources (see Fig. 11.1) and might include:

- Unstructured text: Clinician notes, nursing documentation, discharge summaries, other components of electronic health records (EHRs) etc.
- Structured text: Demographics, vital signs, lab values, medication records etc.
- Image data: Radiographs, CT/MRI scans, ultrasound images, patient image files etc.
- Audio data: Breath sounds, heart sounds, alarm signals etc.
- Time series data: Physiological waveforms like electrocardiography, capnography, oxygen saturation, invasive arterial line recordings etc.

The theoretical framework of multimodal AI is based on the concept of data complementarity which postulates that combination of complementary information from different modalities enables a more complete understanding of complex medical phenomenon (Soenksen et al., 2022). This approach addresses limitations of unimodal AI systems as multimodal systems are often more resistant to noise and fluctuations in individual data streams. Studies have also shown that multimodal AI systems are more accurate than their unimodal counterparts with average improvements of 6.2 percentage points in area under the curve (AUC) metrics (Schouten et al., 2025). Multimodal approach is more generalizable to diverse clinical settings (Soenksen et al., 2022).

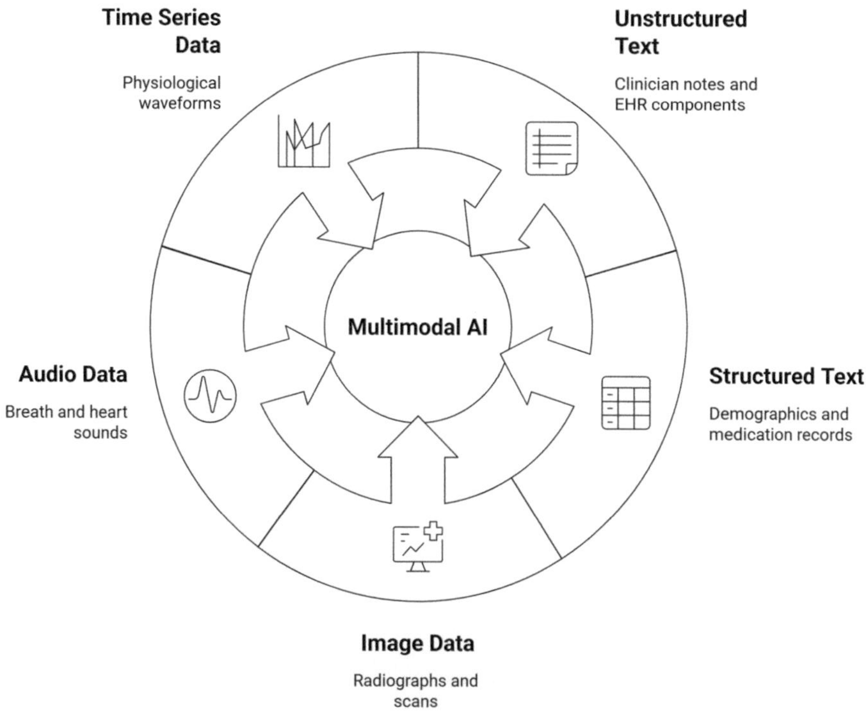

Fig. 11.1 Data modalities in pediatric emergency and critical care

11.2.2 Data Fusion Strategies

Broadly, three data fusion strategies are employed in multimodal AI systems (Fig. 11.2) (Teoh et al., 2024):

- Early fusion: This approach is also known as feature level integration where in raw data from diverse modalities are combined into a single vector and processed jointly. Early fusion methods include concatenation, pooling, or gated units to merge input modalities. This approach enables the machine learning model to train on cross-modal interactions but requires temporal alignment of data streams.
- Late fusion: This approach is also called decision level integration where in separate models are trained for each modality and then their outputs are combined using techniques like weighted averaging, meta models etc. This approach provides robustness against missing modalities but may not account for cross-modal interactions.
- Hybrid fusion: Also known as intermediate integration, this approach combines features of early and late fusion with provision of modality-specific processing at initial stages and then combining them at intermediate stages of model architecture. In this approach, attention mechanisms or transformer architectures to learn optimal strategies for combining information from different modalities.

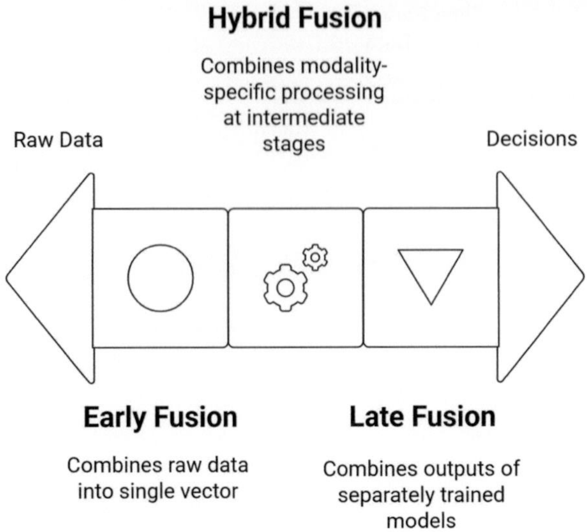

Fig. 11.2 Multimodal data fusion strategies

Table 11.1 Fusion strategies in multimodal AI

Fusion strategy	Advantages	Limitations	Example
Early fusion	Raw data from diverse modalities are combined early in training	Temporal alignment of multimodal data required; sensitive to noise in raw data	Combining SpO_2 waveforms, lab values, respiratory sounds to predict respiratory failure in infants
Late fusion	Handles incomplete datasets by leveraging pre-trained single modality models	Misses out on inter modal interactions	Independent models for vital signs, clinical notes, and lab parameters to predict sepsis, then combined using meta-classifier for computation of final risk score
Hybrid fusion	Balances robustness to missing data and cross-modal training and is able to handle asynchronous data streams more effectively	Architecturally complex model	Processing video data of infant's breathing pattern and audio data of respiratory sounds and then integrating the output with real-time vital sign data to identify impending respiratory failure

The advantages and limitations of different fusion strategies in multimodal AI are summarized in Table 11.1.

11.2.3 Core Components of Multimodal AI

In addition to fusion mechanisms, certain other core components of multimodal AI systems in pediatric critical care deserve mention (AlSaad et al., 2024):

- Data preprocessing and normalization: Modality-specific preprocessing is required in a multimodal system. Images require standardization and augmentation while texts require tokenization or embedding. For time series data, temporal alignment is of paramount importance.
- Modality-specific encoders: Optimization of different types of data requires varying neural network architecture. Medical images are often processed using convolutional neural networks (CNNs), while recurrent neural networks (RNNs) and transformers are suited for processing of sequential data and text data.
- Attention mechanisms: Importance of different data modalities are often weighed dynamically in a multimodal system using attention mechanisms which allows the model to focus on most relevant information for a given clinical task and handle incomplete datasets.

11.3 Applications in Pediatric Emergency & Critical Care

Multimodal AI has the transformative potential to augment decision-making in pediatric emergency and critical care by integrating imaging, physiological signals, structured and unstructured data mimicking cognitive processes of healthcare teams. The applications of multimodal AI in acute pediatric care can be described under the broad domains, laid out in a pivotal report on impact for AI in healthcare by McKinsey & Company—triage & early diagnosis, clinical decision support, diagnostics, prevention & wellness, care delivery and chronic care management (Fig. 11.3) (Transforming Healthcare with AI: The Impact on the Workforce and Organizations | McKinsey, n.d.).

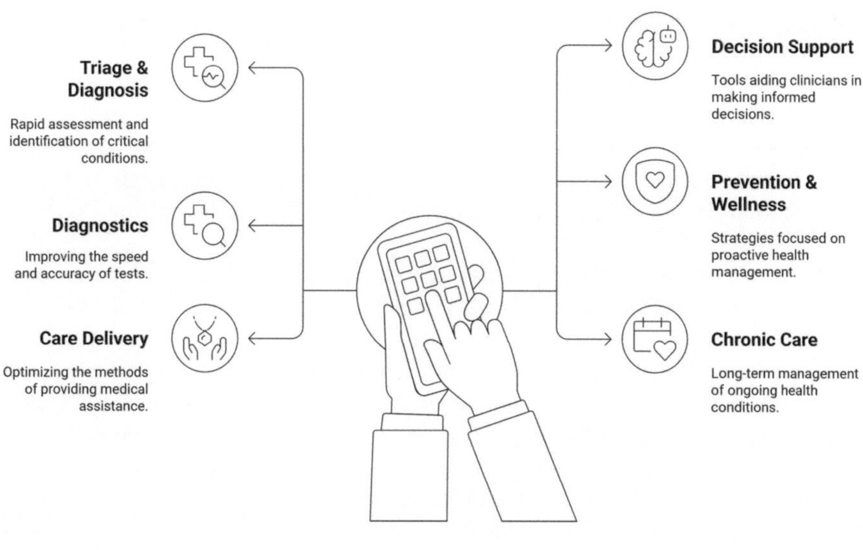

Fig. 11.3 Multimodal AI in pediatric emergency & critical care

11.3.1 Triage & Early Diagnosis

The greatest potential of multimodal AI is seen in its ability of analyzing multiple data streams to objectively triage patients based on acuity and urgency. Multiple studies have documented the use of machine learning prediction models for triage. A study by Wolff et al. with a huge dataset of 189,718 patient visits demonstrated that machine learning models outperform traditional triage models with Random Forest machine learning model performing the best in multi-class performance metrics (Wolff et al., 2019). A similar report of better triage abilities of machine learning models was demonstrated in a study by Goto et al. (2019). Another study demonstrated the proficiency of machine learning models, especially XGBoost, in predicting Korean triage Acuity Scale reliably (Choi et al., 2019). Studies have also developed early critical interventions models and incorporated electronic medical records. It has also been seen that models combining three modalities consistently outperform dual-modal approaches. For preverbal children video data dominates while in older patient texts are given more weightage in dynamic modality weighting strategy employed in multimodal AI.

Many of the pediatric emergencies such as sepsis, respiratory failure, organ dysfunction are initially compensated with subtle and nonspecific clinical signs, making early identification challenging. Multimodal AI has the potential to detect these latent patterns before overt decompensation enabling early identification hours before traditional clinical recognition. Investigators from Children's Hospital of Philadelphia developed eight machine learning models trained on up to 36 features derived from electronic health records, which were able to identify sepsis in infants 4 h prior to usual clinical recognition (Masino et al., 2019). Another example of early diagnosis based on a machine learning model is the use of maternal and neonatal data including clinical, feeding, and laboratory parameters to predict intestinal perforation in case of neonatal enterocolitis. This model utilized Back-propagation neural network (BPNN) and demonstrated high accuracy in estimating intestinal perforation, with regression coefficients between the experimental and predicted data exceeding 0.97 (Irles et al., 2018). Machine learning framework has also been utilized for prediction of pediatric cardiac arrests (Matam et al., 2019). The framework focused on exploiting changing patterns in physiological signals related to deterioration leading to cardiac or respiratory arrests through a machine learning model based on retrospective single-center study using hourly data from HER. This model employed space embedding and time series forecasting methods to achieve a higher accuracy of prediction of cardiac arrests (91%) compared to clinical assessment (6%).

In delivery of acute pediatric care, preverbal and nonverbal children present a diagnostic challenge as decision-making and diagnosis often relies heavily on surrogate data. Advanced multimodal AI systems are now leveraging a combination of video and audio data streams to detect when a preverbal child is in pain, or their condition is deteriorating (Giordano et al., 2024). Such systems can analyze breathing patterns, detect retractions or increased work of breathing through video monitoring while audio analysis of breath sounds or crying can assist in identifying respiratory distress or neurological compromise. In multimodal AI systems, another layer of objective data is added through fusion of physiological signals such as heart rate, respiratory rate, SpO_2 etc., thus enabling early detection and flagging of deterioration in infants and toddlers potentially even before emergence of observable clinical signs.

11.3.2 Clinical Decision Support

Multimodal AI has been leveraged in pediatric critical care to develop regression or neural net-based clinical decision support tools which help with prognostication, predictive parameter thresholds, and treatment prompts. One of the early attempts in this regard was pediatric risk of mortality prediction tool (PROMPT), a deep learning model for real-time mortality prediction in pediatric intensive care units (PICUs). PROMPT uses seven vital signs, age, and body weight at ICU admission. The model achieved an area under the receiver operating characteristic curve (AUROC) between 0.89 and 0.97 for predicting death 6–60 hours in advance. PROMPT showed better predictive performance than the standard pediatric index of mortality (PIM) score (Kim et al., 2019). Deep learning-based early warning systems (DEWS) is another machine learning model based on recurrent neural networks which was trained on four vital signs from a retrospective cohort of over 52,000 patients (Kwon et al., 2018). This system demonstrated significantly higher performance compared to traditional track-and-trigger systems like the modified pediatric early-warning score (PEWS) even on multicentric validation, with better accuracy in predicting deterioration events and fewer false alarms (Shin et al., 2022). AI-powered systems have also been tasked with analysis of vast quantities of physiological data for better informed clinical decision support to improve neonatal outcomes. One such AI-based framework for the real-time monitoring of neonatal vital signs, leveraged LSTM neural networks to process heart rate, respiratory rate, oxygen saturation, and temperature data for early detection of physiological anomalies. This model integrates clinician feedback for real-time adaptation and has transparency for improved interpretability (Sravani et al., 2025).

In India's healthcare infrastructure which has physician availability 30% below WHO recommendations and nurse availability 50% below recommended levels, AI-powered decision support systems can offer crucial assistance to overburdened healthcare workers. A pilot AI-powered clinical decision support platform operated by community health workers has dramatically improved pediatric care access in Mumbai's slums. This multimodal system processed clinical assessment data, demographic information, and environmental factors to provide triage recommendations and treatment guidance. The intervention increased the proportion of childhood illness episodes treated in the community from 4% to 76%, significantly reducing hospitalizations and healthcare costs (Patil et al., 2023).

11.3.3 Diagnostics

Intermediate fusion transformers have been utilized for integration of multimodal imaging data from structural and functional MRI. This model has been utilized in diagnosis of epilepsies in pediatric acute care settings (Huang & Shu, 2025). Another example of use of multimodal AI in diagnostics is the application of deep convolutional neural networks and infrared thermography for detection of health status of neonates. This model utilized data augmentation technique such as brightness enhancement, color transformation, resolution and contrast changes to address the issue of limited medical data and achieved 99.58% accuracy, 99.73% specificity, 99.43% sensitivity, and 0.996 AUC for the 30,400 thermal images employed (Ornek et al., 2019).

11.3.4 Prevention & Wellness

Multimodal AI has revolutionized the wearable health technology sector. AI algorithms have the ability to analyze massive amounts of data collected by biosensors of wearable devices to predict health outcomes and can accurately predict acute events like cardiac arrest, arrhythmia, asthma exacerbations, thereby giving prehospital and emergency care lead time to proactive measures (Shajari et al., 2023). A specific example of actionable data emanating from wearables for monitoring children with congenital heart disease and integrating the data into clinical workflow with the help of AI has been envisioned (Tandon et al., 2024).

Beyond use in at-risk cohorts, the wearable health technology is being increasingly used to monitor physiology for preventive care. Typical examples include infant pulse oximetry monitors used as foot or wrist worn devices. FDA approved Owlet Smart Sock or Masimo stork wrap around infant's foot to transmit continuous SpO_2 and heart rate readings to a smart phone app. Through use of transmittance pulse oximetry and accelerometers, these devices reduce motion artifacts and provide real-time alerts for issues such as sleep apnea and hypoxia. Systems such as Owlet's camera or the Nanit Pro monitor use video monitoring to track infant's chest movements or sleep postures which are combined with wearable readings for detecting abnormal physiology.

These pediatric wearables offer exciting possibilities, where AI-driven analytics could make them the cornerstone of pediatric preventive care. The current challenge is clinical validation and studies are required to determine whether use of such devices reduces emergency visits or even sudden infant death syndrome (SIDS) rate. Improvements in biosensors and multimodal AI fusion algorithms can potentially promote pediatric wellness through wearable tech.

11.3.5 Care Delivery

Use of multimodal AI in emergency healthcare has been shown to transform care delivery in emergency departments through consistent prioritization and appropriate resource allocation. Studies have reported consistent decrease in wait times, overcrowding and improved capability to manage high patient volumes during mass casualty events through use of AI in emergency departments (Ouanes & Farhah, 2024).

11.4 Technical Challenges

Multimodal AI has enormous potential to optimize treatment pathways in pediatric emergency and critical care but there are significant technical and integration challenges impeding its adoption in acute pediatric care. These challenges are often amplified by developmental variability of children and paucity of pediatric datasets.

11.4.1 Data Quality Challenges

Pediatric acute care settings often generate incomplete or noisy data due to factors such as uncooperative pediatric patients, movements, equipment malfunctions and the time constraints of emergency settings (Di Sarno et al., 2024). Furthermore, it is important to note that most commercial AI solutions have developed and validated on adults due to scarcity of pediatric datasets for training machine models. It is estimated that only 20% of AI-based devices authorized by FDA for use in pediatrics have been trained on pediatric data. This compromises their integration into multimodal AI algorithms for pediatric use as it may result in erroneous predictions due to physiological and disease profile differences. Finally, inclusion of local pediatric datasets emanating from Indian cohorts for training of AI algorithms is needed to avoid less sensitive or even biased analysis of multimodal data streams as lack of representativeness can skew results and even introduce harm.

11.4.2 Data Integration Challenges

Heterogeneity of data of pediatric datasets is the most formidable challenge for integration of multimodal data (Ganatra, 2025). This heterogeneity arises from age-dependent physiological parameters, developmental variations, and condition-specific presentations. This complexity is compounded by a lack of standardization of data formats across different healthcare systems. Integration into generalizable multimodal AI systems is challenging due to varying terminologies, units of measurements, and data structures. Another challenge is data alignment and temporal synchronization due to varying sample rates, temporal resolutions, and collection methodologies.

11.4.3 Real-Time Processing Challenges

Fusion of multimodal data streams such as high-resolution medical images, continuous physiological signals, and natural language processing of clinical notes and their real-time processing requires substantial computational power and specialized hardware (Ye et al., 2024). Lack of such infrastructural requirements is a huge challenge for AI implementation. Also, concerns have been raised regarding scalability and performance optimization in form of latency and response times of multimodal AI systems in face of huge patient loads in populous countries like India.

11.5 Ethical, Regulatory, and Practical Concerns

11.5.1 Pediatric Vulnerability and Parental Acceptance

Implementation of multimodal AI in healthcare creates complex ethical dynamics more so in pediatric cohorts because of their developmental status and legal vulnerabilities. Consent or assent of children for healthcare decisions usually depends upon parents and in case of use AI-driven healthcare studies indicate that parental acceptance of AI varies significantly based on educational level and understanding of technology.

11.5.2 Algorithmic Bias

Another critical ethical challenge in the use of multimodal AI is the algorithmic bias which can stem from inadequate representativeness of training data in terms of age, ethnicity, races, socioeconomic demographics etc. Inappropriate generalization from adult datasets has the potential to perform poorly in pediatric populations, hence, ACCEPT—AI framework calls for transparency in age-specific model performance along with emphasizing the need for age-appropriate data labelling and clinically relevant representation of children (Muralidharan et al., 2023).

11.5.3 Data Privacy and Security Concerns

Ethical challenges of data privacy in pediatrics merit greater consideration because of the vulnerability of the population involved as well as the long-term implications of data use. Data breaches, unauthorized access, and cyber exposure during use of pediatric data for machine learning need to be guarded against with the use of data anonymization, encryption, and federated learning (Jamil Abusamra et al., n.d.).

11.5.4 Regulatory Framework

The regulatory framework for the use of multimodal AI in healthcare is evolving, more so, in acute pediatric care. Current regulatory frameworks do not adequately address pediatric-specific considerations in AI device approval unlike the approval process in the field of pharmaceuticals. Off-label use of AI systems based on adult data without adequate validation raises concerns of safety and efficacy of AI systems when used in pediatric emergency and critical care settings. Given the global nature of AI development, there is an urgent need for harmonization of policies internationally regarding data protection and pediatric-specific requirements.

11.5.5 Liability Framework

Use of multimodal AI in healthcare, especially in pediatric settings, creates complex liability questions. Determining responsibility for an error in a pediatric emergency due to deployment of AI can be challenging. Several models have been proposed in the currently evolving liability framework. The vicarious liability model holds healthcare providers or institutions liable for AI system errors while the product liability model holds manufacturers responsible for defective AI systems (Cestonaro et al., 2023).

11.5.6 Trust & Interpretability

One of the most important practical challenges in deployment of multimodal AI is lack of understanding amongst healthcare professionals about the functioning of AI algorithms and deep learning models. This brings about issues of trust and interpretability as healthcare providers need to understand how AI systems make decisions, particularly when those decisions affect vulnerable pediatric populations. This opacity stemming from the "black box" nature of multimodal AI algorithms limits acceptance and workflow integration (Jamil Abusamra et al., n.d.). Explainable AI models instead of overly technical explanations should be based on context specific, concise explanations such as highlighted image regions, segmented text snippets or vital trends, to enable healthcare providers to take informed decisions. Specialized training to healthcare providers in pediatric emergency and critical care to improve their understanding of AI system capabilities and limitations and interpreting AI outputs in pediatric contexts.

11.5.7 Infrastructural and Financial Barriers

The biggest barrier to widespread adoption of multimodal AI in pediatric emergency and critical care, particularly in low- and middle-income countries, is the significant financial and infrastructural requirements. Infrastructural requirements

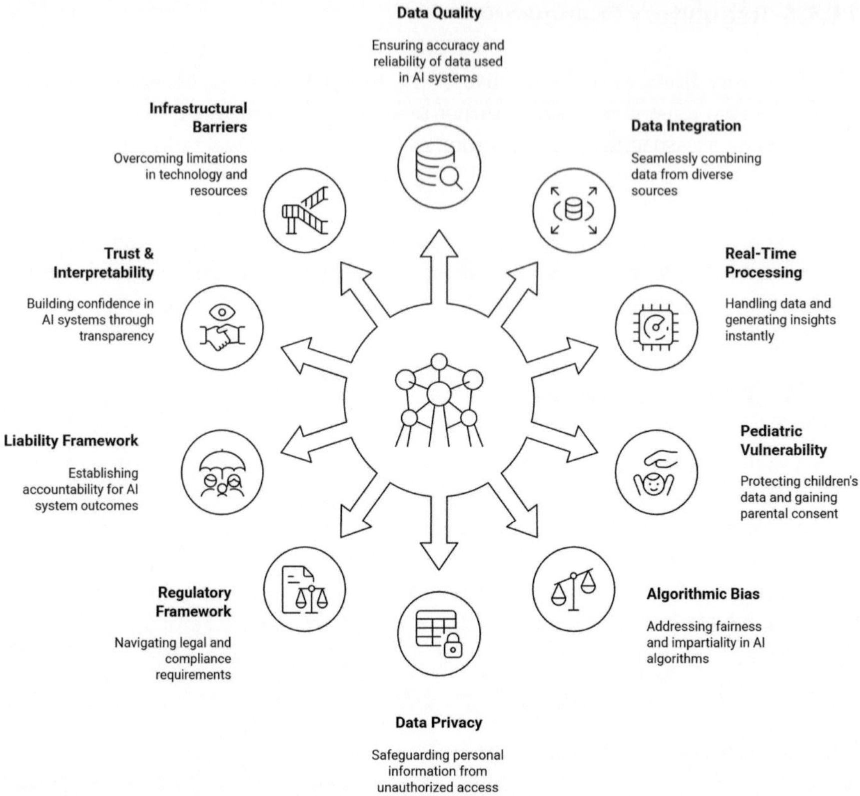

Fig. 11.4 Challenges in implementation of multimodal AI

include high-performance computation hardware, secure data storage, robust network connectivity, augmentation of electronic health record systems and interoperable platforms which involve substantial costs. Beyond hardware, software, and infrastructural requirements, the process of development, validation, and maintenance of AI models along with cybersecurity and processes involved in regulatory compliance add to the financial model of AI deployment in pediatric care. Targeted funding, public-private partnerships and scalable solutions need to be explored to ensure equity in access to advanced AI-driven care for critically ill children.

Challenges in implementation of multimodal AI in pediatric emergency and critical care are summarized in Fig. 11.4.

11.6 Future Directions

The nascent but rapidly evolving field of multimodal AI in pediatric emergency and critical care has multiple innovations on the anvil. These endeavors will improve upon current generations of predictive and decision-support models, to focus on greater contextual understanding, enhanced generalizability, improved interpretability, and equitable global deployment.

11.6.1 Federated Learning

Federated learning is the new approach which machine learning models are employing to promote collaborative model training across multiple institutions through data sharing without compromising patient privacy. In this approach, local datasets are used to train algorithms and only model updates, instead of raw patient data, are shared and aggregated to improve global performance. In addition to ensuring ethical issues related to privacy, federated learning increases the generalizability of multimodal AI in pediatric critical care by including data from underrepresented populations and resource limited settings. Future work is expected to focus on personalized federated learning, where global models are adapted to local contexts without sacrificing accuracy. Recent work on FL-PedBrain demonstrated that federated learning can achieve performance comparable to centralized training while maintaining data privacy (Lee et al., 2024).

11.6.2 Multimodal Explainable AI (XAI)

Development of XAI is being prioritized to create interpretable models that can provide clear reasoning for clinical decisions, particularly in emergency situations (Salih et al., 2024). Emerging techniques include attention heatmaps that highlight critical features in imaging, temporal saliency graphs for time-series data, and natural language explanations for text data to allow users to understand the contribution of different modalities in a clinical decision suggested by an AI model. Causality-based AI models are also being developed to align model reasoning with clinical cause effect relationships.

11.6.3 Edge AI and Real-Time Inference

In order to address the latency in real-time multimodal data integration, edge AI is being introduced which has the capability to process multimodal data at the bedside, thereby reducing the response time for a critical intervention. Lightweight edge computing architecture can continuously process streaming data (e.g., ECG, SpO_2, respiratory waveforms) and issue alerts even in low-bandwidth environments. Edge AI can be particularly valuable for prehospital care, such as in ambulances or remote clinics, where early triage and stabilization are critical.

11.7 Conclusion

The deployment of multimodal AI into pediatric emergency and critical care has the transformative potential for changing how complex clinical data is synthesized to make life-saving decisions and interventions. Multimodal AI, with its ability to process heterogeneous data from diverse data streams such as imaging, laboratory results, clinical texts, time series waveform data etc. mimics and can even augment the cognitive processes of healthcare teams. Applications of multimodal AI are being investigated across the continuum of acute pediatric care delivery—improving triage accuracy in crowded emergency departments, enabling early detection of clinical deterioration, enhancing diagnostic precision through integrated imaging and contextual data analysis, and providing dynamic clinical decision support for early interventions.

However, workflow integration of these advancements requires careful consideration of technical, infrastructural, and ethical challenges. Addressing data quality and algorithmic biases arising out of incomplete pediatric datasets, privacy of data, regulatory—legal frameworks, transparent explainability of AI models need astute attention for its seamless integration in current workflows. Addressing the equity gap is equally critical to ensure that innovations in multimodal AI do not remain confined to resource-rich environments but are suitable for integration in pediatric critical care workflow of low- and middle-income countries where pediatric mortality is highest. Attempts at federated learning, XAI, edge computing models are all efforts in the direction of making multimodal AI a trusted collaborator which aims to augment human expertise rather than replacing it.

For multimodal AI to fulfill its promise of transforming pediatric emergency and critical care for the betterment of the most vulnerable patients, moving forward, an interprofessional approach involving pediatricians, data scientists, engineers, ethicists, and regulators will be key to address all technical and ethical concerns.

References

AlSaad, R., Abd-alrazaq, A., Boughorbel, S., Ahmed, A., Renault, M.-A., Damseh, R., & Sheikh, J. (2024). Multimodal large language models in health care: Applications, challenges, and future outlook. *Journal of Medical Internet Research, 26*, e59505. https://doi.org/10.2196/59505

Cestonaro, C., Delicati, A., Marcante, B., Caenazzo, L., & Tozzo, P. (2023). Defining medical liability when artificial intelligence is applied on diagnostic algorithms: A systematic review. *Frontiers in Medicine, 10*, 1305756. https://doi.org/10.3389/fmed.2023.1305756

Choi, S. W., Ko, T., Hong, K. J., & Kim, K. H. (2019). Machine learning-based prediction of Korean triage and acuity scale level in emergency department patients. *Healthcare Informatics Research, 25*(4), 305–312. https://doi.org/10.4258/hir.2019.25.4.305

Di Sarno, L., Caroselli, A., Tonin, G., Graglia, B., Pansini, V., Causio, F. A., Gatto, A., & Chiaretti, A. (2024). Artificial intelligence in pediatric emergency medicine: Applications, challenges, and future perspectives. *Biomedicine, 12*(6), 1220. https://doi.org/10.3390/biomedicines12061220

Ganatra, H. A. (2025). Machine learning in pediatric healthcare: Current trends, challenges, and future directions. *Journal of Clinical Medicine, 14*(3), 807. https://doi.org/10.3390/jcm14030807

Giordano, V., Luister, A., Vettorazzi, E., Wonka, K., Pointner, N., Steinbauer, P., Wagner, M., Berger, A., Singer, D., & Deindl, P. (2024). Comparative analysis of artificial intelligence and expert assessments in detecting neonatal procedural pain. *Scientific Reports, 14*(1), 20374. https://doi.org/10.1038/s41598-024-71278-6

Goto, T., Camargo, C. A., Faridi, M. K., Freishtat, R. J., & Hasegawa, K. (2019). Machine learning-based prediction of clinical outcomes for children during emergency department triage. *JAMA Network Open, 2*(1), e186937. https://doi.org/10.1001/jamanetworkopen.2018.6937

Huang, W., & Shu, N. (2025). AI-powered integration of multimodal imaging in precision medicine for neuropsychiatric disorders. *Cell Reports Medicine, 6*(5), 102132. https://doi.org/10.1016/j.xcrm.2025.102132

Irles, C., González-Pérez, G., Carrera Muiños, S., Michel Macias, C., Sánchez Gómez, C., Martínez-Zepeda, A., Cordero González, G., & Laresgoiti Servitje, E. (2018). Estimation of neonatal intestinal perforation associated with necrotizing Enterocolitis by machine learning reveals new key factors. *International Journal of Environmental Research and Public Health, 15*(11), 2509. https://doi.org/10.3390/ijerph15112509

Jamil Abusamra, H. N., Ali, S. H. M., Khidir Elhussien, W. A., Ahmed Mirghani, A. M., Alameen Ahmed, A. A., & Abdelrahman Ibrahim, M. E. (n.d.). Ethical and practical considerations of artificial intelligence in pediatric medicine: A systematic review. *Cureus, 17*(2), e79024. https://doi.org/10.7759/cureus.79024

Kim, S. Y., Kim, S., Cho, J., Kim, Y. S., Sol, I. S., Sung, Y., Cho, I., Park, M., Jang, H., Kim, Y. H., Kim, K. W., & Sohn, M. H. (2019). A deep learning model for real-time mortality prediction in critically ill children. *Critical Care, 23*(1), 279. https://doi.org/10.1186/s13054-019-2561-z

Kunitomo, K., Harada, T., & Watari, T. (2022). Cognitive biases encountered by physicians in the emergency room. *BMC Emergency Medicine, 22*(1), 148. https://doi.org/10.1186/s12873-022-00708-3

Kwon, J.-M., Lee, Y., Lee, Y., Lee, S., & Park, J. (2018). An algorithm based on deep learning for predicting in-hospital cardiac arrest. *Journal of the American Heart Association, 7*(13), e008678. https://doi.org/10.1161/JAHA.118.008678

Lee, E. H., Han, M., Wright, J., Kuwabara, M., Mevorach, J., Fu, G., Choudhury, O., Ratan, U., Zhang, M., Wagner, M. W., Goetti, R., Toescu, S., Perreault, S., Dogan, H., Altinmakas, E., Mohammadzadeh, M., Szymanski, K. A., Campen, C. J., Lai, H., et al. (2024). An international study presenting a federated learning AI platform for pediatric brain tumors. *Nature Communications, 15*(1), 7615. https://doi.org/10.1038/s41467-024-51172-5

Masino, A. J., Harris, M. C., Forsyth, D., Ostapenko, S., Srinivasan, L., Bonafide, C. P., Balamuth, F., Schmatz, M., & Grundmeier, R. W. (2019). Machine learning models for early sepsis recognition in the neonatal intensive care unit using readily available electronic health record data. *PLoS One, 14*(2), e0212665. https://doi.org/10.1371/journal.pone.0212665

Matam, B. R., Duncan, H., & Lowe, D. (2019). Machine learning based framework to predict cardiac arrests in a paediatric intensive care unit: Prediction of cardiac arrests. *Journal of Clinical Monitoring and Computing, 33*(4), 713–724. https://doi.org/10.1007/s10877-018-0198-0

Miller, G. A. (1994). The magical number seven, plus or minus two: Some limits on our capacity for processing information. 1956. *Psychological Review, 101*(2), 343–352. https://doi.org/10.1037/0033-295x.101.2.343

Muralidharan, V., Burgart, A., Daneshjou, R., & Rose, S. (2023). Recommendations for the use of pediatric data in artificial intelligence and machine learning ACCEPT-AI. *npj Digital Medicine, 6*, 166. https://doi.org/10.1038/s41746-023-00898-5

Ornek, A. H., Ceylan, M., & Ervural, S. (2019). Health status detection of neonates using infrared thermography and deep convolutional neural networks. *Infrared Physics & Technology, 103*, 103044. https://doi.org/10.1016/j.infrared.2019.103044

Ouanes, K., & Farhah, N. (2024). Effectiveness of Artificial Intelligence (AI) in clinical decision support systems and care delivery. *Journal of Medical Systems, 48*(1), 74. https://doi.org/10.1007/s10916-024-02098-4

Patil, M., Qureshi, A., Naydenova, E., Bang, A., Halbert, J., Vos, M. D., Nair, P., Patil, M., & Medvedev, M. M. (2023). Assessing a digital technology-supported community child health programme in India using the social return on investment framework. *PLoS Digital Health, 2*(11), e0000363. https://doi.org/10.1371/journal.pdig.0000363

Salih, A. M., Menegaz, G., Pillay, T., & Boyle, E. M. (2024). Explainable artificial intelligence in Paediatric: Challenges for the future. *Health Science Reports, 7*(12), e70271. https://doi.org/10.1002/hsr2.70271

Schouten, D., Nicoletti, G., Dille, B., Chia, C., Vendittelli, P., Schuurmans, M., Litjens, G., & Khalili, N. (2025). Navigating the landscape of multimodal AI in medicine: A scoping review on technical challenges and clinical applications. *Medical Image Analysis, 105*, 103621. https://doi.org/10.1016/j.media.2025.103621

Shajari, S., Kuruvinashetti, K., Komeili, A., & Sundararaj, U. (2023). The emergence of AI-based wearable sensors for digital health technology: A review. *Sensors (Basel, Switzerland), 23*(23), 9498. https://doi.org/10.3390/s23239498

Shin, Y., Cho, K.-J., Lee, Y., Choi, Y. H., Jung, J. H., Kim, S. Y., Kim, Y. H., Kim, Y. A., Cho, J., Park, S. J., & Jhang, W. K. (2022). Multicenter validation of a deep-learning-based pediatric early-warning system for prediction of deterioration events. *Acute and Critical Care, 37*(4), 654–666. https://doi.org/10.4266/acc.2022.00976

Soenksen, L. R., Ma, Y., Zeng, C., Boussioux, L., Villalobos Carballo, K., Na, L., Wiberg, H. M., Li, M. L., Fuentes, I., & Bertsimas, D. (2022). Integrated multimodal artificial intelligence framework for healthcare applications. *npj Digital Medicine, 5*, 149. https://doi.org/10.1038/s41746-022-00689-4

Sravani, G., Khaleel, S., Haritha, H., Sudhakar, S., & Vardhan, C. M. V. (2025). Artificial intelligence for real-time monitoring of neonatal vital signs: Enhancing decision-making in critical care units. *Journal of Neonatal Surgery, 14*(15S), 15S.

Tandon, A., Avari Silva, J. N., Bhatt, A. B., Drummond, C. K., Hill, A. C., Paluch, A. E., Waits, S., Zablah, J. E., Harris, K. C., & on behalf of the Council on Lifelong Congenital Heart Disease and Heart Health in the Young (Young Hearts); Council on Lifestyle and Cardiometabolic Health; Council on Clinical Cardiology; and Council on Cardiovascular and Stroke Nursing. (2024). Advancing wearable biosensors for congenital heart disease: Patient and clinician perspectives: A science advisory from the American Heart Association. *Circulation, 149*(19), e1134–e1142. https://doi.org/10.1161/CIR.0000000000001225

Teoh, J. R., Dong, J., Zuo, X., Lai, K. W., Hasikin, K., & Wu, X. (2024). Advancing healthcare through multimodal data fusion: A comprehensive review of techniques and applications. *PeerJ Computer Science, 10*, e2298. https://doi.org/10.7717/peerj-cs.2298

Transforming healthcare with AI: The impact on the workforce and organizations | McKinsey. (n.d.). Retrieved July 8, 2025, from https://www.mckinsey.com/industries/healthcare/our-insights/transforming-healthcare-with-ai

Wolff, P., Ríos, S. A., & Graña, M. (2019). Setting up standards: A methodological proposal for pediatric Triage machine learning model construction based on clinical outcomes. *Expert Systems with Applications, 138*, 112788. https://doi.org/10.1016/j.eswa.2019.07.005

Ye, J., Woods, D., Jordan, N., & Starren, J. (2024). The role of artificial intelligence for the application of integrating electronic health records and patient-generated data in clinical decision support. *AMIA Summits on Translational Science Proceedings, 2024*, 459–467.

12 Multimodal AI and Telemedicine in Remote Health Monitoring

Kalaivane Kannadasan

12.1 Introduction

12.1.1 Background

Telemedicine has come increasingly to the forefront in reshaping the way that healthcare is being provided as a function of meeting the need for a distance-based avenue of access to receive assistance with healthcare services that are normally delivered in a clinical setting. The COVID-19 pandemic has had the possible effect of revolutionizing such a trend by dis-enabling the most structural forms of care through lockdown, breakdown of health systems, and suspending bodily contact. Therefore, remote health monitoring and digital health have become the future theme across the globe.

Aside from this digitalization, the development of artificial intelligence (AI) is becoming a required technological output in the healthcare industry with applications that will make diagnosis easier, make the healthcare industry more streamlined and enhance clinical decision-making. Incorporation of AI in telemedicine infrastructure has promoted the development of a new level of intelligent telemedicine of reactive, adaptive, and scalable to remote healthcare populations.

12.1.2 Multimodal Artificial Intelligence in Healthcare

Multimodal AI recognizes computational systems that can understand and synthesize from many types of sources, such as structured health records, textual symptom descriptions, visual images, audio input (e.g., describing cough sound), video

K. Kannadasan (✉)
Public Health Medicine Specialist, Jempol Health District Office, Ministry of Health, Putrajaya, Malaysia

U. Venkatesh et al. (eds.), *Multimodal AI in Healthcare*, https://doi.org/10.1007/978-981-95-9027-8_12

consultations, and bio signal monitoring from wearables. Such systems also have significant value to remote care settings in their ability to derive coordinated clinical decisions from different types of sources, and in general settings where access to full clinical diagnostics can be severely limited in real time (Stryker, 2025).

In a remote monitoring scenario, multimodal AI can integrate data such as:

- Physiological signals (e.g., heart rate, oxygen saturation)
- Textual entries from patient self-reports or chatbots
- Speech data for respiratory symptom analysis
- Facial and body imagery for dermatological or mobility assessments

This layered interpretation impersonates the multifactorial approach of human clinical reasoning, thereby offering an opportunity to extend medical assessment and intervention capabilities beyond healthcare settings (Huang et al., 2025).

12.1.3 Relevance and Significance

The universal applicability of multimodal AI in telemedicine is highlighted by the use of the field in several healthcare systems. Integrated systems, like the NHS (National Health Service) App in the United Kingdom, or AI-based triage to remote care in the United States, show how machine learning and natural language processing can use their capabilities to direct remote care. Simultaneously, resource-constrained environments are experimenting with lightweight AI tools to support community health workers, enhance triage accuracy, and monitor chronic diseases.

The impact of multimodal AI is particularly noteworthy in:

- Chronic disease management: enabling longitudinal data tracking
- Pandemic response: ensuring continuity of care during outbreaks
- Health equity: improving access in geographically isolated or underserved populations

However, its adoption is also accompanied by challenges, including data privacy, digital literacy gaps, algorithmic bias, and regulatory ambiguity which must be addressed to ensure ethical, equitable, and effective implementation (Jothi Prakash & Varsha, 2025).

12.1.4 Chapter Objectives and Structure

This chapter explores the intersection of multimodal AI and telemedicine in remote health monitoring, providing a comprehensive examination of current innovations, implementation challenges, and policy implications. Specifically, the chapter aims to:

- Define the conceptual of multimodal AI and its role in telehealth systems
- Review global case studies and health system applications
- Present empirical findings from a real-world evaluation of a remote monitoring initiative
- Propose a system architecture for integrating multimodal AI in telemedicine workflows
- Discuss ethical, legal, and social considerations
- Provide strategic recommendations for implementation and policy formulation

The chapter is structured as follows: Section 12.2 elaborates on the conceptual framework of multimodal AI and telemedicine; Sect. 12.3 provides an overview of international use cases; Sect. 12.4 discusses on the structure of a multimodal AI telemedicine system; Sect. 12.5 explores regulatory and ethical considerations; Sect. 12.6 offers a policy roadmap; Sect. 12.7 presents an original research findings from a real-world deployment (Case study from Malaysia); and Sect. 12.8 concludes with future directions for research and practice.

12.2 Conceptual Framework

12.2.1 Telemedicine: Evolution and Definition

Telemedicine can be defined as the exploitation of telecommunications technology in order to provide clinical health services across a distance. Although it has developed over a period of several decades, the rise of the smartphones, the broadband connection, and the digital health platforms has given telemedicine an exponential rise. It currently has the modes of providing patients with an opportunity to communicate with their providers through the means of synchronous (real-time video consultation), asynchronous (store-and-forward), and hybrid communication.

Telehealth is a larger subset of telemedicine, and also encompasses health education, administrative and remote public health meetings. The move to digitally oriented health formats has established the groundwork in the domain of intelligent improvements, especially the integration of AI solutions.

The Van Dyk Model of Telehealth provides a comprehensive and organized approach to the telehealth services conceptualization as to how it can be successfully implemented, integrated, and only maintained in healthcare systems. The model is suggested by Linda Van Dyk (2014), who unites the information provided by other telehealth implementation models in the four most important domains: strategy and readiness, design and implementation, operations and change management, and monitoring and evaluation (van Dyk, 2014).

The first area is strategy and readiness, which underlines the significance of making telehealth initiatives aligned with the overall organizational objectives, stakeholder involvement, system preparedness, legal and regulatory adherence, and financial availability. The second area is concerned with the actual features of design and user interface elements, namely, service design, technology infrastructure, personnel training, and pilot testing. The third domain addresses operationalization and change management, highlighting the need for integrating telehealth into existing clinical workflows, defining clear roles and responsibilities, ensuring data privacy, and supporting both provider and patient adaptation. The final domain, monitoring, evaluation, and sustainability, involves tracking performance indicators, assessing user satisfaction, evaluating cost-effectiveness, and planning for long-term scalability (van Dyk, 2014).

This model edifies that successful telehealth implementation extends beyond technology deployment; it requires a systemic, multi-level approach that considers organizational culture, capacity, user readiness, and policy support. Its holistic viewpoint makes it particularly valuable for guiding telehealth strategies in diverse healthcare settings, especially where resource constraints and health equity are ongoing concerns.

12.2.2 The Role of Artificial Intelligence in Remote Monitoring

AI in healthcare refers to the development of algorithms that mimic cognitive functions such as learning, perceptive, and problem-solving. In the context of remote health monitoring, AI supports functions such as:

- Symptom triaging (e.g., chatbots, self-assessment tools)
- Pattern recognition in bio signals (e.g., ECG, oxygen saturation)
- Risk stratification based on clinical history
- Predictive analytics for adverse event forecasting

AI-enabled telemedicine has improved healthcare accessibility, particularly for chronic conditions, elderly populations, marginalized populations and individuals in geographically isolated regions.

12.2.3 Understanding Multimodal Artificial Intelligence

Multimodal AI refers to systems capable of processing and interpreting multiple types of data inputs simultaneously. In healthcare, these modalities may include:

- Structured data (e.g., laboratory results, vitals)
- Unstructured text (e.g., physician notes, patient chats)
- Imaging data (e.g., X-rays, skin photographs)
- Audio inputs (e.g., breathing sounds, voice tone)
- Video feeds (e.g., patient facial expressions or movement)

By integrating these modalities, multimodal AI systems enable a more all-inclusive assessment of patient health. The coactive processing of multimodal data can reflect and even encompass human diagnostic capabilities, making it particularly suitable for remote health applications where traditional diagnostics may be inadequate (Bajwa et al., 2021).

12.2.4 Key Theoretical Models Supporting Adoption and Evaluation of Telehealth Modality

Telemedicine multimodal AI system development and implementation can be investigated with robust application of theories of health informatics, behavioral science and implementation science. These kinds of frameworks are pivotal in offering the required support by guiding, where such tools are not merely technically well-established but neither least suited to application tasks, systems prospects, or variation in circumstances of operation. One of the most well-known models is the Technology Acceptance Model (TAM), which presupposes imagining the user behavior concerning the introduction of using technologies based on two significant constructs, i.e., considered usefulness and ease of use. TAM is a micro-technology theory that exists in the field of computer science which asserts that the amount of adoption and continuing use of a technology is a function of users' perceptions of a technology which they find performs at a good level and of substance, and of its ease of use. The model is especially applicable to telehealth, where speed, interface, and the perceived effect of the given system on care delivery affect user trust and satisfaction (Schorr, 2023).

Enhancing the TAM, the Unified Theory of Acceptance and Use of Technology (UTAUT) is a more extensive explanation of the concept that does add newer determinants to the concept, including social influence, expectancy regarding performance, expectancy regarding effort, and facilitation conditions. UTAUT can be applied to learning socio-technical interactions during telemedicine adoption and adaptability, particularly to diverse healthcare environments in which the adoption perceptions of users depend on organizational culture, peer pressure, and the appearance of technical assistance. Both the TAM and UTAUT will play a critical role in informing the user interface design, training requirements, and implementation mechanisms in the achievement of AI-enhanced health platform adoptions as well as lifelong use (Shachak et al., 2019).

Another valuable tool in the broad toolkit of implementation science is the Delphi Method in the early stages of systems development. It is a systematic iterative process where system requirements, ethical considerations, clinical significance, and workflows are agreed upon collectively by a group of experts. The Delphi Method along with multidisciplinary experience including clinicians, the technology and health modality and patients, is helpful in ensuring that artificial intelligence-based telehealth models are not only clinically relevant but are also legally and ethically valid. It is particularly necessary in distant health monitoring, where the results based on the algorithmic analysis can directly affect the patient's care (Nasa et al., 2021).

Patient-Reported Experience Measures (PREMs) are required to assess the system performance according to the perceptions of the patient. PREMs are used to relate the subjective levels of user experience such as sense of usability, trust, responsiveness, and level of communication. Applied to multimodal AI, PREMs assist in understanding whether a patient feels safe, understood, or supported when engaging with the platforms, which are supported by AI. Considering patient feedback to system enhancement also demonstrates that the technical complexity does not dominate over sensitivity and accessibility, in especially vulnerable populations with smaller digital literacy (Harrison et al., 2024).

Lastly, the effectiveness support and adoption of AI-enhanced telehealth models and their long-term sustainability must focus on the implementation of the models through the application of implementation science frameworks, including the Consolidated Framework for Implementation Research (CFIR) or the RE-AIM framework (Reach, Effectiveness, Adoption, Implementation and Maintenance). These models are used to close the pilot success to real-world implementation divided by dealing with obstacles like stakeholder involvement, organizational willingness, situational challenges, and ease of policy adjustment. They underline the importance of constant monitoring, adjustment, and capacity-building to make sure that multimodal artificial intelligence systems will transform according to the evolving clinical, technological, and sociocultural environments (Glasgow et al., 2022; Rauner and Stummer, 2025).

Overall, a synthesis of the theoretical frameworks gives a multidimensional strategy in designing, implementing and assessing multimodal AI use in telemedicine. They also provide utility tools so as to make sure that hardware is innovative and also sufficient, fair, extensible, and receptive to the dynamic realities of healthcare delivery systems.

12.2.5 Benefits and Challenges of Multimodal Integration

12.2.5.1 Benefits

The implementation of multimodal AI in remote health studies is also linked to numerous advantages and privileges that would likely turn around how we gauge, provide, fund, and empower quality, efficacious as well as fair health services. One of the most powerful properties that enable derivation of clinical actionable information is the advantage of context-dependent interpretation of varying sources of data such as biometric data, behavioral data and context features. It is a multidimensional way of thinking and can lead to a higher level of knowledge about the health status of the patient and to better clinical judgment. That continuous observation and tracking capacities of such systems obviously exist and they must be supplemented by early warning systems, which appropriately detect exposure of deterioration in the different clinical state variables to an extent that they should not evolve into untenable conditions. For example, in diabetes care, multimodal AI can combine continuous glucose monitor readings, dietary logs, and lab values to tailor insulin titration and lifestyle guidance. In hypertension, wearable blood pressure sensors, medication adherence data, and patient-reported stress levels can be integrated to forecast risks of hypertensive crises. Similarly, in heart failure, fusing wearable vitals such as, heart rate, oxygen saturation, weight changes with EHR data allows early detection of fluid overload and timely remote intervention, particularly valuable in rural or home settings. Hence, multimodal AI also enables the provision of individual care and multiple personalized physiological, behavioral, and social information profiles to generate individualized recommendations and interventions. Beyond chronic disease monitoring, multimodal AI in telemedicine holds promise for elderly patients with multimorbidity or frailty. Fall detection through motion sensors, cognitive assessments using speech or facial analytics, and AI-powered medication reminders can reduce risks and support independent living. Such features are particularly relevant as many health systems transition toward aging societies. Additionally, AI triage algorithms have been applied in the chemical diagnostic process and help in accuracy in diagnosis, support the reduction of errors in the perception of symptoms and help to prioritize the provision of care in a situation of resource scarcity or overcrowding. These benefits collectively position multimodal AI as a powerful enabler of proactive, data-informed, and patient-centered healthcare (Maleki Varnosfaderani & Forouzanfar, 2024).

12.2.5.2 Challenges

Although it has quite good potential, there is no implementation of multimodal AI on remote health systems without inquisitions. The most notable barrier in terms of technicality is the multisource information and platform and device incompatibility and lack of interoperability with electronic health records. Data formats and partial datasets and fragmentation of systems are a hindrance to the smooth integration that happens to provide useful AI performance. In practice, multimodal AI must also manage heterogeneous data streams collected from different devices and platforms, ranging from low-cost wearables to phone messages-based symptom logs. This challenge is amplified in under-resourced or low-bandwidth environments, where inconsistent formats and fragmented health information systems can hinder seamless integration. The other major issue is a bias in training data that leads to biased forecasts and lower accuracy on some groups, especially those who are scarcely represented in the data, whether minorities or individuals with rare disorders. The use of audio, video, and biometric data would generate justified privacy and ethical concerns, especially where information privacy policies are loose or not formalized well enough. People may dislike such technologies, as they believe that they are observed, their data are abused or even information has been stolen. However, overreliance on AI poses risks. If input data are incomplete, biased, or lack contextual nuance, AI-generated recommendations may be inaccurate. Multimodal AI, while powerful, cannot substitute clinical judgment. Human-in-the-loop oversight remains essential to validate outputs, provide context-sensitive care, and preserve accountability in clinical decision-making. Lastly, acceptance and digitization literacy mainly to the older generation and the marginalized is another barrier. Unless supported by specialized training, persuasion, and specialist design, such populations can be deprived of the returns of health digital innovation.

Such advantages and drawbacks are problems that cannot safely and fruitfully bring the transformation of multimodal AI systems into the formal system of the public health system or the channel of clinical care. It is necessary to ensure a balance between innovation, ethics, equity, and readiness of the systems to reach the highest potentials of this emerging technology in healthcare systems across the globe (Parvin et al., 2025).

12.3 Global Landscape and Use Cases

12.3.1 International Trends in AI-Driven Telemedicine

The acceptance of AI in telemedicine systems has made headways of remarkable proportions in the healthcare systems around the globe. Despite varied and heterogeneous scopes and depth of implementation, one of them becomes apparent: the application of multimodal AI as the complement to decision-making in an approach to implementation that continually engages digital individuals with healthcare and enhances health outcomes and clinical outcomes. The first to adopt them from their respective countries are the United Kingdom, the United States, and India, which has been offering a clue on the strategy of its deployment and also the convergence of their policies.

12.3.2 United Kingdom: The NHS and Intelligent Telehealth

The United Kingdom through its National Health Service (NHS) has spearheaded the metamorphosis of digital health. The NHS App features an array of services, such as the book of appointments, prescription services and COVID-19 vaccination certificates, and chipping away at what will become AI-enforced services. Some of the initiatives aimed at testing AI-enabled symptom checkers and decision support systems are implemented by the NHS in particular, in which patient-reported symptoms (text and audio), past clinical assessment, and risk factors are translated into predictions (Peek et al., 2023).

12.3.3 United States: Remote Monitoring and Predictive Analytics

In the United States, telemedicine has seen rapid expansion through providers such as Teladoc Health, Kaiser Permanente, and Mayo Clinic, particularly for chronic disease management. These platforms utilize multimodal remote patient monitoring (RPM) systems that combines:

- Biometric data from wearable devices (e.g., heart rate, glucose levels)
- Patient-entered survey responses
- Clinical records from integrated electronic health record (EHR) systems
- Audio/video consultations

Machine learning models process this data to detect early signs of health deterioration, trigger alerts for intervention, and provide predictive analytics for hospital readmission risks. For example, Livongo (now part of Teladoc Health) uses AI to interpret glucose levels, analyze behavioral data, and user feedback to deliver personalized diabetes management interventions in real time (Paul et al., 2025; Simpson et al., 2022).

12.3.4 India: AI and Telemedicine for Resource-Constrained Settings

India presents a unique context where digital health technologies address significant disparities in access to care. The eSanjeevani platform, launched by the Ministry of Health and Family Welfare, provides real-time teleconsultation services across rural and semi-urban regions. To enhance effectiveness, AI tools have been piloted to assist community health workers (CHWs) in screening, triage, and remote monitoring tasks.

The project integrates AI algorithms for:

- Visual interpretation of dermatological images (via smartphone cameras)
- Audio-based respiratory analysis
- NLP-driven regional language symptom reporting

These systems combine structured and unstructured data in low-resource settings, with the goal of supporting frontline health providers and reducing diagnostic delays. However, challenges related to digital literacy, language diversity, and infrastructure reliability remain substantial (Dastidar et al., 2022).

12.3.5 Comparative Insights and Lessons Learned

A synthesis of global experiences reveals several critical enablers of success:

- Integrated infrastructure: seamless interoperability between devices, apps, and EHR systems
- Data localization and personalization: inclusion of cultural, linguistic, and behavioral context
- Strong governance: regulatory clarity on AI tools, privacy standards, and ethical guardrails
- Capacity building: training for healthcare providers in digital tools and patient communication

Conversely, the most common barriers include:

- Fragmentation of health data systems

- Variability in algorithmic performance across demographic groups
- Ethical concerns around AI decision-making without human oversight
- Low adoption rates in vulnerable populations due to digital exclusion

These insights underline the importance of patient-centric design, diverse evaluation, and participatory implementation in deploying multimodal AI in telemedicine.

12.4 Architecture of a Multimodal AI-Driven Telemedicine System

12.4.1 Rationale for System Design

Traditional telemedicine systems in Malaysia and similar middle-income settings are often built around singular modalities such as text-based symptom checklists or simple self-reporting interfaces. However, real-world remote care demands a wider, more responsive infrastructure that can accommodate heterogeneous patient inputs and automated decision support.

A multimodal AI system expands telehealth capability by allowing simultaneous processing of multiple data types, namely, voice, image, biometric sensor data, and user-reported symptoms, enabling comprehensive patient assessment. The structure is designed to support patient safety, real-time responsiveness, and clinical integration in remote health monitoring (Huang et al., 2025).

12.4.2 System Overview

A telemedicine multimodal AI application system is developed to deliver continuous, meaningful and patient-centered remote care by integrating heterogeneous data sources and having intelligent analytics across a staged architecture. This model is based on five layers which cannot fulfill their vital role in the remote care continuum without each other. These layers help to facilitate real-time data collection, intelligent information processing and personalized feedback, and seamless interactions with the user, thereby creating a holistic digital health environment (Huang et al., 2025).

12.4.2.1 Data Acquisition Layer

Data acquisition layer is the second intermediate layer of implementation concerned with the multimodal data acquisition purposes. These include wearable sensors that will capture physiological variables of heart rate, oxygen saturation, breathing rate, and temperature. The mobile integration offers utility in terms of symptom logging, voice and video recording and user-surveillance reports. Furthermore, the system is also available in rural or distantly amongst available settings in the form of interned coverage-limited settings where data can be distinguished through chatbots or

SMS-based interfaces. Visual data including camera photographs of rash or swelling are also helpful to the diagnosis. Such mixed use of formal and informal data helps gaining a dimensional and evolving view of the health echelon of a patient (Boikanyo et al., 2023).

12.4.2.2 Data Fusion and Preprocessing Layer

Once data is retrieved, the data management layer in the system combines and cleans data for AI-based analysis by the data fusion and preprocessing layer. This layer integrates the data streams by means of time-synchronized general-purpose architectures, ensuring the coherency of multiple modalities. The natural language processing (NLP) regarding the textual and speech inputs determines the clinical relevant content, and convolutional neural network (CNN) boosts the visual signal quality and abnormal conditions of image data. Input data assimilation is a standardization of the input data from the wearable biometric sensors that takes into account device variability and user baselines. This preprocessing ensures high-quality data which is interoperable and can be analyzed reliably in real time (Zhao et al., 2024).

12.4.2.3 AI Analytics and Decision Support Layer

The system can also be based on AI analytics and decision support layer. This intelligence layer has taken a very advanced machine learning architecture—and deep learning layers can detect even the best multimodal data schemes. Not only can specific predictive analytics modules identify the risk of deterioration, but they can also record deviation beyond the baseline, not to mention that they can also potentially identify the patient earlier. Symptom clustering engines combine two or more datasets such as biometric data, self-reported symptoms, and visual symptoms to generate triage scores. Even the aspect complements clinical decision making because the information systems in the system to identify anomalies compare existing information with the most recent one. The items manufactured in this layer are introduced in order to inform escalations of risk and risk-specific recommendations that would assist in timely, and precision and efficiently administered care (Zhao et al., 2024).

12.4.2.4 User Interface Layer

The user interface layer provides interaction between the system and users and is catered to three audiences: patients, family members or caregiver, and the healthcare provider. The patients consider accessibility to be a key factor that we should incorporate; we should offer them multilingual support, voice-command processing, icons and self-explanatory navigations in visual format that is easily understandable even when the patient lacks adequate literacy or computer knowledge. They distributed it to the caregivers as simplified summary dashboards and automatic alert systems to monitor the health status of their dependents. Aggregated triage scores, triage alerts, patient schedules, and embedded communication features can be accessed on a clinician dashboard. Design is participatory and not discriminatory: every age and literacy and state of culture engage in a significant way (Kim et al., 2023).

12.4.2.5 Integration and Feedback Loop Layer

The last layer of the system is the integration and feedback loop layer which integrates the telemedicine platform to the remainder of the health systems infrastructure. It means live connectivity to an institutional or nationwide health information system that provides data continuity, and leads to intelligent care management. All this will be supported by transmission of the two-way forms of communication, safe transfer of phylogeny of providers and patients, a safe audit path that will be in a position to follow the clinical accountability and successful clinical service. Furthermore, it includes a feedback mechanism to the system to learn and revise risk algorithms and provide new advice to the clinician as the machine learning knows more with time. This layer has rendered the system dynamic, accountable and concerned with clinical and patient-reported outcomes (Alenoghena et al., 2022).

12.4.3 Visual Representation of the System

To develop a better understanding of this architecture, visual representation can draw the data flow of all five layers and paint a picture of how raw inputs are transformed into usable knowledge. This diagram [Fig. 12.1] illustrates interconnectivity of layers, and it is critical to note that none of the components in these layers will be siloed but rather depend on the other elements allowing a continuous loop of acquisition, interpretation, and response.

12.4.4 Adaptability and Localization

The distributed and extensible quality of this architecture enables implementation into many possible healthcare settings, including digital urban hospitals where high-speed network connectivity and Internet of Things (IoT) connections interoperate, as well as rural clinics with sparse connectivity. In the context of low resource facilities, the continuity of care is guaranteed with the help of SMS-based symptom check-in and the purpose of offline-capable mobile apps. The system can be localized to be used in local or underserved populations via local dialects to voice input, culturally relevant health content, or bandwidth-strict data delivery. Such flexibility will make sure that remote care solutions are not only effective technically but on the social and cultural level they are also inclusive.

12.4.5 Future Enhancements

In the future, various improvements can be incorporated to make the architecture even more robust, private, and useful to the clinicians. To enhance the training of AI

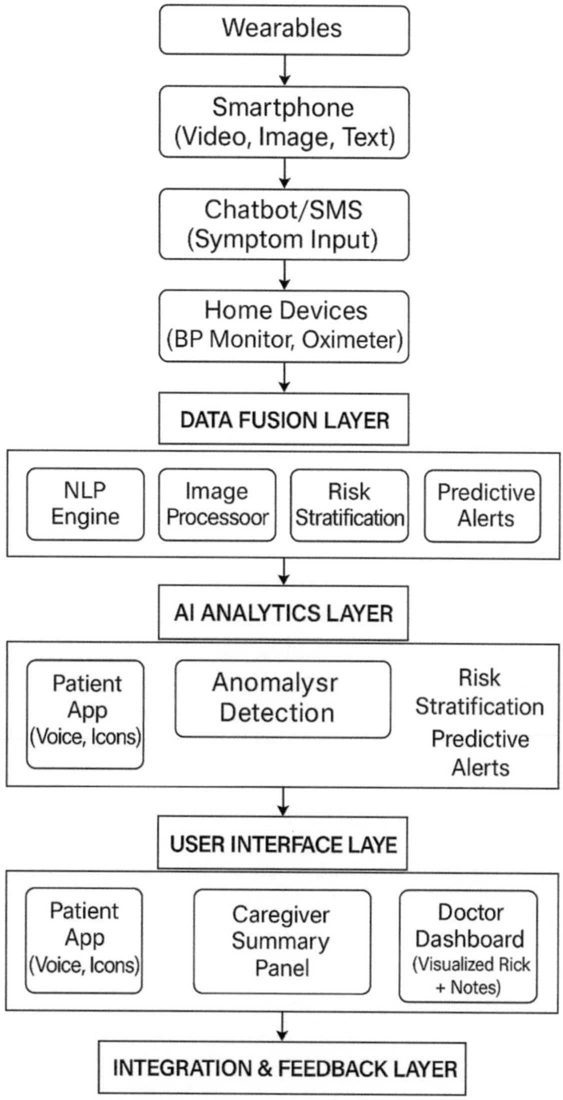

Fig. 12.1 Core components of multimodal AI-driven telemedicine system

and guarantee the privacy of patients, federated learning models can be implemented, so that sensitive data problems do not get decentralized. Transparency and trust among clinicians can be improved by incorporating Federated Learning (FL) and explainable AI (XAI) functionalities that present the rationales of the AI-generated recommendations and their interpretation. A mode of optional offline-first can be implemented to assist in supporting rural deployment, by enabling the system to write data locally and periodically synchronize at the point of a restored connectivity. Finally, the digital capabilities of such phenotyping may be added allowing the pattern of behavior to be constantly assessed in order to determine mental health condition, but this would help expand the system to the psychological and behavioral health monitoring, so that truly holistic remote treatment is delivered (Mohammadi et al., 2024).

12.5 Ethical, Regulatory, and Equity Considerations

12.5.1 The Imperative for Responsible AI in Telemedicine

The application of multimodal AI to telemedicine offers us revolutionary opportunities in the question of how to make more access to healthcare, to practice more in the area of diagnostics, and to find methods of directing resources. However, these advances in technology also present other serious ethical, regulatory, and equity challenges. Even when the AI-based telemedicine turns into one of the solutions that will make minute care more economically positive and cost-effective, large-scale, and needs-centered, it should be presented in a vein of fairness, responsibility, transparency, and inclusiveness. Specifically, this applies to low- and middle-income countries (LMICs) where unstable regulatory environments and structural bottlenecks are bound to widen potentially already huge digitized gaps. In this regard, responsible innovation gives something where there exists more technological prudence of a person caring and loyalty to ideals of human rights, which will also regard even human dignity, reading and writing as part of the caring axis of digital (Bajwa et al., 2021).

12.5.2 Ethical Dimensions of Multimodal AI

12.5.2.1 Informed Consent and Autonomy

Multimodal AI appearance keeps and expertise quite individual and even sensitive information biometric measurements, audio-video, behavioral and geolocation data. Ensuring informed consent is reliable in this case is becoming even more complex, particularly with users likely to be unaware of the nature of the type of data being processed, its use, and the manner in which AI algorithms take their decisions. The process of consent must be understandable, transparent, and culturally aware to guarantee the autonomy of the user. This includes making sure that material on consent is available in more than just one language, it is plain language, and the user has an opportunity to choose whether to share or not share a certain data modality. Other than that, multilayer consent formulas can make the user empowered, namely by giving him or her a sort of choice regarding what kind of information to employ, thus engagement in AI-based health-tracking is rated and conscious.

12.5.2.2 Algorithmic Bias and Fairness

Another major ethical implication with AI algorithms, especially when programs are trained over datasets that do not accurately represent varied groups, is bias. Intersectional bias is even more likely in multimodal AI, when the conclusions are based on numerous types of data and demographics. As an illustrative case, a ruralized, digitally illiterate elderly woman can be automatically mismatched or underserved when its intimidation data is loaded with urban, tech- friendly users. The most effective strategies to reduce these risks are representative and simplistic datasets in design, fairness-conscious machine learning methods, and regular bias audits of demographic subgroups. The inability to solve these problems can further increase health inequity and undermine a trust in digital health systems (Ferrara, 2023).

12.5.2.3 Human Oversight and Explainability

AI-influenced decisions relating to the escalation of a patient case based on the abnormal breathing pattern or set of concomitant symptoms must be clinically interpretable and be subjected to a human review. Explainability will be important in producer confidence, facilitate clinical accountability, and clinical compliance. Healthcare professionals must be able to understand the rationale behind AI-generated recommendations to validate them and provide appropriate follow-up care. Therefore, systems should be designed with human-in-the-loop (HITL) architectures, especially for high-risk decisions. This approach ensures that clinicians retain ultimate decision-making authority while benefiting from AI-assisted insights, thereby safeguarding patient outcomes and preserving the integrity of care (Mienye et al., 2024).

12.5.3 Legal and Regulatory Frameworks

12.5.3.1 Data Protection and Privacy

Multimodal AI systems inherently involve the processing of vast and varied data streams, including physiological, behavioral, and sometimes psychosocial data. In Malaysia, data privacy is governed primarily by the Personal Data Protection Act (PDPA) 2010, which applies to private-sector entities but does not fully regulate government health data repositories. Key principles that must be upheld include data minimization, purpose limitation, secure data storage, and the use of encryption. Where possible, sensitive data should be anonymized or pseudonymized. Globally recognized frameworks such as the EU's General Data Protection Regulation (GDPR) and the OECD's AI Principles offer comprehensive standards that can inform the development of national AI governance strategies, particularly around data ethics, user consent, and cross-border data sharing (Mohammadi et al., 2025).

12.5.3.2 Liability and Accountability

The delegation of clinical decision support to AI systems introduces legal uncertainty regarding responsibility in the event of adverse outcomes. If a patient experiences harm due to an incorrect or delayed alert generated by an AI algorithm, it may be unclear whether the liability rests with the software developer, the healthcare provider, or the institution deploying the system. Existing medical malpractice laws in many jurisdictions, including LMICs, are not equipped to address these new paradigms of shared decision-making. To address this, regulatory bodies should develop certification pathways for AI-based medical tools, define standards for algorithm validation and transparency, and clarify the legal status of AI systems, particularly in distinguishing between "assistive" and "autonomous" functions in clinical workflows (Smith & Fotheringham, 2020).

12.5.3.3 Regulatory Readiness in LMICs

Several LMICs such as Southeast Asia have no specific regulatory measures to address the safe and ethical use of AI in healthcare. Since such technologies have been piloted and scaled, governments have to invest in institutional capacity to regulate AI systems. These involve development of regulatory sandboxes, which can test the innovation in more controlled settings, having digital ethics committees reviewing AI-based health research, and multi-sectoral stakeholders in co-developing the governance policies. Close collaboration between regions and harmonization of AI regulations may further support the adoption of automated technologies safely and efficiently and their preservation of the rights of citizens (Smith & Fotheringham, 2020).

12.5.4 Addressing Digital Health Inequities

12.5.4.1 Access Barriers

Although AI-based telemedicine has potential to deliver care to remote and underserved regions, it also poses the threat of increasing disparities in case it is not developed with a view toward equity. People with no access to smartphones, reliable Internet or digital skills can be systematically barred to the merits of such systems. To overcome this, the systems designed by the developers ought to be compatible with an environment with limited bandwidth, operate on SMS or USSD entries, and work on offline modes where data may be uploaded occasionally. Maximizing access by individuals, including community health kiosks or shared tablets at clinics can also serve to overcome the digital divide, particularly with adults aged 65 years and older, with low income, as well as patients living in rural settings (Rauner & Stummer, 2025).

12.5.4.2 Language and Cultural Adaptation

The impact of language diversity, and the cultural background is frequently neglected in terms of designing AI tools, but they are crucial to the possibility of meaningful interaction. Natural language processing (NLP) modules, using mostly English or Western clinical lexicons, are potentially incapable of picking up region-specific idioms, nonverbal cues, or culturally sensitive conceptualizations of illness. In order to deal with it, AI systems should be trained using the local data and support local languages and dialects. Culturally appropriate visual indicators and voice-to-text options can also increase the access and interactions among users of different levels of literacy (Wei, 2025).

12.5.4.3 Participatory Design

However, inclusion of end users when designing AI-enabled healthcare even the less privileged ones should be considered as among the most effective measures in place to ensure equity in AI. Participatory design means involving the patients, caregivers, and frontline providers to develop the system, starting with the initial tests of concepts, to pilot tests. This could be the organization of community focus groups, a feedback loop of real-time users into the software and the establishment of community advisory boards to offer accountability and direction. Being user-voiced in the development of the innovation lifecycle can turn systems into more inclusive, responsive, and context-specific (Marko et al., 2025).

12.5.5 Ethical Governance and Global Standards

The ethical regulation of AI in the medical sector is to be organized at the intergovernmental level, at the university, at the industrial center, and in civil society, to facilitate a trustful approach and secure the general well-being of people. International organizations like the World Health Organization (WHO), UNESCO, and the IEEE have issued guiding principles that put human rights, transparency, and social responsibility in the development of AI. The most interesting recommendations involve the creation of autonomous audit protocols over AI applications, certification systems over digital health applications, and ethical review boards that pay attention to the control of data and accountability policies by algorithms. To facilitate the development and scale of multimodal AI systems, countries that develop or scale these systems need to localize these international standards to their own sociopolitical, legal, and cultural locations. By doing this, AI innovation will not be bypassed with the purpose of defeating the objectives of equitable, safe, and people-centered healthcare (Parvin et al., 2025).

12.6 Strategic Implementation and Policy Recommendations

12.6.1 Integrating Multimodal AI into Health Systems

A key opportunity to change the situation in healthcare delivery is the potential of providing health-remote support via a combination of modalities through AI, given that there is a lack of service access in some parts of the population. However, effective application or implementation requires more than a technological readiness: it must be framed within a broader ecosystem of country health priorities, available digital infrastructure, and patterns of patient-centered care. The implementation plan must be incremental, based on evidence, and driven by inclusion, equity and sustainability (Huang et al., 2025). To achieve this, a strategic approach should emphasize three critical domains:

1. Technology-readiness and system integration
2. Human capacity building and workflow alignment
3. Policy, regulatory, and financing frameworks

   Aligning these pillars ensures that multimodal AI systems are not only technically sound but also functionally embedded within public health infrastructure.

12.6.2 Technology Infrastructure and Interoperability

In order to facilitate the scalable usability of multimodal AI in telemedicine practice, one of the first priorities of health systems and governments is to focus on the digital infrastructure. The system would include profiles of the cloud-based analytics environment and the corresponding elasticity tool, the secure storage warehouse and the real-time analytics being run on the data. Most significantly, these platforms should be interoperable with existing health information systems such as electronic medical records (EMRs), disease registries and health surveillance systems, all examples of applications that not only will require the transfer of data continuously, but must occur between systems as well.

Open-source concepts, open data requirements that are driving accelerated development and even alleviating vendor lock-in will be imperatively essential. Through that standard and others, the free exchange of a wide range of AI tools is enabled within a common ecosystem, which enables flexibility by the users and across industries within the state and the commercial sector. Moreover, modular architecture is localized and scaled up due to its customization. Especially of chronic diseases, who will regard component underlying AI architecture executed to allow remote monitoring, can simply be re-designed and re-applied in the event of requirements to be specifically to maternal health, or to noncommunicable disease or heredity prevention. The measurement model promotes a gradual change, which may respond to maturity of policy and capacity of the health system (Maleki Varnosfaderani & Forouzanfar, 2024).

12.6.3 Capacity Building and Change Management

Advanced digital systems are only as effective as the people who operate and interact with them. Thus, human capital development is essential for the meaningful integration of AI into healthcare. Health professionals must be equipped with digital literacy, training in AI interpretation, and the ability to adapt to remote consultation workflows. This includes clinicians, public health officers, and administrative staff who will use or oversee the AI-driven systems.

The workforce should also include AI safety officers or digital health stewards embedded within health ministries, hospitals, and research institutions to monitor algorithmic behavior, ensure ethical compliance, and manage data governance. Training programs and continuing professional development (CPD) opportunities should include AI modules and be incentivized through accreditation points or career advancement tracks.

In parallel, medical and nursing curricula must be updated to include foundational education on AI in health, digital ethics, and virtual patient engagement. Public awareness campaigns are equally important to foster digital trust and promote informed adoption among communities. By framing AI as a supportive tool rather than a replacement for care, health systems can ensure greater acceptance, particularly in populations traditionally resistant to technology (Bajwa et al., 2021).

12.6.4 Regulatory and Governance Frameworks

12.6.4.1 National AI in Health Strategy

The safe and ethical use of AI in health requires comprehensive governance. Countries should develop a National AI in Health Action Plan that clearly defines the scope, regulation, and oversight mechanisms for AI applications. Key components include:

- Risk stratification of AI applications based on their intended use and clinical implications
- Regulatory pathways for the approval and certification of clinical-grade AI tools
- Post-deployment audit frameworks for tracking safety, usability, and unintended harms over time

This strategic planning ensures that AI-enabled systems are subject to the same rigor as other clinical interventions, building confidence among stakeholders and end-users.

12.6.4.2 Data Governance and Digital Sovereignty

Considering the sensitivity of the health data, strong data governance systems have to support all the AI systems. Data localization is a policy that ought to be adopted in the countries so that health information is located on the grounds of the countries and increases digital sovereignty, mitigating risks related to foreign access or misuse. Moreover, in these times of emergence, protocols to share data across a boundary can be used to promote collaborative research and epidemiological monitoring during a public health crisis. Institutional-level data stewardship roles need to be specified, and there must be officers in charge of data security, ethical adherence, and consent.

12.6.4.3 Equity-Driven Policy Design

Digital health policy has to be guided by equity. Universal design principles should be integrated into the procurement and development of systems by governments, to make AI tools accessible to a wide range of literacy, language, and disability levels. There should be a set of minimum digital access standards like national 4G access or its presence in rural localities. Also, a digital health intervention must be designed to receive Health Equity Impact Assessments (HEIA) to anticipate and overcome disparity prior to implementation.

12.6.5 Financing Models and Public–Private Partnerships

The artificial intelligence-based telehealth system should be financed carefully and creatively to ensure enduring use. Mixed financing through a blend of government funding, business capital, and charity aid will limit financial pressure to health systems whilst enhancing innovation. Governments can look into exploring the value-based models of digital health reimbursement piloting, whereby practitioners will be rewarded by patient outcomes, instead of the amount of services given.

Also, start-ups, academic institutions, and social enterprises aiming to develop AI solutions can be favored by introducing innovation grants, challenge funds or implementing a regulatory sandbox to find solutions based on local requirements. The space is especially strong in a place such as public-private alliances (PPPs), which lets the public sector capitalize on the technology and expertise held by the private sector while keeping governmental control. Nevertheless, the protection of the interests of the population and preventing commercialization of basic health services require that PPPs should be regulated by clear licensing contracts, equal exchange of intellectual property, and the rights to control data to PPPs.

12.6.6 Monitoring and Evaluation (M&E)

Implementation and policy learning cannot be done without a monitoring and evaluation (M&E) framework that guides the adaptive implementation. Quantitative measures must be monitored regularly and they must include patient uptake, system responsiveness, health outcomes, and provider satisfaction. Moreover, qualified action (user experience, cultural appropriateness or perceived trust) can be introduced to routine reviews.

In order to review the effectiveness of its systems and suggest improvements, as well as to prioritize the updates of the features according to the recommendations of

Table 12.1 Summary of strategic recommendations

Priority area	Recommendation
Digital infrastructure	Interoperable, modular platforms with cloud-based analytics
Workforce development	Upskilling programs and integration into clinical training
Governance	Regulatory standards, ethical oversight, and AI certification
Equity	Universal access mandates and participatory system design
Financing	Value-based models and innovation-friendly PPPs
M&E	Continuous learning through real-time data and expert input

stakeholders, it is possible to use Delphi-based expert panels. Additionally, M&E systems are expected to be entrenched with each implementation stage not only as a post-factum audit instrument but as a live learning engine that communicates system correction, resource deployment, and policy adaptation. Through investments in robust assessment capability, governments and implementing bodies can ascertain that multimodal AI should be responsible, contextual, and ready to meet new public health demands (Table 12.1).

12.7 Case Study: Malaysia's Experience with Multimodal AI in Remote Health Monitoring Through the SELangkah Virtual CAC

The experience of Malaysia during the COVID-19 pandemic can serve as a valuable illustration of an example of the use of digital innovation, including aspects of multimodal AI, to quickly contribute to the welfare of overburdened public health systems. This also saw the introduction of one of the most outstanding inventions, the SELangkah Virtual COVID-19 Assessment Centre (Virtual CAC), a telehealth application designed to handle low-risk COVID-19 patients in home quarantine. The platform was originally conceived to support contact tracing and was broadened to be used as a full-fledged self-monitoring system that effectively supported remote consultations, syndrome-tracking, and escalation channels.

A Kannadasan (2024) study titled "*Assessing the Impact on Patient Experience and Out-of-Pocket Expenditure of a Virtual COVID-19 Assessment Centre in Hulu Langat, Selangor*" (2025), evaluated the usability, acceptability, and cost-effectiveness of this virtual care model. The public health- and digital health-based study provides important insight into the efficacy of a hybrid system employing multimodal AI principles in a real-world crisis scenario.

12.7.1 Integrated Features and Public Health Utility

SELangkah Virtual CAC was one of the pioneering multimodal implementations of AI in public health. The platform combined heterogeneous data inputs including patient self-reported symptoms, oxygen saturation, and geospatial location to support decision-making. Automated rule-based red-flag symptom alerting indicated escalation and supported frontline healthcare personnel to remotely observe patients via teleconsultations and dashboard alerts.

Public health-wise, the platform succeeded in significantly reducing the burden in overcrowded health facilities, especially in periods of infection peaks. It also reduced the risk of transmission by allowing low-risk patients to remain at home under remote monitoring.

12.7.2 Digital Inclusion and Usability Challenges

Despite its strengths, the study by Kannadasan et al. identified notable disparities in user experience based on age, education level, and occupational background. Elderly users, individuals with low digital literacy, and those unfamiliar with mobile health apps often struggled to navigate the system. Some users misunderstood key features such as symptom escalation protocols or were unaware that the system could be used to book teleconsultations.

While the platform incorporated AI-driven features to streamline care, its effectiveness was limited by user engagement and comprehension. For instance, the reliance on self-input data meant that clinical decisions were only as good as the data entered by patients. This raised concerns about the validity of the inputs and the potential for missed deterioration, especially among patients with limited understanding of clinical red flags.

The findings emphasized that multimodal AI cannot function in isolation, hence it should be embedded in a user-friendly, culturally appropriate interface supported by adequate onboarding and technical assistance. For Malaysia's multiethnic, multilingual population, the need for inclusive design including multilingual support, simplified interfaces, and visual guidance was especially pronounced.

12.7.3 Economic Implications and Out-of-Pocket Expenditure

A key dimension explored by Kannadasan et al. was the economic impact on patients, particularly in terms of out-of-pocket (OOP) expenditure. Although the virtual monitoring service was offered free of charge by the government, patients incurred a range of indirect costs. These included the purchase of thermometers and pulse oximeters, mobile data charges for app usage and video consultations, and transportation for follow-up visits or confirmatory testing when their condition escalated.

More critically, income loss emerged as a prominent concern among daily wage earners and informal sector workers, who could not work during home quarantine. Although the virtual care model reduced the need for physical visits and potential hospitalization, the absence of financial support mechanisms to cover incidental costs undermined its affordability for certain population groups.

The study noted that users initially perceived virtual care as cost-saving but later reported cumulative financial burdens, particularly in households with multiple infected members. This gap between perceived and actual costs illustrates the importance of evaluating the full economic footprint of remote health models.

12.7.4 Systemic Strengths and Limitations of AI Application

The SELangkah system demonstrated the potential of AI-driven triaging to streamline pandemic response. However, the study found that the system's capabilities remained largely rule-based, without leveraging advanced predictive analytics or adaptive learning features. For instance, the system did not integrate wearable data for passive monitoring or use historical health data to personalize care pathways.

Multimodal AI in its full expression would involve continuous data fusion from multiple sources such as vital signs, behavioral patterns, symptom trends, and environmental exposures to enhance predictive accuracy. The SELangkah platform represents a promising foundation, but future iterations would benefit from deeper integration with wearable technologies and AI models capable of learning and adapting over time.

12.7.5 Policy Gaps and Health System Integration

The findings from Kannadasan et al. also highlighted the need for supportive policy frameworks to scale and sustain remote health monitoring systems. While Malaysia's rapid deployment of the Virtual CAC model was commendable, its long-term success requires structural alignment with primary healthcare services. Integration with electronic health records, shared care protocols, and chronic disease management plans would help transform virtual care from a crisis response tool into a routine care modality.

In terms of policy implications, the study advocates for targeted digital literacy programs, especially for high-risk groups such as the elderly and rural populations. It also recommends introducing financial protection strategies such as subsidies for monitoring devices or zero-rated mobile data plans—to reduce the hidden costs of digital health usage. From a governance perspective, ensuring data privacy, consent, and ethical AI application remains paramount as digital platforms become more entrenched in national health strategies.

12.7.6 Financial Equity

To address the hidden financial burdens identified in this study, the establishment of a dedicated financial safety net is essential. Although digital platforms like the SELangkah Virtual CAC reduce direct healthcare costs and facility burdens, they inadvertently impose indirect expenses on patients, including the cost of medical devices, data usage, and income loss due to isolation. These costs disproportionately affect low-income households and informal workers, undermining the equity goals of digital health initiatives. Moving forward, Malaysia could consider introducing a form of social health insurance or a digital health protection scheme specifically designed to cover essential out-of-pocket expenditures related to remote care. Such a scheme could ensure coverage for home monitoring equipment, Internet access required for telehealth services, and basic compensation for income disruption during mandatory isolation. Embedding these protections within the national health financing framework would help ensure that remote health monitoring is not only technologically feasible but also financially equitable and sustainable.

12.7.7 Significance and Way Forward

This study is significant as it provides empirical evidence on the feasibility, usability, and economic burden of a real-time AI-assisted virtual care system in a middle-income country. It bridges a critical gap in the literature by examining not only the technological performance of telehealth platforms but also the patient-level realities, of what it costs, how it is experienced, and who benefits or is left behind.

Moving forward, Malaysia's experience offers a valuable blueprint for other countries aiming to operationalize AI in public health. The SELangkah Virtual CAC model shows that innovation can occur rapidly under crisis conditions but sustaining and scaling such innovations requires systemic investment in digital infrastructure, user capacity building, and inclusive policy design.

As Malaysia transitions towards becoming an aging nation, the insight from this study highlights the urgency of designing health systems that are not only technologically advanced but also human-centered and financially protective. Multimodal AI holds transformative potential, but its success lies in how well it is integrated into people's lives not just health systems. The path ahead lies in co-developing technology with communities, ensuring no one is excluded from the promise of digital health.

12.8 Conclusion and Future Directions

12.8.1 Summary of Key Insights

The integration of multimodal AI into telemedicine systems represents a transformative opportunity for remote health monitoring, one that extends the reach, responsiveness, and personalization of healthcare services. By synthesizing diverse inputs such as voice, text, images, and biometric signals, multimodal AI can enhance diagnostic accuracy, enable proactive care, and support patients beyond the boundaries of conventional health facilities.

This chapter has explored the conceptual, technological, and policy of multimodal AI in telemedicine, offering insights from global use cases as well as real-world evidence from Malaysia's Virtual CACs. Key findings highlight the potential for AI to:

- Improve user experience through adaptive, multilingual, and accessible interfaces
- Reduce healthcare burden via predictive analytics and automated triage
- Address digital equity through targeted system design and policy interventions
- Enhance public health outcomes by integrating real-time monitoring into population-level strategies

12.8.2 Addressing Remaining Challenges

While multimodal AI in remote health monitoring presents significant potential for transforming healthcare delivery, several challenges must be systematically addressed to ensure ethical, equitable, and effective integration into health systems. Technical barriers remain prominent, including issues of data interoperability between different devices and platforms, the persistence of algorithmic bias arising from nonrepresentative training datasets, and the need for greater transparency in AI decision-making processes. These limitations can undermine the reliability, fairness, and scalability of AI solutions, particularly in contexts with diverse populations and fragmented digital infrastructure (Bajwa et al., 2021).

In parallel, workforce readiness continues to pose challenges. Clinicians and frontline health workers often express hesitation in trusting AI-generated recommendations, particularly when system outputs lack explainability or are perceived to threaten clinical autonomy. Addressing this requires targeted efforts in digital upskilling, AI literacy training, and integration of human-in-the-loop models that support, not replace the clinical judgment.

Regulatory gaps also hinder the safe deployment of AI in health. Many jurisdictions, especially in low- and middle-income countries, lack clear policies for AI certification, validation, and accountability. There is also ambiguity around legal liability when AI-driven recommendations contribute to adverse outcomes. Moreover, data governance structures remain underdeveloped, with inadequate safeguards for privacy, security, and ethical use of sensitive health data, particularly in cross-border and cloud-based systems (Pham, 2025).

Finally, ethical considerations must be front and center. Ensuring meaningful informed consent in complex multimodal systems is challenging, particularly when users may not fully understand how their data, such as voice, video, or biometric inputs that is being processed or shared. Ensuring fairness, equity, and accountability requires robust ethical review processes, inclusive design standards, and transparency in algorithm development and deployment (Pham, 2025).

Addressing these multidimensional challenges necessitates cross-sectoral collaboration. Health authorities, technology developers, regulatory bodies, academic researchers, and civil society organizations must work in concert to co-create frameworks, tools, and standards that guide responsible AI development. Only through inclusive dialogue and shared responsibility can multimodal AI be harnessed to enhance healthcare in a way that is both scientifically sound and socially just.

12.8.3 Future Directions for Research and Practice

In the future, development of multimodal AI in remote health monitoring will continue in technological advancement, human emphasis, and experimentation of policy. More flexibility, inclusivity, and applicability must be the possible focus of future study and practice to exploit its opportunities.

The other area of enhancement is integration of XAI. The fact of explainability will also be essential owing to the rising ways in which AI can be deployed in clinical workflows to ensure transparency, clinician trust, and comprehension by the patients. XAI approaches are able to provide descriptions of promoted AI warnings or triage suggestions easy to understand, support collective rule of thumb and governance.

In addition, a future possibility lies in the sphere of federated learning models when sharing AI development. Through such models the different institutions or countries can learn the shared algorithms without having to centrally process sensitive information therefore preserving privacy and the generalizability is enhanced. It should be particularly applicable to LMICs, in which the policies on information sharing might either be fragmented or immature.

The applications of the multimodal AI in behavioral and mental health could also require further research. There is an early induced state of depression, anxiety, and cognitive decline that can be identified using a voice tone analysis, facial expression, and interaction logs of video-based interaction. Such innovations would assist significantly in offering timely intervention in mental health of a region that can be an underserved area with urban and rural contexts.

The other major research direction is to develop localized AI models. Multilingual, multicultural, and multifaceted behaviors of AI can be greatly enhanced and much more applicable when trained on data of a large and diverse range of linguistic, cultural, and socioeconomic environment backgrounds. Localization ensures the AI use capability to recognize the symptoms and health behaviors exhibited culturally uniquely with the view of fostering a more accurate diagnosis and interaction with patients.

Digital health sandbox frameworks also need to be established to help them innovate and hold accountability within the minds of the policy-makers, developers, and researchers to test AI technology in low-risk real-time settings. These closed loans facilitate both prompt feedbacks, iterative learning and curative control, surveyable information and authentic evidence on the scaling up of productive and ethical remedies.

Notably, implementation research should be integrated at every system lifecycle phase such as testing, implementation, scaling up, and design. Such methodology would ensure that the technology is constantly grown in line with the requirements of the users, situation-based issues, and structural impediments. Careful consideration should be shown to the experiences of group members that are vulnerable and digitally marginalized so that health disparities do not get escalated.

In general, multimodal AI in remote health monitoring in the future will not be concentrated solely on the capabilities of the algorithm sophistication, but in the readiness of marrying the technology and human values, a systems comprehension, and engagement. The emergence of a new frontier will also not be about more intelligent machines other than environments that are more inclusive and intelligent.

12.8.4 Final Reflections

The concept of multimodal AI is currently no silver bullet, but it is an extraordinarily powerful step toward providing people with greater access to good-quality care, particularly when shielded by responsible arcs and equitably distributed in sparsely staffed and remote settings. Its inclusion in telemedicine gives it a template in building strong and patient-focused, data-driven health systems. Given that nations are yet to continue rebuilding after the turmoil that the COVID-19 pandemic caused and are searching how to implement AI in the tapestry of telemedicine, the suggestion to implement AI in the tapestry of telemedicine is not only timely but works as well.

I believe that ethical implementation of these technologies demands us to create a future in which healthcare is proactive, inclusive, intelligent, and unfragmented. This chapter aids this vision not only by explaining what we can do, but what we must do.

References

Alenoghena, C. O., Onumanyi, A. J., Ohize, H. O., Adejo, A. O., Oligbi, M., Ali, S. I., & Okoh, S. A. (2022). eHealth: A survey of architectures, developments in mHealth, security concerns and solutions. *International Journal of Environmental Research and Public Health, 19*(20). https://doi.org/10.3390/ijerph192013071

Bajwa, J., Munir, U., Nori, A., & Williams, B. (2021). Artificial intelligence in healthcare: Transforming the practice of medicine. *Future Healthcare Journal, 8*(2), e188–e194. https://doi.org/10.7861/fhj.2021-0095

Boikanyo, K., Zungeru, A. M., Sigweni, B., Yahya, A., & Lebekwe, C. (2023). Remote patient monitoring systems: Applications, architecture, and challenges. *Scientific African, 20*, e01638. https://doi.org/10.1016/j.sciaf.2023.e01638

Dastidar, B. G., Suri, S., Nagaraja, V. H., & Jani, A. (2022). A virtual bridge to universal healthcare in India. *Commun Med (Lond), 2*(1), 145. https://doi.org/10.1038/s43856-022-00211-7

Ferrara, E. (2023). Fairness and bias in artificial intelligence: A brief survey of sources, impacts, and mitigation strategies. *The Sciences, 6*(1), 3. https://doi.org/10.3390/sci6010003

Glasgow, R., Battaglia, C., McCreight, M., Aydiko, R., Maw, A., Fort, M., Holtrop, J., Gomes, R., & Rabin, B. (2022). Use of the reach, effectiveness, adoption, implementation, and maintenance (RE-AIM) framework to guide iterative adaptations: Applications, lessons learned, and future directions. *Frontiers in Health Services, 2*, 959565. https://doi.org/10.3389/frhs.2022.959565

Harrison, R., Adams, C., Newman, B., Mimmo, L., Mitchell, R., Manias, E., Alston, M., & Hadley, A.-M. (2024). Measuring healthcare experiences among people with intellectual disability: A rapid evidence synthesis of tools and methods. *Value in Health, 27*(11), 1605–1619. https://doi.org/10.1016/j.jval.2024.05.018

Huang, L., Duan, Q., Liu, Y., Wu, Y., Li, Z., Guo, Z., Liu, M., Lu, X., Wang, P., Liu, F., Ren, F., Li, C., Wang, J., Huang, Y., Yan, B., Kioumourtzoglou, M.-A., & Kinney, P. L. (2025). Artificial intelligence: A key fulcrum for addressing complex environmental health issues. *Environment International, 198*, 109389. https://doi.org/10.1016/j.envint.2025.109389

Jothi Prakash, B. S., & Varsha, R. G. (2025). AI-driven telemedicine: Bridging healthcare and Technology for the Future. *International Journal for Research in Applied Science and Engineering Technology, 13*. https://doi.org/10.22214/ijraset.2025.66171

Kannadasan, K., Mohd Hairi, F., Dahlui, M., Azzeri, A., & Suli, Z. (2024). Patient-reported experiences with virtual Covid-19 assessment Centres in Hulu Langat, SELANGOR. *Malaysian Journal of Public Health Medicine, 24*(3), 122–138. https://doi.org/10.37268/mjphm/vol.24/no.3

Kim, J. C., Saguna, S., & Åhlund, C. (2023). Acceptability of a health care app with 3 user interfaces for older adults and their caregivers: Design and evaluation study. *JMIR Human Factors, 10*, e42145. https://doi.org/10.2196/42145

Maleki Varnosfaderani, S., & Forouzanfar, M. (2024). The role of AI in hospitals and clinics: Transforming healthcare in the 21st century. *Bioengineering (Basel), 11*(4). https://doi.org/10.3390/bioengineering11040337

Marko, J. G. O., Neagu, C. D., & Anand, P. B. (2025). Examining inclusivity: The use of AI and diverse populations in health and social care: A systematic review. *BMC Medical Informatics and Decision Making, 25*(1). https://doi.org/10.1186/s12911-025-02884-1

Mienye, I. D., Obaido, G., Jere, N., Mienye, E., Aruleba, K., Emmanuel, I. D., & Ogbuokiri, B. (2024). A survey of explainable artificial intelligence in healthcare: Concepts, applications, and challenges. *Informatics in Medicine Unlocked, 51*, 101587. https://doi.org/10.1016/j.imu.2024.101587

Mohammadi, S., Balador, A., Sinaei, S., & Flammini, F. (2024). Balancing privacy and performance in federated learning: A systematic literature review on methods and metrics. *Journal of Parallel and Distributed Computing, 192*, 104918. https://doi.org/10.1016/j.jpdc.2024.104918

Mohammadi, M., Tajik, E., Martinez-Maldonado, R., Sadiq, S., Tomaszewski, W., & Khosravi, H. (2025). Artificial intelligence in multimodal learning analytics: A systematic literature review. *Computers and Education: Artificial Intelligence, 8*, 100426. https://doi.org/10.1016/j.caeai.2025.100426

Nasa, P., Jain, R., & Juneja, D. (2021). Delphi methodology in healthcare research: How to decide its appropriateness. *World Journal of Methodology, 11*(4), 116–129. https://doi.org/10.5662/wjm.v11.i4.116

Parvin, N., Joo, S. W., Jung, J. H., & Mandal, T. K. (2025). Multimodal AI in biomedicine: Pioneering the future of biomaterials, diagnostics, and personalized healthcare. *Nanomaterials (Basel), 15*(12). https://doi.org/10.3390/nano15120895

Paul, M. M., Khera, N., Elugunti, P. R., Ruff, K. C., Hommos, M. S., Thomas, L. F., Nagaraja, V., Garrett, A. L., Pantoja-Smith, M., Delafield, N. L., Lizaola-Mayo, B. C., Kresin, M. M., Seetharam, M., Nagarakanti, S. R., & Kaur, M. (2025). The state of remote patient monitoring for chronic disease Management in the United States. *Journal of Medical Internet Research, 27*, e70422. https://doi.org/10.2196/70422

Peek, N., Sujan, M., & Scott, P. (2023). Digital health and care: Emerging from pandemic times. *BMJ Health & Care Informatics, 30*(1). https://doi.org/10.1136/bmjhci-2023-100861

Pham, T. (2025). Ethical and legal considerations in healthcare AI: Innovation and policy for safe and fair use. *Royal Society Open Science, 12*. https://doi.org/10.1098/rsos.241873

Rauner, Y., & Stummer, H. (2025). The socio-technical adoption and diffusion of digital health innovations: The development of the STAD-HC model based on telemedicine in Germany. *Digital Business, 5*(2), 100135. https://doi.org/10.1016/j.digbus.2025.100135

Schorr, A. (2023). The technology acceptance model (TAM) and its importance for digitalization research: A review. In *International Symposium on Technikpsychologie (TecPsy)* (pp. 55–65). https://doi.org/10.2478/9788366675896-005

Shachak, A., Kuziemsky, C., & Petersen, C. (2019). Beyond TAM and UTAUT: Future directions for HIT implementation research. *Journal of Biomedical Informatics, 100*, 103315. https://doi.org/10.1016/j.jbi.2019.103315

Simpson, K., Nham, W., Thariath, J., Schafer, H., Greenwood-Eriksen, M., Fetters, M. D., Serlin, D., Peterson, T., & Abir, M. (2022). How health systems facilitate patient-centered care and care coordination: A case series analysis to identify best practices. *BMC Health Services Research, 22*(1), 1448. https://doi.org/10.1186/s12913-022-08623-w

Smith, H., & Fotheringham, K. (2020). Artificial intelligence in clinical decision-making: Rethinking liability. *Medical Law International, 20*, 096853322094576. https://doi.org/10.1177/0968533220945766

Stryker, C. (2025). *What is multimodal AI?* https://www.ibm.com/think/topics/multimodal-ai

van Dyk, L. (2014). A review of telehealth service implementation frameworks. *International Journal of Environmental Research and Public Health, 11*(2), 1279–1298. https://doi.org/10.3390/ijerph110201279

Wei, X. (2025). Cultural sensitivity in AI language learning: Using NLP to enhance language understanding across cultural contexts. *Theoretical and Natural Science, 79*, 167–172. https://doi.org/10.54254/2753-8818/2025.20110

Zhao, F., Zhang, C., & Geng, B. (2024). Deep multimodal data fusion. *ACM Computing Surveys, 56*. https://doi.org/10.1145/3649447

Part IV

AI in Surgery & Procedural Care

Current Implications and Future Directions of Artificial Intelligence in Surgery and Related Fields

13

Dharmendra Kumar Pipal, Vibha Rani Pipal, Rajendra Kumar Pipal, Seema Yadav, Swati Prasad, Rajesh Kannan, Alan Phillip, and B. Nikhil

13.1 Introduction

Artificial intelligence (AI): AI is leading the path to a new era in the scenario of medicine and particularly of surgical and perioperative medicine, even in the fields of surgery and perioperative medicine, as general surgery, minimally invasive surgery, orthopedics, gynecology, obstetrics, and anesthesia. Its integration into clinical practice is now of increasing importance, and presents an opportunity to make the surgical rules, decision-making, patient monitoring, and prediction of treatment outcome more precise. AI is capable of doing these things with amazing technologies such as machine learning algorithms, computer vision, and robotic-assisted systems and data analytics.

Generally, AI is applied in a couple of areas in general surgery and minimally invasive procedures like preoperative planning, intraoperative navigation, and postoperative outcome prediction. AI-assisted imaging and decision support tools help surgeons locate critical structures, minimize intraoperative errors, and increase operative efficiency. Workflow optimization and predictive analytics in the OR also enhance the resources and management of cases.

D. K. Pipal (✉) · S. Prasad · R. Kannan · A. Phillip · B. Nikhil
Department of General and Minimal Access Surgery, All India Institute of Medical Sciences, Gorakhpur, India

V. R. Pipal
Department of Obstetrics and Gynaecology, All India Institute of Medical Sciences, Gorakhpur, India

R. K. Pipal
Department of Orthopaedics, All India Institute of Medical Sciences, Gorakhpur, India

S. Yadav
Department Anaesthesia, Critical Care and Pain Management, All India Institute of Medical Sciences, Gorakhpur, India

U. Venkatesh et al. (eds.), *Multimodal AI in Healthcare*,
https://doi.org/10.1007/978-981-95-9027-8_13

In the field of orthopedics, AI is used to improve the diagnostic process in imaging, personalised surgical planning in joint replacement, and robotic-assisted surgical procedures. These applications improve the ability to line up the bones, decrease the operative time and help in the optimization of postoperative rehabilitation strategies. AI algorithms are also useful in fracture detection, early diagnosis of osteoarthritis and risk stratification for surgical intervention.

In gynecology and obstetrics, AI is being deployed in an increasing number of use cases, such as to monitor the fetus and forecast when and if complications will occur as well as providing a guide to the minimally invasive procedures. Assisted reproductive technologies make use of the AI in the selection of embryos, prediction of the success of IVF, and the development of individual treatment plans. AI-generated imaging tools create more intraoperative spatial awareness so that the surgeon does not cause injury to any critical structure in the procedure (also promotes safety).

In the anesthesia field and in perioperative medicine, artificial intelligence is helping with drug dosage, real-time vital signs monitoring, and perioperative risk prediction for patients of hypotension and hypoxia or postoperative complications. AI-enabled decision support systems enable safer anesthesia, increased efficiency, and personalized perioperational caring.

Advantages of AI in medicine include better precision, efficiency, and workflow; better decision-making and monitoring for patients; individual care; reduction of human error; and better training tools for clinicians. It can even be contended that AI can also assist in the extension of advanced care to restricted environments and function to reduce the range of clinical results.

Challenges and limitations are still tremendous. AI requires large, high-quality dataset for training and validation of models, and models can be limited by bias or poor generalizability. Integration with existing hospital systems is complicated, and some algorithms are "black boxes," which make it difficult for clinicians to trust them. Ethical issues, legal issues, data privacy issues, and cost issues also restrict large-scale adoption. Furthermore, practitioners may be unwilling to employ new technologies if they are not adequately trained in their use or have not proven to be beneficial.

Looking forward, the use of AI in the field of medicine has an enormous potential. As the accuracy of algorithms, real-time visual guidance, and predictive models based on an individual's health history continue to improve, it will lead to a level of autonomy in the medical intervention that will be more efficient, safe, and effective. For this to be successful, multidisciplinary partnership and good regulatory frameworks and ethical governance will all be required in order to ensure that AI is used to improve care in a meaningful, safe, and fair way.

13.2 Personalized Training Module, Based on AI

Artificial intelligence is being used in the field of surgical education and training for improving the quality, assessing the skills, and development. This emerging issue could help to improve surgical training, patient outcomes, and the medical profession. Surgical training programs will be a leader in this change as they introduce new ways of methods to their total curriculum. Considerably, there should be the joining of AI experts, teachers, and experts in order to take the best use of the emerging technologies. This will both improve surgical training and the care of the patient, as it will ensure that ethics and efficiency is put into use.

Surgical educational programs have been pushed ahead with the integration of AI, which has had a profound impact on training methods and evaluation systems. To be updated with the surgical education, artificial intelligence thus leads to the development of adaptive learning systems, which help in changing according to the latest surgical procedures, technology, and best practices. The emphasis on the current research applications of AI and the future effects on AI in surgical education by Ward et al. (2021) provides credence to this idea.

Artificial intelligence (AI) can make it easier to develop curricula with data through the help of performance indicators and student feedback in optimizing training programs in real time (Han et al., 2019). Weidener and Fischer (2023) have proposed the integration of artificial intelligence (AI) into the medical education program, in an attempt to improve the knowledge, understanding, and confidence required to implement AI in the clinical setting. Park et al. (2022) highlight the need for incorporation of artificial intelligence in surgical education and the need for real life surgical simulators. There is a lot of attention for the integration of AI in surgical training. Research performed by Moglia et al. (2022) is a good example of the application of deep learning models to predict the progress of surgical skills with robotic augmentation. The results of this study may be used in order to bring surgical education to the specific needs of the patient. As per Oleck N. C (2023), ChatGPT may be of assistance to help plastic/reconstructive surgery trainees prepare for oral board exams as is demonstrated by Oleck et al. in their work. Artificial intelligence application for surgical education has helped improve the learning and training outcome.

13.3 Artificial Intelligence: Intraoperative Imaging

The combination of artificial intelligence (AI) to diagnostic radiology and surgical imaging has changed the way computed tomography (CT), magnetic resonance imaging (MRI), and real-time intraoperative imaging systems are interpreted and clinically used. Using pattern recognition, automated feature extraction, and deep learning algorithms, AI has the potential to improve home value in preoperative evaluation and intraoperative decision-making with an increase in sensitivity, specificity, and image-based predictive accuracy.

13.3.1 AI and Prediction of Lung Nodules and Malignancies

One of the best examples of AI implementation in the field of medical imaging is lung cancer diagnosis. Liu et al. (2022) proposed a convolutional neural network

(CNN)-based system using high-resolution computed tomography (CT) data to differentiate the benign and malignant pulmonary nodules. The algorithm was used to automatically extract such radiomic features as the shape of the nodule, spiculation, and internal texture, and predict the likelihood of malignancy. When validated against a radiologist control group, the accuracy of the AI model displayed an AUC of 0.94, indicating it to be better than human readers in borderline lesions. Clinically, this advancement is useful for thoracic surgeons in making decisions criteria for surgery—that is, how to go about resecting those indeterminate nodules; which ones should be resected and which should be observed.

On this basis, Nam et al. (2023) created a multicentric randomized controlled trial with 1080 individuals in a setting of health-screening. The sensitivity of the pulmonary nodules in the chest radiographs was higher by 21% with AI ($P < 0.001$) than without AI. Importantly, there was a significant reduction in interobserver variability as well, underlining the mutual potential application of AI in the standardization of lung cancer screening and to reduce variations in diagnosis between experienced and inexperienced doctors. This is especially important in the perioperative setting where correct localization of the lesion has implications by way of surgical approach and extent of resection.

13.3.2 Characterizing and Making Surgical Decisions by Artificial Intelligence and CT

The *European Journal of Radiology* (2024), Kudo et al., have examined quantitative analysis of small solid pulmonary nodules (<10 mm) using an AI-based approach. Their deep learning algorithm was taught on 15,000 annotated CT images and came out with an accuracy of 92.6% for invasive adenocarcinoma, as compared with 78% for conventional radiologist-based interpretation. This improved risk stratification allows for precision surgical planning—decision-making of whether a patient needs a lobectomy, segmentectomy, or wedge resection. Such stratification has a direct effect on intraoperative decision making and long-term survival by proposing oncologically safe, but minimally invasive interventions.

13.3.3 Multimodal Integration and Oncologic Planning with the Help of AI

Beyond detection, the IBM Watson for Oncology (2023) has taken the role of a clinical decision support platform with radiologic imaging, pathology, and genomic data. By matching patient-specific tumor biomarkers and imaging features against evidence databases from all over the world, Watson is able to produce customized treatment recommendations. In surgical oncology, this capability is used for improving preoperative staging of the tumor, for predicting the involvement of the nodes to recommend adjuvant therapy—so combining intraoperative imaging information and the oncologic strategy.

13.3.4 AI-Aided Localization as Well as Intraoperative Navigation

Peters et al. (2024) investigated performance in AI-assisted detection of pulmonary nodules (on CT) of 24 radiologists with different experience levels. With the help of AI, the detection rate of the novice radiologist increased by 19–23%, and that of the senior radiologist increased by 19–23%, while there was a 17% increase in accuracy of lesion localization ($p < 0.01$). These outcomes have a direct impact on surgical benefits—more precise lesions mapping plays a key role in the improvement of video-assisted thoracoscopic surgical procedures (VATS) and robotic-assisted surgical resections, which can shorten the operating time and enable the complete excision of early-stage nodules.

13.3.5 AI-Augmented Detection and Impact on Clinical Outcome Globally

As reported by RSNA News (2023), high-accuracy AI machines are now in the position to detect the malignancy of lung lesions with over 95% detection accuracy using multicenter datasets. The technique is now being applied in commercial systems including Siemens' AI-Rad Companion and GE's AIR Recon DL in order to provide automated segmentation in real-time and intraoperative image-guided surgery. The RSNA report emphasized on the role of AI in reducing the false-negative rates and time to diagnosis, resulting in better surgical readiness and early intervention results.

13.3.6 Deep Learning for Surgical Aspects of Imaging and Registration

Zhao et al. (2024) gave a well-written review of deep learning in lung cancer imaging, with convolutional- and transformer-based deep learning architectures, which allow for three-dimensional reconstruction of anatomical structures for intraoperative use. Their analysis proved that the AI-based segmentation models proved to be better than manual delineation in terms of margin prediction and vascular mapping which is an integral part of thoracic surgery. These results show the importance of AI becoming more than a tool for preoperative diagnostics and can also be used intraoperatively for an image-guided resection.

Shah et al. (2023) also demonstrated in Frontiers in Surgery that the combination of intraoperative imaging with surgical navigation using AI will improve the instrument tracking by a maximum of 0.6 mm. The system can dynamically adapt to the tissue deformation and blood flow and is used to offer surgeons visual augmentation in real time. This development is centered on an increase in the use of dynamic imaging, which minimizes the need for static imaging and subsequent complications of incomplete tumor removal or excessive parenchymal loss.

13.3.7 Predictive and Postoperative Risk Stratification

In one of the studies presented in *Journal of Thoracic Oncology* in 2024, researchers Xu et al. proposed a predictive model of artificial intelligence based on radiomics of preoperative CT scan and clinical parameters predicting postoperative complications of prolonged air leakages, pneumonia, or respiratory failure. The model achieved an AUC >0.88 that was better than the traditional risk calculators. Such predictive knowledge has the potential for improved surgical decision-making, while enabling peroperative care to be optimized on an individual patient basis and for resources optimization.

Finally, Choi et al. (2024) commented on the difficulty of the clinical integration of AI—privacy of data, transparency of algorithms, and validation with regulations. Their review suggested the use of explainable AI (XAI) frameworks and international validation standards for the ethical, reproducible, and safe deployment in thoracic imaging and surgery.

In summary, AI has become a step from a diagnostic tool to a central part of surgical intelligence in lung cancer management including all phases of management from screening, lesion characterization, intraoperative guidance, and postoperative prediction. "Continual advances in the art of deep learning, multimodal data amalgamation and explainable AI will bring about an evolution in the way we operate for the better in the next decade, promising to increase the precision of surgical procedures, improving patient safety and oncologic outcome."

13.4 Role of AI in Minimal Access Surgery

13.4.1 Image Processing and Analysis in Surgery by Artificial Intelligence

The innovation of intraoperative image processing and analysis of artificial intelligence (AI) algorithms has revolutionized modern surgical practice with a tremendous boost in the quality, clarity, and interpretability of real-time surgical images. Despite its utility, the conventional imaging techniques are sometimes restricted by low resolution, noise interference, and the incapacity to define very small anatomic or pathogenic features. Deep learning and convolutional neural networks (CNNs) have enabled automated and intelligent processing of visual data in intraoperative imaging, resolving a number of different challenges in a manner that is effective.

Deep learning algorithms are great at feature extraction, where the algorithm discovers and learns complex patterns from large datasets of surgical pictures autonomously and without any involvement from the operator. These algorithms might help to reduce the visual noise, enhance edges, increase the importance of relevant features, and increase contrast, hence leading to better discrimination between normal and diseased tissues. Methods such as semantic segmentation and object detection allow the identification and localization of important anatomical landmarks, tumors, blood arteries, and nerves, which play an important role in planning and performing accurate surgical procedures to be performed immediately.

On top of this, AI-empowered image augmentation technologies are also increasingly being combined with intraoperative imaging technologies, such as endoscopy, fluoroscopy, laparoscopy cameras, and robotic-assisted operating systems. These systems enable real-time image processing, which gives dynamic image feedback to surgeons, aiding them in intricate processes. This is particularly helpful in minimally invasive operations, in which the field of vision is narrow and the margin for error is very small.

The therapeutic importance of these developments is huge. Augmented intraoperative imaging provides enhanced situational awareness, surgical navigation, decreased risk of intraoperative harm, and enhanced decision-making. As such, surgeons are potentially able to perform treatments with increased confidence and accuracy, leading to a reduction in surgical time, fewer issues, quicker recovery times, and better outcomes for the patient in surgery.

In addition, the continuous ability to learn of AI systems means they can be trained and updated based on information specific to the institution or patient, again increasing the flexibility and accuracy of the systems over time. As research and clinical trials continue to confirm the success of AI-enhanced intraoperative imaging, the use of this technology in a range of surgical disciplines, including general surgery, neurology, orthopedics, and cardiac surgery, will be expected to take off dramatically.

In summary, intraoperative image processing with AI is a revolution in the way of surgery practice with unprecedented surgical powers of picture augmentation, interpretation, and surgery guiding. These technological innovations offer improvement in the accuracy and safety of surgical treatments and are possible for the future of intelligent, data-driven surgery.

13.4.2 Increased Accuracy by Real-Time Segmentation and Improvement of Pictures

Tanzi L et al. (2021) have put forward the concept to enhance the precision of in vivo robot-assisted radical prostatectomy (RARP) using deep learning and augmented realities. Furthermore, they developed a two-level automated method for matching the three-dimensional virtual temporary model of a patient's organ with the two-dimensional endoscopic image of his organ. This procedure is a way to offer support for surgeons during treatment. In the study effort, the objective of semantic segmentation was accomplished by the use of a convolution neural network (CNN) architecture. Subsequently, an examination of the output was made to give the essential parameters for the attachment of the three-dimensional model. During the process of robot-assisted radical prostatectomy, this characteristic is exploited in order to assure a three-dimensional depiction of the prostate is superimposed exactly. The U-Net was used as the main network and the MobileNet as a framework for segmentation design. They took advantage of encoder-decoder architecture. U-Net was the core network. This was achieved by means of a dataset made up of five endoscopic videos (A, B, C, D, and E), which were selected and annotated by their team of specialists. The dataset was used. In the next step, the best combination of the neural network and segmentation architecture was tested in both performance categories of the overlay. In the process of their research, they discovered that the U-Net architecture is the one that was the most effective in segmentation. Although both these networks got results that were nearly comparable in terms of intersection over union (IoU), MobileNet displayed about two times as many actions per second as ResNet did. This was despite the fact that the two networks came up with the same results. Compared to the previous investigation, the segmentation technique is able to show superior performance, since it was able to reach an average IoU for the catheter of 0.894 ($s = 0.076$). In contrast to the former study, which resulted in an IoU of 0.339 (sigma = 0.195), this has been shown to be significantly different ($p < 0.001$) to the results obtained in the process of which the improvements in terms of equilibrium distance of the anchor point of the predicted models and actual models brought improved performance of the three-dimensional overlay. As a consequence of the modifications, this improvement may tie in with the modifications. This was seen in particular. The distance was reduced from 12.569 (sigma = 4.456) to 4.160 (sigma = 1.448). Overall performance greatly improved. Geodesic distance of the predicted model and actual model's rotations decreased from 0.266 (sigma = 0.131) to 0.169 (sigma = 0.073). This structure provided the system with the best precision operation balance. In order to carry out the assessment of the network, a number of different training datasets that were obtained from a number of different films were used. This was done in order to get generalizable conclusions. Because of their ability to properly build a pipeline that makes use of the output of the segmentation, they were able to correlate a three-dimensional model with a two-dimensional video stream from the very beginning. The old strategy, which used only computer vision programs, is compared with this pipeline in order to see the differences.

The evaluation conducted by Garrow C. R (2021) was based on the use of machine learning (ML) models and data streams for the automated surgical phase detection. This technology is important for improving workflow, surgical education, intraoperative support, patient safety, and efficiency, allowing the evaluation and decoding of huge datasets. This research included 25 full-texts with a total of 2254 analyzed titles and abstracts. In the world of machine learning models, hidden Markov models and artificial neural models were the more used models. A general trend to increasing complexity as time went on was found. As two examples of the types of data used, this study made use of feature learning over surgical films and manual annotation of tool use. The most common that had an accuracy rate of over 90% was laparoscopic cholecystectomy. Based on the model, data type, and complexity of operation, it can be concluded from the authors of this article that the application of machine learning in the identification of the surgical phase may be achieved with a good degree of accuracy in the application. Different forms can be used successfully for intraoperative data. Examples of such forms are movies and apparatus. Many machine learning models need to be annotated by experts for training purposes. These models have the potential to improve surgical processes through the promotion of consistency, efficiency, and objectivity. This has a potential to enhance the outcome for the patients in the future.

13.4.3 Minimal Access Surgeries and Robotic Surgeries: Uses of AI

Artificial intelligence, also known as AI, has had considerable impacts on various fields of human life such as surgery. The two major parts of artificial intelligence are the research and design of algorithms for a robot to carry out cognitive functions such as problem-solving and decision-making (Hashimoto et al., 2018). With the advent of robotic surgery, medicine has altered. Surgical robots are "master-slave" robots, which have no autonomy but are used by humans. Machine learning and artificial intelligence have recently made themselves known to the world of enhancing capabilities of these robots and offer comfort during surgical experience. Surgical robots use the data received from sensors in images to complete their operational tasks.

13.4.4 Role of AI in Improving the Quality of Blurry Images

Through the use of tiny incisions for cameras and other devices, robotic surgery offers an opportunity to make difficult operations in patient anatomy more accessible. The identification of structures and instruments is improved with the use of real-time artificial intelligence picture augmentation. The quality of images may be affected by changing visual surroundings during intraoperative procedures. In an attempt to provide better intraoperative vision during knee arthroscopy, Ali et al. (2023) developed an online preprocessing system with the aim of denoising, deblurring, and color correction of the real-time camera images. Their method outperformed that of the existing enhancement approaches and decreased the amount of time required for the display calculation of pictures.

Electrocautery equipment is frequently used for robotic surgeons to use for the purpose of dissection or ligation. However, this technique produces smoke, which has the potential to get trapped within the anatomical region of interest, therefore causing moments of blockage of the FOV until it is evacuated by suction. An improved and smoke-free surgical view was realized as a result of the work by Wang et al. Hanoi (2023), who proposed the convolutional neural network (CNN) coupled with a swin transformer. This CNN showed positive results in clearing smoke from intraoperative surgical video. During situations when a surgeon has to move quickly while maintaining optimum sight, as in the case of severe intraoperative bleeding, this is very necessary.

13.4.5 Safe Dissection of Loose Connective Tissues Automated Segmentation

One surgeon might accept the power of deep learning systems in being able to predict delicate and difficult anatomical features, such as LCTFs, in intraoperative recordings. This technology is helpful in decision-making in real time by identifying a safe diversification plane which in turn reduces unintended events. In order for performance as well as safety to be improved in surgical domains, more advanced approaches for image segmentation will become increasingly accessible.

The blend of artificial intelligence (AI) in surgical practice is to be able to upgrade the professional experience and cognitive abilities of the surgeon by better prediction of anatomical professionals. Kumazu Y (2021) created a deep learning model with the goal of automatically identifying a safe dissection plane by segmentation of loose connective tissue fibers (LCTFs). The goal was to avoid damaging the integrity of the tissue. A robot-assisted gastrectomy was carried out by competent surgeons, and the annotations were applied to the video frames showing the surgery being performed. A U-Net-based deep learning model was created to provide segmentation results. The model's performance was evaluated using 20 randomly selected frames and a two-item questionnaire with problems regarding sensitivity and misrecognition. Twenty of the surgeons completed the questionnaire. In order to arrive at these findings, a comparison between the results obtained with the recollection and F1/Dice test and those with a ground truth was performed. The recall scores for the model were calculated and the result showed a mean of 0.606 and maximum of 0.861, which were significantly better than the average. The F1/Dice scores had the mean score of 0.549, the minimum score was 0.335, and the maximum was 0.691. This implies the presence of substantial spatial overlaps between the elements. The mean score for sensitivity assigned by surgeon assessors was 3.52 and 88.0% of them have assigned the highest possible score of 4. The scores ranged from 2.45 to 3.95. The mean value of the sensitivity score was considered to be the sensitivity score. The average score was 0.14 for misrecognition, the range of which was 0–0.7, indicating a limited acknowledgment of errors as a result of overdetection. Artificial intelligence can be programmed to successfully predict minute anatomical components to a level of precision that is persuasive to highly skilled surgeons. This can be achieved through the ongoing training process. This approach may be used to find harmless planes for dissection, thus avoiding a major number of unfortunate events.

13.4.6 Real-Time Instrument Delineation: Upgrading Augmented Reality with Deep Learning

The development of augmented reality (AR) for robotic and minimally invasive surgery has opened the way for revolutionary possibilities in intraoperative guidance; however, understanding clinical-based implementation of AR has been hampered by technological, computational, and ergonomic constraints. Two of the most important obstacles are (1) the correct registration of preoperative 3D anatomical models with the intraoperative scene and (2) the visual occlusions of surgical instruments due to the 3D overlay. In robotic surgery of the kidney, such as robot-assisted partial nephrectomy (RAPN) or robot-assisted kidney transplantation (RAKT), the visual precision and constant visibility of the tools are important factors in guaranteeing the safety and efficiency of the surgery.

Traditional AR systems are based on manual matching of 3D reconstructions with endoscopic views—a process that is susceptible to human error as well as to in vivo variation caused by respiratory motion, tissue deformation, or repositioning of the patient. Furthermore, although the active instruments are visible during 3D anatomical overlays that create enhanced spatial awareness, depth perception is lost and delicate maneuvers are performed in surgery with the risk of instrument damage. Addressing these challenges requires the use of advanced deep learning (DL) and computer vision methodologies that are able to address the challenges of simultaneous model registration, instrument segmentation, and real-time visualization.

De Backer, R., Alscular, L., de Vree, E. & van Baemen, Y. (2023): The AR-ID Framework of Robotic Kidney Surgery

A landmark study by De Backer et al. proposed the concept of augmented reality instrument delineation (AR-ID) with deep learning as a solution to deal with both the problems of misalignment and occlusion in AR-guided urological procedures. This research demonstrated for the first time the feasibility of real-time instrument delineation incorporated with 3D AR visualization during robot-assisted partial nephrectomy (RAPN) and robot-assisted kidney transplantation (RAKT).

The AR-ID used convolutional neural networks (CNNs) pretrained with a large and manually sorted data containing 65,927 labeled instances of instruments from 15,100 frames of robotic surgeries. The model was able to identify all of the nonorganic surgical instruments present in the operative field, and successful differentiation of the instruments from the organic tissues and 3D overlays. This enabled surgeons to have clear visualization of instruments even though AR anatomic projections were displayed.

One of the primary things that De Backer et al. demonstrated from their work is how robust and cross-institutional the systems are. The framework was trialled in different hospitals and by different surgical teams which demonstrated a high degree of transferability and reproducibility in a real clinical setting. The hardware requirements were quite modest—consisting of a GPU-enabled laptop (costing between 1000 and 1500 euros), a video capture card (costing between 100 and 400 euros), and an auxiliary display (costing between 100 and 200 euros)—which makes the system cost-effective and scalable.

Practical implementation of the AR-ID resulted in a 0.5 s latency time, which is adequate for intraoperative visualization but is not yet acceptable to use during intraoperative windows exclusively in real time such as in the TilePro display. Future work suggested by the authors include pipeline fusion into a single computational architecture, which may have the potential of eliminating latency and improving synchronization between AR overlays and endoscopic video streams.

Importantly, the system does not currently have a quantitative per-instrument accuracy measurement, which limits the system's ability to perform performance auditing or reliability grading in complex performing tasks that have multiple instruments. This will have to be worked out through the introduction of confidence-based segmentation ranking and live performance data. Moreover, persistent problems such as dynamic model deformation and motion artifacts caused by respiration, still prevent a perfect congruence between the static 3D model and the dynamic field of surgery. These limitations in the future may be reduced by a combination of optical flow estimation and tissue tracking with a numerical model, together with a deep learning algorithm.

Thus, the study by De Backer et al. is an important milestone, not only for AI-assisted urologic surgery, but for establishing a proof-of-concept framework for safe, inexpensive, and adaptive AR integration for robotic operating environments.

Peek et al., Automated 3D Model Registration in Minimally Invasive Surgery
Building on the similar concepts of AR integration, Peek et al. (2024) proposed the novel concept of a sophisticated automated three-dimensional registration algorithm for intraoperative AR navigation in minimally invasive pulmonary resection. Their technique used the aid of deep-learning to conduct a point cloud surface mapping in order to convert the intraoperative camera feed into a geometric 3D interpretation of the anatomy of the patient. This was then algorithmically registered to the preoperative 3D model to permit automatic and real-time spatial registration without manual intervention.

This system is particularly important in that it directly solves the first obstacle that De Backer et al. identified—manual and error-prone 3D alignment. Peek et al. presented that submillimeter accuracy in alignment was possible using surface-based auto-registration techniques that have allowed for frame rates that support real-time visualization. Although their research was done in the setting of thoracic rather than renal surgery, the general structure of point cloud correlation and real-time model warping have very broad translational scope. The approach could be applied to dynamic abdominal or retroperitoneal organs with the Farrick and McKinley addition of elastic registration algorithms that can compensate for intraoperative motion/deformation.

The results of Peek et al. constitute one example of how AI-based registration and spatial calculation can eliminate the need for manual calibration procedures and free the surgeon of cognitive burden for constantly adaptive AR navigation of minimally invasive or robotic procedures. Combined with delineation modules based on instruments like AR-ID, these techniques can potentially result in a complete automated self-correcting AR guidance ecosystem.

Ahmed et al. Segmentation of Surgical Tools with Deep Learning
Complementing these advances in the procedure, Ahmed et al. (2024) published a comprehensive systematic review of 48 peer-reviewed studies involving deep learning for surgical instruments detection and segmentation in robotic-assisted surgery operations. Their review found a strong trend toward convolutional neural networks

(CNNs), derivatives of U-Net architecture, and transformer-based architectures for real-time instrument recognition, component-level segmentation, and motion tracking.

Ahmed et al. stressed that proper delineation of instruments provides the computational basis for the integration of AR in robotic surgery, as the visible and located tools are crucial in the integration of virtual 3D anatomical reconstructions in live surgical footage. Importantly, it was noted that the development of increasingly annotated surgical datasets, like that developed by De Backer et al., is a key enabling factor for model reliability and generalizability.

Furthermore, optimization of the latency, dataset standardization, and multi-domain model training were highlighted by the authors to ensure AI-assisted segmentation systems are able to operate robustly in different conditions of lighting, occlusion, and camera angle. This is very much in line with the limitations in the system found in the work of De Backer et al., and therefore points to a consensus across the world that the next generation of AR systems needs to be both technically autonomous and clinically explainable in order to get regulatory and practical approval.

Synthesizing and Emerging Trends

Violence treatment on the whole, the papers of De Backer et al. (2023), Peek et al. (2024), and Ahmed et al. (2024) describe an evolution toward the use of deep learning for augmented reality surgical systems. Together, these studies show how instrument delineation in real-time, automated 3D registration and data-driven segmentation can come together to form intelligent intraoperative visualization platforms that may help to increase the precision of surgical procedures, mitigate cognitive burden, and improve surgical outcomes.

For this AR-guided robotic kidney surgery, these are the kinds of developments which open up this future where the system will be able to automatically align the preoperative anatomical reconstructions with the preoperational anatomical reconstructions, segmentation, and tracking of the instruments without occlusion, as well as motion or deformation artifacts, corrections, and quantitative confidence feedback to the operating surgeon. To realize this vision, it will be necessary to integrate robotic consoles with high-performance computing hardware, design single AI frameworks with combined scene reconstruction, semantic segmentation, and real-time registration, and meet clinical safety and latency requirements.

All in all, these innovations are ushering in a new paradigm of AR moving away from static faraway spacecraft to something like a pre-rendered data-driven AR ecosystem, which can adapt to the surgical environment in real time. Such systems, empowered by deep learning, promise to bring a significant step to the precision, safety, and efficiency of robotic-assisted urological procedures, an important step toward the realization of intelligent, context-aware, surgery.

13.5 Artificial Intelligence in Gynaecology Surgery: Where Are We, Where Do We Need to Go?

The area of women's health is an important and complex one, since it comprises gynecological illnesses, reproductive health problems, ailments that are affected by hormonal fluctuations, and serious diseases for instance malignancies of cervix or ovaries. The practice of urogynecologic surgery is one of the key aspects of this practice; this is one of the most notable aspects of this specialty due to the difficulty of the diversity of anatomical abnormalities and to the different requirements of each patient. Recent development of information technology, especially artificial intelligence (AI), has created tremendous possibilities for improving gynecologic surgery, as well as a variety of research and education.

13.5.1 Impact of Preoperative Planning and Simulation

Accurate diagnosis, correct planning, and patient-specific simulation contribute a significant part in the surgical outcomes of gynecologic procedures. By combining AI and more conventional imaging techniques, such as MRI, CT, and ultrasound, imaging diagnoses have been dramatically improved. While deep learning and adaptive augmented reality models for better robotic surgery result in three-dimensional radiological images to plan surgery precisely. AI-assisted 3D printing techniques can help in improving the precision of surgeries and also to enhance the probability of error in the surgeries (Moawad et al., 2019). In order to guide the surgical process, minimize the length, increase accuracy, and reduce the problems. 3D printed models may be created using the preoperative MRI scans. This model can give the insight of anatomic depth and width as well as the involvement of the surrounding tissues (Kannaiyan et al., 2024). As the treatment of benign tumors does not entail a treatment as complicated or mal as the one used for malignant tumors, the use of artificial intelligence and robots in these procedures has another cost-benefit analysis. With aims to give the best patient care, the use of AI and robotic systems must be made on the basis of costs and benefits.

Gynecology Surgical Technologies Based on Artificial Intelligence Challenges
Despite the advancements, gynosurgical technologies encounter a hurdle. Addressing shortage of clinical care, increasing the accuracy and reliability of algorithms, and incorporating different sources of clinical data should be top priorities of future research. In order to train AI algorithms, it is imperative to have high quality, varied, and consistent datasets because a lack of data from different samples of patients can weaken the reliability and ability of AI algorithms to be applicable to a wider range of cases. Research into better algorithms, better hardware, and better data streaming and compression techniques is required, as AI systems have complex computing problems with complex processing of operational video data while keeping the latency low. Clinicians are often skeptical of algorithms and their ability to believe in them. There is room for research in the interpretability of AI models using

principles of tractability and intuitive visualization, using explainable and advanced HCI to yield better decision-making processes.

13.5.2 Intraoperative Navigation and Guidance

With the help of brand-new technologies that contribute to better visualization, improved workflow, and improved safety for the patient, artificial intelligence is changing intraoperative gynecologic surgery. A variety of gynecologic operations, such as myomectomies, hysterectomies, and operations related to gynecologic cancer, have shown promising results when performed using robotic-assisted operative systems. AI-driven robotic platforms help surgeons by offering clearer views of important structures such as the blood vessels, nerves, and the reproductive organs (Hanassab, 2024). Artificial intelligence (AI) has enhanced communication in the operating room by incorporating information from different sources such as robotic devices, patient monitors, and intraoperative imaging (Sparling et al., 2023). By removing the mental burden, this solution guarantees decision-making efficiency and ultimately enables the surgical team to focus on the things that matter. Furthermore, AI can also be used to monitor data intraoperatively as well as predict possible complications before they occur. In the case of gynecologic surgery, it means the ability to identify the early signs of an excessive bleeding of meninges, monitor minor changes of patient vitals, and predict susceptibility to alterations of the surrounding structures (Khan & Khare, 2024).

13.5.3 Course After Operation and Administration

Electrical stimulation, pelvic floor biofeedback therapy, pelvic floor muscle training (PFMT), assisted pelvic floor muscular exercise, pelvic floor rehabilitation are all important components of pelvic floor rehabilitation and are effective treatment methods for pelvic floor diseases. Kegel exercises in which the patient contracts the pelvic floor muscles on purpose may help the patient better control the urge to urinate. Biofeedback treatment gives the patient the chance to see visual indications of contractions of the pelvic floor musculature. Electrical stimulation, via low current, assists in the reestablishment of muscle strength in the pelvic floor muscles and also helps to regenerate the nerves by stimulation of parts of the nerve fibers within the pelvic floor muscles.

Once a woman has had her lochia drained and her uterine, organ, and tissue functions have returned to normal once, the ideal time to treat her pelvic floor is 6 months after giving birth. In addition to promoting the good activation of the pelvic floor, this has the benefit of promoting the speed of blood circulation, repair and regeneration of the structure and the functionality of the nerves of the perineum, and also reducing the fibrosis of the tissue of the maternal pelvic floor. In addition to simply improving general health, this method lowers the rate of disorders which have an influence on the pelvic floor. Diseases affecting the pelvic floor in females can be diagnosed in a variety of ways such as magnetic resonance imaging (MRI), computed tomography (CT), cystourethrography, and pelvic floor ultrasonography.

While magnetic resonance imaging (MRI) demonstrates structure and tissues of the pelvic floor, cystourethrography demonstrates structure and function of the lower urinary tract. The radioactivity of MRI makes it limited in its use. As a result of its usefulness and advancement in the field of 3D reconstruction, ultrasonography has recently gained popularity. Although the widespread use of ultrasound is for clinical diagnosis, the accuracy of the results is potentially affected by the physician's subjective opinion and medical analysis experience of films. Improvement in the image-processing technologies is exploited in medical image processing due to the development of the computer technology.

The clinical identification of illnesses of pelvic floor dysfunction is increasingly relying on the application of ultrasound technologies. AI algorithms have been widely applied in healthcare medical image-processing research owing to their great performance capabilities in edge recognition, denoising, lesion segmentation, and feature extraction. However, there is limited research of its use in ultrasound image processing in diseases that affect the pelvic floor. This study investigated the effects of pelvic floor rehabilitation training on the recovery of postpartum tissue structure and function using ultrasound pictures of patients with pelvic floor dysfunction, and the algorithm was used to improve the ultrasound images. It is believed that this technology will be the benchmark for the diagnosis and treatment of the sound clinical-linked illnesses.

Yin P. and colleagues designed a clinical study from 2019 to 2020 to learn the effectiveness of pelvic floor rehabilitation training in mothers in the postpartum period diagnosed with pelvic organ prolapse (POP). The research consisted of 60 hospital female patients with a mean age of 34.6 years ± 11.5 years and 25–65 years old. The cases were clinically diagnosed by all patients to have moderate to severe pelvic organ prolapse indexed as stage I to II on the basis of pelvic organ prolapse quantification (POP-Q) system. The stages represent various degrees of dysfunction of the pelvic floor with the anatomical lowering of the pelvic organs out from their normal position. To maintain homogeneity and minimize the confounding factors, the study did not include participants who had acute irritation of the urinary or the reproductive tracts, pelvic malignancies, history of pelvic surgery, sciatica, or those with any neurological disorder which may independently affect the function of the pelvic floor. Participants that met the eligibility criteria were randomly assigned to two groups: an experimental group that received specific training in rehabilitation of the pelvic floor and a control group that did not receive this intervention. The intervention was a series of protocols aimed toward promoting the pelvic support structures with prescribed pelvic floor muscle training and postpartum recovery. The researchers incorporated artificial intelligence (AI) algorithms for studying ultrasound imaging data of the pelvic floor. This method of analysis made it possible to measure and represent precisely the changes of basic anatomical and functional parameters such as pelvic floor muscle strength, levator ani muscle thickness, and perineal fissure width. Compared with the control group, the experimental group obtained significant experiments in these parameters which can prove improvement of muscle recovery and anatomical restoration after AI-assisted analysis. Artificial intelligence made it possible to process and interpret the ultrasound image better and with clearer and more detailed images of the structures in the pelvic floor, which greatly improved the accuracy of the diagnosis and evaluation.

The research findings of Yin and Wang (2022) indicated that combining pelvic floor rehabilitation training with artificial intelligence–assisted ultrasound image analysis is a feasible strategy for enhancing postpartum recovery in women with pelvic organ prolapse. Their results highlight the potential for integrating automated AI technologies into standard postpartum care to improve the quality and suitability of rehabilitation. However, the authors acknowledged several limitations, including a small sample size and a short follow-up duration. They emphasized the need for future studies involving larger and more diverse populations, with long-term outcome assessments, to validate and generalize their findings.

Artificial intelligence is influencing postoperative care in three major ways: personalized follow-up management, early identification of complications, and data-driven clinical decision-making. Through wearable devices, electronic health records, and predictive analytics, AI can support tailored recommendations related to pain management, dietary adjustments, and rehabilitation interventions. AI-enabled systems may also prescribe individualized physical therapy exercises to strengthen pelvic muscles and reduce the risk of urinary incontinence or prolapse recurrence following pelvic floor repair and other gynecological procedures, underscoring the importance of remote AI-supported monitoring systems (Polineni et al., 2022). Additionally, AI systems may assist in detecting postoperative complications—such as infections, thrombosis, or organ dysfunction—based on preoperative patient status, surgical duration, and intraoperative blood loss (Jiang et al., 2023).

13.6 Role of AI in Obstetrics

13.6.1 Fetal Cardiotocography (CTG)

By improving the assessment of cardiotocographs (CTGs) in labor, artificial intelligence (AI) will assist in minimizing complications and inconsistencies in intrapartum monitoring. Through more standardized and objective assessments, AI-based systems may also have the potential to reduce medicolegal disputes and reduce financial burdens on healthcare systems, particularly in resource-limited healthcare settings.

Notable examples of such innovations are the INFANT research protocol and Computer-Aided Fetal Evaluator, both of them employing complex algorithms in improving CTG interpretation. Similarly, the System 8000 shows important parameters of fetal monitoring, like CTG quality, peak of uterine contractions, baseline heart rate of fetus, variability, decelerations, and accelerations (Brocklehurst, 2016).

Meta-analysis showed a 50% reduction in the incidence of neonatal seizure to be reduced by continuous monitoring using CTG. Since 1989, numerous research works (both retrospective cohort and randomized controlled trials) have been carried out to examine the utilization of AI in the interpretation of CTGs. However, despite these promising results in large randomized controlled trials and in about 50,000 participants, results with regard to accurate risk identification and prevention of adverse neonatal outcome (Dawes et al., 1991) have been inconsistent.

13.6.2 Roesemann, C Cardiotocography (CTG) and Clinical Significance

Cardiotocography (CTG) is one of the most important noninvasive diagnostic tests used in the field of obstetrics which is useful in monitoring the fetal and uterine contractions heartbeat (FHR) at the same time. It is the foundation of fetal monitoring during pregnancy and labor and gives information on the condition of the oxygenation, the general condition of the autonomic nervous system of the fetus. As CTG will pick up abnormal fetal heart patterns that may represent hypoxia and distress, it allows the clinical trough intervention at the appropriate time—to conventionally induce labor or to consider the delivery of the baby by caesarean section, reducing kb morbidity and mortality in the infant. The device traces two continuous tracings—one recording the activity of the uterus and the other showed the fluctuation of fetal heart rate. Together, these parameters give information how well the fetus is coping with the stress of the uterine contractions of labor.

13.6.3 Fundamentals and Variables of CTG Interpretation

CTG interpretation is largely based on the detailed evaluation of five crucial parameters as follows: baseline fetal heart rate, baseline variability, accelerations/decelerations, and uterine contractions.

Vitals on the body during pregnancy—signs and symptoms: Initial heart rates of a fetus are considered "baseline" fetal heart rate, which start at 110–160 beats per minute (bpm). A finding of a constant rate of less than 110 bpm is suggestive of fetal bradycardia, and a rate of more than 160 bpm could be indicative of fetal tachycardia due to maternal fever, infection, or fetal distress.

Sands FHR is the swing in the FHR between the baseline and is typically between 5 and 25 bpm. Normal variance is a normal balance between the activity of the sympathetic and parasympathetic nervous systems, and low variance may be an indication of fetal hypoxia, central nervous system depression, or the effects of sedative medications.

Fetal heart rate tracing—constantly monitors FHR by a baby growing—falling off. Accelerations: transient (increased FHR) increases in heart rate (generally 15 bpm or more lasting for 15 s) and the presence of acceleration is reassuring of good fetal oxygenation.

Decelerations, on the contrary, are temporary losses in FHR, and depending on their nature, they can have various connotations. Early decelerations correspond to uterine contractions and are usually benign in nature whereas variable decelerations are due to compression of the umbilical cord, whereas the late decelerations—occurring after contractions—signal uteroplacental insufficiency and fetal hypoxia.

In addition, separate evaluation is made of uterine contractions both in terms of frequency and intensity as excessive uterine activity (tachysystole) can cause decreased fetal oxygenation due to decreased perfusion of the placenta.

13.6.4 Conditions Detected by CTG

CTG analysis is very useful in the diagnosis of a number of maternal and fetal conditions that may have an impact on the fetus well-being. It is often used in high-risk pregnancies like those which are complicated by preeclampsia, gestational diabetes, intrauterine growth restriction (IUGR), post-term pregnancy, and oligohydramnios. In cases of fetal hypoxia or asphyxia, CTG usually will have a combination of depressing late decelerations and a loss of baseline variability, both of which reflect a worsening of the oxygen supply to the fetus. Umbilical cord compression often causes variable decelerations, and maternal fever or infection is a cause of fetal tachycardia. Similarly, placental insufficiency with limited exchange of nutrients and oxygen may be manifested by a loss of accelerations and late decelerations. By decoding these patterns, medical staff will be able to determine if conservative management or intrauterine resuscitative measures or urgent delivery is needed.

13.6.5 Limitations of Traditional Presentation of the CTG

Despite the usefulness of CTG in clinical settings, the interpretation of CTG has been criticized for many years due to its subjectivity and interobserver variability of analysis. Studies have demonstrated that the same computerized membrane chart-topographic (CTG) actually could be perceived in different ways by different clinicians, which causes miscommunication among them in the diagnostic and management process. The predictive value of CTG for fetal acidosis is very poor; if a high false-positive rate has meant that a large number of unnecessary cesarean sections or other interventions have been carried out. Moreover, CTG waveforms may be influenced by maternal medication, fetal sleep cycles, or technical artifacts, which make interpretation challenging. Due to all these challenges, the focus has changed toward the creation of computerized and AI-based systems to increase the precision of diagnosing the disease and to decrease the human bias.

13.6.6 Development of Computerized AI-Assisted CTG Analysis

Computerized CTG (cCTG) systems were introduced; however, to attempt to standardize the CTG and to make it dependent on a lesser number of observers. Early systems (e.g., Sonicaid Fetal Monitor, Oxford, and Dawes and Redman criteria) automatically calculated parameters such as baseline rate, short-term variability, and the number of accelerations or decelerations from mathematical algorithms. Although new diagnostic systems improved access to objectivity and reproducibility, rigid rule-based logic, and inability to completely describe the complex nonlinear relationships in fetal physiology still limited the use of these systems.

This has been a general area revolutionized with the development of artificial intelligence (AI) using machine learning (ML) and deep learning (DL) techniques. Massive data on CTG recordings gathered together with their clinical results can be used to train artificial intelligence (AI) algorithms to identify subtle and sophisticated patterns, which are difficult to capture for humans. Machine learning models like SVMs, random forests, and decision trees have been used in training models to classify CTG traces as normal, suspicious, or pathological. Later deep learning techniques, such as convolutional neural networks (CNNs) and recurrent neural networks (RNNs), can be applied for analyzing the CTG signal directly as a time series input from which features are extracted automatically and trends in time, typical for fetal distress are detected from the input data.

13.6.7 Clinical Decision-Making Using AI

AI-powered CTG analysis has several important advantages over traditional ways. It helps in improving objectivity and reproducibility and removes the effect of human subjectivity. Additionally, artificial intelligence models can also aid in assessing and warning users of signs of early delivery in a timely fashion to help clinicians make timely decisions. Some of the hybrid AI-based systems involve the CTG data along with other clinical variables of the mother (e.g., blood pressure, temperature, gestational age) to predict an unfavorable outcome more accurately. AI also facilitates the remote monitoring process, which is beneficial in specific geographic locations with limited access to resources or that are remote from a person who specializes in that area where the same level of constant supervision would be unlikely.

Studies have demonstrated an exceeded predictive accuracy of AI models compared to an expert for predicting outcomes such as fetal acidemia, low Apgar score, and emergency cesarean delivery. Additionally, the emergence of a thing known as Explainable AI (XAI) is helping in overcoming the challenge of transparency as clinicians will now be able to understand the reasoning behind AI predictions and be clinically accountable.

13.6.8 Emerging Issues and Future Trends

For example, in recent years, large open-access CTG databases have been built, such as the CTU-UHB dataset and PhysioNet Fetal monitoring repository, which have been able to aid the development of accelerated AI training and validation. The merging of CTG systems based on artificial intelligence with electronic health records (EHRs) and wearable fetal monitoring devices is driving more and more opportunity for continuous home-based fetal monitoring. In addition, with the advancements in cloud computing and Internet of things (IoT) for edge AI, CTG data can also be processed in real time even in remote locations. Next-generation innovations can involve more personalized monitoring of the fetus where AI algorithms could be installed with the personal maternal/fetal characteristics for more personalised diagnosis. However, the wide clinical rollout remains an obstacle since standardization in data, regulatory approval, and ethical aspects of data privacy and clinical attribution are still relevant considerations.

13.6.9 Intern Space Monitoring, Labor Management with Special Staff Concern, Built-in Maternal Health Monitoring

Artificial intelligence (AI) systems that analyze maternal health data have significantly enhanced the ability to predict labor outcomes and identify potential complications. By processing complex clinical variables—such as fetal heart rate patterns, uterine contractions, and cervical dilation—AI models can forecast the onset and duration of labor, thereby enabling clinicians to anticipate adverse events like preterm labor or fetal distress. He et al. (2023) highlight that such predictive analytics support timely decision-making, reduce unnecessary interventions, and optimize the scheduling of obstetric procedures.

AI-enabled fetal monitoring systems further integrate data from multiple sources to detect trends in fetal heart rate, movements, and uterine activity. According to Iftikhar et al. (2020), these tools can identify early signs of fetal compromise, including abnormal heart rate patterns, intrauterine growth restriction, or umbilical cord-related complications, offering real-time insights into fetal well-being.

On the maternal side, AI is increasingly used to interpret biomarkers, laboratory findings, and clinical signs aimed at early detection of conditions such as infections, gestational diabetes, and preeclampsia. Continuous maternal monitoring through AI-powered remote systems facilitates prompt intervention, improves outcomes, and expands access to specialist care. As noted by Yaseen and Rather (2024), AI-based telemedicine solutions play a vital role in monitoring high-risk pregnancies, enabling virtual consultations and sustained surveillance outside traditional healthcare settings.

13.6.10 Postpartum Care

In order to evaluate the health of a mother, artificial intelligence is applied to be able to check vital signs, tests, and calls. In order to provide appropriate intervention, this type of real-time monitoring will be able to detect early problems if there is any problem with the patient such as preeclampsia, gestational diabetes, or infection. Monitoring technologies that are powered by artificial intelligence also make it possible to do continuous surveillance of maternal health indices that are outside of clinical settings. Through the process of facilitating the virtual consultations and remote monitoring of the high-risk pregnancies, this increases access to specialist treatment and improves the results for the patients.

13.6.11 Challenges

Compliance with the Health Insurance Portability and Accountability Act (HIPAA) is required since the use of artificial intelligence in health care creates issues regarding the privacy and security of data. In order to retain the patient's information, it is necessary to restructure the infrastructure; it also educates the medical team and goes against the conventional procedures of obstetricians and gynecologists. In order to ensure that applications of artificial intelligence in the healthcare industry are developed and deployed in an ethical way, it is necessary to address ethical issues such as informed consent, openness, and possible bias. Additionally, there is a need to respect the rights of the patient and treat him or her equally as well. This entails a change in the way of conventional practice and dealing with these issues (Patel et al., 2024a; Basil et al., 2022).

13.7 AI and Orthopedics

Orthopedic surgery is a very specialized area that requires high precision and accuracy in the management of bone, joint, and connective tissue. AI has become the technological revolution in orthopedics as it improves the practice of surgery, personalization, and patient outcomes. The combination of AI-driven analytics, machine learning, and robots has been the catalyst that has brought orthopedic surgery to the age of unparalleled accuracy, predictability, and improved recovery patterns.

13.7.1 AI-Facilitated Surgical Strategy Planner and Predictive Result

13.7.1.1 Individual Surgery Roadmap Generation

AI has revolutionized preoperative planning and made precise and patient-specific plans for surgery. The AI algorithms are customized on the specific plan of the operation by building a customized surgical plan by synthesizing large-scale datasets such as imaging studies, previous surgical records, and anatomic variation optimizing surgical precision. Machine learning and deep learning models provide the simulation of the optimal incisions, positioning of the implants, and anatomical restoration even in the area of the first incision. This predictive model decreases the intraoperative unpredictability and man-hands-on intraoperative adjustment. Therefore, AI-based blueprints not only contribute to the confidence of decision-making of the surgeon, but facilitates the workflow, providing a better level of standardization and accuracy of the procedure.

13.7.1.2 Less Human Planning Modification (Lambrechts et al., 2022)

The results of a study performed by Lambrechts et al. is also aimed at determining the effectiveness of the AI-generated surgical strategies compared to the ones developed by a surgeon. Their research showed that the human plan modifications were reduced by 39.71%, which means that the AI-based blueprints have to be modified much less before surgery. Moreover, plans that had to be revised showed 47.95% increase in accuracy, which proved that AI can match preoperative plans with realities of intraoperatives. This data implies that AI reduces the variation in planning as well as action, eliminates human thinking errors, which results in a more stable surgical process. The authors further noted that not only does this decrease the time of preoperative planning, it also improves the reproducibility, hence better patient outcomes and procedure's reliability.

A comparative study in the surgical specialty of orthopedics carried out by Zhou et al. (2023) studied the effect of 3D AI-assisted preoperative planning. Their findings demonstrated 44.7% improvement on geometric and procedural accuracy than cases of traditional manual procedures. The AI models made use of convolutional neural networks (CNNs) to optimize orientation of implants, alignment of the bone, and sizing of components in total joint arthroplasty. The result was a better biomechanical restoration and a great decline in the number of corrections during the course of operation. The researchers came to the conclusion that the computational models of AI may be used to make the geometrical arrangement reproducible and enhance the efficiency of the overall surgery, which may ideally decrease the malalignment and misplaced implant problems.

The study by Mozafari et al. was a systematic review on the AI-based preoperative planning in total hip arthroplasty (THA). The review was published in Frontiers in Artificial Intelligence (2024) and presented data about the results of various studies, demonstrating that AI did lead to a significant improvement in the accuracy of positioning of the femoral and acetabular component and a 30% reduction in the geometric deviation in comparison to manual planning. In their AI assisted platforms, modeling with 3D CT and computer-aided optimization of parameters were integrated to ensure better cup inclination, leg-length symmetry and recreation of hip biomechanics. The importance of interdisciplinary cooperation between surgeons and biomedical engineers was also highlighted by the authors. AI-based simulations made it possible to evaluate virtual plans between them and reduce the number of planning flaws, while also improving the stability of the postoperative phases and the patient's satisfaction.

Moving not only to the orthopedics field, Morris et al. performed the survey of cross-specialty applications of AI in surgical practice including neurosurgery, hepatobiliary and oncologic surgery. Their results showed that the use of artificial intelligence (AI) based intraoperative navigation and real-time imaging analysis had significant positive effects on the tumor resection fidelity and implant fidelity of the tumor resection. Operations facilitated by AI demonstrated a progressively greater effect in terms of byte reduction of hospitalization duration and postoperation revision by 27% and 32% respectively. The research highlighted the problem with predictive AI algorithms working in tandem with the adaptive decision-making process in the OR, taking into account the feedback of the intraoperative experience and adapting the plans accordingly. The authors concluded that the constant learning ability of the AI enables to fill in the gap between the preoperative intention and the intraoperative performance and improve the efficiency, safety and outcomes of surgery.

13.7.1.3 Overall Implications

All of the studies (Lambrechts et al., Morris et al) show evidence that combatively, AI-based preoperative planning systems increase the surgical intervention accuracy, repeatability, and safety. The complete reliability of interpreting the data and the integration of predictive analytics also minimize human error and the variability of surgery and optimize results of the surgery, which also favors AI in reducing human error. The combination of 3D imaging, machine learning, and real-time simulation is a radical break toward intelligent, adaptive surgery, in which the surgeon will be working in an augmented ecosystem of data-driven precision. With continuous development of AI technology, its application in any specialty continues to standardize the work of complicated procedures, improve patient outcomes, and redefine the planning of surgery as a constantly changing evidence-based process.

13.7.2 Artificial Intelligence-Based Robotic Systems in Arthroplasty

The introduction of AI-based systems using robotized technology has changed radically the procedure of orthopaedic arthroplasty, in particular the total knee arthroplasty (TKA), and the total hip arthroplasty (THA). The MAKO robotic arm-assisted technology is, among the others, one of the examples of the crossroads of artificial intelligence, preoperative imaging, and intraoperative robotic guidance at Stryker.

13.7.2.1 Artificial Intelligence Plus Imaging to Bring Precision during the Surgical

The MAKO system is based on three-dimensional anatomy modeling using artificial intelligence algorithms based on CT to generate a patient-specific surgical plan (Morris et al., 2024). Surgeons are thus able to plan these optimal implant locations to simulate the kinematics of the joint and to predict potential conflicts of the soft tissues. The system can be used for in-operative real-time haptic feedback and corrections to the angles of bone resection and implant placement. This artificial intelligence-directed process can improve the accuracy of doing surgery to a great extent and removes the variability in work by surgeons with varying degrees of experience.

13.7.2.2 Dependence and Precision Improved

Nam et al. (2022) found an increase of 32.14% with the use of MAKO-assisted TKA than conventional manual methods in a prospective study. In particular, the mechanical alignment deviation of robotic-assisted surgeries was less than 1.5 deg. when compared to the deviation of 2.5 to 3+ in manual procedures. This enhancement was explained by the fact that the AI-assisted intraoperative feedback allows to carry out dynamic changes during bone cuts and the implantation of implants. Likewise, Seidenstein et al. (2021) showed in a comparative study comparing the outcome of radiography in 200 patients that the robotic-assisted TKA aligning lesser than 3 and less than 2° was 100% and 93%, respectively, compared to 75% and 60% of conventional manual TKA. The paper has shown how AI-based predictive modeling has been used to enhance the work of the prosthesis to prevent overturning and minimizing the imbalance of the soft tissues.

13.7.2.2.1 Recent Clinical Evidence (2023–2024)

Multicentric and randomized trials in recent years have confirmed that the AI-controlled robotic arthroplasty will turn precision into clinically beneficial influences:

1. This study is a multicenter, randomized study comparing MAKO-assisted TKA with conventional TKA. The patients undergoing the robotic-assisted process had less postoperative pain (VAS 2.3 ± 0.8 vs. 3.9 ± 1.1; $p < 0.001$) and had less length of stay (2.1 vs. 3.6 days; $p < 0.01$). These positive effects were described by the authors as a result of the reduced incidence of trauma to the soft tissues and the optimization of the bone cuts through the use of AI for intraoperative corrections.
2. Lee et al. (2024) assessed the functional outcomes of 200 patients and found that robotic-assisted TKA improved Knee Society Scores (KSS) more than the robotic-assisted one increasing by 18.7 scores at 6 months compared to conventional TKA. Also, WOMAC pain scores dropped by 24, which indicates a reduction in the stress of the joint and the improvement of the initial mobility. This paper has highlighted the role of AI in the predictive modeling of the kinematics done postoperatively that offers personalized joint balancing and also functional restoration.
3. In the case of robotic-assisted THA, the rehabilitation period needed to be shortened by 20%. Patel et al. (2024b) reviewed robotic-assisted THA and found that postoperative pain decreased by 34% and the rehabilitation period had to be shortened by 20%. The use of the AI into the orientation of the components and the optimization of the trajectory played an important role in the equalization of the leg length, compensations of the pelvic tilt, and better joint stability that lead to a quicker functional recovery and patient satisfaction.

13.7.2.2.2 Synthesis and Implications

Not only does the introduction of AI to robotic assisted arthroplasty guarantee the added mechanical preciseness, it is also directly proportional to the patients having improved outcomes, such as reduced pain levels, quicker functional outcomes, and reduced hospitalization. Analyzing intraoperative information and changing the surgery parameters in real time, the AI-driven systems make it possible to perform personalized surgery, making the results uniform and preventing complications after the surgery. Such developments constitute a great paradigm shift in the field of orthopedics with precision medicine as a result of the use of robotic systems that improve efficiency and accuracy of surgery.

13.7.3 Recovery After Surgery and Predictive Analytics

AI has continued to be helpful outside of the operating room to predict potential complications, optimize rehabilitation timeline, and individualise postoperative treatment. Machine learning models use the patient-specific parameters including gait patterns, inflammatory biomarkers, past-recovery data, etc. to come up with adaptive rehabilitation plans. It is individual in approach and enables faster ambulation, reduced opioid use, and better functional outcome in the long run.

Longitudinal data analyses will enable AI systems to predict the progressions of recovery, reckoning the patients who would not recover quickly or whose implants may fail and thus intervene early and increase the overall success of the surgical procedure.

13.7.4 Challenges and Limitations

Along with the apparent advantages, there are many difficulties with application of AI in orthopedics:

1. High implementation cost

   Robotic systems, like MAKO, are expensive at a cost of a lot of money. The MAKO robot is priced at around 1.25 million, the annual service agreements are around 100,000, and the prices of the implants are approximately near 5500. With the addition of the imaging and operating equipment, overall costs could surpass 3–4 million, which becomes a huge hindrance to smaller or rural hospitals.
2. Disparity and accessibility of health care

   In resource-limited institutions, these technologies are not an option for the institution and this marks the increase in disparity in access to health care. A study by Nuffield Trust (2020) and Chartis Center (2020) identifies the financial hardships of rural hospitals and over 450 that are at risk of being closed in the United States.
3. Decreased intraoperative flexibility

   Robotic systems come with strict preset protocols and provide no flexibility for the surgeon in the case of unexpected change in anatomy.
4. Trust and acceptance issues

   According to patients in the United Kingdom are only 11% comfortable with robotic medical procedures which are supposed to be better dealt with through patient education and transparency.
5. Further future projections: augmented reality (AR)

The future of orthopedic surgery is the integration of AI and AR. AR enhances the visualization of the operating room with real-time visualizations of anatomy with overlays and enhanced spatial information. Research involving insertion of screws in the illustrated a high rate of accuracy of 98%, and comparative studies in 2023 flagged a lower rate of errors of 2% compared to 7% using AR-guided spine surgery.

13.7.5 Inference and Conclusion

Both artificial intelligence and robotics have resulted in a new paradigm in orthopedic surgery in particular during total joint arthroplasty. The MAKO and other systems are the embodiment of AI-based preoperative planning, intraoperative accuracy, and postoperative analytics combined to have a positive impact on the outcomes. The steadfast evidence that is seen in better accuracy, less pain, quicker recovery, and better functional scores is a justification for the possibility of AI to transform.

Nonetheless, there is a need for large-scale use that is dependent on the decrease in cost, equitable access, and ongoing confirmation in multicentric randomized trials. The combination of the terms AI, AR, and predictive analytics is the next level of evolution toward individualized, accurate, and patient-centric orthopedic services.

13.8 Specific Applications for Pain Medicine

13.8.1 Opioid Surveillance and Risk Management

Artificial intelligence (AI) has managed to bring a revolution to opioid monitoring with the creation of predictive data-driven strategies. The AI can be used to identify potential patients at risk of being misused and dependent or overdose or adverse events through the integration of electronic health records (EHRs), prescription drug-monitoring programmes (PDMPs), and population-level datasets.

13.8.1.1 Risk of Opioid Misuse and Dependence Identification

Cao B, Liu Y, and colleagues (2022) concluded machine learning using large administrative health datasets to estimate individual-level risk of opioid-use disorder (OUD). Their model was shown to be very sensitive and specific in a population-based cohort showing potential for its use for early identification and targeted prevention of OUD. The authors emphasized that although promising, implementation needs to overcome ethical, privacy, and generalizability issues before clinical implementation. AI algorithms determine predictors of opioid misuse (early opioid misuse). As one example, the machine learning trained by Lo Ciganic et al. (2020) to predict incident opioid-use disorder (OUD) in patients on Medicare had C statistics of approximately 0.87 0.88. Such prediction instruments form the basis of patient education, dose optimization, and systematic monitoring of patients in order to avoid the transition to chronic dependence.

The use of opioid overdose and respiratory depression prediction algorithms are expected to pick up emergency cases and alert the concerned authorities in advance of any escalation of risks. Opioid overdose and respiratory depression prediction algorithms are expected to catch the emergency cases and alert the real authorities before any increase of the risk. High morphine milligram equivalents (MME), polypharmacy, history of previous overdose, and comorbidities are some of the variables analysed with AI models. Using the Medicare data, high-accuracy opioid overdose predictions (C statistics >0.90) were made by Lo Ciganic et al. (2019) using gradient boosting and deep learning. This was later externally validated using Medicaid data in two U.S. states (Pennsylvania and Arizona) by Lo Ciganic et al. (2022) (C statistics of a bit less than 0.84, 0.82, and 0.81). Such advances of predictive modeling may be used to perform timely interventions (e.g., naloxone co-prescription, dose adjustments), and therefore improve patient safety.

13.8.1.2 Data Detected: Aberrant Prescribing and Diversion

AI tracks the prescriber behavior as it is reflected by the identification of aberrant prescribing and possible diversion networks. Patterns not taken up by prescribers or patients are detected by NLP and anomaly-detecting algorithms. To reduce the sociodemographic bias, it is important to take into account the socioeconomic variables and demographic factors to avoid inequities, as noted by Opioid misuse is reduced on a community basis by responsible prescribing, which is enhanced by integrating into PDMPs.

13.8.1.3 Function, Poor Recovery, and Chronic Opioid Use Prediction

AI frameworks identify trash patients who have been on chronic opioid use (COU) after surgery or short-lived treatment. One of the predictors is the previous opioid exposure, psychological distress, baseline pain scores, and socioeconomic hardship (Lo Ciganic et al. 2022; Cao et al., 2023). Predictive analytics can be more effective than the traditional models of regression to predict the high-risk patients where the multimodal analgesia can be administered at an early stage in order to avoid that they will become dependent on the therapy in the long term.

13.8.1.4 Opioid-Induced Adverse Events Prediction

Nonfatal opioid complications (sedation, delirium, falls, and constipation) are more predicted with machine learning algorithms especially in high-risk or elderly groups (Policy Lab at Rutgers University, 2024). Proper predictions help clinicians to vary opioid therapy, evaluate nonopioid options, and apply supportive measures—thus reducing morbidity and readmission. Analyses at population level also provide information to be used in implementing interventions at the population level through addressing risk factors in the community.

13.8.1.5 Implementation, Policy, and Ethical Issues

The adoption of AI in clinical workflow and PDMPs will enable real-time monitoring of patients and the whole population at large. To give an example, predictive analytics with effective interventions was prioritized at the Policy Lab at Rutgers University (Policy Lab at Rutgers University, 2024; Sharma et al., 2024; *Deep learning model to predict persistent opioid use*, 2021). The application of ethics requires the decrease of bias, accountability, and disclosure with diverse populations. The use of AI-inspired recommendations should be used to augment and not replace clinical judgment in order to enhance patient centred care without compromising safety and equity.

13.8.2 Optimization of Accessibility and Outcome

AI in pain psychology has a lot of promise to help those who suffer from chronic pain to manage their feelings of worry and depression. The ability of machine learning to understand differences in pain and mood helps behavioral algorithms to be preset according to the needs of any person using this technology.

AI has the potential to help with the individualized mental treatment as well. Through the study of behavioral trends and the construction of customized worksheets, cognitive behavioral treatment for chronic pain may be able to achieve better results. Given that there is a shortage of pain psychologists throughout the world, AI-based virtual assistants and digital CBT platforms provide resources that help with scaling mental health interventions and make mental health interventions accessible by enabling patients to monitor mood, adherence, and pain response in real time. This approach helps to improve engagement and provide emotional resilience to chronic pain patients.

13.8.3 Neuromuscular Equipment Modulation

13.8.3.1 It Is Important to Optimize Stimulus of Mood

Spinal cord stimulation (SCS) is also more than just a means for treating chronic pain, and it can have an impact on mood and emotion. Research has revealed that SCS can reduce the occurrence of depressive symptoms and also improve psychosocial performance. The impacts of pulse generator-based SCS were reviewed by Xinyu Dong et al. (2021) and Jeon (2012), based on which the quality-of-life factors such as distress experienced by a person have been improved. Wolter et al. (2015) emphasized that psychological components, such as depression, anxiety, and the expectations of the patient, significantly influence the results of spinal cord stimulation (SCS), and they should be thoroughly evaluated preoperatively for the best possible success rates. Cameron (2004) reviewed long-term safety data and reported that, although SCS proves to be generally safe and effective, nevertheless, problems related to lead migration, infection, and malfunction of the hardware are notable issues that warrant careful surgical technique and postoperative observation.

Similarly, Eldabe et al. (2016) conducted a review based on data from 22 studies and concluded that despite excellent pain relief in many patients, the risk of problems remains, thus making careful selection of patients, clinicians, and devices significant for better clinical outcomes. Likewise, set up that burst SCS minimized psychological distress as well as pain relief.

Both Deer et al. (2023) and Tito et al. (2024) demonstrate how crucial it is for purposes of spinal cord stimulation (SCS) therapy, namely device longevity and cost optimization. Deer et al. (2023) has analyzed more than 106,000 SCS systems and shown that rechargeable systems showed considerably greater clinical life spans of patients and lower replacements rates than primary cells, leading to improved long-term patient outcomes and lower revision surgeries. Complementing this, Tito et al. (2024) stressed that improving battery life and using a direct-to-implant approach had a significant and positive impact on reducing overall healthcare spending in Italy, which was used to support the economic and clinical importance of optimizing the durability of SCS devices.

This can be facilitated by the use of machine learning (ML) to create a feedback loop to join dorsal column neural sensations with patient-reported mood measurements to tune the stimulation. Digital feedback mechanisms, such as chatbots, have the potential to capture mood measurements in real time, which further enables automation, refinement of the therapy, and better effects. The given approach has a great potential as mood improvement can be monitored and actively manipulated without the use of invasive intervention, but further large-scale research would be needed to confirm the effects thereof.

13.8.3.2 Optimization of Parametric Stimulation

SCS devices have several forms of stimulation, such as high-frequency stimulation, burst stimulation, and differential multiplex stimulation. ML algorithms have the opportunity to start with evoked compound action potentials (ECAPs), subjective pain scores, and behavioural performance to optimize individual parameters. In particular, in that case, burst SCS was associated with reduced affective aspects of pain.

Based on the optimization of parameters, AI is able to reduce the differences between individual patients and tailor the therapy to them in the most effective and comfortable way possible. Nevertheless, powerful datasets are needed between ECAPs and functional outcomes in order to derive predictive models. Moreover, differences of impedance of tissues, differences of their lead placement, and diversity of the anatomy are also an obstacle for the development of generally applicable algorithms (Wolter et al., 2015).

13.8.3.3 Optimization of Stimulation to Offer Tolerance of Treatment

The limitation of SCS is known to be treatment tolerance, wherein initial success can weaken with time. According to Wolter et al. (2015), one of the patients, the analgesic loss occurs up to 12–24 months after implantation. Constant feedback can be afforded by AI-enabled monitoring based on wearable or implantable sensors collecting physiological data (e.g., sleep patterns, heart rate, or respiration) to change the stimulation settings dynamically.

The mitigating capacity on tolerance can be self-implemented through the adaptive models that ensure long-term human efficacy and reduce the level of discomfort of the patients. Still, close validation and direct control of the clinicians are critical because automated adjustments should be both safe and reliable considering the interindividual variations.

13.8.3.4 Resolving the Lead Migration by AI

The common problem with the failure of SCS is lead migration. Migration rates were determined to be 13–22% by Cameron (2004) and Eldabe et al. (2016). The combination of sensors that are implemented with AI allows determining the absence of alignment with the baseline and difference between mechanical failure and absence of therapeutic effects from the implementation of sensors on SCS. Early intervention allows the clinician the option of treating without using a surgical method and minimal revision surgery is required.

Types of sensors can be micro-inertial sensors, strain sensors, that can be used to measure the orientation of the lead. Machine learning methods help to decipher these signals and give clinicians important deviations with the lowest rate of false alarms. These systems should be able to balance between being technically complex, power consuming, and lasting long term.

13.8.3.5 Deal with Energy and Charge Distribution

In SCS devices, the battery life is one of the important factors. According to Deer et al., over 106,000 implanted SCS systems were evaluated and the authors revealed that rechargeable devices can have a lifetime of up to 9 years, this is four times as long as non-rechargeable systems. The economic advantage of the longer battery life and direct to implant approaches have been announced by Tito et al. (2024).

AI has a power-saving capacity, because they can detect when the patient is active and change the outputs of a stimulator dynamically without the impact of pain management. Also, it is possible to study different types of leads, such as paddle and percutaneous leads, and it is possible to make the choice to one that offers greater energy-efficiency and the distribution of energy. These initiatives enable the patients to increase in the outcome by increasing the sustainable means of the device in the long run.

13.8.4 Summary

SCS has not only developed to only be effective in the management of the pain, but also affects emotional and psychosocial outcomes; this has a positive contribution on the overall quality of life of chronic pain patients. Adaptive and personalized therapy, optimization of stimulation parameters, reducing treatment tolerance, lead migration, and increased energy could be enhanced with the help of artificial intelligence and machine learning. Neural signals, physiological markers, and patient feedback to drive AI-driven adaptable closed-loop systems in real time can increase their efficacy as well as safety of therapy.

Although promising, there are problems in validating mood and emotional modulation, sensor reliability, and device biocompatibility, as well as therapeutic efficacy in case of energy optimization. These issues will need to be worked out to realize the full potential of AI-enhanced SCS. All in all, AI-enabled neuromodulation is a groundbreaking method in chronic pain treatment, since it is more accurate, responsive, and patient-focused and has greater chances of outcome improvements in the long-term.

13.9 Conclusion

Artificial intelligence has become the integrative element of contemporary surgery that has given an even integration of precision, prediction, and personalization into specialties. With extreme intelligence and the ability to process data in real time, using analytics and even fusing data from multiple modalities, AI allows us to improve human experience and resolve the shortcomings of the old-time techniques—no errors, standardization of results, and opening up possibilities. The implications it has today are far-reaching: lesser dangerous processes, lesser recovery time, and equal training. However, the actual value awaits a time when AI turns out to be a copilot instead of an assistant, and we can have a future when all geographical and economic constraints are taken aside and one proactive, adaptive, and lifelong care is delivered to patients.

In the field of general surgery and thoracic procedures, the performance of AI has already brought about results in the field of detecting lung nodules (>95% accuracy), malignancy stratification (AUC 0.94), and live vascular mapping regardless of scope issues such as the bias of the dataset and PACS integration. In the future, predictive avatars of tumors will follow patients over their lives via wearables, which will trigger anticipatory intervention years before the recurrence.

In minimally invasive and robotic surgical procedures, machines like MAKO and AR-ID are available that offer power of less than millimeter precision, smoke-free vision and instrument demarcation with minimal restriction only by cost (>$1 M) and rigidity. The horizon offers self-sovereign nano-robots with 5G telesurgery that enables elite surgeries in clinics being far away with self-corrected haptic intelligence.

In orthopedics, AI roadmap designs help in reducing the number of plan adjustments (by an average of 40%), less than 1.5° alignment, and shorter time in hospitalization (limited by accessibility issues). Smart implants that autoregulate through biosensors and 20-year predictive wear models that make regenerative biologics are part of the future developments.

With regard to gynecology and obstetrics, AI can be used to complement CTG interpretation, analysis of pelvic ultrasound and robotic hysterectomy, which are impaired by issues related to diversity of the data and its lack of trustworthiness. Wearable maternal-fetal networks that will anticipate complications days before that happen and the rehabilitation of women via AI-driven home rehabilitation through smartphone biofeedback are only days away.

In terms of anesthesia and perioperative care—there are predictive models of complications (AUC >0.88), there are predictive models of opioid risks, restrict, EHR silos. The following generation is that of closed micro-dosing anesthesia and protocols that protect the organs even before the vital signs get worse.

Since it is related to surgical education, adaptive platforms provide customization of training and identify skills on the fly, but video annotation is limited. Northward and westward, the future is one of indefinite hyperrealism of simulacra plugging decades of brilliance into faster, globally available curricula.

AI streamlines SCS in terms of pain medicine as well as neuromodulation, tracks lead motion, and anticipates chronic use—but tolerance does not decrease. New technologies include mood + pain adaptive implants with neural loop and real time which could end opioids using.

Lastly, in terms of safety, equity, and ethics, on the front—AI is able to standardize results and warn of danger—but there are differences caused by cost and bias. The whole vision is having federated, open source AI under a set of universal ethics, to which surgical excellence will be a universal human right to which precision is not an indulgence, but a universal promise, which will be kept for all patients, everywhere.

References

Ahmed, F. A., Yousef, M., et al. (2024). Deep learning for surgical instrument recognition and segmentation in robotic-assisted surgeries: A systematic review. *Artificial Intelligence Review, 57*, 10979. https://doi.org/10.1007/s10462-024-10979-w

Ali, S., Jonmohamadi, Y., Fontanarosa, D., Crawford, R., & Pandey, A. K. (2023). One step surgical scene restoration for robot assisted minimally invasive surgery. *Scientific Reports, 13*, 3127. https://doi.org/10.1038/s41598-022-26647-4

Basil, N. N., Ambe, S., Ekhator, C., & Fonkem, E. (2022). Health records database and inherent security concerns: A review of the literature. *Cureus, 14*, e30168. https://doi.org/10.7759/cureus.30168

Brocklehurst, P. (2016). A study of an intelligent system to support decision making in the management of labour using the cardiotocograph – The INFANT study protocol. *BMC Pregnancy and Childbirth, 16*, 10. https://doi.org/10.1186/s12884-015-0780-0

Cameron, T. (2004). Safety and efficacy of spinal cord stimulation for the treatment of chronic pain: a 20-year literaturereview. *J Neurosurg*. 100(3):254–67. https://doi.org/10.3171/spi.2004.100.3.0254. PMID: 15029914

Cao, B., Liu, Y., et al. (2022). Individualized prospective prediction of opioid use disorder in a large population-based administrative health dataset. *PLOS Medicine*. https://www.ncbi.nlm.nih.gov/pmc/articles/PMC9720482/

Cao, B., et al. (2023). Machine learning predicts risk of opioid use disorder for individual patients. *Canadian Journal of Psychiatry*.

Chartis Center for Rural Health. (2020). *The state of rural hospitals in the U.S.*

Choi, H. K., et al. (2024). Challenges in clinical integration of artificial intelligence for lung nodule management. *Journal of Medical Artificial Intelligence, 7*, 15. https://doi.org/10.21037/jmai-24-15

Dawes, G. S., Moulden, M., & Redman, C. W. (1991). System 8000: Computerized antenatal FHR analysis. *Journal of Perinatal Medicine, 19*, 47–51. https://doi.org/10.1515/jpme.1991.19.1-2.47

De Backer, P., et al. (2023). Real-time instrument delineation for augmented reality in robot-assisted kidney surgery using deep learning. *European Urology Open Science, 50*, 12–24. https://doi.org/10.1016/j.euros.2023.01.004

Deep learning model to predict persistent opioid use. (2021). *Computers in biology and medicine*. https://www.sciencedirect.com/science/article/pii/S153204642100054X.

Deer, T. R., et al. (2023). Clinical longevity of 106, 462 rechargeable and Primary Cell Spinal Cord stimulators: real world study in the medicare Population. *Neuromodulation, 26*(1), 131–8. https://doi.org/10.1016/j.neurom.2022.04.046. Epub 2022 Jun 9. PMID:35690511.

Dong, X., Deng, J., Hou, W., Rashidian, S., Rosenthal, R. N., Saltz, M., Saltz, J. H., & Wang, F. (2021). Predicting opioid overdose risk of patients with opioid prescriptions using electronic health records based on temporal deep learning. *Journal of Biomedical Informatics, 116*, 103725.

Eldabe, S., Buchser, E., Duarte, RV. (2016). Complications of spinal cord stimulation and peripheral nerve stimulation: A review of 22 studies. *Pain Medicine, 17*(2), 325–36. https://doi.org/10.1093/pm/pnv025. PMID:26814260.

Garrow, C. R., Kowalewski, K. F., Li, L., Wagner, M., Schmidt, M. W., Engelhardt, S., et al. (2021). Machine learning for surgical phase recognition: A systematic review. *Annals of Surgery, 273*(4), 684–693. https://doi.org/10.1097/SLA.0000000000004425

Han, E. R., Yeo, S., Kim, M. J., Lee, Y. H., Park, K. H., & Roh, H. (2019). Medical education trends for future physicians in the era of advanced technology and artificial intelligence: An integrative review. *BMC Medical Education, 19*, 460. https://doi.org/10.1186/s12909-019-1891-5

Hanassab, S., Abbara, A., Yeung, A. C., Voliotis, M., Tsaneva-Atanasova, K., Kelsey, T. W., et al. (2024). The prospect of artificial intelligence to personalize assisted reproductive technology. *Npj Digital Medicine, 7*, 55. https://doi.org/10.1038/s41746-024-01006-x

Hashimoto, D. A., Rosman, G., Rus, D., & Meireles, O. R. (2018). Artificial intelligence in surgery: Promises and perils. *Annals of Surgery, 268*(1), 70–76. https://doi.org/10.1097/SLA.0000000000002693

He, X., Zeng, X., Troendle, J., et al. (2023). New insights on labor progression: A systematic review. *American Journal of Obstetrics and Gynecology, 228*, S1063–S1094. https://doi.org/10.1016/j.ajog.2022.11.1299

IBM Watson Health. (2023). *IBM Watson for Oncology: Clinical decision-support platform integrating imaging and genomic data for oncologic planning*. https://www.ibm.com/products/watson-for-oncology

Iftikhar, P., Kuijpers, M. V., Khayyat, A., Iftikhar, A., & DeGouvia De Sa, M. (2020). Artificial intelligence: A new paradigm in obstetrics and gynecology research and clinical practice. *Cureus, 12*, e7124. https://doi.org/10.7759/cureus.7124

Jeon, Y. H. (2012). Spinal cord stimulation in pain management: A review. *Pain Practice, 25*, 143.

Jiang, Y., Wang, C., & Zhou, S. (2023). Artificial intelligence-based risk stratification, accurate diagnosis and treatment prediction in gynecologic oncology. *Seminars in Cancer Biology, 96*, 82–99. https://doi.org/10.1016/j.semcancer.2023.09.005

Kannaiyan, A., Bagchi, S., Vijayan, V., Georgiy, P., Manickavasagam, S., & Kumar, D. S. (2024). Revolutionizing women's health: Artificial intelligence's impact on obstetrics and gynecology. *Journal of South Asian Federation of Obstetrics and Gynaecology, 16*, 161–168. https://doi.org/10.5005/jp-journals-10006-2394

Khan, I., & Khare, B. K. (2024). Exploring the potential of machine learning in gynecological care: A review. *Archives of Gynecology and Obstetrics, 309*, 2347–2365. https://doi.org/10.1007/s00404-024-07479-1

Kudo, Y., et al. (2024). AI-driven characterization of solid pulmonary nodules on CT imaging for enhanced malignancy prediction in small-sized lung adenocarcinoma. *European Journal of Radiology, 173*, 111149. https://www.pubmed.ncbi.nlm.nih.gov/38760224/

Kumazu, Y., et al. (2021). Automated segmentation by deep learning of loose connective tissue fibers to define safe dissection planes in robot-assisted gastrectomy. *Scientific Reports, 11*, 21198. https://doi.org/10.1038/s41598-021-00557-3

Lambrechts, A., Wirix-Speetjens, R, Maes, F., Van, Huffel S. (2022). Artificial intelligence based patient-specific preoperative planning algorithm for total knee arthroplasty. *Front Robot AI*. 9:840282. https://doi.org/10.3389/frobt.2022.840282. Erratum in: Front Robot AI. 29:899349. https://doi.org/10.3389/frobt.2022.899349. PMID: 35350703; PMCID: PMC8957999

Lee, S., et al. (2024). Comparative functional outcomes of robotic-assisted and conventional total knee arthroplasty: A 6-month prospective study. *International Orthopaedics*. https://doi.org/10.1007/s00264-024-05942-3

Liu, J. A., et al. (2022). Development of AI algorithms for CT-based lung nodule malignancy prediction. *AJR American Journal of Roentgenology, 219*(6), 1427–1437. https://doi.org/10.2214/AJR.22.27487

Lo Ciganic, W. H., Huang, J. L., Zhang, H. H., et al. (2019). Evaluation of machine learning algorithms for predicting opioid overdose risk among Medicare beneficiaries with opioid prescriptions. *JAMA Network Open, 2*(3), e190968.

Lo Ciganic, W. H., Huang, J. L., Zhang, H. H., et al. (2020). Using machine learning to predict risk of incident opioid use disorder among Medicare beneficiaries: A prognostic study. *PLoS One, 15*(7), e0235981.

Lo Ciganic, W. H., Donohue, J. M., Yang, Q., et al. (2022). Developing and validating a machine learning algorithm to predict opioid overdose in Medicaid beneficiaries: A prognostic modelling study. *The Lancet Digital Health, 4*(6), e455–e465.

Moawad, G., Tyan, P., & Louie, M. (2019). Artificial intelligence and augmented reality in gynecology. *Current Opinion in Obstetrics and Gynecology, 31*(5), 345–348. https://doi.org/10.1097/GCO.0000000000000559

Moglia, A., Morelli, L., D'Ischia, R., Fatucchi, L. M., Pucci, V., Berchiolli, R. N., et al. (2022). Ensemble deep learning for the prediction of proficiency at a virtual simulator for robot-assisted surgery. *Surgical Endoscopy, 36*(9), 6473–6479. https://doi.org/10.1007/s00464-021-08999-6

Morris, M. X., et al. (2024). Current and future applications of artificial intelligence in surgery. *Frontiers in Surgery.* https://doi.org/10.3389/fsurg.2024.1393898/full

Mozafari, J. K., et al. (2024). The role of artificial intelligence in preoperative planning for total hip arthroplasty: A systematic review. *Frontiers in Artificial Intelligence*. https://doi.org/10.3389/frai.2024.1417729

Nam, D., et al. (2022). Accuracy of robotic arm–assisted total knee arthroplasty compared with conventional techniques. *Journal of Arthroplasty, 37*(3), 495–503. https://doi.org/10.1016/j.arth.2021.09.010

Nam, J. G., Park, S., Hwang, E. J., et al. (2023). AI improves nodule detection on chest radiographs in a health screening population: A randomized controlled trial. *Radiology, 307*(2), e221894. https://doi.org/10.1148/radiol.221894

Nuffield Trust. (2020). *Rural hospital financial sustainability in the NHS.*

Oleck, N. C., Naga, H. I., Nichols, D. S., Morris, M. X., Dhingra, B., & Patel, A. (2023). Navigating the ethical landmines of ChatGPT: Implications of intelligent chatbots in plastic surgery clinical practice. *Plastic and Reconstructive Surgery Global Open, 11*, e5290. https://doi.org/10.1097/GOX.0000000000005290

Park, J. J., Tiefenbach, J., & Demetriades, A. K. (2022). The role of artificial intelligence in surgical simulation. *Frontiers in Medical Technology, 4*, 1076755. https://doi.org/10.3389/fmedt.2022.1076755

Patel, D. J., Chaudhari, K., Acharya, N., et al. (2024a). Artificial intelligence in obstetrics and gynecology: Transforming care and outcomes. *Cureus, 16*(7), e64725. https://doi.org/10.7759/cureus.64725

Patel, R., Gomez, M., et al. (2024b). AI-integrated robotic total hip arthroplasty improves pain and functional recovery: A multicenter evaluation. *Journal of Orthopaedic Research, 42*(7), 1183–1192. https://doi.org/10.1002/jor.25783

Peek, J. J., et al. (2024). Automated three-dimensional model registration for intraoperative augmented reality navigation in minimally invasive pulmonary resections. *International Journal of Computer Assisted Radiology and Surgery, 19*(4), 665–678. https://doi.org/10.1007/s11548-024-03308-7

Peters, A. A., et al. (2024). Impact of AI assistance on pulmonary nodule detection and localization in chest CT: Comparative study among radiologists of varying experience levels. *Radiology, 311*(1), 112–124. https://www.pubmed.ncbi.nlm.nih.gov/39341945/

Policy Lab at Rutgers University. (2024). *A roadmap for integrating AI in opioid policy and monitoring*.

Polineni, T. N. S., Pandugula, C., & Ganti, V. K. A. T. (2022). AI-driven automation in monitoring post-operative complications across health systems. *Global Journal of Medical Case Reports, 2*, 1225. https://doi.org/10.31586/gjmcr.2022.1225

Radiological Society of North America. (2023). *High-accuracy AI improves lung-cancer detection*. https://www.rsna.org/news/2023/august/high-accuracy-ai-lung-cancer-detection

Seidenstein, A., et al. (2021). Radiographic outcomes of robotic arm–assisted versus conventional total knee arthroplasty. *Bone & Joint Journal, 103-B*(5), 923–930. https://doi.org/10.1302/0301-620X.103B5.BJJ-2020-2299.R1

Shah, A., et al. (2023). Deep learning in intraoperative imaging and surgical navigation: Current state and future directions. *Frontiers in Surgery, 10*, 1123456. https://doi.org/10.3389/fsurg.2023.1123456

Sharma, Y., Nguyen, T., et al. (2024). Machine learning–based prediction of opioid-induced complications in high-risk populations. *Bioelectronic Medicine, 3*, 56.

Sparling, J. L., Hong Mershon, B., & Abraham, J. (2023). Perioperative handoff enhancement opportunities through technology and artificial intelligence: A narrative review. *The Joint Commission Journal on Quality and Patient Safety, 49*, 410–421. https://doi.org/10.1016/j.jcjq.2023.03.009

Tanzi, L., Piazzolla, P., Porpiglia, F., & Vezzetti, E. (2021). Real-time deep learning semantic segmentation during intra-operative surgery for 3D augmented reality assistance. *International Journal of Computer Assisted Radiology and Surgery, 16*(9), 1435–1445. https://doi.org/10.1007/s11548-021-02432-y

Tito, F., et al. (2024). Optimizing healthcare expenditure for spinal cord stimulation in Italy: The value of battery longevity improvement and a direct-to-implant approach. *Journal of health economics and outcomes Research., 11*, 149.

Wang, F., Sun, X., & Li, J. (2023). Surgical smoke removal via residual Swin transformer network. *International Journal of Computer Assisted Radiology and Surgery, 18*(8), 1417–1427. https://doi.org/10.1007/s11548-023-02835-z

Ward, T. M., Mascagni, P., Madani, A., Padoy, N., Perretta, S., & Hashimoto, D. A. (2021). Surgical data science and artificial intelligence for surgical education. *Journal of Surgical Oncology, 124*(2), 221–230. https://doi.org/10.1002/jso.26496

Weidener, L., & Fischer, M. (2023). Artificial intelligence teaching as part of medical education: Qualitative analysis of expert interviews. *JMIR Medical Education, 9*, e46428. https://doi.org/10.2196/46428

Wolter, T., et al. (2015). The impact of psychological factors on outcomes for spinal cord stimulation. *Pain Physician Journal, 16*(3), 265–275.

Xu, W., et al. (2024). AI-based prediction of postoperative complications following thoracic surgery using radiomics and clinical data. *Journal of Thoracic Oncology, 19*(5), 723–734. https://doi.org/10.1016/j.jtho.2024.02.012

Yaseen, I., & Rather, R. A. (2024). A theoretical exploration of artificial intelligence's impact on feto-maternal health from conception to delivery. *International Journal of Women's Health, 16*, 903–915. https://doi.org/10.2147/IJWH.S454127

Yin, P., & Wang, H. (2022). Evaluation of nursing effect of pelvic floor rehabilitation training on pelvic organ prolapse in postpartum pregnant women under ultrasound imaging with artificial intelligence algorithm. *Computational and Mathematical Methods in Medicine, 2022*, Article 1786994. https://doi.org/10.1155/2022/1786994

Zhao, Y., et al. (2024). Deep learning for lung cancer detection: A review. *Artificial Intelligence Review*. https://doi.org/10.1007/s10462-024-10807-1

Zhou, L., et al. (2023). 3D AI-based surgical planning improves precision in complex orthopaedic reconstructions. *BMC Surg*. 23, p. 237

Fusion of Artificial Intelligence in Surgical Health Care

14

Gupta Ravi, Gaurav Aditya, and Jagani Harsha Sai

14.1 Introduction

In the surgical field, the integration of multimodal artificial intelligence (AI) is a hallmark of a revolutionary shift in development in healthcare systems worldwide. This chapter will focus on the exploration of the fusion of artificial intelligence, which is a synergistic combination of AI techniques such as machine learning, natural language processing, computer vision, and deep learning, in the surgical field to enhance preoperative diagnostic and prognostic assessment as well as intraoperative safety of procedure with quality decision making. Similarly, the use of AI in surgery has improved resident training and postoperative care. This chapter highlights that combining the data from multiple sources in the form of patient history, investigations, genomics, and imaging, that is, computed tomography scan and magnetic resonance imaging scan (CT and MRI scans), enhances the accuracy of diagnosing and prognostication of diseases along with reducing human error. AI systems enable us to improve the patient care by making diagnosis faster, individualizing the treatment plan. Ethical aspects and patient privacy are also important points addressed in this chapter related to the integration of AI in the surgical discipline. Each section will explore specific applications of AI and machine learning in surgical subspecialties, offering insights into how these technologies are revolutionizing surgical precision and efficiency (Amin et al., 2024). A consolidated overview of these applications across the surgical care continuum is presented in Table 14.1. This process is visually summarized in Fig. 14.1.

G. Ravi (✉) · G. Aditya · J. Harsha Sai
Department of General Surgery, All India Institute of Medical Sciences, Gorakhpur, India

U. Venkatesh et al. (eds.), *Multimodal AI in Healthcare*,
https://doi.org/10.1007/978-981-95-9027-8_14

Table 14.1 Key applications of artificial intelligence across the surgical care continuum

Surgical phase	AI applications	Key benefits
Preoperative planning	CT/MRI interpretation using ML Digital pathology and automated grading Risk stratification tools (MySurgeryRisk, POTTER) 3D reconstruction of liver, pancreas, breast vascular anatomy	Early diagnosis and prognostication Accurate lesion detection Better surgical planning Improved patient selection and reduced complications
Intraoperative navigation and guidance	Computer vision for structure recognition Real-time nerve identification (e.g., colorectal nerve preservation) Segmentation overlays in robotic/ MIS systems Hazard prediction during dissection	Safer surgical procedures Better identification of vital structures Reduced bile duct injuries, nerve injuries Enhanced resident learning curve
Minimally invasive and robotic surgery	Surgical phase recognition Image-guided robotic assistance AI-driven haptic feedback Autonomous/semiautonomous tasks (e.g., STAR robot)	Increased precision Lower cognitive load for surgeons Standardized surgical quality Improved instrument dexterity
Postoperative care and outcome prediction	Predictive models for mortality, sepsis, ICU stay, readmission Wearable sensors for remote monitoring NLP-based symptom analysis Real-time early warning systems	Faster detection of complications Personalized recovery pathways Better resource allocation Reduced postoperative morbidity
Training and surgical education	VR/AR simulation with AI feedback Skill evaluation via video-based analytics Generative AI for case scenarios Automated competency assessment	Objective performance evaluation Shortened learning curve Personalized training modules Safe, reproducible skill practice
Ethical and regulatory framework	Explainable AI models Bias detection systems Data encryption and privacy safeguards Shared-liability mechanisms	Safe and transparent AI use Reduced algorithmic bias Protection of patient data Ethical accountability in AI-assisted surgery

14.2 Preoperative Planning

Preoperative planning in surgery includes clinical history, imaging, and pathological diagnosis. Incorporation of AI has further refined the preoperative evaluation in identifying the high-risk patients, early detection of complications, and timely intervention. Preoperative imaging is one area where AI has had a lot (Feng et al., 2021). Diagnosis of hepatocellular carcinoma is basically based on CT and MRI imaging. Incorporation of AI in imaging systems has led to differentiation between different types of lesions in the liver, which further helps the clinician to make decisions on

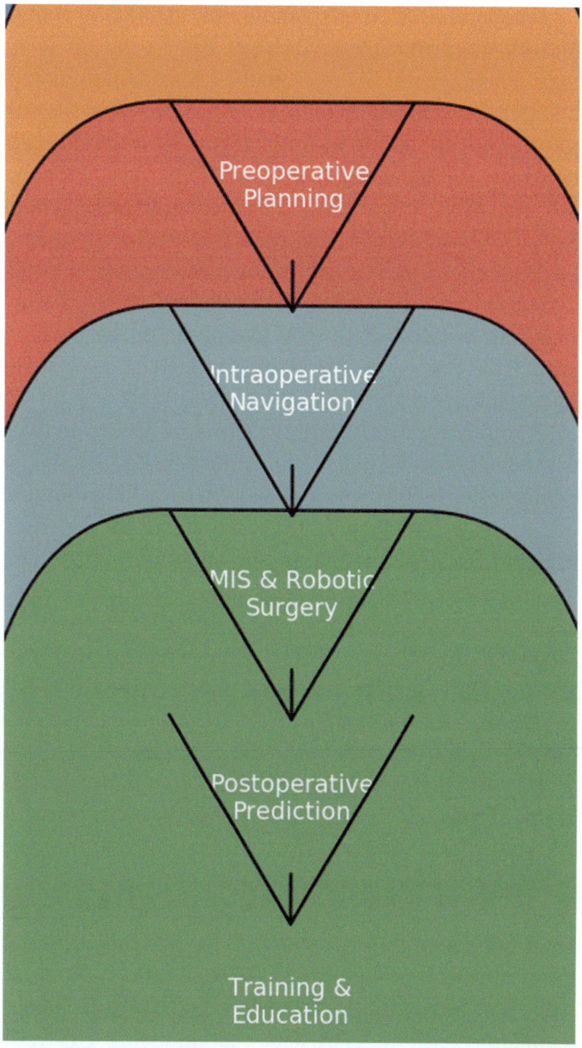

Fig. 14.1 AI integration across surgical continuum

the treatment part (Feng et al., 2021). In breast cancer patients, autologous breast reconstruction is the Achilles' heel of surgical intervention. Its outcome depends on the anatomy of the deep inferior epigastric artery. AI and machine learning (ML) algorithms for the assessment of CT scans have improved the selection of perforators on which flap will be based, further leading to improved outcomes in breast reconstructive surgery (Cevik et al., 2023). Preoperative 3D reconstruction of liver anatomy in preoperative planning has improved the decision-making in planning of hepatectomy and liver transplantation (McGivern et al., 2023). Similarly, 3D reconstruction of the vascular anatomy of the pancreas helps to determine the resectability in pancreatic neoplasms (Bari et al., 2021).

Preoperative accurate pathological evaluation is important to guide the treatment and to prognosticate the disease. Liking the histopathological images, including their characteristic like surrounding histopathological findings with clinical history and genetic status with help of AI has provided the survival outcome and response to neoadjuvant and adjuvant therapy. AI in digital pathology has strengthened the accuracy of diagnosing the disease. It has also enhanced the accuracy in predicting the response to treatment and the detection of gene mutation from histopathological images. Detection of breast cancer in the lymph node by using AI has been studied by Bejnordi et al. and the result were similar to human control (McGenity et al., 2024). In prostate cancer, automated Gleason grading has been developed to differentiate between high- and low-grade prostate cancer. A similar type of grading system has been made for other cancers like breast and brain cancer (Jafari-Khouzani & Soltanian-Zadeh, 2003).

Preoperative endoscopy evaluation is needed in most gastrointestinal diseases. It is used to take a biopsy, evaluate the disease location, and many times for therapeutic purposes. Incorporating AI has led to making the endoscopic job easy. Assessment of the image guides the area from where the biopsy should be taken to have the highest yield. Chromoendoscopy and narrow band imaging (NBE) is used to map the suspected area on endoscopy and with AI it has now become easy to identify the suspected area and to guide the clinician for biopsy. Capsule endoscopy is a wireless method that evaluates complete gastrointestinal tract by taking multiple images per second. These images are stored in a computer, which are analyzed to make a diagnosis. AI has improved the detection rate of lesions and erosion and has increased the accuracy of this system (Aoki et al., 2019).

It is impossible to envision surgery without anesthesia care. Preoperative evaluation, optimization, and risk stratification are crucial for better surgical outcomes. AI has been incorporated in evaluating the risk prediction, depth of anesthesia monitoring, control of anesthesia, ultrasound guidance, and pain management. The widely used American Society of Anesthesiologists (ASA) categorization is not free from subjective judgment flaws. AI and ML platforms that get data from huge databases of patient outcomes can find and reliably forecast risk based on the characteristics that Electronic Health Records (EHRs) make available. The MySurgeryRisk technology utilizes EHR data encompassing 285 variables and has demonstrated superior accuracy in predicting perioperative risk compared to professional judgment (Brennan et al., 2019). To provide accurate mortality prediction, it uses big data from EHRs and eliminates the need for manual variable input. Using intraoperative data, it has been demonstrated that ML can reliably predict death, sepsis, and acute kidney injury (Brennan et al., 2019). POTTER, or Predictive OpTimal Trees in Emergency Surgery (ES) Risk, is an app that was made to be an easy-to-use and interactive interface for the algorithms that are used to figure out how risky a surgical patient is (Bertsimas et al., 2018). Using data from 382,960 ES patients, we constructed sophisticated decision-making algorithms and created POTTER, where the provider's answer to a question determines what the next question will be. POTTER is a highly accurate and user-friendly ES risk calculator that can continuously increase accuracy through ML. It can be connected with EHR data to identify and avoid postoperative risks such as SSI, sepsis, pneumonia, urinary tract infection, cardiac problems, and prolonged intensive care unit (ICU) stay. POTTER is a new, interpretable, and highly accurate predictor of in-hospital mortality in senior ES patients up to age 85 (Maurer et al., 2023).

14.3 Intraoperative Navigation and Real-Time Guidance

The introduction of laparoscopic surgery has caused a major change in the way how surgery is executed, moving from traditional open procedures to minimally invasive surgery (MIS) in many different types of surgeries. MIS has the advantage of early recovery in the postoperative period and early discharge of the patients. With these advantages, MIS has been widely accepted, but it has a steep learning curve. Incorporation of AI has led to the identification of vital structures during surgery. This helps surgeons in identifying these vital structures and avoiding injuries. Intraoperative navigation with the use of AI has improved the identification of vital structures and also has helped in the training of residents, with a decrease in the learning curve. Intraoperative navigation has been well incorporated in liver and brain surgery. AI, with its ability to recognize images and process data in real time, is a promising way to make MIS safer and more accurate.

During colorectal cancer surgery, the nerves are important anatomical structures. Injuries to the lumbar splanchnic, hypogastric, and pelvic visceral nerves (S3, S4) can lead to problems with sex or urination. In colorectal surgery, with the use of AI, preservation of the splanchnic and hypogastric nerves is done to improve the outcome (Ryu et al., 2025). Ryu S et al. developed a surgical AI prototype named Eureka (Anaut, Inc., Tokyo, Japan) and used it to study colorectal surgery. In 51 left-sided colorectal surgeries, they use AI for the detection and preservation of the autonomic nerve. At the same time, they use this tool for the training of surgical residents also (Ryu et al., 2025). AI has emerged as a tool to guide in complex oncological procedures. Surgical robots provide mechanical enhancements, including enhanced instrument dexterity, hand–eye coordination, and a three-dimensional perspective; however, in numerous surgical procedures, no significant clinical advantage over traditional laparoscopic surgery has been established to date. Researchers have been working hard in recent years to develop image recognition algorithms using laparoscopic imaging data. This is because they think that adding surgical guidance (like segmentation overlays of certain structures at certain points in a procedure) to minimally invasive surgical systems could greatly improve the quality and outcome of surgery and reduce the differences in quality between surgeons. A study by Fiona R. Kolbinger et al. (2024) reported that the use of AI in robot-assisted rectal surgery improves the surgical outcome by preserving vital structures without compromising the oncological principles.

Laparoscopic cholecystectomy is the most common MIS procedure performed globally. Being the most common surgical procedure performed, since 20 years risk of bile duct injury has remained the same. Significant anatomic distortion from inflammation or abnormal anatomy often leads to major bile duct injuries because it makes it hard to understand the biliary anatomy during the procedure. For a surgeon to do a safe dissection, they need to be able to read the surgical field and make important decisions all the time. Intraoperative guidance with AI in identifying the critical structure has a scope in minimizing the rate of bile duct injury (Endo et al., 2023).

Liver surgery has always been associated with significant morbidity and mortality because of complex anatomy. At high-volume centers, pure laparoscopic donor hepatectomy (PLDH) has become the standard method of organ procurement in living donor liver transplantation (LDLT). Because PLDH affects both the donor and recipient's outcomes after surgery, the procedure needs a precise technical method, which is associated with a long learning curve. Preoperative evaluation of biliary anatomy is crucial for better outcomes for the donor as well as the recipient. Preoperative MRI is essential to identify such complex biliary anatomy. At the same time, intraoperative use of cholangiography or the indocyanine green (ICG) near-infrared fluorescence method is crucial for guidance of liver resection (Oh et al., 2024).

The minimally invasive technique is also becoming more common in esophageal surgery. In comparison to the abdomen, in the thoracic cavity, structures are closer to vital structures like lungs, heart, recurrent laryngeal nerve, and thoracic duct. In malignant esophageal disease, the radical surgery includes a complete lymphadenectomy. The mediastinal lymph nodes are in close relation to the bronchus and recurrent laryngeal nerve in the upper and mid part of the esophagus. Similarly, near the lower thoracic esophagus thoracic duct is an important structure. Injury to the nerve leads to the risk of hoarseness of voice, aspiration pneumonia. Thoracic duct injury has complications like chylothorax, which has a high rate of morbidity and is difficult to treat (Kröger et al., 2025).

Breast surgery has also incorporated AI with the coming era. AI has emerged as a powerful tool in the intraoperative guidance of early breast cancer lesion surgery. Surgery remains the gold standard treatment for early breast cancer. Real-time guidance with the use of AI helps in localizing the tumor and deciding the optimal procedure on a case-by-case basis. Breast conserving surgery provides reduced morbidity with a good cosmetic outcome in cases of early breast cancer without compromising the long-term outcomes (Weitz et al., 2024).

14.4 AI in Minimally Invasive and Robotic Surgery

The role of AI in the advancement of MIS and robotic surgery is undeniable; it has improved the aspects of surgical training, intraoperative assistance, postoperative assessment, and clinical decision-making. MIS is highly dependent upon high-resolution video, limited tactile feedback, and complex psychomotor skills, hence making MIS and robotic platforms ideal for AI integration. Large datasets, including intraoperative photos and video, can be used to train ML and deep learning (DL) systems. Early AI applications were focused on simulation and skill assessment, but recently the focus has been shifted toward developing real-time navigation, anatomical identification, and semiautonomous surgical actions aimed to improve surgical safety (Hassan et al., 2023; Iftikhar et al., 2024; Kenig et al., 2024; Kolbinger et al., 2024; Kröger et al., 2025).

Computer vision (CV) is a key concept for the application of AI in MIS. High-quality laparoscopic and robotic videos allow deep-learning models to identify anatomical structures, tissue planes, and safe surgical zones. Arakaki et al. report accurate identification of key structures such as cystic duct, common bile duct, seminal vesicles, recurrent laryngeal nerve, and vascular anatomy using AI and segmentation models like DeepLab and YOLO architectures (Arakaki et al., 2025).

One major advancement is the Critical View of Safety (CVS) assessment during laparoscopic cholecystectomy (LC), where AI systems have achieved up to 90% success rate in recognizing cystic structures and safe dissection zones (Arakaki et al., 2025). AI can also detect hazards such as bleeding and injury and can warn the operating surgeon about potential risks. Limitations in this aspect include visual obstructions such as smoke, blood, and fat, which reduce accuracy and global application (Arakaki et al., 2025). Robotic systems generate rich quality data, which can be used in advanced AI integration. According to Iftikhar et al., AI algorithms now support image recognition, motion optimization, and haptic feedback augmentation for robotic arms, which can help reduce tremor, improve instrument path planning, and enhance the precision (Iftikhar et al., 2024). Integration of AI into LC has opened a new frontier for achieving the CVS, which is considered the gold standard end point of safe dissection during LC. Importantly, AI tools are developed to complement rather than replace surgeon expertise; they may act as early alerts or second-opinion systems during critical dissection phases. The criteria for achievement of CVS can be judged more objectively using AI during LC. In a recent unpublished study, certain novel parameters were developed, including critical angle ratios, critical area ratios, and critical distance ratios for a more objective assessment of CVS, which can be further integrated with AI for intraoperative assessment of CVS before proceeding to irreversible steps of LC, that is, clipping and division of two cystic structures cystic artery and cystic duct. In this study, the parameters critical angle ratios and critical area ratios were found to be significantly associated with satisfactory achievement of CVS. A critical angle ratio (<0.80) and critical area ratio (>0.33) were associated with satisfactory CVS, with a p value of 0.19 and 0.049, respectively. These markers can be incorporated into AI assistance during LC (Figs. 14.2 and 14.3) (Gupta et al., 2025).

Morris et al. highlight that integrating AI with robotic systems enables real-time detection of vascular anatomy, tumor margins, and tissue perfusion (Morris et al., 2024). In various surgical disciplines, AI assists surgeons with suturing and anastomosis planning, autonomous tissue retraction, precise biopsies, ablation, and optimizing instrumentation through reinforcement learning (Iftikhar et al., 2024; Kenig et al., 2024). Advanced autonomous systems such as the smart tissue autonomous robot (STAR) demonstrate that supervised autonomy is possible in performing tasks like bowel anastomosis with precision comparable to expert surgeon (Iftikhar et al., 2024). In robotic surgery, AI can help in recognizing surgical phases, predict upcoming steps, and support intraoperative decision-making. Arakaki et al. describe

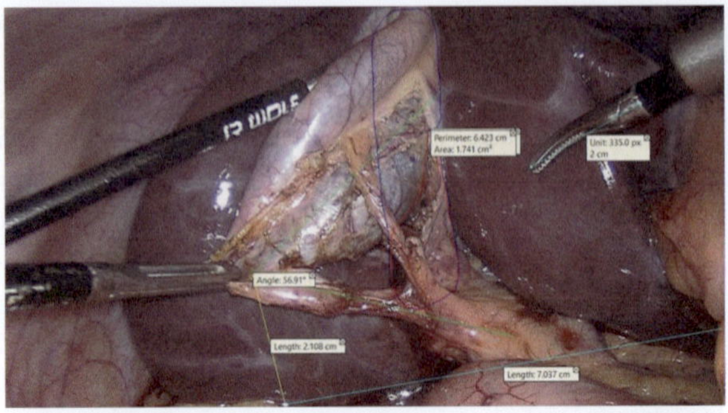

Fig. 14.2 Anterior surgical view demonstrating the critical angle, cystic plate area, and two structures entering the gallbladder for achieving a critical view of safety (CVS)

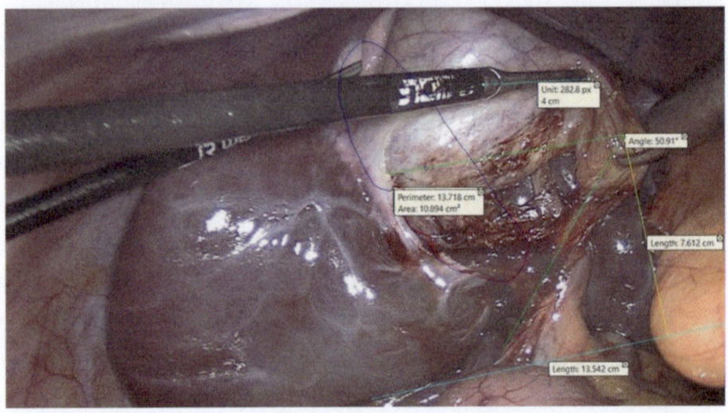

Fig. 14.3 Picture showing critical angle, cystic plate area, and two structures going to gallbladder, posterior view

automated surgical phase recognition models with high specificity and sensitivity using AI Confidence Scores (AICS) (Arakaki et al., 2025). These systems evaluate tissue handling and dissection strategies. Moreover, workflow prediction improves teamwork, reduces operative time, and facilitates instrument readiness, particularly in colorectal and urologic MIS, including camera navigation, vessel control, anastomosis, and lymphadenectomy to allow synchronized action among the surgical team (Morris et al., 2024).

Robotic surgery lacks tactile feedback, creating risks during delicate dissection. AI can increase haptic feedback by analyzing instrument–tissue interactions. Systems have been created to predict suture breakage, too much traction, and tissue stress. They use vibrotactile alerts to stop mistakes (Iftikhar et al., 2024). These technologies can reduce cognitive load and enhance precision during confined-space surgeries such as pelvic, vascular, or thoracic procedures.

AI is making MIS and robotic surgery better in many ways, such as training, perception, workflow prediction, haptic feedback, and semiautonomy. Various advancements are ongoing to improve surgical precision, safety, and standardization.

14.5 Postoperative Care and Outcome Prediction

AI has become an important part of modern surgery because it makes diagnoses more accurate, procedures safer, and predictive analytics better across the whole perioperative spectrum. Most often talked about in terms of training, simulation, and navigation during surgery. Its effect is becoming more noticeable in postoperative care and predicting outcomes. The postoperative phase is a critical interval wherein the early detection of complications, physiological monitoring, and risk stratification can influence patient recovery, morbidity, and survival. In various surgical fields, including general surgery, cardiac surgery, neurosurgery, and orthopedic spine surgery, numerous predictive models have been established that consistently surpass conventional scoring systems, facilitating more personalized, data-informed decision-making (Leon et al., 2025; Li et al., 2025; Maurer et al., 2023; McGenity et al., 2024; Morris et al., 2024).

AI models can learn to detect various complex patterns by analyzing thousands of variables simultaneously, including laboratory values, intraoperative events, imaging, hemodynamic, and patient-specific factors. Unlike conventional statistical tools, ML algorithms and neural networks identify subtle interactions that may not be apparent to clinicians. The integration of AI with postoperative care thus represents a major shift toward proactive and targeted recovery pathways, early complication detection, and optimized resource allocation.

Traditional models such as ACS-SRC, POSSUM, RACHS-1, and ASA-PS have served as essential tools but are limited. Hassan et al. highlighted that these models often do not detect hidden relationships among variables and may underestimate complications, particularly in high-risk groups (Hassan et al., 2023). Mohammadi et al. demonstrated that in congenital cardiac surgery, AI models have consistently outperformed RACHS-1 across outcomes including mortality, prolonged ventilation, ICU stay, and complications (Mohammadi et al., 2024). Similar findings were seen in general and reconstructive surgery, where ML performed better in predicting infections, readmission, thromboembolism, and organ dysfunction (Hassan et al., 2023).

Hassan et al. reported models achieving AUC values up to 0.98 for stroke, 0.76–0.90 for surgical site infections, and >0.80 for major morbidity, surpassing logistic regression (Hassan et al., 2023). ML tools were better in identifying more risk factors than regression models.Jiang et al. described an AI platform achieving an AUC of 0.88 for predicting major complications in metastatic spine surgery, which is an exceptionally high-risk population (Jiang et al., 2025). Predictors included blood loss, neurological status, tumor burden, and nutrition, enabling earlier triage and tailored surveillance. Mohammadi et al. evaluated 35 studies describing AI models in predicting mortality, prolonged ICU stay, ventilation, arrhythmias, pulmonary hypertension, and interstage mortality with AUCs of 0.70–0.997 (Mohammadi et al., 2024). In these studies, AI has greatly surpassed STS-EACTS and RACHS-1 frameworks. AI predicted postoperative infection, reoperation, ICU stay, and neurologic deterioration with AUCs between 0.74 and 0.97 (Hassan et al.,

2023). Orthopedic applications showed better prediction for thromboembolism, wound complications, and mortality.

Apart from prediction, AI enhances postoperative surveillance via continuous monitoring, wearables, and telemedicine. Byrd et al. reported integration of vital signs, labs, and imaging to detect infection, sepsis, hemorrhage, and organ failure early (Iv & Tignanelli, 2024). Wearable sensors track mobility, respiration, sleep, and heart rate, enabling a personalized recovery plan and reducing readmissions. Kenig et al. noted variations in validation, widespread use of retrospective datasets, and limited external validation. There are many lacunae in most of the available models, like a lack of long-term data on outcomes, a lack of standardization, and fragmented data. Ethical issues such as accountability, privacy, and transparency require proper supervision. Byrd et al. emphasized that safe AI integration requires surgeon education, prospective trials, and multidisciplinary oversight (Iv & Tignanelli, 2024).

With its ability to enable earlier detection of complications, risk prediction, continuous monitoring, and improved decision-making, AI is already improving postoperative care. Across general surgery, cardiac surgery, neurosurgery, orthopedics, and spine surgery, AI has consistently outperformed traditional tools. Continued validation and ethical implementation will determine AI's future impact on postoperative care.

14.6 Training and Surgical Education

AI is greatly influencing the way surgical knowledge is taught, practiced, and assessed. The growing integration of machine learning (ML), computer vision, and natural language models into various educational platforms is transforming the previous practice of apprenticeship-based culture into a data-driven, continuously evolving learning experience. By using simulation, real-time feedback, and analytics, AI can help trainees improve their techniques while ensuring patient safety in training programs (Satapathy et al., 2023). The influence of AI has now extended from preclinical simulation and intraoperative guidance to much more complex systems that personalize learning for every trainee. AI provides an objective performance assessment as well as feedback. According to Satapathy et al., AI-powered virtual platforms allow safe and repetitive practice with no increased risk to patient safety, providing individualized progress monitoring (Satapathy et al., 2023). AI algorithms can detect a trainee's strengths as well as weaknesses and can individualize modules for better learning. Leon et al. emphasized that these systems introduce adaptive feedback, which can replace subjective assessment with real-time analysis of surgical skills of the trainee. Such a data-driven framework can bridge the gap between classroom instruction and operating table performance (Leon et al., 2025). Simulation is considered one of AI's most successful and widely used applications in surgical education. Leon et al. described how ML can improve the virtual-reality (VR) simulators by providing quantitative metrics such as instrument trajectory and tissue interaction patterns (Leon et al., 2025). In these models, systems like the virtual operative assistant (VOA) can classify trainee performance and provide real-time, reliable feedback. Such tools can possibly shorten the learning curve, allowing individual skill development before live operating table exposure. Similarly, Silva et al. noted that AI-driven VR modules improve psychomotor and decision-making skills in laparoscopic and endoscopic training by creating interactive feedback-rich environments that mimic operative stress (Silva et al., 2024). Augmented-reality (AR) overlays, discussed by Satapathy et al., can further help improve spatial understanding by displaying real-time anatomical markers, improving simulation practice (Satapathy et al., 2023).

An important recent advancement is generative AI, which can produce text, images, and videos that enhance theoretical and practical learning. Rao et al. highlighted the role of large language models (LLMs) such as ChatGPT and generative adversarial networks (GANs) in creating interactive case scenarios, procedure steps, and patient-specific simulations (Rao et al., 2024). These models answer surgical questions, summarize key concepts, and even generate examination material at the trainee's level. GANs have been used to produce synthetic anatomical and pathological images, addressing privacy issues linked to real patient data (Rao et al., 2024). Nevertheless, the authors cautioned against uncritical reliance on such systems because of "AI hallucination," biases, and a lack of interpretability. Generative AI, therefore, functions best within blended learning frameworks, augmenting, not replacing, human teaching and supervision (Rao et al., 2024).

AI has become integral to modern robotics and MIS. Brian et al. reported that machine-vision algorithms incorporated in robotic platforms can analyze surgical video feeds to evaluate skills in suturing, knot tying, and instrument control (Brian et al., 2024). These systems provide instant feedback and automate competency assessment, helping mentors to standardize performance criteria. Leon et al. further described AI-based intraoperative tools capable of identifying critical anatomical structures during laparoscopic cholecystectomy or thyroidectomy and warn the operating surgeon about unsafe manoeuvres (Leon et al., 2025). By coupling AI with AR, surgical trainees can visualize hidden anatomy, appreciate three-dimensional cues, and get live guidance projected within their operative field. Such innovations turn every operation into a potential teaching opportunity, bridging simulation and real-world practice (Jafari-Khouzani & Soltanian-Zadeh, 2003; Oh et al., 2024).

AI is also changing how residents are chosen and how they are evaluated over time. Leon et al. talked about using natural language processing to look at application essays, letters of recommendation, and performance portfolios to see if someone would be a good fit for surgical training (Leon et al., 2025). Machine learning algorithms can find candidates who are likely to make little progress and suggest personalized interventions. Simultaneously, Silva et al. illustrated that AI-assisted analytics facilitate the mapping of competency milestones across programs, aligning evaluations with entrustable professional activities (EPAs) and fostering transparent benchmarking (Silva et al., 2024). These methods change subjective grading into standardized, evidence-based evaluation, which makes people more responsible while still being fair in hiring and testing.

Because of all its benefits, AI's use in surgical education needs to be closely monitored. Satapathy et al. underscored significant issues such as data privacy, algorithmic bias, and excessive dependence on technology, which may compromise students' autonomy and decision-making (Satapathy et al., 2023). Leon et al. reiterated these warnings, emphasizing that unvalidated or obscure "black-box" algorithms might distort feedback and diminish the skills of future surgeons (Leon et al., 2025). Rao et al. expounded on the notion that the utilization of AI devoid of oversight will result in misinformation and reliance on technology (Rao et al., 2024). Thus, strong ethical frameworks that stress openness, validation, and human supervision are necessary. AI should enhance rather than supplant expert mentorship, safeguarding clinical judgment, empathy, and situational awareness (Jafari-Khouzani & Soltanian-Zadeh, 2003; Morris et al., 2024; Oh et al., 2024; Power, 2024; Pressman et al., 2024).

AI has come a long way since it was first tested. It is now a key part of surgical training and education. AI can provide personalized, more objective, and scalable learning by combining data analytics, simulation, and generative capabilities. But it is clear that it will only work if it is done in a responsible way with the right amount of openness, ethical leadership, and close human guidance. In the future, the surgical curriculum should use a modern method that combines AI-assisted analytics with traditional apprenticeship to train surgeons who are both good with technology and caring in the clinic (Jafari-Khouzani & Soltanian-Zadeh, 2003; Morris et al., 2024; Oh et al., 2024; Power, 2024; Pressman et al., 2024). So, AI is not a replacement for surgical education; it is a way to speed up its progress so that the next generation of surgeons is better prepared, safer, and more adaptable than ever before.

14.7 Challenges and Ethical Considerations

AI is now a big part of modern surgery, affecting everything from planning before the surgery to keeping an eye on the patient after the surgery. AI uses machine learning (ML) and natural language processing (NLP) to help surgeons make decisions, diagnose patients, and evaluate them during surgery. But there have been a lot of questions about privacy, responsibility, and ethics. The growing use of large language models (LLMs) and autonomous robotics has led to more discussions about responsibility, consent, and bias. These advancements require an ethical framework that includes autonomy, beneficence, non-maleficence, and justice (Cobianchi et al., 2022).

Pressman et al. underscored principlism—autonomy, beneficence, non-maleficence, and justice—as fundamental tenets for AI ethics in surgery (Pressman et al., 2024). Autonomy necessitates patient awareness and informed consent; beneficence aims to promote the patient's best interests; non-maleficence requires the prevention of harm; and justice guarantees equitable access. AI has been shown to make things more accurate and faster, but these rules say not to trust algorithms without question, especially those that even developers do not fully understand (Dagnino & Kundrat, 2024; Ryu et al., 2025). AI relies heavily on datasets, like imaging and intraoperative video, which can show private patient information. This is another big problem. Chappell and Teven emphasized the importance of employing encryption and adhering rigorously to privacy regulations, including HIPAA, to reduce these risks (Chappell & Teven, 2023). Sharing data without permission or breaking into it can hurt people emotionally and financially. For AI to be used ethically, there must be strict cybersecurity, permission to use data, and clear rules about who owns the data (Rao et al., 2024; Ryu et al., 2025). Bias is one of the most common ethical problems. Algorithms that learn from small datasets may make differences in race, gender, or income level worse. Pressman et al. discovered bias referenced in approximately 75% of surgical AI studies (Pressman et al., 2024). These unfair situations go against justice and the principle of "do no harm." Using different datasets, checking algorithms, and self-explanatory AI models that show how decisions are made are all possible solutions (Dagnino & Kundrat, 2024; Rao et al., 2024).

Informed consent becomes exceedingly intricate when patients and clinicians are unable to fully comprehend AI's decision-making process. Chappell and Teven contended that surgeons are obligated to explicitly convey the degree and ambiguity of AI involvement, especially concerning non-FDA-approved systems (Chappell & Teven, 2023). The "black box" quality of deep learning models can make it harder to hold people accountable, which could hurt their freedom. Pressman et al. (2024) proposed the utilization of explainable AI (XAI) systems, engineered for interpretability, in surgical applications.

AI's increasing independence is putting traditional ideas of responsibility to the test. If an AI-assisted robot hurts someone, it is hard to figure out who is to blame: the surgeon, the maker, or the programmer (Ryu et al., 2025; Satapathy et al., 2023). Power called this the "moral crumple zone," where people are held responsible for mistakes made by machines (Power, 2024). To avoid ethical and legal confusion, shared-liability frameworks are needed. Furthermore, sufficient training must enable surgeons to critically assess AI outputs and make informed decisions instead of excessively depending on them. Maintaining professional judgment is crucial for ensuring patient safety and trust (Ryu et al., 2025; Satapathy et al., 2023). AI outputs must be correct for surgery to be safe. Pressman et al. found that accuracy was the most common ethical issue in recent literature (Pressman et al., 2024). Sometimes, LLMs make up false or "hallucinated" content, which can lead to misunderstandings or wrong advice. So, we need to keep testing and validating algorithms in the real world. Surgeons must validate AI recommendations through evidence-based practice and ensure human oversight in all decision-making processes (Dagnino & Kundrat, 2024; Satapathy et al., 2023).

AI should promote global equality instead of disparities. AI-assisted systems are available in many high-income countries, but poorer areas have trouble getting them because of money and infrastructure problems. Chappell and Teven stressed that fairness means everyone should have equal access to AI technologies that improve results for all groups of people (Chappell & Teven, 2023). Capelli et al. advocated for the establishment of an international regulatory framework to guarantee equitable distribution of AI technologies ("(PDF) White Paper," 2025). For sustainable development, we need cheap models, shared data resources, and open-source tools to make AI in surgery available to everyone (Ryu et al., 2025; Satapathy et al., 2023; Silva et al., 2024).

Even though AI has the potential to change surgical outcomes in a big way, the ethical side of AI in surgery cannot be ignored. The literature consistently underscores critical challenges: data privacy, algorithmic bias, informed consent, accountability, and equitable access (Dagnino & Kundrat, 2024; Rao et al., 2024; Ryu et al., 2025; Satapathy et al., 2023; Silva et al., 2024). To deal with these issues, we need an ethical approach that is based on principlism and constant supervision. Regulations must require openness and sharing of responsibility, and training should keep human judgment and machine ability separate. Power said that the future of surgical AI should not take away from the role of humans, but rather strengthen it. Technology should help the ethical and caring surgeon, not take their place.

14.8 Future Directions

AI is becoming a powerful tool in every part of surgical care. It is quickly changing the field of surgery by giving surgeons more precise data, better visualization, and the ability to make decisions based on individual needs. AI has the potential to change preoperative planning, intraoperative guidance, postoperative recovery, and global surgical education by combining image analysis, robotics, predictive modeling, and machine learning. The role of AI has evolved from evaluating preoperative imaging to analyzing complex data, intraoperative videos, and real-time imaging. Machine learning models can now look at complicated datasets to come up with the best ways to do surgery, guess what problems might come up during the procedure, and guess what will happen after the procedure (Li et al., 2025). Li et al. (2025) talked about how combining ML with imaging and patient data has made it possible to make 3D models of weak structures like ducts and vessels. These tools help surgeons get ready and make safety margins better. In oncologic surgery, AI aids multidisciplinary decision-making by offering prognostic insights extracted from extensive datasets. For instance, predictive modeling now helps tumor board meetings by predicting how often a tumor will come back and helping doctors decide between minimally invasive and open approaches (Amin et al., 2024).

CV and real-time analytics have changed the way that guidance works during surgery. AI algorithms in robotic systems can find important anatomical features, mark safe dissection planes, and stop accidental injuries by sending smart alerts (Morris et al., 2024). Surgeons can automatically find anatomical landmarks with real-time video analysis, which improves their spatial awareness during complicated laparoscopic or robotic procedures. Miranda et al. talked about how augmented reality overlays that use AI to help with visualization can combine preoperative CT or MRI data with live surgical video to give a more detailed picture of the anatomy (Morris et al., 2024). The next big thing is reinforcement learning, which is when systems get better on their own by getting feedback on how well they work. This kind of adaptive intelligence could soon let robots do simple tasks like suturing or pulling back soft tissue while a person watches (Hamilton, 2024). This collaboration between people and machines makes things more accurate and less tiring for surgeons.

AI is also changing the way surgical skills are taught, tested, and made the same. Traditional surgical education depends on mentor observation, but AI now offers objective, quantitative assessment. AI algorithms create unbiased performance metrics by looking at motion trajectories, how well instruments are handled, and how long it takes to finish a task (Amin et al., 2024). Amin et al. elucidated that interactive simulators integrated with AI dynamically modify case scenarios according to trainee advancement, thereby customizing learning trajectories (Amin et al., 2024). AI-driven video analysis platforms also let you watch your own surgery again and find ways to improve your technique. Future robotic consoles could have built-in AI tutors that give real-time feedback on how to do things and help you learn new skills. This would make global surgical training standards more consistent.

More and more, AI is being used to keep an eye on patients after surgery and predict how well they will do. Machine learning models trained on electronic health records can find early warning signs of problems like infections, bleeding, thromboembolism, or anastomotic leaks before the patient's condition gets worse (Li et al., 2025). Predictive analytics now help surgeons figure out how risky a patient is, how much monitoring they need after surgery, and how to best plan for their discharge. Li et al. reported the successful use of deep learning algorithms to predict readmission and mortality, improving both safety and resource allocation (Li et al., 2025). Wearable sensors and remote monitoring devices connected to AI platforms provide ongoing postoperative data, enabling supervision of recovery at home. Natural language processing (NLP) tools make virtual follow-up even better by looking at patient-reported outcomes and finding worrying symptom patterns without needing to see the patient in person (Morris et al., 2024).

The combination of AI and precision medicine is the start of real personalized surgery. AI helps surgeons plan treatments that are tailored to each patient's unique biological profile by combining genomic, radiomic, and phenotypic data (Li et al., 2025) (Amin et al., 2024). In oncologic surgery, this integration facilitates the identification of resection margins and the prediction of responses to neoadjuvant or adjuvant therapy. Hamilton came up with the idea of "digital twins," which are virtual copies of patients that use their own anatomical and genomic data to simulate surgical procedures before the actual surgery (Hamilton, 2024). This method aids in predicting intraoperative difficulties and postoperative results. AI engines will soon be able to help with intraoperative decision-making in real time by changing strategies based on tissue perfusion, margin adequacy, or other physiological parameters.

Even though AI integration has a lot of potential, it also brings up moral and legal issues. Regulation is needed in important areas like transparency, data privacy, and algorithmic accountability. To keep patients safe and trust them, surgical teams must be the ones who make the final decisions about AI (Morris et al., 2024). Miranda et al. pointed out problems like bias from datasets that don't represent everyone, unequal access around the world, and unclear responsibility when AI systems break down (Morris et al., 2024). Ethical guidelines now stress explainable AI, which means systems that give reasons for their suggestions that doctors can understand. Federated learning addresses privacy issues by enabling training on decentralized data networks without the need to transfer patient records. To make sure that algorithms are developed fairly, it is important to standardize data formats and make secure registries (Li et al., 2025; Amin et al., 2024).

Modern surgical practice relies more and more on collaboration between different specialties, and AI can help bring these areas together. Creating "surgical AI ecosystems" that link data streams from radiology, pathology, anesthesia, and intraoperative settings will lead to better decision-making (Li et al., 2025). Li et al. proposed the idea of surgical informatics frameworks that combine different types of data, such as imaging, operative video, sensor datasets, and patient outcomes, into single predictive models. These kinds of platforms speed up continuous learning, which means that each surgical case can improve and build on future algorithms (Li et al., 2025). NLP is also changing how we use data by automatically pulling structured information out of reports and operative notes. This harmonization cuts down on manual data entry, makes the registry more complete, and makes it possible to do large-scale cohort research with little administrative work (Morris et al., 2024).

The development of AI in surgery will probably lead to the creation of "smart operating rooms" where sensors, robots, and analytics platforms can all talk to each other easily. AI will not take the place of surgeons; instead, it will act as a cognitive copilot, helping people make decisions with speed and accuracy that cannot be matched by hand (Amin et al., 2024; Hamilton, 2024). Hamilton and Amin et al. stressed that human empathy, judgment, and creativity are still very important, especially when things go wrong during surgery (Amin et al., 2024; Hamilton, 2024). So, in the future, surgical intelligence and computational intelligence will work together in a way that helps both. Advanced systems might be able to guess what the surgeon will do next, change the lighting, change the camera angle, or show important metrics on their own. Over time, these environments that are aware of their surroundings could become self-learning systems that tailor their help to each surgeon's needs.

Ultimately, the incorporation of AI will redefine surgical excellence—not through automation alone but through seamless collaboration between human expertise and machine precision. By integrating these technologies responsibly, surgery will transition toward safer, more efficient, and truly personalized care.

References

Amin, A., Cardoso, S. A., Suyambu, J., Abdus Saboor, H., Cardoso, R. P., Husnain, A., Isaac, N. V., Backing, H., Mehmood, D., Mehmood, M., & Maslamani, A. N. J. (2024). Future of artificial intelligence in surgery: A narrative review. *Cureus, 16*(1), e51631. https://doi.org/10.7759/cureus.51631

Aoki, T., Yamada, A., Aoyama, K., Saito, H., Tsuboi, A., Nakada, A., Niikura, R., Fujishiro, M., Oka, S., Ishihara, S., Matsuda, T., Tanaka, S., Koike, K., & Tada, T. (2019). Automatic detection of erosions and ulcerations in wireless capsule endoscopy images based on a deep convolutional neural network. *Gastrointestinal Endoscopy, 89*(2), 357–363.e2. https://doi.org/10.1016/j.gie.2018.10.027

Arakaki, S., Takenaka, S., Sasaki, K., Kitaguchi, D., Hasegawa, H., Takeshita, N., Takatsuki, M., & Ito, M. (2025). Artificial intelligence in minimally invasive surgery: Current state and future challenges. *JMA Journal, 8*(1), 86–90. https://doi.org/10.31662/jmaj.2024-0175

Bari, H., Wadhwani, S., & Dasari, B. V. M. (2021). Role of artificial intelligence in hepatobiliary and pancreatic surgery. *World Journal of Gastrointestinal Surgery, 13*(1), 7–18. https://doi.org/10.4240/wjgs.v13.i1.7

Bertsimas, D., Dunn, J., Velmahos, G. C., & Kaafarani, H. M. A. (2018). Surgical risk is not linear: Derivation and validation of a novel, user-friendly, and machine-learning-based predictive OpTimal trees in emergency surgery risk (POTTER) calculator. *Annals of Surgery, 268*(4), 574–583. https://doi.org/10.1097/SLA.0000000000002956

Brennan, M., Puri, S., Ozrazgat-Baslanti, T., Feng, Z., Ruppert, M., Hashemighouchani, H., Momcilovic, P., Li, X., Wang, D. Z., & Bihorac, A. (2019). Comparing clinical judgment with the MySurgeryRisk algorithm for preoperative risk assessment: A pilot usability study. *Surgery, 165*(5), 1035–1045. https://doi.org/10.1016/j.surg.2019.01.002

Brian, R., Murillo, A., Gomes, C., & Alseidi, A. (2024). Artificial intelligence and robotic surgical education. *Global Surgical Education – Journal of the Association for Surgical Education, 3*(1), 60. https://doi.org/10.1007/s44186-024-00262-5

Cevik, J., Seth, I., & Rozen, W. M. (2023). Transforming breast reconstruction: The pioneering role of artificial intelligence in preoperative planning. *Gland Surgery, 12*(9), 1271–1275. https://doi.org/10.21037/gs-23-265

Chappell, A. G., & Teven, C. M. (2023). How should surgeons consider emerging innovations in artificial intelligence and robotics? *AMA Journal of Ethics, 25*(8), E589–E597. https://doi.org/10.1001/amajethics.2023.589

Cobianchi, L., Verde, J. M., Loftus, T. J., Piccolo, D., Dal Mas, F., Mascagni, P., Garcia Vazquez, A., Ansaloni, L., Marseglia, G. R., Massaro, M., Gallix, B., Padoy, N., Peter, A., & Kaafarani, H. M. (2022). Artificial intelligence and surgery: Ethical dilemmas and open issues. *Journal of the American College of Surgeons, 235*(2), 268–275. https://doi.org/10.1097/XCS.0000000000000242

Dagnino, G., & Kundrat, D. (2024). Robot-assistive minimally invasive surgery: Trends and future directions. *International Journal of Intelligent Robotics and Applications, 8*(4), 812–826. https://doi.org/10.1007/s41315-024-00341-2

Endo, Y., Tokuyasu, T., Mori, Y., Asai, K., Umezawa, A., Kawamura, M., Fujinaga, A., Ejima, A., Kimura, M., & Inomata, M. (2023). Impact of AI system on recognition for anatomical landmarks related to reducing bile duct injury during laparoscopic cholecystectomy. *Surgical Endoscopy, 37*(7), 5752–5759. https://doi.org/10.1007/s00464-023-10224-5

Feng, B., Ma, X.-H., Wang, S., Cai, W., Liu, X.-B., & Zhao, X.-M. (2021). Application of artificial intelligence in preoperative imaging of hepatocellular carcinoma: Current status and future perspectives. *World Journal of Gastroenterology, 27*(32), 5341–5350. https://doi.org/10.3748/wjg.v27.i32.5341

Gupta, R., Gaurav, A., Gupta, G., Pipal, D. K., Singh, M., Kumar, R., Chowdhary, S. A., & Rath, R. S. (2025). *Factors affecting the quality of critical view of safety assessed with intraoperative doublet photography during laparoscopic cholecystectomy*. Unpublished master's thesis. All India Institute of Medical Sciences, Gorakhpur.

Hamilton, A. (2024). The future of artificial intelligence in surgery. *Cureus, 16*(7), e63699. https://doi.org/10.7759/cureus.63699

Hassan, A. M., Rajesh, A., Asaad, M., Jonas, N. A., Coert, J. H., Mehrara, B. J., & Butler, C. E. (2023). Artificial intelligence and machine learning in prediction of surgical complications: Current state, applications, and implications. *The American Surgeon, 89*(1), 25–30. https://doi.org/10.1177/00031348221101488

Iftikhar, M., Saqib, M., Zareen, M., & Mumtaz, H. (2024). Artificial intelligence: Revolutionizing robotic surgery: Review. *Annals of Medicine and Surgery (2012), 86*(9), 5401–5409. https://doi.org/10.1097/MS9.0000000000002426

Iv, T. F. B., & Tignanelli, C. J. (2024). Artificial intelligence in surgery—A narrative review. *Journal of Medical Artificial Intelligence, 7*(0). https://doi.org/10.21037/jmai-24-111

Jafari-Khouzani, K., & Soltanian-Zadeh, H. (2003). Multiwavelet grading of pathological images of prostate. *IEEE Transactions on Bio-Medical Engineering, 50*(6), 697–704. https://doi.org/10.1109/TBME.2003.812194

Jiang, W., Zhang, J., Shi, W., Cao, X., Zhao, X., Zhang, B., Yu, H., Wang, S., Qin, Y., Lei, M., Cao, Y., Zhu, B., & Liu, Y. (2025). An artificial intelligence platform for predicting postoperative complications in metastatic spinal surgery: Development and validation study. *Journal of Big Data, 12*(1), 120. https://doi.org/10.1186/s40537-025-01155-0

Kenig, N., Monton Echeverria, J., & Muntaner Vives, A. (2024). Artificial intelligence in surgery: A systematic review of use and validation. *Journal of Clinical Medicine, 13*(23), 7108. https://doi.org/10.3390/jcm13237108

Kolbinger, F. R., Bodenstedt, S., Carstens, M., Leger, S., Krell, S., Rinner, F. M., Nielen, T. P., Kirchberg, J., Fritzmann, J., Weitz, J., Distler, M., & Speidel, S. (2024). Artificial intelligence for context-aware surgical guidance in complex robot-assisted oncological procedures: An exploratory feasibility study. *European Journal of Surgical Oncology, 50*(12), 106996. https://doi.org/10.1016/j.ejso.2023.106996

Kröger, J., Jorek, N., Seitel, A., Mayer, L., Salg, G. A., Crnovrsanin, N., Pianka, F., Pausch, T., Maier-Hein, L., Michalski, C., & Nienhüser, H. (2025). Application of artificial intelligence in esophageal surgery: A systematic review. *Journal of Robotic Surgery, 19*(1), 694. https://doi.org/10.1007/s11701-025-02854-9

Leon, S., Lee, S., Perez, J. E., & Hashimoto, D. A. (2025). Artificial intelligence and the education of future surgeons. *American Journal of Surgery, 246*, 116257. https://doi.org/10.1016/j.amjsurg.2025.116257

Li, H., Han, Z., Wu, H., Musaev, E. R., Lin, Y., Li, S., Makatsariya, A. D., Chekhonin, V. P., Ma, W., & Zhang, C. (2025). Artificial intelligence in surgery: Evolution, trends, and future directions. *International Journal of Surgery (London, England), 111*(2), 2101–2111. https://doi.org/10.1097/JS9.0000000000002159

Maurer, L. R., Chetlur, P., Zhuo, D., El Hechi, M., Velmahos, G. C., Dunn, J., Bertsimas, D., & Kaafarani, H. M. A. (2023). Validation of the AI-based predictive OpTimal trees in emergency surgery risk (POTTER) calculator in patients 65 years and older. *Annals of Surgery, 277*(1), e8–e15. https://doi.org/10.1097/SLA.0000000000004714

McGenity, C., Clarke, E. L., Jennings, C., Matthews, G., Cartlidge, C., Freduah-Agyemang, H., Stocken, D. D., & Treanor, D. (2024). Artificial intelligence in digital pathology: A systematic review and meta-analysis of diagnostic test accuracy. *npj Digital Medicine, 7*(1), 114. https://doi.org/10.1038/s41746-024-01106-8

McGivern, K. G., Drake, T. M., Knight, S. R., Lucocq, J., Bernabeu, M. O., Clark, N., Fairfield, C., Pius, R., Shaw, C. A., Seth, S., & Harrison, E. M. (2023). Applying artificial intelligence to big data in hepatopancreatic and biliary surgery: A scoping review. *Artificial Intelligence Surgery, 3*(1), 27–47. https://doi.org/10.20517/ais.2022.39

Mohammadi, I., Rajai Firouzabadi, S., Hosseinpour, M., Akhlaghpasand, M., Hajikarimloo, B., Zeraatian-Nejad, S., & Sardari Nia, P. (2024). Using artificial intelligence to predict post-operative outcomes in congenital heart surgeries: A systematic review. *BMC Cardiovascular Disorders, 24*(1), 718. https://doi.org/10.1186/s12872-024-04336-6

Morris, M. X., Fiocco, D., Caneva, T., Yiapanis, P., & Orgill, D. P. (2024). Current and future applications of artificial intelligence in surgery: Implications for clinical practice and research. *Frontiers in Surgery, 11*, 1393898. https://doi.org/10.3389/fsurg.2024.1393898

Oh, N., Kim, B., Kim, T., Rhu, J., Kim, J., & Choi, G.-S. (2024). Real-time segmentation of biliary structure in pure laparoscopic donor hepatectomy. *Scientific Reports, 14*(1), 22508. https://doi.org/10.1038/s41598-024-73434-4

Power, D. (2024). Ethical considerations in the era of AI, automation, and surgical robots: There are plenty of lessons from the past. *Discover Artificial Intelligence, 4*(1), 65. https://doi.org/10.1007/s44163-024-00166-9

Pressman, S. M., Borna, S., Gomez-Cabello, C. A., Haider, S. A., Haider, C., & Forte, A. J. (2024). AI and ethics: A systematic review of the ethical considerations of large language model use in surgery research. *Healthcare (Basel, Switzerland), 12*(8), 825. https://doi.org/10.3390/healthcare12080825

Rao, L., Yang, E., Dissanayake, S., Cuomo, R., Seth, I., & Rozen, W. M. (2024). The use of generative artificial intelligence in surgical education: A narrative review. *Plastic and Aesthetic Research, 11*(0), N/A–N/A. https://doi.org/10.20517/2347-9264.2024.102

Ryu, S., Imaizumi, Y., Goto, K., Iwauchi, S., Kobayashi, T., Ito, R., & Nakabayashi, Y. (2025). Artificial intelligence-enhanced navigation for nerve recognition and surgical education in laparoscopic colorectal surgery. *Surgical Endoscopy*. https://doi.org/10.1007/S00464-024-11489-0

Satapathy, P., Hermis, A. H., Rustagi, S., Pradhan, K. B., Padhi, B. K., & Sah, R. (2023). Artificial intelligence in surgical education and training: Opportunities, challenges, and ethical considerations – Correspondence. *International Journal of Surgery (London, England), 109*(5), 1543–1544. https://doi.org/10.1097/JS9.0000000000000387

Silva, C., Nascimento, D., Dantas, G. G., Fonseca, K., Hespanhol, L., Rego, A., & Araújo-Filho, I. (2024). Impact of artificial intelligence on the training of general surgeons of the future: A scoping review of the advances and challenges. *Acta Cirurgica Brasileira, 39*, e396224. https://doi.org/10.1590/acb396224

Weitz, M., Pfeiffer, J. R., Patel, S., Biancalana, M., Pekis, A., Kannan, V., Kaklamanos, E., Parker, A., Bucksot, J. E., Romera, J. R., Alvin, R., Zhang, Y., Stefka, A. T., Lopez-Ramos, D., Peterson, J. R., Antony, A. K., Zamora, K. W., & Woodard, S. (2024). Performance of an AI-powered visualization software platform for precision surgery in breast cancer patients. *NPJ Breast Cancer, 10*(1), 98. https://doi.org/10.1038/s41523-024-00696-6

(PDF) White paper: Ethics and trustworthiness of artificial intelligence in clinical surgery. (2025). *ResearchGate*. https://doi.org/10.20517/ais.2023.04

Part V

AI for Public Health & Behavioural Intelligence

15 Artificial Intelligence in Primary Health Care

Vineet Kumar Pathak, Ajeet Singh Bhadoria,
Shubham Gupta, Mahek Rai, and Priyanka Parhad

15.1 Introduction

Artificial intelligence (AI) is here to revolutionize healthcare delivery throughout the globe. By 2025, AI applications had clearly moved beyond the experimental stage and into practical, real-world use in the medical field. This shift was highlighted when the U.S. FDA approved over 700 AI-enabled medical devices by late 2023, with radiology tools accounting for a striking 77% of that total (Health, 2025).

Primary health care, which serves as the fundamental backbone and first point of contact for health systems, stands to gain significantly from these AI innovations. The primary care system is often up against serious challenges, including a lack of specialist access, high patient volumes, and limited resources, particularly in rural and underserved areas. AI technologies offer a promising way to strengthen primary care by improving diagnostic accuracy, streamlining workflows, and extending service delivery to remote regions.

The World Health Organization (WHO) acknowledges how AI stands as proponent for medical diagnosis and treatment and public health applications, while its design and use must be guided by ethical principles and human rights to deliver benefits across all populations (Ethics and Governance of Artificial Intelligence for Health, 2021). This chapter delivers applications of AI in primary health care through discussions about innovative implementations citing international

V. K. Pathak (✉) · S. Gupta · M. Rai
Department of Community Medicine, IMS, BHU, Varanasi, India
e-mail: pathakvineet@bhu.ac.in

A. S. Bhadoria
Department of Community and Family Medicine, AIIMS, Rishikesh, India

P. Parhad
Centre for Community Medicine, All India Institute of Medical Sciences, New Delhi, India

U. Venkatesh et al. (eds.), *Multimodal AI in Healthcare*,
https://doi.org/10.1007/978-981-95-9027-8_15

examples and enhancements with essential policy and ethical frameworks for implementation. The analysis focuses on detailed evaluation of three essential AI applications, including medical imaging, decision support, and patient triage systems, while assessing their implementation and infrastructure requirements with obstacles in primary care implementation.

15.1.1 Key AI Technologies and Primary Care Applications

The healthcare sector today uses AI broadly in two main ways, which include (1) machine learning (ML) and deep learning for pattern recognition and (2) natural language processing (NLP) and expert system-based approaches.

These technologies power various applications that align with primary care needs:

Clinical decision support and diagnosis: The system uses patient data to analyze and generate potential medical diagnoses to detect health conditions with risk factors. The differential diagnosis system Isabel demonstrated its effectiveness in improving clinician diagnostic skills and detecting previously undetected cases (Impact Studies | Isabel Peer Reviewed Articles, 2021). In the medical field, large language models (LLMs) and generative AI tools such as ChatGPT are used to create medical knowledge synthesis and clinical query responses. Research indicates that LLMs show potential to simplify complex medical information with a decreased physician's mental workload (Waldren, 2024). The current use of LLMs needs careful attention because these systems produce fabricated outputs known as "*AI hallucinations*" and require validation before they can be used to guide medical decisions. The application of AI decision support systems in primary care helps physicians determine which patients need immediate medical attention versus home-based care and provides potential diagnoses for ambiguous symptoms. The AI network operated by Apollo Hospitals in India collaborated with an AI network to create an ML model that processed clinical data from 400,000 patients to predict heart attack risk by identifying risk factors and creating a scoring system for preventive interventions. Predictive models enable primary care providers to concentrate on preventive care and early intervention for patients who have high risk profiles (AI in Healthcare Is India's Trillion-Dollar Opportunity | World Economic Forum, 2022).

- *Medical imaging and diagnostics:* The development of computer vision technology allows AI to diagnose medical conditions with high precision, which helps primary care facilities lacking immediate specialist access such as radiologists or ophthalmologists. AI tools in radiology allow primary care physicians to access automated abnormality detection through the interpretation of X-rays and scans. Annalise CXR represents an AI tool that analyzes chest X-rays to detect 124 different findings, starting from lung nodules through fractures (AI Chest X-Ray Tool Made Available to Radiologists at over 40 NHS Trusts, 2024). These interpretation tools enable specialist professionals to save time, while doctors achieve faster diagnostic processes. The AI Diagnostic Fund allowed more than 40 English hospitals to adopt Annalise's chest X-ray AI system for lung cancer disease detection speedup purposes. One NHS site demonstrated AI advantages through a 9-day reduction in X-ray to lung cancer treatment time and a 27% improvement in detecting early-stage cancer cases. The combination of AI technology with point-of-care diagnostic imaging allows primary care clinics to employ portable ultrasound and dermatology devices that utilize AI for pathological identification. IDx-DR represents a primary care flagship application that uses artificial intelligence to screen diabetic retinopathy. IDx-DR uses a basic retinal image from primary care settings to analyze diabetic retinopathy presence and specialist referral necessity (FDA Approves First Software That Can Interpret Images without Doctor's Help, 2018). IDx-DR demonstrated 87% sensitivity and 91% specificity in detecting more-than-mild diabetic retinopathy during its primary care office trial (Abràmoff et al., 2018). The FDA granted FDA-authorized autonomous AI diagnostic system status to IDx-DR in 2018 because it could function independently from clinician interpretation for screening purposes. This milestone established that AI technology enables specialist-level ophthalmology screening capabilities to be implemented in primary care facilities, which expands medical services at lower costs. Primary care medical diagnostic tools use artificial intelligence to analyze TB chest X-rays as well as cervical cancer through automated Pap smear analysis and skin lesion classification for dermatologic referrals. Deep learning algorithms in medical image analysis enable the detection of conditions early in primary care and community screening environments.

- *Patient self-assessment and triage tools:* AI symptom checker applications now enable patients to determine their care requirements through patient self-assessment and triage tools. Users of Symptomate (by Infermedica) can provide their symptoms along with answers to questions, which leads the AI to generate possible conditions and care recommendations from self-care to emergency treatment. The tool uses and analyzes medical information through NLP and combines it with probabilistic methods from reviewed medical knowledge bases. The tools operate worldwide through websites and mobile applications to perform triage functions beyond the clinical settings. Symptom checkers enable primary care systems to lower inappropriate patient visits while helping patients access suitable care pathways. The performance of these tools has shown inconsistent results. The 2022 systematic review of digital symptom checkers reported the top diagnostic accuracy of 19% to 38%, while the triage advice accuracy reached 49% to 90%. The variability often depended on the nature of the condition; these tools often tend to perform better at triaging acute conditions with clear symptoms, such as respiratory infections, but are less accurate in diagnosing complex or chronic diseases that are presented with ambiguous or overlapping symptoms creating a state of confusion. Symptomate achieved better performance than other competitors according to tests using clinical vignettes, yet it remains less reliable than a trained doctor (Aissaoui Ferhi et al., 2024). Primary care providers use symptom checking apps as patient decision tools rather than definitive diagnostic tools while emphasizing that such applications should support professional medical advice. Symptom checkers serve an essential AI function for primary care demand management by providing patients with information while promoting early care access for concerning symptoms and enabling clinician data collection (NHS general practices use AI triage apps to gather patient histories before consultations). With enhancements, it is expected that AI models will improve in their accuracy of diagnostic recommendations. Telemedicine platforms are now integrated with symptom checkers through AI triage, which automatically connects users and doctors via teleconsultation for severe symptoms which need immediate attention. The implementation of AI symptom assessment tools function as a connecting link between the public domain and primary care services to provide continuous advice and decrease unnecessary clinic visits, but their safety designs and effectiveness require ongoing assessment to build trust among users (Wallace et al., 2022).

- *Administrative and operational AI tools:* The implementation of AI extends beyond clinical practice; it supports administrative operations and efficiency in primary care settings. Natural language processing (NLP) technology helps automate documentation through AI "scribing" that transcribes and summarizes patient records for electronic storage purposes. Existing products use audio recording during office visits to create a draft version of clinical notes and referral letters to help physicians spend less time on paperwork through this system. The AI system analyzes patient behavior and identifies no-show patterns to detect patients who require follow-up care and can manage appointment schedules. The analysis of electronic health records (EHRs) by machine learning algorithms enables the detection of care gaps which results in automated health maintenance reminders and registry population. Primary care physicians utilize generative AI to generate standard documents including insurance pre-authorization requests and patient education materials through commands to ChatGPT for creating referral letters with essential points. The time-saving applications need human verification to prevent mistakes from occurring. The application of AI in public health and population primary care involves predictive models that analyze community data to forecast outbreaks and detect vulnerable neighborhoods, thus helping primary health centers direct their resources in advance. The back office and organizational side of primary care benefits from AI technology, which reduces administrative work (a survey revealed physicians believe AI's most significant benefit is its ability to reduce clerical work so doctors can dedicate more time to patient care (Physicians' Greatest Use for AI? Cutting Administrative Burdens | American Medical Association, 2025). Table 15.1 presents an overview of major AI applications in primary care that compares worldwide and Indian implementations along with their performance levels and necessary infrastructure and achieved results.

15.2 Case Studies and Examples from India and Abroad

Diabetic Retinopathy Screening Given that studies indicate the prevalence of diabetic retinopathy in India is around 17%, with many cases going undiagnosed in primary care settings, early detection through screening is critical to preventing

Table 15.1 Key AI applications in primary care, with global and Indian examples

Application	Global example (effectiveness and outcome)	Indian example (effectiveness and outcome)	Infrastructure requirements
Diabetic retinopathy screening—In India, an estimated 17% of the large diabetic population has retinopathy, much of it undiagnosed in primary care settings	*IDx-DR*—AI analysis of retinal images for diabetic retinopathy. Sensitivity ~87%, specificity ~91% in trials. First FDA-approved autonomous diagnostic AI; in primary care use it flags diabetics needing ophthalmologist referral, preventing vision loss	AI-driven retinal screening by start-ups like *Remidio* and *Artelus* using portable fundus cameras. Pilots in India have extended screening to rural clinics, enabling early detection of diabetic eye disease without on-site specialists (Kapoor et al., 2024). For example, Aravind Eye Hospital partnered on AI screening programs to reach underserved diabetic patients	Fundus camera for retinal images, trained health workers to capture images, reliable electricity and ideally Internet (for cloud AI or updates). Some solutions run offline on an integrated device
Chest X-ray analysis (TB/lung)—India carries the world's highest TB burden with over 2.5 million cases annually	*Annalise CXR*—deep learning for chest X-ray. Detects 100+ findings (e.g., nodules, TB, fractures). Used in UK/Australia; NHS deployment showed earlier cancer diagnosis (27% more early-stage lung cancers) and cut time to treatment by ~9 days by expediting radiology workflows. Also aids ICU care by spotting line/tube misplacements	*Qure.ai's qXR*—AI for chest X-rays used in India's TB screening. Implemented in municipal and rural programs to flag TB suspects. In a 2023 study, adding qXR increased TB case detection yield by 15.8% over standard screening (catching cases radiologists missed). It also reduced time to diagnosis in some tribal community pilots from ~6 weeks to 1 week. Now being rolled out in >100 Indian districts with government and NGO support to bolster TB eradication efforts (Vijayan et al., 2023)	Digital X-ray machines (or CR systems) to generate images; computing hardware or cloud connectivity to run the AI; integration into screening workflow (AI software at radiology centers or on portable X-ray vans). Training for radiographers to handle software outputs

(continued)

Table 15.1 (continued)

Application	Global example (effectiveness and outcome)	Indian example (effectiveness and outcome)	Infrastructure requirements
Symptom checker and triage	*Symptomate*—a patient-facing symptom checker (web/app) that evaluates inputs and provides likely conditions and triage advice. Performs consistently well in independent vignette tests (often ranking correct diagnosis in top suggestions). However, overall diagnostic accuracy of symptom checkers is still low (~30% on first guess) and variable. They mainly excel at triage (e.g., identifying emergency vs. routine cases) with up to ~90% accuracy [10]. Used in Europe and the United States by health systems to guide patients online (e.g., NHS trials for digital 111 services)	No widely adopted indigenous symptom checker in primary care yet. Some Indian telehealth providers and insurers offer basic chatbot triage (often powered by global engines like Babylon or local start-ups), but accuracy in the Indian context is unproven. Language and cultural relevance are challenges—most apps operate in English. The government's telemedicine service (eSanjeevani) currently relies on human doctors rather than AI for triage (eSanjeevani). Pilot projects are exploring multilingual symptom checkers for primary health centers, but as of 2025 these remain in testing phases	Smartphones or computers for patients to access the tool; an underlying medical knowledge database covering local disease patterns; NLP that supports local languages. Internet connectivity to run cloud-based AI. Clinical oversight to periodically audit advice given. Public awareness and trust are also needed for patients to use such tools

(continued)

Table 15.1 (continued)

Application	Global example (effectiveness and outcome)	Indian example (effectiveness and outcome)	Infrastructure requirements
Clinical decision support (CDS)	*Computerized guidelines/diagnosis support*—for example, the United Kingdom's primary care uses CDS systems integrated with EHR (like reminders from NICE guidelines, or diagnostic aids such as Isabel). These systems can improve adherence to best practices and catch potential diagnostic misses. Studies in the United States showed using a diagnosis checklist tool improved physicians' diagnostic accuracy by up to differential ~7–8% per case and in some educational settings by as much as 30% (Sibbald et al., 2022). Newer AI like Google's Med-PaLM (an LLM tuned for medicine) have even passed medical licensing exams and are being evaluated for answering doctors' questions, though not yet deployed clinically	*Arezzo CDSS pilot*—NITI Aayog and Elsevier conducted a pilot in 2021 using the Arezzo AI-based decision support system in primary health centers. Arezzo delivered personalized treatment pathways for each patient by integrating national clinical guidelines with patient data on a tablet app (HAICReportNITIAayog, 2021). Frontline health workers (nurses/auxiliary midwives) followed the AI's prompts for screening and treatment decisions. The pilot demonstrated improved guideline adherence but also revealed challenges: for instance, local language translation of medical content was a significant hurdle in implementation. The system required substantial customization to Indian protocols. Scale-up will depend on training, acceptability to clinicians, and proving impact on patient outcomes in primary care	Tablets or computers at the primary care point of care; standardized digital clinical protocols; integration with patient record systems (if available); connectivity to update guidelines and collect data. Training of healthcare staff to work with the decision support interface. Change management to ensure the tool is accepted as a help rather than seen as a hindrance or replacement for clinical judgment

vision loss. India is home to a significant population of people with diabetes, making this a high-priority area for intervention. IDx-DR technology makes it possible for family practice clinics across the United States to run independent DR screening tests. The AI system analyzes retinal images obtained by primary care doctors or nurses to produce immediate results about referable retinopathy detection. The initial screening process for diabetic patients no longer requires specialist ophthalmologists. IDx-DR achieved the same accuracy as specialists in detecting referable DR in a pivotal multicenter study that also linked its deployment to better screening rates for diabetic patients who rarely underwent yearly eye exams. Several AI projects are currently working to detect diabetic retinopathy in rural areas of India where the condition frequently remains untreated. Google Research together with Aravind Eye Hospital validated their AI algorithm on thousands of Indian retinal images to achieve detection performance matching that of retina specialists for DR. The Indian start-up Remidio incorporated AI technology into its affordable fundus camera solutions for primary health centers to use. Primary care nurses operated Remidio's AI-powered fundus camera to examine diabetic patients in Karnataka villages under a pilot project. This led to referral of patients detected with diabetic retinopathy to ophthalmologists. In patients whom diabetic retinopathy was not detected, they were advised to retest after 1 year or as per doctor's protocol. This approach enables early eye care detection through a system that functions without medical professionals present at the site. The Indian start-up Artelus has implemented its AI software on tablet-based fundus cameras throughout primary care facilities to screen tens of thousands of patients for DR as well as other eye diseases. The efforts resulted in better patient access to screening, and AI-detected conditions that nonspecialist clinicians overlooked, which led to proper referrals. These case studies demonstrate AI capabilities to bridge specialist shortages in primary care, yet demonstrate the necessity for staff training and verification processes to validate AI-detected cases through ophthalmological verification.

Tuberculosis (TB) Detection via X-rays India accounts for over a quarter of the global disease burden of tuberculosis with many cases presenting for the first time at a primary care facility. Here, leveraging AI for TB screening is a crucial public health strategy, especially given the lack of radiologists in rural areas. Among the most notable cases is the use of Qure.ai's qXR tool in public health programs in Nagpur and certain parts of the country. Chest X-ray camps were set up for screening of at-risk populations by PATH and municipal health authorities. qXR was used to immediately analyze the X-rays for TB signs on the field away from hospital centers. The AI's findings were used to flag individuals, and data was shared to district tuberculosis officers (DTOs) who then supervised Asha workers to collect sputum samples for GeneXpert testing to confirm tuberculosis. An analysis of this program showed that qXR caught additional TB cases—specifically, a 15.8% increase in TB case detection was attributed to AI identifying abnormal X-rays that human readers had not tagged for follow-up. This meant dozens of extra patients diagnosed and treated who might otherwise have been missed. Another outcome was a reduction in diagnostic delay. In certain pilot sites (e.g., tribal areas of Maharashtra), using an AI-equipped portable X-ray unit cut the average time to confirm TB from over a month to about 1 week. Globally, similar use of AI for TB is seen—for instance, in 2021, the WHO endorsed the use of certified AI tools for screening TB chest X-rays in lieu of human readers in resource-limited settings, after studies in Africa showed some AI systems could match radiologist sensitivity.

These experiences show us that AI can enhance primary care and public health programs by scaling expert interpretation without active intervention. The challenges encountered included integrating the software into the existing workflow. Initially, some staff were unfamiliar with the AI interface and ensuring quality X-ray image capture so that the AI's accuracy does not drop if images are poor, so training radiographers was also important. This Nagpur project and others prompted the Indian government to include this AI solution in the National TB Elimination Program (NTEP). By 2024, qXR and similar tools were being deployed in over 100 districts as part of active case finding campaigns under the program. A key lesson from these case findings is that AI is not only a plug-and-play solution—it requires groundwork (digital equipment, training, evaluation of results)—but when done properly, it can help strengthen the primary care of the country by enabling earlier diagnosis of diseases like TB at the community level.

Primary Care Triage and Virtual Assistants In the United Kingdom, one high-profile example was that of the NHS partnering with Babylon Health to provide an AI-triage chatbot for the NHS 111 (nonemergency medical advice) service. Patients in the program could input symptoms via a smartphone application and AI would suggest either self-care, pharmacist advice, GP appointment, or emergency care as needed based on the training model. While thousands used the service, independent audits raised concerns of the AI's triage being both overly cautious or occasionally missed serious diagnoses. This emphasized the need for rigorous testing. Another symptom checker, in contrast—Ada Health—was evaluated by the NHS and was found to be reasonably safe giving triage advice, but still not a perfect diagnostic tool. These global studies showed that AI can handle large volumes of patient queries (Babylon's system handling million interactions), potentially reduced call center load in the program. Although, these also illustrate liability and safety concerns: the NHS has to reorient these services to have more clinician oversight for further training. In India, the use of AI chatbots in primary care is at a pretty nascent stage. One case is a state-led project in Telangana where a chatbot was tested for COVID-19 telescreening: citizens answered questions about symptoms and exposure, and the system (using an AI from Haptik) would classify risk and advise on testing or isolation. This helped offload the call centers during the pandemic. In routine care, a few start-ups have developed Hindi or multilingual symptom checkers (e.g., a Bengaluru-based start-up built a WhatsApp chatbot in local language to advise mothers on child health issues). These have seen limited trials. The Indian context poses additional challenges as seen in these case studies: language diversity (AI needs to understand patients describing symptoms in various languages/dialects) and low e-health literacy in some populations (patients might not accurately input information). As a result, the more common approach in India has been telemedicine apps that connect patients to human doctors (like eSanjeevani or private apps), with AI playing a background role (such as sorting patients by urgency based on a simple algorithm, or providing the doctor with a draft note). The case studies globally and in India suggest that AI-driven triage is promising for increasing access, but a hybrid model (AI plus human) is currently safer and more acceptable. Notably, Poland's Symptomate system (used internationally) has not yet been localized for Indian health care, but the company Infermedica announced plans to incorporate epidemiological data from Asia to improve its tool's relevance. Future case studies might soon emerge from India as these tools are piloted in primary care outreach programs.

AI-Enabled Decision Support for Frontline Health Workers The base of health care lies at the roots of primary health care. In many countries, primary care relies on nurses, community health workers, and general practitioners who are required to follow standard protocols and guidelines. Case studies show AI can help reinforce adherence to these protocols through algorithms and systemic checks. In Canada, an AI-based clinical decision support embedded in primary care EMRs was studied—it would prompt physicians if, say, a diabetic patient had not had a foot exam or if a hypertensive patient's BP was above target without medication change. This system led to a modest improvement in guideline adherence (e.g., more referrals to diabetic councillors, more timely medication dose adjustments). In Indian context, the Arezzo pilot mentioned in Table 15.1 is a telling case study. It was deployed in Uttar Pradesh, Arezzo provided an application with integrated *Standard Treatment Workflows* (STWs) for conditions like antenatal care, child illness, and common community infections. Auxiliary nurse midwives (ANMs) used tablets running the AI CDSS during their village visits and clinic hours in the field. For instance, an ANM enters a pregnant woman's details and symptoms; Arezzo guides her through the recommended ANC checklist and flags danger signs for high-risk pregnancy (HRP) (e.g., high blood pressure or edema) leading to a prompt referral. The feedback from health workers was that it boosted their confidence levels and ensured no critical step was missed. However, it was also later revealed—the software was in English and had to be translated to Hindi, during which some medical terms were hard to translate precisely. Additionally, network connectivity in rural areas was problematic meaning sometimes the app could not sync or update in real time. Overall, the pilot did show an increase in completeness of care (more women received the full panel of antenatal services when guided by the app, compared to baseline), indicating that the AI can act as a "digital assistant" to standardize care delivery with continuum of care. Another related example from abroad is the use of AI in community health in Africa: in Uganda, a decision support app for community health workers (powered by a simple AI algorithm) helped them classify childhood illnesses, which resulted in improvement of appropriate referral rates for pneumonia and communicable diseases like malaria. These case studies collectively highlighted that details of implementation matter—success requires customizing the AI tools to local guidelines, training the users, and having fallback plans if the AI or device fails given harsh local conditions or otherwise. When and if done right, AI decision support can extend the reach of quality and tailored primary care through semi-skilled health workers, which is particularly relevant for India's large cadre of ASHAs and ANMs, helping them serve a population of 1.45 billion people.

15.3 Opportunities and Challenges in the Indian Primary Care Context

Currently, India presents a unique environment for AI in health care. On one hand, we have to deal with a vast population facing diverse health needs and a shortage of doctors (especially specialists) in primary care; on the other, a burgeoning tech industry and government push toward integrating digital health into common practice. This juxtaposition creates significant opportunities for AI in Indian primary health care, but also distinct challenges that must be navigated from the grassroots level.

15.3.1 Opportunities

- The doctor-to-population ratio in primary care remains low in India because of disparities in geography and basic amenities with some rural areas having only one doctor for more than 10,000 people. AI systems function and cater a solution to human resource shortages by enabling task-shifting, training, and support operations. The CDSS pilot demonstrates how primary care nurses and health workers like CHOs can use AI diagnostic tools to diagnose and manage more medical conditions than usual while referring patients to doctors only when needed. The consistent operation of AI systems enables us to screen lab results and images without fatigue, which reduces workload. AI automation of routine tasks through AI-driven systems enables frontline providers in India to dedicate their time to patient care because they handle multiple responsibilities.
- The majority of India's population resides in rural areas where specialist medical services remain unavailable till date. The implementation of such AI technologies enables remote diagnosis and patient assessment to help expert medical capabilities to reach distant clinics and deliver specialist insights. The implementation of AI screening for eye disease in rural clinics demonstrates how a single ophthalmologist's expertise encoded in an algorithm can extend to distant locations. Mobile screening units powered by AI technology can travel through rural villages to detect medical conditions which require treatment. The initiative supports India's mission to provide healthcare services to all citizens. The ongoing transformation of 150,000 health and wellness centers (HWCs) under Ayushman Bharat will integrate AI tools to deliver screening services for noncommunicable diseases (NCDs) at community-based facilities (Kumar, 2018). The extensive population of India enables the development of AI models that can serve as solutions for 40% of the world's population because they are trained with data from diverse populations.
- AI enables India to skip traditional infrastructure limitations by creating digital solutions that bypass physical barriers. AI systems combined with basic diagnostic tools can provide temporary solutions to areas without specialist doctors through the implementation of an AI ECG interpretation algorithm for primary health centers that lack cardiologists to detect abnormal ECG readings that

require tele-consultation. The large number of smartphones in rural India enables the deployment of mobile health AI applications for patient education and disease surveillance and decision support. The Ayushman Bharat Digital Mission (ABDM) has established a unified digital health ID and health record system, which provides a foundation for AI applications to analyze nationwide health data and detect real-time care gaps.
- NITI Aayog predicts that AI in health care will drive significant economic expansion because it could generate $1 trillion for India's economy by 2035 across different sectors with health care being a main sector. The health AI start-up sector in India has experienced growth because of these opportunities, which include Qure.ai and Niramai alongside other companies that work on genomics and drug discovery. The combination of these innovations occurs in primary care because it uses AI for disease screening and AI for monitoring chronic conditions. The national AI strategy "AI for All" supports healthcare solutions, while multiple public–private partnerships currently operate. The India AI program (I-Hub) established in 2023 works to develop AI innovation with health care as its main focus (India's Path to AI Autonomy–Atlantic Council, 2025). A tenacious IT workforce in India helps to enable the creation of AI oriented solutions that can address local requirements and train them to be capable of being exported to other developing nations.

15.3.2 Challenges

- *Data quality and availability:* AI systems thrive on data to build and train models—but in Indian primary care, data is often fragmented or inconsistent in quality. Many primary healthcare centers still use paper records, and digital data may not be standardized if at all it exists. The ABDM addresses interoperability, but as of 2025 it is still in its early stages. Moreover, like most AI models are trained on Western datasets, it is increasingly difficult to train them all over again. For example, an AI symptom checker trained on European patients may not account for disease prevalence or presentation variations in India. This can lead to reduced accuracy (a phenomenon where algorithms do not generalize well, known as "algorithmic bias"). Ensuring AI tools are trained or at least calibrated for the local population data is the key. A related challenge is lack of annotated data: developing a high-quality medical AI tool (like a new model for detecting tropical diseases) requires thousands of labeled examples, which are scarce in the Indian context outside a few centers of excellence. There are efforts to build repositories (e.g., the government's initiative to create an India-specific medical image database), but this is an ongoing challenge. If data is key, we are yet to unlock the model.
- *Infrastructure gaps:* The digital infrastructure like computers, network servers and databases at many primary care facilities is not robust or even integrated. The deployment of AI systems faces challenges because of power outages, insufficient Internet bandwidth, and outdated devices at the very least. The TB screen-

ing project encountered connectivity problems at first with X-ray facilities because they needed offline modes to function. The maintenance of equipment presents a challenge because equipment failures, such as digital X-ray malfunctions or tablet malfunctions, can stop AI programs from operating; a simple glitch can halt the workflow. The implementation of AI at large scale requires establishing reliable power systems, network connectivity, and device availability for all 180,000 HWCs (or AAMs). The government's broadband expansion initiative and solar-powered PHC program will help but infrastructure disparities persist during the short-term affecting all avenues of life.

- *Skilled workforce and training:* To use AI efficiently by healthcare workers need training, both for the use of the tools and in interpreting their results.
- Currently, most medical and nursing curricula in India do not include AI, and digital literacy varies widely. There is a risk of either overreliance on AI (trusting it blindly) or under-utilization (distrust or lack of comfort). The case studies showed some health workers were initially intimidated by technology. Thus, change management is a big challenge: it involves upskilling the workforce and fostering a mindset that AI is a tool to complement, not replace, their expertise. Efforts are being made—for example, AIIMS and other institutes have started short courses on digital health for doctors, and the WHO is developing training modules for health workers on AI use.
- *Localization (language and culture):* The linguistic diversity of India requires any patient-facing AI system to support multiple languages. The effectiveness of English-based voice or text AI systems does not translate to understanding patients who speak Assamese or use local expressions. The Arezzo pilot demonstrated that converting clinical algorithms into Hindi required extensive translation work. Symptom checkers require the ability to detect local disease terminology, such as "daayu," which means joint pain in certain dialects to achieve true effectiveness. People from different cultures use their health beliefs to shape their symptom reporting methods. AI interfaces require cultural design elements to achieve equitable use because they need to include simple interfaces for low-literacy users and pictorial guidance options. The lack of localization to state and cultural norms in AI systems would result in serving primarily urban English-speaking populations, thus increasing existing health disparities leaving behind the vernacular.
- *Regulatory and ethical frameworks:* The current healthcare system in India is operating on no specific regulatory framework without any guidelines to govern AI applications. The present approval and oversight operate without a standardized system because India does not have an FDA-style validation system for medical devices and technologies that use AI technology. The current regulations and environment hold no accountability for safety risks to patients while making it difficult to determine who bears responsibility. The responsibility for patient harm resulting from wrong AI tool suggestions at government clinics remains unclear between doctors and tool developers and health system management. The market could become overwhelmed with untested AI health applications because there is no regulatory framework in place. The government has estab-

lished general guidelines (NDHM's principles of security and privacy for digital health), and NITI Aayog has proposed sandbox frameworks for testing AI in controlled environments. Healthcare providers remain cautious about AI outputs because they lack strong standards for implementation. The draft Personal Data Protection law and the new Digital Personal Data Protection Act 2023 (if enacted) will establish requirements for consent and data handling that AI developers need to follow. Most AI algorithms operate as "black boxes," which makes it difficult to achieve transparency in their operations. The system needs mechanisms to prevent discrimination against specific population groups because it fails to detect diseases properly in women and minority populations. The WHO (World Health Organization) requires healthcare organizations to maintain accountability for algorithmic bias and conduct safety audits according to their guidance. The implementation of these ethical principles in India faces an open challenge because patients lack health literacy and are unaware when AI systems participate in their care but trust-building remains essential to the end user.

- *Financial and sustainability concerns:* Although AI solutions promise cost savings in the long run, the upfront investment is really significant. Many primary health centers operate on tight budgets without financial freedom and a chain of red tapings. Procuring AI-enabled devices, maintaining software licenses, and training staff would require funding and a continuous flow. If AI tools are provided through private players, issues of cost, and scalability arise—who pays for each use, what is the cost-effectiveness of the tool used? In some cases, state governments have sponsored pilots through major projects, but scaling nationally would still require integration into government programs. Demonstrating cost-effectiveness is key to unlocking public funding and raising demand: for example, if an AI can prevent enough hospitalizations by early detection, its cost could be justified. Some early economic analyses by NITI Aayog and others are promising (they suggest AI-led interventions in preventive care could give a huge ROI by reducing severe disease burden and improve years of productive life lost, but more India-specific health economics studies are needed to justify the claims). Sustainability also means local capacity: building native and not relying on foreign AI solutions indefinitely which might be costly, so nurturing local development the way India did for generic drugs could be strategic for the future.

15.4 Strategic Integration Roadmap for AI in Primary Care

Deploying AI in primary care needs to be done in a phased and context-specific manner. Based on international experience and the requirements of India, this section provides a strategic plan for bringing AI into primary care. The plan includes the establishment of the groundwork required, piloting and scaling up the innovations, and ensuring long-term sustainability and governance.

- *Developing the digital foundation:* The first step involves developing the digital foundation of the primary care centers. The digital infrastructure requires both hardware elements (power, Internet connectivity, stable power supply, diagnostic equipment that provide digital data, such as digital stethoscopes, X-ray machines, or smartphone sensors) and software platforms (basic digital data capture systems or electronic health record systems at clinics). The Ayushman Bharat Digital Mission is a core effort to create digital infrastructure through Health ID allocation and Health Information Exchange establishment. The phased rollout of infrastructure in PHCs and HWCs should facilitate the use of AI applications with tablet computers with decision support software and cloud-based transmission of scan to AI services. The creation of interoperable data formats is a sine qua non for AI data intake and processing at big data scales. Union Budget and state budgets must allocate funds for primary care digitization. Public–private collaborations may assist this endeavor through telecom operator village outreach initiatives and corporate social responsibility hardware donations. AI utilization will remain limited to compartmentalized pilot zones until a strong ground is laid.

- *Capacity building and training:* While the infrastructure is being implemented, human capacity must receive equal focus. Training modules must be created to enhance healthcare professionals on digital platforms and basic AI concepts. For residents and medical students, clinical AI modules may be introduced so that new physicians are AI-literate right from the beginning. For current primary care workers (doctors, nurses, ANMs, ASHAs), short courses and on-the-job training may be conducted with the emphasis on learning to use relevant specific AI applications in their line of work. For example, if a new smartphone-based AI screening application for oral cancer is developed, dental surgeons and health professionals would need to be educated not just about how to use the app, but also about the interpretation of its result (e.g., what a "high risk" score indicates and what the next step is). Educating them on careful critique of AI suggestions—that ultimate decisions lie with human experts—would also be needed. Another dimension is sensitization: dealing with anxieties about job replacement by AI. Employees must be reassured (and demonstrated through experience) that AI is coming to help, not punitively monitor or replace them. There are usually champions or "superusers," who can be found at some locations—computer-literate staff who are in a position to train and enable others. Eventually, an AI-savvy workforce will be better positioned to optimize these technologies.
- *Pilot implementation and evaluation:* AI solutions need to be tested initially in pilot projects in controlled environments prior to large-scale implementation. Pilot sites of varying settings should be chosen, including rural PHC and urban primary care clinics and tribal area clinics, in order to gain insights from various settings. Each pilot's evaluation design should have definite goals that should answer if AI triage decreases patient waiting time and referral load and if AI screening increases disease detection rate. Pilot evaluation should have a sequential structure which, first of all, examines usability (ease of use by health workers and technical issues) prior to considering outcomes (changes in health indicators and cost savings). The process of evaluation entails collaboration between academic institutions and independent evaluators to obtain rigorous findings by way

of ICMR clinical efficacy studies and health economic cost-effectiveness analyses. The evaluation criteria need to measure both clinical precision and workflow effect and patient satisfaction and any potential unintended consequences (e.g., physicians over-relying on the AI system and overlooking pertinent information it did not flag). The assessment process must involve gathering opinions from end-users in pilot stages so that their comfort levels and improvement recommendations can be learned. The outcome of an initial AI CDSS pilot would reveal the necessity for more regional language support and an easy-to-use interface, which can be corrected prior to widespread implementation. The success of pilots will create evidence and support for wider adoption but failed pilots with significant issues might suggest a need to redirect or abandon the approach. Evidence-based filtering is an essential process to avoid the wastage of resources to ineffective technology.

- *Scaling up and integration into health programs:* The Indian health system needs to have a regulatory framework in place, which should be accompanying its efforts toward AI implementation. Development of such a framework requires involvement of the representatives of Ministry of Health and NITI Aayog and CDSCO and the experts specialized in AI and ethics. An Indian regulatory framework should lay down testing guidelines for the validation of AI-based medical devices through standards originating from global best practices. The US FDA has drawn up an action plan for AI/ML medical software by laying down change control mechanisms to track continuous learning algorithms. Rules have to be framed by the government that every clinical AI software shall utilize Indian data for training or must provide performance figures relating to Indian subgroups. Certification procedure under the name of "Indian Digital Health Device" with accredited laboratory testing for safety and accuracy assessment under STQC or such organizations must be followed. The regulation system should incorporate post-market surveillance obligations since AI technologies require developers to report periodically from the field performance along with adverse event reports akin to pharmacovigilance. The regulation system should create guidelines regarding liability by setting that human providers should have full accountability for decisions but companies will be responsible for product liability when AI devices go wrong. All AI interventions must abide by future data protection regulations by maintaining personal health data storage security and seeking patients' informed consent. The WHO has defined six ethical principles for AI that act as guidelines, which include inclusion and safety and transparency and accountability. The government needs to create an AI in health advisory body for evaluating new technologies while making recommendations and formulating guidelines for their approval. Health care practice standards must be updated periodically to incorporate AI references, so healthcare professionals know how to utilize authorized AI tools effectively. For instance, TB program guidelines must specify that government-approved AI X-ray devices must have at least Y sensitivity for the purposes of screening. Incorporating this provision will authenticate the use of AI tools and give healthcare professionals clear performance thresholds.

- *Regulatory framework and certification:* Concurrent with the implementation process, India must create a regulatory framework for AI in the healthcare sector. This would most likely include a multi-stakeholder process involving the Ministry of Health, NITI Aayog, CDSCO (India's drug/device regulator), and technical/ethical experts in AI. The framework must establish standards for validation of AI-based medical devices—possibly taking a global best practice approach. For example, the U.S. FDA has released an action plan for medical AI/ML software, such as the idea of "predetermined change control" for continuously learning algorithms. India may impose a requirement that any clinically used AI be trained at least on some Indian data or that it report performance metrics on Indian subgroups. A certification procedure (such as an "Indian Digital Health Device" certification) might be implemented where devices are tested by approved labs (perhaps by STQC or other institutions) for safety and precision. Considering that AI can improve with time, the regulatory body must also require post-market monitoring: developers could be obligated to periodically report real-world performance and adverse events similar to pharmacovigilance. And, too, guidelines on responsibility must be established—maybe establishing that, overall, the human provider is liable for decisions, but in the event that an AI machine goes wrong, the company has product liability. On the moral side, regulation should impose privacy safeguards—adherence to the new data protection regulations (e.g., keeping individual health information safe, getting informed consent for AI interventions where appropriate). WHO's six ethics principles for AI (transparency, accountability, inclusion, safety, etc.) can be a guide (Future-Leaders-Healthcare-Estates-Facilities-Management-Joint-Workforce-Strategy.Pdf, 2021). India could also gain by establishing an AI in health advisory body that regularly examines new AI technologies, issues recommendations for approvals (like the United Kingdom's NICE does for new health tech), and publishes guidelines. As part of the regulatory environment, revising medical practice guidelines to refer to AI where applicable would be useful—for example, as part of TB program guidelines stating that "an AI X-ray device approved by the government can be utilized for screening with a sensitivity of at least Y," which makes its use legitimate and establishes a standard.
- *Policy and governance steps:* The following steps will help ensure continued integration of AI by way of policy and governance structures at the highest level. Policy steps may include financing incentives (grants or innovation challenges for coming up with India-specific AI solutions for top primary care priorities such as maternal health or infectious disease). The government must include financial support for established AI tools used in public sector healthcare services through the same subsidies as favoring essential medicines in order to avoid public health care lagging behind private health care. Ethical utilization and equality need policies to implement bias testing on AI tools, which need to confirm their performance in various genders and castes and regions in order to avoid healthcare imbalances. Regular audits by independent bodies should form part of a governance structure, which would carry out annual reviews of AI in primary care through the use of a committee of the sort as an AI ethics commit-

tee. Public engagement is a fundamental governance element through the representation of communities on oversight committees as well as through public education concerning AI in health care in order to maintain trust. Patients must be informed regarding AI-driven decisions by way of comments entered into their medical records (e.g., "This X-ray was first interpreted using an AI algorithm and subsequently read by a radiologist"). The NHS Code of Conduct for data-driven health technologies could be adapted to create a "Code of Conduct for AI in Indian Healthcare" that all stakeholders would pledge to follow through its 10 principles including transparency and accountability and explainability.

- *Continuous learning and adaptation:* Finally, integrating AI is not a one-time project but an ongoing process. The more data is gathered, the more the AI models need to be upgraded to better (e.g., an AI with 100,000 Indian patient records may be upgraded to a superior version when it reaches one million records). This calls for constant learning mechanisms—perhaps the formation of centralized anonymized datasets or biobank for AI, which researchers and corporations can leverage to retrain and test algorithms (under proper governance). It also implies being agile: if a specific AI technology is overtaken by an improved method (let us assume it happens in 5 years, new quantum-computing-based AI will appear), the healthcare system needs to be prepared to assess and implement the new and eliminate the old. Basically, an innovation-savvy environment is necessary, where primary care professionals are receptive to experimenting with novel tools (once tested) and where there is research and implementation funding. There need to be feedback loops: frontline staff need ways to feed back problems or ideas back to developers, so that products become better in user-oriented directions. India can also make global contributions through publishing and documenting results of its primary care AI implementations—building the evidence base and learning from others.

15.5 Policy and Ethical Considerations

AI deployment within primary care needs to be supported by sound policy structures and strict adherence to ethical guidelines. This makes certain that technological advancement is a public health benefit without infringing on the rights of patients or their safety. Some of the major policy and ethical considerations are below, drawing on international standards (WHO, FDA, NHS, etc.) and adapting them to primary care and the Indian context.

- *Safety and efficacy of the patient:* First and foremost, any AI applied in medicine needs to be safe and effective—basically an implementation of the "do no harm" medical ethics principle. Regulatory bodies, such as the FDA, demand safety/efficacy evidence to grant approval for devices; for AI, this translates into conclusive validation testing. In general practice, where AI may inform clinical choice for multiple patients, even a tiny error rate can impact a lot of people. Thus, prospective clinical verification and post-market monitoring are a must.

Policymakers must require independent testing (e.g., an AI diagnostic must be compared against the state of the art in a representative patient population). If an AI symptom checker mistakenly tells a patient with a chest pain to stay at home, the consequences could be disastrous—therefore, there need to be safety nets: that is, AI triage systems may be programmed to err on the side of caution (over-triage rather than under-triage) in order to reduce risk. The human-in-the-loop argument is frequently invoked: AI must assist, rather than completely replace, clinical judgment within primary care. Policies might mandate that AI high-stakes decisions (serious illness diagnosis, initiation of high-risk treatment) always be validated by a human clinician. This is in accord with the recommendation that "AI should assist, not automate, healthcare decision-making." National guidelines might list where the use of AI is acceptable and where it is not—for example, permitting AI for screening but not for writing out a prescription without physician approval.

- *Accountability and liability:* Accountability becomes a complicated process when there is involvement of AI systems in the delivery of care. Determination of accountability is complicated when AI systems are involved in the delivery of care. Establishing liability for AI errors requires policymakers to define clearly. The manufacturer is responsible for product defects when there are concealed flaws in medical devices that cause patient injury even when physicians utilize them appropriately. The practitioner would be responsible for injury caused by violating obvious AI warnings. The medical community needs both well-established guidelines as well as new legal frameworks to manage this scenario. The code of conduct for NHS AI needs the developers to reveal algorithm limitations while medical professionals are fully accountable for their ultimate decisions. The Indian government needs to come out with firm guidelines regarding the implementation of AI in public health care through amendments in the Clinical Establishments Act or new Medical Council regulations. The patients should have access to reporting channels as well as redress when AI processes result in negative events. A nationwide registry of AI-related mishaps with anonymization would be useful for pattern detection toward system improvement.
- *Ethical use:* Fairness principles along with equity measures and bias removal methods form the basis of ethical usage of AI systems. AI systems created from city hospital data can also neglect giving proper care to rural patients and minority groups thereby increasing healthcare inequalities. AI implementation has to remain absolutely ethical in its nature in order to offer services unbiased and free of prejudice. AI system development has to be tested with all those demographic categories that encompass age, gender, and ethnicity and socioeconomic class in order to ensure potential biases are brought to the surface. In the absence of represented data, AI algorithms may learn and spread bias causing severe underestimation of maternal deaths in rural communities. Likewise, rural tuberculosis stigma can cause lower data availability and hence misrepresented sensitivities. Nontypical presentation of angina among women can result in missed myocardial infarction which can be fatal if interventions are delayed. The U.S. algorithms exhibited lesser recommendations for high-level care to Black patients

due to previous data indicating inadequate access to care for these patients; such biases must be actively identified in the case of Indian AI deployments (e.g., avoiding gender bias in estimating the risk of child malnutrition in children from diverse populations). AI algorithms must be subjected to bias audits as part of certification under policies, which make this mandatory. AI systems must be usable by people with disabilities in terms of voice interaction and be able to support multiple languages so that they can be made available to low-literacy users. As per the WHO, the first AI ethics principle requires safeguarding human autonomy in practice that is interpreted in healthcare form as preventing depersonalized care interaction that converts patients into machine contact rather than empathetic systems. Patients must be informed of how to utilize chatbots since they are dealing with artificial intelligence rather than human beings as per examples worldwide. AI programs must have the participation of communities explaining their medical functions in health care while eliminating misconceptions that artificial systems ought to make medical decisions. Ethical AI practices must be implemented through absolute openness regarding the functioning of the AI system and an assurance to avoid unjust care rationing. Use of algorithms to decide on poor patient outcomes does not justify withholding such patients necessary medical referrals since the practice would be unethical. The use of policies must explicitly prohibit the utilization of AI systems for practices contrary to care and justice ethical principles.

- *Privacy and data security:* Privacy of personal health information and data security remain a key concern. Deploying AI systems necessitates large sets of data which poses privacy threats to users. Health data will likely qualify as sensitive personal data within India's evolving data protection system, which calls for explicit patient consent for data use. Application of AI systems for predicting outbreaks and identification of patients requiring intervention calls for robust de-identification and privacy safeguards for longitudinal records of individuals and communities kept in primary care environments. The policies must adhere to HIPAA guidelines when international organizations engage while taking privacy by design models for all health AI products. The WHO recommendations need patient consent and complete transparency regarding the practice of data usage. The AI firm must create data-sharing arrangements that affirm ownership of PHC data by health services while ensuring safe storage in India based on pending regulations and banning selling data and abusing it. The patients must retain the right to opt for whether or not their information will be processed by AI systems when they do not wish to engage (with the exception of surveillance practices that utilize aggregated and anonymized data). The implementation of AI technology provides new software vulnerabilities, which could be used by hackers to steal information through breaches. The policy must include procedures for security verification of AI software and regular updates and breach notification protocols for affected individuals.
- *Transparency and explainability:* Clinicians and patients are more likely to trust and adopt AI if they have some understanding of how it works or why it outputs certain results. There is a growing movement for explainable AI (XAI) in health

care—making AI's decision process more interpretable. For applications that are critical, policies may demand a threshold of explainability. If, for example, an AI marks a chest X-ray as TB-positive, it may be asked to highlight the regions of the image that contributed to that determination (as some algorithms already do by generating heatmaps). This not only instills trust, but enables clinicians to check plausibility. If an AI reports a diabetic patient as being at risk for complications, it would be able to refer to risk factors (e.g., "last 3 HbA1c results high, renal function deteriorating"). The NHS code of conduct has transparency as a core principle—the patients must be aware they are receiving treatment with assistance of AI and the clinicians should be aware of the evidence upon which the AI is working. India's policy may also require AI tools to report to the end users their performance data (sensitivity, specificity, limitations). A novel approach may be an online public registry of certified AI tools with information on them available to healthcare providers and even patients, making it more transparent.

- *Ethical patient-facing AI use:* The ethical framework for patient-facing AI use in primary care must directly engage with the public via symptom checkers and chatbots. The applications must adhere to ethical communication norms. The system must provide proper guidance while also providing safety precautions and informing users that it cannot substitute emergency professional medical treatment (in a similar way app disclaimers are typical). The moral issue with algorithmic nudging happens when health apps are sponsored because it may result in skewed suggestions that lead to patients being directed toward specific hospitals or brands. Policies should be implemented in such a way that it avoids conflicts of interest since government-employed AI-based triage systems must be impartial without any commercial incentives. Digital health interventions must ask users to give informed consent prior to data collection and guidance provision and elucidate the system's operation. Special care is needed in AI mental health chatbot design in primary care settings to be able to manage crisis situations ethically by identifying suicidal ideation and invoking human intervention rather than relying on algorithms.
- *Alignment with global standards and best practices:* The use of global standards and best practices in India will speed up development and ensure quality as the nation works within a global system. The 2021 WHO report on ethics of AI creates a holistic framework that should be adopted by India by adhering to guidelines for safeguarding autonomy and enhancing human flourishing and ensuring transparency and engendering responsibility and accountability and enabling inclusiveness and equity and responsive and sustainable AI. The policy milestones can be formulated based on these guidelines. The responsible party identification requirement is needed for all AI systems to address problems. The U.K. NHS has an AI ethics program that gives AI developers deployment guidelines for NHS systems in the form of evidence-based requirements for usability and effectiveness and monitoring plans. The public health system would do well to create similar guiding documents for innovators who wish to collaborate with them. The U.S. FDA has created an AI/ML-enabled medical device list in the

process of crafting new regulation strategies for adaptive algorithms. The Indian regulatory agency needs to establish fast-track approval processes for AI systems that meet set criteria to encourage innovation but must enforce algorithm change control measures to avoid unmonitored AI drift once they are deployed.

- *Community and stakeholder engagement:* Ethical use of AI in primary care demands more than top-down regulation because it necessitates direct involvement with the stakeholders who will be affected. Public engagement with digital health policies enables individuals to voice their concerns and expectations regarding such policies. Concerns regarding misuse of data and a high priority for face-to-face care mean that policies should direct a hybrid model rather than AI-only services. Guidelines for the use of AI by the medical community will be more well-received when general practitioners are engaged in their creation. Professional organizations such as the Indian Medical Association and Associations of Family Physicians must be involved in debates on AI utilization to formulate their own statements on positions as has been done by the British Medical Association on safety and efficacy and ethical and equitable deployment of AI. Stakeholder involvement results in policies that are practical as well as endorsed by those who must implement them. The process has an educational role that advances stakeholder awareness of AI potential and limits.

15.6 Conclusion

The use of artificial intelligence technology facilitates core enhancements to primary healthcare systems through improved diagnostic ability and optimized public health intervention strategies. The chapter has explained in detail how AI technologies, such as machine learning and NLP, are relevant to primary care screening functions and triage processes and decision support systems. The use of AI in the form of international and Indian case studies is indicative of its ability to improve healthcare outcomes through disease identification at earlier stages and workflow optimization and patient empowerment features. The benefits of AI are most apparent when healthcare professionals leverage AI systems as tools to improve their work instead of carrying out their responsibilities autonomously.

The use of AI technology in India offers a chance to revolutionize service delivery to populations that are not yet served and bridge the chronic shortage of doctors in rural areas. Implementing AI systems successfully involves overcoming key challenges that include infrastructure and training needs and standards and quality of data and ethical considerations. The strategy proposed gave a roadmap that included investment in digital infrastructure and skills followed by pilot testing of innovations prior to scaling successful components and ongoing ecosystem governance and optimization. The key ingredient to this roadmap is rigid conformity to robust policy frameworks together with ethical standards that safeguard patient rights and safety and equity. The WHO with NHS and FDA show us that responsible innovation by way of proper regulation is achievable. The key takeaway for medical students and health policymakers from this study illustrates that the success of AI in health care requires synchronized efforts of tech experts and clinicians, as well as policymakers at the same time.

The professional obligation in the age of AI requires ongoing learning since training tools today will undergo drastic changes in a matter of a few years. Implementation of technology necessitates policymakers to recognize that it does not have a magic solution since they have to pay equal attention to developing an enabling environment and enhancing capacity and building trust within the community. Clinicians should embrace new technology tools that enhance their professional ability while critically examining AI suggestions by validating them against medical standards and specific patient requirements.

References

Abràmoff, M. D., Lavin, P. T., Birch, M., Shah, N., & Folk, J. C. (2018). Pivotal trial of an autonomous AI-based diagnostic system for detection of diabetic retinopathy in primary care offices. *npj Digital Medicine, 1*, 39. https://doi.org/10.1038/s41746-018-0040-6

AI chest X-ray tool made available to radiologists at over 40 NHS trusts. (2024). Retrieved October 26, 2025, from https://www.digitalhealth.net/2024/05/ai-chest-x-ray-tool-made-available-to-radiologists-at-more-than-40-nhs-trusts/

AI in healthcare is India's trillion-dollar opportunity | World Economic Forum. (2022). Retrieved October 26, 2025, from https://www.weforum.org/stories/2022/10/ai-in-healthcare-india-trillion-dollar/

Aissaoui Ferhi, L., Ben Amar, M., Choubani, F., & Bouallegue, R. (2024). Enhancing diagnostic accuracy in symptom-based health checkers: A comprehensive machine learning approach with clinical vignettes and benchmarking. *Frontiers in Artificial Intelligence, 7*, 1397388. https://doi.org/10.3389/frai.2024.1397388

eSanjeevani. Retrieved October 26, 2025, from https://esanjeevani.mohfw.gov.in/#/

Ethics and Governance of Artificial Intelligence for Health: WHO Guidance (1st ed). (2021). World Health Organization.

FDA approves first software that can interpret images without doctor's help. (2018). Retrieved October 26, 2025, from https://www.statnews.com/2018/04/11/fda-ai-software-interpret-images/

Future-Leaders-Healthcare-Estates-Facilities-Management-Joint-Workforce-Strategy.pdf. (2021). Retrieved October 26, 2025, from https://www.iheem.org.uk/wp-content/uploads/2021/02/Future-Leaders-Healthcare-Estates-Facilities-Management-Joint-Workforce-Strategy.pdf

Health, C. for D. and R. (2025). *Artificial intelligence-enabled medical devices*. FDA. https://www.fda.gov/medical-devices/software-medical-device-samd/artificial-intelligence-enabled-medical-devices

Impact Studies | Isabel Peer-Reviewed articles. (2021). Retrieved October 26, 2025, from https://www.isabelhealthcare.com

India's path to AI autonomy—Atlantic Council. (2025). Retrieved October 26, 2025, from https://www.atlanticcouncil.org/in-depth-research-reports/issue-brief/indias-path-to-ai-autonomy/

Kapoor, N., Sanjana, S. N., Davalagi, S. B., Balu, P. S., & Sethia, S. (2024). AI horizons in Indian healthcare: A vision for transformation and equity. *Indian Journal of Community Medicine: Official Publication of Indian Association of Preventive & Social Medicine, 49*(Suppl 2), S210–S216. https://doi.org/10.4103/ijcm.ijcm_806_24

Kumar, A. (2018). *National strategy for artificial intelligence*. Available at https://www.niti.gov.in/sites/default/files/2023-03/National-Strategy-for-Artificial-Intelligence.pdf. Last seen on 20.03.2026

NITI Aayog, & Department for International Trade (UK-DIT). (2021). *A feasibility study to assess the usability, usefulness, and adherence to standard treatment guidelines in Indian healthcare settings with the use of Elsevier's "Arezzo®"—A declarative artificial intelligence–based clinical decision support system and pathway technology (Healthcare Artificial Intelligence Catalyst [HAIC] Pilot Study)*. NITI Aayog.

Physicians' greatest use for AI? Cutting administrative burdens | American Medical Association. (2025). Retrieved October 26, 2025, from https://www.ama-assn.org/practice-management/digital-health/physicians-greatest-use-ai-cutting-administrative-burdens

Sibbald, M., Monteiro, S., Sherbino, J., LoGiudice, A., Friedman, C., & Norman, G. (2022). Should electronic differential diagnosis support be used early or late in the diagnostic process? A multicentre experimental study of Isabel. *BMJ Quality & Safety, 31*(6), 426–433. https://doi.org/10.1136/bmjqs-2021-013493

Vijayan, S., Jondhale, V., Pande, T., Khan, A., Brouwer, M., Hegde, A., Gandhi, R., Roddawar, V., Jichkar, S., Kadu, A., Bharaswadkar, S., Sharma, M., Vasquez, N. A., Richardson, L., Robert, D., & Pawar, S. (2023). Implementing a chest X-ray artificial intelligence tool to enhance tuberculosis screening in India: Lessons learned. *PLOS Digital Health, 2*(12), e0000404. https://doi.org/10.1371/journal.pdig.0000404

Waldren, S. E. (2024). The promise and pitfalls of AI in primary care. *Family Practice Management, 31*(2), 27–31.

Wallace, W., Chan, C., Chidambaram, S., Hanna, L., Iqbal, F. M., Acharya, A., Normahani, P., Ashrafian, H., Markar, S. R., Sounderajah, V., & Darzi, A. (2022). The diagnostic and triage accuracy of digital and online symptom checker tools: A systematic review. *npj Digital Medicine, 5*(1), 118. https://doi.org/10.1038/s41746-022-00667-w

Role of Artificial Intelligence in Strengthening the Primary Healthcare System

16

Krupal Joshi and Krishna Jasani

16.1 Introduction

All individuals, all over the world, are entitled to achieve the highest feasible level of health. This cardinal principle forms the basis of primary health care (PHC), which is the foundation of equitable and inclusive health systems. According to the World Health Organization (WHO), PHC is defined as "a whole-of-society approach to health that seeks to ensure the highest attainable level of health and well-being and their equitable distribution by focusing on people's needs as early as possible along the continuum from health promotion and disease prevention to treatment, rehabilitation, and palliative care, and as close as possible to people's daily environment" (World Health Organization, 2019a).

As the first point of contact for individuals within the health system, PHC plays a critical role in addressing the full spectrum of health needs—from health promotion to end-of-life care—through approaches that are person-centered and contextually responsive. It is widely recognized as the most cost-effective, accessible, and equitable strategy for achieving universal health coverage (UHC). Notably, scaling up PHC interventions in low- and middle-income countries (LMICs) could potentially save 60 million lives and increase average life expectancy by 3.7 years by the year 2030 (World Health Organization, 2019a).

Nevertheless, PHC systems in many countries, especially in low- and middle-income ones, continue to face numerous and complex challenges. Providers in these primary healthcare areas suffer from critical professional shortages, particularly in rural and underserved areas, and this increases their workload and leads to stress

K. Joshi (✉) · K. Jasani
Department of Community and Family Medicine, All India Institute of Medical Sciences, Rajkot, India

U. Venkatesh et al. (eds.), *Multimodal AI in Healthcare*,
https://doi.org/10.1007/978-981-95-9027-8_16

and burnout. Inadequate space for clinics, frequent power interruptions, unhygienic conditions, and lack of essential medicines and medical equipment further exacerbates the poor provision of services (World Health Organization, 2019b; Bigdeli et al., 2014).

In addition, education or ongoing professional development confines providers to addressing changing health needs such as noncommunicable diseases, mental disease, and geriatric care (Cometto et al., 2020).

Administrative inefficiencies are also a major challenge. The existence of multiple disintegrated health information systems coupled with extensive paperwork decreases the time for direct patient engagement (Cometto et al., 2020). Moreover, inadequate associative collaborations and insufficient postoperative support hinder the seamless and organized integration of care. These sociocultural difficulties alongside limited education about health services, societal stigma, as well as deep-rooted patriarchal customs hinder constructive interactions between service providers and users and community involvement (Rifkin, 2009). Compounding these issues is the widespread resistance to adopting digital health solutions, which is frequently rooted in low digital literacy among health workers and a lack of reliable technical infrastructure (Labrique et al., 2018). In this complex landscape, AI presents a significant opportunity to address some of these challenges by automating tasks, providing diagnostic assistance, and improving healthcare access.

16.2 AI in Healthcare

There is no consensus on a definition of artificial intelligence (AI), but WHO has proposed "The performance by computer programs of tasks that are commonly associated with intelligent being" (World Health Organization, 2021a). AI encompasses a broad spectrum of technologies and applications—ranging from machine learning and natural language processing to robotics and computer vision—and is increasingly being utilized across medical disciplines (Esmaeilzadeh, 2024) (Fig. 16.1).

Artificial intelligence (AI) systems and AI-powered tools have been utilized in healthcare to support a wide range of functions and objectives (Fig. 16.2). The intended purpose of an AI application typically corresponds to a specific healthcare need or goal it aims to address, while the associated task refers to the particular function or process the AI system is designed to automate or facilitate.

Digital health tools have significantly transformed healthcare delivery by enabling providers to gain a more comprehensive and integrated view of patient health. These tools facilitate real-time access to patient data, thereby enhancing the ability of healthcare professionals to make informed clinical decisions. Concurrently, they empower patients by providing them with detailed health statistics and

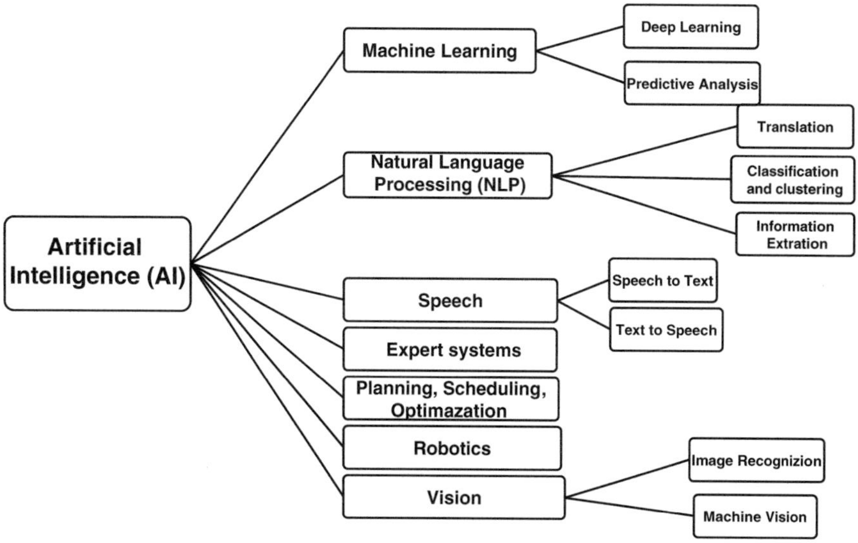

Fig. 16.1 Spectrum of technologies and applications of artificial intelligence

personalized health insights during their clinical encounters. These technological strides offer powerful chances to enhance treatment results and overall effectiveness. Yet, anxiety is mounting around the psychological dimensions of these tools, particularly as patients, the public, and even clinicians increasingly engage with social media and smart mobile applications (World Health Organization, 2021a, b).

Furthermore, the convergence of various platforms—health information systems, wearable technologies, telemedicine and mobile health apps, telehealth networks, medical imaging, and a range of AI-based solutions—has created enormous oceans of big data (Briganti & Le Moine, 2020). This information-saturated space is now fertile ground for machine learning and artificial intelligence in health systems. These systems take advantage not just of the clinical encounters, but also of research databases, patient-generated data, and advanced algorithms that scour petabytes of data and allow them to adapt and to create responsive, adaptive strategies for patient care (Hu et al., 2016).

In addition, electronic health records (EHRs) represent an important component of this data infrastructure, including a wide range of patient-specific health information including medical history, diagnosis, medical regimes, and clinical results. When integrated effectively, these datasets can be distributed through advanced AI functions for the patient's care (Al Kuwaiti et al., 2023). In this evolving digital landscape, AI continues to establish itself as a pivotal enabler for the application of big data in healthcare, offering the potential to revolutionize both clinical practice and health system management.

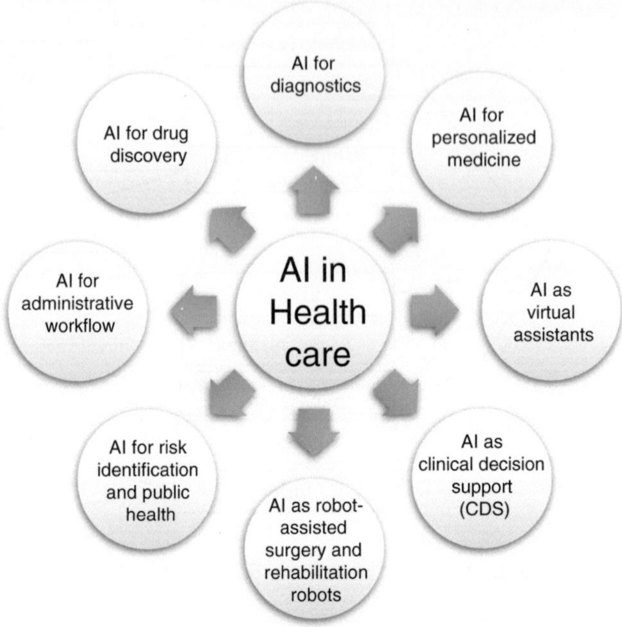

Fig. 16.2 Role of artificial intelligence in health care

16.3 Applications of Artificial Intelligence in Strengthening Primary Health Care

Within primary care, AI-powered decision support tools can assist clinicians in diagnostics and treatment planning, thereby improving accuracy and efficiency. Additionally, automation of routine administrative functions can reduce provider burden, while AI-driven supply chain systems enhance the availability of essential drugs and equipment. AI-powered telemedicine platforms have the potential to greatly enhance access to specialist consultations and healthcare services, especially in remote or underserved regions. By leveraging predictive analytics from extensive datasets, we can improve workforce planning, catch disease outbreaks early, and implement health interventions based on solid data. When we weave AI innovations into the existing primary healthcare framework, health systems, particularly those in resource-limited environments—can make significant strides in service delivery, boost patient outcomes, and enhance overall system performance (Labrique et al., 2018) (Table 16.1).

Table 16.1 Role of artificial intelligence in primary health care: applications, opportunities, and implications

Role of AI in primary health care	Description
AI for risk prediction and public health surveillance	AI can transform the way public health officials track and react to health threats. AI has the ability to revolutionize public health surveillance by analyzing data automatically, identifying potential outbreaks, and providing early warnings. For instance, amid the COVID-19 pandemic, the U.S. Centers for Disease Control and Prevention (CDC) utilized AI to assist in monitoring how the virus spread. They integrated information from electronic health records (EHRs), media reports, and social media messages to discover early warnings of outbreaks. This helped health agencies respond more quickly and make better-informed decisions using real-time evidence. AI systems are able to search big data that humans would never be able to analyze in time, rendering them critical agents for early disease outbreak and health hazard detection (Al Kuwaiti et al., 2023)
	AI also plays an important role in predicting the future trends of noncommunicable diseases (NCDs), like heart disease, diabetes, and cancer. These diseases are a major cause of death worldwide. AI models process a broad array of data, such as individual behaviors, demographic information, and environmental aspects. This enables public health authorities to know which groups are most at risk and where interventions should be concentrated. For example, AI-integrated mobile and point-of-care applications can facilitate timely screening and risk stratification for noncommunicable diseases such as hypertension and diabetes, as well as infectious diseases like tuberculosis and cervical cancer. These AI systems can analyze real-time data from portable diagnostic devices, electronic health records, and even voice or image inputs to support frontline health workers in making early, evidence-based decisions. Such innovations not only improve diagnostic accuracy but also bridge human resource gaps in peripheral health systems, reduce diagnostic delays, and enhance the efficiency of community-level interventions. Moreover, AI can review death certificate data for identifying early signals of increasing drug overdose fatalities before the official coding is done. This affords officials an early start in dealing with emerging health challenges, which can save thousands of lives. The capacity to predict NCD patterns allows for improved planning and investment, ultimately minimizing disease burden (Fisher & Rosella, 2022)

(continued)

Table 16.1 (continued)

Role of AI in primary health care	Description
	In addition to traditional health information, AI reaches into behavioral epidemiology by monitoring data from mobile apps and social media. These platforms provide real-time insights on how people live. AI programs track patterns of physical activity, eating habits, mobility, and social contacts. For example, information from fitness apps can indicate the level of physical activity in a population and identify areas where a try at health promotion is needed. This also enables health authorities to assess whether certain programs or policies actually change health habits. Should an intervention promote increased walking or a healthier diet, AI can quantify its effect by gauging social media talk and application use. This ability assists in generating more focused, effective health promotion tactics (Dignum et al., 2020; Mac Aonghusa & Michie, 2020)
	Mental health monitoring is another field in which AI is strong. Sentiment analysis, which is a machine learning-based method of determining feelings and opinions posted on the web, assists in monitoring mental health trends in groups of individuals in general. From statements and responses posted on social media, AI can identify warning signs of escalating anxiety, depression, or stress for certain groups. Real-time surveillance enables health authorities to respond sooner to mental health emergencies and adjust response programs as needed. It also illuminates the impact of events at a population level, for example, economic recession or social unrest, on mental wellness. Together, these AI-driven tools provide a better insight into the mental health landscape and help public health response and guide resource management more effectively (Saha et al., 2022; Wang et al., 2024)
AI in public health communication	AI is transforming how public health officials communicate with the public. Advanced algorithms scan big sets of data, including demographic data like location, age, and gender, and behaviors of users. It allows messages to be addressed to specific groups, thereby making them more relevant and even easier to understand. For example, using techniques like k-means clustering, AI can identify groups of people having similar attributes. This allows health campaigns to target their messages based on cultural values and language use, thus being more effective. Lasso regression also helps to reveal the most influential factors of health behavior, and based on this, it helps in prioritizing the most effective way of communication. This level of targeting makes the health message more comprehensible, especially in groups that would otherwise not understand or trust them (Bashingwa et al., 2023)
	AI also plays a vital role in fighting misinformation. During health crises like the COVID-19 pandemic, false claims and rumors spread quickly. To counter this, organizations such as the World Health Organization used AI-powered chatbots on popular platforms like WhatsApp. These chatbots provided accurate, easy-to-understand health advice and dispelled harmful misinformation in real time. They could respond instantly to hundreds of queries, giving users trusted information when they needed it most. Chatbots help prevent false health advice from spreading by directing people to reputable sources. They are especially effective because they are available 24/7, do not judge or dismiss users, and can handle multiple conversations at once. The use of AI in these tools has shown that it can significantly improve public understanding of health issues. It also saves time for health professionals by managing common questions and concerns online, allowing them to focus on more complex cases. Overall, AI is changing how health information is shared, making messages more targeted, clear, and trustworthy, especially in times of crisis (World Health Organization, 2022). Chatbots have proven effective in improving public understanding and directing individuals to trustworthy sources

Role of AI in primary health care	Description
AI in telemedicine for primary health care	AI plays a key role in improving telemedicine for primary healthcare services. It makes virtual doctor visits more effective by allowing quick and accurate assessments of patient needs. With AI-driven tools, healthcare providers can greatly improve how they handle remote consultations, making them more efficient and reliable. Chatbots fueled by artificial intelligence are frequently utilized to assist patients prior to a visit with a doctor. They inquire about symptoms, collect pertinent health data, and decide if a same-day visit is necessary or if the patient might wait. This purpose saves time for doctors and avoids unnecessary appointments, especially when patients are high-volume
	AI also mechanizes triage, helping to sort patients according to primarily the urgency of their health conditions. In doing so more urgent cases are identified earlier, enabling providers to attend to patients who need urgent care. Additionally, remote monitoring equipment in real time closely monitors patients afflicted by long-term ailments such as diabetes or cardiovascular diseases. These equipment monitor data from wearable devices and alert healthcare providers if a patient's health declines. This kind of monitoring detects issues early, often before they become critical. Monitoring catches troubles early, frequently before they become dire
	The developments in question have especially been recognized as useful in places that are rural and lacking in resources. Individuals living at a great distance from primary health centers usually endure long trips just to get their simple checkups done. The telemedicine powered by AI is the solution to this as it gives them the opportunity to access medical care straight from their homes. The health workers in the mentioned hard-to-reach areas can have the aid of the AI to continue carrying out their care for the patients, thus minimizing the possibility of severe health problems arising and of the patients having to go to the hospital. This procedure turns primary health services into providers that are more flexible, more accessible, and more responsive especially for those who are the most dependent on remote health care solutions

(continued)

Table 16.1 (continued)

Role of AI in primary health care	Description
AI for administrative workflow optimization	AI systems are now taking over common administrative tasks in many primary care sites. This includes tasks such as welcoming the patient as part of the registration process or coordinating the patient's presence during routine patient healthcare, as well as completing the billing and scheduling process. Smart software automates and takes the burden on many work processes, saves time spent with patient experience for paper documentation paperwork processes, contributes to less time spent waiting for patients, and less demands for the work resource contained with a staff member's work. AI automates routine work processes, for example, AI kiosks allow patients to check-in at registration either by a tablet or by using a kiosk, with the ultimate goal of reducing the front desk registration and check-in paperwork paraphernalia normally taken care of by the front desk staff. Automated billing systems process payments quickly and accurately, cutting down on errors and delays. Scheduling tools optimize appointment times, minimizing gaps and overlaps that could cause frustration for both staff and patients. These advancements not only save time but also improve the accuracy of administrative data, making clinic operations smoother (Juluru et al., 2021)
	A further advancement involves voice-enabled AI documentation tools. With these, physicians can utilize voice commands to capture notes during or after a patient visit. Rather than typing reports or filling out forms after-hours, doctors can use natural speech that the software will turn into coherent documentation while maintaining an explicit level of detail. In a recent study, the voice documentation tool allowed physicians to spend significantly less time on paperwork and more time on patient diagnosis. The use of voice documentation by physicians results in a dramatic decrease in the time spent on clerical work and at the same time an increase in the time spent on patient evaluation and treatment of physicians. The improvement in organizational efficiency brings about better consultation quality, since the doctors are able to maintain full attention during the patient visits without being distracted by visiting administrative pressures (Juluru et al., 2021)
	Such innovations are pioneering the way of working for primary healthcare staff in several aspects. They take away administrative burdens and, thus, the staff can devote the time saved to quality care and making difficult decisions. Staff can now respond to patient needs more quickly, handle a larger number of patients, and provide a better service, which means that primary health care is more capacity-filled, more appropriately, flexible, and accessible in this case
AI as virtual health assistants	Utilization of chatbots and virtual assistants powered by AI can enhance access to PHC via health education; responding to simple health queries; appointment scheduling; and triaging. In the underserved areas, the above serve as first-line triage systems, providing advice and facilitating self-care (Fan et al., 2021)

AI for diagnostics in primary care	AI algorithms support frontline health workers in interpreting clinical data, including radiographic images, sensor data from wearable devices, and electronic health records (EHRs), to detect early signs of diseases and risk factors. For example, AI tools such as Qure.ai are capable of analyzing chest X-rays to detect conditions like pneumonia or tuberculosis. Likewise, image recognition algorithms can detect diabetic retinopathy from retinal scans, or identify skin abnormalities using dermatoscopic images to provide timely diagnosis and referrals (Castiglioni et al., 2021)
	Academically qualified social health activists (ASHAs) are a critical frontline function in the primary healthcare system of India, the vital intermediary between the community and the health facility. Yet, training constraints, clinical skills deficits, and the lack of access to timely direction may limit the latter's potential to properly triage or direct care trajectories. Mobile apps with AI engines and decision support systems are increasingly being hailed as useful facilitators that can fill these gaps. These devices, which tend to be offline-capable and in local languages, can help ASHAs pick up danger signs at antenatal, postnatal, or child health visits. For instance, an AI-powered application would walk an ASHA through a systematic symptom checklist, process real-time inputs, and provide recommendations on referring a mother for potential preeclampsia or seeking emergency care for a newborn showing signs of sepsis. These systems also allow for prioritization of follow-ups, reminders, and alerts for high-risk individuals, thus facilitating community-level early intervention. Embedding AI into ASHA workflows not only enhances decision-making and care coordination but also increases trust and participation among communities served by them
AI for personalized primary care	In PHC, AI is the one that enhances the timeliness and accuracy of the delivery of precision medicine through the assessment of individual-level data—genes, lifestyle, and clinical histories, which consequently leads to the creation of data-informed care plans. This also responds to chronic disease management, which involves patient-specific drugs, preventive measures, and lifestyle modification tactics, especially for noncommunicable diseases (NCDs) like diabetes and hypertension, among others (Johnson et al., 2021)
AI for clinical decision support (CDS)	AI tools provide clinical decision support to primary care practitioners in real time and based on evidence, by pulling together clinical guidelines, patient data, and risk analysis. These kinds of systems can assist in prioritizing cases, suggest investigations, and identify patients who require urgent referral to a higher level of care. A good example of this includes AI algorithms that will scan if a pregnancy is indicated as high risk or forecasting the probability of sepsis, based on clinical input (Khosravi et al., 2024)
	AI has transformative possibilities in enhancing maternal and child health (MCH) outcomes, particularly in low-resource environments. Antenatal care (ANC) and postnatal care (PNC), which are integral parts of primary health services, can be supplemented by AI in terms of early identification of risks and timely intervention. For example, AI algorithms learned from electronic health record (EHR) data have the ability to forecast high-risk pregnancies on the basis of factors like maternal age, obstetric history, hemoglobin counts, trends in blood pressure, and ultrasound scan results. Such prediction algorithms can notify frontline health workers at PHCs to refer high-risk cases for specialized care, thereby lowering maternal and neonatal morbidity. Likewise, computer-augmented mobile applications and decision-support systems can help accredited social health activists (ASHAs) and auxiliary nurse midwives (ANMs) detect neonatal danger signs—for example, poor feeding, hypothermia, respiratory distress, or jaundice—during home visits. Such systems, commonly with visual or voice-enabled interfaces in local languages, increase early detection and prompt referral, which are essential for maximizing neonatal survival rates in underserved and rural areas

(continued)

Table 16.1 (continued)

Role of AI in primary health care	Description
AI in drug discovery and rational use	While the vast majority of drug discovery occurs in tertiary care and research facilities, the primary health care (PHC) sector also shares the benefits of drug discovery, particularly through AI-enabled platforms that promote rational drug use. These platforms can make recommendations on optimal drug combinations, alert users to potential drug interactions, and provide real-time adherence monitoring (David et al., 2020)
AI for assistive technologies in rehabilitation	Although more common in tertiary care, AI-powered assistive technologies are being adapted for PHC-level rehabilitation services. Robotic systems and AI-guided devices can facilitate physical therapy for elderly or poststroke patients, enabling home-based rehabilitation under remote supervision (Panesar et al., 2019)
AI in environmental health and resource allocation	AI-powered tools have been employed to monitor urban air quality using machine learning and remote sensing data. In health systems planning, AI has contributed to optimising COVID-19 vaccination campaigns by analyzing demographic, geographic, and health system data to determine ideal vaccination site locations (Mellado et al., 2021)

16.4 Country-Specific Innovations in AI for Primary Healthcare Delivery

The global landscape of artificial intelligence (AI) integration into primary health care (PHC) reveals a diverse array of innovations, driven by local contexts, technological readiness, and health system priorities. Real-world implementations in both high-income and low- and middle-income countries (LMICs) offer valuable insights into how AI can bridge gaps in access, quality, and efficiency of primary care services.

Numerous governments worldwide have formally approved or piloted AI-based solutions to strengthen primary healthcare delivery. Rwanda's Ministry of Health partnered with Babylon Health to provide AI-driven virtual triage under the national insurance scheme. In India, Google's ARDA tool for diabetic retinopathy screening was piloted with MoHFW collaboration. Thailand's Ministry of Public Health implemented AI tools for medicine forecasting at rural PHCs, and Kenya's Ministry of Health has deployed AI-assisted cervical cancer screening tools in PHC clinics. During the COVID-19 pandemic, Brazilian state health systems adopted the AI-based digital nurse "Laura" to reduce PHC burden. China's National Health Commission endorsed AI tools like Tencent Miying to enhance diagnostic capabilities in township health centers. These examples highlight how government-led integration of AI can address critical gaps in primary care services (Table 16.2).

Table 16.2 Examples of country specific initiative/tool in AI for primary health care delivery

Country	Initiative/tool	Application area	Government role	Reference
Rwanda	Babyl AI Chatbot	Symptom triage and virtual consultations	Officially integrated with national health insurance; partnership with ministry of health	Rwanda MoH, 2021; Babylon Health Reports
India	Google ARDA	Diabetic retinopathy screening in PHCs	Piloted in PHCs with MoHFW support; in collaboration with Aravind Eye Hospital	MoHFW India, 2023; Aravind Eye Care
India	Ayushman Bharat Digital Mission (ABDM)	Foundational digital ecosystem with AI integration potential	National Health Authority-led initiative to digitize PHC services	ABDM Framework Document, NHA 2023
Thailand	AI-based Medicine Forecasting	PHC logistics and inventory management	Implemented by ministry of public health to optimize medicine supply in rural clinics	UNESCAP Report 2021; Thai MoPH

(continued)

Table 16.2 (continued)

Country	Initiative/tool	Application area	Government role	Reference
Kenya	VIA-AI (Visual Inspection AI)	Cervical cancer screening at PHC level	Piloted by ministry of health in PHC settings, with international collaboration	Kenya MoH 2022; Qure.ai
Brazil	Laura Digital Nurse	COVID-19 risk triage and patient guidance	Adopted by state public health systems (SUS) during pandemic	Fiocruz, 2021; Brazilian State Health Departments
China	Tencent Miying AI Platform	Imaging diagnostics in township health centers	Supported by national health commission to strengthen rural diagnostic capacity	NHC China Report, 2020

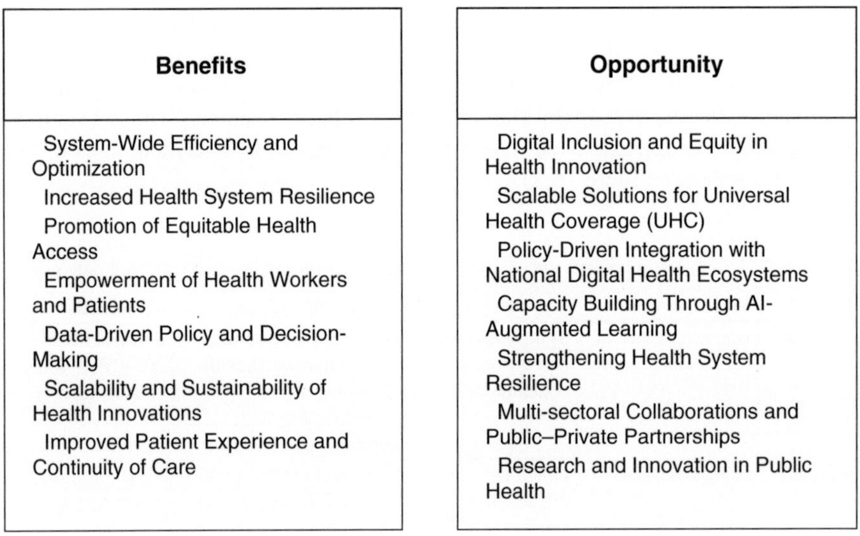

Fig. 16.3 Strategic benefits and emerging opportunities of artificial intelligence in primary health care

16.5 Benefits and Opportunities of Adopting Artificial Intelligence in Primary Health Care

The adoption of artificial intelligence (AI) in primary health care (PHC) systems represents a paradigm shift in how essential health services are delivered, monitored, and optimized. While applications of AI have been explored extensively, it is equally important to understand the broader systemic and strategic benefits that accompany AI integration in PHC—particularly in the context of low- and middle-income countries (LMICs), where primary care remains the bedrock of health service delivery (Fig. 16.3).

16.5.1 Benefits of Adopting Artificial Intelligence in Primary Health Care

16.5.1.1 System-Wide Efficiency and Optimization

- The adoption of AI facilitates the optimization of PHC systems by automating routine processes, enhancing scheduling mechanisms, and streamlining patient flows. AI algorithms can support the intelligent allocation of appointments, predict patient-load trends, and improve referral linkages between different levels of care.
- These efficiencies lead to decreased waiting times and duplication of services, as well as a more effective use of existing human resources and materials—facilitating an overall more adaptive and responsive healthcare system (Panesar et al., 2019).

16.5.1.2 Increased Health System Resilience

- AI improves the resilience of PHC systems, by providing real-time monitoring, alerts, and predictions. In public health emergencies, such as pandemics, natural disasters, or epidemics, AI tools can assist with dynamic modeling of transmissibility and risk, and enable rapid deployment of resources. With this type of preparedness, the care pathway can continue, and the health system can absorb, adapt, and recover from shock and disruption (Panesar et al., 2019).

16.5.1.3 Promotion of Equitable Health Access

- AI-enabled solutions, specifically when implemented using digital platforms, support the reduction of health access inequalities by bringing health services to marginalized, geographically remote, or underserved populations.
- AI reduces the spatial, infrastructure, and human resources barriers of health access utilizing virtual consultations, automated triage, and community-based data. AI will support realization of universal health coverage (UHC) by ensuring coverage types reach all population levels (Johnson et al., 2021).

16.5.1.4 Empowerment of Health Workers and Patients

- The introduction of AI helps frontline healthcare personnel to a greater extent with the provision of clinical decision support tools, automated note-taking systems, and learning resources.
- This brings down the mental effort required, boosts the self-assuredness in clinical decision-making, and lets the doctors deal with more challenging patient issues. Meanwhile, the patients utilizing the AI-supported applications for monitoring their health, getting aware of their health, and participating in their care plan are energized. Trust is a by-product of empowerment and thus, health systems are more open to the public and health-seeking behavior is encouraged (Mellado et al., 2021).

16.5.1.5 Data-Driven Policy and Decision-Making

- The use of artificial intelligence in healthcare creates the possibility of obtaining data of the highest quality that is both timely and useful by carrying out the processing of numerous different and varied sources such as electronic health records (EHRs), mobile health applications, and community health data sources.
- The AI-powered analysis or dashboard tools will be available through which policymakers and health administrators can monitor health trends, evaluate program performance, and identify or create services to minimize inequities in access to care. As a result, this will facilitate clinical and context-specific responsiveness, enabling fast decision-making (Johnson et al., 2021).

16.5.1.6 Scalability and Sustainability of Health Innovations

- When proven, AI solutions can be rolled out at scale at a marginal cost, so the cost diminishes to where it is no longer prohibitive for large-scale implementation. In addition, they can be scaled up between various healthcare settings and population segments, making their adoption more sustainable.
- Similarly, AI applications are updated and enhanced constantly using local data, keeping them context-applicable while remaining informed by national and international health priorities (Johnson et al., 2021).

16.5.1.7 Improved Patient Experience and Continuity of Care

- Embracing AI enables seamless, patient-centered care pathways that connect services across providers and levels of care. Personalized recommendations, automated follow-up reminders, and interoperable health records along the care continuum (and especially in the case of chronic disease) improve the patient experience and continuity of care. Therefore, AI has great potential to enhance adherence to treatment, exacerbate the fragmentation of care, and ultimately improve long-term health outcomes (Johnson et al., 2021).

16.5.2 Opportunities of Adopting Artificial Intelligence in Primary Health Care

16.5.2.1 Digital Inclusion and Equity in Health Innovation

- The rise in use of mobile phones, Internet, and digital literacy in LMICs holds the prospect of creating AI-facilitated health solutions. AI technologies, such as speech recognition, NLP, and voice-controlled interfaces, can reach and serve various populations if factors such as culture, language, and access are built into their design, even low-literacy populations or those from vernacular-speaking areas. Evidence is surfacing to show how inclusive design strategies to AI will not only provide digital health breakthroughs, but also assist the digital health experience avoid harmful and/or complicate health equity by ensuring AI works for equity and not widens health gaps (Fisher & Rosella, 2022).

16.5.2.2 Scalable Solutions for Universal Health Coverage (UHC)

- The scalability of AI may be one of its most important advantages over other technologies. Once developed, trained, and validated, deploying the AI algorithm at additional health systems can occur very rapidly, and at minimal cost.
- That allows important health services to be made available to rural, remote, and otherwise underserved populations. By automating triaging of symptoms, making remote diagnostic screening possible, and automating follow-up and tracking, AI makes it easy for governments and public health authorities to scale primary health care across an exceptionally cost-effective model that can be hastened to achieve UHC targets (World Health Organization, 2021a, b).

16.5.2.3 Policy-Facilitated Integration with National Digital Health Systems

- The value AI adds to PHC is maximized when it has connected infrastructure to national digital health strategies. One example is India's Ayushman Bharat Digital Mission (ABDM), which is designed to create integrated digital health systems that include unique health IDs, electronic health records, and interoperability of health networks.
- The definition of AI features, such as clinical decision support, predictive analytics, disease surveillance, and others, bring about consistent data sharing and enable programmatic decision-making in real time. This data alignment advances key policy goals for system-wide alignment to drive sustainability (Hu et al., 2016).

16.5.2.4 Capacity Building Through AI-Augmented Learning

- AI can transform health workforce development through sophisticated deployment of adaptive learning platforms. AI-augmented training can distribute training content and adapt to the existing knowledge, speed and learning styles of the trainee.
- For community health workers and primary healthcare providers, these devices often deliver ongoing commercial development of training content in real time, in local languages and on mobile devices. These training systems support the development of clinical competencies and facilitate the decentralization of quality care in the resource-limit environment (Hu et al., 2016).

16.5.2.5 Strengthening Health System Resilience

- AI is critical to provide resilience in PHC systems, including predicting disease outbreaks, reallocating human resources, and ensuring continued care during challenging times.
- AI can aid moving resources, establishing online visits with doctors, and communicating critical information during pandemics, natural disasters, or issues related to the climate so that a person can receive care even during difficult times. It makes the health system stronger and more flexible (Hu et al., 2016).

16.5.2.6 Research and Innovation in Public Health

- Artificial intelligence-driven analytics open doors to new insights in public health studies by enabling real-time scrutiny of massive complex datasets. These insights assist with disease transmission modeling identifying high-risk populations, monitoring how interventions are effective, and enhancing service delivery.
- Furthermore, AI applications can test the extent to which primary healthcare programs are implemented and the number of individuals they target. This assists in producing valuable evidence to refine policies and determine where resources should be allocated (Al Kuwaiti et al., 2023).

16.5.2.7 Multisectoral Collaborations and Public–Private Partnerships

- Creating and implementing AI in PHC frequently requires collaboration between governments, universities, technology businesses, and civil society organizations. These partnerships between sectors of society foster new ideas, pool expertise and resources, and expedite the creation of AI innovations for the local context. To ensure that these AI innovations are in the public health interest and respect people's rights, it is important to create fair, transparent, and ethical means of leveraging these collaborations (Hu et al., 2016).

16.6 Risk and Challenges and Ethical Considerations

Artificial intelligence (AI) is transforming primary health care (PHC) at an unprecedented rate via predictive disease models, diagnostic support, enhanced patient engagement and improved health systems. However, AI integration in PHC also creates a number of risks, practical challenges and ethical considerations to discuss in the pursuit of responsible, fair and sustainable AI solutions (Fig. 16.4).

16.6.1 Data Privacy and Cybersecurity

- Healthcare AI applications often involve large-scale datasets, which can contain sensitive personal health information (PHI). Violations of patient data privacy can destroy patient trust and statute regulations such as GDPR, India's proposed Digital Personal Data Protection Bill. AI is susceptible to hacking, leaks, and sabotage (Esmaeilzadeh, 2024; Price & Cohen, 2019).

Potential Solutions

- Implement end-to-end encryption and secure data storage protocols.
- Ensure compliance with international data privacy regulations such as Health Insurance Portability and Accountability Act (HIPAA).
- Develop robust cyber-resilience plans and regular security audits.
- Introduce federated learning and differential privacy models to minimize data exposure.

Fig. 16.4 Key risks and challenges associated with the integration of artificial intelligence in primary healthcare delivery

By prioritizing patient privacy and investing in secure systems, healthcare organizations can mitigate the risks associated with AI integration.

16.6.2 Accountability and Responsibility

- There are important questions about accountability when AI is integrated into clinical workflows. At least in the context of AI tools used near the point of care (e.g., for risk stratification, diagnoses support, or referral guidance), it is important to be clear on who takes responsibility for the outcome of the patient. The problem is compounded in PHC practice environments where vendors are likely to rely on decision-support algorithms, potentially in the absence of sufficient human or animal health training. Without transparent mechanisms of accountability, with bad outcomes, both health workers and patients may be confused and lose trust (World Health Organization, 2021a, b).

Potential solutions

- Integrate human-in-the-loop (HITL) systems where primary care providers retain ultimate authority over clinical decisions supported by AI tools.
- Establish standard operating procedures (SOPs) in PHC settings that outline the appropriate use and limitations of AI recommendations.

- Create context-specific regulatory guidance that defines roles and responsibilities of PHC staff, health administrators, and technology developers.
- Promote explainable AI tools tailored for PHC use, enabling providers to understand and communicate how decisions are made.

16.6.3 Time to Production and Scalability

- Many AI tools show promise in research or pilot settings but face challenges in scaling due to insufficient infrastructure, lack of clinical validation, and limited integration with existing health systems (Esmaeilzadeh, 2024).

Potential solutions
- Foster partnerships between health systems, academia, and information technology (IT) industries.
- Conduct large-scale implementation research to evaluate real-world effectiveness.
- Standardize AI validation protocols and certification mechanisms.

16.6.4 Interoperability Issues

The employment of AI applications in primary health care (PHC) is, however, frequently challenged by fragmented health information systems and the absence of smooth information exchange between facilities. Not only are a large proportion of PHC centers siloed (i.e., that the storage of patient records is kept separate), but many utilize no digital records at all or incompatibly, significantly reducing the capability of AI systems to access full, longitudinal patient records—essential for making accurate clinical insights and decisions (Esmaeilzadeh, 2024).

Potential solutions
- Encourage the use of standardized digital record systems at all levels of PHC. This will make it easier to share data.
- Match AI applications with nationally approved interoperability frameworks. This will help integrate them into existing PHC workflows.
- Build and improve national and regional health information exchanges (HIEs). This will allow secure, real-time access to patient data across PHC networks.
- Support training for PHC staff to ensure they can use and understand AI-enabled systems that work together.

16.6.5 Data Scarcity and Bias

- In PHC, AI technology can amplify health inequities if it is based on datasets that fail to capture the diversity of patients it cares for. Rural populations, tribal populations, and other disadvantaged groups are frequently underrepresented in health data. This can lead to biased algorithms that may misdiagnose symptoms, overlook culturally relevant risk factors, or provide less precise recommendations. These inequalities can exacerbate differences in access, diagnosis, and treatment within the PHC system (World Health Organization, 2021a, b; Esmaeilzadeh, 2024).

Potential solutions

- Strengthen data collection systems in primary health settings to ensure inclusion of underrepresented and vulnerable populations.
- Promote participatory data collection approaches involving community health workers and local governance structures.
- Utilize fairness-aware algorithms tailored to diverse demographic and epidemiological contexts common in PHC.

16.6.6 Financial and Regulatory Barriers

- The incorporation of AI in primary healthcare systems is usually hampered by budget constraints at the care point. Budgetary constraints in primary care facilities, particularly in rural and underserved communities, limit buying, training, and maintenance required by AI solutions. Additionally, the absence of explicit regulations regarding AI in primary health care makes clinical accountability, data handling, and ethics uncertain. This hinders the process of implementation and upscaling (World Health Organization, 2021a, b; Wahl et al., 2018).

Potential solutions

- Careful planning, collaboration, and strategic investment must come together to overcome these financial obstacles. Government assistance, public–private partnerships, and innovative financing models can make the integration of AI in health care more accessible so that everyone can enjoy AI throughout the healthcare continuum.
- Create flexible and inclusive regulatory pathways that reflect the realities of community-based healthcare delivery.
- Connect AI adoption with value-based or outcome-based payment models to encourage effective and fair use of AI in primary health care.

16.6.7 Ethical and Bias Concerns

- Ethical issues regarding the use of AI are highly significant due to the continuous engagement of patients with the healthcare professionals. AI systems can perpetuate existing health inequities when they are taught from biased or unrepresentative data. This especially impacts marginalized and underserved communities. It could result in biased clinical decisions, reduced quality of care, and erosion of confidence in the healthcare system. Further, insufficient transparency about how recommendations are generated by AI tools can undermine patient autonomy, constrain informed decision-making, and erode the provider–patient relationship in primary care (World Health Organization, 2021a, b; Esmaeilzadeh, 2024).

Potential solutions

- Bring PHC-centric AI tools in line with ethical frameworks like the WHO's Ethics and Governance of Artificial Intelligence for Health to protect justice, equity, and human dignity.
- Ensure algorithmic transparency and interpretability to support shared decision-making between primary care providers and patients.
- Engage frontline health workers, community representatives, and patients in the development and deployment of AI tools to ensure cultural relevance and ethical alignment.
- Conduct periodic ethical impact assessments to evaluate fairness, inclusiveness, and accountability in PHC settings.

16.6.8 Resistance to Adoption

Healthcare workers might resist adopting AI because of concerns about job replacement, distrust of outputs from AI, or inadequate digital literacy. Patients might also doubt machine-generated suggestions.

Potential solutions

- Provide ongoing training and skill enhancement for health workers.
- Showcase the impact of AI through real-world examples.
- Do not expect AI tools to replace, but rather augment, functions.
- Create community engagement through awareness campaigns and codesign.

While AI holds great potential to enhance primary healthcare delivery, especially with vulnerable populations, it also has some notable limitations that we are aware of, in order to provide a balanced perspective. One important limitation is that many of the front-line PHC workers (e.g., ASHAs, ANMS) have limited digital literacy, and this may restrict effective utilization of AI-enabled tools. Additionally, many rural areas have limited Internet access and unstable power supply, creating feasibility concerns for AI-enabled telemedicine and data analytics. Data security and privacy, as well as the compatibility of AI tools with existing health information systems, and the interpretability of AI's suggested actions further complicate the landscape around adoption. Several health practitioners may struggle to accept, or act on, AI outcomes without being able to see the reasoning behind the predictions and being able to provide a clinical rationale for action. Thus, effective AI integration into PHC work streams will need strong technological solutions, targeted capacity development, enabling infrastructure, and context-specific implementation plans. Addressing these limitations requires a collaborative effort that prioritizes justice and blends technology with moral standards, rules, and policies inclusive of all. By addressing the aforementioned risks early on, we can leverage AI as a powerful instrument to enhance primary healthcare systems and advance universal health coverage (World Health Organization, 2021a, b; Esmaeilzadeh, 2024).

16.6.8.1 Limitations and Challenges of AI Implementation at the PHC Level

While artificial intelligence (AI) holds transformative potential for strengthening primary health care, particularly in rural and underserved settings, several practical, infrastructural, and systemic limitations need to be addressed for effective and sustainable implementation. These limitations are outlined below:

- *Limited digital literacy and training among health workers*
  Most frontline health workers at the PHC level, including accredited social health activists (ASHAs), auxiliary nurse midwives (ANMs), and medical officers, often have limited exposure to digital tools, let alone advanced AI-powered systems. Without appropriate digital literacy and hands-on training, there is a risk that these tools will be underutilized or misused. Furthermore, the lack of user-friendly interfaces and support in local languages can further inhibit adoption among nonspecialist health workers.
- *Inadequate infrastructure*
  A foundational barrier to AI adoption in PHCs is the inconsistent availability of basic infrastructure. Many rural health centers suffer from poor internet connectivity, unreliable electricity, and lack of access to compatible digital hardware (such as smartphones, tablets, or diagnostic devices). These infrastructural gaps make it challenging to deploy real-time AI systems, teleconsultation platforms, or cloud-based data storage and analysis tools, all of which require stable connectivity and power.
- *Low interoperability with existing health systems*
  AI solutions often struggle to integrate seamlessly with existing electronic health record (EHR) systems or national health information platforms. Lack of interoperability between AI tools and government databases (e.g., HMIS, AB-HWC portals) leads to fragmented data systems, duplication of work, and inefficiencies in decision-making. Without standardized data formats and APIs, AI cannot function optimally across varied platforms used within public health systems.
- *Lack of contextual relevance*
  Many AI models are trained on datasets from urban, high-resource settings or from different countries altogether. These models may not account for sociocultural, epidemiological, or demographic differences prevalent in rural India or other low-resource settings. As a result, predictions and recommendations generated by such models may not always be valid or relevant at the PHC level.
- *Limited explainability and clinical interpretability*
  A major limitation of AI in health care is the "black box" nature of many algorithms—where outputs are produced without clear explanation of how the decision was made. The fact that the AI system is not interpretable means that providers at the primary healthcare level, who do not often have specialist skills, will find it hard to understand, trust, or act on the system's recommendations. In contexts where responsibility and human judgment matter, this poses a risk to patient safety and clinical governance.

- *Privacy, security, and ethical concerns*
  Applying AI tools involves gathering and analyzing personal health information. There may be no standard guidelines or infrastructure in PHC for data security and patient confidentiality. This, in turn, poses ethical questions regarding informed consent, misuse of data, and surveillance. In addition, AI systems could perpetuate biases unwittingly if they are trained using unrepresentative or biased datasets.
- *Sustainability and cost constraints*
  Even though AI tools are frequently advertised as ultimately cost-effective, the technological infrastructure, hardware, software licenses, and human resources needed to build, deploy, and sustain new AI tools requires significant upfront and on-going investment. For most primary health care (PHC) centers, working in often resource-limited budget contexts, it may prove difficult for them to continue an AI intervention or technology after an initial developer or donor subsidizes the continuation of AI intervention or digital health technology.
- *Regulatory and policy gaps*
  The rapid pace of AI development has outstripped the evolution of appropriate legal and regulatory frameworks in many low- and middle-income countries. There are often unclear guidelines on approval, certification, quality assurance, and liability for AI-based medical tools, which creates uncertainty and reluctance among health administrators and providers to adopt these technologies at scale.

16.7 SWOT Analysis of Artificial Intelligence in Primary Health Care

The incorporation of AI in primary healthcare systems introduces an intriguing combination of opportunities and challenges. By performing an exhaustive SWOT (Strengths, Weaknesses, Opportunities, and Threats) analysis, the stakeholders—such as policymakers, health planners, and experts in technology—can strategically evaluate how AI can enhance the accessibility, quality, and efficiency of PHC services (Fig. 16.5).

16.7.1 Strengths

- *Improved decision support:* AI systems have the ability to enhance diagnostic accuracy and clinical decision-making based on algorithmic interpretation of symptoms, images, and data trends, especially in low-resource health settings with poor specialist access.
- *Greater efficiency and process automation:* AI can automate routine and administrative tasks like scheduling patients, data entry, and inventory forecasting, thus diminishing the burden on primary care staff and enabling them to work directly with patients.

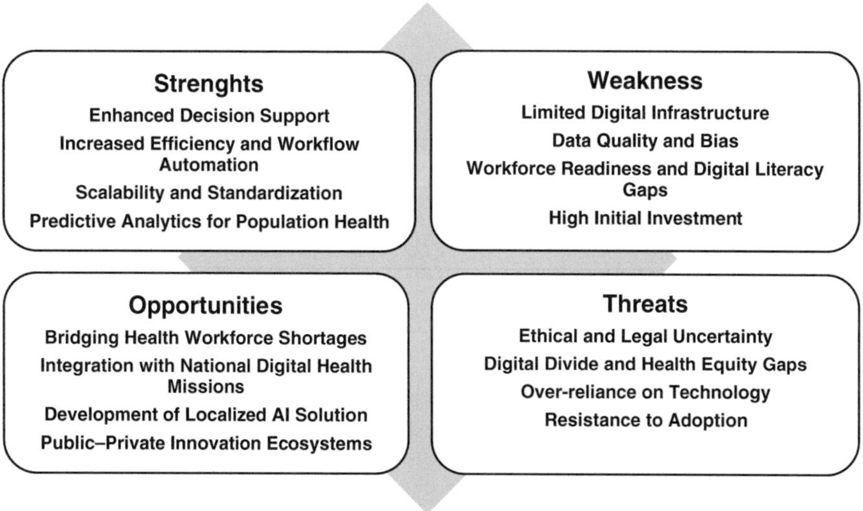

Fig. 16.5 SWOT analysis of artificial intelligence for delivering primary healthcare

- *Scalability and standardization:* AI models are capable of providing high-quality output at scale, facilitating standardized care protocols in decentralized and heterogeneous PHC environments, thereby reducing quality variations in care.
- *Predictive analytics for population health:* Machine learning algorithms can identify at-risk populations, forecast disease outbreaks, and support targeted interventions for chronic disease management, immunization planning, and maternal-child health services.

16.7.2 Weaknesses

- *Limited digital infrastructure:* Many PHC systems in low- and middle-income countries (LMICs) lack the foundational digital health infrastructure (e.g., electronic health records, reliable Internet) necessary for AI deployment and integration.
- *Data quality and bias:* AI models are very much dependent on high-quality, representative data. Variable data collection practices and nonstandardized formats may constraint model performance and exacerbate systemic biases.
- *Workforce readiness and digital literacy gaps:* The current health workforce could not have training to properly interpret and use AI output, risking underutilization or inappropriate application of AI tools.
- *High initial cost:* The expense of developing, deploying, and sustaining AI solutions, such as hardware, software, and training, might be too high for health systems with limited budgets.

16.7.3 Opportunities

- *Bridging health workforce shortages:* AI-enabled tools can extend the capabilities of community health workers and mid-level providers, enhancing task-sharing and compensating for gaps in human resources, particularly in rural or underserved areas.
- *Integration with national digital health missions:* Alignment with government-led digital health initiatives, such as India's Ayushman Bharat Digital Mission or the WHO's Digital Health Strategy, can catalyze AI adoption in PHC through standardized platforms and frameworks.
- *Development of localized AI solutions:* There is growing potential for locally developed, culturally and linguistically tailored AI tools that align with the epidemiological and sociocultural context of the populations served.
- *Public–private innovation ecosystems:* Partnerships between government, academia, and the private sector can foster innovation in AI for PHC, with co-development of tools that are context-sensitive and ethically robust.

16.7.4 Threats

- *Ethical and legal uncertainty:* Inadequate regulatory frameworks for AI in health raise concerns about data privacy, algorithmic transparency, patient consent, and liability in case of errors.
- *Digital divide and health equity gaps:* If not implemented inclusively, AI tools may exacerbate existing inequities, particularly for populations lacking digital access or literacy, thus widening health disparities.
- *Overreliance on technology:* Overdependence on AI systems might compromise clinical judgment, particularly if users are not adequately trained or if system flaws are not identified and addressed on time.
- *Non-adoption:* Professional and cultural resistance by health workers, coupled with fear of losing their job or autonomy, can be a source of regressing to non-adopting earlier practices.

16.8 Conclusion: Reframing Artificial Intelligence in Primary Healthcare—From Threat to Enabler

With advances in artificial intelligence (AI) technologies, primary care networks and public health have been afraid of their capacity to replace current patterns of work, minimize human interaction, or push healthcare workers to the periphery. Stopping job loss, automating choices, or excessive reliance on computer output is by no means far-fetched, particularly within resource-scarce environments where trust in digital solutions remains in the embryonic stage.

In primary health care, specific apprehensions include:

- The automation of screening and diagnostic procedures (e.g., for tuberculosis, anemia, or diabetic retinopathy) potentially support frontline providers and decrease the workload.
- The use of AI-powered virtual assistants and chatbots reducing the need for in-person consultations, particularly in rural or underserved areas.
- The deployment of AI-driven clinical decision support tools that may be perceived as undermining clinical autonomy or local contextual judgment.
- The risk of oversimplifying complex public health decisions through cost-driven algorithmic recommendations, which may overlook social determinants of health.
- Deskilling of health workers as AI systems take over increasingly complex functions, leaving only routine or administrative tasks for human personnel.

But used judiciously and responsibly, AI is a vast potential enabler—not a force for disruption—of the PHC workforce. AI is not intended to be a replacement for healthcare workers; it is instead a force multiplier—one that can expand their ability to work smarter, expand their reach of effectiveness, and boost their productivity for anything they do. By coordinating mundane or clerical work—like finding specialists and scheduling appointments, and entering data, or sorting logistics—AI can free healthcare providers, primary care doctors, nurses, and community health workers, to have deeper interactions with patient-facing care and community outreach.

Additionally, AI applications can aid PHC caregivers in the provision of timely and improved treatment by surfacing clinical knowledge, identifying risky patients, predicting outbreaks, and optimizing resource deployment. AI-based decision support systems, for instance, can help accredited social health activists (ASHAs) or members of the community health workforce detect early signals of maternal complications or noncommunicable diseases in even the most remote contexts, with minimal supervision.

First and foremost, governments and public health organizations should take an active role in co-defining the AI narrative, one not of supplanting human intelligence, but of a partner in supplementing strong, universal and equitable primary healthcare services. In practice, supporting training schemes to upskill the health workforce to work in concert with AI is just one example of recognizing and establishing a paradigm of a positive convergence between human judgment and digital technology.

At the broader public health level, it will be important to reposition AI as a vehicle for innovation and inclusion. When placed within participatory, community-based systems, AI can speed progress toward UHC by increasing service coverage, enhancing surveillance, and strengthening the capabilities of health workers—most notably in lower-resourced contexts.

References

Al Kuwaiti, A., Nazer, K., Al-Reedy, A., Al-Shehri, S., Al-Muhanna, A., Subbarayalu, A. V., Al Muhanna, D., & Al-Muhanna, F. A. (2023). A review of the role of artificial intelligence in healthcare. *Journal of Personalized Medicine, 13*(6), 951. https://doi.org/10.3390/jpm13060951

Bashingwa JJH, Mohan D, Chamberlain S, et al. Can we design the next generation of digital health communication programs by leveraging the power of artificial intelligence to segment target audiences, bolster impact and deliver differentiated services? A machine learning analysis of survey data from rural India. BMJ Open. 2023;13(3):e063354. Published 2023. https://doi.org/10.1136/bmjopen-2022-063354

Bigdeli, M., Peters, D. H., & Wagner, A. K. (2014). *Medicines in health systems: Advancing access, affordability and appropriate use*. World Health Organization.

Briganti, G., & Le Moine, O. (2020). Artificial intelligence in medicine: Today and tomorrow. *Frontiers in Medicine, 7*, 27. https://doi.org/10.3389/fmed.2020.00027

Castiglioni, I., Rundo, L., Codari, M., Di Leo, G., Salvatore, C., Interlenghi, M., et al. (2021). AI applications to medical images: From machine learning to deep learning. *Physica Medica, 83*, 9–24. https://doi.org/10.1016/j.ejmp.2021.03.005

Cometto, G., Buchan, J., & Dussault, G. (2020). Developing the health workforce for universal health coverage. *Bulletin of the World Health Organization, 98*(2), 109–116. https://doi.org/10.2471/BLT.19.234138

David, L., Thakkar, A., Mercado, R., & Engkvist, O. (2020). Molecular representations in AI-driven drug discovery: A review and practical guide. *Journal of Cheminformatics, 12*(1), 1–22. https://doi.org/10.1186/s13321-020-00445-9

Dignum, F., Dignum, V., Davidsson, P., et al. (2020). Analysing the combined health, social and economic impacts of the coronavirus pandemic using agent-based social simulation. *Minds and Machines, 30*, 177–194. https://doi.org/10.1007/s11023-020-09527-6

Esmaeilzadeh, P. (2024). Challenges and strategies for wide-scale artificial intelligence (AI) deployment in healthcare practices: A perspective for healthcare organizations. *Artificial Intelligence in Medicine, 151*, 102861. https://doi.org/10.1016/j.artmed.2024.102861

Fan, X., Chao, D., Zhang, Z., Wang, D., Li, X., & Tian, F. (2021). Utilization of self-diagnosis health chatbots in real-world settings: Case study. *Journal of Medical Internet Research, 23*(1), e19928. https://doi.org/10.2196/19928

Fisher, S., & Rosella, L. C. (2022). Priorities for successful use of artificial intelligence by public health organizations: A literature review. *BMC Public Health, 22*, 2146. https://doi.org/10.1186/s12889-022-14525-9

Hu, J., Perer, A., & Wang, F. (2016). Data-driven analytics for personalized healthcare. In C. B. M. Weaver (Ed.), *Healthcare information management systems* (pp. 529–554). Springer. https://doi.org/10.1007/978-3-319-20765-0_35

Johnson, K. B., Wei, W. Q., Weeraratne, D., Frisse, M. E., Misulis, K., Rhee, K., et al. (2021). Precision medicine, AI, and the future of personalized health care. *Clinical and Translational Science, 14*(1), 86–93. https://doi.org/10.1111/cts.12880

Juluru, K., Shih, H.-H., Keshava Murthy, K. N., Elnajjar, P., El-Rowmeim, A., Roth, C., et al. (2021). Integrating AI algorithms into the clinical workflow. *Radiology: Artificial Intelligence, 3*(6), e210013. https://doi.org/10.1148/ryai.2021210013

Khosravi, M., Zare, Z., Mojtabaeian, S. M., & Izadi, R. (2024). Artificial intelligence and decision-making in healthcare: A thematic analysis of a systematic review of reviews. *Health Services Research and Managerial Epidemiology, 11*, 23333928241234863. https://doi.org/10.1177/23333928241234863

Labrique, A. B., Wadhwani, C., Williams, K. A., Lamptey, P., Hesp, C., Luk, R., & Aerts, A. (2018). Best practices in scaling digital health in low- and middle-income countries. *Globalization and Health, 14*(1), 103. https://doi.org/10.1186/s12992-018-0424-z

Mac Aonghusa, P., & Michie, S. (2020). Artificial intelligence and behavioral science through the looking glass: Challenges for real-world application. *Annals of Behavioral Medicine, 54*(11), 942–947. https://doi.org/10.1093/abm/kaaa062

Mellado, B., Wu, J., Kong, J. D., et al. (2021). Leveraging artificial intelligence and big data to optimize COVID-19 clinical public health and vaccination roll-out strategies in Africa. *International Journal of Environmental Research and Public Health, 18*(14), 7890. https://doi.org/10.3390/ijerph18147890

Panesar, S., Cagle, Y., Chander, D., Morey, J., Fernandez-Miranda, J., & Kliot, M. (2019). Artificial intelligence and the future of surgical robotics. *Annals of Surgery, 270*(2), 223–226. https://doi.org/10.1097/SLA.0000000000003264

Price, W. N., II, & Cohen, I. G. (2019). Privacy in the age of medical big data. *Nature Medicine, 25*(1), 37–43. https://doi.org/10.1038/s41591-018-0272-7

Rifkin, S. B. (2009). Lessons from community participation in health programmes: A review of the post Alma-Ata experience. *International Health, 1*(1), 31–36. https://doi.org/10.1016/j.inhe.2009.02.001

Saha, K., Yousuf, A., Boyd, R. L., Pennebaker, J. W., & De Choudhury, M. (2022). Social media discussions predict mental health consultations on college campuses. *Scientific Reports, 12*, 123. https://doi.org/10.1038/s41598-021-04101-2

Wahl, B., Cossy-Gantner, A., Germann, S., & Schwalbe, N. R. (2018). Artificial intelligence (AI) and global health: How can AI contribute to health in resource-poor settings? *BMJ Global Health, 3*(4), e000798. https://doi.org/10.1136/bmjgh-2018-000798

Wang, S., Liang, C., Gao, Y., et al. (2024). Social media insights into spatiotemporal emotional responses to COVID-19 crisis. *Health & Place, 85*, 103174. https://doi.org/10.1016/j.healthplace.2023.103174

World Health Organization: WHO. (2019a). *Primary health care*. Who.int; World Health Organization: WHO. https://www.who.int/health-topics/primary-health-care#tab=tab_2

World Health Organization. (2019b). *Primary health care on the road to universal health coverage: 2019 global monitoring report. Executive summary* (Licence: CC BY-NC-SA 3.0 IGO). World Health Organization.

World Health Organization. (2021a). *Ethics and governance of artificial intelligence for health: WHO guidance* (Licence: CC BY-NC-SA 3.0 IGO). World Health Organization.

World Health Organization. (2021b). *Global strategy on digital health 2020–2025* (pp. 7–13). World Health Organization.

World Health Organization. (2022). *Chatbots against COVID-1b9: Using chatbots to answer questions on COVID-19 in the user's language*. World Health Organization.

Multimodal AI in Suicide Risk Prediction: Behavioral, Physiological, and Digital Biomarkers

17

Richa Tripathi and Mohd Rashid Alam

17.1 Introduction

17.1.1 Global Burden of Suicide

Suicide is a major public health concern. It is defined as an act of killing oneself with implicit or explicit evidence that the person intended to die. Suicide has accounted for a total of 746,000 deaths in 2021, with 519,000 males and 227,000 female deaths. In 2021 data, the average age at suicide increased over time, reaching 46.9 years for females and 47.0 years for males. While females have higher rates of suicide attempts requiring medical care, completed suicides are more prevalent among males (Singh, 2022). The highest suicide rates were recorded in Eastern Europe, southern sub-Saharan Africa, and central sub-Saharan Africa. Mortality due to suicide has become a public health concern in India. India is observing a high number of suicide rate of 14.04 per lakh population, making it rank 49th worldwide. The highest number of suicides has also been reported annually from India, which cannot be ignored (Yadav et al., 2023).

Suicide is also a significant burden on the world economy. Deaths due to suicide have caused an economic loss equal to 0.12% of the total GDP in 54 African countries in the year 2019. In developed countries, in the same year, the estimated loss was around US$5.53 billion. A global study focusing on self-harm among young people aged less than 24 years estimated the total economic burden at over $251 billion, in which India has contributed the greatest (Nigam et al., 2024).

Understanding these global impacts is important for encouraging more financial, academic, and clinical investment in suicide prevention efforts. Suicide prevention is now a global priority in the United Nations sustainable development goals and is

R. Tripathi · M. R. Alam (✉)
Department of Psychiatry, All India Institute of Medical Sciences, Gorakhpur, Uttar Pradesh, India

U. Venkatesh et al. (eds.), *Multimodal AI in Healthcare*,
https://doi.org/10.1007/978-981-95-9027-8_17

included in the World Health Organization's Comprehensive Mental Health Action Plan 2013–2030 (Pirkis et al., 2024). In order to achieve these goals and reduce suicide rates in an effective manner, a change in approach for screening and early detection becomes mandatory.

17.1.2 Limitations of Traditional Suicide Prevention Approaches

Traditional suicide prevention strategies largely rely on clinical presentation of the individual and their expression of distress in mental status examination and history. However, the data show that many individuals who have completed suicide do not express their suicidal thoughts in their hospital visits. A study indicated that only 16–20% individuals consulted healthcare providers in previous week of their suicide and 34–38% in the previous month. Most individuals expressed psychological distress in their visits, but suicide ideations were either not assessed or documented (Raue et al., 2014). This occurs mostly due to hesitation of clinicians to initiate discussion about suicide, probably due to thinking that talking about suicide may increase suicidality, and similarly, patients often do not express themselves unless asked directly. The problem multiplies considering the absence of reliable short-term predictors of suicide, time constraints in OPD visits, and suboptimal professional training in suicide risk assessment. Apart from this, current guidelines do not recommend routine screening for suicidality in asymptomatic individuals. Other limitations include a lack of effective and practical national prevention strategies, a lack of awareness around the decriminalization of suicide, and poor interdisciplinary collaboration (Ryan & Oquendo, 2020).

17.1.3 Emergence of Artificial Intelligence (AI) in Mental Health

AI chatbots are being increasingly used for emotional support by individuals with psychological distress. Moreover, AI is working as an assistant for clinicians in analyzing unstructured and large datasets, analyzing cognitive functioning such as attention, concentration, calculation, and memory. Plus, AI-based models have the capability to recognize physiological arousal related to different emotions in the body, like autonomic hyperactivity, facial expressions, change in voice, and psychological signs of distress. Newer AI technologies, such as machine learning models, convolutional neural networks (CNNs), and support vector machines (SVMs), can analyze neuroimaging scans, EEG waveforms, and specific biomarkers for early detection of neurodevelopmental as well as neurodegenerative disorders (Gkintoni et al., 2025). AI tools can also assist mental health professionals by performing assessments, therapy, and monitoring in patients. AI tools like chatbots, mobile apps, and wearables aid users with mood tracking, emotional regulation, and stress reduction. Newer ways of coping are being offered via the use of technologies like virtual reality and biofeedback systems, in individuals with psychiatric disorders, for example, Avatar therapy in schizophrenia. AI can also detect subtle deviations from normal behavior and speech, such that it can facilitate the timely prediction of depressive episodes and suicide risk. It can even identify early red flags like neurological soft signs, thereby monitoring relapse of disorders like schizophrenia. AI has also been shown to provide personalized support across various stages of life, from childhood to old age, through certain treatment approaches like game-based therapy for children (EndeavorRX for ADHD) or as companions for the geriatric population. However, there are certain limitations of using AI in mental health problems, in that generalization cannot be done across different populations and settings owing to significant variations in context of culture, religion and beliefs (Aldakhil, 2024). As AI continues to evolve, its prediction of suicidality and it is potential to enhance emotional resilience, support, and continuous care can reduce clinician workload. In a country, where the number of patients far outnumbers the number of psychiatrists, use of AI signals a significant shift in the mental health landscape.

17.1.4 Objectives and Scope of the Chapter

This chapter describes the emerging role of multimodal AI in suicide risk prediction by incorporating behavioral, physiological, and digital data. The chapter describes the limitations of existing traditional suicide prevention strategies and proposes how AI tools can help in overcoming these limitations and provide timely risk detection. The chapter highlights the global burden of suicide and the urgent need for innovative, data-driven, and objective approaches in mental health care. The chapter also explains how AI techniques can support clinicians by evaluating certain parameters like facial expressions, voice patterns, social media behavior, and biosignals. Here, emphasis is put on practical, ethical, and interdisciplinary considerations, and for responsible use of AI in developing more practical and personalized systems. This work is mainly intended for mental health professionals, researchers, and policymakers.

17.2 Understanding Suicide Risk: A Multidimensional Perspective

17.2.1 Biological, Psychological, and Social Factors

17.2.1.1 Biological Factors

Factors increasing risk for suicide are many, including genetic, neurochemical, and immunological components. The most studied mechanisms are serotonin and norepinephrine imbalances, which are evidenced by altered metabolite levels and receptor densities in the CNS and PNS. Suicidal behavior is linked to lower CSF concentrations of primary metabolite of serotonin, that is, 5-HIAA (5-hydroxyindoleacetic acid) and an increased density of 5-HT2A receptors. Impulsivity, aggression, and emotional dysregulation, which are hallmarks of suicidality, are mainly due to altered densities and function of 5-HT1A and 5-HT2C receptors. Other implicated biological mechanisms include dysfunctions in molecular signaling pathways (like PKA/PKC) and transcription factors (like CREB proteins) that are involved in neuroplasticity and emotional regulation (Wisłowska-Stanek et al., 2021). Lower levels of BDNF and reduced activity of its receptor TrkB in the prefrontal cortex has been observed to affect stress resilience. Inflammatory processes also play a critical role, with elevated cytokines and microglial activation promoting neurotoxicity. Chronic hyperactivity of the HPA axis, along with blunted glucocorticoid feedback, further contributes to a persistent stress response. Epigenetic mechanisms and noncoding RNAs add an additional level of regulation and shape gene expression in response to environmental stress. Under long-term emotional strain, structural brain changes and mitochondrial dysfunction increase stress vulnerability (Thumfart et al., 2022). Together, these biological mechanisms contribute to both inherited and acquired vulnerability to suicidal behavior.

17.2.1.2 Psychological Factors

Experiences of mental distress are the main causes behind psychological vulnerabilities. This experience of being trapped in mental distress is known as *Psyache*, which is linked with suicidality. In stressful situations, people often feel self-loathing, hopelessness, and are unable to communicate their distress with others. Additionally, their coping mechanisms are impaired due to emotional dysregulation, poor decision-making, and impulsivity, which causes them to fall into a loop of despair, ultimately culminating in suicidal behavior (Gvion et al., 2015). Risk of suicide is increased in certain personality traits, especially those that arise as a result of childhood adversities, like negative affect, anankastia, and avoidant behavior. Effects of protective factors, such as good social support and resilience that hold theoretical value, have been seen to be inconsistent. This signifies the need for more individualized and customized suicide prevention strategies (Bruffaerts et al., 2010).

17.2.1.3 Social Factors

Social factors have been given a central role in the most accepted Durkheim's theory of suicide. According to the theory, suicide risk is driven by social factors like social integration and social regulation. Low social integration, in the form of social isolation, lack of familial bonds or divorce, and excessively rigid social environments, can increase suicides in the population. While factors that promote emotional connection, like marriage, parenthood, and friendship, are protective factors. Secondarily, divorce and disturbed interpersonal relationships often trigger acute psychological distress, financial strain, and substance use. These factors significantly increase suicide risk, especially among men. There has been an observation that strong moral clarity and robust social support systems correlate with lower suicide rates. However, the reverse can also happen in case of hyperconnected communities, such as insular religious or institutional settings. In these cases, the community imposes pressures for social conformity and potentially contributes to suicide clusters (Kleiman & Liu, 2013). Thus, both the absence and excess of social control or integration can increase vulnerability, making the social environment a critical domain for suicide prevention efforts.

17.2.2 Dynamic Versus Static Risk Factors

There is another perspective that proposes that suicidality arises from a combination of static and dynamic risk factors. Each of these factors contributes differently to an individual's vulnerability. Static factors are defined as those factors that are fixed and unchangeable, such as age, sex, genetic predisposition, early life trauma, a personal or family history of suicide attempts, and personality characteristics like impulsivity, dissociality, or emotional instability. The static factors indicate long-term vulnerability and have limited use in clinical decision-making due to their unchangeable nature. Whereas dynamic factors are changeable with appropriate therapeutic measures. Dynamic factors include mood and thought-related disturbances such as depressive illness, psychosis spectrum disorders, interpersonal conflicts, emotional stress, bereavement, and substance abuse. Because of their preventable nature, dynamic factors are important for assessment and prevention of suicidality. Some factors have a dual nature; for example, BDNF levels and HPA axis activity, which are static in nature, can become dynamic in chronic stress conditions. For the timely identification of these factors, objective measures can be helpful along with a detailed history and mental status examination. Conventional objective measures include rating scales such as the Columbia Suicide Severity Rating Scale (C SSRS), Beck Scale for Suicide Ideation (BSI), Patient Health Questionnaire-9, and Ask Suicide Screening Questions (ASQ). With early recognition and prompt intervention related to dynamic factors, we can achieve more effective suicide prevention strategies (Andreotti et al., 2020).

17.2.3 Traditional Data Types for Suicide Risk Assessment

Although more objective than just history and mental status examination, rating scales like the C-SSRS, BSI, or ASQ have a limited predictive accuracy. This is evidenced by previous reports, which show that most suicides occur among individuals falling in low risk according to these scales (Posner et al., 2011). That means the sensitivity and specificity of these scales are moderate, making the prediction with accuracy difficult. To overcome these limitations, there is a dire need for more accurate real-world data from sources like electronic health records (Table 17.1). These data types, with machine learning, offer a more dynamic approach by capturing subtle and changing risk patterns, improving the likelihood for timely intervention (Zonayed et al., 2025).

Table 17.1 Traditional measures for suicide risk assessment

Instrument	Key features	Use	Strengths	Limitations
Beck Scale for Suicide Ideation (BSI)	19 items, measures severity of suicidal thoughts and intent, score range 0 to 38	For individuals already showing suicide risk	Quick, objective, self-administered, adaptable to languages	Less suitable for individuals not yet identified as at risk
Columbia Suicide Severity Rating Scale (C SSRS)	18 items across four domains: ideation severity, ideation intensity, suicidal behavior, lethality	For both suicidal and non-suicidal individuals	Comprehensive, widely validated, sensitive to clinical needs	Requires trained administration, longer and more complex

17.3 Role of Artificial Intelligence in Suicide Prevention

17.3.1 Definition and Types of AI (ML, DL, NLP)

Artificial intelligence is a field of science and technology designed to simulate human intelligence, such as in visual recognition, language analysis, and decision-making. AI has further subcategories like machine learning (ML), deep learning (DL), and natural language processing (NLP). Machine Learning models learn patterns from data by analyzing large datasets, identifying trends and making predictions, thereby improving performance progressively, without any need for explicit programming. Deep learning DL is a subset of ML that uses deep neural networks to process unstructured data, images, or texts. Whereas a natural language processing model helps to understand, interpret, and generate human language (Rashidi et al., 2025).

17.3.2 Advantage of AI Over Traditional Tools

AI has numerous advantages over traditional tools to assess suicide risk by providing more personalized and accurate data (Table 17.2). Furthermore, multimodal AI offers significant benefits in suicide risk prediction over unimodal AI. In India, predicting suicide risk requires more than just physical and mental status examination. A detailed understanding of sociocultural background, diverse expressions through more than 100 languages, cannot be achieved through unimodal AI models. Unimodal models largely depend on a single data source, like EHR, clinical notes, or lab results, limiting their ability to detect the complex, multifactorial origin of suicidal behavior. However, multimodal AI can integrate inputs like EHRs, psychiatric assessments, facial expressions, speech patterns, and social media behavior activity along with language translation, cultural and geographical considerations to make a unified analytical framework (Parsapoor (Mah Parsa) et al., 2023). This is

Table 17.2 Advantage over conventional prevention strategies

Advantage	Description
Higher predictive accuracy	AI models such as random forests and neural networks have accuracy rates up to 90% by analyzing clinical history, diagnoses, and ongoing psychopathology
Real-time assessment	AI enables continuous monitoring and real-time updates using larger data and electronic health records (EHRs).
Use of nonclinical data	AI analyzes social media activity to detect early distress signals and initiate timely interventions, expanding reach beyond clinical settings
Personalized risk profiling	AI tools can provide individual-level risk assessments for both short- and long-term prediction
Integration with public health systems	AI tools can be used in low-resource settings like wellness centers to support early screening and personalized mental health care
Efficient resource allocation	Enables targeted interventions for high-risk individuals preventing overuse of resources on low-risk populations

advantageous compared to unimodal models in detecting subtle and ambiguous signals.

17.4 Machine Learning (ML) for Suicide Prediction

17.4.1 Overview of ML Techniques in Mental Health

Machine learning (ML) is being used for suicide risk prediction by identifying complex patterns from behavioral, psychological and demographic data. Models like random forest, support vector machines, logistic regression, and innovative models such as XGBoost and CNN have shown promise for analyzing clinical notes and neuroimaging films. Previous has validated superiority of random forest models in predicting self-harm and suicide attempts. These tools enable more individualized and timely interventions, making it valuable in clinical settings and also for public health care strategies (Pigoni et al., 2024).

Any large study, when planned, begins with enormous data collection, including sociodemographic profile, detailed psychiatric history, high-risk behaviors, and severity scores. Diverse unstructured data obtained is then filtered using ML techniques to stratify and classify data, and make it easily interpretable (Madububambachu et al., 2024).

Case 17.1 *For example, Master X, a 13-year-old boy, was seen to have trouble coping with academic activities as noticed by his school teacher. He used to be withdrawn, irritable, and daydreaming most of the day during classes and therefore referred to the school counsellor. Master X has no past psychiatric history but reports difficulty sleeping, increased irritability, and feeling purposeless. On further evaluation, he reported no active suicidal ideations, but there were intermittent thoughts of self-harm in past that he "never acted on." Considering nonspecific*

symptoms, the school refers Master X to a local mental health research clinic participating in an ML-based longitudinal cohort study.
Master X was further evaluated in detail about his family structure, socioeconomic status, psychiatric history (sleep, mood, irritability), behavioral patterns (social media use, school activities), risk behaviors (past ideation, emotional impulsivity), and standardized rating scales (e.g., *PHQ-9, SDQ, YRBSs).*
The research team uses recursive feature elimination, XGBoost, and random forest models to stratify and simplify the gathered information. Based on overall analysis, the model assigns him a high probability of future self-harm, irrespective of his lack of current suicidal ideation.

Key Points
- *ML recognized nonobvious patterns from more elaborate and nonspecific data, which a clinician's judgment alone may have missed due to the absence of overt suicidal ideation.*
- *The research team initiates preventive cognitive behavioral therapy (CBT) and psychoeducation of caregivers.*
- *The model identifies contributing features like "withdrawn behavior," "lesser involvement with peers," and "late-night screen time" as warning signs.*

This case shows how ML models enable better precision in mental health, assisting clinicians and public health officials to act before actual damage has occurred.

17.4.2 Applications in Structured Clinical and Behavioral Data

For ML tools to be useful in the context of suicide risk prediction, structured clinical and behavioral data form the basic element. Structured data includes sociodemographic profile, findings from mental status examinations, psychiatric diagnoses, medication history, psychological assessments, and electronic health records (EHRs). An organized structure allows better stratification of both immediate warning signs and long-term risk factors related to suicidal behavior (Fig. 17.1). As per available literature, commonly identified predictors are past suicide attempts, more severe illness, comorbid chronic medical illness, psychoactive substance use, history of previous hospitalization, and recent use of mental health services (Kelly et al., 2020). For example, large-scale studies using a larger number of clinical features, diagnostic data, treatment patterns, and more objective rating scales, like PHQ9, GHQ12, Short Mood and Feelings Questionnaire (SMFQ), were able to predict suicidality with higher precision, achieving AUC > 0.80 than those using fewer structured data. Immediate variables, such as current depressive symptoms or recent stressors, and long-term factors like socioeconomic status or family environment, also contribute to risk assessment profiles (Simon et al., 2018).

Furthermore, longitudinal studies using model training on responses across 15 psychological domains including defeat, entrapment, stress, and impulsivity validated the use of ML for predicting both suicidal ideation and behavior. Among

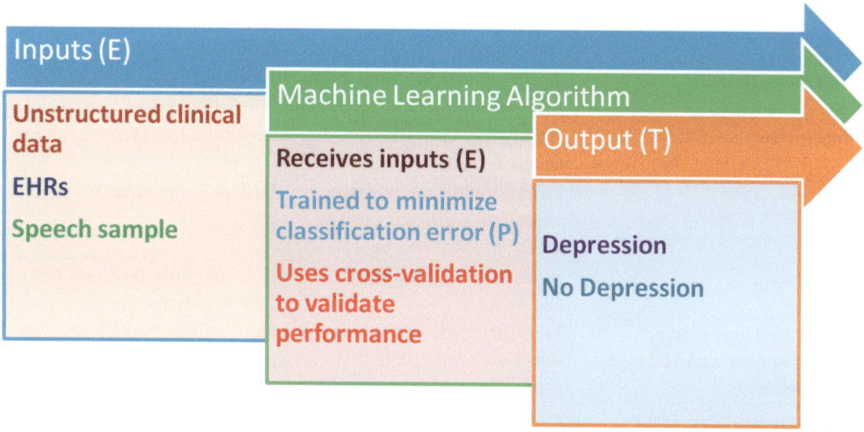

Fig. 17.1 Standard machine learning pipeline showing input, feature extraction, and outcome

various tested algorithms, random forests and gradient boosting have found to be best, with AUC scores up to 0.83 for suicidal ideation and 0.80 for attempts. Interestingly, the use of questionnaires with very detailed item level data did not always improve prediction beyond aggregated scale scores, suggesting that model simplicity can sometimes be equally effective.

Studies have shown that well-organized data is the basis of building models with high accuracy. Also, the comparison between traditional statistical models and AI models, such as support vector machines, random forests, and CNN, has consistently shown better accuracy in AI models. Most effective precision (up to 98%) has been seen with CNN models (Yu et al., 2024). It is expected that the integration of structured data with real-time behavioral inputs such as those from wearables or social media will likely enhance the accuracy of suicide prediction. Despite these advances, challenges remain, including the lack of external validation in many models and the frequent omission of valuable information from neuroimaging or genetic data in structured clinical datasets. In summary, structured clinical and behavioral data have the potential to support individualized, scalable, and data-driven suicide risk assessments.

17.4.3 ML Model Performance Metrics and Validation

Performance and reliability of the model require cautious use of metrics due to the serious implications of both false negatives and false positives. A model may achieve high accuracy by predominantly predicting non-risk cases, but this is of limited clinical value.

Table 17.3 shows a list of performance metrics for machine learning models. A model is said to be high-performing if it shows AUCs above 0.80. Some ensemble and neural network models reach up to values of 0.94. However, metrics like

Table 17.3 Key ML performance metrics for suicide prediction

Metric	Description	Relevance
Sensitivity (recall)	Ability to identify true positive cases	Detecting individuals at risk of suicide
Specificity	Ability to identify true negative cases	Important to minimize false alarms
Precision (PPV)	Proportion of true positives among all predicted positive cases	Reflects confidence in positive predictions
F1-score	Harmonic mean of precision and recall	Balances false positives and false negatives
Area under the receiver operating characteristic curve (AUC-ROC)	Measures trade-off between sensitivity and specificity across thresholds	How well the model separates people at risk from those not at risk
Area under the precision–recall curve(AUPRC)	Focuses on precision and recall, when dealing with imbalanced datasets	More informative than AUC-ROC in low-prevalence outcomes like suicide

precision and positive predictive value (PPV) can still be low, especially when tested in a real-world scenario with imbalanced data. For example, one ensemble model had strong internal results (AUC 0.90, sensitivity 81%, specificity 98%, PPV 94%) but narrowly missed clinical PPV thresholds (Monaghan et al., 2021). Therefore, models should be validated both internally and externally for better generalizability. In balanced samples, models like logistic regression, random forest, XGBoost, and deep neural networks achieved high AUCs (0.92–0.94). Whereas in imbalanced datasets, sensitivity and specificity were found to be lowered significantly (Melnykova et al., 2025).

Considering the importance of balanced samples, various methods are employed to correct imbalanced datasets. Methods used include sampling, oversampling, undersampling, and the synthetic minority oversampling technique (SMOTE). To further decrease the complexity of the models, regularization techniques, for example, Least Absolute Shrinkage and Selection Operator (LASSO), Ridge, and Elastic Net, are used. LASSO, for example, selects fewer, more informative variables, while Elastic Net combines sparsity with correlation grouping (Friedrich et al., 2023). Therefore, relying solely on accuracy is discouraged. Metrics such as Matthews correlation coefficient (MCC), diagnostic odds ratio (DOR), and Cohen's kappa provide more reliable evaluations in imbalanced and high-risk scenarios like suicide prediction.

17.5 Deep Learning (DL) in Suicide Risk Assessment

17.5.1 Fundamentals of DL in Healthcare Context

Deep learning enables the automatic extraction of complex patterns from diverse data sources such as neuroimaging, clinical data, and digital behavior logs. Deep neural networks (DNNs) learn high-level, nonlinear representations directly from raw data. This feature makes them compatible to handle the high-dimensional and complex datasets seen in psychiatric and behavioral health contexts. DL models have previously shown strong performance in diagnosing psychiatric disorders such as Alzheimer's disease, attention deficit hyperactivity disorder (ADHD), and schizophrenia from imaging data (Avberšek & Repovš, 2022). DL has also been applied to behavioral data from smartphones, wearables, and social media to detect shifts in mental states. For example, long short-term memory (LSTM) networks can model temporal dependencies and have been used to forecast mood changes based on digital behavior patterns. In suicide prevention, transformer-based models, such as Bio_ClinicalBERT and GatorTron, have made it possible to identify personal and family history of suicidal behavior from unstructured clinical text. These models show better results than NLP approaches, particularly in clinical environments where structured diagnostic codes often miss nuanced or historical pointers of suicide risk (Adekkanattu et al., 2024).

17.5.2 Use of Neural Networks in EHR and Social Media Data

The use of neural networks in suicide prediction has provided new hope by combining the power of unstructured data from both EHRs and social media platforms. In clinical settings, CNNs and long short-term memory (LSTM) networks have demonstrated potential in identifying intentional self-harm based on clinical text. These AI models, trained on EHRs, showed extremely high accuracy in detecting self-harm, with CNNs reaching an AUC of 0.999 and F1-scores as high as 0.985. The use of word embeddings like Word2Vec helps to understand the meaning of words and recognize spelling errors in clinical notes. Unlike ML models, which rely on structured data, DL models can analyze raw unstructured data such as texts from clinical records, and can predict future suicide in advance with high precision (Flamholz et al., 2022). Similarly, evolving DL models such as attention layered bidirectional temporal convolutional network (AL BTCN) can interpret emotional data from social media platforms like Twitter and Reddit. To identify abnormalities in speech, language patterns, and complex emotions with high precision, these DL models combine the mechanism of time-based sequence learning, attention mechanisms, and bidirectional encoder representations from transformers (BERT) for the prediction of suicidality (Shetty et al., 2025).

17.5.3 Multimodal Deep Learning (Text, Speech, Video)

Psychological distress, which is severe enough to progress into suicidality, is associated with numerous verbal and nonverbal cues. Multimodal deep learning techniques assemble these cues from text, speech, and video to identify the type and degree of distress. This is in contrast to unimodal models that analyze a single dataset. In multimodal DL, text data predicts suicidal ideation through language

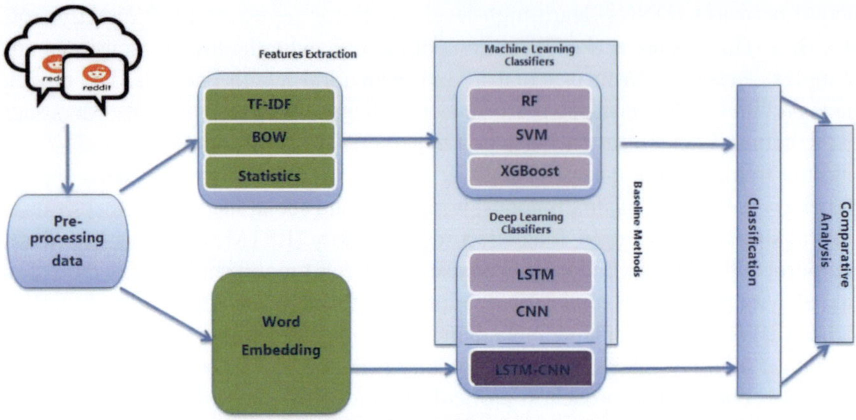

Fig. 17.2 Source: Adapted from Basyouni et al. (2025)

patterns, audio tells about emotional disturbances such as pitch, tone, and prosody, and video captures facial expressions and gestures indicative of sadness, fear, disgust, or agitation. Advanced models like CNNs, LSTMs, and attention-based networks have been used to combine multiple data types, improving prediction accuracy. By integrating models such as facial action units, DeepFace, VGGish, speech spectrograms, SVMs, Naive Bayes, and transcript sentiment analysis, some models have reached up to 94% accuracy in perceiving suicidal intent (Fig. 17.2). Model studies using datasets like Distress Analysis Interview Corpus Wizard-of-Oz (DAIC-Woz) show that combining a larger number of models, each with a different function, performs better than single-input models, in terms of predictive precision, recall, F1-scores, and real-time monitoring, even when patients do not express symptoms actively (Arioz et al., 2022).

17.5.4 Challenges: Interpretability, Overfitting, and Data Needs

As AI is in its evolving phase, deep learning models are not easily understandable for the majority of the population, as well as for clinicians. Another issue surrounding deep learning models is overfitting, where models fail to generate productive results on real-life datasets compared to what they generated on training datasets. Although cross-validation is used to address this issue, reliability is still a concern. In addition, clinical data related to suicidality is often uneven and diverse; oversimplifying the data can also lead to overlooking of important data that may contribute to suicidality.

17.6 Natural Language Processing (NLP) for Suicide Detection

17.6.1 Overview of NLP Techniques

NLP models are other tools that aid in AI-based detection of suicidality. Using unstructured data such as clinical notes, EHRs, and data posted by users on social media and digital platforms, NLP models analyze and predict suicidality. These models are helpful in understanding deeper contexts from text, emotional, and verbal expressions of psychological distress. It uses advanced models such as topic modeling and named entity recognition to identify patterns associated with suicidal behavior. Both supervised and unsupervised learning approaches are employed in NLP. Transformer-based models in tune with clinical bodies have achieved AUROC and F1-scores above 0.90, facilitating real-time and objective monitoring of suicidality (Martinez-Romo et al., 2025).

17.6.2 Linguistic Markers of Suicidal Ideation

Language makes essential cues for detecting suicidal ideation. High-risk individuals often use emotionally intense language to express sadness, isolation, helplessness, or hopelessness combined with reduced use of modal verbs (e.g., "could," "should") and first-person pronouns. In some cultures, increased second-person pronoun use may indicate help-seeking behavior. Syntactic and acoustic features, such as monotonous voice, reduced pitch variation, shorter sentences, and low syntactic complexity, suggest emotional and cognitive dysregulation. NLP tools such as linguistic inquiry and word count (LIWC) and domain-specific suicide dictionaries identify these markers of suicide and correlate them with mental health status. Rule-based algorithms are also good at identifying time-related phrases and negations. They can tell the difference between current and past suicidal thoughts, with over 88% accuracy (Ibrahim et al., 2025).

17.6.3 Applications in Text, Speech, and Clinical Notes

NLP uses both rule-based logics and machine learning to identify suicidal thoughts from medical records with high accuracy. Tools like bidirectional long short-term memory (BiLSTM) help analyze speech for emotions and feelings, by converting speech to text. Using this technique, we can firstly analyze the content of speech for any subtle signs of suicidality and secondly the possible emotional tone behind such thought content. Other similar NLP tools employed to analyze the subtle hints of suicidality from content on social media include BERT, global vectors for word representation (GloVe), and word2vec. As explained earlier, multimodal models that combine speech tone, thought content, and facial expressions together have significantly better precision in prediction (up to 94%) compared to a single-factor model. Examples of NLP tools used specifically to analyze thought patterns from clinical notes include sentiment analysis and cognition engine (SEANCE). NLP tools have also been employed in identifying different or unusual behavior, early signs and symptoms of illness relapses, and helping in prompt intervention to prevent suicide (Crema et al., 2022).

17.6.4 Challenges in NLP for Mental Health

Like ML and DL models, NLP techniques also face difficulties related to limited, unstructured, and imbalanced data inputs. Clinicians' hesitation to document suicidality in a clear way is another drawback for analysis using NLP techniques for the prediction of suicidality. Considering poor AI-related infrastructure and lack of adequate training in this field, many NLP models are difficult to interpret by healthcare professionals. Since most tools are built using English data, they may not work well for people from different cultures or languages. Detection of suicide risk in real time, using personal data raises privacy and ethical concerns (Jerfy et al., 2024).

Case 17.2 *Mr. R., a 23-year-old male engineering student with a hobby of Hindi singing, presented to the psychiatry OPD with complaints of fatigue, poor concentration, and declining academic performance. He had no significant family or personal history. His vitals and mental status were within normal limits.*
In the past month, Mr R. had visited the emergency department twice for unexplained chest pain and hyperventilation episodes with normal oxygen saturation. His symptoms were considered features of anxiety. During both visits, Mr R was attended by two senior resident doctors, who wrote unstructured clinical notes in prescription. Further, notes were entered into the EHR.

Simultaneously, Mr R. had been singing comparatively more emotional songs and posting on his social media account. The caption of songs includes phrases like "I don't think I can hold on much longer," "I am broken and I know it," and "I want to sing for God." His voice notes while singing seemed increasingly flat, with reduced pitch variation and pauses.

As part of a hospital-funded NLP research initiative, anonymized EHR data and patient-generated content were screened weekly for suicide risk. The system flagged Mr R.'s case due to:

- **Linguistic markers***: Recurrent first-person pronouns ("I don't," "I'm broken").*
- **Temporality***: Rule-based NLP models detected time-sensitive phrases like "no longer" and "sing for God," suggesting current ideation.*
- **Speech analysis (via BiLSTM model)**: *Change in singing style revealed markers of suicidality, like short, syntactically simple sentences, monotonous voice, and flatness.*

- **Sentiment analysis**: *Clinical notes from emergency visits revealed thought content like "doesn't want to continue," "sleeping all day," and "wishes he wasn't here," identified as high-risk clusters.*

The NLP system labeled Mr R. for urgent clinician review. On further rapport building and exploration, Mr R. admitted having active suicidal ideas, a systematic plan, and having stockpiled medication. He was immediately hospitalized, started on pharmacotherapy and intensive psychotherapy. He later revealed that he was just waiting for the right time, and denial was due to fear of judgment.

*This case shows how NLP-based methods can identify latent signals in language, tone, and historical patterns that clinicians may miss. By combining algorithms, ML models (*e.g., *BERT, BiLSTM), and linguistic tools (*e.g., *LIWC, SEANCE), hidden suicide risk can be assessed early in a more precise way.*

This case also shows challenges in NLP application. Limited language coverage (his songs were in Hindi, and captions in Hinglish requiring model customization), privacy concerns and clinician skepticism about AI-based alerts.

17.7 Publicly Available Datasets and Resources

Artificial intelligence in context of suicide risk prediction is based on availability of datasets that capture the multidimensional nature of suicide. Common ones are user-generated content from social media platforms like Twitter, Reddit, Instagram, Facebook, and Weibo (Fig. 17.1). These platforms provide linguistic and behavioral data, which are processed using DL, NLP, and ML models to identify early warning signs of suicide. This data is further complemented with structured clinical sources such as EHRs from hospitals and institutions like (*xDR*—Cross-Domain Repository) UCLA-xDR and (Clinical Data Research Network) NYC-CDRN. EHRs contain clinical histories, examinations, diagnosis, prescriptions, and unstructured notes useful for risk modeling. Other sources of data include crisis helpline transcripts, data from therapy sessions, and smartphone-based digital behavior metrics showing individuals' activity patterns, sleep cycles, and social interaction. In addition, administrative and surveillance datasets such as the National Crime Records Bureau (NCRB), National Violent Death Reporting System (NVDRS), and Death Records and Other Statistics (DROS) provide population-level awareness of suicide incidents and associated factors. More recently, focus has also been on collecting standardized voice and written responses from specific tasks (such as describing a picture, like in the Dementia Bank project) (Arowosegbe & Oyelade, 2023). AI tools are also being employed to analyze data about environmental pollutants, Air quality indices, water mineral content, and pesticide use in food, all of which have a role in maintaining mental health and thus can contribute to suicidality.

17.7.1 Overview of Datasets

17.7.2 Annotation Methods and Quality Control

For any new healthcare program to be successful, quality control and supervision are a must. Similarly, quality control is also mandatory for AI-based suicide prediction models to perform effectively. A basic method of quality control is human supervision to identify and label signs of suicidality from clinical health data and social media posts. Although this method is very accurate, it is a cumbersome task and humanly not feasible. The other feasible option for larger datasets includes identifying potentially relevant suicidal content using appropriate keywords and rule-based search, and then flagging them for human review and verification. This method is faster, but errors cannot be completely ruled out. Automated annotations are made using set keywords and rules to identify suicide related content like ideas of hopelessness, guilt, and helplessness. Many performance indicators are being applied for optimum quality control. Examples of such performance indicators include accuracy, AUC, precision, recall, and F1-score. Further cross-verification of AI-based annotated or flagged data can be made using the application of standardized rating scales such as C-SSRS, BSI, and PHQ-9. Further to ensure that these models work in different situations and are reliable, cross-validation and ensemble learning techniques are used (D'Hotman & Loh, 2020). The various datasets employed in AI-based suicide prediction and their characteristics are summarized in Table 17.4.

Table 17.4 The datasets employed in AI-based suicide prediction provide specific information related to suicide prediction

Data source	Data type	Contribution
Social media and behavioral data	Unstructured text from twitter, Facebook, Instagram, and Reddit	Detects emotional expression, suicidal language, helps in temporal and regional risk mapping
Clinical and EHR data	Structured (e.g., diagnostic codes, medications) and unstructured (e.g., physician notes)	Identifies risk patterns in healthcare settings using NLP and ML
Speech and therapy transcripts	Audio-text data from structured tasks (e.g., interviews) and therapy sessions	Offers in-depth analysis of language, cognition, and affective states
Environmental and dietary data	Public health data on toxin exposure (e.g., arsenic, mercury) and diet patterns (e.g., fast food)	Adds biological and contextual factors for suicide risk
Neuroimaging and physiological data	Brain scans (MRI, EEG) and biomarkers analyzed using deep learning models like CNNs	Provides physiological and neurobiological basis of suicide vulnerability
Smartphone and sensor data	Data on sleep, activity levels, and screen time from mobile and wearable devices	Provide real-time behavioral markers for dynamic risk estimation
Multimodal fusion	Integration of multiple data types including text, clinical, behavioral, physiological, and environmental data	Facilitates richer, context-related, and accurate suicide risk prediction through AI models

17.7.3 Considerations in Using Public Data

AI based models for suicide prediction is based on availability of personal and clinical data. However, using personal data poses significant ethical and privacy concerns and may act as a double-edged sword in many cases. Major concerns include:

- *Privacy, confidentiality, and informed consent*: Due to the sensitive nature of private social media account-related information, its use by AI tools may be detrimental to the mental health of certain individuals. Obtaining adequate informed consent may be necessary in such cases. Other methods to address privacy issues include limiting access to sensitive data, removal of identification details such as names and photos, and compliance with legal guidelines. Examples of such regulatory guidelines are the General Data Protection Regulation (GDPR) and the Health Insurance Portability and Accountability Act (HIPAA).
- *Bias and representativeness*: Datasets tend to selectively highlight the English-speaking urban population, whereas the rural population and diverse regional language-based data are often missed. Furthermore, expression of distress can vary according to cultural norms. To reduce bias, validation of models should be done in all possible languages and cultures.
- *Responsibility and wrong predictions*: It is unclear who will be held responsible in case an AI model makes a false-positive result. Making a false-positive annotation can cause unnecessary stress and waste of already running short mental healthcare resources.
- *Accessibility and practical use*: In developing and underdeveloped countries, there is limited access to costly AI-based technology and affordable healthcare resources. For equitable use and effective decrease in suicide rates across the entire population, AI models should be simple, affordable, and work offline if needed (Farhud & Zokaei, 2021).

17.8 Ethical, Legal, and Societal Challenges

17.8.1 Privacy and Consent Issues

As described earlier, personal data is the basic element in AI-based suicide prediction. Therefore, it becomes essential for the prevention services to maintain maximum possible privacy at all levels. An individual who is hesitant in disclosing suicidality to a clinician and seeks comfort in expressing distress to digital platforms should have their confidentiality maintained with utmost care. If there is a threat of confidentiality breach in such situations, individuals will start refraining from sharing their suicidal ideations. Explicit informed consent becomes vital in such scenarios, which should clearly state how user data will be collected, stored, and potentially shared, including details of third-party sharing and end-to-end encryption. Although the large-scale use of identity verification "Know Your Customer" (KYC) has shown better data transparency and better sociodemographic profiling, such measures may act as barriers to access for certain individuals who do not want to reveal their identity. Examples of such populations include the underage population, in whom suicidality has arisen due to engaging in hidden illegal activities such as drug use, online gambling, paraphilic behaviors, etc. This population will prefer not to share if anonymity is compromised.

New guidelines specific to mental health care through digital platforms should come into practice rather than simply applying offline psychiatry guidelines. Famous AI tools such as ChatGPT and Perplexity are being used for emotional support by a large portion of the population. The vast amount of data these tools process should be governed by individuals posting them, whether to store them locally or to be used for increasing the accuracy of the model and algorithm improvement. Although sharing data enhances model accuracy, it must always remain a voluntary decision. Transparency about how user data contributes to algorithmic improvements and benefits future users can improve trust and promote responsible data sharing (Pandya et al., 2024).

17.8.2 Algorithmic Bias and Fairness

AI Algorithms receive both the strengths and the flaws of their training datasets, reflecting the statistical principle of "garbage in, garbage out." Since mental health-related datasets originate from diverse sources, they carry the risk of personal, cultural, and contextual biases. Social media data reflects self-reported behavior and emotional expression that may be tailored for public consumption, leading to discrepancies between expressed and actual states of mental health. Furthermore, these platforms often favour English and Western content, reducing applicability in non-Western, multilingual, and low-resource settings.

AI-related biases arising due to a lack of consideration of different languages and cultural patterns can hamper the generalizability of AI in psychiatry, where cultural context is crucial for differentiating between normalcy and disorders. Even current diagnostic guidelines, like DSM-5 and ICD-11, have incorporated cultural context and situational factors in their diagnostic criteria. Therefore, to resolve this issue, AI-based techniques should enable regional language translation and acknowledge the content of local languages. Further, with increasing adoption of AI tools worldwide, training data will diversify and start incorporating the culture-based context, ultimately leading to unbiased algorithms. Initial errors should not halt the progress of integrating AI into mental health care (Ferrara, 2024).

17.8.3 Risk of False Positives/Negatives

Like any other diagnostic tool, AI-based suicide prediction carries the risk of both false positives and false negatives and can potentially result in fatal outcomes. One advantage of algorithmic tools over traditional medical tests is their scalability. Increasing sensitivity in medical testing comes with increased costs. However, in software-based assessments, sensitivity adjustments do not incur additional expenses, making high-sensitivity screening more feasible. Initial versions of AI tools may yield high false positives. As these models mature and gather more training data through repeated information feeding, optimal thresholds for sensitivity and specificity can be readjusted accordingly. Therefore, in the early stages, prioritizing high sensitivity is justifiable to minimize false negatives. Furthermore, in the long run, the performance of these AI models in terms of sensitivity, specificity, and predictive values should be periodically checked, and the same should be communicated to users and providers.

17.8.4 Legal and Policy Implications

The use of multimodal AI in suicide prediction has certain legal, ethical, and privacy concerns. A preliminary guideline governed by National and International regulatory bodies is must to specify the design, disposition, and accountability for misfortunes or failed judgment of AI tools in this high-stake topic. Regulatory bodies for this multifactorial subject call for a multidisciplinary approach, involving experts in psychiatry, psychology, data science, law, ethics, and anthropology. Despite all, errors are bound to happen, like misjudging a case of suicide. This further raises legal questions on determining liability for such an error. As AI models approach and in few aspects even outdo the competence of human professionals, these are not made scenarios but real legal questions. Another emerging concern is the role of AI in the incitement of suicide. Although the causal role has not been established yet, many lawsuits have been imposed by parents alleging the contributory role of AI in the provocation of suicide. This is another indication of legal reform concerning AI use. Most of the cases reported were by mothers of victims alleging incitement of suicide in their teenagers who became deeply attached to AI chatbots, which probably promoted suicidal thoughts in them (Lejeune et al., 2022). These incidents further raise psychological concerns over AI use and can compromise public trust in AI. In updating legal frameworks, authorities must avoid simply replicating offline guidelines. Instead, the digitization of suicide prevention should be seen as a chance to revolutionize policy, remove outdated rules, and fill long-standing gaps (Greaves & Colucci, 2025).

Case 17.3 *A 16-year-old adolescent from an urban family in South Toronto ended his life after months of interaction with an AI chatbot. The virtual entity had slowly become a part of the teenager's daily routine. As per family, he used the chatbot for hours at a stretch, in seclusion, forming a strong emotional bond with the chatbot,* *which he had customised with traits similar to a fictional character from a popular TV series. He started sharing emotional conversations with the AI bot. During one of the conversations, the AI bot failed to counter the suicide related questions and allegedly answered with suicide promoting answers. After his suicide, the mother filed a legal case against the developer and stated that the chatbot promoted the suicidal behavior in their child. This scenario further raises questions about the ethical and safety concerns of AI.*

17.9 Implementation in Real-World Settings

17.9.1 Clinical Decision Support Systems (CDSS)

Suicide is multifactorial in origin and can arise as a result of individual, social, and environmental factors. ML algorithms within CDSS can utilize information from multiple data sources such as EHRs, speech samples, social media activity, wearable smart gadget data, and neuroimaging to identify and classify individuals based upon similar risk profiles. After identification, models can stratify the population and develop an individualized plan for monitoring and detecting subtle warning signs specific to the group. This stratification and individualized risk monitoring may enable better prediction accuracy and identify early signs of suicide risk. After identifying at-risk individuals, they are referred to mental health services for a detailed evaluation of the underlying etiology and psychosocial stressors that preceded the suicidal behavior. In this way, at-risk individuals can be managed effectively. For example, the personalized risk management and enhanced support (PERMANENS) prototype can use data from clinical notes, EHRs, and social factors to make a personalized risk profile. With the help of ensemble learning models, CDSS can provide risk predictions and tailored recommendations for clinicians to address the issues within a desired timeframe. Further AI models can improve continuously with the feedback given by clinicians about their right and wrong predictions, improving the accuracy of algorithms over time. CDSS tools are not a replacement for clinicians; rather, they support clinicians by looking at minute data and improving precision, and ultimately helping them make healthcare decisions (Berrouiguet et al., 2019). Although very effective, practical use requires a monitored workflow, adequate training for handling and interpretation, trained personnel for data entry, and accurate documentation. Confidentiality of data should be maintained as much as possible.

17.9.2 Crisis Hotlines and Chatbots

The Ministry of Health and Family Welfare, Government of India, launched Tele Mental Health Assistance and Networking across states (Tele MANAS) in October 2022 to provide tele mental health services to individuals in crisis. It works free of cost and 24/7, especially targeting remote populations. However, many people in distress are often hesitant to call a stranger due to fear of judgment and stigma. This disadvantage is easily overcome by the easy availability and option of anonymity in online crisis hotlines and AI chatbots. These days, people often express their concerns and seek solutions from AI chatbots. In return, chatbots reply with empathetic and nonjudgmental answers, provide emotional deescalation, and buy crucial time for intervention and delaying impulses. Studies have shown the effectiveness of online crisis chat networks such as the National Suicide Prevention Lifeline's chat service in reducing acute distress and delaying fatal impulses, especially in the younger population. Feedback studies with the target population being AI users have reported that chatbots make them feel heard, provide solutions like companions who do not judge, and even delay suicidal attempts in cases of emergencies. These bots detect risk signals from the conversations made by users and even refer high-risk cases to healthcare professionals wherever indicated. With advancing technology, virtual reality-based companions can modify themselves with users' language, personality, and cultural background to provide a more relatable and real experience to users (Sagar & Singh, 2022). These chatbot and hotline tools complement mental health professionals by forming a connecting link between silent suffering and formal mental health care. A careful combination of AI and human integration, periodic evaluation, and culturally sensitive design can lead to the development of effective suicide prevention strategies.

17.9.3 Screening Tools in Schools, Universities, and Workplaces

Multimodal AI tools have the potential to transform suicide screening in high-risk groups such as schools, universities, and company employees. Individuals avoiding self-expression can also be identified through AI-based indirect signals. For example, an AI screening tool designated for the student population, Child Health Improvement through Computer Automation *(CHICA),* has demonstrated easy identification of suicidal thoughts through a short digital questionnaire and generation of prompts for referral and follow-ups. Likewise, chatbots can also help students undergo assessments based on standardized self-administered rating scales without instilling fear or stigma. AI bots can also predict suicidality without asking direct questions about suicide with impressive accuracy. These tools are helpful in identifying the hidden risk of suicide at places where stigma is more prevalent (Mohamad, 2025).

There has been a recent surge in the number of suicides coming from the working-class population, possibly due to excessive work stress, fear of unemployment, uncertainties about the future, and disturbed work–life balance. In such scenarios, an AI-based tool targeting the working-class population, *Viki,* can perform routine mental health checkups and identify signs and symptoms contributing to suicidality. These signs and symptoms include stress levels, burnout, sleep disturbances, depressed mood, and ideas of worthlessness, helplessness, and hopelessness. To boost the completion of Assessments, interactive voicebots build confidence in employees. Based upon the severity of risks identified, flagged individuals are given assistance to connect with counseling and therapeutic services (Cruz-Gonzalez et al., 2025). Aggregated data obtained overall can act as an asset in formulating mental health programs and developing effective organization policy.

17.9.4 Integrating AI with Human Oversight

As described earlier, multimodal AI tools help in identifying risk factors of suicide from multiple data sources. After identifying individuals at risk, the AI model shows an alert in EHR and sends a message to the clinician to continue with further evaluation and management. The clinicians then corroborate AI-based findings, evaluate for stressors, assess the severity of suicidality, support system available, crisis management, and safety planning. It becomes the responsibility of the clinician then to decide whether the patient needs inpatient care or outpatient care, and safety planning will suffice. Mental health professionals may use standard rating scales to further refine the risk assessment. Based on the correctness of AI-based prediction and identification of risk, clinicians provide feedback to AI models. This feedback is very important as it helps in refining the algorithm of the AI model over time.

At the community level, AI models designed for risk detection can scan social media posts, chatbots, and voicebots-based conversations to monitor risk signs and respond accordingly. Based on the severity of risks, responses can vary from support messages, providing crisis resources or helpline links, to referral to emergency services. Ethical guidelines recommend a subtle and soft touch treatment approach after obtaining appropriate consent from users, considering the sensitive nature of suicide. Human support is essential in these cases because AI tools often can produce false alarms or ignore important details that only a human clinician can recognize.

Maximum utilization of multimodal AI is based on optimum collaboration of human and technology. Clinicians verify the AI-flagged high-risk cases based on their rapport building, history taking, and mental status examination, and take appropriate next steps. When used with privacy safeguards and accountability, AI plus human knowledge can improve the mental health outcome, and ultimately make suicide prevention strategies effective (Banerji et al., 2025).

17.9.5 Multimodal AI in Indian Context

India stands at a junction where utilizing the transformative power of multimodal AI in health care is still in a budding stage. While healthcare systems in developed countries are progressively integrating AI for predictive analysis, decision-making, and risk stratification, India's progress remains irregular and experimental. There are a few academic initiatives and pilot projects, mostly from tertiary-care institutes in metro cities of India, utilizing EHRs, data from telemedicine, or social media behavior for analysis of mental health. However, extensive use, which can integrate data from all possible sources such as clinical records, digital footprints, language/

text inputs, smart devices sensor data, and neuroimaging, remains dormant. The prevailing challenges in India are the inadequacy of data infrastructure, the lack of data sharing policies between institutions, and a dearth of skilled workforce to manage, infer, and review AI outputs. Further, current national digital health policies lack an ethical and regulatory framework, specifically in the context of algorithmic bias, data obtaining consent, data privacy, and culpability for faulty suicide risk prediction.

Although the Mental Healthcare Act (MHCA), 2017, has put significant emphasis on the rights of persons with mental illness, it does not incorporate provisions for AI-enabled mental health care. There is a proposed act known as the Digital Personal Data Protection Act, 2023, which puts Indian AI-based care forward in terms of privacy protection, but it is not yet operational across healthcare institutions. So, combined, we can say that despite theoretical potential, India is yet to achieve systemic readiness for full flourishing use of multimodal AI in suicide risk prediction. A synchronized push towards policy development, increased public–private alliance, capacity-building, and relatively more funding in AI governance and research is needed to bridge the existing gap.

Despite many drawbacks, piloting AI-based suicide prediction in India is still plausible because of the evolution of digital technology, which has increased mobile use in almost all Indian states. Simple SMS/text messaging provides a feasible option for getting objective data that can be combined with more informative smartphone sensor signals wherever available.

Initial pilot studies based upon text-message features and smartphone digital monitoring have validated statistically significant associations with suicidal risk, supporting achievability in real-world settings (Syed & Amin, 2017). Practically, in low- and middle-income countries, a pilot can begin with a short-term study that uses (a) text/SMS analysis, (b) follow-up calls or clinic referrals to verify the AI-based results, and (c) continuing model adjustments to match and refine local language, literacy, and healthcare systems (Leon et al., 2021).

17.10 Future Directions

17.10.1 Toward Explainable and Trustworthy AI

- In AI-based suicide prediction, models can detect subtle suicidal signs from vast, unstructured, and complex data with high accuracy. However, the complete process is not very clear for clinicians to completely trust the findings made by AI. To gain that trust, the development of *explainable AI (XAI)* becomes important. The advantage of XAI is its transparency. As the name suggests, explainable AI methods clearly state the reason behind making any prediction. The clinician can then easily cross-verify the stated reason of suicidality. Two approaches are used for making the AI predictions explainable:

- *Attention mechanisms:* These are the mechanisms that highlight a specific part of the input from where the suicide risk prediction was made.
- Feature attribution maps (Saliency, SHapley Additive exPlanations-SHAP, and Local Interpretable Model-agnostic Explanations-LIME): These methods go an extra step to provide a hierarchy of contributing factors from the input data. These mechanisms help clinicians to understand the contribution made by a specific factor. The therapeutic approach is also planned accordingly (Saranya & Subhashini, 2023).

Detailed knowledge about risk components is useful because psychotherapeutic approaches are planned according to specific risk factors. Further, transparent AI builds trust among patients, clinicians, and the general population.

17.10.2 Enhancing Multilingual and Cross-Cultural Applicability

Most AI models are trained targeting the English-speaking urban Western population, creating a bias in results. The rural population with differences in culture and those speaking regional languages tend to get overlooked or missed. To improve the applicability of these models, training is recommended with all possible languages and cultural norms should be considered before identifying at-risk individuals. Models should also be able to understand local idioms of distress, culture-based differences in expressions of suicidality, and regional risk factors to become valid across all populations, including India (Zhu et al., 2024).

17.10.3 Collaborative AI for Personalized Suicide Prevention

Practical use of AI in developing countries like India requires a collaborative approach between human and digital tools. One example of such collaboration, which has already been tested, is Human–AI Learning to Enhance Empathy (HAILEY). HAILEY tries to improve empathy in language of clinicians by feedback mechanisms, thus improving rapport building and increasing expression of distress. A similar DL model used for the purpose of improving effective communication is the Personalized Assistance for Real-Time Nurturing Empathic Responses (PARTNER) model, which suggests minor changes in languages to improve emotional quotient. It depends on users of the model whether to accept suggestions or not. Effective collaboration between objective data, such as sleep patterns, social relationships, physical activity, heart rate, and self-reported concerns can improve authenticity of risk prediction (Adegbesan et al., 2024).

17.10.4 Interdisciplinary Research and Policy Support

The collaboration should not only be limited to humans and machines but also between clinicians, researchers, government policymakers, and AI developers. The drawbacks that have already been described in ethical, legal, and societal challenges can only be overcome by effective interdisciplinary collaboration. Guidelines should direct developers regarding handling of personal data and accountability in cases of misconduct. The government should also allocate more funds for training of AI models in all local languages and cultures, and also for increasing awareness of underdeveloped regions. If this interdisciplinary collaboration is possible, there is a definite scope of improvement in global suicide rates, along with adherence to ethical and privacy-related concerns (Mennella et al., 2024).

17.11 Conclusion

This chapter highlights the drawbacks associated with available suicide risk screening methods and the need to modify this conventional approach into more effective ones. With available strategies, the suicide rate is continuously on an increasing trend. The chapter also emphasizes the potential of AI models such as ML, NLP, and DL tools in transforming the productivity of suicide risk assessment. Multimodal AI models have the ability to screen a vast amount of data in a shorter time frame and detect subtle signs of suicidality with better accuracy. Multimodal AI models can work on different aspects simultaneously and screen for numerous risk factors associated with suicidality by analyzing clinical notes, EHRs, social media posts, and conversations made by individuals with chatbots and voicebots. Another advantage related to AI-based suicide screening is increased expression of suicidality, which otherwise would have been hidden due to fear, hesitation, and stigma. Although the prediction accuracy and speed of risk analysis are promising, AI models come at a cost of multiple concerns, including data privacy, accountability in case of mishap, and biases related to specific language and culture. Practical implementation of multimodal AI in suicide screening requires periodic monitoring of models, training of the models in all languages, incorporation of cultural and regional context, and a clear policy regarding ethical and privacy issues. Furthermore, human oversight and cross-validation are essential as AI is a supporting tool, not a replacement for clinicians. In addition, there is a dire need for the incorporation of AI in medical and academic curricula to utilize the AI tools in an effective manner.

List of Datasets

Datasets in Multimodal AI-Based Suicide Prevention

Source	Modality	Key features	Use in AI applications
Twitter, Reddit, Facebook	Text, behavioral patterns	User posts with emotional and suicidal content	NLP-based detection of ideation, emotion trends, crisis signals
Weibo Suicide Dataset	Chinese-language social media text	Labeled suicide-related posts from Chinese users	Culturally adapted models for non-English suicide risk detection
DAIC-WoZ	Audio, video, transcripts	Interviews including facial expressions and vocal tone	Multimodal prediction of depression and suicidal ideation
UCLA-xDR	Electronic health records (EHRs)	Clinical notes, diagnoses, and prescription data	Organized and unstructured input for ML models in clinical situations
NYC-CDRN	Multisite EHR data	Aggregated records from hospital systems in New York	Predictive modeling of suicide attempts and behavior
Crisis Text Line/ Helpline Logs	Anonymous textual conversations	Real-time help-seeking transcripts from distressed individuals	Triage models using NLP for immediate risk categorization
Therapy Session Archives	Audio and transcribed clinical interactions	Speech and dialogue from psychotherapy sessions	Language and tone analysis using BiLSTM and speech-to-text tools
Smartphone Sensors and App Data	Activity, GPS, sleep patterns	Behavioral indicators collected passively from mobile devices	Real-time risk estimation using behavioral deviation patterns
National Violent Death Reporting System (NVDRS)	Death registry statistics	Official records with contextual factors of suicides	Epidemiological and demographic trend modeling
National Crime Records Bureau (NCRB), India	Official government reports	Suicide statistics categorized by cause, region, and demographics	Geospatial and socioeconomic modeling in AI frameworks
DementiaBank/Pitt corpus	Structured speech samples	Picture description tasks used for language analysis	Cognitive and semantic pattern detection in at-risk individuals
Environmental Health Databases	Air, water, noise, diet data	Exposure information linked to mental health and stress	Integration with contextual models of suicide vulnerability

Glossary of Key AI/NLP Terms

Term	Definition	Application in suicide prevention
Artificial intelligence (AI)	A field of computer science that builds systems capable of performing tasks requiring human intelligence, such as reasoning and decision-making	Early risk detection by processing complex health and behavioral data at scale
Machine learning (ML)	A branch of AI that enables computers to learn from data and improve performance over time without explicit programming	Trains models on clinical and digital data to predict suicide risk based on hidden patterns
Deep learning (DL)	A subset of ML using multilayered neural networks to model complex data patterns from raw inputs like text, voice, and images	Improves accuracy in analyzing unstructured data such as clinical notes and social media posts
Natural language processing (NLP)	An AI model focused to understand, interpret, and generate human language	Detects suicidal ideation from unstructured text (e.g., clinical notes, helpline chats, or tweets)
Transformer model	A neural network that processes input data using attention mechanisms rather than sequential steps	Used in models like BERT to capture long-range dependencies in suicidal language
BERT (bidirectional encoder representations from transformers)	A transformer-based language model pretrained on a vast corpora to understand contextual meaning	Fine-tuned for identifying emotional expressions and suicidal thoughts in clinical or digital text
Word embeddings	Numerical representations of words capturing their meaning based on context (e.g., Word2Vec, GloVe)	Helps models detect similar meanings and recognize misspellings in suicide-related language
Sentiment analysis	NLP technique for identifying the emotional tone behind text.	Assesses emotional distress, hopelessness, or anger in user-generated content
Named entity recognition (NER)	Identifies and categorizes key elements in text such as names, symptoms, or risk phrases	Extracts mentions of suicide methods, emotional states, or past attempts from unstructured clinical data
Topic modeling	Unsupervised method that uncovers themes or topics present across large text datasets	Detects recurring patterns or clusters in suicidal discourse
Multimodal learning	Integration of data from multiple sources like text, audio, video, and physiological signals	Combines facial expression, tone of voice, and language for holistic suicide risk analysis
Long short-term memory (LSTM)	A type of recurrent neural network designed to capture time-based patterns in sequential data.	Tracks mood shifts or behavior over time from digital and speech inputs

(continued)

Term	Definition	Application in suicide prevention
Attention mechanism	A method in neural networks that focuses on the most relevant parts of input data when making predictions	Enhances model interpretability by identifying which words or features influenced risk classification
Feature engineering	The process of selecting and transforming data variables into inputs that improve model performance	Extracts critical predictors of suicide (e.g., sleep disturbance, isolation, prior attempts)
Cross-validation	A technique used to evaluate model performance by testing it on different subsets of data	Prevents overfitting and ensures model reliability across populations
Area under the curve (AUC)	A metric that summarizes the performance of a classification model across all thresholds	Commonly used to report model effectiveness in suicide risk prediction studies
Precision and recall	Precision is the ratio of true positives among predicted positives; recall (sensitivity) is the ratio of true positives among actual positives	Balancing both is essential to avoid missing at-risk individuals or over-flagging false alarms
SMOTE (synthetic minority oversampling technique)	A method used to balance datasets where one class (e.g., suicide cases) is underrepresented	Helps improve model accuracy in detecting rare but critical cases of suicide risk
Zero-shot learning	A learning approach where the model applies knowledge from known tasks to new, unseen tasks	Allows detection of suicidal language even without prior exposure to specific expressions or phrases
Explainable AI (XAI)	Techniques that make the decision-making process of AI models understandable to humans	Builds clinician trust and supports ethical implementation in suicide risk detection tools
Anhedonia	The loss of interest or pleasure in previously rewarding activities	A psychological marker often detected through language and used to assess suicide risk via NLP
Psychache	A term describing unbearable psychological pain linked to suicidal ideation	Linguistic cues related to psychache are critical for text-based suicide prediction systems

References

Adegbesan, A., Akingbola, A., Ojo, O., Jessica, O. U., Alao, U. H., Shagaya, U., Adewole, O., & Abdullahi, O. (2024). Ethical challenges in the integration of artificial intelligence in palliative care. *Journal of Medicine, Surgery, and Public Health, 4*, 100158. https://doi.org/10.1016/j.glmedi.2024.100158

Adekkanattu, P., Furmanchuk, A., Wu, Y., Pathak, A., Patra, B., Bost, S., Morrow, D., Wang, G., Yang, Y., Forrest, N., Luo, Y., Walunas, T., Jenny, W.-H., Gellad, W., Bian, J., Bao, Y., Weiner, M., Oslin, D., & Pathak, J. (2024). Detection of personal and family history of suicidal thoughts and behaviors using deep learning and natural language processing: A multi-site study. *Research Square*. https://doi.org/10.21203/rs.3.rs-4014472/v1

Aldakhil, A. F. (2024). Investigating the impact of an AI-based play activities intervention on the quality of life of school-aged children with ADHD. *Research in Developmental Disabilities, 154*, 104858. https://doi.org/10.1016/j.ridd.2024.104858

Andreotti, E. T., Ipuchima, J. R., Cazella, S. C., Beria, P., Bortoncello, C. F., Silveira, R. C., & Ferrão, Y. A. (2020). Instruments to assess suicide risk: A systematic review. *Trends in Psychiatry and Psychotherapy, 42*, 276–281. https://doi.org/10.1590/2237-6089-2019-0092

Arioz, U., Smrke, U., Plohl, N., & Mlakar, I. (2022). Scoping review on the multimodal classification of depression and experimental study on existing multimodal models. *Diagnostics, 12*(11), 2683. https://doi.org/10.3390/diagnostics12112683

Arowosegbe, A., & Oyelade, T. (2023). Application of natural language processing (NLP) in detecting and preventing suicide ideation: A systematic review. *International Journal of Environmental Research and Public Health, 20*(2), 1514. https://doi.org/10.3390/ijerph20021514

Avberšek, L. K., & Repovš, G. (2022). Deep learning in neuroimaging data analysis: Applications, challenges, and solutions. *Frontiers in Neuroimaging, 1*. https://doi.org/10.3389/fnimg.2022.981642

Banerji, C. R. S., Shah, A. B., Dabson, B., Chakraborti, T., Hellon, V., Harbron, C., & MacArthur, B. D. (2025). Clinicians must participate in the development of multimodal AI. *eClinicalMedicine, 84*. https://doi.org/10.1016/j.eclinm.2025.103252

Basyouni, A., et al. (2025). A suicidal ideation detection framework on social media using machine learning and genetic algorithms. *ResearchGate*. https://doi.org/10.1109/ACCESS.2024.3454796

Berrouiguet, S., Billot, R., Larsen, M. E., Lopez-Castroman, J., Jaussent, I., Walter, M., Lenca, P., Baca-García, E., & Courtet, P. (2019). An approach for data mining of electronic health record data for suicide risk management: Database analysis for clinical decision support. *JMIR Mental Health, 6*(5), e9766. https://doi.org/10.2196/mental.9766

Bruffaerts, R., Demyttenaere, K., Borges, G., Haro, J. M., Chiu, W. T., Hwang, I., Karam, E. G., Kessler, R. C., Sampson, N., Alonso, J., Andrade, L. H., Angermeyer, M., Benjet, C., Bromet, E., de Girolamo, G., de Graaf, R., Florescu, S., Gureje, O., Horiguchi, I., et al. (2010). Childhood adversities as risk factors for onset and persistence of suicidal behaviour. *The British Journal of Psychiatry, 197*(1), 20–27. https://doi.org/10.1192/bjp.bp.109.074716

Crema, C., Attardi, G., Sartiano, D., & Redolfi, A. (2022). Natural language processing in clinical neuroscience and psychiatry: A review. *Frontiers in Psychiatry, 13*. https://doi.org/10.3389/fpsyt.2022.946387

Cruz-Gonzalez, P., He, A. W.-J., Lam, E. P., Ng, I. M. C., Li, M. W., Hou, R., Chan, J. N.-M., Sahni, Y., Guasch, N. V., Miller, T., Lau, B. W.-M., & Vidaña, D. I. S. (2025). Artificial intelligence in mental health care: A systematic review of diagnosis, monitoring, and intervention applications. *Psychological Medicine, 55*, e18. https://doi.org/10.1017/S0033291724003295

D'Hotman, D., & Loh, E. (2020). AI-enabled suicide prediction tools: A qualitative narrative review. *BMJ Health & Care Informatics, 27*(3), e100175. https://doi.org/10.1136/bmjhci-2020-100175

Farhud, D. D., & Zokaei, S. (2021). Ethical issues of artificial intelligence in medicine and healthcare. *Iranian Journal of Public Health, 50*(11), i–v. https://doi.org/10.18502/ijph.v50i11.7600

Ferrara, E. (2024). Fairness and bias in artificial intelligence: A brief survey of sources, impacts, and mitigation strategies. *The Sciences, 6*(1), 3. https://doi.org/10.3390/sci6010003

Flamholz, Z. N., Crane-Droesch, A., Ungar, L. H., & Weissman, G. E. (2022). Word embeddings trained on published case reports are lightweight, effective for clinical tasks, and free of protected health information. *Journal of Biomedical Informatics, 125*, 103971. https://doi.org/10.1016/j.jbi.2021.103971

Friedrich, S., Groll, A., Ickstadt, K., Kneib, T., Pauly, M., Rahnenführer, J., & Friede, T. (2023). Regularization approaches in clinical biostatistics: A review of methods and their applications. *Statistical Methods in Medical Research, 32*(2), 425–440. https://doi.org/10.1177/09622802221133557

Gkintoni, E., Panagioti, M., Vassilopoulos, S. P., Nikolaou, G., Boutsinas, B., & Vantarakis, A. (2025). Leveraging AI-driven neuroimaging biomarkers for early detection and social function prediction in autism spectrum disorders: A systematic review. *Healthcare, 13*(15), 1776. https://doi.org/10.3390/healthcare13151776

Greaves, J., & Colucci, E. (2025). Crisis-line workers' perspectives on AI in suicide prevention: A qualitative exploration of risk and opportunity. *BMC Public Health, 25*(1), 2229. https://doi.org/10.1186/s12889-025-23298-8

Gvion, Y., Levi-Belz, Y., Hadlaczky, G., & Apter, A. (2015). On the role of impulsivity and decision-making in suicidal behavior. *World Journal of Psychiatry, 5*(3), 255–259. https://doi.org/10.5498/wjp.v5.i3.255

Ibrahim, S. T., Li, M., Patel, J., & Katapally, T. R. (2025). Utilizing natural language processing for precision prevention of mental health disorders among youth: A systematic review. *Computers in Biology and Medicine, 188*, 109859. https://doi.org/10.1016/j.compbiomed.2025.109859

Jerfy, A., Selden, O., & Balkrishnan, R. (2024). The growing impact of natural language processing in healthcare and public health. *Inquiry: The Journal of Health Care Organization, Provision, and Financing, 61*, 00469580241290095. https://doi.org/10.1177/00469580241290095

Kelly, L. M., Rash, C. J., Alessi, S. M., & Zajac, K. (2020). Correlates and predictors of suicidal ideation and substance use among adults seeking substance use treatment with varying levels of suicidality. *Journal of Substance Abuse Treatment, 119*, 108145. https://doi.org/10.1016/j.jsat.2020.108145

Kleiman, E. M., & Liu, R. T. (2013). Social support as a protective factor in suicide: Findings from two nationally representative samples. *Journal of Affective Disorders, 150*(2), 540–545. https://doi.org/10.1016/j.jad.2013.01.033

Lejeune, A., Glaz, A. L., Perron, P.-A., Sebti, J., Baca-Garcia, E., Walter, M., Lemey, C., & Berrouiguet, S. (2022). Artificial intelligence and suicide prevention: A systematic review. *European Psychiatry, 65*(1), e19. https://doi.org/10.1192/j.eurpsy.2022.8

Leon, N., Namadingo, H., Cooper, S., Bobrow, K., Mwantisi, C., Nyasulu, M., Sicwebu, N., Crampin, A., Levitt, N., & Farmer, A. (2021). Process evaluation of a brief messaging intervention to improve diabetes treatment adherence in sub-Saharan Africa. *BMC Public Health, 21*(1), 1576. https://doi.org/10.1186/s12889-021-11552-8

Madububambachu, U., Ukpebor, A., & Ihezue, U. (2024). Machine learning techniques to predict mental health diagnoses: A systematic literature review. *Clinical Practice and Epidemiology in Mental Health, 20*, e17450179315688. https://doi.org/10.2174/0117450179315688240607052117

Martinez-Romo, J., Araujo, L., & Reneses, B. (2025). Guardian-BERT: Early detection of self-injury and suicidal signs with language technologies in electronic health reports. *Computers in Biology and Medicine, 186*, 109701. https://doi.org/10.1016/j.compbiomed.2025.109701

Melnykova, N., Patereha, Y., Skopivskyi, S., Farion, M., Fedushko, S., & Drohomyretska, K. (2025). Machine learning for stroke prediction using imbalanced data. *Scientific Reports, 15*(1), 33773. https://doi.org/10.1038/s41598-025-01855-w

Mennella, C., Maniscalco, U., Di Pietro, G., & Esposito, M. (2024). Ethical and regulatory challenges of AI technologies in healthcare: A narrative review. *Heliyon, 10*(4), e26297. https://doi.org/10.1016/j.heliyon.2024.e26297

Mohamad, K. S. B. (2025). *Advances in AI and machine learning for suicide risk detection* (SSRN Scholarly Paper No. 5481828). Social Science Research Network. https://doi.org/10.2139/ssrn.5481828

Monaghan, T. F., Rahman, S. N., Agudelo, C. W., Wein, A. J., Lazar, J. M., Everaert, K., & Dmochowski, R. R. (2021). Foundational statistical principles in medical research: Sensitivity, specificity, positive predictive value, and negative predictive value. *Medicina, 57*(5), 503. https://doi.org/10.3390/medicina57050503

Nigam, A., Vuddemarry, M., & Zadey, S. (2024). Economic burden of suicide deaths in India (2019): A retrospective, cross-sectional study. *The Lancet Regional Health – Southeast Asia, 29*, 100477. https://doi.org/10.1016/j.lansea.2024.100477

Pandya, A., Lodha, P., & Ganatra, A. (2024). Is ChatGPT ready to change mental healthcare? Challenges and considerations: A reality check. *Frontiers in Human Dynamics, 5*. https://doi.org/10.3389/fhumd.2023.1289255

Parsapoor (Mah Parsa), M., Koudys, J. W., & Ruocco, A. C. (2023). Suicide risk detection using artificial intelligence: The promise of creating a benchmark dataset for research on the detection of suicide risk. *Frontiers in Psychiatry, 14*, 1186569. https://doi.org/10.3389/fpsyt.2023.1186569

Pigoni, A., Delvecchio, G., Turtulici, N., Madonna, D., Pietrini, P., Cecchetti, L., & Brambilla, P. (2024). Machine learning and the prediction of suicide in psychiatric populations: A systematic review. *Translational Psychiatry, 14*, 140. https://doi.org/10.1038/s41398-024-02852-9

Pirkis, J., Dandona, R., Silverman, M., Khan, M., & Hawton, K. (2024). Preventing suicide: A public health approach to a global problem. *The Lancet Public Health, 9*(10), e787–e795. https://doi.org/10.1016/S2468-2667(24)00149-X

Posner, K., Brown, G. K., Stanley, B., Brent, D. A., Yershova, K. V., Oquendo, M. A., Currier, G. W., Melvin, G. A., Greenhill, L., Shen, S., & Mann, J. J. (2011). The Columbia–Suicide Severity Rating Scale: Initial validity and internal consistency findings from three multisite studies with adolescents and adults. *The American Journal of Psychiatry, 168*(12), 1266–1277. https://doi.org/10.1176/appi.ajp.2011.10111704

Rashidi, H. H., Pantanowitz, J., Hanna, M. G., Tafti, A. P., Sanghani, P., Buchinsky, A., Fennell, B., Deebajah, M., Wheeler, S., Pearce, T., Abukhiran, I., Robertson, S., Palmer, O., Gur, M., Tran, N. K., & Pantanowitz, L. (2025). Introduction to artificial intelligence and machine learning in pathology and medicine: Generative and nongenerative artificial intelligence basics. *Modern Pathology, 38*(4), 100688. https://doi.org/10.1016/j.modpat.2024.100688

Raue, P. J., Ghesquiere, A. R., & Bruce, M. L. (2014). Suicide risk in primary care: Identification and management in older adults. *Current Psychiatry Reports, 16*(9), 466. https://doi.org/10.1007/s11920-014-0466-8

Ryan, E. P., & Oquendo, M. A. (2020). Suicide risk assessment and prevention: Challenges and opportunities. *Focus, 18*, 88–99. https://doi.org/10.1176/appi.focus.20200011

Sagar, R., & Singh, S. (2022). National Tele-Mental Health Program in India: A step towards mental health care for all? *Indian Journal of Psychiatry, 64*(2), 117. https://doi.org/10.4103/indianjpsychiatry.indianjpsychiatry_145_22

Saranya, A., & Subhashini, R. (2023). A systematic review of explainable artificial intelligence models and applications: Recent developments and future trends. *Decision Analytics Journal, 7*, 100230. https://doi.org/10.1016/j.dajour.2023.100230

Shetty, N. P., Singh, Y., Hegde, V., Cenitta, D., & K, D. (2025). Exploring emotional patterns in social media through NLP models to unravel mental health insights. *Healthcare Technology Letters, 12*(1), e12096. https://doi.org/10.1049/htl2.12096

Simon, G. E., Johnson, E., Lawrence, J. M., Rossom, R. C., Ahmedani, B., Lynch, F. L., Beck, A., Waitzfelder, B., Ziebell, R., Penfold, R. B., & Shortreed, S. M. (2018). Predicting suicide attempts and suicide deaths following outpatient visits using electronic health records. *American Journal of Psychiatry, 175*, 951–960. https://doi.org/10.1176/appi.ajp.2018.17101167

Singh, O. P. (2022). Startling suicide statistics in India: Time for urgent action. *Indian Journal of Psychiatry, 64*(5), 431–432. https://doi.org/10.4103/indianjpsychiatry.indianjpsychiatry_665_22

Syed, S., & Amin, I. (2017). Prediction of suicide causes in India using machine learning. *Journal of Independent Studies and Research–Computing, 15*. https://doi.org/10.31645/jisrc/(2017).15.2.01

Thumfart, K. M., Jawaid, A., Bright, K., Flachsmann, M., & Mansuy, I. M. (2022). Epigenetics of childhood trauma: Long-term sequelae and potential for treatment. *Neuroscience & Biobehavioral Reviews, 132*, 1049–1066. https://doi.org/10.1016/j.neubiorev.2021.10.042

Wisłowska-Stanek, A., Kołosowska, K., & Maciejak, P. (2021). Neurobiological basis of increased risk for suicidal behaviour. *Cells, 10*(10), 2519. https://doi.org/10.3390/cells10102519

Yadav, S., Aathavan, K. K., Cunningham, S. A., Bhandari, P., Mishra, U. S., Aditi, A., & Yadav, R. (2023). Changing pattern of suicide deaths in India. *The Lancet Regional Health – Southeast Asia, 16*, 100265. https://doi.org/10.1016/j.lansea.2023.100265

Yu, X., Tang, L., Long, L., & Sina, M. (2024). Comparison of deep and conventional machine learning models for prediction of one supply chain management distribution cost. *Scientific Reports, 14*(1), 24195. https://doi.org/10.1038/s41598-024-75114-9

Zhu, L., Mou, W., Lai, Y., Lin, J., & Luo, P. (2024). Language and cultural bias in AI: Comparing the performance of large language models developed in different countries on Traditional Chinese Medicine highlights the need for localized models. *Journal of Translational Medicine, 22*(1), 319. https://doi.org/10.1186/s12967-024-05128-4

Zonayed, M., Tasnim, R., Jhara, S. S., Mimona, M. A., Hussein, M. R., Mobarak, M. H., & Salma, U. (2025). Machine learning and IoT in healthcare: Recent advancements, challenges and future direction. *Advances in Biomarker Sciences and Technology, 7*, 335–364. https://doi.org/10.1016/j.abst.2025.08.006

MIX
Papier aus verantwortungsvollen Quellen
Paper from responsible sources
FSC® C105338

If you have any concerns about our products,
you can contact us on
ProductSafety@springernature.com

In case Publisher is established outside the EU,
the EU authorized representative is:
Springer Nature Customer Service Center GmbH
Europaplatz 3, 69115 Heidelberg, Germany

Printed by Libri Plureos GmbH
in Hamburg, Germany